LABOR
RELATIONS

Third Edition

LABOR
RELATIONS

ARTHUR A. SLOANE
Professor of Industrial Relations
University of Delaware

FRED WITNEY
Professor of Economics
Indiana University

Prentice-Hall, Inc., Englewood Cliffs, New Jersey

Library of Congress Cataloging in Publication Data

SLOANE, ARTHUR A
    Labor relations.

    Includes bibliographies and index.
    1. Collective bargaining—United States.
2. Industrial relations—United States. I. Witney,
Fred, joint author. II. Title.
HD8072.S6185 1977   331.89′2973   76–13649
ISBN 0–13–519595–0

Printed in the United States of America

10 9 8 7 6 5 4 3 2

PRENTICE-HALL INTERNATIONAL, INC., *London*
PRENTICE-HALL OF AUSTRALIA PTY. LIMITED, *Sydney*
PRENTICE-HALL OF CANADA, LTD., *Toronto*
PRENTICE-HALL OF INDIA PRIVATE LIMITED, *New Delhi*
PRENTICE-HALL OF JAPAN, INC., *Tokyo*
PRENTICE-HALL OF SOUTHEAST ASIA PTE. LTD., *Singapore*

TO
LOUISE, AMY, AND LAURA
AND
JUDY, EILEEN, AND FRANK

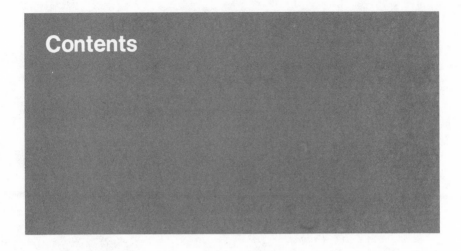

Contents

Chapter 3

The Legal Framework   104

Chapter 4

Union Behavior: Structure, Government, and Operation   141

PART III
COLLECTIVE BARGAINING

Chapter 5

At the Bargaining Table   187

Chapter 6

Administration of the Agreement   217

Chapter 7

Wage Issues under Collective Bargaining   275

Chapter 8

Economic Supplements under Collective Bargaining   335

Chapter 9

Institutional Issues under Collective Bargaining   376

Chapter 10

Administrative Issues under Collective Bargaining   405

PART IV
SOME FINAL THOUGHTS

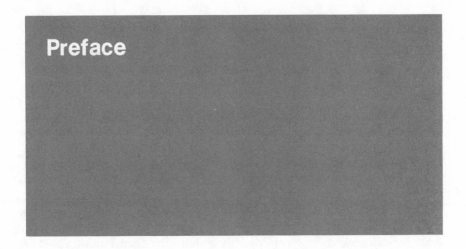

Preface

There are no prerequisites to this book beyond an interest in labor–management relations. We have designed it to serve as an aid to all readers who desire a basic understanding of unionism in its natural habitat. With such a thrust, however, the volume focuses on certain areas, which necessarily minimizes the treatment of others.

Labor Relations brings in, for example, sufficient economic material to allow a fundamental appreciation of the union–management process and stops at that point. We have, throughout, tried to implement our belief that all of the various topic treatments should, as in the case of a woman's ideal skirt-length, be short enough to be interesting and long enough to cover the subject.

On the other hand, our offering in no way *restricts* itself to what is commonly described as "collective bargaining." Its focus is on the negotiation and administration of labor agreements, with emphasis on the development and application of the more significant bargaining issues as they now appear between the covers of the contracts. Further, our own teaching experiences have shown us that these topics cannot profitably be studied in isolation. Labor relations, in the sense in which we use the term, can best be viewed as an interaction between two organizations—management and the labor union—and the parties to this interaction are always subject to various, often complex, environmental influences. Only after the reader gains an understanding of the evolving management and labor institutions, and only after the environment surrounding their interactional process has been appreciated, can he or she attempt to understand bargaining itself in any meaningful way.

The book, consequently, begins with a broad overview of the general nature of the labor–management relationship as it currently exists in the United States (Part I). It then moves to a survey of the historical, legal, and structural environments which so greatly influence contractual contents and labor relations behavior (Part II). Finally, it presents a close examination of the negotiation, administration, and major contents of the labor agreement itself (Part III). Through description, analysis, discussion questions and, in the later stages of this volume, selected arbitration cases drawn from our own experiences, we hope to impart understanding of all these aspects of labor relations.

Numerous changes, primarily additions, mark this third edition. Even in the few years since the 1972 publication of our first revision, developments in the field have dictated the inclusion of new material relating to public-sector unionism, arbitration law, seniority rights, occupational safety and health, governmental wage and price controls, "multinationals," and women in labor unions. We have also, with the benefit of some hindsight, substantially enlarged upon our prior treatment of black worker unionism, arbitration costs and delays, Boulwarism, and supplementary unemployment benefits (among other topics), and we have considerably updated the discussion of a host of other issues ranging from union finances to pension entitlement. Fourteen new and recent arbitration cases are presented, as are a significantly revised bibliography and an amended mock negotiation problem. Nonetheless, we have exercised self-restraint in the rewriting; only changes which could be defended on grounds of general improvement of *Labor Relations* have been incorporated. We are strong believers in the old Puritan dictum that "Nothing should ever be said that doesn't improve upon silence," while also sharing with the late Calvin Coolidge the conviction that "If you don't say anything, no one will ever call upon you to repeat it."

We want to take this opportunity to thank Professor I. B. Helburn (University of Texas at Austin), Professor Robert D. Miller (Hillsborough Community College), and Professor Dale Yoder for their helpful review of the manuscript. We stand indebted to many people for their help in this revision. Students, friends from the ranks of both management and labor, and colleagues at other educational institutions have all offered not only encouragement but also a wide variety of highly constructive suggestions. We have accepted all of the encouragement and many of the suggestions with thanks.

ARTHUR A. SLOANE
FRED WITNEY

LABOR
RELATIONS

PART I
SETTING
THE STAGE

Chapter 1
Organized Labor
and the Management Community:
An Overview

Our society has historically placed a high premium on property rights. Because of this, and perhaps also because the American soil has nurtured a breed of highly individualistic and aggressive businessmen, employers in this country have accepted unionism through the years approximately as well as nature tolerates a vacuum.

The evidence for this phenomenon is not in short supply. Symbolic of management sentiments in the mid-nineteenth century were, for example, the comments of the editors of the *New York Journal of Commerce* relating to current demands of the printers in that locality:

> Who but a miserable craven-hearted man, would permit himself to be subjected to such rules, extending even to the number of apprentices he may employ, and the manner in which they shall be bound to him, to the kind of work which shall be performed in his own office at particular hours of the day, and to the sex of the persons employed, however separated into different apartments or buildings? For ourselves, we never employed a female as a compositor and have no great opinion of apprentices, but sooner than be restricted on these points, or any other, by a self-constituted tribunal outside of the office, we would go back to the employment of our boyhood, and dig potatoes, pull flax, and do everything else that a plain, honest farmer may properly do on his own territory. It is marvelous to us how any employer, having the soul of a man within him, can submit to such degradation.[1]

Five decades later, George F. Baer, president of the Philadelphia and Reading Railroad, relied on God rather than ridicule in setting forth views that were no less representative of many employers of *his* time. In a 1903 letter, Baer replied to a citizen who had requested him "as a Christian gentleman" to make concessions to the striking workers on his railroad, as follows:

> I see you are evidently biased in your religious views in favor of the right of the working man to control a business in which he has no other interest than to

[1] *New York Journal of Commerce*, February 7, 1851, as quoted in Neil W. Chamberlain, *The Labor Sector* (New York: McGraw-Hill, 1965), p. 341.

secure fair wages for the work he does. I beg of you not to be discouraged. The rights and interests of the laboring man will be protected and cared for, not by the labor agitators, but by the Christian men to whom God in His infinite wisdom has given control of the property interests of the country. Pray earnestly that the right may triumph, always remembering that the Lord God Omnipotent still reigns and that His reign is one of law and order, and not of violence and crime.[2]

Sinclair Lewis used the medium of fictional satire to make his points, but real-life counterparts of his small-town businessman George F. Babbitt were sufficiently in supply to make *Babbitt* an instant success when it was published in 1922. Babbitt's opinions on the subject of organized labor were quite forthright, if not entirely consistent:

> A good labor union is of value because it keeps out radical unions, which would destroy property. No one ought to be forced to belong to a union, however. All labor agitators who try to force men to join a union should be hanged. In fact, just between ourselves, there oughtn't to be any unions allowed at all; and as it's the best way of fighting the unions, every businessman ought to belong to an employer's association and to the Chamber of Commerce. In union there is strength. So any selfish hog who doesn't join the Chamber of Commerce ought to be forced to.[3]

In our own day, management views on the subject are considerably more sophisticated and far less emotion-laden. Over the past few decades, major changes have affected the employment relationship and contributed to the lessening of overt antiunionism. The findings of the behavioral sciences, particularly industrial sociology and applied psychology, have led to an employee-centered management approach that was unknown to an earlier era. Far greater worker expectations have been fostered by a new social climate derived from the ending of mass immigration, growing levels of education, and the spread of the world's most ambitious communications network. Moreover, the old-time owner–manager, holding a major or exclusive proprietary interest in his business, has now been substantially displaced. He has been succeeded by the hired administrator, oriented toward management as a profession, as much an employee as the people far below him in the company hierarchy, and increasingly aware that profitability is not the only test of his company's performance today (and that community responsibilities are also prime considerations). Finally, the right of workers to organize and bargain collectively, free of employer restraint or coercion, has been protected by statute since the mid-1930s.

[2]Herbert Harris, *American Labor* (New Haven, Conn.: Yale University Press, 1939), pp. 126–27.

[3]Sinclair Lewis, *Babbitt* (New York: Harcourt, Brace & World, 1922), p. 44. (Rights for the British Commonwealth excluding Canada have been granted by Jonathan Cape Limited, Publishers, London, England.)

In this new setting, progress in union–management relations has undeniably been made. Considerably more enlightened management policies toward organized labor are in effect today than was the case even 25 years ago. A large measure of contractual stability has been achieved in many situations. Violence in labor disputes has all but disappeared. The incidence of strikes has been almost steadily decreasing, and strikes now consume a minuscule portion of total working time—less than 0.20 percent in most recent years. A greater willingness by both parties to resort to facts rather than to power or emotion as a basis for bargaining is in evidence. And, indeed, unions have now been completely accepted by some managers, with outspoken attacks on organized labor in general being relatively rare from *any* employer quarter.

For all these sanguine developments, however, the fact remains that unions are still far from welcome in the eyes of the employer community. If the attacks on unionism are more muted and less belligerent than they were in the past, they nonetheless exist on a wide scale. More than a decade ago, one observer of the labor scene summed up what he saw as the modal situation at that time in words that we believe to be wholly appropriate even now:

> Even if the manager does not view the union as a gang, he often still feels that they strike a discordant note in the happy home. Once there, unrest develops. A peer group outside the home becomes more important to the children than the parents; the father's powers are challenged; the child begins to think his goals are not synonymous with those of the parents (he may even want his allowance raised); and, perhaps worst of all, he wants to have his voice heard in how the home should be run.[4]

In the face of this management enmity, on the other hand, unionism has shown absolutely no tendency to retreat. Owing primarily to the inroads of automation and the resulting employment decline, as well as to changing market demands affecting the manufacturing sector, organized labor has, it is true, expanded its membership only moderately in the past few years. And despite some claims by labor relations analysts that the fast-growing white-collar-worker sector will soon become more hospitable to collective bargaining, it is equally true that union penetration in this area thus far has fallen considerably short of its potential. But it is no less a matter of record that almost seven times as many workers are union members today as was the case in 1932, and it is quite apparent that the 21 million employees who currently constitute the labor movement in this country exhibit no notable signs of disenchantment with it. Whatever one's speculation about the problems awaiting unionism as the nature of our labor force changes (and, as

[4]Albert A. Blum, "Management Paternalism and Collective Bargaining," *Personnel Administration*, XXVI (January–February 1963), p. 38.

will be shown, the speculation is both optimistic and pessimistic from the union viewpoint), the labor union seems to be very much here to stay.

In this introductory chapter, then, we shall want to examine several questions. Why do workers, apparently in complete disregard of their employers' wishes, join and remain in unions? Why, for that matter (beyond the extremely general reasons suggested by the preceding paragraphs), do employers so steadfastly continue to oppose the concept of unionism? Assuming that managers have no choice other than to deal with a labor organization, what alternative methods for this collective bargaining are open to them? And what, if any, trends in their concrete dealings with unions have managements exhibited in recent years? Before we discuss these questions, however, we must assess the current status and strategic power of the American labor movement itself.

THE STATE OF THE UNIONS TODAY

Completely reliable statistics relating to union membership in this country have never been available. Some unions in reporting their figures have traditionally exaggerated, to gain respect and influence for the union itself within the total labor movement, to make the union officers look better by showing a rise in enrollments during their term of office, or merely to hide a loss of membership. Other unions have been known to report fewer members than they actually have, for financial reasons (for example, to avoid paying per capita taxes to labor federations to which they may belong, particularly the AFL-CIO), or because of bookkeeping practices that exclude workers currently on strike (or those on layoff from work) from the list of present members.

The figure of 21 million workers, offered above as constituting the present extent of union organization, is commonly accepted as an appropriate one, however. This total includes some 19.5 million U.S. members of national and international unions[5] and roughly 1.5 million American members of independent local unions (those not affiliated with any national or international union). It excludes the approximately 1.2 million Canadians who belong to internationals with headquarters in the United States.[6]

In 1975, in terms of relative labor-force penetration, the 21 million in the unionized work force represented approximately 21.8 percent of all civilian members of the labor force in the country and accounted for almost three out of every ten employees in nonagricultural establishments (where union organizing has historically been concentrated). They also constituted somewhat less than 35 percent of "organizable" American industrial em-

---

[5]The terms *national* and *international* will be used interchangeably in this volume as, indeed, they are used in practice.

[6]Unofficial data furnished by U.S. Department of Labor, Bureau of Labor Statistics.

ployees (our nonprofessional and nonsupervisory employees, although some union representation from both the professional and supervisory sectors does exist).[7]

More specifically, just about one-half of the nation's 30 million blue-collar workers (craftsmen, operatives, and kindred workers) are now in unions. These include at least 80 percent of such workers in transportation, construction, and municipal utilities and somewhat over two-thirds of all blue-collar employees in manufacturing and mining. Almost all manual workers in many manufacturing industries—steel, automobile, rubber, aerospace, meat packing, agricultural implements, brewing, paper, the needle trades, and a few others—have now been organized. So, too, has a substantial percentage of the blue-collar employees in the printing, oil, chemical, shoe, electrical, electronic, and pharmaceutical industries.

States and cities with a high percentage of their workers in these industries show, not surprisingly, a high proportion of unionized employees. Indeed, five states alone—New York, California, Pennsylvania, Illinois, and Ohio—account for almost half of all union members in this country (while employing just over one-third of the U.S. nonagricultural work force). There are, in fact, more union members in New York alone than there are in eleven southern states, including Texas, combined. And Washington, Michigan, and Massachusetts also have ratios of union membership to nonagricultural employment that place them well above the national average of just under 30 percent. Several major cities, too, that are heavily dependent on the industries cited—Pittsburgh, Detroit, and Seattle, among others—currently have at least 90 percent of their manufacturing-plant workers covered by union contract. Cities without large representation from these industries tend to show considerably lower figures.

Union strength, then, is highly concentrated in areas that are strategic to our economy. If organized labor has thus far been notably unsuccessful in its attempt to organize such white-collar (and fast-growing) sectors as trade, services, and finance, and such remaining great pockets of non-unionism in manufacturing as the textile industry, unions *have* been cordially greeted by the workers in much of large-scale industry. Indeed, the labor movement today bargains with many of the most influential managements in the country, those that regularly take the lead in price and wage movements. By and large, as Slichter, Healy, and Livernash have pointed out, trade unions have dominant representation "where technology is most advanced, where capital is used most abundantly, where the productivity of labor is highest, and where technological progress is most rapid. . . . In other words, trade union membership is concentrated and strongest where strength counts most of all."[8]

[7] *Ibid.*
[8] Sumner H. Slichter, James J. Healy, and E. Robert Livernash, *The Impact of Collective Bargaining on Management* (Washington, D.C.: The Brookings Institution, 1960), p. 2.

Union membership related directly to industrial category also illustrates the high percentage of labor organization accounted for by the groups cited above, and the relatively small successes enjoyed by labor organizers in white-collar industries. The figures in the following partial industrial listing relate to the *total* work forces in each industry. In fairness to unions, it should be recognized that each industry includes a varying but never inconsequential number of employees who would consider joining the ranks of organized labor, if at all, only in their wildest dreams (managers and other administrators, higher-echelon specialists, and in some cases political officeholders). But the discrepancy between the blue- and white-collar sectors is vivid nonetheless.[9]

Industry	Percentage Unionized
Railroads	78.6%
Automobiles	66.2
Primary metals	59.8
Postal	52.2
Paper	48.7
Other transportation	42.9
Telephone communication	40.1
Stone, clay, and glass	39.6
Construction	39.2
Fabricated metals	38.2
Local government	19.6
State government	13.3
Wholesale, retail trade	10.2
Hospitals	8.4
Services, finance	7.8

Further evidence of the importance of the blue-collar industry groups to the labor movement is given in a listing of the largest unions. Ranked according to their size in 1976, the six largest internationals show their heavy dependence on blue-collar workers even in their titles. Accounting for just about one-third of all union members, these internationals are:

Union	Members
Teamsters (Independent)	2,100,000
Automobile Workers (Independent)	1,400,000
Steelworkers (AFL-CIO)	1,400,000
Electrical Workers (AFL-CIO)*	800,000
Carpenters (AFL-CIO)	775,000
Machinists (AFL-CIO)	700,000

*International Brotherhood of Electrical Workers.

Source: Authors' estimates based on data published by the U.S. Department of Labor.

[9] Figures furnished by the U.S. Department of Labor.

WHITE-COLLAR EMPLOYEES

If the labor movement is predominantly a blue-collar one, however, this is no longer true of the U.S. labor force itself. In 1956, the number of white-collar workers exceeded that of blue-collar workers in this country for the first time in our nation's history. And the gap has been steadily widening ever since: Such sectors as trade, services, finance, and government have continued to expand, while the blue-collar sectors—particularly manufacturing, mining, and transportation, but with the construction sector as a conspicuous exception—have actually, in the face of improved technologies and changing consumer demands, shown employment declines.

More than any other factor, this changing complexion of the labor force has given organized labor cause for concern. Over the past two decades, its inability to recruit white-collar workers on any significant scale has forced it to watch the unionized percentage of the total civilian work force slip somewhat—from over 24 percent to the approximate current figure of 21.8.

This is not to say, of course, that unions do not exert a major collective bargaining influence on behalf of some groups of white-collar workers. Such white-collar types as musicians and actors have for years been willing joiners of labor organizations. In recent years, two unions in particular have shown significant gains in this quarter: the State, County and Municipal Employees, whose estimated 650,000 members now place it just below the very largest labor organizations in the country; and the American Federation of Teachers, which grew from 60,000 members in 1960 to roughly 445,000 fifteen years later. Also exhibiting no small amount of organizational success have been the Retail Clerks (now at an estimated 500,000 membership), the Retail, Wholesale and Department Store Employees (190,000), and such somewhat smaller white-collar internationals as the Letter Carriers (170,000) and the Postal Clerks (160,000). And although substantial numbers of workers within some of these unions (in particular, the Retail Clerks, the State County and Municipal Employees, and the Letter Carriers) perform such clearly blue-collar assignments as stock-handling, pothole-patching, and post-office building maintenance, the percentage of pure white-collar types in each appears to have steadily climbed since the 1960s. Moreover, many of labor's largest internationals—most notably the Teamsters and the Steelworkers—do represent large numbers of white-collar employees in addition to their traditional types of constituents.

Nonetheless, there has been no particularly impressive change in total union penetration of the white-collar field in recent years. In 1956, some 2.42 million white-collar workers were in unions; a decade later, the figure had risen only to approximately 2.7 million, despite the growth of this sector by several million more jobs, to over 26 million by the late 1960s. And by 1976, with an even more rapid growth in total white-collar employment in the intervening years, the union rolls had advanced only to the 3.6-million mark, a point clearly far short of the saturation level. Nor had even these modest gains of organized labor been evenly spread throughout the white-collar world. Most of them had been gained strictly from the public-service sector, where, as we shall see, in many cases favorable legislation had made the enrollment of new members comparatively easy.

SOME PROBABLE EXPLANATIONS

Why has the white-collar world been so relatively unreceptive to the union organizer, when its blue-collar counterpart has been so hospitable to him? Many theories have been advanced, by almost as many theorists. All bear some risk of oversimplification, given both the variety of ever-changing needs and wants that play on human behavior and the heterogeneity of the white-collar population itself (including as it does such dissimilar occupational categories as engineers, professional salesmen, medical and other health workers, clerical and office employees, members of the teaching profession, and government workers). But among the many explanations for labor's general failure to date in penetrating the White-Collar Frontier, the following may well be the most accurate. Taken collectively, they also constitute some rather formidable grounds for union pessimism in the years ahead.

1. The public has in recent years been inundated with news of seemingly irresponsible union strikes and commensurately unstatesmanlike settlements, union leaders' criminality, and featherbedding situations. The resulting poor image of the labor movement, as conveyed by the mass media, may well have alienated hundreds of thousands—and, conceivably, even millions—of potential white-collar union joiners. In an age when even the occupant of the White House can be determined by public image, this factor—although it is not only unquantifiable but even basically unprovable—cannot be overlooked.

This topic should in any event receive far more attention than it has heretofore been given. Certainly, as has long been observed by thoughtful students of labor relations, unions most often get into the headlines for activities that cover them with discredit. A union leader's criminality will invariably do the trick. And so, too, will news of any seemingly irresponsible union strike, or almost any charge, if made with sufficient vigor, that unionized employees are receiving pay for work that is not performed (or "featherbedding").

Thus, there may well be significant numbers in the general population who believe that "Construction Strike Threat Looms" is a regular, if somewhat repetitious, column appearing in their local newspaper. (*Looms*, from all available evidence, is the only verb utilized in such situations, a phenomenon similar to that pertaining to "Prison Riots," which can only be "Quelled.") And one can only guess at how many Americans think that

"Featherbedding" is part of the official job designation of the "Railroad Firemen." It is also true, as the late A.J. Liebling once commented, that the public is regularly informed that "Labor *Demands*" but that "Management *Offers*"; and few can argue with a further observation of this famous journalist that when General Motors workers go out on strike for more wages, this is major news throughout the nation (if not the world), whereas the president of General Motors takes his considerably larger income home quietly.

From the labor point of view there is, of course, an intrinsic unfairness in such a factor. It is conflict, as more than one newsman has observed, that makes the headlines. The large majority of union agreements that are peacefully renegotiated year after year go virtually unnoticed by the reporters of the news, but the few strikes of any dimensions are treated with the journalistic zeal of a Tolstoy. The overwhelming proportion of union officials continue to lead their lives in full compliance with the laws of the land, but this seems insignificant to the news compilers in the face of the conviction of a single Jimmy Hoffa or Tony Boyle, with whose blemished records all informed citizens have become amply familiar. And charges that unions demand pay for work that is not performed totally dwarf the large body of evidence that featherbedding is engaged in by only a small segment of unionized employees.

Yet what editor can justify headlines proclaiming that "Local 109 of the Hatters Is a Very Statesmanlike Local," that "Business Agent Duffy Gabrilowitz of the Plumbers Union Is One Hundred Percent Honest," or that "Management Says That Pulp, Sulphite, and Paper Mill Workers Are Giving a Fair Day's Work for a Fair Day's Pay"? Only, we suspect, a newsman with a strongly developed suicidal urge. Accordingly, the large segment of the population that allows its opinions of unionism to be molded only by those labor activities receiving wide publicity is understandably—if, for organized labor, unfortunately—less than enthusiastic about the institution. An incalculable but undoubtedly formidable number of white-collar workers— unlike their blue-collar counterparts, who are generally in a better position by virtue of proximity to perceive strengths as well as weaknesses in unionism —fall into this population category.

2. The labor movement has in recent years been distinguished in the main by uninspiring, rather bureaucratic leadership that seems only dimly aware of the white-collar problem and totally unimaginative about discovering any solutions. The complaint of labor scholar J.B.S. Hardman that "superannuated leaders, who have outlived their usefulness, are probably met more frequently in the labor movement than in any other militant social movement,"[10] although it was made almost fifty years ago and intended to apply exclusively to the late 1920s, could fit into any typical outsider's critique

[10]J.B.S. Hardman, *American Labor Dynamics* (New York: Harcourt, Brace & Co., 1928), p. 95.

of labor's current performance without doing violence to the basic theme. Hardman's words constitute, as Jack T. Conway could point out a few years ago, "the lingering lament of an aging officialdom, which too frequently symbolizes—to the public and to its membership—dried-up idealism and a stalled drive for reform."[11]

Nor has this condition entirely escaped the attention of labor leaders themselves. The secretary-teasurer of the United Automobile Workers, Emil Mazey, for example, has offered the observation that "some of the board members of some of the unions, when they have a board meeting, they look like a collection of a wax museum."[12] And, indeed, the UAW, which withdrew from the AFL-CIO in May 1968, at least ostensibly because of its unhappiness with what it perceived to be the federation's leadership apathy, has charged that the AFL-CIO "has become isolated from the mainstream and too often acts like a comfortable, complacent custodian of the status quo."[13] By the same token, the AFL-CIO's leadership has pointed out that UAW leadership is on vulnerable ground in making such charges, since the UAW represents a smaller proportion of the work force in its own industry than it did at the time of the AFL-CIO merger in 1955.

However one judges the respective merits of the federation and UAW cases, the tremendous amount of time and energy poured into this particular battle in the past few years by the two sides constitutes to many people, as James P. Gannon has commented, "the nonproductive, self-serving task of publicly flogging each other."[14] And since so little concrete progress in revitalizing labor's sagging fortunes has supplemented this activity, the appearance is clearly not far removed from the reality.

For those who continue to believe strongly in the potential of the labor movement as a force for accomplishment in our society, there is something quite sad about the current state of union leadership. All the trappings of success surround it—as Raskin has accurately pointed out, "The hair shirt has given way to white-on-white broadcloth, imported fabrics, and custom tailoring"[15]—and the expense-account perquisites of labor's major officials are totally indistinguishable in their lavishness from those of the leaders of the business community. But somewhere in the transformation from crusader for the underdog to accepted member of the Establishment, both the sense of mission and the creative spark to implement it seem to have been severely dampened by affluence. The senior citizens who constitute the bulk

[11]Jack T. Conway, "Challenges to Union Leadership in an Era of Change," in *Proceedings of the Twenty-First Annual Winter Meeting, Industrial Relations Research Association*, December 29–30, 1968, p. 183.

[12]*Wall Street Journal*, March 26, 1964, p. 8.

[13]*Business Week*, May 31, 1969, p. 77.

[14]James P. Gannon, "The Labor Movement: Sinew Turned Fat," *Wall Street Journal*, June 3, 1969, p. 22.

[15]A. H. Raskin, "The Unions and Their Wealth," *Atlantic Monthly*, April 1962, p. 89.

of current labor leadership appear, in short, to be resting quite comfortably on their hard-earned laurels, lacking motivation to reenter the organizational arena and expend the energy, money, and, perhaps above all, imagination that is required by such an elusive potential constituency as the white-collar sector. As Wilfrid Sheed has written in *The Atlantic*, "The widespread impression that Labor consists of aging white men guarding their gains may be an exaggeration verging on libel; but it *is* widespread."[16]

3. White-collar workers possess certain unique general properties that may tend to work against unionization in any event. Any citation of these ingredients automatically incurs all the risks of generalization alluded to earlier, but there is agreement among scholars of the white-collar population that they definitely exist.

a. White-collar employees have long felt superior to their blue-collar counterparts and have tended to believe that joining a union (an institution traditionally associated with manual workers) would decrease their occupational prestige. This goes well beyond the issue of labor's currently poor image cited above. A certain autonomy at work, however little it may be in many cases, is imparted to the holder of the white-collar job as it is not to the factory or even construction worker. Prior educational achievements, modes of dress and language, relative cleanliness of the work situations, and even job locations within the enterprise also typically give the white-collar job-holder much more in common with management than with the blue-collar employee. Income based on salary rather than wages further weakens the potential bonds between the two submanagerial classes. Nor, clearly, can the sheer fact that society generally looks down upon manual work and places its premium upon mentally challenging employment be disregarded in explaining the superiority complex of the white-collarite.

In an economy such as ours—where for most people the more basic needs have now been relatively well satisfied—the role of such status considerations can be considerable. To ask the white-collar worker to identify by unionization with the steel worker, automobile assembly-line employee, truck driver, and hod carrier—and to follow in the traditions of Samuel Gompers, John L. Lewis, Sidney Hillman, and Philip Murray (to say nothing of Jimmy Hoffa and Tony Boyle)—is consequently, by its very nature, no small undertaking.

b. However tenuous it may be, the white-collar worker can at least perceive some opportunity to advance into managerial ranks, whereas the blue-collar employee is typically limited in his most optimistic advancement goal to the "gray area" of the foremanship. Unlike the wearer of the white collar, the blue-collar worker senses (usually quite accurately) that educa-

---

[16]Wilfrid Sheed, "What Has Happened to the Labor Movement?" *The Atlantic*, July 1973, p. 69.

tional and social deficiencies have combined to limit his promotional avenues within the industrial world, and he can adjust to the fact that he is permanently destined to be apart from and directed by the managerial class. Since such a fate is often not nearly as clear to the white-collar worker (partially for the reasons cited in the previous paragraphs), he is understandably more reluctant to join the ranks of unionism and thus support what is potentially a major constraint on employer freedom of action.

c. The considerably higher proportion of women in white-collar work than in blue-collar work has served as a dampening force for organization. By and large, women have always been notoriously poor candidates for unionism. In many cases, the job is thought of as temporary—either pre-marital or to supplement the family breadwinner's paycheck (often on a sporadic basis)—and, consequently, the union's argument of long-run job security has had little appeal.[17] In other cases—perhaps as high as 25 percent at the time of this writing—the job is a part-time one, also to the detriment of the union organizer. Nor can the labor movement's traditional aura of militant masculinity be eliminated as a possible causal factor in explaining the female response to organizational attempts, although here one moves wholly into the realm of speculation.

d. Finally, many white-collar workers with professional identifications—engineers, college professors, and institutionally employed doctors, for example—continue to believe that for them there is still much more to be gained from individual bargaining with their employer than from any form of collective bargaining. Viewing the latter as an automatic opponent of individual merit rewards, they tend to perceive the relatively few unionists within their professions as either mediocrities in need of such group support, or masochists.

SOME GROUNDS FOR UNION OPTIMISM

If it is thus tempting to begin sounding the death knell for the labor movement on the grounds that its failure to penetrate the critical Collar Frontier can be explained by a combination of factors that seem to be at least collectively insurmountable, realism dictates that several other factors also be pondered. And these additional considerations can lead one to an entirely different conclusion regarding the future of organized labor in the white-collar area.

1. The same newsprint, television, and radio announcements that have brought news of union misdoings to the white-collar population have also

---

[17]As Kassalow points out, this can further work against unionism by making the promotional chances of the more stable male white-collar employees that much more visible to them. See Everett M. Kassalow, "New Union Frontier: White Collar Workers," *Harvard Business Review*, XL (January–February 1962), 41–52.

informed this primarily nonunion audience of highly impressive income improvements in the unionized sector. For example, few nonunionists are entirely unaware of the gains in the heavily organized construction sector that by 1975 were adding $3.25 per hour and more to the wages of skilled craftsmen over the next two years, or significantly more than the $2.75 to $3.50 commonly received as total hourly wages by workers in wholesale and retail trade, finance, insurance, real estate, and many other parts of the white-collar world. The imminence of a situation where soon the lowest wage for even a common laborer in the construction industry would be $16,000 or more could only have been received with considerable envy by the unrepresented insurance-company debit agent whose current earnings, despite his college degree, placed him at not much more than half this figure. And knowledge of the fact that substantial overtime opportunities at hefty premiums were also available to such unionists—as they were most frequently not to white-collar workers—could only increase the latter's flow of adrenalin.

In fairness, it must be recognized that the historically overtight labor markets and fractionalized bargaining structure of construction makes it a labor union extreme from the viewpoint of wage aggrandizement. But the kind of invidious comparisons engendered by the construction totals clearly extend to other situations. Consider, for example, the following gross average weekly earnings of nonsupervisory production workers for February 1975: petroleum and coal products, $250.28; mining, $239.10; primary metal industries, $239.00; transportation equipment, $226.20; transportation and public utilities, $225.94; machinery (except electrical), $214.24; chemicals and allied products, $207.14; ordinance and accessories, $206.82.[18] In contrast to these figures—all of which pertain to heavily unionized areas—the comparable statistic for wholesale and retail trade was $122.58 ($103.67 for retail trade alone); finance, insurance, and real estate (lumped together by the Bureau of Labor Statistics) registered $151.03; services yielded an average weekly gross earnings of $133.62; and the predominantly nonunionized "textile mill products" and "apparel and other textile products" areas showed averages of $117.78 and $104.88, respectively.[19]

Nor can the white-collar population indefinitely be expected to be indifferent to truck-driver incomes (symbolically, the *International Teamster* magazine could report some years ago that "recently a professor at ivy-covered Williams College in New England returned to the Teamsters as an over-the-road driver because he could double his salary at Williams")[20] and to various other highly remunerated (and overwhelmingly unionized) workers such as longshoremen, tool and die makers, and airline mechanics. For that matter,

[18]*Monthly Labor Review*, Vol. 98, No. 4 (April 1975), 105.
[19]*Ibid.*
[20]*International Teamster*, September 1960, p. 16.

San Francisco sanitation workers were receiving $17,000 in annual base wages alone by the mid-1970s, and even this figure was not as impressive as the $16,640 garnered by Port of New York Authority longshoremen, since the latter income—although slightly lower—was, in most cases, contractually *guaranteed.*

The responsibility for the relatively high standards of living involved here does not rest completely with unionism. Clearly, one must also examine such a variety of other factors as skill levels, industrial ability to pay, community wage structures, imperfections in the product market, and industrial productivity (among others) in explaining these wage levels. And one can readily cite such unionized areas as the New England boot and shoe industry and the meatpacking industry, where the overall situation often allows no real wage improvement at all and, consequently, none is received by organized labor.

But the hazards of accepting the more impressive union bargaining totals at their face value are not particularly relevant in this context. Misleadingly or not, such dollar amounts often symbolize in a highly visible fashion the ability of unionism to effect dramatic wage gains. And, as the gap between the incomes of the blue-collar and white-collar worlds continues to widen, a greater willingness to consider union membership may conceivably be the result. Indeed, appreciation of the fact that snobbishness neither purchases groceries nor pays the rent seems already to have accounted for some of the increased willingness of at least teachers and—by the 1970s— lower echelons of hospital work forces to undertake such a consideration.

2. The definite upsurge in unionism among government employees— although probably attributable far more to enabling legislation at not only the federal but at many state and local levels than to any pronounced rank-and-file militancy—is combining with the (lesser) emergence of collective bargaining in other white-collar areas to gradually weaken the nonmember's traditional association of organized labor with manual work. As previously inferred, the process is still an excruciatingly slow one from labor's viewpoint. But the growing presence of these higher-status, better-educated federal civil servants and state employees (to say nothing of that paragon of brainwork, the local schoolteacher and, in fact, some 80,000 college faculty members, as well as approximately 15,000 physicians at the present time) in union ranks can only be expected to erode the older images in time. Whether this psychological change will be sufficient in itself to win over more than a fraction of the untapped white-collar market for the labor movement is another question. But, certainly, one of the grounds for labor's failure until now will have been dissipated.

3. It is probably also only a question of time before considerably more aggressive, imaginative, and empathetic leadership than organized labor now possesses comes to the fore, which would also make widespread white-collar unionization far more likely.

For all of the apparent apathy and conservatism at the highest levels of labor as it entered the late 1970s, there was no dearth of people in the second and third tiers of union leadership who exhibited these more positive characteristics. Far more attuned to the aspirations and values of our increasingly sophisticated labor force than were their currently more influential colleagues, they had become more and more frustrated by labor's lack of progress in recent years (as well as, often, by the tepid responses of their own memberships to the official goals of their particular unions). They fully appreciated the necessity for an immense outpouring of financial, institutional, and personal effort in the quest for the white-collarite. And, in the best traditions of Samuel Gompers and John L. Lewis, they exhibited no lack of ideas as to how such unionization could be effected, even advocating wholly different organizational structures to attain this goal, should these become necessary. The vicissitudes of union politics clearly ensured that not all, or even many, of these men would ever actually achieve ascendancy in the labor movement. Those who would, however, would undoubtedly abet the chances of white-collar unionization.

4. Finally, the working conditions of white-collar employment are themselves now changing in a direction that may weaken both the superiority complex and pro-management proclivity of the white-collar wearer.

The very individuality of white-collar work is itself now disappearing from much of the industrial scene. An accelerating trend toward organizational bigness has already combined with the demands of technological efficiency to make cogs in vast interdependent machines of many clerks, comptometer operators, technicians, and even engineers, rather than allowing them to remain as individuals working alone or in comfortably small groups in these categories. And, as Kassalow has observed, "More and more while-collar workers are being routinized and bureaucratized. [Many] jobs in instance after instance become less interesting in the wake of modernization. The white-collar worker's relationship with his supervisor also becomes more remote; and, in most instances, he has no individual contact with the public. Further, since such large numbers are employed, there is a considerable blockage of upward mobility."[21]

In the years ahead, there will undoubtedly be many more such jobholders in the white-collar category. The advance of technology (particularly in the form of the computer, whose introduction into offices is now being conducted at an even faster rate than in factory atmospheres) will not only severely constrain much of the analytical and decision-making possibilities of the traditional "brain-workers," but will also cause considerable job uncertainty and most likely also a decrease in the economic value of job skills. The computer itself—since such equipment if idle constitutes an indefensible luxury—may even force many white-collar employees into one

[21]Kassalow, "New Union Frontier."

of the heretofore most distinguishing features of factory employment, shift work. But under any conditions, these changes will serve to alter the complacent self-image of the white-collar worker by blurring the traditionally perceived differences between the nature of his work and that of his blue-collar counterpart.

And, in such an atmosphere, it may well be that the white-collar worker's long-standing feeling of affinity with management as well as his sense of self-actualization on the job will also evaporate, to the point of rendering the white-collarite far more susceptible than he has been in the past to the overtures of the union organizer.

Thus a case can be made for either position. And while it is difficult to deny that future white-collar unionization does face great obstacles, it is probably no less advisable to hedge one's bets before writing off organized labor as an institution doomed to an ultimate slow death because, having long ago captured the now-shrinking blue-collar market, it has realized its only natural potential. If the grounds for union optimism as expressed above must necessarily remain speculative, nonetheless there are enough of them and there is sufficient logic to each of them to justify at least some amount of hopefulness on the part of the labor movement.

LABOR'S PRESENT STRATEGIC POWER

Other formidable obstacles also confront organized labor today. It is undeniable that unions have in recent years fallen from public favor, owing perhaps above all to various public exposures of corruption at the top levels of a few but nonetheless highly visible unions, and also to their own bargaining excesses. These latter topics will be discussed on subsequent pages. Here, it is relevant to note that the publicity involved, temporary or not, has cost the labor movement thousands of friends among the general public (and, presumably, in the ranks of potential union members). It has also led to restrictive federal and state legislation (summarized in Chapter 3) that in some ways can be construed as "antilabor." And, finally, labor has been handicapped to some extent by such current factors as the national trend to smaller, decentralized plants, resulting in more personalized worker treatment; industry's present tendency to locate new plants in smaller, semirural, and often Southern communities, climates not conducive to a hearty reception for the union; and the growing levels of income across the nation, stripping union promises of a "living wage" of some of their effect.

Yet, for all these adverse factors, it is still of some relevance for anyone who attempts to predict the labor movement's future that in their century and three-quarters on the American scene, unions have faced even greater obstacles than these and have ultimately surmounted them. As Chapter 2 relates, the history of U.S. labor is in many ways a study of triumph over economic, social, and political adversity.

However one views organized labor's future, its present strategic power cannot be denied. The labor movement's concentration of membership in the economy's most vital sectors has meant that the 21.8 percent of the labor force that bargains collectively has been an extremely influential minority. One may not agree with the newspaper headlines that a particular strike has "paralyzed the economy," but it appears to be an acceptable generalization that the wages or salaries and other conditions of employment for much of the remaining 78.2 percent of the labor force are regularly affected to some degree by the unionized segment.

Thus, if the exact future dimensions and membership totals of organized labor are today in some doubt, the importance of collective bargaining is not. Neither can one dispute labor's staying power, given the labor movement's deep penetration into virtually all the traditional parts of our economy and its continuing hold upon these areas. The reports of collective bargaining's death are, as Mark Twain cabled from Europe following reports of his own demise, "greatly exaggerated." And if the modern manager is unhappy with unionism, realism dictates not that he wait for it to vanish from the scene, but that he apply his efforts toward improving the collective bargaining process by which he is so likely to be directly affected.

WHY WORKERS JOIN UNIONS

Questions concerning human behavior do not lend themselves to simple answers, for the subject itself is a highly complex one. "Why do workers join unions?" clearly falls within this category.

In his widely accepted theory of motivation, however, the late psychologist A. H. Maslow has provided us with helpful hints, although the theory itself relates to the whole population of human beings rather than merely to those who have seen fit to take out union membership.[22]

Maslow portrays man (a category that presumably also encompasses "woman") as a "perpetually wanting animal," driven to put forth effort (in other words, to work) by his desire to satisfy certain of his needs. To Maslow, these needs or wants can logically be thought of in terms of a hierarchy, for only one type of need is active at any given time. Only when the lowest and most basic of the needs in this hierarchy has been relatively well satisfied will each higher need become, in turn, operative. Thus, it is the *unsatisfied* need that actively motivates man's behavior. Once a need is more or less gratified, man's conduct is determined by new, higher needs, which up until then have failed to motivate simply because man's attention has been devoted

---

[22]A H. Maslow, *Motivation and Personality* (New York: Harper & Row, 1954). Much of Maslow's concept was originally presented in his article "A Theory of Human Motivation," *Psychological Review*, L (1943), pp. 370–96. See also Douglas McGregor, *The Human Side of Enterprise* (New York: McGraw-Hill, 1960), pp. 36–39, for an excellent restatement of Maslow's theory.

to satisfying his more pressing, lower needs. And the process is for most mortals unending, since few people can ever expect to satisfy, even minimally, all their needs.

At the lowest level in this Need Hierarchy, but paramount in importance until they are satisfied, are the *physiological* needs, particularly those for food, water, clothing, and shelter. "Man lives by bread alone, when there is no bread"; in other words, any higher needs he may have are inoperative when he is suffering from extreme hunger, for man's full attention must then necessarily be focused on this single need. But when the need for food and the other physiological essentials is fairly well satisfied, less basic or higher needs in the hierarchy start to dominate man's behavior, or to motivate him.

Thus, needs for *safety*—for protection against arbitrary deprivation, danger, and threat—take over as prime human motivators once man is eating regularly and sufficiently and is adequately clothed and sheltered. This is true because (1) a satisfied need is no longer a motivator of behavior, yet (2) man continues to be driven by needs, and (3) the safety needs are the next most logical candidates, beyond the physiological ones, to do this driving.

What happens when the safety needs have also been relatively satisfied, so that both the lowest need levels no longer require man's attention? In Maslow's scheme of things, the *social* needs—for belonging, association, and acceptance by one's fellows—now are dominant, and man puts forth effort to satisfy *this* newly activated type of want.

Still higher needs that ultimately emerge to dominate man's consciousness, always assuming that the needs below them have been gratified, are in turn *self-esteem* needs, especially for self-respect and self-confidence; *status* needs, for recognition, approval, and prestige; and finally, *self-fulfillment* needs, for realization of one's own potential and for being as creative as possible.

All this constitutes an oversimplification of Maslow's Need Hierarchy. Maslow himself qualified his concept in several ways, although only one of his reservations is important enough for our purposes to warrant inclusion here: He recognized that not all people follow the pattern depicted, and that both desires and satisfactions vary with the individual.

Even in the capsule form presented above, however, Maslow's contribution is of aid in explaining why workers join unions. The many research findings that now exist on this latter topic[23] basically agree that all employees endeavor to gratify needs and wants that are important to them, because of

---

[23]Perhaps the best of these studies are E. Wight Bakke, "To Join or Not To Join," in E. Wight Bakke, Clark Kerr, and Charles W. Anrod, eds., *Unions, Management and the Public* (New York: Harcourt Brace Jovanovich, 1960), pp. 79–85; Joel Seidman, Jack London, and Bernard Karsh, "Why Workers Join Unions," in *The Annals of the American Academy of Political and Social Science*, 274: 84 (March 1951); and Ross Stagner, ed., *Psychology of Industrial Conflict* (New York: John Wiley, 1956).

dissatisfaction with the extent to which these needs and desires have been met. They also agree that, while what is "important" among these needs and wants varies with the individual employee, much of the answer depends upon what has already been satisfied either within the working environment or outside it. Many of these studies also support Maslow's hierarchy for the majority of workers in approximately the order of needs indicated by Maslow.

It should not be surprising that dissatisfaction with the extent of physiological need gratification is no longer a dominant reason for joining unions in this country. In our relatively affluent economy, few people who are working have any great difficulty in satisfying at least the most basic of these needs. In an earlier day, before the advent of minimum wage laws and other forms of legal protection, this was not as true and, as has already been suggested, union promises of a "living wage" were of great appeal to many workers. However, those members of the labor force who today are frustrated in trying to satisfy their minimal needs for food, clothing, and shelter are those who are *unemployed*, not the most logical candidates for union membership. The research substantiates this down-playing of the role of physiological needs rather conclusively. Significantly, one of the most thorough of the studies found that not one employee out of 114 workers in a large industrial local union became a union member primarily for this purpose.[24] (This is hardly to say that union members have lost interest in higher wages and other economic improvements. As will be shown later, the desire for these benefits persists as strongly as ever. The point is, however, that this desire now stems from higher need activation. Money can satisfy more than just the physiological needs.)

On the other hand, research suggests that dissatisfaction with the extent of gratification of (1) safety, (2) social, and (3) self-esteem needs— in approximately that order—has motivated many workers to join unions. To a lesser extent, status and self-fulfillment needs have also led to union membership.

Unions are uniquely equipped, in the eyes of thousands of workers, to gratify safety needs. If very few of the 150,000 labor–management contracts currently in force in the United States are identical, at least this much can be said for virtually all of them: They are generally arrived at through *compromise*, and they define in writing the "rules of the game" that have been *mutually agreed upon* to cover the terms and conditions of employment of *all* represented workers for a specific future period of time. The union thus acts as an equal partner in the bilateral establishment of what the late Sumner H. Slichter called the "system of industrial jurisprudence." And in the interests of minimizing conflict among the workers it represents, it strives to inject uniformity of treatment—particularly in the area of job protection—into the contract.

[24]Seidman, London, and Karsh, "Why Workers Join Unions."

Union membership can consequently provide workers with some assurance against arbitrary management actions. The union can be expected to push for curbs against what it calls "management discrimination and favoritism" in, for example, job assignment, promotional opportunity, and even continued employment with the company. However well-meaning are a management's intentions, the company cannot guarantee that it will not at times act arbitrarily, for in the absence of such checks as the union places on its actions, it is always acting unilaterally. Satisfaction of the safety needs—in the form of considerable protection against arbitrary deprivation, danger, and threat—is thus offered by the union in its stress on uniformity of treatment for all workers. Many employees, particularly after they have perceived "arbitrary" action by management representatives, have found the appeal irresistible.

The social needs are also known to be important, if secondary, motivators of union membership. Especially where the work itself must be performed in geographically scattered locations (as in many forms of railroad employment, truck driving, or letter-carrying) or where the technology of the work minimizes on-the-job social interaction (as on the automobile assembly line), the local union can serve the function of a club, allowing the formation of close friendships built around a common purpose. But even when the work is not so structured, local unions foster a feeling of identification with those of like interests, often in pronounced contrast to the impersonality of the large organization in which the worker may be employed. Increasingly, unions have capitalized upon their ability to help satisfy social needs. As the latter have become more important to members of the labor force (not only because of the declining frustration of the lower needs but also because general leisure time has increased) unions have become increasingly ambitious in sponsoring such activities as vacation retreats, athletic facilities, and adult education programs "for members only." But unions have never been reluctant to publicize the social bonds they allow: It is not by accident that internal union correspondence has traditionally been closed by the greeting "Fraternally yours," that the official titles of many unions have always included the word "Brotherhood," and that several labor organizations continue to refer to their local unions as "lodges."

Social *pressure* has also been instrumental in causing workers to join unions. Employees often admit that the disapproval of their colleagues would result from their not signing union application cards. Normally, the disapproval is only implied. The Seidman, London, and Karsh study, for example, unearthed such explanations from workers who had joined unions as, "I can't think of a good reason, except everybody else was in it," and, "I suppose I joined in order to jump in line with the majority." On occasion, however, the pressure has been considerably more visible, as witness this quotation from the same study: "They approached you, kept after you, hounded you. To get them off my neck, I joined."

Other workers, at higher levels, have explained their union membership as being attributable mainly to their desire to ensure that they will have a direct voice, through union election procedures, in decisions that affect them in their working environment. Such employees tend to participate actively in union affairs and to use rather freely such phrases as, "I wanted to have a voice in the system." The underlying rationale of this behavior is a clear one: Managements do not normally put questions relating to employment conditions to worker vote; unions, however imperfectly, purport to be democratic institutions. To these workers, representation by a labor organization has appeared to offer the best hope in our complex, interdependent, and ever-larger-unit industrial society that their human dignity will not be completely crushed. On this basis, self-esteem needs can, at least to some extent, be appeased.

Finally, a relatively few other employees have found in the union an opportunity for realization of their highest needs—for status and self-fulfillment. They have joined with the hope of gaining and retaining positions of authority within the union officer hierarchy. For the employee with leadership ambitions, but with educational or other deficiencies that would otherwise condemn him to a life of prestige-lacking and unchallenging work, opportunities for further need satisfaction are thus provided.

Unionization, then, results from a broad network of worker needs. The needs for safety, social affiliation, and, to a lesser extent, self-esteem appear to be of primary importance to employees in contemporary America. And it would appear that these needs are being relatively well met by unions, or workers would have exercised their legally granted option of voting out unions in far greater measure than they have done.

This in no way minimizes the role of money and other economic benefits, for these emoluments—which unions have not been reluctant to seek, even with their members' incomes at today's high levels—are clearly related to needs beyond the physiological. Health insurance and pensions lend protection against deprivation, for example, and wages themselves can increase not only safety but status. But it does emphasize the roles of protection against arbitrary treatment, formal group affiliation beyond the framework of the company, and—for some workers—an opportunity for participation in "the system." By definition, management can never itself satisfy either of the first two worker needs. Thus far, in unionized establishments, it has failed to satisfy employees on the last ground.

Two final remarks are in order. First, it has often been hypothesized that many workers join unions for *none* of the reasons cited above, but simply because they work where union membership is required for continued employment after their probationary period (the so-called "union shop" arrangement). Although it is undeniable that some workers do join for this reason, the facts do not support the belief that they are numerous. Beginning in 1947, the American labor laws provided that only if a majority of workers in the bargaining unit voted for the union shop in a secret-ballot election supervised by the government would such a shop be permitted in a labor contract. In the next four years, 46,000 elections were held: 97 percent of them favored the union shop and 91 percent of the workers eligible to vote voted in favor of the arrangement. In 1951, the election provision was repealed as a waste of the taxpayer's money.

Second, although an explanation of why workers join unions can be reduced (as was done here) to relatively uncomplicated statements, for a specific worker the motivations may be considerably more involved, even encompassing several levels of need satisfaction at once. The summary offered, if the research on which it is based is valid, is sufficiently accurate to meet our own needs. By the same token, however, unionization is at times derived from a variety of complex variables, and complete understanding of it must therefore necessarily rest on a situational foundation.

WHY MANAGERS RESIST UNIONS

Some time ago, after years of successfully withstanding union organization attempts, a small-scale New York City dress manufacturer discovered that a majority of his workers had finally become union members. Immediately thereafter, these employees struck for increased job security and improved pension benefits. On the very first morning of the strike, the manufacturer's wife—who was also the firm's bookkeeper—reported to work at her customary hour of 8 A.M. She was amazed to see her husband out on the picket line, addressing the strikers as follows: "Sam, you stand over there; Harry, you stand eight yards in back of Sam; and Leo, you come over here, eight yards behind Harry." The puzzled woman posed the natural question, "Jack, what on earth are you doing?" And the manufacturer replied, "I want they should right away know who's boss!"

The outcome of this particular labor–management struggle is unknown. But the episode nonetheless furnishes a clue as to one reason why managers are considerably less than enthusiastic about unions. As we have already seen, collective bargaining necessarily decreases the area of management discretion. Every contractual concession to the union subtracts from the scope that the company has for taking action on its own. As Bakke put it, in his classic study of many years ago but in words that are every bit as relevant today, "A union is an employer-regulating device. It seeks to regulate the discretion of employers . . . at every point where their action affects the welfare of the men."[25] Yet it is the manager who tends ultimately to be held responsible for the success or failure of the business, and not the union. Hence, company representatives feel it essential that they reserve for them-

[25]E. Wight Bakke, *Mutual Survival: The Goal of Unions and Management* (New York: Harper & Row, 1946), p. 7.

selves the authority to make all major decisions, including those the union might construe to be "affecting the welfare of the men." In short, they feel that they must still be allowed to remain, on all counts, "the boss."

Managers tend to be quite adamant on the subject. One company representative's thoughts are illustrative:

> Restriction on management freedom is a big issue. . . . We've got heavy responsibilities for making quick, accurate, and effective decisions. Sometimes there are considerations that we can't divulge or that wouldn't be understood if we did. We're held responsible for the success of them, but the union isn't. It takes complicated maneuvering to run a business, and all the parts have to be kept working together. You have to have a good deal of free play in the rope for that. Sometimes there is a particular restriction that gets your goat, but on the whole it's the overall sense of being closed in on . . . that gets you. It's the cumulative effect of one area of freedom after another being reduced and the promise of still more that gives us real concern, but you make adjustments and go on to every particular one. It's not impossible, but you wonder how long it can go on and leave you able to meet your responsibilities.[26]

Behind such remarks as these is a managerial awareness, continuously reinforced for all administrators of profit-making institutions by day-to-day realities, that management hardly owes its exclusive allegiance to its employees. Clearly, employee needs are important and, for that matter, can be ignored for any length of time only with complete disregard for the continued solvency of the enterprise. But exactly the same can be said of the pressures exerted on management by the firm's customers, stockholders, competitors, and suppliers. Were those pressures not opposing ones, management's job would be far easier than it is. But because there are so many points of conflict, an aggressive union can make the managerial role a highly difficult one.

The desire to retain decision-making authority is by no means, however, strictly attributable to a managerial desire for peace of mind. Unions undoubtedly do add to the personal unhappiness and consequent morale problems of managers, but the resistance to unionism is often based also on a genuine and deep concern for the welfare of society. Countless managers believe that only if management remains free to operate without union-imposed restrictions can American business continue to advance. And only through such progress, they believe, can it provide employment for our rapidly growing labor force, let this nation compete successfully in world markets, and increase general living standards. By decreasing company flexibility (in the form of work-method controls, decreased work loads, increased stress on the seniority criterion in the allocation of manpower, and various other ways), it is argued, unions endanger the efficiency upon which continued industrial progress depends. And this is no less true, managers contend, just because these union demands are made in the name of such euphemistic goals as "job security," "equitability," and "democracy in the workplace."

[26]*Ibid.*, p. 29.

A related employer fear is also held by many managers, although it is understandably given somewhat less publicity by them than is the previous argument. Such company representatives feel that in the absence of management's unhampered freedom to manage, the optimum utilization of manpower will be lost to society. This argument assumes that there are strong elements of a process of natural selection at work in the industrial world and that, admittedly with some exceptions, those who rise to levels of great authority within it are those who have proved that they are best equipped to hold such places. Any attempt to undercut this authority—on the part of, for example, labor unions—consequently makes society the poorer.

On four different grounds, then—(1) that the manager must be allowed authority commensurate with his responsibility, (2) that unchecked union pressures may totally frustrate the manager in his role as the recipient of cross-pressures from many other institutional and market forces, (3) that unions limit company flexibility and thus endanger economic progress, and (4) that only by allowing managers maximum opportunity to manage is society furnished with an optimum allocation of manpower—union inroads are typically resisted by management. There is, however, a common denominator to all four: Each argument seeks to ward off encroachments on management's *decision-making* powers.

Admittedly, even in the absence of unionism, management's ability to make decisions in the employee-relations area is not an unlimited one. A widespread network of federal, state, and community legislation now governs minimum wages, hours of work, discrimination, safety and health, and a host of other aspects of employee life with complete impartiality as to whether or not the regulated firms are organized or nonunion. Moreover, where employers encounter tight labor markets (those in which new employees are difficult to recruit), they tend to accommodate at least their more visible personnel practices—wages and other economic benefits, in particular—to what the market demands. Finally, the prevalent values of our times must always be considered. The mores of society have an important influence on employers. And it is a hallmark of our ever more sophisticated society that workers expect to be governed by progressive personnel policies that are based on objective standards whenever possible. Most nonunion firms have attempted to conform to these values no less actively than have most unionized enterprises.

The fact remains, however, that managers who are not bound by the restrictions of labor agreements, and who do not have to anticipate the possibility of their every action in the employee relations sphere being challenged by worker representatives through the grievance procedure, have considerably more latitude for decision making than do their counterparts at unionized companies. One need not in any way sympathize with the management fear of unionism to understand this fear. Given the importance of the decision-making prerogative to managements, the managerial resistance to labor organizations—whether it stems directly from management self-interest or from a concern for the welfare of society—can at least be appreciated.

If the previous paragraphs help to explain the major reasons for management's jaundiced view of the labor union, they do not acknowledge other reasons that frequently bolster this view. There are, undoubtedly, several such reasons.

In the first place, many employers tend to look upon the union as an *outsider*, with no justifiable basis for interfering in the relationship between the company and its employees. The local union, with which the firm is most apt to engage in direct dealings, typically represents workers of many competitive companies, and hence by definition it cannot have the best interests of any particular firm at heart. Worse yet, runs this charge, the local is often part of a large, geographically distant international union, by which it is closely controlled, and thus is not allowed to give adequate consideration to unique problems within its locality.[27] Beyond this, the union (whether local, international, or some intermediate body) has objectives and aspirations that are very different from those of the particular company: Where the company seeks to maximize profits within certain limits, the union seeks such goals as the maximization of its own membership and of its general bargaining power. These are objectives that the company can at best greet with apathy and at worst (when the pursuit of such goals is "subsidized" by the company in the form of its own concessions to the union) can view only with unhappiness.

Second, the manager may look upon the union as a *trouble-maker*, bent upon building cleavages between management and workers where none would otherwise exist. Even aside from the previously noted fact that the union grievance procedure allows all management actions affecting areas delineated in the labor contract to be challenged, and therefore regularly provides an opportunity for controversy that is normally absent in nonunion situations, there is some truth in this charge. Particularly where the union occupies an insecure status in the plant (possibly in the absence, for example, of the union shop), its leaders may find it essential to solicit grievances in order to keep the employees willing to pay union dues. But even where the labor organization does have such security, grievances may still be encouraged by union officials. Slichter, Healy, and Livernash pinpoint several possibilities:

> The purpose may be to harass management into accepting interpretations of the agreement that the union wants; or the purpose may be to develop a militant attitude among the members to help the union in negotiating new con-

---

[27]Not all employers lament the "outside" aspects of unionization. Many prefer the more detached viewpoints of international union representatives who *are* removed from the tensions and political considerations involved in day-by-day local labor relations. Some managers welcome, in addition, the stabilization of labor terms among otherwise competitive employers that frequently accompanies wider-scale bargaining.

tracts. Some union representatives may stir up grievances . . . in an effort to advance their political fortunes within the union or to build up interest in it. Finally, elected stewards or committeemen may lack the independence to handle weak cases.[28]

Third, many managers view unions as *underminers of employee loyalty* to the company. In order to understand this point of view, one does not have to fully embrace the philosophy that high worker motivation levels depend upon appreciative employees who view the employer as a benefactor and work for him to a great extent out of gratitude. It is sufficient for the reader to imagine the reactions of any employer who has prided himself on providing good wages and working conditions and showing a personal concern for the individual problems of his employees (perhaps tangibly evidenced by the voluntary payment of medical expenses to meet health emergencies and unsolicited loans to meet other financial crises) upon learning that a majority of his work force has suddenly decided to "go union." This employer may use such epithets as "ingrates" in speaking of his own employees, but it is more likely that the union itself will bear the brunt of his censure. It is human nature to attribute one's defeats to forces beyond one's own control ("an irresponsible union misleading our employees and turning them against the company") rather than to factors looked upon as controllable ("employee attitudes"). The previously cited fact that management can *never* itself provide either full protection against arbitrary treatment or formal group affiliation independent of the company is overlooked by company representatives at such moments. So, too, is a silver lining in the situation—namely, that it is entirely possible for workers to have dual loyalties, to the union *and* to the company.[29] In at least the early stages of the union–management relationship, unions may be resisted for having subverted employee allegiance fully as much as they are opposed on the other grounds that have been noted.

A fourth root of tension, although it is applicable to only a minority of company executives, may arise simply because the previously discussed *reputation* of the labor movement has preceded the arrival of unionism in the plant. This has been a particularly influential factor in the resistance of some managers to collective bargaining in the recent past. Not being forced to deal with a union until now, and, primarily because of this freedom,

[28]Slichter, Healy, and Livernash, *The Impact of Collective Bargaining*, p. 40.

[29]The most exhaustive study on the subject of "dual loyalties" is that of Father Theodore Purcell, conducted in the mid-1950s. Interviewing 202 workers in various departments at Swift and Company, he discovered that whereas at least 79 percent felt a definite allegiance to the union as an institution, 92 percent felt allegiance to the company. "Allegiance" was construed as an attitude of approval of the overall objectives of each institution, rather than strict loyalty. See Theodore V. Purcell, *Blue Collar Man* (Cambridge, Mass.: Harvard University Press, 1960); and also *The Worker Speaks His Mind on Company and Union* (Cambridge: Harvard University Press, 1953), by the same author. More recently, a 1975 poll of several thousand Burlington Northern Railroad employees (made in this case by the management itself) showed that workers with a "favorable attitude" toward their union also had a favorable attitude toward their boss, to a very large extent.

knowing little more about labor unions than they have been told by the mass media, such relatively unsophisticated employers have been alarmed by the widely publicized reports of irresponsible union strikes, union-leader criminality, and featherbedding charges that have found their way onto newspaper front pages and television screens over the past decade. These managers have asked, in effect, "How can you expect us to welcome an institution whose representatives engage in such activities?"

Fifth, and rounding out the list of major causes of the corporate executive's opposition to organized labor, are the *major values of the labor movement* as these are perceived by management. Some of these values—a stress on seniority, work-method controls, and decreased work loads—have already been mentioned in the context of "threats to decision making." There are, however, many other such shared union values that rankle management at least as much.

"Security," for example, has far more favorable connotations to unionists than it does to company representatives. Higher managers by definition have a history of successful achievement behind them and hence are willing to take chances because they are relatively optimistic as to the outcome. The average union member, feeling that the probabilities of his success in risk-taking are low, and, indeed, often believing that he is running in a race that is fixed, presses the union leadership to obtain even greater protection for him in his *current* job.

"Democracy" is a hallmark of the union value structure, and union representatives who bargain with managements are usually elected through a process that at least claims to be democratic. Managers, whose hierarchy is based on merit and experience, are thus forced to bargain, often on issues with major ramifications for the company, with unionists who may have no better credentials for their role than the possession of a plurality of votes in a popularity poll.

And where the company representative speaks glowingly of "individualism" and declares that America's economic triumphs have been based upon it, the union sees itself as part of a social movement and places a premium on "group consciousness."

As for "efficiency," which scores high on the management scale of values, to the union it smacks of a callous disregard for worker dignity and even worker health. Accordingly, it is something to be regarded with deep suspicion by employee representatives and to be resisted whenever resistance is practicable.

Such comments as those above, as with our treatment of "Why Workers Join Unions," can be offered only as generalizations. For a specific union–management relationship, the value differences may hardly be as pronounced; the writers are personally familiar, for that matter, with several relationships in which the unions seem to place far higher values on ability and efficiency than do the managements. Such value conflicts as the ones enumerated are, however, quite genuine in many union–management situations, and thus represent the realities of labor relations rather than its stereotypes. As such, they serve to reinforce management's opposition to unionism, however much this opposition may be anchored to such other reasons as the decision-making issue.[30]

MANAGEMENT PHILOSOPHIES TOWARD UNIONS

Given the many different roots of management opposition and the pervasiveness of so many of these, it is tempting to speculate that, deep in their corporate hearts, the basic attitude of most business enterprises must be one of intransigent hostility. Were this presumed attitude, in other words, to be stated as an official policy, it would read approximately, "We seek to weaken organized labor by any and all means at our command, to frustrate it in its demands, to grant it nothing that is not absolutely necessary, and under no circumstances to make any attempt at accepting the union as a permanent part of our employee relations. If we adhere to this approach consistently and with sufficient patience, our workers will see that the union offers them nothing. And they will ultimately arise and vote the union out at least as enthusiastically as they have voted it in."

There can be no denying that some executives do espouse this policy, and that at an earlier time in American labor history, many managers did so. The irony of contemporary labor relations, however, is that despite management's continuing opposition to unionism and its constant resistance to new labor inroads, much of the employer community has substantially departed from such a provocative stance. It has moved instead to what Professor Lloyd Reynolds of Yale has called a "defensive endurance" philosophy: "If this is what our workers want, I guess we'll have to go along with it." In a word, the union is *accommodated*, however unwelcome and even unpalatable its presence may be. Management remains ever on guard as to "matters of principle," seeks to prevent the union from "intruding" in areas that are "the proper function of management," and frequently is highly critical of certain union actions. *But* the labor organization is taken for granted, harmony with it is sought wherever possible, and the employer can deal with the union on a day-by-day basis without feeling that conciliation has made him a traitor to his class. When one speaks of "maturity" in labor relations, he is frequently thinking of this rapidly growing managerial posture—and organized labor's reciprocation of it.

A specific union–management relationship even in the late 1970s, however, need not necessarily be marked by *either* employer attitude depicted

[30]To this list of why employers resist unionization, some managers would probably add *status*: It is, in certain management circles, quite a mark of distinction to be able to keep a union out. Such a reason is, however, somewhat less visible than are the ones outlined in the body of this section.

above. Variety is still the essence of our labor relations system, and so many variables can influence management policies that it is unrealistic to assume that the only possibilities are (1) intransigence and (2) accommodation. Variations in the abilities of managers to accurately understand the membership goals and leadership desires of the unions with which they are dealing, and in the statesmanship with which companies have met these union aspirations—to say nothing of the nature of these goals and desires themselves—have led to a wide diversity of management positions. So, too, have variations in the managers' own relative degrees of security within the corporate framework, and the economic health of the companies involved. Obviously, variations in union attitudes may be highly relevant. And the same can be said of such other variables as the past labor relationships between the parties, the technological environments of both the industry and the employer, and even the role of the government, where this is a factor. Most of these topics will receive fuller treatment in later chapters of this book. Here it is pertinent to note the many grounds for differing attitudes toward unions among managerial groups.

Thus, although accommodation today is the dominant attitude in many relationships, having followed an era of intransigence, there are many variations on the theme of "management labor relations philosophies." And even among the more general of these different philosophies, at least six separate types (including the two above) can be distinguished.[31]

In reviewing these different possibilities for management policy, let it be clearly understood that in each case the company's ability to adopt the avenue under description depends upon a factor that is beyond its direct control: the union's own basic policy for its dealings with management. The labor organization, obviously, must reciprocate in kind, and in the absence of such reciprocation, at least in the long run, management's chosen approach becomes a completely fruitless one. In short, the company can *work toward* each of the following approaches, but this managerial project will always be subject to some modification, depending upon the union's response.

1. *Conflict,* or the intransigent, uncompromising attitude depicted previously, is now fast fading from the labor relations scene. Nonetheless, this attitude existed on a wide scale prior to World War II. Such a managerial

[31]The late Benjamin M. Selekman was justifiably considered one of the foremost theoreticians in this field, although he generally portrayed "bargaining relationships" and not merely the management portion of these relationships. The exposition that follows bears a strong indebtedness to his work (although it departs from it on several major points), and particularly to his *Labor Relations and Human Relations* (New York: McGraw-Hill, 1947); his "Varieties of Labor Relations," *Harvard Business Review,* XXVII (March 1949), 177–85; and his "Framework for Study of Cases in Labor Relations," in *Problems in Labor Relations,* 3rd ed., coauthored with S. H. Fuller, T. Kennedy, and J. M. Baitsell (New York: McGraw-Hill, 1964), pp. 1–11. See also Frederick H. Harbison and John R. Coleman, *Goals and Strategy in Collective Bargaining* (New York: Harper & Row, 1951).

stance arose to a great extent because many companies were newly organized before that time, and because union organizational campaigns have never been notable for their sensitivity to personal feelings. As Selekman has stated:

> The [union] organizers dramatize and make tangible [their] appeals . . . by personifying whatever stands in the way of these objectives as enemies who must be fought. . . .
>
> The organizer will of course make full use of the actual executives and supervisors in the plant if their past behavior affords substance for the antagonism he is mobilizing. But he will also evoke hostility by stereotyped images of "the other side." Behind any employer, for instance, the average worker is made to see the so-called "profit maker" . . . , the inhuman corporate "interests" generally, or just the harsh figure of authority. . . . Employers who have long prided themselves upon fair dealing with their men only to be shaken by hostility thus unexpectedly turned toward them should probably realize that they too have been temporarily assimilated into these hate images or symbols.[32]

The union, consequently, does more than "undermine employee loyalty to the company" at such a time; it frequently goes well beyond the borders of the factual and bruises management egos in the process. Add managerial fears of decision-making encroachments and of union values that are antithetical to those of management, as well as the other grounds for management's opposition to unionism on top of such an emotion-charged atmosphere, and it should not be surprising that many companies in the period immediately following their unionization embraced a philosophy of "no acceptance" of the union. Only in the face of the law and union power could unions extract concessions from such managements, and then only quite begrudgingly and on as temporary a basis as possible.

Some companies and an ever-growing number of public servants are, of course, even today among the newly organized, since new union conquests hardly ended with the unionization of the major mass-production industries in the 1933–41 period. And it is in the labor relations of these, indeed, that one is most apt today to encounter the conflict philosophy. But this managerial attitude is not confined to new bargaining relationships: A minority of long-organized companies also currently adheres to it, owing to changes in management personnel, changes in union personnel, or various other factors—including the particular management's sheer refusal to abandon the hope that if unions are never really accepted by their companies, they will eventually also lose acceptance from their worker-members. In recent years, various newspaper publishers throughout the country have seemed, to many observers, to epitomize this latter situation. So, too, have the owners and operators in the world of organized professional sports, most particularly baseball.

---

[32]Selekman, *Labor Relations and Human Relations*, p. 20.

Such an attitude does not lead to amicable labor relations. It can also be expected to foster union militancy, as the union reacts by engaging in various pressure tactics (often including slowdowns of production and sudden "wildcat" strikes) to gain through these means what it cannot hope to procure at the bargaining table. Finally, managements embracing a conflict philosophy run a decided risk of being found in violation of the labor laws, particularly those involving "refusal to bargain" and discrimination against employees for the purpose of discouraging membership in a union.

It is primarily for these reasons that many conflict philosophies have either been dismissed as realistic management alternatives in the first place, or given way to:

2. An *Armed Truce* attitude. Here, company representatives are motivated by approximately the following logic: "We are well aware that the vital interests of the company and the union are poles apart, and that they always will be. But this doesn't mean that every action we take in our labor relations should be geared to weakening the union and thus forcing head-on conflict with it. Instead, since we can expect the union to firmly press to extend its fields of interest, our basic mission is to press, just as ambitiously, toward containing it within limits. We will honor the law immaculately, and therefore deal with the union without any subterfuges on the subjects of wages, hours, and conditions of employment; but we will hold our bargaining practice strictly within the boundaries of these legal obligations, and thus define our negotiation scope as rigidly as possible. Moreover, we will interpret any agreements emerging from these negotiations strictly and insist upon the union's observing, in its day-to-day conduct, its contractual obligations 100 percent."

Even today, many union–management relationships have made no more progress than this. The union representatives return the feelings of their management counterparts, and the struggle for power goes on indefinitely. Wages, hours, and other rigidly construed employee-relations areas are dealt with as their issues arise, but the more crucial question of union security versus management rights, being insoluble in such an atmosphere, continually blocks more constructive dealings. With some justification, the General Electric Company is frequently regarded as an excellent example of a company that has espoused this Armed Truce philosophy.

3. *Power Bargaining*, as an alternative, is only slightly more conducive to solving labor relations problems than is the Armed Truce approach. As is *not* the case under either Conflict or Armed Truce, managers in Power Bargaining can "accept" the union and, in fact, tend to pride themselves on their sense of "realism," which leaves them no choice but to acknowledge the union's power. (A prerequisite for this philosophy, obviously, is that the union *have* significant power.) By the same token, such executives press their own company's bargaining power to the maximum that economic and other

conditions at any one time allow. To paraphrase Selekman, the managerial rationale is: "We face strong and deeply entrenched unions squarely and with an accurate perception of their power—and we accept them as sovereign spokesmen for their side. We are practical men and economic realists, not crusaders with a naïve faith in idealistic trimmings. Our task is not to pursue the fruitless approach of directly opposing and limiting the union, but to increase and then use our own power to offset that of the other side where we can."

Might does not necessarily make right, but it can lead to agreement at the bargaining table. And on this basis it can be argued that continued controversy is minimized in Power Bargaining. However unenthusiastically, managements in such a relationship can live with their unions, for at least the short run, in most areas affecting employee relations.

On the other hand, any relationship focused upon a balance of power is a highly tenuous one. It always contains the danger of regression to one of the earlier approaches when the power ratios change. As such, Power Bargaining has not been widespread at any one time in American labor relations, although many industries marked by small employers and highly centralized unions have at one time or another seen it. In such cases, the employers have typically associated in an attempt at a united front to counter the union's strength.

In short, for the reasons indicated, most managements in the current economy view all three previous alternatives as unsatisfactory. Since, needless to say, their unions wholeheartedly agree with them on this point, the climate for a more harmonious relationship—in the form of Accommodation—exists.

4. *Accommodation*, however, is hardly the same as cooperation. As pointed out earlier, management remains constantly vigilant as to "principle" and, as does the union, clings to such values as "orbits of respective equities and privileges." In this regard, Accommodation differs little from Armed Truce. Moreover, the management gaze is still riveted upon the traditional agenda of collective bargaining—wages, hours, and conditions of employment—and there is a self-conscious employer unwillingness to *officially* discuss anything that cannot rather rigidly be construed as falling within these topics.

The property of Accommodation that makes it unique lies in the area of everyday practice rather than in formal declarations. Once again, Dr. Selekman has provided a definitive description—in this case, of what results in daily affairs when a management philosophy of "meeting the union halfway" is reciprocated by the labor organization:

> ... Within these bounds [of "principles," "equities," and "privileges"] the leaders, the ranks, and the organizations ... interact within comfortable, "customary," familiar patterns of behavior. They have evolved their routines of

> recognizing functions and settling differences. They have learned how to adjust one to another . . . , to accept the reduction of conflict as an accomplishment without demanding its total elimination. They have proved themselves willing to . . . conciliate whenever necessary, and to tolerate at all times.[33]

Note that such a definition in no way implies that the company need go out of its way to *help* organized labor. For that matter, opposition to the concept of unionism in general may still remain the hallmark of management's philosophy, as it frequently does. In an atmosphere of Accommodation, however, the roles of both emotion and raw power are minimized, in favor of the company's *adjusting* to the union *as it is*. Extreme legalism in at least the basic areas of wages, hours, and conditions is supplanted by compromise, flexibility, and "toleration." As such, Accommodation constitutes a considerably more positive approach to labor relations than do any of the previous alternatives.

There is ample evidence that the mainstream of American management has today entered the Accommodation stage in its dealings with unions. The process of adjustment is still, as Slichter, Healy, and Livernash point out in their authoritative study, "neither complete nor uniform": Mutual accommodation of the parties' goals and policies has gone farthest in such areas as employee benefits, discipline, work scheduling, and development of grievance procedures, and least far in the areas of production standards, promotion principles, work assignment, and subcontracting.[34] And, not surprisingly, there is still wide variation in the nature and quality of contract administration among companies, and even among plants within the same company. But the growth of Accommodation has quite visibly resulted in the significant development of mutually acceptable policy and in more orderly day-to-day union–management relations, results that even the great diversity of labor relations cannot obscure.

To show how far the Accommodation relationship can go to promote the mutual benefit of all concerned, one need only refer to a dramatic development in the basic steel industry. In the spring of 1973, the basic steel corporations and the United Steelworkers of America agreed that the 1974 contract negotiations would be terminated *without a strike*.[35] Instead of a strike, they agreed that any issue not settled by the parties in collective bargaining would be submitted to final and binding arbitration. Note that this development resulted as the voluntary creation of the parties and was not imposed by the government. What is of material importance is that the negotiators settled all issues, and no arbitration took place! In commenting

---

[33]Selekman, Fuller, Kennedy, and Baitsell, *Problems in Labor Relations*, p. 7.

[34]Slichter, Healy, and Livernash, *The Impact of Collective Bargaining*, p. 958.

[35]For a detailed description of the program, see AFL-CIO, *American Federationist*, July 1973, pp. 1–7.

on the success of the experiment, I.W. Abel, president of the union, stated:

> The Experimental Negotiating Agreement (ENA), utilized in the negotiations
> with the 10 major basic steel companies, proved so successful that it was decided
> by both sides to use the new bargaining procedure in the 1977 negotiations.
> ENA, in short, did what it was designed to do and what we hoped it would
> do—prevent the "boom–bust" cycles that plagued past basic steel talks and
> employment following peaceful settlements.[36]

5. *Cooperation*, involving full acceptance of the union as an active
partner in a formal plan, is for exactly that reason decidedly rare. It necesi-
tates a management (as well as a union) that is willing to extend matters of
everyday union–management relations beyond the traditional areas to such
broader fields as technological change, waste, and business solvency. And
this, in turn, calls for corporate executives who genuinely believe that unions
can make definite and positive contributions to the success of the firm,
through furnishing management with information it would not otherwise
have, through winning over worker support for management goals, and in
various other ways.

In a formal plan for cooperation, the management supports not only
the right but the *desirability* of union participation, and the union recipro-
cates by actively endorsing the company's right and need for an adequate
return on its investment. The two labor relations parties *jointly* deal with
both personnel and production problems as they occur. Suggestions pertaining to cost reduction and productivity improvement are typically solicited
from all worker levels. And whatever economic gains in increased efficiency
may be realized from such cooperative projects are normally shared by the
company with the work force.

Most companies that have adopted this approach to labor relations
have, by and large, been well publicized, either as participants in rather
formalized "Scanlon Plans" or, as in the case of the Kaiser Steel Corporation, independently. But the very fact that so much publicity has been given
to these plans based on the cooperative approach graphically symbolizes
how few in number they have been thus far. Moreover, the approach is still
so incompatible with present-day management (and, often, union) value
systems that, to date, most such plans have been implemented only as a last
resort, when the company was faced with a severe financial crisis. The word
"cooperation" is frequently used in management addresses to worker groups,
but in the managers' lexicon of the 1970s, it obviously has a meaning that is
considerably more restricted than the one depicted here.

As different as each of the previous five approaches to labor relations
is from the four others, there is a common denominator: Whichever one is
selected is, subject to its ability to meet management goals, at the outset

[36]United Steelworkers of America, *Steel Labor*, December 1974.

strictly the company's business. Ultimately, a Conflict approach may lead to a strike involving government intervention, or an amassing of strength in a Power Bargaining situation may have other legal ramifications, and in any of the five cases, the union may, of course, react in such a way to make the approach unsuitable. The company can hardly do much with Accommodation if the union is Conflict-oriented. But at least at the outset, the company is perfectly free to experiment with any of the various approaches.

6. The same cannot be said of one other approach, *Collusion.* If, up until now, the enumerated management alternatives can be viewed as leading to successively more union–management harmony (from conflict on the one hand to cooperation on the other), this one can be looked upon as generating "too much harmony." Our public policy, needless to say, is designed to prevent it from serving as a workable labor relations alternative.

To Selekman, Collusion constitutes:

> . . . "cooperation" [which] generates problems that extend beyond the specific structure of relationship to affect adversely the legitimate interests of other employers, other workers, and the consuming public. For the collusive parties to collective bargaining connive to control their market, supplies, or prices, or to engage in practices of mutual interest to serve their exclusive advantage. They cooperate but through a form of jointly established monopoly which is frankly unconcerned with every legitimate interest except their own. The courts . . . and the watchfulness of competitors, rival unions, and public representatives no doubt will continue to curb these questionable deals.[37]

To such curbs might be added the sheer unwillingness of both companies and their unions, in all but a relatively few black-mark situations, to attempt such arrangements in the first place. Employer bribes to union officials to agree to substandard or "sweetheart" labor contracts and various other illegal pursuits have hardly been unknown to American labor history. But such collusion has been almost exclusively confined to narrow sectors of local-market industries, with marginal and intensely competitive employers for whom a small difference in labor cost can mean the difference between solvency and insolvency, and where visibility to the public law-enforcement agencies is relatively slight. Having named the least ethical sectors of the garment trades, building trades, trucking, waterfront, and entertainment industries, one has almost exhausted the list.

LABOR RELATIONS IN THE PUBLIC SECTOR

If the unionized percentage of the mid-1970s' total civilian labor force has registered some slippage in the past two decades, and if the figures from the overall white-collar frontier in the recent past can be described as essen-

---

[37]Selekman, Fuller, Kennedy, and Baitsell, *Problems in Labor Relations*, p. 8.

tially unchanged, organized labor can point with satisfaction to its organizational successes in the fastest-growing employment sector of all, that of the public employee.

In 1940, according to the official figures of the U.S. Department of Labor, the nation's governmental work force at all levels (federal, state, and local) numbered 4.2. million, or 9.6 percent of total payroll employment. By 1960, the figure had exactly doubled, to 8.4 million. And, rising even more dramatically when compared to overall labor force figures in the years since, it reached the 12.5-million mark by the end of the 1960s and climbed to well above 14 million (and over 18 percent of total payroll employment in the country) by 1975, with no signs of abatement at the time of this writing.

Undoubtedly, many factors explain this strong upward curve. But Loewenberg and Moskow seem to have their fingers on the foremost three of them in pointing out that (1) all else being equal, a growing population (the U.S. figures grew by 55 percent between 1940 and 1970, for example) requires an even larger growth in public services; (2) technological progress and relative affluence have produced a whole new gamut of challenges (for instance, air-lane regulations, water pollution, mass urban transport); and (3) changes in concepts of what government can do or should do vary over time, but generally in a more ambitious direction.[38]

No reliable figures for union membership among government employees are available for the period before 1956, when civil servants in the Bureau of Labor Statistics began collecting this kind of data. But where the BLS's information reveals 915,000 governmental unionists in 1956 (heavily concentrated in the federal service, and particularly among its postal, shipyard, and arsenal employees), the same agency reported almost 1.5 million organized workers only eight years later, and by 1975 was estimating that 2.4 million public employees—widely distributed throughout all levels of government and embracing a spectrum that included such disparate types as engineers, zoo keepers, firemen, jail guards, teachers, sewage workers, and common laborers—were in union ranks.

It should thus come as no surprise to the reader that the greatest rate of growth in the entire labor movement has occurred among unions that represent, either exclusively or primarily, public employees. The American Federation of State, County and Municipal Employees (AFSCME), gaining 1,000 new members a week by 1975 and up to a total membership of some 650,000 (from only 210,000 in 1961), is, in fact, now the fastest growing union in the nation. An almost comparable success story has been registered by the American Federation of Teachers, which increased in size (as noted earlier) from 60,000 members in 1960 to approximately 445,000 by 1975. And the

[38] J. Joseph Loewenberg and Michael H. Moskow, *Collective Bargaining in Government* (Englewood Cliffs, N.J.: Prentice-Hall, 1972), p. 3.

labor movement can also take considerable encouragement from the 362.2 percent gain in members recorded by the American Federation of Government Employees during the 1960s (from 70,300 in 1960 to 324,000 ten years later), although by the mid-1970s this organization—with little growth in its primary potential membership market of defense and Pentagon installations—was essentially unchanged in size from its 1970 figure.

Even the foregoing statistics understate the degree of recent union penetration of the public sector, however. It was generally estimated by the time of this writing that at least another 3 million employees belonged to professional and civil-service associations that were outside the official ranks of organized labor but in many cases distinguishable from bona fide unions only by their titles. Into this latter category would certainly fall the fast-growing and increasingly militant 1.5-million-member National Education Association, the heavy majority of whose members are now covered by collective bargaining agreements. So, too, would the Assembly of Government Employees (estimated strength of over 500,000 members in various state-employee subunits), the American Nurses Association (representing the interests of almost 250,000 employees), and the Fraternal Order of Police (with over 100,000 members), all of these also having shown rapid rises in organizational size over the past few years.

One must freely acknowledge that organized labor still has a long way to go before its penetration of the public sector can be deemed to be anywhere near complete. Based only on official union-membership figures, the 2.4 million unionized public employees probably constitute no more than 16 percent of the total membership potential. And even if all 3 million association members are included (and, as indicated above, not all of them should be, since an indeterminate although doubtless minority percentage of them are not bargained for collectively), the figure still comes to not much more than one-third of the total public-sector employee population. But the gains of the recent past are nonetheless highly impressive and deserve exploration.

The Growth of Public-Sector Unionism: Some Explanations

In all likelihood, three factors have been particularly responsible for this new union thrust.

First and probably foremost, *legal developments* since 1960 have given organized labor both a protection and an encouragement that were previously conspicuous by their absence. At the federal level, a highly influential event was President John F. Kennedy's issuance of Executive Order 10988, constituting the first recognition ever on the part of the federal government that its employees were entitled to join unions and bargain collectively with the executive agencies for which they worked. Three types of union recognition were provided—informal, formal, and exclusive—depending upon the percentage of employees in the bargaining unit represented by the union. And if the latter could gain exclusive recognition (by showing that it represented at least 10 percent of the employees involved and then being selected or designated by a majority of employees within the bargaining unit), the employing agency was compelled to meet and confer regularly with such a union on matters affecting personnel policy and practices and working conditions.

The order did remove many key topics from the scope of this collective bargaining—among them, mandatory union membership, agency budgetary negotiations, and new technology—and it had certain deficiencies in the dispute-settlement area (in case of a bargaining impasse, should mediation efforts fail, the only available procedure was an appeal to a higher level of the agency's own management). But E.O. 10988, nonetheless, by attempting to provide organizational and bargaining rights for employees of the federal government in essentially the same way as these rights had been established for employees in the private sector almost three decades earlier by the Wagner Act, provided a significant stimulus to union growth not just in the federal-employee province but, in short order, also at the state and local government levels. As former president John F. Griner of the American Federation of Government Employees could succinctly observe, "No matter that the collective bargaining rights (under E.O. 10988) were modified, truncated, almost emasculated. E.O. 10988 was the . . . Magna Charta. The workers saw their opportunity. They grasped it. They joined the union in droves."[39]

The White House, moreover, liberalized its "Magna Charta" a very few years later. Richard M. Nixon's Executive Order 11491, effective as of January 1, 1970, abolished both informal and formal union recognition on the grounds that these two types had proved to have had little meaning. It provided, instead, that any union could gain exclusive recognition if selected by a majority of the bargaining-unit employees in a secret-ballot election. It also created a three-member Federal Labor Relations Council (composed of the chairman of the Civil Service Commission, the secretary of labor, and an official from the president's Executive Office) to decide major policy matters and administer and interpret the order itself, substituting these officials for the large potpourri of department heads who had handled—often quite inconsistently—these activities under E.O. 10988. And it gave the assistant secretary of labor for labor–management relations authority to settle disputes over the makeup of bargaining units and representation rights, to order and supervise elections, and to disqualify unions from recognition because of corrupt or undemocratic influences; formerly, these matters had been handled by the particular federal agency involved, and its ultimate judgment on them was not subject to appeal.

[39]Loewenberg and Moskow, *Collective Bargaining*, p. 57.

Finally, E.O. 11491 established an impartial Federal Services Impasses Panel to settle disputes arising during contract negotiations, by final and binding arbitration if necessary. As stated above, the old order had provided for no such impartial procedure in the case of bargaining deadlocks (except for mediation), effectively placing unions at the ultimate mercy of the federal agency with which they were negotiating (and thus allowing one labor leader to compare the whole process to "a football game in which one side brings along the referee"). Since federal employees lack the right to strike, the new system for arbitration by neutrals seemed both equitable and realistic.

At the state level, although the influence of the developments in Washington can be clearly detected, the trend toward giving legal protection to civil servants in their efforts to organize and bargain collectively has been even more pronounced. Prior to the enactment of the Kennedy order, only one state, Wisconsin in 1959, had extended such a right to public employees. By the time of this writing, virtually all other states had sanctioned collective bargaining for at least some types of public workers. Indeed, twenty of them had enacted legislation conferring such protection upon all (or almost all) state and local employees, and laws in six states (Alaska, Hawaii, Montana, Oregon, Pennsylvania, and Vermont) even allowed—in different degrees—some strikes, while court decisions in three other states (Michigan, New Hampshire, and Rhode Island) had effectively also made the strike weapon a viable tool for some public workers in those jurisdictions.

And no signs of a reversal are on the horizon of either this trend or the significant increase in state and local employee union membership that it has generated.

A *second* factor behind the explosion in public-sector unionism has been the public servant's increasing unhappiness as his *remuneration package has fallen* farther and farther *behind* that of private employment.

Wages in the two sectors had historically been quite comparable, but by the mid-1960s the gap, even going beyond that of the general union–nonunion discrepancy already touched on in this chapter, was fully in evidence. In San Francisco, for example, journeymen electricians earned on the average $12,979 in 1966, whereas city librarians with M.A. degrees there could expect a top salary of $12,150. In the same year, city laborers in Boston averaged a significant $737 less than manufacturing laborers. And in Detroit in 1967, city stock clerks received for their annual average incomes a full $1,085 less than did stock clerks in the automobile industry.[40] As a general statement, public employees in these years earned from 10 to 30 percent less than their exact counterparts, who perhaps worked down the street from them, in private industry.[41]

[40]Thomas R. Brooks, *Toil and Trouble*, 2nd rev. ed. (New York: Dell Publishing, 1971), p. 306.
[41]*Ibid.*

Even more jarring to the civil servant, however, was the lag in working conditions underpinning this wage package, since these conditions had for years been far *superior* in the public sector. For his traditionally comparable pay, the public servant had been asked to work shorter hours (with appreciably more liberal holiday and vacation entitlements than his private counterpart), had been given a degree of job security that almost no other worker possessed, and could look forward to a pension entitlement that in most instances would dwarf that of the private-industry employee—if, in fact, the latter even had a pension expectation. By the 1960s, all these relative advantages had eroded, as public-sector fringe benefits and working conditions saw little further liberalization, while these areas in private industry first caught up with and then slowly eclipsed the public emoluments. If the public employee was not completely disgruntled in the face of this development, he was certainly—to paraphrase the late P.G. Wodehouse—a long distance from being gruntled. Increasingly, he turned to his newly legalized avenue of collective bargaining to redress what was viewed as a clear injustice.

Third, and finally, one cannot disregard the *general spirit of the times* in explaining the rise of public unionism. These same growth years were marked throughout American society by a degree of social upheaval rare in the nation's history. No part of the established order was seemingly immune from attack, as blacks, Latin-Americans, women, homosexuals, student activists, an increasingly broad spectrum of citizens opposed to the Vietnam War, and even older people organized—often, militantly—to exert in support of their respective causes a collective pressure that could hardly be overlooked. The results were, as in the case of the black demands upon organized labor that will be dealt with in Chapter 2, generally mixed. But sufficient progress was certainly made to bring home to many public employees who had eschewed organization until that point the advantages to be gained by collective action.

To this trio of key explanations, the reader might care to add others of his (or her) choosing: the increasing vulnerability to unionization of many public-sector managers because of archaic personnel policies; a fear on the part of government workers in the latter, inflation-dominated years of this period that their jobs would be the first to be eliminated in the face of growing taxpayer resistance to the higher costs of public administration (an issue that will be touched upon shortly); the changing complexion of the government work force itself, with an ever-higher percentage of younger and often more aggressive jobholders; and perhaps the sheer numerical growth in public employees, making them a more tempting target for the union organizer. In any case, however, the reasons for the demonstrable, if to date incomplete, successes of labor in the public-employee arena appear at the very least to have been understandable. As such, they seem destined to continue, certainly through the late 1970s and probably well beyond.

The Public-Employee Unionist: The Strike Issue

"If you treat public employees bad enough," said George Meany in late 1974, on the occasion of the founding convention of the AFL-CIO's new Public Employee Department, "they'll go on strike and they'll get the support of the union movement." Meany, a man rarely accused of mincing words, also told the same audience that public workers involved in labor disputes should feel free to strike "any damn time you feel like going on strike."[42] This was not the first time in 1974 that the AFL-CIO chief executive had registered these sentiments. Nor did he depart from the views expressed by many other, if less influential, labor chieftains in advancing them. But the setting this time—the new department symbolized the conquests of the recent past by uniting under its aegis 24 AFL-CIO-affiliated unions representing more than 2 million workers—gave a special impact to his words.

Ironically, had Meany said exactly the same thing only a few years earlier, he would very likely have been either publicly vilified as a nihilistic demagogue or dismissed as a droll master of hyperbole (this being the same Meany who on an earlier occasion had offered his observation that "most college professors, when given a choice of publish or perish, tend to make the wrong decision"). For, throughout labor's long history in this country, public policy toward the public-sector strike had been clear, unequivocal, and resoundingly negative. Calvin Coolidge had deemed such work stoppages "anarchy"; Franklin D. Roosevelt had called them "unthinkable";[43] all relevant government regulations (including E.O. 11491) for federal employees had historically banned the public-worker strike; and as Barrett and Lobel have asserted, "In the mid-1960s, it would be accurate to say that public policy in all states clearly prohibited work stoppages of public employees by statute, court decision, or attorneys' general opinion."[44] Indeed, public-employee organizations themselves showed their general agreement with this constraint by including, in almost all cases, total bans on work stoppages in their own constitutions.

What was past was definitely not prologue in this case, however. If, prior to 1960, public-sector strikes were all but unknown, and if, even as late as 1960, only 36 such strikes were recorded, the 1970 totals showed 412 of them,[45] including an unprecedented eight-day strike by the nation's postal employees and another nationwide one by airport flight controllers. The trend was accelerating by the mid-1970s (in a single three-week period in July 1974, for example, the American Federation of State, County and Muni-

[42]*Wall Street Journal*, November 7, 1974, p. 29.

[43]Jerome T. Barrett and Ira B. Lobel, "Public Sector Strikes—Legislative and Court Treatment," *Monthly Labor Review*, Vol. 97, No. 9 (September 1974), 19.

[44]*Ibid.*

[45]U.S. Department of Labor, Bureau of Labor Statistics, *Report 1727*, 1972.

cipal Employees alone was involved in approximately 30 strikes), and the harsh punishments all but universally called for by the various laws were essentially being ignored by civic authorities. (For example, in the federal government, any striker is subject to up to five years in jail plus a fine and dismissal, but, as A.H. Raskin has pointed out in speaking of the aforementioned postal and flight controllers' stoppages, "No striker ever got close to Leavenworth or Lewisburg,"[46] and no striker has since.) It was, indeed, in recognition of this fact—that except in the rarest of instances, the antistrike laws could be violated with impunity, given the political realities—that the several states mentioned earlier had legalized the public strike for at least some workers. Most significantly, it was because of this awareness that the new AFL-CIO department was all set to mount a major legislative drive in the 94th Congress to legalize all public-sector strikes except for those creating a demonstrable peril to the public health or safety.

Thus, the years immediately ahead should see a resolution of this inevitably emotion-laden issue. And, given the proven ineffectuality of the present strike bans, this resolution will quite probably be on the side of the right to strike except for (1) such clearly indispensable civil servants as policemen and firemen, and (2) cases where the peril to health and safety is otherwise shown to exist; in these cases, most likely, binding arbitration by third parties will be utilized to resolve bargaining impasses.

Supporters of such a development—and in their ranks are many neutrals—contend that this right to strike would only recognize reality. They argue also that only the strike threat can guarantee that public officials will bargain in good faith. And they point out that the many private-sector unionists who perform jobs identical to those in the public arena (for example, transit employees, teachers, and maintenance workers), since they do have the right to strike, possess an inequitable bargaining advantage over their government counterparts.

Arguments on the negative (or antistrike) side focus on these factors: (1) In the private sector, the employer can counter the strike weapon with a lockout of his own, but he can hardly do this as a government official, and hence the legalized public strike would create a large labor relations imbalance; (2) public pressures on the public official to end a strike are infinitely greater than those on the private administrator, and thus the former is forced to capitulate more quickly, to the ultimate detriment of the community; and (3) the monopolistic nature of virtually all public-sector employment makes almost all of it "essential," and thus the public should be guaranteed against its legalized interruption.

Whatever the merits of these latter contentions and supplementary

[46]*New York Times*, Sept. 22, 1974, p. 2-E.

antistrike ones,[47] the momentum definitely belonged to those taking the other side of the argument as this was being written.

Public Employees and the Budget

"In many cases," observed the editors of *Business Week* in the middle of the 1970s, "when labor goes to the public well, the public takes a bath because of poor city management and militant unionism."[48] The editors were thinking in particular of New York City ("where all urban troubles seem to begin," they said). For, at the time, that city was apparently being prevented from using its single remaining option in closing a horrendous $641-million budgetary gap—that of cutting labor costs—by the bitter negative reaction on the part of New York's municipal unions to such a program. "This," asserted the journalists, "is labor relations at its worst," for the situation was seemingly a direct product of—among other things—"political posturing, budget gimmickry, labor relations amateurism and a deeply held belief by [New York City's] workers that job security is tantamount to a constitutional right."[49] Yet they could have used other, if less extreme situations; as examples: as San Francisco's Mayor Joseph Alioto had proclaimed in the face of this New York City trauma, "The seeds of New York are in every American city,"[50] and states, too, had increasingly encountered these same problems.

It was the deep recession of these months—the first since the 1930s resulting in the need for a major contraction of labor costs—that had brought all of them to a head. AFSCME's president Jerry Wurf seemed to be on solid ground in pointing out that "until the recession became very severe, the claimed inability to meet demands was always a fiction we could not take seriously. When pressed, the money was always forthcoming. But states and local governments have become very susceptible to recessions. For the first time, their money problems are real."[51]

At least in the nation's largest cities, it can be argued, public-employee unions had in a relatively few years become victims of their own successes. As a critical local political bloc, they had achieved stunning economic benefit victories in the comparatively recent past. By 1975, policemen and firemen in Chicago could count on an $18,000 annual income (with commensurate fringes) even without promotion; teachers in New York City could realist-

---

[47]See John F. Burton, Jr., and Charles Krider, "The Role and Consequences of Strikes by Public Employees," in Loewenberg and Moskow, *Collective Bargaining*, pp. 274–88, for a lucid treatment of many of these considerations.

[48]*Business Week*, July 21, 1975, p. 50.

[49]*Ibid.*

[50]*Time*, July 14, 1975, p. 13.

[51]*Business Week*, July 21, 1975, p. 51.

ically and fairly quickly expect to be earning almost the same amount; and the sanitation workers in Mayor Alioto's own city of San Francisco (at $17,000) have already been cited. It was, in the lush decade preceding the mid-1970s, not only an easy task for politicans to give away public monies in the pursuit of "labor peace" but also an altogether enjoyable one if, in the process, political support could be concurrently garnered.

The pronounced downturn in economic activity, however, brought an abrupt end to this practice by causing tax revenues to plummet. And simultaneously, a major period of inflation was making the cost of running public operations more costly. Above all, embittered taxpayers—increasingly upset by ever-higher tax burdens and also mindful of the ravages of inflation on their own budgets—were demanding a far greater level of efficiency in government than had previously been the case. The citizenry may or may not have agreed with Oscar Levant's observation that "a politician is a man who will double-cross a bridge when he comes to it," but it was painfully obvious to all public figures that the expectations of constituents were now a great deal higher than they had been when the money flowed freely, and that the easygoing days of labor relations had ended. It was hoped that that situation would be replaced by a more responsible bargaining system, administered by parties whose maturity had been hastened by adversity, and fairer to all concerned.

Labor Relations in the Public Sector: An Assessment

To experienced neutral Sam Zagoria, the boom in public-sector unionism constitutes "a quiet revolution of government . . . [with] workers . . . effectively building some new passageways into the executive and council chambers where public policy is determined."[52] To former government manager Frederick O.R. Hayes, it "is only one manifestation of the powerful social forces that have swept the nation during the last decade. . . . Community participation and militant unionism in the public sector are clearly bedfellows."[53] Union leader Wurf views it as proof that "the day when the service worker was destined to be a grub is gone forever";[54] and former secretary of labor Peter Brennan has observed that it "may be the single most important development in labor–management relations in the past generation."[55]

Probably all these comments are valid, and our society is not necessarily the loser for their being so. Public employers, long the wielders of unques-

---

[52]Sam Zagoria, *Public Workers and Public Unions* (Englewood Cliffs, N.J.: Prentice-Hall, 1972), pp. 1–2.
[53]*Ibid.*, p. 99.
[54]*Business Week*, July 27, 1974, p. 54.
[55]*U.S. News & World Report*, October 14, 1974, p. 66.

tioned authority and unilateral decision-making powers, are now being forced by unions and quasi unions to share these perquisites much as private employers were in the turbulent decades of the 1880s and 1930s. However one feels about unionism, it is undeniable that in the private sector labor has encouraged not only more enlightened and responsible management but also a meaningful sense of worker participation, while generally producing conditions of employment that both parties can comfortably live with. There is no reason to believe that these consequences—for all the obvious (if lessening) differences between public and private employment and for all the major problem areas in the public arena at the moment (most conspicuously, of course, those involving the strike and the budget)—will not, for government work, ultimately be the same.

SOME CONCLUDING REMARKS ON THE CURRENT QUALITIES OF LABOR–MANAGEMENT RELATIONS

"Anyone," the noted arbitrator Theodore W. Kheel once remarked, "who starts a sentence by saying that 'the trouble with labor or management is' is bound to be partially right but mostly wrong."[56] Such sweeping generalizations as the one cited are highly hazardous in most areas of life, but in a field as varied as labor relations, they are wholly unwarranted.

It is hoped that in pointing up the various "multiplicities"—of causes for workers joining unions, of reasons why managers resist unions, and of employer philosophies themselves—the dangers of being too cavalier in *interpretation* have also been implied. Maslow's Need Hierarchy does not always fall neatly into place in linking Specific Employee X to his labor organization. And when one analyzes the motivations of "workers" as a general grouping, he may be equally far off base unless he recognizes that a variety of different need-motivated reasons may be simultaneously at play. The management resistance to union inroads is, in turn, also derived from a wide array of specific causes, even though the desire to retain decision-making authority in managerial hands lies at the heart of most of them. And employer philosophies concerning unionism can run a gamut from intransigent hostility on the one hand to complete "togetherness" in the form of collusion on the other, although neither of these extremes is common. The various frameworks presented in this chapter can serve as useful guides for specific analyses, but a little knowledge has at times been known to be a dangerous thing. Let the student beware!

Moreover, if variations in (1) worker expectations from their unions, (2) employer grounds for resisting unionism, and (3) company attitudes

---

[56]Theodore W. Kheel, "A Labor Relations Policy for 1964," *Personnel Journal*, April 1964, p. 181.

in implementing this resistance account *by themselves* for much present-day diversity in labor relationships, other factors augment this diversity. To recall only a few that were cited in this chapter, the current financial states of the individual companies (and industries and, increasingly, public employers) may serve as an influential variable. So, too, may technological change confronting both the industry and the employer, past relationships between the parties, the goals of the leaders themselves on both sides of the bargaining table, management's degree of perception regarding labor situations, and, of relevance for some relationships, the prospects for government intervention, including an assessment of the form this is likely to take.

And this is to say nothing of the differences between one union *as an institution* and another, a topic that has been intentionally deferred for extensive treatment in Chapter 4. Let it suffice to state here that unions exhibit a heterogeneity all their own. In a very important sense, indeed, there has never been a literal "labor movement" in this country. The AFL-CIO is a loose federation with very limited power. Bargaining is carried out by the highly diverse international unions, each with its particular traditions, structure, and government, and by the constituent locals and other subgroups of the internationals. Even today, despite a strong trend toward international union control over local union activities, a few international unions perform little more than bookkeeping functions, with the locals exercising almost complete autonomy. Other internationals are highly centralized, and local independence in any sphere is virtually nonexistent. Organized labor is broad enough, too, to contain (1) the Teamsters Union, which has long represented to many people a prime form of "business unionism," with its leaders utilizing the union as "a marketing cooperative to sell so many head of labor to employers at the highest market price"[57] and in no way being concerned with general social reform; (2) the United Automobile Workers, whose long-time president Walter P. Reuther was frequently thought of as the nation's foremost "social unionist"; and (3) the garment unions, which have—through ambitious union-financed projects ranging from cooperative housing to adult education programs—made unionism for their constituents a "way of life." In short, there are unions and there are unions.

Any of the variables enumerated above can be crucial to the molding of a specific labor–management relationship. At any one time, several of them are apt to be at work in influencing the nature of this relationship. And, given this situation, the great variety in the subject areas, wordings, and lengths of the nation's 150,000 labor–management contracts, which serve as tangible (if, as will be seen, not always completely accurate) symbols of labor relationships, is understandable.

[57]Lester Velie, *Labor U.S.A.* (New York: Harper & Row, 1959), p. 14.

Certainly, there is no reason to expect a contract for the five waitresses in a New Hampshire restaurant to bear any resemblance to the International Brotherhood of Teamsters' nationwide trucking agreement. Any great similarity between the General Electric Company–International Union of Electrical Workers document and that negotiated by the Lace Workers and their marginal employer in Honeysuckle, Mississippi, would likewise constitute a striking coincidence.

Can *any* remarks, then, in the face of all of these variables, be applied to the majority of the contracts in this country? Some statements *can* still be made, and even as ambitious a phrase as "the *vast* majority of all agreements" will support them.

For all their variations, almost all labor contracts today validate a particular institutional status for the union, and well over two-thirds of them incorporate the union-shop arrangement, requiring union membership for continued employment. The vast majority of the agreements reveal what the parties have agreed to as being "vested exclusively in the company," either explicitly (in a so-called "management rights" article) or implicitly (in indirect language scattered throughout the contract). They announce, in more or less detail, the increasingly broad range of wage, hour, and other economic-related employment conditions under which the employees have agreed to be governed. They incorporate a variety of administrative clauses dealing with work rules and job tenure. And they outline the procedures for settling the disputes that will inevitably arise during the life of the agreement, as well as providing for a renegotiation of the contract when its duration has been exhausted.

These are no small accomplishments. Real or imaginary threats to job security, to the union's existence, to what managers deem their freedom to run their own businesses, and to what employees refer to as fair conditions are regularly involved. Yet the signing of any contract requires some form of mutual agreement and, most often, some major concessions by both the management and the union. It is tribute to the increasing maturity of both parties that so much progress has been made in this direction over the past few decades. This is particularly true when one considers not only the drastic technological and economic changes that have taken place in our society since the Great Depression, but also the many direct grounds for open conflict between labor and management that have existed ever since.

A host of other accomplishments, which will be given liberal treatment in the pages that follow, also bear testimony to the ability of the labor relations system to adjust itself to accommodate new needs and desires. The spread of the seniority principle, under which the employee with the longest service receives preference in various employment matters, has minimized employee demands for both "justice" and "objective personnel management." On these morale-building grounds, it has also had considerable appeal—when used in moderation—to many managements. Moreover, the almost complete acceptance by the parties of binding arbitration by a neutral as the final step in the grievance procedure, thus normally ruling out work stoppages during the term of the agreement, has also injected much stability into labor relations. And the same can be said of the growth of long-term contracts—now commonly three years in duration instead of the traditional one-year basis. Nor can one overlook the contractual adjustments to the spread of the many new employee fringe benefits that have arisen in this period. Bilateral statesmanship must receive some credit, too, for the satisfactory contractual resolution, at least over time, of many knotty problems involving technological change and unionized workers.

The labor contract, admittedly, forms only the bare skeleton of the total relationship between a union and a management. As is also true of both the marriage contract and the citizen's income tax report, it is little more than a legal prerequisite to harmony; by itself, it does not produce rapport. To evaluate accurately any labor relationship, one must know the degree of mutual trust and good will that lies behind the written agreement, to say nothing of the extent to which supplementary documents and verbal understandings may affect the wording printed on the contract pages. Finally, no contract is any better than its *administration:* The contract incorporates a body of rules, but this does not guarantee that both parties will always interpret these rules in the same way. Moreover, the fact that agreements can never hope to explicitly cover all contingencies means that there will always be at least the chance for future disagreement. In short, a variety of problems affecting the relationship can surround even the most harmonious-appearing labor contract.

Judged by any available standard, however, the considerable progress and increasing maturity that is at least *symbolized* by the contractual contents has marked *all* portions of union–management relations over the past very few decades. One can accept the Slichter, Healy, and Livernash verdict that the process of accommodation is "neither complete nor uniform," and recognize that judgment involving the public sector must as yet remain suspended, without in any way negating the more basic conclusions of these three scholars that:

> . . . the American collective bargaining system must be regarded as one of the most successful economic institutions in the country. In the great majority of plants it has produced rules and policies that are fair to both sides and that permit managements to conduct operations efficiently. Although there is wide variation in the results of bargaining, the concentration of settlements that are good compromises is large . . . [and] experience to date evidences a degree of social progress that few would have predicted [at the end of the 1930s].[58]

[58]Slichter, Healy, and Livernash, *The Impact of Collective Bargaining*, pp. 960–61.

The reader is invited to postpone his own agreement (or disagreement) with these opinions until the contents of the various areas cited in the preceding paragraphs are treated more fully. Part III's six chapters are totally reserved for this latter purpose: Chapter 5, for an examination of management and union behavior at the bargaining table; Chapter 6, for the treatment of contract administration; Chapters 7 and 8, for description and analysis of the major economic issues with which collective bargaining is now involved; and Chapters 9 and 10, for a relatively detailed inspection of the basic institutional and administrative issues in the current labor–management sphere.

If one does acquiesce at this early point, however, is there also justification for assuming that the mainstream of our labor relations system today stands on the threshold of a great new era to which strikes will be entirely foreign and where harmony will be the universal guiding rule?

Despite all the progress to date, such a prophecy would, we think, be extremely naïve. It can be expected that managements will continue to oppose the concept of unionism and to resist new union inroads as energetically as ever, for the roots of this opposition are essentially rational ones *as judged by management values.* By the same token, there is little reason to believe that unions will not continue to press for an ever-greater narrowing of the scope of management discretion, in the interests of obliging worker wants and needs as they view them. Indeed, in the years immediately ahead, the stresses between the parties seem destined to grow: The recent intensification of industrial price and technological competition (and, in the public sector, of severe budgetary pressures) has already pitted an accelerated employer search for greater efficiency against an equally determined union campaign for increased job security.

Since a labor relations millennium is far distant, it seems a safe prediction that occasional impasses will continue to be reached by labor and management, and that these will result in strike actions, as they have in the past.

There is both an irony and a serious threat for our system of free collective bargaining in the inevitability of future strikes. If labor relations progress has clearly been evident, the community has also increased its expectations from union–management relations. Indeed, as Livernash has pointed out, "Our level of aspiration rises perhaps more rapidly than realized progress. In this situation, there is always some feeling of impatience with the degree of progress of private institutions and a desire for increased governmental control."[59]

Our system of industrial jurisprudence, the public sector patently excepted, has thus far remained essentially in private hands despite an ever

---

[59]Arthur A. Sloane and E. Robert Livernash, *Note on Collective Bargaining in the United States* (Cambridge, Mass.: Harvard University, 1961), p. 35.

deeper penetration of government regulations (described in Chapter 3). This toleration for private decision making is consistent with the dominant values of our society, particularly with its premium on maximum freedom of action for both individuals and organizations. But the possibility that a tripartite labor relations system, with the government as a full-fledged participant, will ultimately supplant the present bipartite system can never be overlooked. Whether or not what is still "free collective bargaining" will be allowed to continue will depend to no small degree on the ability of the current system to continue its progress sufficiently and in time to satisfy the increasingly high level of public expectation. The fact that there is still much room for improvement in labor–management relations makes the entire system as it currently exists a vulnerable one.

DISCUSSION QUESTIONS

1. George P. Schultz and John R. Coleman have argued that "there is at least some excuse for the inability of all of us to understand unionism as fully as we might like to: There is just too much to understand." How much knowledge and understanding of labor–management relations *does* it appear realistic to expect from the course in which this book is currently being used, and *why*?

2. "Unions have outlived their usefulness, if indeed they ever had any, for at least the many employees whose managements deal with them on the basis of enlightened, worker-oriented policies." Discuss.

3. From your own experience (first- or second-hand), which case regarding future union penetration of the white-collar field is more persuasive with you: the relatively "pessimistic" one, as advanced in this chapter, or the more "optimistic" one, which has also been presented on the previous pages?

4. The authors' own qualified endorsement of A. H. Maslow's theory of motivation notwithstanding, how valuable do you personally view this theory in understanding why workers join unions?

5. From the viewpoint of society, is there anything to be said for the union's role as an "employer-regulating device," seeking (in Bakke's words) "to regulate the discretion of employers . . . at every point where their action affects the welfare of the men"?

6. "Even if some of the day-by-day values of management and labor are not fully compatible, in the last analysis the *basic goals* of the two parties are identical." Evaluate.

7. What *primary* standards do you feel should be adopted by anyone attempting to evaluate the current performance of labor–management relations in this country, and why?

8. San Francisco Mayor Joseph Alioto, referring to an illegal strike of 10,000 New York City sanitation men in 1975 as a protest against the layoff of 3,000 of their fellow workers, has argued that all municipal strikes should be banned. "I mean," he has said, "fire anybody who strikes—really fire them." How do his views accord with yours?

SELECTED REFERENCES

BOK, DEREK C., and JOHN T. DUNLOP, *Labor and the American Community.* New York: Simon & Schuster, 1970.

COLE, DAVID L., *The Quest for Industrial Peace.* New York: McGraw-Hill, 1963.

HARBISON, FREDERICK, H., and JOHN R. COLEMAN, *Goals and Strategy in Collective Bargaining.* New York: Harper & Row, 1951.

HORTON, RAYMOND D., *Municipal Labor Relations in New York City: Lessons of the Lindsay-Wagner Years.* New York: Praeger, 1973.

LOEWENBERG, J. JOSEPH, and MICHAEL H. MOSKOW, *Collective Bargaining in Government.* Englewood Cliffs, N.J.: Prentice-Hall, 1972.

MASLOW, A. H., *Motivation and Personality.* New York: Harper & Row, 1954.

PURCELL, THEODORE V., *Blue Collar Man.* Cambridge, Mass.: Harvard University Press, 1960.

REYNOLDS, LLOYD G., *Labor Economics and Labor Relations,* 4th ed., pp. 141–58. Englewood Cliffs, N.J.: Prentice-Hall, 1964.

SELEKMAN, BENJAMIN M., *Labor Relations and Human Relations.* New York: McGraw-Hill, 1947.

SERRIN, WILLIAM, *The Company and the Union.* New York: Alfred A. Knopf, 1973.

SLICHTER, SUMNER H., JAMES J. HEALY, and E. ROBERT LIVERNASH, *The Impact of Collective Bargaining on Management,* pp. 1–26. Washington, D.C.: The Brookings Institution, 1960.

WOLFBEIN, SEYMOUR L., ed., *Emerging Sectors of Collective Bargaining.* Braintree, Mass.: D. H. Mark Publishing Company, 1970.

ZAGORIA, SAM, *Public Workers and Public Unions.* Englewood Cliffs, N.J.: Prentice-Hall, 1972.

PART II
THE ENVIRONMENTAL FRAMEWORK

Chapter 2
The Historical
Framework

As is true of other established disciplines, there is still some controversy as to the returns inherent in the study of history. For every Shakespeare asserting that "what is past is prologue," or Santayana who proclaims that "those who do not understand history are condemned to repeat its mistakes," there is a Henry Ford declaring that "history is a pack of tricks that we play on the dead," and that the field is, in fact, "bunk."

No one can claim to understand present-day institutions, however, unless he has at least some basic knowledge of their roots. It would make a considerable difference to those who are either hopeful or fearful that labor unions will ultimately fade from the industrial scene, for example, if unions were purely a phenomenon of the last few years (and thus potentially destined for extinction when environmental conditions change), rather than being—as they are—organizations of relatively long standing in the economy. Similarly, only by recognizing what workers have expected of their unions in the past is one entitled even to begin to pass judgment on the present performance of organized labor. This chapter thus attempts to provide the reader with a necessary working knowledge of American labor history.

THE EIGHTEENTH CENTURY: GENESIS OF THE AMERICAN LABOR MOVEMENT

If labor unions connote *permanent* employee associations that have as their primary goal the preservation or improvement of employment conditions, there were no such institutions in America until the closing years of the eighteenth century. Concerted actions of workingmen in the form of strikes and slowdowns were not unknown to the colonial period, but these disturbances were, without exception, spontaneous efforts. They were conducted on the spur of the moment over temporary grievances, such as withholding of wages. Generally unsuccessful, they were never undertaken by anything resembling permanent organizations.

Given the dimensions of the labor movement today and the variety of seemingly compelling reasons why workers have attached themselves to it, this total absence of labor unions for well over a century calls for an immediate explanation.

In those years of simple handicraft organization, there were, in fact, at least four forces at work that served to weaken any motivation that workers might otherwise have had for joining together on a long-term basis.

In the first place, the market for the employer's product was both local and essentially noncompetitive. Workingmen were thus allowed close social ties with the owner, often performing their work in the owner's home. In addition, they could maintain a comparatively relaxed pace of production in such an atmosphere.

Second, both the laws of supply and demand and government regulations allowed employees a large measure of job security at this time. Labor of all kinds, and particularly skilled craft labor, was in short supply in the colonies. In addition, a series of colonial labor laws calling for apprenticeship service prior to many kinds of employment and carefully circumscribing the conditions under which employees could be discharged offered further protection to jobholders.

Third, the existence of ample cheap land in the West meant that the dissatisfied artisan or mechanic could always move on should either local adversity or the spirit of adventure strike him. Many workers did migrate to the ever-expanding frontier, allowing even more advantageous employment conditions for those who remained: Incomes increased all the more in the East, to the point where, by some estimates, wages were twice those paid to workers in Britain.

Finally, the low ratio of labor to natural resources in the frontier nation helped ensure that price rises would lag behind the wage increases. Assistant Secretary of the Treasury Coxe, sounding very much like a twentieth-century Chamber of Commerce manager, could—even as late as 1790—assert with considerable justification that "though the wages of the industrious poor are very good, yet the necessaries of life are cheaper than in Europe, and the articles used are more comfortable and pleasing."[1]

Ironically, however, the development of the frontier laid the groundwork for the birth of bona fide labor organizations. An expanded system of transportation built around canals and turnpikes was simultaneously linking the new nation's communities and allowing the capitalists of the late eighteenth century to enlarge their product markets into the beginnings of nationwide ones. The merchant who was unwilling or unable to respond to the challenge was left by the wayside as competitive pressures forced each businessman to find cost-cutting devices in the newly unsheltered atmosphere. The more

[1] Lloyd Ulman, *American Trade Unionism—Past and Present* (Berkeley, Calif.: Institute of Industrial Relations, 1961), p. 367.

imaginative employers located such devices: To decrease labor costs, they introduced women and children to their workplaces, farmed out work to prison inmates, and generally cut the wages of males who remained in their employ. For good measure, they frequently increased the hours in the workday (at no increase in pay), minutely subdivided the work into more easily assimilated (but commensurately more repetitive and monotonous) operations, and hired aggressive overseers to enforce newly tightened work standards.

The less-skilled workingman could react to these unwelcome changes by moving to the frontier. Not having invested much in the way of time or education in learning his current job, he might also attempt to move occupationally to more desirable kinds of work. The skilled worker, on the other hand, had mastered his craft through years of apprenticeship and was no longer occupationally mobile.

Some skilled craftsmen did move to the frontier. But the extension of the product market meant that their new masters were still not free to ignore labor cost-cutting methods; suits tailored in Ohio competed now with those made in Boston. Nor could the craftsmen count any longer on advancing into the class of masters themselves; the scope of manufacturing was necessarily greater, and to enter the employer ranks it now took capital on a scale not ordinarily available to most wage earners. Basically, the skilled workers' alternatives were to passively accept the wage cuts, the competition of nonapprenticed labor, and the harsh working conditions, or to join in collective action against such employer innovations. Increasingly, by the end of the eighteenth century, they chose the latter course of action.

THE FIRST UNIONS AND THEIR LIMITED SUCCESSES

These early trade unions—individually encompassing shoemakers, printers, carpenters, tailors, and artisans of similar skill levels—waged blunt attacks on the changes brought about by the extension of markets. Their members agreed upon a wage level and pledged not to work for any employer who refused to pay this amount. They also bound themselves not to work alongside any employee who did not receive the basic minimum or who had not served the customary period of apprenticeship for the trade. In addition, most of these craft unions attempted to negotiate closed-shop agreements, whereby only those who were union members in the first place would be employed at all. Whatever agreement was subsequently struck with the employer, little trust was placed in him by the representatives of his workers; the union sent a "walking delegate" to walk around from shop to shop on a regular basis and thus ensure that the wages and conditions of the contract were being honored. Later, "tramping committees" of union delegates performed the same function.

Generally proving themselves willing to strike, if need be, in support of their demands, the early unions were at times surprisingly successful in achieving them. And although work stoppages of the day were typically both peaceful and short in duration, the new worker aggressiveness they symbolized was sufficient to bring on considerable countervailing action from the employers.

The masters turned to two sources: organization in employers' associations, and aid from the courts. Societies of otherwise competitive master masons, carpenters, shoemakers, printers, and other employers of skilled labor were quickly established in most urban areas where union activity was pronounced, for the purposes of holding down wages and destroying labor combinations wherever these existed. Attacking on a second front, the masters also turned to the judges and urged prosecution of their workers' organizations as illegal conspiracies in restraint of trade. The jurists were quickly convinced: The Journeyman Cordwainers (shoemakers) of Philadelphia were found guilty of joining in such a conspiracy by striking in 1806, and within the next decade a variety of similar court cases had also resulted in shattering defeats for the worker organizations. Not until 1842, indeed, with the famous *Commonwealth* v. *Hunt* decision in Massachusetts that strikes could be legal if they were undertaken for legal purposes, did the judges even begin to modify the harsh tenets of the "Cordwainer doctrine" when requested to rule on union affairs by employers.

If the criminal conspiracy doctrine and the varying successes of the employer associations crimped the growth of the incipient labor movement, moreover, an economic event temporarily sent unionism into almost total collapse. In 1819, a major nationwide depression occurred and, as was to be no less the case in later nineteenth-century periods of economic reversal, labor organizations could not withstand its effects. Union demands that might be translated into employer concessions when the demand for labor was high could be safely dismissed by the masters with jobs now at a premium. Employers once again cut rates with impunity and showed little hesitation in dismissing workers who had joined unions in earlier years. Under the circumstances, the worker cry was "Every man for himself," rather than "In union there is strength," and virtually no union could, or did, survive such mass desertion.

REVIVAL, INNOVATION, AND DISILLUSIONMENT

The return of economic health to the country by late 1822 was paralleled by a revival of unionism. Their bargaining power restored, skilled employees in the trades that had previously been organized once again turned to union activity.

More significantly, the process of unionization now spread to new frontiers, both geographic and occupational. Aroused by the same merchant-capitalist threats to living standards and status that had previously given incentive for collective bargaining to their East Coast counterparts, craftsmen in such newly developed cities as Buffalo, Pittsburgh, Cincinnati, and Louisville established trade union locals at this time. And new (and widely publicized) victories of the skilled worker unions both in the older and the newer cities had by the mid-1830s generated the formation of unions among such previously nonunion groups as stonecutters, hatters, and painters. By 1836, there were 58 different local trade unions in Philadelphia, 52 in New York, 24 in Baltimore, and 14 in Cincinnati.

These years also saw other innovations made by organized labor. Prior to 1827, each local craft union had operated on its own as a totally separate organization. In that year, however, representatives of fifteen different trades in the city of Philadelphia formed the country's first central labor union, for joint action on a citywide basis. The original goal of the Philadelphia group was a ten-hour day for its trade union members, but this was soon displaced as a major demand: In 1828, the organization converted itself into a political party, endorsing "workingmen's candidates"—with only limited success—for public office.

Workingmen's parties were also organized in other eastern states in this period of Jacksonian democracy. Political associations of workers seeking such goals as universal free education and the abolition of imprisonment for debt arose in New York, Massachusetts, and Delaware. Most of their objectives were soon realized, but the workingmen's parties themselves—often torn by internal dissension and always confronted by competition from the two major national parties—were generally short-lived.

The original form that the Philadelphia "city central" had taken—as a purely economic joint undertaking of several trade unions in a single city—had a more lasting influence on workers in other locations. Similar bodies were quickly set up throughout the East and, despite the frequent divergence of opinion among the various trades represented, showed remarkable staying power. By the mid-1830s, at least twelve cities had such "city centrals," most of which provided their affiliated local unions with financial and moral encouragement in times of strikes and coordinated such ancillary activities as the promotion of union-made goods.

Even the beginnings of national worker organization were attempted at this time. In 1834, delegates from the city centrals of several eastern cities met in New York to form the National Trades' Union. This pioneering workers' project quickly proved fruitless—industry had not yet itself significantly organized on a national basis, and would not for three more decades—but the scope of the NTU's activities nonetheless symbolizes the ambitiousness of the worker representatives involved.

Indeed, the initiative displayed by leaders of both the city centrals and the local unions had led to impressive union membership totals by 1836. It has been estimated that there were in the country as a whole in that year

300,000 unionized workers, constituting 6.5 percent of the labor force.[2] One can only guess to what heights the total figures would have risen had not the following year brought a national economic depression that was even more severe than the business slump of 1819.

The hard times that began in 1837 were to last for almost thirteen years. In the face of them, trade union activity vanished almost as completely as it had two decades earlier. Moreover, a new factor now arose to compound union ills: The 1840s saw waves of immigrants—themselves often the victims of economic adversity in such countries as Ireland, Germany, and England— enter the United States. American business conditions by themselves had been sufficient to wipe out most unions of the day, but this new source of job competition and low wages ensured that not even the strongest of unions could endure.

Now so severely frustrated in their economic actions and distrustful of the free enterprise system for having failed to safeguard their interests, some workers transferred their energies to a series of ambitious political schemes for redesigning the economy. "Associationists" set up socialistic agricultural communities; George Henry Evans preached the virtues of "land reform" through direct political action by workingmen ("Vote Yourself a Farm"); and still other advocates of a new social order promulgated producers' cooperatives—employee-owned industrial institutions—as the workingman's salvation.

None of these programs succeeded, however. As Dulles has astutely observed, they did not "in any way meet the needs of labor. In spite of the enthusiastic propaganda, the answer to industrialization did not lie in an attempt to escape from it."[3]

THE LAYING OF THE FOUNDATION FOR MODERN UNIONISM AND SOME MIXED PERFORMANCES WITH IT

With the return of prosperity in 1850, unions once again became a factor to be reckoned with. Profiting from the past, they eschewed political diversions, concentrated on such now-traditional goals as higher wages, shorter workdays, and increased job security, and regained much of their former membership.

The first major national unions, often superseding the economic functions of the city centrals, were also established at this time. Although the "Golden Age" of American railroading still lay ahead, the construction of the first complex rail systems was now accelerating. As a result, not only were

[2]Foster Rhea Dulles, *Labor in America*, 2nd rev. ed. (New York: Thomas Y. Crowell, 1960), p. 59.
[3]*Ibid.*, p. 81.

product markets once more widening, but so too were labor markets, bringing workers within the same crafts and industries into direct economic competition with each other. National coordination to standardize wages, working conditions, membership rules, and bargaining demands was deemed necessary by labor leaders; the alternative was cutthroat competition among individual local unions, eager for new members and expanded work opportunities and therefore willing to undercut the terms of other locals (to the employer's distinct advantage). The National Typographical Union, the country's oldest permanent national, dates from 1850. By 1860, at least fifteen other crafts had organized on a national basis. In addition to the Typographers, the Machinists and the Iron Molders have continued as labor organizations to this day, although the last-named is currently anything but a giant in labor circles.

The 1861 advent of the Civil War brought a new spurt in union membership growth, to a post-1836 high of over 200,000 unionists by the end of hostilities in 1865. Some of this organizational success was due to the labor shortages brought on by military mobilization: The economy's demand for labor commensurately increased, thus enlarging labor's bargaining power and union economic gains. There were undoubtedly at least two other reasons, however: (1) Wartime inflation always threatened to counteract the wage increases achieved by unions, and many workers (somewhat unsuccessfully) looked to collective bargaining as a force for staving off this menace; and (2) organized labor was further helped by the pro-labor sentiments of President Lincoln, who firmly resisted employer and public pressure to intervene in the occasional wartime strikes and instead offered as his opinion that "labor is the superior of capital and deserves much the higher consideration."

At war's end, however, the labor movement still comprised less than 2 percent of the country's labor force (as against 6.5 percent in 1836) and had yet to make any real penetration into the factories of the land and their huge organizing potential. But the foundation for the unionism of the next seventy years had now been laid. Few skilled-worker types were totally unrepresented by unions in 1865: More than 200 local unions, individually encompassing such widely divergent craftsmen as cigar makers, plumbers, and barrel makers, were founded in the war years alone. In addition, the logical necessity of forming *national* unions had now been almost universally recognized by labor leaders, and some thirty new ones had been added to the several that had preceded the war. And labor had achieved, through Lincoln, at least a measure of government support for its right to strike.

Labor's momentum, moreover, was sustained in immediate postwar years. The war-generated nationwide prosperity continued virtually unabated until 1873 and, aided by its favorable economic conditions (as in earlier business booms), labor's bargaining strength again increased. New members were attracted by announcements of new union gains, but there were now also other reasons for the increased membership totals. The broader organizational foundations that had been laid prior to 1865, particularly in the multiplication of national unions, allowed both more efficient and more varied organizing campaigns. Moreover, the post-Civil War period unleashed formidable threats to the workingman in the form of (1) accelerated waves of immigrants (increasingly, now, from southern and eastern Europe) who were willing to work for low wages; (2) changing technology, with the machine downgrading many skill requirements and allowing the employer to substitute unskilled labor for craftsmen and women for men; and (3) the continued widening of the gap between wages and prices that had begun in the wartime years. Workers thus had more incentive to join in collective bargaining, and acted upon it.

On the other hand, not every union shared in these gains. Particularly unsuccessful, in fact, was the new Molders national union, whose embittered president, William Sylvis, now turned away from "pure and simple" collective bargaining to espouse cooperative foundries. He was totally convinced that workers "must adopt a system which will divide the *profits* of labor among those who produce them," and was soon instrumental in the establishment of a number of producers' cooperatives.

These undertakings proved no more successful than they had in the 1840s, however. By 1870, most of the worker-owned associations had been forced by competitive pressures to cut wages, hire lower-cost labor, and—in general—act very much like the management-run businesses that Sylvis had so lamented.

Sylvis then transferred his energies to a new organization, which had been founded in 1866. The National Labor Union, riding the crest of union optimism at the close of the war, constituted the first major attempt at uniting all national unions, city centrals, and locals into a single central federation of American labor since the ill-fated National Trades' Union of 1834. Its first leaders, drawn mainly from the building and printing trades, had unsuccessfully urged legislative enactment of the eight-hour working day. They had also sought, again without tangible success, such further political goals as currency reform and women's suffrage.

Sylvis drew the organization even further from economic action to such new political objectives as the reservation of public lands for actual settlers only and abolition of the convict labor system. But the National Labor Union could not sustain membership enthusiasm with a credo that was so far removed from worker pocketbooks; one by one, its constituent labor organizations deserted it, and by 1872 the NLU had passed from the scene.

The failures of the cooperative and political movements were harbingers of more wide-sweeping labor disasters. Business collapsed in 1873, beginning a new period of deep depression that lasted for more than five years. In its wake, most of the local unions (as well as the city centrals) once more disappeared. Many of the nationals fared no better, but the greater financial resources and more diversified memberships of these broader organizations did allow them to offer greater resistance to the slump; not only did eleven of the nationals, in fact, weather these years, but eight new nationals were established during this time. Consequently, for the first time, a depression did not completely stop unionization. Nonetheless, five-sixths of total union membership did erode in the 1873–78 period; only 50,000 unionists remained in 1878.

Encouraged by the depression-caused weakening of union bargaining power, employers also turned—in the 1870s—to weapons of their own, in an all-out frontal attack on what was left of organized labor. Acting both singly and through employer associations, they engaged in frequent lockouts, hired spies to ferret out union sympathizers, circulated the names of such sympathizers to fellow employers through so-called black lists, summarily discharged labor "agitators," and engaged the services of strikebreakers on a widespread scale.

The results of these efforts varied. Most of the labor organizations that were strong enough to withstand the depression could also frustrate the employer onslaughts. But there were at least two notable effects of the management campaign. First, several unions of this period became secret societies to avoid employer reprisal. Such esoteric groups as the Knights of St. Crispin (shoemakers) date from this era. Second, retaliating in kind to the quality of employer opposition (as well as to the widespread unemployment of the times), both unionists and nonunionized workers engaged in actions that for bitterness and violence were unequalled in American history. A secret society of anthracite miners, the Molly Maguires, terrorized the coal fields of Pennsylvania in a series of widely publicized murders and acts of arson. Railroad strikes paralyzed transportation in such major cities as Baltimore, Pittsburgh, and Chicago and, with mob rule typically replacing organized leadership as these ran their course, were most often ended only with federal troops being called out to terminate mass pillaging and bloodshed. Public opinion was almost always hostile to such activities, and lacking this support the demonstrations could not succeed. It is probably also true that employers were more easily enabled, by the general resentment directed toward worker groups for these actions, to gain still another weapon in their battle against unions: The labor injunction, first applied by the courts during a railway strike at this time, was to be quite freely granted—as Chapter 3 will bring out—by the judges for more than five decades thereafter.

THE RISE AND FALL OF THE KNIGHTS OF LABOR

Prosperity finally returned to the country in 1878, and with it union growth once again resumed. Over the next ten years, 62 new national unions (or "international" unions, as many of these were now calling themselves, in recognition of their first penetration of the Canadian labor market) were established. Locals and city centrals also resumed their proliferation. Even more significantly, the early 1880s marked American labor's most notable attempt to form a single, huge "general" union, the Noble and Holy Order of the Knights of Labor.

The Knights had actually been established before the depression. In 1869, a group of tailors had founded the organization's first local in Philadelphia. Its avowed goal was "to initiate good men of all callings"—unionists as well as those not already in unions, craftsmen and (unlike virtually all other labor organizations of the day) totally unskilled workers. It particularly desired such a broad base of membership to "eliminate the weakness and evils of isolated effort or association, and useless and crushing competition resulting therefrom." But the Knights' definition of "good men of all callings" was not all-inclusive; the founders specifically wanted "no drones, no lawyers, no bankers, no doctors, no professional politicians."

Surviving the depression as a secret society, the Knights abolished their assortment of rituals and passwords in the late 1870s and thenceforth openly recruited in all directions.

Such aggressiveness, combined with what now was the normal increase in union bargaining strength amid general economic prosperity, allowed a slow but steady growth of the order's membership. There were roughly 9,000 Knights in 1878, and over 70,000 by 1884. Then, following a major 1885 strike victory against the Wabash Railroad, the growth became spectacular: Workers of all conceivable types clamored for membership, and by mid-1886 there were 700,000 people in the wide-sweeping organization.

The aftermath of the Wabash strike was to be the high-water mark for the Knights, however. The leaders of the order proved wholly unable to cope with the gigantic membership increase, and as the new Knights sought to duplicate the Wabash triumph with one ill-timed and undisciplined strike after another, a steady stream of union defeats ensued. The very diversity of backgrounds among the members also drained the effectivess of the organization: The old skilled trade unionists found little in common with the shopkeepers, farmers, and self-employed mechanics who shared membership with them, and they rapidly deserted the order. Nor did the presence of thousands of unskilled and semiskilled industrial workers, often of widely varying first-generation American backgrounds, add anything to group solidarity. Greatly discouraged by the schisms within their organization, many such workers soon followed the path set by the skilled tradesmen and left it.

Although each of the factors above was undoubtedly influential in the Knights' rapid decline after 1886—to 100,000 members by 1890 and to virtual extinction by 1900—still another factor was probably even more responsible for the fall of the order: The system of values held by the Knights' leadership was considerably at variance with the values of rank-and-file Knights. For all their diversity and essential lack of discipline, the latter could (employers and the self-employed always excepted) at least unite on the desirability of higher wages, shorter hours, and improved working conditions. Under Knight president Terrence V. Powderly, however, these goals were significantly minimized in favor of such "social" goals as the establishment of consumer and producer cooperatives, temperance, and land reform. Even the strike weapon, despite its great success against the Wabash management and its popular appeal to Knight members, was viewed with disdain by Powderly to the end; he considered it both expensive and overly militant. Why was this Knight different from all other Knights? The historical records lack a definitive explanation. But whatever the reason, the philosophical gap between leadership and followers was thus a wide one, and Powderly was forced to pay the supreme penalty for perpetuating it: ultimately, he was left with no one to lead.

By the late 1880s, a wholly new organization—the American Federation of Labor—had won over the mainstream of the Knights' skilled trade unionists, and the once vast array of other membership types, disillusioned, was again outside the ranks of organized labor. Taft has written an appropriate epitaph:

> The Knights of Labor can best be regarded as a producers', and not specifically as a wage earners', organization. It had no program around which workers in industry could rally for a long campaign. . . . The Knights of Labor expired because it could not fulfill any function.[4]

THE FORMATION OF THE AFL AND ITS PRAGMATIC MASTER PLAN

Almost from its inception in 1881, the American Federation of Labor was a highly realistic, no-nonsense organization.

Even in that year, the more than 100 representatives of skilled-worker unions who gathered at Pittsburgh to form what was originally entitled the Federation of Organized Trades and Labor Unions included many dissident Knights, disenchanted with Powderly's "one big union" concept and political-action emphasis. The rebels were already convinced that the future of their highly skilled constituents lay completely outside the catch-all Knights. They recognized that such craftsmen possessed considerably greater bargaining power than other, less-skilled types of Knights members because of their relative indispensability to employers. Consequently, they were anxious to exercise this power *directly* in union–management negotiations. Powderly's idealistic and somewhat hazy legislative goals might be appropriate for workers who could not better their lot in any other way, but they seemed to many FOTLU founders to be a poor substitute for strike threats and other forms of economic action when undertaken by unionists who were not so easily replaceable. Well versed in American labor history, these early advo-

[4]Philip Taft, *Organized Labor in American History* (New York: Harper & Row, 1964), p. 120.

cates of an exclusive federation of craft unions were also well aware of the fates of earlier organizations that had subordinated economic goals to political ones.

However logical these arguments for a more homogeneous and "pure collective bargaining" federation of skilled craft unions may seem to present-day readers, the FOTLU was not immediately a smashing success. It was initially torn by both personality and philosophical schisms. More important, the built-in weaknesses of the Knights had not yet become widely apparent to the large body of American craftsmen; paradoxically, the craft confederation's ultimate triumph had to await the first real victories—and then the rapid downfall—of the Powderly organization.

Indeed, the basic issue that was to split irrevocably the craft unions from the Knights involved the jurisdiction of the national unions themselves. The dramatic spurt in Knights membership following the 1885 Wabash victory threatened to entirely submerge the craft "trade assemblies" and the parent national craft unions, which had thus far retained their separate identities within the order, in a throng of numerically superior semiskilled and unskilled workers. Nor would Powderly, never the compromiser and now at the pinnacle of his short-lived success, grant any assurances that the Knights would not violate the jurisdictions of the existing national unions. Rubbing salt into the nationals' wounds, the Knights' leadership even went so far now as to organize rival national unions and to try to absorb both these and the established nationals into the "mixed" assembly and district structures of the order.

The rupture was soon complete. In late 1886, representatives of 25 of the strongest national unions met at Columbus, Ohio, transformed the somewhat moribund FOTLU into the American Federation of Labor, unanimously elected Samuel Gompers of the Cigar Makers as the AFL's first president, and thereby ushered in a new era for the American labor movement. Despite their moment of glory, the Knights were soon to begin their rapid decline—with some of the impetus toward their dissolution, to be sure, being directly lent by the secession of the skilled-worker nationals. For the next fifty years, the basic tenets of the AFL were to remain unchallenged by the mainstream of labor in this country.

Samuel Gompers, the Dutch-Jewish immigrant who was to continue as president of the federation for all except one of the next 38 years, has frequently been referred to as a supreme pragmatist, a leader convinced that any supposed "truth" was above all to be tested by its practical consequences. Careful consideration of the basic principles upon which he and his lieutenants launched the AFL does nothing to weaken the validity of this description. Essentially, Gompers had five such principles.

In the first place, the national unions were to be autonomous within the new federation: "The American Federation of Labor," Gompers proudly announced, "avoids the fatal rock upon which all previous attempts to effect the unity of the working class have split, by leaving to each body or affiliated organization the complete management of its own affairs, especially its own particular trade affairs."[5] The leader of a highly successful national himself— as were such other AFL founders as Peter McGuire of the Carpenters and P. F. Fitzpatrick of the Molders—Gompers felt particularly strongly that questions of admission, apprenticeship, bargaining policy, and the like should be left strictly to those directly involved with them.

Second, the AFL would charter only one national union in each trade jurisdiction. This concept of "exclusive jurisdiction" stemmed mainly from the unpleasant experiences of the nationals with rival unions chartered by the Knights. It was also, however, due to Gompers' deep concern that such competitive union situations would give the employer undue bargaining advantages by allowing him to pit one warring union against another.

Third, the AFL would at all costs avoid long-run reformist goals and concentrate instead only upon immediate wage-centered gains. As noted above, its founders were determined not to suffer the fates of earlier, reform-centered organizations: "We have no ultimate ends," asserted Gompers' colleague Adolph Strasser on the occasion of his testimony before a congressional committee at this time. "We are going on from day to day. We are fighting only for immediate objects—objects that can be realized in a few years."

Fourth, the federation would avoid any permanent alliances with the existing political parties and, instead, "reward labor's friends and defeat labor's enemies." Gompers was willing, however, to accept help for the AFL from any quarter, with only one major exception: He had at one time been a Marxian Socialist, but familiarity had bred contempt and, long before 1886, he had permanently broken with his old colleagues. At the 1903 AFL convention, he was to announce to the relative handful of Socialists present: "Economically, you are unsound; socially, you are wrong; and industrially, you are an impossibility."[6] To the end, Gompers' philosophy was firmly embedded in the capitalistic system.

Finally, Gompers placed considerable reliance on the strike weapon as a legitimate and effective means of achieving the wages, hours, and conditions sought by his unionists. Shortly before his election to the AFL presidency in May 1886, he had been one of the leaders of a general strike designed to obtain the eight-hour day. More than 300,000 workers had participated in this action, and almost two-thirds of them had achieved their objective through it. Gompers' own Cigar Makers, too, had rarely hesitated to resort to strikes when bargaining impasses had been reached. And, generally speaking, these demonstrations of economic strength had also been successful.

---

[5]Taft, *Organized Labor*, p. 117. Quoted from a speech by Gompers to the Web Weavers Amalgamated Association, March 5, 1888.

[6]*AFL Convention Proceedings*, 1903, p. 198.

Profiting from the lessons of history, Gompers' federation thus represented a realistic attempt to adjust to an economic system that had become
deeply embedded in the United States. National union autonomy, exclusive
jurisdiction, "pure and simple" collective bargaining, the avoidance of political entanglements, and the use of strikes where feasible—these proven sources
of union strength were to be the hallmarks of the new unionism. The federation would provide the definition of jurisdictional boundaries for each
national and give help to all such constituent unions in their organizing, bargaining, lobbying, and public relations endeavors. But it would otherwise
allow a free hand to its national union members as they pursued their individual goals. And the stress was to be on the needs of skilled workers, not
those of "good men of all callings," as the Knights had placed it: Some
semiskilled and unskilled workers within a relatively few industries (such as
mine workers and electricians, because of the strategic power of their national
unions) were encouraged to join, but basically the AFL made no great efforts
to organize workers with less than "skilled" callings and was to admit them
only if they organized themselves and had no jurisdictional disputes with craft
unions.

So successful did this master plan prove to be that, except for slight
modifications that will be described later, it was not until the mid-1930s that
its logic was in any way seriously questioned.

THE EARLY YEARS OF THE AFL
AND SOME MIXED RESULTS

Even in the short run, the policies of the AFL were so attractive to the
nationals that within a few years virtually all of them had become members
of the new organization. The only notable exceptions were the brotherhoods
of railroad operating employees, whose relative unwillingness to strike and
emphasis on elaborate accident and health insurance plans had traditionally
set them apart from other organizations of craftsmen. Given this reception,
the Gompers federation grew steadily, if not spectacularly: It had counted
140,000 members in 1886; by 1893, the figure had risen to 278,000.

It is also noteworthy that the economic depression that swept the country
between 1893 and 1896 did not drastically deplete union membership totals,
as had been the case in earlier hard times. The new principles of Gompers,
reflected at both the federation and national levels, gave labor significant
staying power. Moreover, the now centralized control held by the nationals
over their locals both lessened the danger that local monies would be dissipated in ill-advised strikes and provided the locals with what were normally
sufficient funds for officially authorized strikes.

On the other hand, organized labor still had a severe problem to contend
with in the 1890s: the deep desire of the nation's industrialists, now themselves strongly centralized in this era of trusts and other forms of consolida-

tion, to regain unilateral control of employee affairs. Not since the 1870s had the forces of management been as determined, as formidable, or, particularly in the case of two widely heralded strikes of the time, as successful in opposing unionism.

The first of these two union disasters involved the long-established Amalgamated Association of Iron and Steel Workers and the Homestead, Pennsylvania, plant of the Carnegie Steel Company (predecessor of the United States Steel Corporation). Here, in 1892, the company attempted to reduce wages as part of its renegotiation of an expiring agreement with the union. When the workers refused to agree to the pay cut, the Carnegie management locked them out and imported some 200 Pinkerton detectives to safeguard 2,000 strikebreakers who had been hired to replace the Amalgamated members. In a subsequent pitched battle between detectives and unionists, ten men were killed, several on each side. But the company successfully resumed operations with the strikebreakers, aided by the presence of the state militia, and thus dealt a crushing blow to the once powerful Amalgamated: The union's morale was badly broken, and not for 45 more years would Carnegie, or most of the other fast-growing mills in the Pittsburgh area, again operate under a union contract. Adding insult to injury, the Carnegie management also permanently blacklisted many of the defeated strikers and thereby denied them reemployment throughout the industry.

The Pullman, Illinois, strike of 1894 was unlike Homestead in that it involved the fast-growing American Railway Union, not an AFL affiliate. Otherwise, however, it differed essentially only in degree of violence and exact method of company victory. As in 1892, it was precipitated when the company (here, the Pullman Palace Car Company) attempted unilaterally to cut wages. The workers, not originally ARU members, then walked off their jobs and requested the railway union to intervene in their behalf. The union, welcoming the opportunity for new members, promptly instituted a boycott against all Pullman cars throughout the country. In Chicago, violence ensued when the railroad executives there imported Canadian strikebreakers. Considerable railroad property was destroyed and most train operations were completely halted. When total mob rule then threatened, the U.S. Department of Justice intervened and obtained a federal court injunction outlawing further union activities. President Grover Cleveland also dispatched federal troops to the scene, despite the objections of the governor of Illinois. Only after a month of further violence, plant destruction, and the killing and wounding of several soldiers and rioters was the boycott finally ended. But, as at Homestead, the defeat was a crushing one for the union. The railroads refused to reinstate the strikers and, within a few years, the union had permanently vanished from the scene.

Other managers, impressed by the triumphs of the Carnegie and railroad managements, and at times alarmed by what they felt was the too-belligerent stance of the AFL unions, also became more aggressive in their battles with labor. Employers in the metal trades formed a Metal Trades Association to defeat the Machinists in their quest for a nine-hour day, and then adopted a policy of "no outside interference" with their company operations. Builders in Chicago, no less strongly united, completely ousted their workers' union representatives and regained full control of construction activities following a one-year 1899 strike. And the employers in the job foundry industry banded together in the National Founders' Association, which successfully terminated not only long-standing Molders Union work rules but, for all practical purposes, the existence of the union itself. In addition, the general public tended to be no more sympathetic, normally, to the aims of the labor movement; symbolically, the eminent president of Harvard University, Charles W. Eliot, reportedly "went so far as to glorify the strikebreaker as an example of the finest type of American citizen whose liberty had to be protected at all costs."[7]

Moreover, magnifying union problems at the turn of the century were the effects of Frederick W. Taylor's influential "scientific management" movement. While many of his contemporaries lamented worker inefficiency with no more practical results than they produced when they decried the weather, Taylor was determined to take positive action. He made his life a crusade to eradicate excessive fatigue, wasted time, and lost motion from the workplace by discovering and then implementing what he called "the one best way" of performing a given operation. Two parts of the total Taylor program were particularly assailed by labor leaders: (1) the systematic breakdown of all jobs into elementary task elements, and then their recombination into highly standardized "best way" procedures—which often made the new jobs so easily mastered by workers that even skilled factory employees were threatened with becoming as interchangeable and consequently as replaceable as their products; and (2) the stress on incentive methods of wage payment— which threatened to undermine group solidarity by rewarding individual initiative and to make working conditions less palatable by giving companies an excuse for instituting what workers called "speedups." Union fears proved to be justified, as the Taylor movement spread across the factory employer community. Owing at least in part to the influence of "scientific management," too, any hopes that organized labor might have harbored for enrolling the growing army of American factory workers had to be postponed, essentially for another 35 years.

Despite all these adverse factors, union membership growth in this period was unparalleled. From 447,000 unionists in 1897, the figure increased almost fivefold to 2,073,000 in 1904—a rate of expansion that has never been equalled since. The figures reflect the national prosperity of the day and the success of

[7]Joseph G. Rayback, *A History of American Labor* (New York: Macmillan, 1959), p. 215.

many of the national unions (their problems notwithstanding) in organizing their official jurisdictions along the lines of the AFL principles.

But the labor movement could not indefinitely withstand the continuing employer opposition, now augmented by a series of devastating court injunctions on the one hand and rival union challenges from leftist workingmen's groups on the other. Total union membership dropped to 1,959,000 in 1906, and even its ultimate growth to 3,014,000 by 1917 was quite uneven and—considering the fact that 90 percent of the country's labor force still remained unorganized—unspectacular.

Intensified employer campaigns for the open (nonunion) shop, led by the National Association of Manufacturers, resulted in a number of notable union strike losses after 1904 in the meat-packing and shipping industries, among others. Violence often occurred—most drastically at the Colorado Fuel and Iron Company's Ludlow location, when in 1913 eleven children and two women were found burned to death in strikers' tents that the state militia, summoned by the company, had set afire. These were also the peak years of yellow-dog contracts (under which employees promised in writing never to engage in union activities); labor spies; immediate discharge of workers at the slightest evidence of union sympathies; and the use of federal, state, and local troops on a wholesale scale to safeguard company interests in the face of strike actions.

The courts, too, were not particularly restrained in their conduct toward unions. Injunctions banning specific union activities often appeared to unionists to be issued quite indiscriminately. As early as 1906, Gompers had been sufficiently aroused by such court orders to petition the president and Congress for relief from injunctions. His claim that the court orders represented unconstitutional usurpations of legislative power went unheeded, however, and although the AFL leader was enough moved by the rebuff to set up a lobbying agency within the federation, the injunctions continued to be forthcoming. Indeed, the judges now went considerably beyond even their restraining orders in their labor relations decisions: In 1908, the Supreme Court invalidated the pioneering Erdman Act of 1898, which had banned interstate railroads from discriminating against their union-member employees, on the grounds that the act had "unconstitutionally invaded both personal liberty and the rights of property." Nine years later, the Court upheld the validity of the yellow-dog contract.

Still another threat to the established unions, in the years between 1904 and 1917, came from workers themselves. Sometimes impatient with what they considered to be the slow pace of AFL union gains, and sometimes wholly antagonistic toward the very system of capitalism, radical labor groups arose to challenge the Gompers unions for membership and influence. This was the heyday of immigration into the United States—some 14 million newcomers, mainly from Europe, arrived in the first two decades of the twentieth century—and the European political socialism that many of the radical groups espoused found some recruits in this quarter. But the most significant of these radical organizations was essentially a native American one, the colorful Industrial Workers of the World.

The IWW was founded in 1905 by a wide array of dissidents: western metal miners, loggers, and out-and-out drifters; Socialist Labor party members; and a few disenchanted AFL union leaders from locals of longshoremen and barbers, among others. Its militant organizers placed no faith in the free enterprise system and asserted in the very first line of the IWW preamble that "the working class and the employing class have nothing in common." They also put a premium on inviting all types of workers to join (including, with a hospitality reminiscent of the Knights of Labor, farmers, industrial workers, and intellectuals); were willing to support what they called a "genuine labor party"; and strongly advocated militant direct economic action.

The "Wobblies," as IWW members were termed, achieved several tangible victories. They made major inroads among the miners and lumber workers of the West. Most notably, they assumed leadership of a spontaneous 1912 walkout of Lawrence, Massachusetts, textile workers and led them to victory in the form of wage-cut restorations, despite considerable management opposition and police intervention. But an equally bitter fight, marked by much violence, was lost the following year by the IWW-sponsored silk mill workers in Paterson, New Jersey, and from then on Wobblie membership—never more than perhaps 70,000—rapidly declined. By 1917, strongly opposing U.S. entry into World War I, the IWW had lost virtually all public support, and the federal government was in the process of obtaining convictions against its leaders for sedition. Yet, despite its ultimate failure and comparatively small membership, the IWW did demonstrate in its few years of gains that many unskilled and even migratory workers were now beginning to look to collective bargaining to safeguard their interests—indeed, given no alternative by the AFL, that they would support a bargaining agency as removed from their other values as the revolutionary IWW. Gompers' original principles were still quite adequate to meet the needs of the basic labor movement, but the day would come when the concept of skilled-worker paramountcy would be more seriously challenged.

For the time being, however, Gompers and the AFL could point with satisfaction to some signal gains. As previously noted, these did not lie primarily in the area of overall organizational growth: In the face of the onslaughts from the employers and the courts, as well as the abortive threats of radical dual unionism, AFL union membership rose only slowly in the pre-World War I years. Rather, the gains rested to a great extent on the outstanding organizing and bargaining successes of a few specific AFL member nationals, particularly in the building trades, the ladies' garment industry, and coal mining. Ironically, two of these unions (the International Ladies'

Garment Workers and the United Mine Workers) owed much of their new strength to membership policies that took in many semiskilled and even unskilled workers, although skilled-worker needs were still emphasized (and although both these unions were definite exceptions to AFL union practice in their actions).

The AFL's further grounds for satisfaction rested on another irony: Despite the continuation of the policy against active involvement in politics, AFL lobbying activities at both the federal and state levels had been instrumental in the enactment of significant progressive labor legislation. Among other such achievements, by 1917 some thirty states had introduced workmen's compensation systems covering industrial accidents, and almost as many had provided for maximum hours of work for women. On the federal level, the 1915 LaFollette Seamen's Act had greatly ameliorated conditions on both American vessels and foreign vessels in American ports, and the 1916 Owen-Keating Act had dealt a severe blow to child-labor abusers. But Gompers was destined not to be successful in what had appeared at first to be an even greater triumph: Although the Clayton Act of 1914 had seemed to exempt labor from antitrust laws and the penalties of the injunction, in 1921 the Supreme Court was to interpret the Clayton Act in such a way as to render it toothless in labor disputes.

WARTIME GAINS AND PEACETIME LOSSES

From 1917 to 1920, the time of World War I and the months of prosperity following it, the AFL grew rapidly. The 3 million workers in the AFL unions on the eve of hostilities increased to 4.2 million by 1919 and to 5.1 million only one year later.

During the war, military production, the curtailment of immigration, and the draft combined to create tight labor markets and thus gave unions considerable bargaining power and commensurate gains. Real wages for employees in manufacturing and transportation increased by more than 25 percent during the war.

Even more significantly, labor received for the first time official government support for its collective bargaining activities. The rights to organize and bargain collectively, free of employer discrimination for union activities, were granted AFL leaders by the Wilson administration for the length of the war. In return, Gompers and his colleagues pledged that their unions would not engage in strikes and promised full cooperation with the war effort. Wilson was, of course, not the first chief executive to accept the idea of collective bargaining—Lincoln having done so almost six decades earlier—and the World War I president's actions were undoubtedly based to a great extent on military expediency. But where Lincoln had merely abstained from intervention on the side of the employers, Wilson's program was considerably more positive from the viewpoint of the labor movement. Although it ended with the Armistice, it undoubtedly helped to stimulate the growth of union membership during the war.

But the immediate postwar months were even more conducive to union growth than the war years. The economy's production needs remained high, now to satisfy pent-up consumer demands, and the cost of living hit an all-time high. Company profits also burgeoned, freed of artificial wartime restraints. No longer obliged to honor the no-strike pledges, unions aggressively struck in pursuit of worker wages attuned to both profits and cost of living, and, with their bargaining power now so high, they generally succeeded. As in earlier times of demonstrated labor triumphs, victory brought further conquest: New recruits flocked into the labor movement to gain their share in prosperity through collective bargaining.

Despite this auspicious entrance into the 1920s, however, the decade was to be one of great failure for unionism. Total union membership rapidly dwindled from the 1920 peak of 5.1 million to 3.8 million three years later and, steadily if less dramatically declining even after this, hit a twelve-year low of 3.4 million at the close of the decade. The drop is even more remarkable given the fact that the economy generally continued to flourish during this period; in every prior era of national prosperity, unions had *gained* considerable ground.

Nonetheless, there were understandable reasons for the poor performance of unionism in the 1920s. A combination of five powerful factors, most of them as unprecedented as organized labor's boom-period decline, was now at work.

First, after the beginning of the decade, prices remained stable, and with workers generally retaining their relatively high wage gains of the 1917–20 period, the cries of labor organizers that only union membership could stave off real wage losses fell on deaf ears.

Second, employers throughout the nation not only returned to such measures for thwarting unionization as the yellow-dog contract and the immediate discharge of union "agitators," but now embarked on an antiunion, open-shop propaganda campaign so extensive that one contemporary observer was moved to remark that never before in its history had:

> ... America seen an open shop drive on a scale so vast as that which characterizes the drive now sweeping the country. Never before has an open shop drive been so heavily financed, so efficiently organized, so skillfully generaled. The present drive flies all of the flags of patriotic wartime propaganda. It advances in the name of democracy, freedom, human rights, Americanism.[8]

The campaign, typically conducted under the slogan of the "American Plan," portrayed unions as alien to the nation's individualistic spirit, restric-

[8]Savel Zimand, *The Open Shop Drive* (New York: Bureau of Industrial Research, 1921), p. 5.

tive of industrial efficiency, and frequently dominated by radical elements who did not have the best interests of America at heart. Particularly in regard to the last of these charges, the public appeared to be impressed: It was still mindful of the IWW, and now its attention was also called, freely by the newspapers, to the relatively few other significant leftist inroads into labor circles. To many citizens, too, organizations that could even remotely be construed as going against individualism and the free enterprise system in this day of laissez-faire Republicanism were also highly un-American.

Third, but often tied into their "American Plan" participation, many companies introduced what became known as "welfare capitalism." Intending to demonstrate to their employees that unions were unnecessary (as well as dangerous), they established a wide variety of employee benefit programs: elaborate profit-sharing plans, recreational facilities, dispensaries, cafeterias, and health and welfare systems of all kinds. Employee representation plans were also instituted, with workers thus being offered a voice on wages, hours, and conditions—the companies being thereby enabled to satisfy many grievances before they became major morale problems. Although the managements could withdraw the benefits at any time, and although the employee representatives normally had only "advisory" voices, union ills were undeniably compounded by these company moves.

In the fourth place, the courts proved themselves even less hospitable to labor unions than they had been in labor's dark days preceding World War I. Having denied in 1921 that the Clayton Act exempted unions from the antitrust laws and the injunction, the Supreme Court proceeded to invalidate an Arizona anti-injunction law the same year and then struck down state minimum-wage laws as violations of liberty of contract in 1923. Encouraged by the implied mandate from Washington, lower-court judges now issued injunctions more freely than ever.

Fifth, and finally, some of the union losses were due to unimaginative leadership in the labor movement itself. Gompers died in 1924, and his successor, William Green, lacked the aggressiveness and the imagination of the AFL's first president. Labor's troubles were clearly not to be viewed with equanimity, but Green and most of his AFL union leaders were, as Rayback has tersely commented, "content to rest upon past performances, to confine membership to the elite among workingmen, and to remain the junior partner of management in the nation's economic system."[9]

On the eve of the Great Depression in late 1929, then, organized labor remained almost exclusively the province of the highly-skilled-worker minority, apathetic in the face of the loss of one-third of its members in a single decade, militantly opposed by much of the employer community, severely crimped by judicial actions, and often suspected by the general public

[9]Rayback, *History of American Labor*, p. 303.

of possessing traits counter to the spirit of America. It appeared to have a superb future behind it.

THE GREAT DEPRESSION AND
THE AFL'S RESURGENCE IN SPITE OF ITSELF

The stock-market collapse of October 1929 ushered in the most severe business downturn in the nation's history. Between 1929 and the Depression's lowest point in 1933, the gross national product dropped from over $104 billion to around $56 billion, and a staggering 24.9 percent of the country's civilian labor force was out of work by 1933, compared to an unemployment rate of only 3.2 percent in 1929.[10]

Figures specifically relating to organized labor were equally gloomy. Between 1929 and 1933, the average twelve-month membership loss rate for organized labor accelerated to 117,000, and by 1933 union membership stood at 2,973,000—only 200,000 above the 1916 level. [11]

Given this severe loss of dues-payers, plus the necessity of sustaining strikes against the inevitable wage cuts of workers still employed, it is not surprising that many unions soon became as impoverished as their constituents. Symbolically, Ulman reports that "one forlorn strike against a small steel mill had to be called off after the contents of the strikers' soup kitchen had been depleted by a group of hungry children."[12]

It is surprising, however, that the mood of the workers themselves seemed to be one of bewildered apathy. The atmosphere was now marked by constant mortgage foreclosures (resulting in thousands moving into shanty towns on city dumps, which were bitterly called "Hoovervilles" after the incumbent president). It was characterized by the constant fear of starvation on the part of many of those not working, and the fear of sudden unemployment on the part of many of those still employed. Virtually all remnants of welfare capitalism were being abruptly terminated. Under these conditions, one might have expected a reincarnation of such militant organizations as the IWW, seeking to overthrow the capitalistic system that was now performing so poorly. Some workers did indeed turn to such radical movements as communism, but, in general, the nation seemed to have been shocked into inaction.

It is still more surprising, even considering its uninspiring performance in meeting the challenge of the 1920s, that the leadership of the AFL did not noticeably change its policies in these dark days. Through 1932, Green and the AFL executive council remained opposed to unemployment com-

[10]Stanley Lebergott, *The Measurement and Behavior of Unemployment* (Princeton, N.J.: National Bureau of Economic Research, Inc., 1957), p. 215.

[11]Ulman, *American Trade Unionism*, p. 397.

[12]*Ibid.*, pp. 397–98.

pensation, old-age pensions, and minimum-wage legislation as constituting unwarranted state intervention. They asked only for increased public-works spending from the government. So far was the AFL from the pulse of the general community at this time that, although the great bulk of union officials were and had long been Democratic party supporters, it refused, with scrupulous official neutrality, to endorse either candidate in the 1932 presidential election which swept Democrat Franklin D. Roosevelt into office with what was then the largest margin in American history.

Roosevelt's one-sided victory symbolized the country's (if not the AFL's) willingness to grant the federal government more scope for participation in domestic affairs than it had ever been given before. The business community, upon which the nation had put such a premium during the prosperous years of the 1920s, was now both discredited and demoralized. It had become painfully apparent, too, to the millions who had been steeped in the values of American individualism, that the individual worker was comparatively helpless to influence the conditions of his employment environment. In short, the depression allowed labor unions—which had been so greatly out of favor with their countrymen only a few years earlier—a golden opportunity for revival and growth, now with government encouragement.

Even before the election, such a climate had resulted in one notable gain for unions. The Norris–La Guardia Act of 1932 satisfied a demand Gompers had originally made in his petition to the president and Congress some 26 years earlier: The power of judges to issue injunctions in labor disputes on an almost unlimited basis was now revoked. Severe restrictions were placed on the conditions under which the courts could grant injunctions, and such orders could in no case be issued against certain otherwise legal union activities. In addition, the yellow-dog contract was declared unenforceable in federal courts.

The 1932 act marked a drastic change in public policy. Previously, except for the temporary support that unions received during World War I, collective bargaining had been severely hampered through judicial control. Now it was to be strongly encouraged, by legislative fiat and—after Roosevelt took office in early 1933—by executive support.

Roosevelt and the first "New Deal" Congress wasted little time in making known their sentiments. The National Industrial Recovery Act of mid-1933, in similar but stronger language than that already existing in the Norris–La Guardia Act, specifically guaranteed employees "the right to organize and bargain collectively through representatives of their own choosing . . . free from the interference, restraint or coercion of employers." Green, in what for him was unusual enthusiasm, immediately praised the act as giving "millions of workers throughout the nation . . . their charter of industrial freedom" and launched a moderate drive to expand AFL membership among craft workers. More remarkable, however, was the response to the NIRA by rank-and-file workers themselves: Almost overnight, thousands of laborers in such mass-production industries as steel, automobiles, rubber, and electrical manufacturing spontaneously formed their own locals and applied to the AFL for charters. By the end of 1933, the federation had gained more than a million new members.

The largest single gains at this time were registered by those established AFL internationals that had lost the most members during the 1920s and could capitalize upon the new climate in public policy to win back and expand their old clientele. Both the men's and women's clothing unions fell into this category. Most impressive of all, however, was the performance of the United Mine Workers under their aggressive president, John L. Lewis. Lewis dispatched dozens of capable organizers throughout the coal fields, had signs proclaiming that "President Roosevelt wants you to join the union" placed at the mine pits, and not only regained virtually all his former membership but organized many traditionally nonunion fields in the Southeast. There were 60,000 Mine Workers at the time of the NIRA's passage; six months later, the figure had grown to over 350,000.

The employers, however, did not long remain docile in the face of this new union resurgence. Terming collective bargaining "collective bludgeoning," many of them responded to the NIRA by restoring or instituting the employee representation plans of the previous decade. Such "company unions," although bitterly assailed by bona fide unionists as circumventing the law's requirements concerning "employer interference," spread rapidly. By the spring of 1934, probably one-quarter of all industrial workers were employed in plants that had them. Many other managements simply refused, the law notwithstanding, to recognize any labor organizations. On many occasions, this attitude led to outbreaks of violence, ultimately terminated by the police or National Guard units.

The National Industrial Recovery Act was itself declared unconstitutional by the Supreme Court early in 1935, but Congress quickly replaced it with a law that was even more to labor's liking. The National Labor Relations Act, better known (after its principal draftsman in the Senate) as the Wagner Act, was far more explicit in what it expected of collective bargaining than was the NIRA, in two basic ways. First, it placed specific restrictions on what management could do (or could not do), including an absolute ban on company-dominated unions. And second, it established the wishes of the employee majority as the basis for selection of a bargaining representative and provided that in cases of doubt as to a union's majority status, a secret-ballot election of the employees would determine whether or not the majority existed. To implement both provisions, it established a National Labor Relations Board, empowered not only to issue cease-and-desist orders against employers who violated the restrictions, but also to determine appropriate bargaining units and conduct representation elections.

Considerably less than enthusiastic about the Wagner Act, many employers chose to ignore its provisions and hoped that it would suffer the same fate as the NIRA. They were to be disappointed: In 1937, the Supreme Court held that the 1935 act and its congressional regulation of labor relations in interstate commerce were fully constitutional.

THE CIO'S CHALLENGE TO THE AFL

Meanwhile, however, the AFL itself almost snatched defeat from the jaws of victory. The leaders of the federation clashed sharply as to the kind of reception that should be accorded the workers in steel, rubber, automobiles, and similar mass-production industries who had spontaneously organized in the wave of enthusiasm following the NIRA's passage. The federation had given these new locals the temporary status of "federal locals," which meant that they were directly affiliated with the AFL rather than with one of the established national unions. The workers involved, however, wanted to form their own national industrial unions covering all types of workers within their industries, regardless of occupation or skill level. And this, obviously, meant a radical departure from the fifty-year AFL tradition of discouraging non-skilled workers and essentially excluding noncraft unions (the mining and clothing industries, as noted earlier, always excepted because of their particular situations).

John L. Lewis, who had shown such initiative in expanding the ranks of his Mine Workers in the preceding months, led the fight for industrial unionism within the federation. Allied with Sidney Hillman of the Clothing Workers and David Dubinsky of the Ladies' Garment Workers, he argued that changing times had now made skilled-craft unionism obsolete, that the AFL could no longer speak with any political power as long as it confined itself to what was (with the acceleration of mechanization and the replacement of craftsmen by semiskilled machine operators) a steadily dwindling minority of the labor force, and that, should the federation fail to assert its leadership over the new unionists, rival federations would arise to fill the vacuum. With perhaps the greatest oratorical powers ever possessed by an American labor leader, Lewis ridiculed the AFL president for not being able to decide the issue: "Alas, poor Green. I knew him well. He wishes me to join him in fluttering procrastination, the while intoning *O tempora, O mores!*" And in a dramatic speech at the 1935 AFL Atlantic City convention, he warned that should the federation fail to "heed this cry from Macedonia that comes from the hearts of men" and refuse to allow industrial unionism or to organize the millions still unorganized, "the enemies of labor will be encouraged and high wassail will prevail at the banquet tables of the mighty."

Lewis spoke to no avail. The convention was dominated by inveterate craft-unionists, many of whom possibly believed that Macedonia was somewhere east of Akron and who at any rate were opposed to admitting what Teamster president Daniel Tobin described as "rubbish" mass-production laborers. The demands of industrial unionism were defeated by a convention vote of 18,024 to 10,933. And Lewis, never one to camouflage his emotions for the sake of good fellowship with his AFL colleagues, left Atlantic City only after landing a severe uppercut to the jaw of Carpenter Union president William L. Hutcheson in a fit of pique.

Within a month, Lewis had formed his own organization of industrial unionists. The Committee for Industrial Organization (known after 1938 as the Congress of Industrial Organizations) originally wanted only to "counsel and advise unorganized and newly organized groups of workers; to bring them under the banner and in affiliation with the American Federation of Labor."[13] But the AFL, having already made its sentiments so clear, was to deny the new organization the latter opportunity; almost immediately, Green's executive council suspended the CIO leaders for practicing "dual unionism," and ordered them to dissolve their group. When these actions failed to dissuade the CIO, the AFL took its strongest possible action and expelled all 32 national member unions.

Lewis and his fellow founders—themselves heads of such nationals, in addition to those in the garment industries, as the Textile Workers, the Hatters, and the Oil Field Workers—were spectacularly successful in realizing their objectives. Armed with ample loans from the rebel nationals, aggressive leadership, experienced organizers, and, above all, confidence that mass-production workers enthusiastically *wanted* unionism, the AFL offshoot was able to claim almost 4 million recruits as early as 1937.

By 1941, even more remarkable conquests had been registered. One by one, virtually all the giant corporations had recognized CIO-affiliated unions as bargaining agents for their employees: all the major automobile manufacturers, almost all companies of any size in the steel industry, the principal rubber producers, the larger oil companies, the major radio and electrical equipment makers, the important meatpackers of the country, the larger glass makers, and many others. Smaller companies that had also been unionized in this period could at least take comfort in the fact that they were in good company.

Still, the CIO's organizing campaigns were not welcomed by many of these companies with open arms. United States Steel recognized the CIO's Steel Workers Organizing Committee without a contest in 1937 (ostensibly because it feared labor unrest at a time when business conditions were finally improving). But the other major steel producers unconditionally refused to deal with unionism, the law notwithstanding. In 1941, the National Labor

[13] *Minutes of Committee for Industrial Organization*, Washington, D.C., November 9, 1935.

Relations Board ordered these companies to recognize what had by then become the United Steelworkers of America, but four years of company intimidation, espionage, and militia-protected strikebreaking—highlighted by a Memorial Day 1937 clash between pickets and police that resulted in the deaths of ten workers, injuries to many more, and substantial damage to property—had then elapsed. In other industries, characterized by similar antiunion sentiments, the workers were forced to resort to sit-down strikes— protest stoppages in which the strikers remained at their places of work and were furnished with food by allies outside the plant. Such stoppages, now illegal as trespasses upon private property, were of considerable influence in gaining representation rights for the unions in the historically nonunion automobile, rubber, and glass industries.

Nor, more significantly, was the AFL itself placid in the face of its new competition. Abandoning its traditional lethargy, it now terminated its "craftsmen only" policy and chartered industrial unions of its own in every direction. AFL meatcutters emerged to challenge CIO packinghouse workers for members of all skill levels within the meat-packing industry. AFL paper-mill employees competed against CIO paper workers. AFL electricians tried to recruit the same workers, from all quarters of the electrical industry, as did the CIO electrical-union organizers. And the story was much the same in textiles and automobiles. Moreover, many of the long-established AFL unions now broadened their jurisdictions; most notable were the Teamsters, whose president had apparently become oblivious to his former charge that mass-production workers were "rubbish," and who now waged aggressive organizational campaigns among workers in the food and agricultural pro-cessing industries. Aided by the same favorable climates of worker opinion and public policy that had originally inspired Lewis, and now also helped by improving economic conditions, the AFL actually surpassed the CIO in membership by 1941. By that time, however, the CIO had paid its parent the supreme compliment: It had modified its framework to include craft unionism as well as industrial unionism, and the lines separating the two rival federations had become permanently clouded.

At the time of Pearl Harbor, in December 1941, total union membership stood at 10.2 million, compared to the less than 3 million members of only nine years earlier. The CIO itself—representing some 4.8 million workers at this time—was destined to achieve little further success, as measured by sheer membership statistics; it would enroll only 6 million employees at its zenith in 1947 and then gradually retreat before the onslaught of a further AFL counterattack. But if Lewis' organization failed to live up to its founder's expectations as the sole repository of future union leadership, neither could it in any meaningful way be described as a failure. When America entered World War II in late 1941, the labor movement was not only a major force to be reckoned with but, for the first time, was to a great extent representative of the full spectrum of American workers. And for this situation, the CIO's challenge to the AFL's fifty years of dominance deserves no small amount of credit.

WORLD WAR II

As in the case of World War I, the years after Pearl Harbor saw a further increase in union strength. Although the country's economic conditions had improved considerably in the late 1930s, only after the start of hostilities and the acceleration of the draft did a tight labor market arise to weaken employer resistance to union demands.

Other factors favorable to organized labor were also present. The federal government, sympathetic enough with the goals of unionism for almost a decade, now went even further in its tangible support: In return for a no-strike pledge from both AFL and CIO leaders, labor was granted equal representation with management on the tripartite War Labor Board, the all-powerful institution that adjusted collective bargaining disputes during this period. It was also given an unprecedented form of union security—the still-utilized "maintenance of membership" arrangement, requiring all employees who are either union members when the labor contract is signed or who voluntarily join the union after this date to continue their membership for the length of the contract (subject to a short "escape" period). Finally, unions further profited in the membership area from the fast growth of such wartime industries as aircraft and shipbuilding and the reinvigoration of such now crucial sectors as steel, rubber, the electrical industry, and trucking. By the end of the war in 1945, union ranks had been increased by more than 4 million new workers, or by almost 40 percent.

By and large, labor honored its no-strike pledge during hostilities. Somewhat less than one-tenth of 1 percent of total available industrial working time was lost to the war effort through union economic action. But with the cost of living continually rising, and with the War Labor Board nonetheless attempting to hold direct wages in check (not always successfully, and frequently at the cost of allowing such "nonwage" supplements as vacation, holiday, and lunch-period pay), the incidence of strikes did increase steadily after 1942. Particularly galling to the general public were several strikes by Lewis' own Mine Workers, all in direct defiance of President Roosevelt's orders and all given substantial publicity by the mass media.

Managers themselves, regaining much of their lost stature with the stress on war production at this time, could also point to other evidence that labor had become "too powerful." The competition between the AFL and CIO, officially postponed for the duration of the war, in practice continued almost unabated. Such rivalry on occasion temporarily curtailed plant output, as unions within the two federations resorted to "slowdowns" and "quickie strikes" to convince employers of their respective jurisdictional claims. Instances of worker "featherbedding"—the receipt of payment for unperformed work—marked several industries, notably construction. And members of the Communist party, originally welcomed by some CIO unions because of their demonstrated organizational ability, had now gained substantial influence if not effective control within several of these unions, including both the United Automobile Workers and the Electrical, Radio, and Machine Workers.

The public's attention was also called, by forces unhappy with the labor movement's rapid growth, to union political strength. The AFL had not yet abandoned its traditional policy of bipartisanship, but Lewis had led the CIO actively into political campaigning and had, in fact, resigned his federation presidency (while retaining his Mine Workers leadership) when the CIO rank and file had refused to bow to his wishes and vote for Republican Wendell Willkie in 1940. Under Lewis' successor, Philip Murray, and particularly through the direct efforts of Clothing Worker president Sidney Hillman, the CIO had become even more aggressive and influential—within the Democratic party. It now held considerable power within most northern Democratic state organizations, and such was its influence at the national Democratic level that when a fabricated story swept the country to the effect that Roosevelt had ordered his 1944 party convention to "clear everything with Sidney," it was widely believed. So effective had Hillman's CIO Political Action Committee become by this time that attacks upon it emanated from the highest of places: The Republican governor of Ohio claimed that the PAC was "trying to dominate our government with radical and communistic schemes," and the House Un-American Activities Committee (with a membership unfriendly to Roosevelt) called it "a subversive . . . organization."[14]

The American man in the street seemed to be impressed. By the end of the war in 1945, public opinion polls showed more than 67 percent of the respondents in favor of legislative curbs on union power.

PUBLIC REACTION AND PRIVATE MERGER

Organized labor fell even further from public favor in the immediate postwar period. Faced with income declines as overtime and other wartime pay supplements disappeared, with real wage decreases as prices rose in response to the huge pent-up consumer demand, and with layoffs as factories converted to peacetime production, workers struck as they had never done before. Although the violence of earlier-day labor unrest did not recur often, the year 1946 saw new highs established in terms of number of stoppages (4,985), number of employees involved (4.6 million), and man-days idle as a

---

[14]Rayback, *History of American Labor*, p. 386.

percentage of available working time (1.43).[15] The month of January 1946 alone was marked by almost 2 million workers on strike. And by the end of the year, noteworthy stoppages (many of them simultaneously) had occurred in virtually every sector of the economy, including the railroads, autos, steel, public utilities, and even public education.

Such strikes were not well received by a frequently inconvenienced public that had already voiced reservations about union strength. The sentiments that the Wagner Act and other public policies of the 1930s had been too "one-sided" in favor of labor grew rapidly and soon became compelling. In 1947, a newly elected Republican Congress passed, over President Truman's veto, the Taft-Hartley Act.

Taft-Hartley drastically amended the Wagner Act to give greater protection to both employers and individual employees. To the list of "unfair" labor practices already denied employers were added six "unfair" *union* practices, ranging from restraint or coercion of employees to featherbedding. Employees could now hold elections to decertify unions as well as to certify them. Provisions regulating certain internal affairs of unions, explicitly giving employers certain collective bargaining rights (particularly regarding "freedom of expression" concerning union organization), and sanctioning government intervention in the case of "national emergency strikes" were also enacted.

A fuller discussion of Taft-Hartley is reserved for later pages; however, it might be added here that the 1947 act was at least as controversial as the Wagner Act had been. Its proponents, consistent with the views of Senator Taft, asserted that it "reinjected an essential measure of justice into collective bargaining." Less friendly observers of Taft-Hartley, including the spokesmen of organized labor, were less happy and hurled such epithets as "slave labor act" at it. That the act has proved generally satisfactory to the majority of Americans, however, may be inferred from the fact that in the 1970s, Taft-Hartley, essentially unchanged from its original edition, remained the basic labor law of the land.

Speaking with the self-assurance always allowed one who can draw on hindsight, it is tempting to argue that the AFL-CIO merger of 1955 was inevitable. The issue that had led to the birth of the CIO was, as noted, blunted even by the late 1930s, when the AFL rapidly chartered its own industrial unions and the CIO began to recognize craft unions as part of its structure. By 1939, indeed, 10 of the 29 existing CIO unions were craft organizations, and the AFL encompassed possibly as many noncraft workers as it did craftsmen. But sixteen more years were still to elapse before merger became

---

[15] *Monthly Labor Review*, LXIV, No. 5 (May 1947), 782. Recalling this wave of strikes, one former War Labor Board member has commented that a further major factor was release from controls, "together with the economic uncertainty and even fear of a new depression. Controls were more and more difficult to maintain as time went on. It's hard to say how much longer the lid could have been kept on if the war hadn't ended, but strikes upon gaining freedom were very much to have been expected."

a reality, and significant differences of values, political opinions, and personalities still had to be bridged in this period.

In the first place, the new unions that had been formed, first by the CIO and later by the AFL, were often meeting head-on in their quests for new members and enlarged jurisdiction. Any merged federation would have to resolve not only this kind of overlap but also the membership raiding that was frequently carried on by such rival unions. For a long while, compromise seemed impossible: The AFL tended to regard all jurisdictions as exclusively its own and to insist that the CIO unions be fully absorbed within its framework; on its part, the CIO strongly suggested that its affiliates would participate in a merger only if their existing jurisdictions were given official protection.

Second, the conservative AFL leaders displayed deep hostility toward the communist-dominated unions within the CIO. Such unions reached a peak in the immediate postwar months, when a special report of the Research Institute of America listed eighteen of them in this category. And Taft has gone so far as to assert that for a short while in that period, "it was a question whether the anti-Communists in the CIO could muster a majority."[16]

Finally, personalities played a role. Murray, still influenced by his predecessor as CIO president, Lewis, and Green were mutually suspicious leaders. Each was quite unwilling to take the initiative in any merger move that would involve subordination of influence to the other.

By 1955, however, most of these cleavages had been resolved. Murray, his patience with the communist unions exhausted as they became more aggressive and (in particular) strongly opposed the government's Marshall Plan, had taken the lead in expelling most such unions from the CIO in 1949 and 1950.[17] Virtually all other communist-influenced unions, presumably taking the hint, had voluntarily left the federation shortly thereafter. Murray's move cost the CIO an estimated 1 million members, but new unions were quickly established to assume the old jurisdictions, and Murray claimed to have regained most of the lost membership within the next two years.

Further preparing the way for ultimate merger were the 1952 deaths of Murray and Green, both suddenly and only eleven days apart. The two successors—Walter Reuther of the United Auto Workers, for Murray, and AFL secretary-treasurer George Meany, for Green—were relatively divorced from the personal bitterness of the earlier presidents.

And beyond these factors were growing sentiments on the part of both AFL and CIO leaders that only a united labor movement could (1) stave off future laws of the Taft-Hartley variety, (2) avoid the jurisdictional squabbles that were increasingly sapping the treasuries of both federations, and (3) allow

[16]Taft, *Organized Labor*, pp. 623–24.

[17]Support for the 1948 presidential candidacy of Henry A. Wallace by these unions was another leading issue in this split.

organized labor to reach significant new membership totals for the first time since 1947.

In December 1955, culminating two years of intensive negotiations between representatives of the two organizations, the AFL-CIO became a reality. The new constitution respected the "integrity of each affiliate," including both its "organizing jurisdiction" and its "established collective bargaining relationships." Consolidation of the rival unions was to be encouraged, but was to be on a voluntary basis. And it was agreed that the new giant federation would issue charters "based upon a strict recognition that both craft and industrial unions are equal and necessary as methods of trade union organization." Twenty years later, as will be seen, complete harmony between the AFL and CIO wings had yet to be achieved. But with the act of merger, the open warfare that had first revitalized and then damaged the labor movement passed from the scene.

ORGANIZED LABOR SINCE THE MERGER

Although some observers predicted that the original 15-million membership total (two-thirds of it provided by the AFL) of the AFL-CIO would rapidly double, the figure had actually declined, by the beginning of 1976, to 13.6 million.

It is true that the united federation had expelled the International Brotherhood of Teamsters in 1957 for alleged domination by "corrupt influences," thereby depriving itself of 2.1 million members in terms of 1976 statistics. And the 1968 departure from the AFL-CIO fold by the 1.4-million-member United Automobile Workers, an action due especially to Walter Reuther's unhappiness with what he perceived to be a lack of federation leadership aggressiveness, but also complicated by Meany–Reuther personality differences, must also be recognized in explaining the federation's growth failures. But the fact remains that organized labor *overall* has been anything but impressive in terms of membership growth since the merger. The current 21-million figure for all union members (counting those in unions currently outside the ranks of the AFL-CIO—Teamsters, Automobile Workers, Mine Workers, railroad operating employees, and others) is, in fact, less than 3 million higher than it was in the mid-1950s. And since the nation's total labor force has been growing at a much faster clip than organized labor's membership since the merger, labor has clearly been losing ground on a relative basis. At the time of this writing, as mentioned earlier in this book, unionists made up slightly under 30 percent of America's total nonagricultural employment, the lowest percentage since 1942.

Several formidable obstacles undoubtedly serve to explain this situation. Paramount among them is, of course, the fact that blue-collar workers, traditionally comprising that sector of the labor force most susceptible to the overtures of the union organizer, have now been substantially organized. And this sector has, it will be recalled, been declining as a source of jobs in recent years, due mainly to the onslaughts of automation and to changes in demand. It remains to be seen whether or not new approaches, fresh leadership, and environmental changes adversely affecting worker morale can gain for organized labor the allegiance of the growing white-collar sector. As the statistics in the preceding chapter indicated, however, unions to date have not been spectacularly successful in recruiting this wave of the future (their performance in the public sector excepted).

Beyond this, labor's fall from public favor, which began in the 1940s and led initially to the enactment of Taft-Hartley, had yet to be arrested three decades later. Congressional disclosures of corruption in the Teamsters and several smaller unions (among them, the Laundry and Bakery Workers) in the late 1950s hardly improved labor's image. The AFL-CIO quickly expelled the offending unions, but the public seemed to be far more impressed by the disclosures than by the federation's reaction to them, as indeed had been the case following the CIO's expulsion of its communist-dominated affiliates.

Union resistance to technological change, sometimes taking the form of featherbedding and insistence on the protection of jobs that seemed no longer to be needed (those of diesel firemen and certain airline and maritime employees, for example), also was anything but calculated to regain widespread public support. Nor was it easy to generate sympathy outside the labor movement on behalf of plumbers who threatened to strike for wage rates in excess of $15 per hour, electricians demanding a 20-hour workweek, and New York City transit workers seeking a 50 percent wage increase, a 32-hour workweek, and some 75 other demands. These few examples were among the extremes; most unionists showed considerably more concern for the welfare of their industries in the postmerger years. But such actions as the ones illustrated, being more newsworthy, attracted more attention. It is conceivable that, through this combination of factors ranging from corruption to excessive demands, countless potential union members had been alienated.

The continuing lack of public confidence in unionism had also led, in the relatively recent past, to new legislation restricting labor's freedom of action. In particular, the Landrum-Griffin Act of 1959 stemmed from this climate and, directly, from the union-corruption revelations of Congress that were cited above. Among its other provisions, Landrum-Griffin guarantees union members a "Bill of Rights" that their unions cannot violate and requires officers of labor organizations to meet a wide and somewhat cumbersome variety of reporting and disclosure obligations. It also lays out specific ground rules for union elections, rules that have been deemed too inhibiting (as have most other parts of the act) by many labor leaders.

It is perhaps also true that labor's conspicuous recent lack of success has stemmed from what Lester views as four more grounds for union concern: (1) The business leader is no longer the tyrant that he frequently was before the mid-1930s; (2) industrial employees are no longer treated as inferior citizens; (3) unionism's success has decreased its needs; and (4) an affluent society like our present one generates moderation and a middle-class outlook that is at odds with the laboring-class viewpoint espoused by unions.[18] But such statements as these, as thoughtful as they all may be, tend also to be somewhat more conjectural than the earlier reasons offered for the unremarkable growth figures of American unionism over the past twenty years.

At the very least, it was obvious that organized labor could not count the immediate postmerger period among its golden years, and that many of the conditions that could explain unionism's lack of success in these years persisted at the end of this period.

UNIONISM AND THE BLACK WORKER

Inevitably, in the 1970s, organized labor was also forced to devote considerable attention to an issue that was far less parochial in its thrust: the increasingly intense quest of the black community for genuine equality of opportunity. Employment expectations that were initially (if indirectly) raised by the landmark Supreme Court school-desegregation decision of 1954 had been considerably heightened by the broad equal-employment-opportunities legislation of the Civil Rights Act of 1964. And, since even by the end of the sixties the gap between expectation and reality remained significant, the labor movement found itself under growing attack as frustrated blacks charged it with bigotry and racism, collusion with an equally insensitive managerial community to exploit the black worker, and total inadequacy in the field of integrative social action.

Not all blacks, of course, shared this dim opinion. The Urban League's late, highly respected Whitney Young undoubtedly echoed the sentiments of a significant sector of the black world in stating that "when we look at the whole picture, labor is strongly on the side of social justice and equal rights. . . . All unions ought to be educating their members to the dangers of bigotry, and to the fact that racism damages white workers as well as blacks. But on the whole, organized labor is as good a friend of black efforts for equality as exists in our imperfect society."[19] Nor would objective blacks deny not only that AFL-CIO leadership, and particularly Meany and Reuther, had been in the forefront of efforts to enact the equal-employment-opportunities provisions into the Civil Rights Act of 1964 itself, but that for a time these federation chieftains had waged this campaign almost entirely alone. As the head of the NAACP's Washington Bureau, Clarence Mitchell, could later testify in this regard, "Organized labor gave unfailing, consistent

---

[18]Richard A. Lester, "The Changing Nature of the Union," *New York University Thirteenth Annual Conference on Labor* (New York: Mathew Bender & Co., 1960), pp. 19–30.

[19]"John Herling's Labor Letter," *Washington Daily News*, November 30, 1968, p. 4.

and massive support where it counted most. . . . The members of organized labor were always present at the right time and in the right places.[20] And most blacks would presumably acknowledge that the approximately 2.5-million-member black contingent within the ranks of unionism in the middle of the 1970s constituted—in aggregate figures—not only roughly the same proportion as that for blacks in the total U.S. population, but substantial progress from 1928, when black membership was 2.1 percent, and even from 1956, when the figure had climbed to 8.6 percent.[21]

To the growing body of black militants, however, the Youngs and Mitchells could quickly be dismissed as Uncle Toms, whose laudatory statements only proved that they had been captured by the Labor Establishment. And the significant numerical growth in black unionists in no way touched the heart of the problem—that even where the admissions bars were down, a highly disproportionate number of blacks' jobs were at the bottom of the skills ladder, situations shunned by whites and entirely lacking in career progression opportunities. Above all, they could point with considerable bitterness to the building trades, where a decade after the passage of the Civil Rights Act, less than 5 percent of all black apprentices were enrolled in skilled-craft training programs (the remainder being in the so-called "trowel trades"—general laborers, cement masons, and kindred occupations, whose pay scales averaged much less and whose status was lowest). This was an especially jarring situation to blacks, given the increasing number of projects financed with public money.

Thus, while black militants had espoused picketing and (on occasion) disrupted production as a protest against alleged discrimination in the automobile, steel, and appliance sectors, it was in the nation's huge construction industry that the most potentially explosive confrontations had occurred. For a while, hopes for blacks had been raised in this sector, several events in 1969 being especially notable. In Chicago, a black Coalition for United Community Action had demanded 25,346 skilled-trades jobs and a 30 percent membership in nineteen building craft unions that had a total 1969 membership of 90,000 in the metropolitan area (according to the coalition, only 2,251 were from minority groups). It succeeded in temporarily closing construction projects involving nearly $100 million in that city, and a compromise agreement was ultimately effected whereby the unions promised "to obtain employment at once" for 1,000 qualified black journeymen (with the coalition aiding in the recruitment). Several thousand more black workers would also be trained and admitted over the next few years under this plan.

In Pittsburgh, where, despite the fact that blacks constituted 23 percent of the population, only four of 25 building-trades unions had black memberships exceeding 2 percent in late 1969 and only one (the low-skilled general

[20]Ray Marshall, *The Negro Worker* (New York: Random House, 1967), pp. 40–41.
[21]Derek C. Bok and John T. Dunlop, *Labor and the American Community* (New York: Simon & Schuster, 1970), p. 120.

construction laborers local) had a black membership above 10 percent,[22] similar black protests—accompanied by some physical clashing with white construction workers—had also resulted in compromise agreements reasonably satisfactory to the black community, at least as starting points. Other cities appeared destined to be forced to deal with similar protests.

But the unlikely prospects for an amicable or imminent resolution of the national construction-employment issue were accurately indicated by the enthusiastic reception accorded the president of the AFL-CIO Building and Construction Trades Department immediately after the Chicago and Pittsburgh confrontations. On this occasion, he defiantiy declared to 300 cheering delegates at the department's convention, "We wish to make it clear that we do not favor acceptance of unreasonable demands. . . . We should make it clear again that the conduct, curriculum, and control of our training programs are going to remain in the hands of our crafts and our contractors. They are not going to be turned over to any coalition."[23]

And vastly compounding the construction-industry problem was the deeply embedded building-trades tradition of restrictive membership, designed not only to limit competition for jobs and to increase the asking price for the existing members' performance of services, but in part also to nurture a certain amount of father–son employment situations. In support of such goals, and also because much employment in the industry had been intermittent and seasonal, hiring had historically been done through the union hiring hall. Racial intolerance itself had, indeed, not often been easily provable in the face of these other exclusionary considerations—as, presumably, in the case of the Philadelphia building trades local whose leader a few years ago countered black charges of discrimination with the outraged declaration that "we don't take in *any* new members, regardless of color."[24]

Adding a final complexity to the building-trades issue, moreover, was the fact that, by craft-union definition, journeymen cannot be created instantaneously. Skilled ironworkers, plumbers, electricians, steamfitters, and similarly highly remunerated workers by and large have emerged only after rigorous apprenticeship programs, often lasting five or more years (and paying relatively low trainee wages during the period). Only through this process, the unions had argued, could the high standards of the craft be upheld. To many blacks, who had long viewed much of the apprenticeship philosophy as primarily a restrictive device (racial or otherwise) anyhow, the unions owed the black community considerable accelerated upgrading to journeyman status as compensation for years of total exclusion. To many whites already in unions, such a concession would greatly dilute the quality of craftsmanship and thus devastate morale among the present skilled-trades workers.

[22] *Wall Street Journal*, September 26, 1969, p. 1.
[23] *Business Week*, September 27, 1969, p. 31.
[24] Marten Estey, *The Unions* (New York: Harcourt Brace Jovanovich, 1967), p. 68.

The gap separating the two positions was, consequently, a very large one. And given its dimensions, few observers predicted much success even from the federal government's much-heralded Philadelphia Plan, which was also implemented in 1969. This innovative concept established minority-group quotas for six building trades unions working on federal construction jobs in the Philadelphia area, beginning with a 4 percent quota in 1969 and scheduled to rise to a 19 percent average by 1973. It was, however, immediately assailed by unions and some contractors as an illegal system denying to other prospective employees equal protection of the Constitution, as a mechanism that would undermine the crafts and decrease the efficiency of building-trades work, and as an impractical device requiring the hiring of blacks either not available at all or unacceptable as employees if available. Ironically, civil rights groups also quickly attacked the plan as insufficient in ensuring jobs, and also as making no provisions for training or upgrading to journeyman status within the unions. They also viewed it negatively as being geared only to temporary employment. And the influential black spokesman Bayard Rustin, in fact, went so far as to describe the plan as one that "actually does nothing for integration. . . . It is designed primarily to embarrass the unions and to organize public pressure against them."[25]

Although plans similar to Philadelphia's had by the mid-1970s been implemented in Atlanta, San Francisco, St. Louis, Camden, N.J., and Washington, D.C., as well as Chicago (although not Pittsburgh), support for the basic concept involved had long before steadily eroded. It had become a victim not only of the sharp attacks upon it from both sides but of a national white backlash in general. It had also been substantially weakened by the Nixon Administration's preference in the 1970–74 period for a voluntary approach to construction-industry hiring. "It's best," said Secretary of Labor Peter J. Brennan in 1973, "when labor and management honestly agree on a plan and work together to make it succeed,"[26] and under the Nixon "hometown plan" approach to minority hiring, more than 60 such plans—based on having labor, management, and minority leaders work out their own "goals and timetables" for integration—were implemented, with mixed but generally very unimpressive results.

By 1975, the deep national recession, a particularly severe one for construction and whose further employment ramifications for minority-group members will be explored in the last chapter of this book, had further dampened whatever optimism remained for significant building-trades job improvement on the part of blacks. And one could only conclude that if the 1969–75 period could be used as any guide to the future, meaningful progress for blacks in this sector was still many years away.

Nor were the building trades unique in having aroused the ire of blacks. Several of the railway brotherhoods continued to show an almost total

---

[25]Bayard Rustin, "The Blacks and the Unions," *Harper's*, May 1971, p. 79.
[26]*Business Week*, December 1, 1973, p. 86.

absence of blacks on their membership rosters (a situation that could be primarily explained by the strong southern historical ties of these unions), as did some printing and entertainment-industry crafts and the Air Line Pilots Association. And black holders of major union-leadership posts, even in unions with substantial black memberships, remained conspicuous by their absence. Neither the Teamsters nor the Steelworkers, for example, had any blacks on their executive boards despite the large black percentages in both these large internationals; the Automobile Workers, over one-third black, had only two blacks in the 26 positions on its board; and only two of the 35 members of the AFL-CIO's executive council itself were black.

Yet the problem should be viewed in perspective. Generally speaking, industrial unions had rarely practiced membership discrimination either in admission or job assignment. They had recognized that in most industries (as opposed to crafts), large numbers of blacks already existed and that the price of discrimination in such a situation would be the sacrifice of organizing potential. Thus, even prior to the rise of the CIO, the needle-trades unions and coal miners aggressively fought off efforts on the part of their more biased rank and file to restrict membership to whites, and essentially all industrial unions, following the great waves of organization in the 1930s, had espoused a policy of full equality regarding both admission and occupational level for blacks. The attitude of the AFL-CIO has already been cited, in reference to the 1964 Civil Rights Act, and it is no less a matter of record that the federation had consistently upheld as a cardinal principle ever since the 1955 merger, "to encourage all workers without regard to race, creed, color, national origin or ancestry to share equally in the full benefits of union organization."[27] Finally, the effective allowances forged between labor and civil rights groups—which resulted most notably in improved conditions for black Memphis, Tennessee, sanitation workers in 1968, and one year later (under the banner of "Union Power Plus Soul Power Equals Victory") union recognition and considerable economic betterment for black hospital employees in Charleston, South Carolina—cannot be overlooked in any summary of this more positive side of labor's efforts.

Even the federation and industrial unions, however, had been unable to uproot occasional discriminatory practices (as opposed to policies) within the lower levels of their hierarchies. The federation, as Chapter 4 will attempt to show, has limited powers over its affiliates and has stopped short of using its ultimate penalty of expulsion both out of consideration of "overkill" and because of a realistic fear that many craft unions might voluntarily leave the federation fold in sympathy with the disciplined organizations. And the elected leaders of local industrial unions have had, as Bok and Dunlop have accurately pointed out, "much to lose and little to gain by fighting against racial prejudice" where it does exist among their members at these lower

[27] *AFL-CIO Constitution*, Article II, Section 4.

levels, particularly "given the high rate of turnover in local union office, and the natural inclination to remain in power."[28] Again, however, the problem was nowhere near as blatant as in the case of the craft unions.

Perhaps it was asking too much of organized labor to exhibit a record that was above reproach in regard to its treatment of black employees, considering that no other sector of our society had performed any better—or possibly, indeed, as well. But in view of the understandable unhappiness of the black community with labor's performance to date, it was nonetheless obvious in the 1970s that this issue was, for unionism, a great one.

Blacks: A Legal Footnote

Of particular concern to unions and employers had been the tendency of some black workers to bypass the bargaining agent and "take the law in their own hands." That is, to protest against discrimination—real or imagined —some black employees had picketed and otherwise engaged in disrupting activities rather than using union representation to deal with their complaints. This issue was dealt with by the U.S. Supreme Court in 1975.[29] In *Emporium Capwell*, a group of employees of a San Francisco department store believed they were being racially discriminated against in work assignment and promotion, and brought the matter to the attention of their local union. The union investigated the charge, found that indeed the situation was potentially explosive because of the racial issue, and decided to process the complaint through the grievance procedure established by the collective bargaining contract. The grievants, however, refused to participate in the procedure, holding that the contractual provisions were inadequate to handle a grievance of this kind. Taking the matter into their own hands, they began to picket the store, demanding that the president of the company deal with them directly over the issue of racial discrimination. They also distributed handbills urging consumers not to patronize the store. The company warned two of the dissidents that continuance of such conduct would result in their discharge, but the warning was disregarded and the men were, indeed, fired.

The Supreme Court upheld the discharge of the black employees. In its decision, with Justice Thurgood Marshall writing for the majority (the vote was 8-1, with Justice Douglas dissenting), the Court held that the employees were obligated to use the union to seek a remedy through the grievance procedure. Justice Marshall pointed out that labor relations could not be conducted on a sound basis if any group of employees had the right to bypass the exclusive bargaining agent and deal with the employer directly. He stressed that it would place an intolerable burden upon an employer to engage in separate bargaining with various groups of different interests. Also material

[28]Bok and Dunlop, *Labor and the American Community*, p. 135.
[29]*Emporium Capwell Co.* v. *Western Addition Community Organization; NLRB* v. *Same*, U.S. Sup. Ct. Nos. 73–696 and 73–830, February 18, 1975.

to the decision was the observation that if the union failed to represent the black employees fairly and squarely, or if the employer in fact discriminated against them because of their race, the employees had the opportunity to proceed against the union and/or the employer under Title VII of the Civil Rights Act. In other words, the black employees had a remedy in law, should their complaint not be adjusted to their satisfaction.

Although one would sympathize with any minority group whose interests are not protected fairly by a union, or where an employer discriminates against them, the Supreme Court's decision was proper so as to maintain the stability of labor relations. Effective collective bargaining and sound labor relations cannot be implemented if employees have the right to deal with employers apart from the union that represents them.

WOMEN IN LABOR UNIONS

Blacks, assuredly, were not alone in their quest for a greater influence in union affairs. Increasingly, women workers had challenged the Labor Establishment, not so much for employment opportunities in this case as for participation in major union-leadership positions. Through the mid-1970s, such positions were, as they had been throughout labor's long history, held all but exclusively by men.

Consequently, even though women had become significantly more numerous both in the civilian labor force and within union ranks in the years since the merger—by 1975, they made up over 40 percent of the total labor force (up from only about 31 percent twenty years earlier) and about 22 percent of total union membership (as opposed to roughly 18 percent in 1955) —through all this time period, the number of women on the AFL-CIO executive council had stayed at the same level as it had been initially (or at zero). And female occupants of top international-union positions had remained almost as rare. In 1972, for example, women held the national presidencies of only two of the 177 unions in the United States—the Veterinarians, and the Stewards and Stewardesses Division of the Air Line Pilots— or exactly the same number as they had in 1952. They had fared only slightly better in this twenty-year period in gaining the office of national secretary-treasurer, holding thirteen such positions in 1972, as opposed to nine in 1952. And they had actually seen a slippage in their possession of such major appointive positions as research director (down from ten to three) and editor (from six to three), while failing to maintain even one slot as director of organizing activities in these two decades.[30]

It was in recognition of this lack of progress, and a deeply harbored belief that the masculine leaders of labor had not fought aggressively enough for

[30]"Women's Participation in Labor Organizations," *Monthly Labor Review*, Volume 97, No. 10 (October 1974), 8.

higher wages and improved working conditions for their female constituents, that more than 3,000 women members from 58 international unions met at Chicago in March 1974. In general agreement with the sentiments of one speaker (Linda Tarr-Whelan, deputy director for program development for the American Federation of State, County, and Municipal Employees, and as such, symbolically, one of the more prominent female unionists) that "the union presidents understand power,"[31] they formed the Coalition of Labor Union Women (CLUW) to work within the union movement for change.

In particular, they pledged that the new organization's objectives would focus upon increased union efforts to organize women workers; greater participation of women in union affairs, particularly in policy-making positions; positive action by unions against sex discrimination in pay, hiring, job classification, and promotion; and adequate child-care facilities. But while not one union specifically endorsed the new women's group, the founders of CLUW made it very clear that they harbored no thoughts of engaging in a direct confrontation with organized labor. "Working through the union" was the dominant theme of this convention, and no one questioned the declaration of the CLUW's new vice-president, Addie Wyatt, that "our unions are not really our enemies, since we are the unions. Our real job is to see to it that our bosses respond in a more meaningful way to our needs." Nor was any challenge lodged to the assertion of another CLUW leader that "men aren't going to resign their posts. They're just going to have to make room for more people on the boards."[32]

Of course, it remained to be seen if all this oratory would lead to concrete results. At the end of the 1960s, a respected observer had claimed that unions were at that time paying less attention to the special problems of women than they had 60 years earlier; she had also noted that women's pages in labor journals were almost wholly devoted to consumer problems, recipes, and household hints.[33] There was little in the way of evidence to show that much had changed by 1975. And for every union that had clearly in those years devoted more concern to women than it had in the past (the United Automobile Workers, for example, with its increasingly active women's department), there might well have been another (such as the Textile Workers, the Ladies' Garment Workers, and the Amalgamated Clothing Workers, despite the predominantly female memberships of all three of them) that in the mid-1970s appeared to be far less aggressive in pursuing the interests of women than it once was.[34]

Yet one must also recognize the validity of Edna E. Raphael's 1974 state-

[31] *Business Week*, March 30, 1974, p. 102.

[32] *Ibid.*

[33] Alice Cook, "Women and American Trade Unions," *Annals*, January 1968, pp. 124–32.

[34] See Edna E. Raphael, "Working Women and Their Membership in Labor Unions," *Monthly Labor Review*, Volume 97, No. 5 (May 1974), 32, for some elaboration here.

ment that the fast-growing women's liberation movement of the 1970s had already "had an important if only indirect effect on women in the labor movement, through the encouragement it has given to all women to accept themselves as capable and competent to engage in all action on all fronts."[35] As in the case of the black demands for more attention, it was at the very least clear that organized labor could afford to ignore the increasing self-awareness of women only to its definite detriment.

AN ANALYSIS OF UNION HISTORY

It is impossible to explain the history of unionism in this country with a single or all-encompassing theory. Economic, structural, and philosophical factors have all been at work, in varying degrees at various times—as has, occasionally, the sheer force of circumstances.

In earlier years, the highly sporadic growth of the American labor movement depended to a great extent on the basic *health of the economy*, and one can rather closely correlate the years of union success and failure with the periods of good and bad times for general business conditions. Union bargaining power, and thus the basic attractiveness of union membership, was high in the essentially prosperous periods of the years immediately prior to 1819, the 1822–37 era, and in 1850–73 (with the exception of brief recessions in the late 1850s); in each of these intervals, union membership lists significantly rose. By the same token, it was not until the depression of 1873–78 that the labor movement could even moderately withstand the slumping demand for labor services engendered by periods of economic reversal; the depressions of 1819–22 and 1837–50 all but eradicated collective bargaining for their durations.

Nor does such a correlation end with 1878. The record fivefold expansion in union ranks between 1897 and 1904 occurred simultaneously with another economic boom period, and the tight labor markets of the two world wars clearly fostered union growth and labor-organization effectiveness. But after the late 1870s, there are as many exceptions to this rule of "as the economy goes, so goes unionism" as there are illustrations of its accuracy. Organized labor rode out the drastic 1893–96 depression without major depletions of either its ranks or its previously acquired bargaining strength; it was forced into an ignominious retreat in the highly prosperous 1920s; and it enjoyed its greatest successes during the most formidable of all American depressions, in the 1930s. It is clear that the analyst of labor history can take the economic conditions factor only so far.

Room must also be reserved for recognition of the pronounced *structural changes* that unionism has been willing to make throughout its existence to accommodate the changing nature of industry. Some of these attempts were

[35] *Ibid.*

premature and consequently abortive—notably the National Trades' Union of 1834, whose ambitious concept had to await the nationalizing of industry in the 1860s. But just as the widening of product markets had given impetus to the growth of local unions at the turn of the nineteenth century, the extension of labor markets following the construction of comprehensive railroad networks ultimately made the coordination of local unionism through the national union structure no less mandatory. Had labor been either unwilling or unable to establish its countervailing power in this fashion, the existence of the movement on any significant scale might have ended with the rise of the large national corporation in the closing decades of the century. It is equally tempting to speculate as to the sanguine effects for labor of the establishment of the AFL's "exclusive jurisdiction" concept; it is a matter of record, however, that the rival unionism of the pre-1886 period had proven highly detrimental to many national unions.

Above all, it is undeniable that labor faced a critical juncture in the midst of the Great Depression, when the continuing wisdom of its craft-unionism structure was severely questioned—and that, however begrudgingly the peak federation moved to accommodate the millions of industrial-unionist constituents who desired acceptance, an ultimate willingness to adapt to a changing situation was for labor the only logical decision. High wassail did not prevail at the banquet tables of the mighty.

Major *philosophical decisions*, too, have exerted a strong influence on the state and shape of American unionism in the 1970s. In many ways, Samuel Gompers was not only the father of the modern labor movement but its supreme spiritual symbol. A pronounced strain of pragmatism runs, in fact, through all of labor's history, just as it motivated so many of Gompers' actions. The mainstream of labor, with or without Gompers, has always stressed the practical at the expense of the ideal, shunning, as he and his fellow AFL founders did, "objects that cannot be realized in a few years." To George Meany, "ideology is baloney."

Thus, such presumed social panaceas as the socialistic agricultural communities, land reform, and producers' cooperatives that were proposed by the zealous reformers of the 1840s had no great appeal to the typical working-man; their connection with his on-the-job happiness and their relevance to solving the pressing problems of industrialization were too remote to be appreciated. The same can be said of the National Labor Union's advocacy of the termination of the convict-labor system, currency reform, and women's suffrage three decades later, and of Terrence V. Powderly's campaign for cooperatives and temperance. Nor does the notable failure of the IWW and its revolutionary credo that "the working class and the employing class have nothing in common" detract from this common denomination. Such lofty goals as these and their latter-day reincarnations in the various radical groups that have on many occasions dotted the periphery of the labor movement have been received with total apathy by the average rank-and-file unionist.

What *has* historically concerned the union member has been more in the here and now: more economic benefits, improved working conditions, and, above all else, a maximum of job security. These great motivators of support for organized labor accounted directly, it will be remembered, for the rise of the first American unions, and no labor organization of any lasting influence since 1800 has ever lost sight of such mundane, "bread-and-butter," but also (to the union constituent) vitally important goals.

So greatly does this stamp of "pure and simple," "more and more" unionism permeate labor history that whole schools of academic thought in the labor area have been built around it. Most notable of them is the John R. Commons–Selig Perlman, or "Wisconsin School," theory, which holds that the key to understanding union growth and survival rests primarily on understanding the American worker's "consciousness of scarcity" and of limited opportunity, which in turn fostered a deep desire for improved "property rights" on the job itself. To protect the dignity and security of the individual jobholder, collective bargaining appears to this school to have been accepted by employees as a vital first step.

History seems to support this basic Commons-Perlman thesis as at least a major further explanation of American labor history. It has not been by sheer coincidence that all major periods of union growth, excepting only wartime ones, have been marked by widespread job insecurity; this situation was as true of both 1800–19 and 1822–37, when the worker fears stemmed primarily from employer cost-cutting devices necessitated by the new scope of product markets, as it was two decades later, when the menace of inter-worker competition on a geographic basis due to widened labor markets was the major cause of alarm. It was as much in evidence when the immigrant waves from Europe accelerated in the late 1860s as in the 1897–1904 period, marked by its myriad of "scientific management" innovations. And the booming union totals of the 1930s coincided, of course, with the Great Depression. The fact that equally great "consciousness of scarcity" characterized other, *less* successful periods for labor (for example, the 1904–16 period, when European immigration hit its peak) in no way negates the "Wisconsin School" thesis.

But just as some attention must be paid to the economic and structural factors in addition to these philosophical ones in understanding the growth of unionism, and just as Maslow's Need Hierarchy can hardly be ignored in dealing at least with contemporary unionism, so too must one recognize that some key aspects of labor history defy any theoretical generalizations at all. One can attempt to account for the huge success of AFL and CIO organizational drives in the 1930s, for example, in terms of "willingness to adjust to organizational forms" (structural) or "job consciousness" (philosophical)— if not in terms of the "economic conditions" framework—but in doing so he has only a partial explanation. In retrospect, the evidence is clear that *both* of the factors above combined with a variety of special economic, public-policy, and labor-leadership circumstances to foster this great period of union growth, and that in many ways each further factor was unprecedented in its order of magnitude. Similarly, the adverse technological, public relations, and legal obstacles with which labor has been confronted over the past two decades also hinge on unparalleled conditions.

Thus what is past may not necessarily, the declaration of Shakespeare notwithstanding, be prologue. And hopes for a resurgence of union growth that are anchored only to the propositions that labor's growth has "always" been sporadic, that unionism has "always" been able to adapt itself structurally to changing needs, and that worker job consciousness has "always" guaranteed collective bargaining a firm place in our society are not necessarily justified.

What, then, can one say about labor's future in terms of its past? Even with the high degree of uncertainty that such predictions inevitably involve, and despite all the unprecedented circumstances since the 1930s, at least one factor emerges clearly from a reading of labor history in this country, and it suggests that the current reports of unionism's impending doom may indeed be grossly exaggerated. Organized labor has been surrounded by conditions at least as bleak as those confronting it today many times in its 175-year history, and on each occasion it has proved equal to the challenge. It has fully recovered not only from the disastrous economic depressions that at various times have wiped out most of its membership, but from the inroads of reformers who temporarily succeeded in divorcing it almost entirely from its collective bargaining functions. It has overcome devastating victories won by employers, and formidable weapons in the hands of the courts. It has incurred deep-rooted public disfavor before, particularly in the 1870s and 1920s, and ultimately surmounted it. And at perhaps the two most critical junctures of all in its still-short history—(1) in the 1880s with the rapid disintegration of the Knights and their "one big union" concept, and (2) on the eve of the Great Depression, when an apathetic AFL remained almost exclusively the province of the highly skilled amid severe membership losses and concerted attacks from without—a Gompers and a Lewis could emerge to lead unionism to heights previously thought unreachable.

It is entirely possible that labor's remarkable staying power has been due to the single fact that to many workers, from the early nineteenth century to the present, there has really been no acceptable substitute for collective bargaining as a means of maintaining and improving employment conditions. Whatever its deficiencies, the labor union has offered millions of employees in our profit-minded industrial society sufficient hope that their needs, not only as employees but as individuals, would be considered to warrant their taking out union membership. At the very least, these employees have been satisfied that the only theoretical alternative to collective bargaining—individual bargaining—has for them been no alternative at all from a practical viewpoint.

Thus, the strongest of cases can be built, as the earliest pages of this book have indicated, that collective bargaining is here to stay—most probably in the highly pragmatic "bread-and-butter" form from which its successes have always emanated, and quite probably also with future structural modifications (however belated at times these may be in coming) to accommodate future institutional needs—but at least here in some form that is not dramatically different from its present character for the foreseeable future.

From this it necessarily follows that, as Kheel has pointed out, "Our objective must be not to find a substitute for bargaining but to discover ways of making it work better."[36] And the latter can be located only after one fully understands not only the labor relations process but the framework in which it operates, toward which understanding such a book as this is, of course, directed.

DISCUSSION QUESTIONS

1. "Without the rise of the merchant-capitalist in this country, there could have been no genuine labor movement." Comment.

2. It has been said that "unions are for capitalism for the same reason that fish are for water." Elaborate upon this statement, drawing from the historical record.

3. Explain the paradox that until relatively recent years skilled workers who enjoyed comparatively high levels of income and status constituted the main source of union membership.

4. "If the Knights of Labor expired because it could not fulfill any function, the American Federation of Labor succeeded because it could admirably fulfill many functions." Elaborate, qualifying this statement if you believe that qualifications are needed.

5. Richard A. Lester has offered as his opinion that "even with the New Deal . . . union development experienced, not a marked mutation, but a partial alteration and expansion in leadership, tactics, and jurisdiction. The adjustment in basic union philosophy was neither profound nor completely permanent." Do you agree?

6. If a Gompers and a Lewis could emerge to rescue unionism at critical times in the past, cannot a case be made that there is nothing basically wrong with organized labor today that imaginative leadership could not cure? Discuss fully.

7. Evaluate the argument that, at least in part, unionism has become a victim of its own success.

SELECTED REFERENCES

DUBOFSKY, MELVYN, *American Labor Since the New Deal*. Chicago: Quadrangle, 1971.

DULLES, FOSTER RHEA, *Labor in America*, 2nd rev. ed. New York: Thomas Y. Crowell, 1960.

FINLEY, JOSEPH E., *The Corrupt Kingdom: The Rise and Fall of the United Mine Workers*. New York: Simon & Schuster, 1972.

[36]Theodore W. Kheel, "A Labor Relations Policy for 1964," *Personnel Journal*, April 1964, p. 181.

GALENSON, WALTER, *The CIO Challenge to the AFL: A History of the American Labor Movement, 1935–1941.* Cambridge, Mass.: Harvard University Press, 1960.

HENRY, ALICE, *Women and the Labor Movement.* New York: Arno Press, New York Times Co., 1971.

LITWACK, LEON, *The American Labor Movement.* Englewood Cliffs, N.J.: Prentice-Hall, 1962.

LYND, ALICE and STAUGHTON LYND, *Rank and File.* Boston: Beacon Press, 1974.

PIERSON, FRANK C., *Unions in Postwar America.* New York: Random House, 1967.

RAYBECK, JOSEPH G., *A History of American Labor.* New York: Free Press, 1966.

TAFT, PHILIP, *Organized Labor in American History.* New York: Harper & Row, 1964.

TYLER, GUS, *The Labor Revolution.* New York: Viking, 1966.

ULMAN, LLOYD, *American Trade Unionism—Past and Present.* Berkeley, Calif.: Institute of Industrial Relations, University of California, 1961.

——, *The Rise of the National Trade Union.* Cambridge, Mass.: Harvard University Press, 1955.

Chapter 3
The Legal Framework

As previous pages have suggested, today's manager is hardly free to deal with the union as he wishes. A growing body of federal and state laws and the judicial and administrative interpretations of these laws now govern the employer at virtually all points at which he comes into contact with organized labor. Legislation today has much to say about management's role in union organizational campaigns and its bargaining procedures in negotiating contracts once a union has gained recognition. It is also outspoken about the acceptable contents of the company's labor agreements, and even its actions in administering these agreements. As is also true of the union, whose conduct is at least equally regulated by public policy, the employer can scarcely afford to be poorly informed in the area of labor law.

If the laws have become extensive, however, they have also become complex and often nebulous. Labor lawyers have been forced to undertake Herculean tasks, not always successfully, in attempting to assess what is legal and what is not in the sphere of collective bargaining. And inconsistent interpretations of the labor statutes—stemming from the National Labor Relations Board, the various state and lower federal judiciaries, and the Supreme Court itself—continue to mark the field. There is, in fact, some justification for those who have termed the last major piece of federal labor legislation, the Landrum-Griffin Act of 1959, the "Lawyers' Full Employment Act."

But if it is impossible to state definitively the exact constraints on union–management relations that the law now imposes, at least what might appropriately be described as "currently useful generalizations" can be offered. Moreover, not only such basic principles but also their paths of development must be dealt with if the environment in which labor relations operate in the late 1970s is to be fully appreciated. If the lessons of general labor history have greatly influenced the nature of the bargaining process as it exists today, the ever-greater thrust of the laws has had an equally pervasive effect.

THE ERA OF JUDICIAL CONTROL

In view of the present scope of labor legislation, it is somewhat ironic that only four decades ago, employers were virtually unrestrained by law from dealing with unions as they saw fit. There was, as we have seen, almost no statutory treatment of labor–management relations from the days of the American Revolution until the Great Depression of the 1930s. Instead, individual judges exercised public control over these relations. And the courts' view of union activities was, for the most part, as unsympathetic as was that of most businessmen of the times.

The employers' traditional weapons for fighting labor organizations— such as formal and informal espionage, blacklists, and the very potent practice of discharging "agitators"—were normally left undisturbed by the judges. However, if the members of the judiciary believed that union activities were being conducted either for "illegal purposes" or by "illegal means," they were generous in extracting money damages from the unions and in ordering criminal prosecution of labor leaders.

The qualifications for "illegality" varied to some extent from court to court. In general, however, most aggressive union activities of the day— strikes to obtain agreements whereby the employer would employ only union members (the closed shop), picketing by "strangers" (those not in a direct superior–subordinate relationship with the employer), and the secondary boycott (the exercise of economic pressure against one company to force it to exert pressure on another company that is actually the subject of the union's concern)—were held to be illegal. Many courts went even further: Through the 1920s, such remarks as, "Judicial actions against even peaceful picketing are merely declaratory of what has always been the law and the best practice in equity," flowed freely from the judges. And although it was President Calvin Coolidge who asserted that "the business of the United States is business," the remark could readily have emanated from most members of the judiciary well into the third decade of this century. The courts, viewing their primary role as that of protecting property rights, allied themselves with few exceptions squarely with the employer community to neutralize the economic power of organized labor.

Fully as welcome to employers, too, was the extensive court use of the injunction. This device, a judicial order calling for the cessation of certain actions deemed injurious and for which the other forms of court-provided relief appeared to be unsuitable remedies, was often invoked by the judges following employer requests for such intervention. To unionists, such restraining orders seemed to be issued quite indiscriminately. Even the relatively detached observer of legal history, however, would very likely conclude that it did not seem to take much to convince the judges that union activities should be curbed: The jurists issued their restraining decrees almost as reflex actions; and strikes, boycotts, picketing—virtually any form of union "self-help" activity—thus ran the risk of being abruptly ended if in any way present or imminent damage to the employer's property could be shown as being threatened.

THE NORRIS–LA GUARDIA ACT OF 1932

Despite its 1932 date, the Norris–La Guardia Act is of considerably more than historical interest. As is true of the later labor laws that will be discussed in this chapter, most of its provisions are still valid and continue today to govern labor relations in interstate commerce.

At the time of its passage, however, the act was particularly noteworthy. Not only did it constitute the first major interindustry federal legislation to be applied to collective bargaining, but—as stated earlier—it marked a significant change in public policy *from repression to strong encouragement of union activity*. Implemented in the final days of the Hoover administration, it owed its birth mainly to the widespread unemployment of the times and to a general recognition that only through bargaining collectively could many employees exercise any meaningful influence on their working environments. It also stemmed, however, from popular sentiment that justice had not been served by allowing the courts their virtually unlimited authority to issue injunctions in labor disputes.

Accordingly, the act greatly narrowed the scope of the courts for issuing such injunctions. Peaceful picketing, peaceable assembly, organizational picketing, payment of strike benefits, and a host of other union economic weapons were now made nonenjoinable. Also enacted within the new law were procedural requirements for injunctions issued on other grounds.

Even more symbolic of the major shift in public policy was the act's assertion that it was now necessary for Congress to guarantee to the individual employee "full freedom of association, self-organization, and designation of representatives of his own choosing, to negotiate the terms and conditions of his employment . . . free from interference, restraint, or coercion of employers." All the federal labor laws passed since 1932 have embodied this same principle.

Nor was the new treatment of unionism destined to be confined only to the federal arena. Within a short period of time, twenty states (including almost all the major industrial ones) had independently created their own "little Norris–La Guardia Acts" to govern labor relations in intrastate commerce.

Norris–La Guardia and its state counterparts did not by themselves, however, greatly stimulate union growth. They clearly expanded union freedoms and placed legal limits on judicial capriciousness, but they did little to restrain employers directly in their conduct toward collective bargaining. Only the previously cited "yellow-dog" contract arrangement, whereby managements had been able to require nonunion membership or activity as a condition of employment, was declared unenforceable by the 1932 act. Otherwise, employers remained at liberty to fight labor organizations by whatever means they could implement, despite the ambitious language of Norris–La Guardia.

THE WAGNER ACT OF 1935

It remained for the National Labor Relations Act of 1935, more commonly known as the Wagner Act, to alter this situation, by putting teeth in the government's pledge to protect employee collective bargaining rights. The Wagner Act, it will be recalled, accomplished this through two basic methods: (1) It specifically banned five types of management action as constituting "unfair labor practices"; and (2) it set forth the principle of majority rule for the selection of employee bargaining representatives and provided that, should the employer express doubt as to the union's majority status, a secret-ballot election of the employees would determine if the majority existed. It also created an independent, quasi-judicial agency—the National Labor Relations Board (NLRB)—to provide the machinery for enforcing both these provisions.

Employer Unfair Labor Practices

The five employer unfair labor practices, deemed "statutory wrongs" (although not crimes) by Congress, have been modified to some small extent since 1935, as noted below. They remain, however, a significant part of the law of collective bargaining to this day, and they constitute an impressive quintet of "thou shalt nots" for employers who might otherwise be tempted to resort to the blunt tactics of prior eras in an effort to undermine unionism. The Wagner Act (1) deemed it "unfair" for managements to "interfere with, restrain, or coerce employees" in exercising their now legally sanctioned right of self-organization; (2) restrained company representatives from dominating or interfering with either the formation or the administration of labor unions; (3) prohibited companies from discriminating "in regard to hire or tenure of employment or any term or condition of employment to encourage or discourage membership in any labor organization"; (4) forbade employers to discharge or otherwise discriminate against employees simply because the latter had filed "unfair labor practice" charges or otherwise offered testimony against company actions under the act; and (5) made it an unfair labor practice for employers to refuse to bargain collectively with the duly chosen representatives of their employees.

In the years since 1935, the NLRB and the courts (to which board decisions can be appealed by either labor relations party) have had ample opportunity to make known their interpretations of all five of these provisions. In dealing with some of them, both public bodies have been quite consistent in their decisions, and what the framers of the Wagner Act had in mind is no longer seriously questioned by either management or union representatives. In other cases, however, the board members and judges have had some difficulty in issuing rulings that have been perceived by the labor relations parties as being compatible with prior rulings on the same subject. But the judges have at least generally proved themselves to be reluctant to reverse the original NLRB decisions when these have been appealed to the courts, and the inconsistencies would in most cases appear to stem more from the changing membership of the five-member board through the years and from inherent difficulties in the words of the laws themselves than from this "opportunity for appeal" factor.

Relatively clear-cut decisions have been rendered by the NLRB and courts in two of the five areas:

1. The interpreters of the Wagner Act have consistently held a wide variety of employer practices to be in violation of the "interfere with, restrain or coerce employees" section. Among other management actions, bribery of employees, company spy systems, blacklisting of union sympathizers, removal of an existing business to another location for the sole purpose of frustrating union activity, and promises by employers of wage increases or other special concessions to employees should the latter refrain from joining a union have all historically constituted "interference" contrary to the act. The same can be said of board and court treatment of employers who have threatened to isolate ("like a rotten apple," in one case) pro-union workers, engaged in individual bargaining with employees represented by a union, or questioned employees concerning their union activities in such a way as to tend to restrain or coerce such employees. When satisfied that any such violations have occurred, the board has issued "cease and desist" orders against the guilty employer with no hesitation. And when it has found that employees have been discharged unlawfully in the process, the NLRB has most frequently required their reinstatement with full back pay.

Particularly in this area, the courts have proved unwilling, by and large, to reverse board decisions upon appeal, moreover, and the fact that failure to "cease and desist" after the courts have called for this action constitutes contempt of court has at times dissuaded employers from carrying an appeal to the courts in the first place. However, under normal circumstances, the employer who both refuses to comply with an adverse board order and decides not to appeal it (so as not to bring the matter to the court's attention) stands to gain little; the NLRB itself can be counted upon to take the initiative and ask the judges for an order calling for employer compliance with the original board decision.

2. The board and courts have also had no apparent difficulty in deciding what constitutes evidence of employer discrimination related to the fourth unfair labor practice. They long ago concluded that such management actions

as the layoff of an employee shortly after his testimony before the board and the discharge of a woman worker immediately after her husband had filed unfair labor practice charges (on other grounds) against the company could be taken as discriminatory, and have consistently ruled in this direction ever since. The board has further concluded, apparently also without much hesitation, that a company's belief that charges filed by an employee are false in no way justifies its taking punitive action against the employee. On the other hand, considerably fewer cases have had to be decided concerning this fourth unfair practice than any of the others, presumably because employers have themselves recognized that violations here are normally quite obvious to all concerned, and have therefore refrained from taking such action in the first place.

Interpretation seems to have been somewhat more difficult when the issues have involved the three other portions of the employer unfair labor practice section.

1. The restriction on company discrimination "in regard to hire or tenure of employment or any term or condition of employment to encourage or discourage membership in any labor organization" has clearly made it unlawful for employers to force employees who are union members to accept less desirable job assignments than nonunionists, or to reduce the former type of employee's pay because of the union affiliation. Similarly, it is obvious that companies that demand renunciation of union membership as a condition of continued employment, or in order to be promoted within the nonsupervisory ranks, do so only at their peril. But the legality of other types of employer conduct has proved to be anything but as clearcut.

Where, for example, there is conclusive evidence that an employee has falsified his employment application and thus failed to reveal a previous criminal record, can he be properly discharged by the company for this offense? Not always, according to at least one NLRB decision covering exactly this situation. Here, the board cited the company's "antiunion bias," its knowledge of the employee's union activities, and its treatment of nonunion employees who had committed comparable offenses, in deciding that the company's official reason for the discharge was only a pretext for discriminating against union members.[1] Cases of this kind have proved to be thorny ones for the board and the courts and have often caused considerable flows of adrenalin on the part of employers.

2. The proviso restraining company representatives from dominating or interfering with both the formation and the administration of labor unions —included because of Congress's unhappiness with the widespread creation of employer-influenced company unions in the years preceding 1935—has been the basis of much complex litigation since that date. Falcone has tersely

---

[1] *Photoswitch*, 99 NLRB 1366 (1962).

pointed out that "it is generally held that when an employer has control over the union sitting on the other side of the bargaining table, collective bargaining is a farce and a delusion";[2] but determining just when an employer has such control has proved to be no easy matter. Among specific management actions that the board and courts have looked unfavorably upon as evidence of employer control have been the following: the solicitation of company-union membership by supervisory employees, the company's payment of membership dues for all employees joining the union, and an employer gift to a union of $400 and the right to operate a canteen that made a monthly profit of $50 to $100—none of these company moves being especially notable for their subtlety. On the other hand, interpretations have found nothing unlawful in the mere fact that, for example, a labor organization limits its membership to employees of a single employer; the test for unfair practice pivots exclusively upon the question of which party *controls* the organization, and in a case such as this only much closer inspection (and the standards for "control" established by the interpreters) can reveal whether or not the employer is in violation of the law.

3. The fact that the 1935 legislation said little more on the subject of an employer's "refusal to bargain collectively with the representatives of his employees" than can be gleaned from these words perhaps guaranteed that controversies would result from this last section of the Wagner Act's "Rights of Employees" section, and this has indeed been the case. As such new topics for potential bargaining as pensions, health insurance, seniority, and subcontracting have arisen in the years since 1935, the NLRB and courts have been freely called upon to make known their opinions as to what must be bargained by employers, and what need not be. The courts have also been asked for a more precise definition of "bargaining" itself than the act provided. The issue is still far from resolved, and with new possibilities for bargaining constantly emerging, perhaps it never fully will be. But the board and judicial decisions of the past four decades have at least ambitiously attempted to shed light on the scope for employer action in this area, and certain statements can now be made with some authority.

In brief, there are today many "mandatory" subjects of bargaining with which the employer must deal in good faith. Such subjects include wages, hours of employment, health insurance, pensions, safety practices, the grievance procedure, procedures for discharge, layoff, recall and discipline, seniority, and subcontracting. Managers are not required to make concessions or agree to union proposals on any of these (or various other) subjects. They *are* obligated, however, to meet with the union at reasonable times and with the good-faith intention of reaching an agreement. On "nonmandatory" or "voluntary" subjects—those that are lawful but not easily related to "wages, hours and other conditions of employment"—employers are not so obligated and are free to refuse to bargain about them.

[2]Nicholas S. Falcone, *Labor Law* (New York: John Wiley, 1963), p. 213.

Where there is a duty to bargain, the employer must supply—upon union request—information that is "relevant and necessary" to allow the labor representatives to bargain "intelligently and effectively." The NLRB and courts have ruled, for example, that a union is entitled to information in the employer's possession concerning wage rates and increases, on the grounds that it cannot deal intelligently with the subject without such information. Similarly, if a company claims financial inability to honor the union's demands, it must stand ready to supply the union with authoritative proof of this inability.

The employer's duty to bargain also entails the duty to refrain from taking unilateral action on the "mandatory" subjects. Companies that have announced a wage increase without consulting the employees' designated representatives, or have subcontracted work to another employer without allowing their own union a chance to bargain the matter, violate this portion of the law.

Yet the apparent finality of such remarks as these is highly deceptive. Not only is considerable uncertainty left as to what else is a "mandatory" subject for bargaining (beyond the specific topics cited and the few others that the NLRB and judges have thus far dealt with affirmatively) and what is "nonmandatory," but the question of what constitutes "the good-faith intention of reaching an agreement" on the employer's part is left an open one.

It remains to be seen what further subjects the board and courts will ultimately assign to the "mandatory" category. A union demand for moving allowances for workers transferred by the company? A proposal that all production workers be placed on a salaried basis, rather than being paid by the hour? A request by the labor organization that all foreign production of the company's product be terminated? Guarantees by the company that pension funds will be invested in low-cost housing for union employees? Each of these demands has been raised on several occasions in actual bargaining situations in recent years. Except for the first, company negotiators have been notably reluctant to accommodate any of them, or numerous similarly ambitious union proposals. Yet as Fleming, who raises the possibility of all of them ultimately going before the interpreters of public policy, has pointed out, "In the changing and very real world of bargaining, all [of these and similar demands] may be close to the felt needs of the parties . . . [and] deciding which of [them] falls into the mandatory category will not be an easy task. Job security and internal union affairs pose extremely delicate issues."[3]

If disposition of such issues as these must thus await future board and court treatment, it at least appears safe to predict that the books have not yet closed on the list of "mandatory" topics; most of the subjects with which

[3]Robben W. Fleming, "The Obligation To Bargain in Good Faith," in Joseph Shister et al., *Public Policy and Collective Bargaining* (New York: Harper & Row, 1962), p. 83; see also Guy Farmer, *Management Rights and Union Bargaining Power* (New York: Industrial Relations Counselors, Inc., 1965).

employers are now required to deal in good faith are themselves relative newcomers to such status, and the NLRB and jurists today appear to be more activistic in this regard than ever.

Another fact is of significance. When the NLRB or a court determines that an issue does *not* fall within the mandatory category, it means that such an issue will probably not be included in a collective bargaining contract. With respect to these subjects, the parties may agree *voluntarily* to include them, but neither side may force such an issue to an impasse. For example, a union may not strike on an issue that is held to fall within the nonmandatory category. Thus, if such a proposal is not to the liking of one party, it may simply refuse to bargain over the issue, and the other side may not use economic power (such as a strike, lockout, or picketing) to force the issue. Over the years, the NLRB and the courts have found many issues to fall within the nonmandatory category. Employers may not insist that a union withdraw fines previously imposed upon union members who have crossed picket lines during a strike; demand that a national union be a party to the contract where a local union affiliated with the national union is the lawful and certified bargaining representative; require a union to post a performance bond; require that nonunion employees shall have the right to vote on the provisions of the contract negotiated by the union; or demand a strike-vote election among employees before a strike occurs.

Unions may not insist that the employer increase pensions and other benefits of those employees already retired; require a company to contribute to an industrywide promotion fund; make the prices that an employer charges for food in its cafeteria and vending machines subject to joint determination; or require a bank to continue a free investment counseling service for employees whom the bank terminated.

The steadily increasing types of tests adopted by the board and courts for "good faith"—for example, whether or not employer delaying tactics were used in the bargaining, some evidence of management initiative in making counterproposals, employer willingness to accommodate completely routine demands (such as the continued availability of plant parking spaces) —have seemingly been attacked more for their naïveté than for the spirit behind them. As the authors of the highly respected Committee for Economic Development's *The Public Interest in National Labor Policy* have asserted:

> The limitations and artificiality of such tests are apparent, and the possibilities of evasion are almost limitless. . . . Basically, it is unrealistic to expect that, by legislation, "good faith" can be brought to the bargaining table.[4]

At the very least, however, it is obvious that in being forced to plug the existing gaps in the Wagner Act's "refusal to bargain" interpretations, representatives of public policy have projected themselves more and more into

[4]Committee for Economic Development, *The Public Interest in National Labor Policy* (New York: CED, 1961), p. 82.

the labor–management arena in the years since 1935, perhaps to an extent that was never contemplated when the Wagner Act was passed.

Employee Representation Elections

Despite all the interpretative difficulties that have been involved in the employer unfair labor practice provisions, the latter clearly were—and are—wide-sweeping in their implications for collective bargaining. However, they still represent an *indirect* approach to the protection of employee bargaining rights: By themselves, they clearly restrict employer action in the labor relations area, but they say nothing explicit about the key question of initial union recognition.

The authors of the Wagner Act were well aware of this gap and proceeded to deal directly with the issue in another section of the act, that pertaining to the secret-ballot election. As noted previously, the NLRB was authorized to conduct such an election should the company express doubt that a majority of its employees had chosen to be represented by any union at all. Prior to this time, a union could gain recognition from an unreceptive employer only through the successful use of such economic weapons as the strike and boycott.

As this part of the act now stands, the board can conduct a representation election if requested to do so by a single employee, by a group of employees, or by a labor organization acting for employees. In any of these three cases, the petition must be supported by "a substantial number of employees" who desire collective bargaining representation, and it must allege that the employer refuses to recognize such representation. Employers may also petition for such an election, presumably with the objective of proving that the employees do *not* desire union representation or for various reasons of scheduling strategy (such as trying to get the board to hold the election at the time least favorable to the union).

It is also possible for an election to involve two or more unions, each claiming "substantial" employee support. The employees then have the choice of voting for any of the unions on the ballot or for "no union." If none of these choices (including "no union") wins a majority of the votes cast, a runoff election is then conducted between the two choices that have received the highest number of votes.

In administering this portion of the law, the NLRB itself ultimately framed a few further rules designed to foster labor relations stability. Should any union win an NLRB-conducted election and then execute a valid contract with the employer, rival unions may now not seek bargaining rights (through a subsequent election) for a period of three years following the effective date of the contract or for the length of the contract—whichever is the shorter. However, the victorious union is still not guaranteed its bargaining rights for this period of time: If the employees themselves have second thoughts about the desirability of retaining the union's services, they can—

after one year—petition the NLRB for a decertification election. A majority vote in this election rescinds the union's bargaining agency.

Although winning an election is by far the most common way a union secures bargaining rights, there are circumstances under which the NLRB now orders an employer to bargain collectively even though it does not conduct an election. These occur when a union is successful in getting a majority of employees in a bargaining unit to sign union-membership authorization cards, and the employer engages in serious unfair labor practices the effect of which destroys the union's majority. For example, the employer may discharge employees who are union sympathizers. In such situations, the NLRB theory is that a union would win the election were it not for the unfair labor practice, and the holding of the election would not reflect the actual sentiment of the employees. In 1969, the Supreme Court sustained this doctrine in *NLRB* v. *Gissel Packing Company*.[5]

Employers and management groups have bitterly criticized this NLRB policy. They contend that the NLRB should not order collective bargaining on the basis of authorization cards; the test of the union's majority should be determined only through an election. Employers contend that employees may sign cards because of social pressure or could be misled by a union organizer as to the purpose of the authorization card. Of course, employers can avoid the effect of the policy by not engaging in serious unfair labor practices during the time a union conducts its organizing campaign. In the last analysis, therefore, it depends upon employer conduct as to whether the NLRB will order collective bargaining based on authorization cards. Also, if frequency is used as a standard, the issue of bargaining orders based on authorization cards has been exaggerated. In the typical year, the NLRB orders collective bargaining on this basis in only about 1 percent of the cases. In all other cases, the board determines the majority status of unions through the election process.

FROM THE WAGNER ACT TO TAFT-HARTLEY

As established by the Wagner Act, then, the scope of National Labor Relations Board activities was to be twofold. The board was charged with investigating employer unfair labor practices, and it was given the authority to conduct employee representation elections.

The NLRB's members (appointed by the president, subject to confirmation by the Senate) and its various regional officials outside Washington, even in their earliest years of existence, undertook both these assignments zealously. By 1947, they had processed almost 44,000 unfair labor practice cases, running the gamut in their decisions from dismissing complaints as having no merit to issuing "cease and desist" orders against guilty employers. In the area of representation cases, the board was even more active. Almost

5395 U.S. 575 (1969).

balancing effects of T-H

60,000 such cases were dealt with between 1935 and 1947. In addition to determining whether or not elections should be held and conducting such elections if the answer was in the affirmative, the NLRB often had the further duty of deciding the type of unit appropriate for the particular labor relationship (such as employer, craft, or plant).

Although its activities were necessarily controversial, as was the act sanctioning them, there is general agreement today that in this twelve-year period the board performed its basic mission of protecting the right of employees to organize and bargain collectively quite creditably. Even at the time, many contemporaries had been impressed; as in the case of Norris–La Guardia, "Little Wagner Acts" were soon enacted in many states to govern labor relations in intrastate commerce.

The modern labor movement in this country can, in fact, justifiably be said to have begun in 1935. Union membership totals boomed after that year, due in no small measure to the Wagner Act and its state counterparts. Other factors were, of course, also responsible: the improving economic climate, the generally liberal sentiments of the times, the keen competition between the American Federation of Labor and the newly born Committee for Industrial Organization, and dynamic union leadership. And it is equally true that prior legislation—not only Norris–La Guardia, but also the ill-fated National Industrial Recovery Act of 1933—had paved the way for the new era and had independently led to much spontaneous union organization before 1935. But it is no less a fact that employers could still legally try to counteract unionism by almost any means except the yellow-dog contract and the arbitrary injunction process—up to and including sheer refusal to grant the union recognition under any circumstances—before the passage of the Wagner Act. It is extremely doubtful that organized labor could have grown as it did—from 3.6 million unionized workers in 1935 to more than 14 million by 1947—without the Wagner Act's protection.

Certainly public opinion as registered in Congress did not debate this last point. As the man in the street gradually turned against unionism in the mid-1940s, he blamed existing public policy for the union excesses of the times, most notably for the postwar strike waves. As the last chapter has described, his voice ultimately became a compelling one: Congress overrode President Truman's veto and passed the Taft-Hartley Act of 1947, thereby stilling the cries that the Wagner Act had become too "one-sided" in favor of labor.

THE TAFT-HARTLEY ACT OF 1947

With the advent of Taft-Hartley, officially known as the Labor-Management Relations Act, a new period in public policy toward labor unions began: that of *modified encouragement coupled with regulation.*

Much as the Wagner Act was to a great extent designed to correct weaknesses in Norris–La Guardia, which nonetheless was not repealed and remains a part of the legal environment of collective bargaining to this day, Taft-Hartley amended but did not displace the Wagner Act. The Wagner Act, essentially as adjusted by the 1947 legislation, governs labor relations today.

Indeed, the old unfair employer practices were continued virtually word for word by the new legislation. The only significant changes were that the closed shop (and its requirement that all workers be union members at the time of their hiring) was no longer allowed, and the freedom of the parties to authorize the *union shop* (which, as noted earlier, allows the employer to hire anyone but provides that all new employees must join the union after a stipulated period of time) was somewhat narrowed. The intention of this amendment related to the third employer unfair labor practice: In its ban on employer hiring and job-condition discrimination in order to encourage or discourage union membership, the Wagner Act *had* authorized employers to enter into union and closed shop agreements. The changes clearly symbolized public policy's new attitude toward unions.

Far more indicative of the public's less enthusiastic sentiments toward unions, however, were those portions of Taft-Hartley that dealt with (1) *union unfair labor practices*, which were now enumerated and prohibited in the same way that the employer practices had been; (2) *the rights of employees as individuals*, as contrasted with those rights that employees now legally enjoyed as union members; (3) *the rights of employers*, a subject the Wagner Act had glossed over in its concentration on employer duties; and (4) *national emergency strikes.* To some extent, other major parts of the new law—those relating to internal union affairs, the termination or modification of existing labor contracts, and suits involving unions—also demonstrated a hardening of congressional attitudes toward labor organizations. We shall consider these various provisions separately.

Union Unfair Labor Practices

Going the framers of the Wagner Act one better, Taft-Hartley enumerated six labor practices that unions were prohibited from engaging in. Labor organizations operating in interstate commerce were now officially obliged to refrain from (1) restraining or coercing employees in the exercise of their guaranteed collective bargaining rights; (2) causing an employer to discriminate in any way against an employee in order to encourage or discourage union membership; (3) refusing to bargain in good faith with their employer about wages, hours, and other employment conditions; (4) certain types of strikes and boycotts; (5) charging employees covered by union-shop agreements initiation fees or dues "in an amount which the board finds excessive or discriminatory under all the circumstances"; and (6) engaging in "featherbedding," the requirement of payment by the employer for services not performed.

As in the case of the unfair employer labor practices, interpretative difficulties have marked the subsequent treatment of some of these provisions. In addition, the six unfair labor practices directed against unions appear to have varied considerably more widely than in the case of the Wagner Act employer provisions in their effects on labor relations practice.

Two of the six provisions have perhaps had the greatest influence on collective bargaining, and, undoubtedly a salutary one, in the years since the enactment of Taft-Hartley:

1. The ban on union restraint or coercion of employees in the exercise of their guaranteed bargaining rights, which also entails a union obligation to avoid coercion of employees who choose to refrain from collective bargaining altogether. What constitutes such restraint or coercion? The myriad of rulings rendered by the NLRB and courts since 1947 has at least indicated that such union actions as the following will always run the risk of being found "unfair": the stating to an antiunion employee that the employee will lose his job should the union gain recognition; the signing with an employer of an agreement that recognizes the union as exclusive bargaining representative when in fact it lacks majority employee support; and the issuing of patently false statements during a representation election campaign. Union picket-line violence, threats of reprisal against employees subpoenaed to testify against the union at NLRB hearings, and activities of a similar vein are also unlawful.

Despite this ban against union coercion of employees who do not desire to engage in union activities, the Supreme Court in 1967 did hold that a union may assess and collect fines from union members who work during a strike.[6] However, whatever tangible benefit unions received from the ruling proved short-lived, because the same court in 1972 held that strikebreaking union members may not be fined when they resign from the union before crossing the picket line.[7]

This first unfair union practice also extends to the coercion of the employer in the latter's selection of his own bargaining representative. Post-1947 rulings have stated, for example, that unions cannot refuse to deal with former union officers who represent employers, or insist on meeting only with the owners of a company rather than with the company's attorney. On the other hand, unions have every right to demand that the employer representative with whom they deal have sufficient authority to make final decisions on behalf of the company; the interpreters of public policy have clearly understood that to have this any other way would be to frustrate the whole process of bargaining.

2. The Taft-Hartley provision that makes it unfair for a union to cause an employer to discriminate against an employee in order to influence union

[6] *NLRB* v. *Allis-Chalmers*, 388 U.S. 1975 (1967).
[7] *NLRB* v. *Granite State Joint Board*, 409 U.S. 213 (1972).

membership. There is a single exception to this prohibition: Under a valid union-shop agreement, the union may lawfully demand the discharge of an employee who fails to pay his initiation fee and periodic dues. Otherwise, however, unions must exercise complete self-control in this area. They cannot try to force employers to fire or otherwise penalize workers for any other reason, whether these reasons involve worker opposition to union policies, failure to attend union meetings, or refusal to join the union at all. Nor can a union lawfully seek to persuade an employer to grant hiring preference to employees who are satisfactory to the union. Subject only to the union-shop proviso, Taft-Hartley sought to place nonunion workers on a footing equal to that of union employees.

Occupying more or less middle ground in its degree of influence upon the labor relations process stands the third restriction on union practices, pertaining to union refusal to bargain. Here, clearly, Taft-Hartley extended to labor organizations the same obligation that the Wagner Act had already imposed on employers.

To many observers, the law's inclusion of this union bargaining provision has meant very little; unions can normally be expected to pursue bargaining rather than attempt to avoid it. Nevertheless, the NLRB has used it to some extent in the years since Taft-Hartley to narrow the scope of permissible union action. The board has, for example, found it unlawful under this section for a union to strike against an employer who has negotiated, and continues to negotiate, on a multiemployer basis, with the goal of forcing him to bargain independently. It has also found a union's refusal to bargain on an employer proposal for a written contract to violate this part of the law. To the employer community, in short, at least some inequities seem to have been corrected by this good-faith bargaining provision.

The fourth unfair union practice has given rise to considerable litigation. Indeed, of all six Taft-Hartley union prohibitions, the ban on certain types of strikes and boycotts has proven the most difficult to interpret. Even as "clarified" by Congress in 1959, this area remains a particularly murky one for labor lawyers.

Briefly, Section 8(b)(4) of the 1947 act prohibits unions from striking or boycotting if such actions have any of the following three objectives: (1) forcing an employer or self-employed person to join any labor or employer organization or to cease dealing with another employer (secondary boycott); (2) compelling recognition as employee bargaining agent from another employer without NLRB certification; (3) forcing an employer to assign particular work to a particular craft.

Particularly in regard to the secondary-boycott provision, it does not take much imagination to predict where heated controversy could arise. To constitute a secondary boycott, the union's action must be waged against "another" employer, one who is entirely a neutral in the battle and is merely caught as a pawn in the union's battle with the real object of its concern. But when is the secondary employer really neutral and when is he an "ally" of the primary employer? The board has sometimes ruled against employers alleging themselves to be "secondary" ones on the grounds of common owner- ship with that of the "primary" employer and, again, when "struck work" has been turned over by primary employers to secondary ones. But board and court rulings here have not been entirely consonant.

In its other clauses, too, the Taft-Hartley strike and boycott provision has led to intense legal battles. When is a union, for example, unlawfully seeking recognition without NLRB certification and when is it merely picketing to protest undesirable working conditions (a normally legal action)? Is a union ever entitled to try to keep within its bargaining unit work that has traditionally been performed by the unit employees? On some occasions, but not all, the board has ruled that there is nothing wrong with this. The histories of post-1947 cases on these issues constitute a fascinating study in the making of fine distinctions. At least, however, the large incidence of liti- gation might indicate that the parties have not been able totally to overlook the new rights and responsibilities bestowed upon them by Taft-Hartley (whatever these might exactly be).

Last, and least in the magnitude of their effect, stand the relatively unenforceable provisions relating to union fees and dues, and to feather- bedding.

The proscription against unions charging workers covered by union- shop agreements excessive or discriminatory dues or initiation fees included, it will be recalled, a stipulation that the NLRB could consider "all the circum- stances" in determining discrimination or excess. Such circumstances, the wording of the Taft-Hartley Act continues, include "the practices and cus- toms of labor organizations in the particular industry and the wages currently paid to the employees affected." Without further yardsticks and depending almost exclusively on the sentiments of individual employees rather than irate employers for enforcement, this part of the act has had little practical value. In one of the relatively few such cases to come before it thus far, the board ruled that increasing the initiation fee from $75 to $250 and thus charging new members the equivalent of about four weeks' wages, when other unions in the area charged only about one-eighth of this amount, was unlawful. In another case, it was held that the union's uniform requirement of a reinstatement fee for ex-members that was higher than the initiation fee for new members was *not* discriminatory under the act.

The sixth unfair labor practice for unions has proved even less influential in governing collective bargaining: Taft-Hartley's prohibition of unions from engaging in "featherbedding." The board has ruled that this provision does not prevent labor organizations from seeking *actual* employment for their members, "even in situations where the employer does not want, does not need, and is not willing to accept such services." And mainly because of this interpretation, the antifeatherbedding provision has had little teeth; the union would be quite happy to have the work performed, and the question of need is irrelevant. Employer spokesmen for some industries, entertainment and the railroads in particular, have succeeded in convincing the public that their unwanted—but performing—workers are "featherbedding," but under the interpretation of the law as this now exists they are engaging in inaccuracies.

Even these least influential of the six union prohibitions, however, clearly indicate the philosophy in back of Taft-Hartley—in the words of the late Senator Robert A. Taft, "simply to reduce special privileges granted to labor leaders."

The Rights of Employees as Individuals

In other areas, too, the act attempted to even the scales of collective bargaining and the alleged injustices of the 1935–47 period.

Taft-Hartley, unlike the Wagner Act, recognized a need to protect the rights of individual employees against labor organizations. It explicitly amended the 1935 legislation to give a majority of the employees the right to refrain from, as well as engage in, collective bargaining activities. It also dealt more directly with the question of individual freedoms—even beyond its previously mentioned outlawing of the closed shop, union coercion, union-caused employer discrimination against employees, and excessive union fees.

Right-to-Work Legislation. Perhaps most symbolically, Taft-Hartley provided that should any state wish to pass legislation more restrictive of union security than the union shop (or in other words, to outlaw labor contracts that make union membership a condition of retaining employment), the state was free to do so. Many states have proved themselves as so willing: Nineteen states, mainly in the South and Southwest, now have so-called "right-to-work" legislation. Advocates of such laws, which will be discussed at greater length in Chapter 9, have claimed that compulsory unionism violates the basic American right of freedom of association; opponents of "right-to-work" laws have pointed out, among other arguments, that majority rule is inherent in our democratic procedure. There has thus far, however, been an impressive correlation between stands on this particular question and attitudes toward the values of unionism in general. People opposed to collective bargaining have favored "right-to-work" laws with amazing regularity. Pro-unionists seem to have been equally consistent in their attacks on such legislation. It is still unproven, at any rate, that "right-to-work" laws have had much effect on labor relations in the states where they exist.

Direct Presentation of Grievances. Also designed to strengthen the rights of workers as individuals was a Taft-Hartley provision allowing any *employee* the *right to present grievances directly* to the employer without intervention of the union. The union's representative was to be given a chance to be present at such employer–employee meetings, but the normal grievance procedure (with the union actively participating) would thus be suspended. Few employees have thus far availed themselves of this opportunity: The action clearly can antagonize the union, and since the employer's action is normally being challenged by the grievance itself, the employee may have a formidable task ahead.

Restricted Dues Checkoff. Finally, the act placed a major restriction on the fast-growing dues-checkoff arrangement. Through this device (which will also be discussed in more detail later), many employers had been deducting union dues from their employees' paychecks and remitting them to the union. Companies were thus spared the constant visits of dues-collecting union representatives at the workplace, and unions had found the checkoff to be an efficient means of collection. Under Taft-Hartley, the checkoff was to remain legal, but now only if the individual employee had given his own authorization in writing. Moreover, such an authorization could not be irrevocable for a period of more than one year. This restriction has hardly hampered the growth of the checkoff; it is today provided for in over 80 percent of all labor contracts, compared to an estimated 40 percent at the time of Taft-Hartley's passage. The new legal provision has undoubtedly minimized abuse of the checkoff mechanism, however.

The Rights of Employers

In still a third area, Taft-Hartley circumscribed the union's freedom of action in its quest for industrial relations equity. In this case, it explicitly gave employers certain collective bargaining rights.

For example, although employers were still required to recognize and bargain with properly certified unions, they could now give full freedom of expression to their views concerning union organization, as long as there was "no threat of reprisal or force or promise of benefit." Thus an employer may now, when faced with a representation election, tell his employees that in his opinion unions are worthless, dangerous to the economy, and immoral. He may even, generally speaking, hint that the permanent closing of his plant would be the possible aftermath of a union election victory and subsequent high union wage demands. Nor will an election be set aside, for that matter, if he plays upon the racial prejudices of his workers (should these exist) by describing the union's philosophy toward integration, or if he sets forth the union's record in regard to violence and corruption (should this record be vulnerable) and suggests that these characteristics would be logical consequences of the union's victory in his plant—although in recent years the board has attempted to draw the line here between dispassionate statements on the employer's part and inflammatory or emotional appeals.[8] An imaginative employer can, in fact, now engage in almost any amount of creative speaking (or writing) for his employees' consumption. The only major restraint on his conduct is that he must avoid threats, promises, coercion, and direct interference with the worker-voters in the reaching of their decision. Two lesser restrictions also govern, however: The employer may not hold a meeting with his employees on company time within 24 hours of an election; and he may never urge his employees individually at their homes or in his office to vote against the union (the board has held that he can lawfully do this only "at the employees' work area or in places where employees normally gather").

Under this section of Taft-Hartley, employers can also (1) themselves now call for elections to decide questions of representation (as noted earlier); (2) refuse to bargain with supervisors' unions (the Wagner Act protection was withdrawn for these employees, although they are not prohibited from forming or joining unions *without* the NLRB machinery and other safeguards of public policy); and (3) file their unfair labor practice charges against unions.

Such changes, understandably, were favorably received by the employer community.

National Emergency Strikes: An Overview

Of most direct interest to the general public, but of practical meaning only to those employers whose labor relations can be interpreted as affecting the national health and safety, are the national-emergency strike provisions that were enacted in 1947. As in the case of most Taft-Hartley provisions, these remain essentially unchanged to this day.

Sections 206 through 210 of the act provide for government intervention in the case of such emergencies. If the president of the United States believes that a threatened or actual strike affects "an entire industry or a substantial part thereof" in such a way as to "imperil the national health and safety," he is empowered to take certain carefully delineated action. He may appoint a board of inquiry, to find out and report the facts regarding the dispute. The board is allowed subpoena authority and can thus compel the appearance of witnesses. It cannot, however, make recommendations for a settlement. On receiving the board's preliminary report, the president may apply, through the attorney general, for a court injunction restraining the strike for 60 days. If no settlement is reached during this time, the injunction can be

---

[8]See, particularly, the excellent article by Derek C. Bok, "The Regulation of Campaign Tactics in Representation Elections under the National Labor Relations Act," *Harvard Law Review*, LXXVIII, No. 1 (November 1964), for a fuller discussion of these and various related organizational campaign legislative matters.

extended for another 20 days, during which period the employees are to be polled in a secret-ballot election as to their willingness to accept the employer's last offer. The board is then to submit its final report to the president. Should the strike threat still exist after all these procedures, the president is authorized to submit a full report to Congress, "with such recommendations as he may see fit to make for consideration and appropriate action."

By 1976, the national emergency provisions of the law had been invoked 30 times, and 26 injunctions had been issued. On four occasions, the president did not elect to seek injunctions after receiving board of inquiry reports. Injunctions, however, have not always been effective in bringing about settlements; six strikes started or were resumed after the injunction expired.

People with professional expertise in the field of labor relations have not been enthusiastic about this portion of the law through the years. For example, W. Willard Wirtz, Secretary of Labor during most of the 1960s, never visibly wavered from his 1959 assertion that "what Taft-Hartley comes down to is simply a polished-up, embroidered form of relief by court injunction . . . the real question is to get a settlement of the strike issue, and on this the injunction procedure seems to me to hurt, rather than to help."[9] The late George W. Taylor, a highly respected academician-arbitrator, was adamant in his long-standing position, based to a great extent on firsthand observation, that "devices such as the injunction, designed to get production resumed prior to the settlement of a dispute, add additional complexities to the negotiating process which has already bogged down."[10] And virtually every session of Congress over the past thirty years has been asked to consider "national emergency disputes" revision bills from those of its members with special interests and/or proficiency in the area. The procedures themselves, however, continue on the books, in their unadulterated 1947 form.[11]

It would be naïve to predict that this gap between complaint and remedial action will continue in its present dimensions for another quarter century.

[9] *U.S. News & World Report*, XLVII (October 19, 1959), 74.

[10] George W. Taylor, "The Adequacy of Taft-Hartley in Public Emergency Disputes," *Annals of the American Academy of Political and Social Science*, CCCXXXIII (January 1961), 78.

[11] Nor has much applause been heard for the emergency strike machinery of the Railway Labor Act of 1926, which governs the airlines as well as the railroads. General agreement exists that at least since World War II, the mediation, voluntary arbitration, ad hoc emergency board appointments, and sixty-day "cooling-off" periods provided by this legislation have settled few of the major disputes in these two transportation sectors. Even worse, the parties can get the emergency boards established with relative ease—more than 100 such boards have been appointed in railroad disputes alone since 1947—and this fact has been widely blamed for depriving managements and unions involved of incentive to live up to their own collective bargaining responsibilities. Why bargain in good faith when the whole dispute can be dumped handily into the lap of the government boards, whose recommendations, although they may be of great help to one or the other of the parties, are not binding? As in the case of the Taft-Hartley provisions, however, the criticism continues unabated, and the emergency procedures remain wholly intact.

Certainly a public that has greatly increased its level of aspiration as to union behavior, and shouts that "there ought to be a (new) law" almost as a reflex action in the face of public inconvenience, cannot be held at bay indefinitely.

This consideration, however, cannot erase the record. In a period of unparalleled government inroads into a host of other fields of once-private endeavor (clearly including many other areas of union–management relations), our national emergency strike provisions have—with few supporters and no shortage of both influential and active antagonists—at least until now been left entirely alone.

Several reasons have been widely advanced to explain this paradox. A necessary prerequisite for altering existing legislation is the reopening of Taft-Hartley to congressional debate; a cogent case can be made that organized labor, despite its attacks upon the existing legislation, now views such action as a potential Pandora's box that might bring into the spotlight such issues as labor's present exemption from antitrust laws, a nationwide right-to-work law, and even new congressional treatment of industrywide bargaining. Nor has industry, by and large, welcomed congressional exploration of the industrial relations scene in the years since 1947. Management spokesmen have frequently voiced fears of compulsory arbitration, price control, and generally increased government intervention in the sphere of private enterprise. And although conjectures must remain unproven that this combined labor–management trepidation has significantly influenced the federal government in its preservation of the status quo, the joint opposition to changes in laws has undoubtedly had some restraining effect.

It is also a matter of record that agreement has been lacking as to the right solution, even though many have been proposed, primarily by representatives of the academic community. This, too, has presumably acted as a major deterrent to remedial action by our public officials.

And the all-but-patent futility of the task, if balancing the objectives of public policy is considered, must surely be thought of as a further explanation for the continuing gap between words and action in Washington. As Lloyd G. Reynolds, who has suggested that "anyone who could devise an equitable and enforceable method of handling these disputes would deserve a Nobel prize for industrial peace," has forcefully argued:

> The objective of public policy is not just to prevent strikes in essential industries. The objective is rather to prevent strikes by methods which are orderly and uniform in their application, which involve a minimum of direct compulsion, which do not impose greater hardships on one party than on the other, and which leave maximum scope for settlements to be reached through direct negotiation between the parties.[12]

[12]Lloyd G. Reynolds, *Labor Economics and Labor Relations*, 4th ed. (Englewood Cliffs, N.J.: Prentice-Hall, 1964), p. 295.

Any solution falling short of satisfying all these requirements would, to most thoughtful American citizens, be deficient. Recognition that such an ideal may be impossible to achieve, however, has undoubtedly acted as an additional restraining force for public officials.

But to the explanations for the laissez-faire stance adopted, however reluctantly, by both Democratic and Republican administrations, must be added one that has been advanced with considerably less frequency: the extralegal weaponry in the hands of our presidents. It is a major irony that White House improvisation, having realized a significant amount of success in the past, may also have decreased the incentive in Washington to locate something better.

National Emergency Strikes:
The Weapons of Extralegality

It is not generally appreciated, particularly amid the abundance of current pleas to give the president an "arsenal of weapons" for handling national emergencies, that our chief executives do not now lack for alternative courses of action, even if these are not framed explicitly by the laws. Nor have presidents, in general, hesitated to use these weapons when political pressures to "do something" have loomed large enough and prospects of warding off or ending a strike through the machinery of Taft-Hartley (or the Railway Labor Act) have appeared sufficiently dim.

Four examples illustrate these workings of extralegality. The 116-day 1959 basic steel strike was settled above all by high-level mediation efforts and ultimate settlement-term recommendations by Vice-President Nixon with the aid of Secretary of Labor Mitchell. It has been generally agreed that both Nixon's prestige and his pressure ended this dispute after the Taft-Hartley procedures had failed. The prestige was influential, as John P. Horlacher has stated, because:

> ... in conferring with Mr. Nixon, the company and union representatives were not unaware that they were dealing with the man who could be the next occupant of the White House, the man who, in this situation, was obviously functioning as the President's alter ego.[13]

Nixon's pressure was felt through such actions as those later depicted by Mitchell in his comments upon these sessions:

> Reviewing the Waldorf [Astoria Hotel] conference, Mitchell said that Nixon did not threaten the [steel-company] executives but that he did paint "a very realistic picture of what might happen" if they failed to avail themselves of a

[13]John P. Horlacher, "A Political Science View of National Emergency Disputes," *Annals of the American Academy*, p. 90.

chance to settle—"conjuring up many possibilities of the kind of legislation that might result." . . . He left "many things" to their imagination, Mitchell said.[14]

In the Lockheed Aircraft–Machinist dispute of 1962, President Kennedy not only personally requested a sixty-day truce and appointed a three-man extralegal board of public citizens to assist federal mediators in negotiations, but—according to Northrup and Bloom—when Lockheed "declined to accept . . . [this] board's recommendation for an election to determine the union shop issue, the Defense Department announced, in effect, that its defense contracts were being especially reviewed and placed on an *ad hoc* basis."[15]

Confronted with the failure of the Taft-Hartley mechanism a few months later, in the case of the 1962–63 Atlantic and Gulf Coast longshoring strike, Kennedy also appointed an extralegal board, chaired by Sen. Wayne Morse. This board "in effect imposed a settlement too generous for the union to reject and which was reluctantly accepted by the employers."[16]

And President Johnson more or less duplicated his treatment of the 1964 nationwide railroad strike threat by virtually locking up the 1965 steel industry and United Steelworkers' negotiators for five days in quarters near his White House office. He constantly requested the parties during personal visits (at times with the secretaries of labor and commerce) to come to terms in the process, and ultimately provided his own "statistical referee" in the person of the chairman of the Council of Economic Advisers to institute suggestions, which led to White House recommendations accepted by both sides.

Such a list could be extended considerably. Special mediation efforts on the part of highly respected private citizens were utilized with beneficial results in the maritime disputes of 1961 and 1962. Prior to invocation of Taft-Hartley in the 1962–63 Boeing Company–Machinist impasse, an extralegal board made recommendations, a privilege denied official Taft-Hartley boards. In the 1964–65 East and Gulf Coast longshoring dispute, a special panel comprising the secretaries of labor and commerce and (once again) Senator Morse did likewise after the expiration of the eighty-day injunction period, with some (although not complete) effectiveness. And the record hardly lacks for instances of presidential exhortations, made both publicly and privately, for self-restraint in the face of national defense (cold war, Korean, or Vietnamese) exigencies; of executive suggestions that an unhappy Congress could be forced into drastic ad hoc remedial action (most notably carried out in the case of 1963, 1967, and 1970 railroad strike prevention

[14]*Business Week*, January 9, 1960, p. 28.

[15]Herbert R. Northrup and Gordon F. Bloom, *Government and Labor* (Homewood, Ill.: Richard D. Irwin, 1963), p. 369.

[16]*Ibid.*, p. 362.

orders); or of White House expressions of dissatisfaction with existing strike legislation and broad hints of less palatable laws to come should labor statesmanship not prevail on a bipartite basis.

If these extralegal weapons have not been universally successful in achieving their immediate goal of strike settlement or strike avoidance, they have at least combined with the existing labor statutes—and on many occasions with the entirely independent actions of the two contractual parties—to realize this objective. Although some of the settlements may have added to unwanted inflationary movements or may otherwise have had publicly undesirable consequences, the basic mission of dissipating a national emergency dispute has always been accomplished. Extralegal avenues now open to our chief executives have invariably produced labor peace when all else has failed.

National Emergency Strikes:
The Risk of Relative Success

Obviously, however, the problem can hardly be dismissed in as cavalier a fashion as the preceding paragraph might suggest. At least three additional factors must be considered.

First, successful executive improvisation has often been implemented only after the "emergency" has existed for some time. The extralegal avenues performed effectively, for example, only after 116 days of strike activity (plus passage of almost the full Taft-Hartley injunction period) in the case of steel in 1959, after a three-week strike and expiration of the eighty-day period in the 1961 maritime-industry dispute, and after a one-month strike following the injunction period in the case of the 1962–63 Atlantic and Gulf Coast longshoring impasse. Improvisation was tried earlier in these and many other national disputes with a notable lack of success, and the fact that such "emergencies" have not been terminated as rapidly as chief executives would have liked—with attendant adverse consequences for the economy—should not go unnoticed.

Second, although the efficacy of each of the successful extralegal weapons can hardly be debated, the question can be raised whether or not all have been consistent with the dominant values of our private enterprise society: How appropriate, for example, is a threat to deprive an aircraft manufacturer of defense contracts essentially because of its presumably sincere aversion to the principle of the union shop? How advisable is the imposition of ad hoc compulsory arbitration in peacetime, as in the case of the railroads? And would threatened new and essentially punitive legislation, directed primarily against the party deemed by government representatives as the recalcitrant in the bargaining, in any way be guaranteed an objective—or equitable—basis?

Third, the fact that the extralegal actions have until now produced labor peace when all else has failed obviously provides no assurance that the nation will not be confronted ultimately with an "emergency" strike that no existing presidential weapon—legal or extralegal—will be able to terminate easily. It is entirely conceivable that at some future time, a major labor relations impasse will combine with the imperviousness of one or both parties to existing executive weapons and the unwillingness of Congress to supply tailor-made back-to-work legislation, forcing the nation to wait until the strike burdens become completely intolerable. This unhappy state of affairs was almost reached in the case of the 1974 coal strike, which fortunately terminated after a short period of time. A long coal strike then, taking into consideration soaring prices and a high unemployment rate, could have had the most serious consequences for the nation.

In short, the existing weapons of extralegality do not constitute a panacea for the problem of "national emergency" disputes. And if their successful exercise in the past as a frequently used supplement to our official legislation helps explain the remarkable staying power of these all but friendless laws, the existence of the defects in the improvised weapons would still seem to make some overhaul in our present machinery highly desirable. The danger may lie in the strong possibility that the relative efficiency of these weapons in achieving their immediate purpose of ending an "emergency" is depriving us of sufficient incentive to search seriously for a better way to serve the national interest.

Other Taft-Hartley Provisions

Taft-Hartley also devoted attention to *internal union affairs*, the first such regulation in American history. Its impetus came not only from the previously cited Communistic taints attached to several unions but also from the fact that, in the case of a few other labor organizations, lack of democratic procedures and financial irregularities (often involving employer wrongdoing as well) had become glaringly evident. Accordingly, the act set new conditions for unions thenceforth seeking to use the NLRB's services: (1) All union officers were obligated to file annual affidavits with the board, stating that they were not members of the Communist party; (2) certain financial and constitutional information had to be annually filed by unions with the secretary of labor; and (3) unions (as well as corporations) could no longer contribute funds for political purposes in connection with any federal election. The affidavit requirement, judged to be ineffective, was repealed in 1959.[17] The other stipulations were allowed to remain in force until that date, when they were only slightly amended and then substantially enlarged upon (as further discussion will indicate). Essentially, aside from what unionists vocally

---

[17]It was replaced with the proscription against Communists' holding union office for a period of five years after terminating their Communist affiliation. However, the Supreme Court in 1965 held such legislation to be unconstitutional. *United States* v. *Brown*, 381 U.S. 437 (1965).

termed a nuisance value, the provisions are notable for the first recognition of public policy that some internal regulation of the union as an institution was in the public interest—and as a harbinger of more such regulation to come.

Another Taft-Hartley provision that has upset some union leaders involves the *termination or modification of existing labor contracts*. Applicable to both labor organizations and employers, it requires the party seeking to end or change the agreement to give a 60-day notice to the other party. The law further provides that, during this time period, the existing contract must be maintained without strikes or lockouts. In addition, the Federal Mediation and Conciliation Service and state mediation services are to be notified of the impending dispute 30 days after the serving of the notice. Workers striking in violation of this requirement lose all legal protection as "employees" in collective bargaining, although the law also asserts that "such loss of status for such employee shall terminate if and when he is reemployed" by the employer.

In some instances, leaders of labor organizations have found it both difficult and politically unpopular to restrain their constituents from violating this provision. Unionists have also, on occasion, frankly pointed out that the scheduling prerequisites for striking have deprived their organizations of some economic power, at least insofar as the element of surprise is concerned. Yet many representatives of both parties would undoubtedly agree with Falcone that "these provisions have slowed down the calling of strikes, enabled mediators to intervene before it is too late to help and have generally provided an orderly method for resolving disputes and reaching final settlements."[18] From the point of view of the public interest, it is clearly on this basis that the effectiveness of the notice provisions should be judged.

Finally, Section 301 of Taft-Hartley decreed that "*suits for violations of contracts* between an employer and a labor organization representing employees in an industry affecting commerce" could be brought directly by either party in any U.S. district court. Labor agreements, in short, were to be construed as being legally enforceable for the first time in American history. Damage suits are not calculated to increase mutual trust or offset misunderstandings between the parties in labor relations, however, and unions and managements have generally recognized this. Consequently, relatively few such suits have come to the courts in the years since this provision was enacted. Many contracts today, in fact, contain agreements *not* to sue, a perfectly legal dodge of Section 301. The remedy of the suit, for employers confronted with union violations of no-strike clauses or for unions faced with management lockouts inconsistent with no-lockout provisions (for example), nonetheless remains an available one for both parties in the absence of any restrictive convenants.

[18]Falcone, *Labor Law*, p. 275.

Administrative Changes in the Law

Taft-Hartley also enlarged the NLRB from three to five members and, in the interests of a faster disposition of cases, authorized the board to delegate "any or all" of its powers to any group of three or more members. In addition, the office of independent General Counsel was created within the NLRB, to administer the prosecution of all unfair labor practices. This last change was made to satisfy the increasingly bitter charges (particularly from employers) that the same individuals had exercised both prosecution and judicial roles.

As the NLRB machinery now operates, the board members and General Counsel delegate most of their work in processing unfair labor practice charges and conducting representation elections to 31 regional and two sub-regional offices scattered throughout the country. Each office deals with these two problems as they arise in its particular geographic area. The General Counsel supervises the work of the offices, and the board members' efforts are thus saved for those issues appealed to it from the regional level. As will be recalled, board decisions can themselves be appealed to the courts (and ultimately to the Supreme Court).

From what has been said, it is obvious that the NLRB has considerable authority to apply the provisions of the law. What the legislation does is to establish broad guidelines, but it is up to the agency to apply the law to particular situations. In the vast majority of the cases, the courts have sustained the decisions of the board on the grounds that the agency possesses expertise that should be given full faith and credit by the judiciary. It follows, therefore, that how the law will be applied depends to a great extent on who sits on the board. It is a matter of common sense that presidents will choose members who generally represent the socioeconomic philosophy of the nation's chief executive office, and thus, over the years, employers and unions alternatively have been bitterly critical of board policies. In general, unions criticized the policies of the Eisenhower- and Nixon-appointed NLRB members, and employers displayed the same attitude toward the board when directed by appointees of Roosevelt, Truman, Kennedy, and Johnson.

THE LANDRUM-GRIFFIN ACT OF 1959

As might have been expected, the Taft-Hartley Act generated considerable controversy. In the years immediately after its passage, labor leaders bitterly assailed the new law as being—in addition to a "slave labor act"—a punitive one, and invoked such statements in regard to its authors as "the forces of reaction in this country want a showdown with free American labor." Taft-Hartley supporters, on the other hand, have frequently referred to the act as a "Magna Carta" for both employers and employees, and widely praised its efforts to "equalize bargaining power." Unable to see any appro-

equalizing extent of L-G

priateness in these latter remarks, spokesmen for organized labor, until roughly a decade ago, in turn responded by pressing for the repeal of the act—or occasionally, for its drastic amendment—in every session of Congress. Their complete failure to realize this goal and their recent unwillingness even to pursue it attests to the basic acceptance of Taft-Hartley's provisions in the recent past by the American public, as well as to labor's concern that an even less desirable law might be the outcome.

The framers of public policy themselves, however, did not long remain satisfied that existing labor legislation was fully adequate to uphold the public interest. In 1959, the national legislature passed another significant law, the Landrum-Griffin Act (officially, the Labor-Management Reporting and Disclosure Act). This act was the direct outgrowth of the unsatisfactory internal practices of a small but strategically located minority of unions, as revealed by Senate investigations, and it can be said to have marked the beginning of quite *detailed regulation* of internal union affairs, going far beyond the Taft-Hartley treatment of this subject.

Under Landrum-Griffin provisions, as noted earlier, union members are guaranteed a "Bill of Rights" that their unions cannot violate, officers of labor organizations must meet a variety of reporting and disclosure obligations, and the secretary of labor is charged with the investigation of relevant union misconduct.

The "Bill of Rights" for union members is an ambitious and wide-sweeping one. It provides for equality of rights concerning the nomination of candidates for union office, voting in elections, attendance at membership meetings and participation in business transactions—all, however, "subject to reasonable" union rules. It lays down strict standards to ensure that increases in dues and fees are responsive to the desires of the union membership majority. It affirms the right of any member to sue the organization once "reasonable" hearing procedures within the union have been exhausted. It provides that no member may be fined, suspended, or otherwise disciplined by the union except for nonpayment of dues, unless the member has been granted such procedural safeguards as being served with written specific charges, given time to prepare a defense, and afforded a fair hearing. And it obligates union officers to furnish each of their members with a copy of the collective bargaining agreement, as well as full information concerning the Landrum-Griffin Act itself.

Not content to stop here in prescribing internal union conduct, the 1959 legislation laid out specific ground rules for *union elections*. National and international unions must now elect officers at least once every five years, either by secret ballot or at a convention of delegates chosen by secret ballot. Local unions are obligated to elect officers at least once every three years, exclusively by secret ballot. As for the conduct of these elections, they must be administered in full accordance with the union's constitution and bylaws, with all ballots and other relevant records being preserved for a legis. - corruption

period of one year. Every member in good standing is to be entitled to one vote, and all candidates are guaranteed the right to have an observer at the polls and at the ballot-counting.

Landrum-Griffin also made it more difficult for national and international unions to place their subordinate bodies under *trusteeships* for purely political reasons. The trusteeship, or the termination of the member group's autonomy, has traditionally allowed labor organizations to correct constitutional violations or other clearly wrongful acts on the part of their locals. The Senate investigations preceding Landrum-Griffin had found, however, that this device was also being used by some unions as a weapon of the national or international officers to eliminate grass roots opposition per se. Accordingly, the act provided that trusteeships could be imposed only for one of four purposes: (1) to correct corruption or "financial malpractice"; (2) to assure the performance of collective bargaining duties; (3) to restore democratic procedures; and (4) to otherwise carry out "the legitimate objects" of the subordinate body. Moreover, the imposition of a trusteeship, together with the reasons for it, was now to be reported to the secretary of labor within 30 days, and every six months thereafter until the trusteeship was terminated.

The extent of Landrum-Griffin control of the internal affairs of unions is perhaps best illustrated by the act's policing of the kind of person who can serve as a union officer. Persons convicted of serious crimes (robbery, bribery, extortion, embezzlement, murder, rape, grand larceny, violation of narcotics laws, aggravated assault) are barred for a period of five years after conviction from holding any union position other than a clerical or custodial job. The period of exclusion may be shortened if the person's citizenship rights are fully restored before five years or if the U.S. Department of Justice decides that an exception should be made.

A fair question to ask is whether or not this policy should be applied to officers of other kinds of institutions, such as business, government, universities, and churches. On the surface, at least, it would appear that if government controls the moral character of union officers, it should apply the same policy across the board. To do otherwise makes it appear that union officers are being held to a higher standard of personal conduct than is required of, say, corporation officials. Should a corporation official who has been convicted of a serious crime, including violations of the nation's antitrust and pure food and drug laws, be treated in the same way as a union officer? This could be the subject for a lively debate in any student group.

To curb financial corruption, the law requires that union officers must each year file reports with the secretary of labor containing the purpose for which union funds are spent. The objective is to discourage union officers from using the organization's treasury for items of a personal nature. Since financial reports are made available to union members, they can learn whether or not their dues are being used in the interest of the membership. Should it be determined that a union officer has used union funds for personal items, the law authorizes court suits to recover the money from the officer. If a report is not filed, or the information contained is not true, the responsible union officer is subject to criminal penalties. Outright embezzlement of union funds may also result in imprisonment and/or fines. In addition, all union officers must be bonded by a private bonding company in which the union has no interest.

Although most of Landrum-Griffin was aimed at union behavior, the act does include provisions that cover employer activities. The Senate investigations had unearthed rather flagrant instances of *employer wrongdoing* as well: company bribery of union agents and, particularly, situations in which outside agents had been hired by companies to stave off union organizations by illegal means. Such agents, typically self-styled "labor relations consultants," often acted as intermediaries in "buying off" the threat of unionization or, as a last resort, in ensuring that the union would at least extract only a minimum of concessions from the company.

Landrum-Griffin made employers responsible for reporting annually to the secretary of labor all company expenditures directed at influencing employee collective bargaining behavior. Employer bribery of union officers and other such blunt tactics had actually constituted federal crimes since the passage of Taft-Hartley, but the new act expanded the list of unlawful employer actions. Bribes by companies to their own employees so that they do not exercise their rights to organize and bargain collectively were added to the list of crimes. So, too, were many forms of employer payment aimed at procuring information on employee activities related to labor disputes. Violations by employers of their reporting obligations invite the same criminal penalties as are provided for union representatives.

In a way, the law attempted to fill the gap created by union membership apathy. It can be argued that a more effective way to promote union democracy and financial responsibility is by active participation of members in union affairs. The members of any union, local or international, have it in their power to require that their organizations adhere to democratic procedures and financial responsibility through the existing internal machinery of their unions. It is debatable that the federal government should protect union members against abuse by the organization when these members are not particularly concerned as to how their unions in fact operate.

In any event, few would now argue for repeal of the legislation. Even union opposition against Landrum-Griffin has subsided. Control of the internal affairs of unions by government is now an established feature. Possibly, no law will convert unions into models of democracy; still, the effect of the law has eliminated some of the more flagrant abuses of undemocratic practices and financial irresponsibility. For example, in 1969, the United Mine Workers held an election to choose their international officers. This was the first such national election ever conducted in this union. It is not likely that the election would have been held in the absence of the law's requirements.[19] And, undoubtedly, the act has curtailed the activities of the comparatively small number of union officers who would regard the union's treasury as something to be used for their personal aggrandizement. Although there probably still exist some undemocratic practices and some corruption in the house of labor, there have been fewer flagrant instances of such conduct since the passage of the legislation. If nothing else, the law has educated union officers as to their responsibilities to their members. To this extent, the law has apparently accomplished its major objectives, and does for union members what they have failed through apathy to do for themselves.

Landrum-Griffin—Title VII

Quite apart from regulating internal union affairs and imposing obligations on employers, the Landrum-Griffin law in Title VII made some important changes in the Taft-Hartley Act. It authorized the NLRB to decline cases involving small employers engaged in interstate commerce, and permitted the states to take jurisdiction of such cases. The theory here was that the NLRB should conserve its funds and manpower for those cases that have a substantial impact on interstate commerce.

It also closed the so-called loopholes that developed under Taft-Hartley's secondary boycott provisions. As we have seen, one purpose of the Taft-Hartley law was to outlaw secondary boycotts. However, the NLRB and the courts permitted unions to engage in certain types of secondary boycott activity. The reason for this was the character of the language of the 1947 law that regulated these activities. Under the 1959 law, Congress adopted new language that generally closed these loopholes, and under the present state of affairs, a union's opportunity to engage in secondary boycott activities has been virtually eliminated.

Landrum-Griffin also outlawed the "hot cargo" arrangement. Under a hot cargo clause, an employer agrees with a union not to handle products of or otherwise deal with another employer involved in a labor dispute. Accordingly, the hot cargo arrangement is a form of secondary boycott. The difference is that an employer agrees by contractual provision to engage in secondary boycotts upon receiving a signal from its union that another employer should be boycotted. Such arrangements are now illegal, and unions that force an employer to negotiate hot cargo clauses engage in an unfair labor practice. For reasons peculiar to the nature of the construction and

---

[19]However, the election had tragic consequences. On New Year's Eve 1970, Joseph Yablonski (who opposed Tony Boyle, the incumbent president), his wife, and his daughter were murdered. Subsequently, Boyle and other officers of the union were convicted of the crime. In 1972, in a court-ordered election conducted under the supervision of the secretary of labor, Arnold Miller defeated Boyle for the presidency of the union.

garment industries, however, Congress excepted these two industries from the hot cargo proscription.

Title VII imposed another important restriction upon unions. It pinned down and controlled recognition and organizational picketing. At times, unions have found this kind of picketing effective to force employers to recognize unions and to persuade employees to join unions. Such picketing is particularly effective in a consumer business, such as a department store or a restaurant. A picket line thrown around a department store could persuade customers not to buy at the store, and this kind of union pressure could force the employer to recognize the union. Under Taft-Hartley, there was no restriction on this kind of picketing, and unions could picket for recognition and organizational purposes for an indefinite length of time.

Under the 1959 law, the opportunity for unions to picket for such purposes was sharply reduced. Such picketing activities now constitute an unfair labor practice if (1) the employer is lawfully recognizing another union; (2) a valid election has been conducted by the NLRB in the previous twelve months; and (3) no election petition has been filed with the NLRB within 30 days after the picketing began.

This provision is of particular importance to employers who want to be freed from the pressure of picketing. Thus, within 30 days after the start of the picketing, the union must file a petition for an election. If it loses the election, recognition and organizational picketing may not be engaged in for one year. Consequently, the opportunity of a union to picket for an indefinite period of time is eliminated.

However, there is one major qualification to this proscription. A union may picket for informational purposes after 30 days without filing an election petition. Informational picketing is defined by the law as the kind that advises the public that the employer involved does not employ members of the union or have a contract with it. Of course, the picket-sign legends must be truthful. That is, they may not state that the employer does not employ members of the union if in truth he does. Also, informational picketing, as distinct from recognition and organizational picketing, may not interfere with pickup and delivery of products at the site of the company being picketed.

So far, it would appear that the Title VII amendments to Taft-Hartley are oriented against unions: The law of 1959 authorized the NLRB to decline cases of small employers engaged in interstate commerce, thereby eliminating the opportunity for the employees of such employers to exercise their organizational and collective bargaining rights under the federal law. If a state does not have a law similar to Taft-Hartley (and most states do not), these employees have no legal forum to protect them in their efforts to organize and bargain collectively. Unions are forbidden to engage in practically every kind of secondary boycott, and may not negotiate hot cargo agreements. And, as we have seen, the 1959 law sharply limits the opportunity for unions to engage in recognition and organizational picketing.

In only one major way did unions, indeed, benefit from the enactment of Title VII. The Title does redress a pro-management inequity that was created by Taft-Hartley. Under the earlier law, workers out on an economic strike (wages, pensions, seniority, and the like) were not permitted to vote in NLRB elections held during the course of a strike if the employer replaced them with other employees. What was inequitable about this provision is that the replaced economic strikers could not vote, *but the replacements were entitled to vote.* The replacements would, of course, vote to decertify the union, since, if the union maintained bargaining rights, it would insist as a condition of settling the strike that the regular employees be reinstated in their jobs and the replacements ("strikebreakers," "scabs," "finks" in union talk) be fired. Thus, the only way the replacements could be assured of holding their jobs would be to vote the union out. This would not be hard to do, provided the employer hired a sufficient number of replacements during the strike.

Assume that the bargaining unit is composed of 500 employees, all union members. A strike takes place, and the 500 employees go out on strike. The employer then hires 400 replacements, and an election is held by the NLRB to determine whether the union still represents a majority of the bargaining unit. Under this illustration, the 400 replacements vote in the election, but, of the regular employees, only the 100 who have not been replaced can vote. When the votes are counted, it should occasion little surprise that the 400 replacements vote to destroy the union. And, with this result, the employer will no longer need to recognize the union.

Indeed, under the original Taft-Hartley law, some employers provoked economic strikes, hired replacements, and then petitioned the NLRB for an election. It is easy to see why organized labor looked upon this provision as a real threat to its existence.

Unions received some relief from this state of affairs in the 1959 law. Under its terms, replaced economic strikers may vote in NLRB elections, provided the election is held within one year from the start of a strike. If the strike lasts longer than one year, the replaced strikers are not eligible to vote. Under the assumption that most strikes would terminate before one year, it is understandable that the AFL-CIO stated in November 1960 that "although most of the Taft-Hartley amendments were severely damaging to labor unions, [this one] was favorable."

SOME CONCLUSIONS

What are some reasonably safe conclusions based on the long experience of public policy recited on these pages? Can we make some predictions about the future developments in the area of labor law? The first and perhaps the most accurate conclusion that can be made is that public policy toward organized labor and collective bargaining has changed significantly over the years. It has moved from legal repression to strong encouragement, then to modified encouragement coupled with regulation, and, finally, with Landrum-Griffin, to detailed regulation of internal union affairs. It seems a safe prediction not only that further shifts in this public policy can be expected but that these changes, as was not always the case in earlier times, will depend for their direction strictly on the acceptability of current union behavior to the American public.

This point is particularly important to the unionists of today. Especially since 1937, when it held the Wagner Act wholly constitutional, the Supreme Court has permitted the legislative branch of government the widest latitude to shape public policy. Congress and the state legislatures are judicially free to determine the elements of the framework of labor law. To most citizens, such a situation is only as it should be; our judiciary is expected to interpret law but not to make it, and we generally expect actions of the legislative branch to be voided only when the particular statute clearly and unmistakably violates the terms of the Constitution. But since today the polls, and not the courts, do constitute the forum in which our policies toward labor are determined, and since the public has in the recent past apparently increased its level of aspiration as to union behavior, labor organizations have been forced to become increasingly conscious of the images they project. Such a situation accounts to a great extent for the growing union stress on such nontraditional labor concerns as charity work, college scholarships, Boy Scout troops, and Little League teams, which will be discussed in the next chapter. It also accounts for the entire labor movement's uneasiness whenever such newsworthy strikes as the 1966 New York City transit tie-up, or the 1970 federal postal workers' strike, or such notable black marks as James R. Hoffa's jury-tampering and pension-fund defrauding convictions occur. And it undoubtedly has been one major factor in leading to more maturity and self-restraint on the part of some labor leaders at the bargaining table. As Chapter 1 noted, however, whether this progress will continue sufficiently and in time to satisfy the increasingly high level of public expectation and thereby ward off further laws of the Taft-Hartley and Landrum-Griffin variety remains an unanswered question.

Second, every law since Norris–La Guardia has expanded the scope of government regulation of the labor–management arena. To the curbs on judicial capriciousness enacted in 1932 have been added, in turn, restrictions on employer conduct, limitations on union conduct, and governmental fiats closely regulating internal union affairs. Most of the other parts of the later laws—to cite but two examples, Taft-Hartley's modification of the Wagner Act's closed- and union-shop provisions and Landrum-Griffin's new conditions regarding the "hot cargo" clauses—represent ever-finer qualifications of the freedom of action of both parties. Given both the electorate's impatience with the progress of collective bargaining and Congress's apparently deep-seated reluctance to decrease the scope covered by its laws, future legislation can be expected to move *further* in the direction of government intervention. This should hold true whether the future laws are enacted with the implicit goal of "helping" or of "hurting" unions.

Individual value judgments clearly determine the advisability of such a trend. But if one believes that stable and sound industrial relations can be achieved only in an environment of free collective bargaining, wherein labor and management—the parties that must live with each other on a day-to-day basis—are allowed to find mutually satisfactory answers to their industrial relations problems, there is cause for concern. Government policy that limits this freedom strikes at the very heart of the process.

This is not to say that the more recent labor statutes are entirely barren of provisions that are valuable additions to the law of labor relations. The union unfair labor practices relating to restraint and coercion of employees and to union-caused employer discrimination are clearly a move in the right direction. So, too, are Taft-Hartley's curbs on strikes and boycott activity engaged in at times by some unions for the objective of increasing the power of one union at the expense of other labor organizations, despite all the litigation that has surrounded these curbs since 1947. Nor does the requirement that unions bargain collectively embarrass anyone except the union leader who is uncooperative and recalcitrant.

At the same time, however, the government intervention in regard to such issues as union security, the checkoff, and the enforcement of the collective bargaining agreement (to cite but three), and the decreasing scope for union and management bargaining-table latitude in general, do raise the question of ultimate government control over *all* major industrial relations activities. For one who believes in "free collective bargaining," the increasing reach of the statutes may be steering labor policy in a very dangerous direction.

Third, even if one does conclude that the gains of our present dosage of government regulation outweigh its losses and inherent risks, this hardly proves that the current statutes and their interpretations constitute the most appropriate ones to meet each specific labor relations topic now being dealt with.

Finally, and probably also as an inevitable consequence of the increased coverage of public policy, labor laws have become anything but easy to comprehend. The inconsistent NLRB and judicial rulings that have plagued them in recent years may be based to some extent on philosophical and political differences, but they undeniably also stem from the built-in interpretative difficulties in the laws themselves. As Justice Felix Frankfurter could argue in this connection in 1957:

The judicial function is confined to applying what Congress enacted after ascertaining what it is that Congress enacted. But such ascertainment . . . is nothing like a mechanical endeavor. It could not be accomplished by the subtlest of modern "brain" machines. Because of the infirmities of language and the limited scope of science in legislative drafting, inevitably there enters into the construction of statutes the play of judicial judgment within the limits of the relevant legislative materials. Most relevant, of course, is the very language in which Congress has expressed its policy and from which the Court must extract the meaning most appropriate.[20]

What constitutes "refusal to bargain"? When are companies discriminating in regard to "hire or tenure of employment or any term or condition of employment" to influence union membership? What constitutes unlawful union recognition picketing? It is hard to disagree with the commonly heard lament of unionists and labor relations managers that it has become ever more risky to state definitively what is legal in bargaining relationships and what is not; and the most valuable information available to the management or labor union representative who is concerned with labor law may very possibly be the telephone number of an able labor attorney. But, given the dimensions of this law today, however unpalatable many of its tenets may be to one or the other party, and whatever dangers may be inherent in present trends, the managers and unionists who are *not* concerned with public policy remain so only at their peril.

DISCUSSION QUESTIONS

1. Erect as strong a case as you can for the labor injunction. Then build as strong a case as you can *against* the injunction. Which of the two cases is more persuasive to you, and why?

2. "The Norris-La Guardia Act conferred no new rights on workers. It merely adjusted an inherently inequitable situation." Comment.

3. How much truth do you feel lies in the statement that "there was great need for the Wagner Act . . . its sole defect lay in the fact that it was not slightly broadened from time to time to regulate a few union practices of dubious social value"?

4. It has been argued that, whatever deficiencies may have accompanied the Taft-Hartley Act, it did "free workers from the tyrannical hold of union bosses." Do you agree?

5. Do you feel that the Wagner Act or the Taft-Hartley Act has been more influential in leading to the current status of organized labor in this country?

6. "In the last analysis, the public must judge the relative merits of the collective bargaining process." Discuss.

7. If all existing national labor legislation could be instantly erased and our statutory regulation could then be completely rewritten, what would you advocate as public policy governing labor relations—and why?

[20]*Local 1976 Carpenters Union* v. *NLRB*, 357 U.S. 93–100 (1957).

8. Whether or not you agree with the exact scope and specific wording of the present laws, do you consider these laws to be essentially equitable to both management and labor?

SELECTED REFERENCES

AARON, BENJAMIN, and K. W. WEDDERBURN, eds., *Industrial Confict: A Comparative Legal Survey*. New York: Crane, Russak & Co., 1973.

BAKKE, E. WIGHT, CLARK KERR, and CHARLES W. ANROD, *Unions, Management and the Public*, 3rd ed., pp. 644–717. New York: Harcourt Brace Jovanovich, 1967.

COHEN, SANFORD, *Labor Law*. Columbus, O.: Charles E. Merrill, 1964.

CULLEN, DONALD E., *National Emergency Strikes*. Ithaca, N.Y.: New York State School of Industrial and Labor Relations, 1968.

EVANS, ROBERT, JR., *Public Policy toward Labor*. New York: Harper & Row, 1965.

FALCONE, NICHOLAS S., *Labor Law*. New York: John Wiley, 1962.

GREGORY, CHARLES O., *Labor and the Law*, 2nd rev. ed. New York: Norton, 1961.

MCCULLOCH, FRANK W., and TIM BORNSTEIN, *The National Labor Relations Board*. New York: Praeger, 1974.

MUELLER, STEPHEN J., and A. HOWARD MYERS, *Labor Law and Legislation*, 3rd ed. Cincinnati: South-Western Publishing, 1962.

NORTHRUP, HERBERT R., and GORDON F. BLOOM, *Government and Labor*. Homewood, Ill.: Richard D. Irwin, 1963.

TAYLOR, BENJAMIN J., and FRED WITNEY, *Labor Relations Law*, 2nd ed. Englewood Cliffs, N.J.: Prentice-Hall, 1975.

WIRTZ, W. WILLARD, *Labor and the Public Interest*. New York: Harper & Row, 1964.

Chapter 4
Union Behavior:
Structure, Government,
and Operation

Simplicity is not a hallmark of the structure of organized labor in this country. The movement has layers upon layers of governmental instruments, and even though some of these are pivotal in nature, others can most kindly be described as inconsequential. But this complexity does have a basis that is historically rational. Labor's internal system has emerged only through the years. And it is in fact still undergoing what is at times significant face-lifting as the movement continuously exercises what it has believed to be the winning approach ever since Samuel Gompers pointed the way: doing whatever is felt to be necessary to improve the lot of the American workingman, and by whatever means seems to offer the greatest chances of success at the time. The system is, in short, based on pragmatism, and it has consistently attempted to adapt itself to changing conditions as these conditions have arisen.

Given this paramount fact, the reader should hardly be surprised to learn that unionism in this country includes a variety of different functions, levels of authority, and governing practices.

For example the AFL-CIO is a federation that contains many different sectors exercising different duties and authority. Most of the 157 national or international unions in existence in the United States belong to the federation, but 47 of them, including such mighty unions as the International Brotherhood of Teamsters, the United Mine Workers, and, since 1968, the United Automobile Workers, operate independently from the AFL-CIO.[1] National unions are themselves, in turn, subdivided into regions or districts for more efficient management and administration. And although the vast majority of the country's 77,400 local unions belong to national unions, several hundred of them do not, and are thus commonly described as "independent" unions.[2] Finally, some unions are craft in character, others industrial, and some are both craft and industrial.

[1] From figures furnished by the U.S. Department of Labor, Bureau of Labor Statistics.
[2] A number of such "independents" nonetheless belong to the AFL-CIO as federal locals.

Because unions are not similar in terms of heritage, size, geographic location, the personalities of their officers, and the kinds of workers who are members, it should be expected that they will differ widely in terms not only of their governments but of their day-to-day operations. Some unions (perhaps most notably the International Typographical Union and the Newspaper Guild) both before and after Landrum-Griffin have operated very democratically, whereas a few (including most but not all segments of the International Brotherhood of Teamsters) have always maintained a highly autocratic system of internal government. Unions are different in terms of the intensity of their political activities, although events of the past three decades have made virtually all labor organizations conscious of a need to become relatively active in political campaigns and thus in influencing the selection of lawmakers. Some unions have engaged in considerably more "social" activities of the type alluded to in the preceding chapter than have others. Above all, unions vary in terms of their internal rules, dues and initiation fees, and qualifications for membership. Thus, although in the following pages an effort will be made to present a systematic analysis of union behavior, structure, and government, one should recognize that diversity rather than uniformity characterizes the American labor movement. We must be concerned with common principles and trends, but there are many exceptions to them.

THE AFL-CIO

Relationship to National Unions

The decision of the former AFL and CIO to unite forces into a consolidated AFL-CIO in 1955 was made by the affiliated national unions of the two federations; the officers of the AFL and the CIO did not themselves have the power to bring about such a consolidation. This observation demonstrates a very important principle of the structure of the American labor movement— the autonomy of the national unions. The federation can exist only as long as the national unions that belong to it agree to stay in this labor body.

In a sense, the relationship of the national unions to the federation compares closely to the relationship of member nations to the United Nations. No nation *must* belong to the United Nations; any nation *may* withdraw from the international organization at any time and for any reason whatsoever. Nor does the UN have the power to determine the internal government of any of its affiliates, its tax laws, its foreign policy, the size of its military establishment, and similar national specifications. Nations affiliate and remain members of the world body for the advantages that the organization allows in the pursuit of world peace, and for other purposes, but they continue to exercise absolute sovereignty in the conduct of their own affairs.

The same is true of the relationship of the AFL-CIO to its affiliated national unions. A union belongs to the federation because of the various advantages of affiliation, but the national union is autonomous in the conduct of its own affairs. Each union determines its own collective bargaining program, negotiates its contracts without the aid or intervention of the federation, sets its own level of dues and initiation fees, and may call strikes without any approval from the AFL-CIO; nor, conversely, can the federation prohibit a strike that an affiliated member desires to undertake.

Moreover, the federation cannot force a merger of two of its affiliates that have essentially the same jurisdiction. For example, the International Brotherhood of Electrical Workers of the old AFL and the International Union of Electrical Workers of the old CIO have what strikes the disinterested observer as virtually identical jurisdictions in manufacturing. It may seem logical that these two national unions should merge their forces, and in the process further consolidate with the smaller, independent United Electrical Workers; in fact, all three of these unions have in recent years discussed such a consolidation. To date, however, the conversations have produced no action, and perhaps they never will. As Jerry Wurf, president of the American Federation of State, County and Municipal Employees has observed:

> Mergers and consolidations are, of course, easier to talk about than to bring about. At stake are the bread-and-butter questions that always impede institutional change: What will happen to the elected officers, the paid staff, the local and regional structures, and the assets and traditions to which all unions, meek or mighty, cling? There still would be jobs and titles. But even the most selfless politician (and we labor leaders are, after all, political creatures) often sees himself as peerless when it comes to occupying a union presidency. The power, the payroll, the trappings—these are the real obstacles. . . .[3]

On the other hand, two or even more unions within the AFL-CIO may merge voluntarily if they do desire to do so, and, since 1955, at least thirty of them have. Most notable in recent years was the 1969 joining together of four of the five railroad operating brotherhoods into the 220,000-member United Transportation Union, now the largest AFL-CIO affiliate concerned solely with transportation. Consolidations of some importance have also taken place in the past few years in meat-packing and food processing, printing, the postal service, chemicals, and steel.

Steadily rising administrative costs have motivated many of these merger actions; almost half of the federation's 110 national unions have fewer than 50,000 members and thus fall below what AFL-CIO officials have estimated to be the minimum dues-paying base necessary to support effective action. And it is likely that in future years there will be additional voluntary mergers for another reason: the growth of the "conglomerate," a structure of business

[3] *Washington Post*, October 14, 1973, p. C1.

that brings under common management and ownership a variety of formerly independent companies. For example, Ling-Temco-Vought, one of the nation's leading conglomerates, today controls, among other operations, Braniff Airways, Jones and Laughlin, National Car Rental, Wilson and Company (meat-packers), and Wilson Sporting Goods. It employs more than 125,000 workers, about three-quarters of whom are members of a dozen different unions. And it does not require much imagination to recognize that only through the merger route can such unions hope to match the bargaining strength of this employer—or, increasingly, of the many others that are reshaping themselves into conglomerates.

This trend, however, does not make it any less true that authority in the AFL-CIO is decentralized in character: Its authority is distributed among all the affiliated unions, rather than concentrated in any single body. The affiliated unions are masters of their own fates, and each of them can pursue its own objectives, conduct its own affairs, and devise what policies and programs it desires to follow without intervention by either the federation or any other national union. Least of all can any outsider compel them to merge.

Enforcement of Federation Rules

The AFL-CIO's constitution does, however, contain certain rules of conduct that a national union must respect if it desires to remain a member of the federation. Each affiliate must pay to the federation a per capita tax of 10 cents per member per month. No union may "raid" the membership of any other affiliate, nor may it be officered by communists, fascists, or members of any other totalitarian group. Among other rules, an affiliate is obligated to conduct its affairs without regard to "race, creed, color, national origin, or ancestry." Each affiliate is further expected "to protect the labor movement from any and all corrupt influences."

The practical question immediately arises as to what powers the AFL-CIO may exercise when an affiliated national union does not comply with these and various other rules of the federation. If the AFL-CIO had wide-sweeping powers over the national unions, the federation officers could swiftly compel the errant union to correct its improper conduct. It could still belong to the federation, but its violation of the federation's constitution would be abruptly terminated.

The realities of the situation, however, are such that the federation is not empowered to correct violations by exercise of such power. It can do no more than to suspend or expel a national union that persists in the violation of the federation's constitution.

The expulsion weapon has been used in several instances, but never rashly. Before the AFL-CIO expelled the Teamsters Union, for example, that union was put on notice that it stood in flagrant violation of the anticorruption provision of the federation's constitution. AFL-CIO officials instructed the Teamsters that they would face expulsion unless certain of their national officers were removed and the corrupt practices eliminated. Only when the Teamsters adamantly refused to comply did the AFL-CIO convert the threat into actuality and take the ultimate step of expelling the union from its ranks. And even though the UAW actually withdrew from the AFL-CIO in 1968 because of Reuther's claim that the AFL-CIO was not doing enough in organizational work and had not been militant enough in areas of social affairs, the federation technically expelled the UAW only on the entirely understandable ground that it had refused to pay its per capita dues.

Moreover, as a practical matter, the federation is compelled to use even this amount of authority sparingly and with discretion. The expulsion of the Teamsters was prompted by the corrupt practices of union officers who were highly visible to the public. The AFL-CIO could not tolerate such a situation in the light of the existing public clamor against dishonest union leadership and practices; it was fully aware that the retention of the Teamsters would reflect adversely on *every* affiliated union. One would be naïve, however, to believe that all unions scrupulously adhere to the letter and spirit of each rule incorporated in the federation's constitution. It is, for example, common knowledge that many affiliated unions still discriminate against blacks, although—as has been noted earlier—in recent years progress has been made in eliminating such practices, and although certain provisions of the Civil Rights Act of 1964 (which make it unlawful for unions to discriminate because of race, color, or creed) have further helped in this regard. Despite all this improvement, however, some unions still prohibit blacks from joining, fail to represent them fairly and equally in collective bargaining, and otherwise discriminate against them. Such practices, of course, conflict not only with legality but with the AFL-CIO constitutional proscription against racial discrimination; but the federation is faced with a major dilemma under such circumstances: If it were to expel each union found to be in any way discriminating against blacks, the size of the federation would be drastically reduced and its influence as a labor body would be seriously impaired.[4] Indeed, to date no union has been expelled from the federation for racial discrimination; about all the federation officers have done has been to use moral suasion to deal with the problem. Such an approach has not yet been particularly effective in many cases, but to do more than this would jeopardize the entire federation.

Member-union autonomy is also evident from the ease with which national unions have left the federation voluntarily. The peripatetic United Mine Workers well illustrate this situation. After they were expelled from the AFL for spearheading the formation of the CIO through the efforts of their

---

[4]See Ray Marshall, *The Negro and Organized Labor* (New York: John Wiley, 1965); and Thomas R. Brooks, *Toil and Trouble*, 2nd rev. ed. (New York: Dell Publishing Co., 1971), pp. 242–61.

president, John L. Lewis, the Mine Workers became a CIO affiliate when Lewis was elected the latter federation's first president. As part of Lewis' resignation as CIO president following the defeat of Wendell Willkie in 1940, however, the Mine Workers disaffiliated from the CIO and shortly thereafter rejoined the AFL. Yet Lewis *once again* pulled his union out of the AFL, in 1947, after he had attempted to persuade the AFL to pass a resolution to the effect that no union leader should sign the non-Communist affidavit that was then required of union officers by the Taft-Hartley law, and the Mine Workers have continued to be independent to this day.

Nor have the Mine Workers been unique in their actions. Even since 1955, several other affiliates have withdrawn from the AFL-CIO (and, in some cases, returned to it), each time pointing up the fact that the federation has no power whatsoever to force any of its affiliates to remain in its ranks.

Why, then, *do* most national unions seek to belong to the federation? What do they get for their per capita tax money?

Advantages of Affiliation

By far the chief benefit associated with membership is protection against "raiding." One provision of the AFL-CIO constitution states that "each such affiliate shall respect the established collective bargaining relationship of every other affiliate and no affiliate shall raid the established collective bargaining relationship of any other affiliate." This means that once an affiliated union gains bargaining rights in a company, no other union affiliated with the federation may attempt to dislodge the established union and place itself in the plant. Such a stricture frees unions from the task of fighting off raids from sister unions of the federation. Time and money conserved in this way can be either used to organize the unorganized or devoted to other union programs. Unions that violate the no-raiding provision of the constitution may realistically expect to be expelled from the AFL-CIO; and because mutual self-interest of all members is involved, the amount of raiding has in fact decreased sharply since the formation of the federation.

Thus, before a union withdraws voluntarily from the AFL-CIO or engages in conduct that could result in expulsion, the officers of the union must weigh the consequences of operating outside the federation as these consequences concern proneness to raiding. Such considerations have been particularly influential in maintaining AFL-CIO membership for most smaller and weaker nationals, whom protection against raids benefits to a greater degree than it does larger national unions. But considerations of the money, time, and energy involved in counterattacking raiding attempts have also convinced most larger nationals of the wisdom of continued federation membership.

Federation membership involves still other advantages. With the federation as the spearhead, the union movement has comparatively more power in the political and legislative affairs of the nation—a particularly influential consideration, given the thrust of the laws today—and labor's impact upon elections and congressional voting is correspondingly greater than if each national union went its own way. In addition, by coordinating political efforts, the federation can use union funds, and such other sources of political persuasion as letter-writing campaigns, more effectively. Moreover, the AFL-CIO helps national unions in organizing campaigns, although the nationals are expected to bear the chief responsibility for new organization. And affiliated national unions also receive some help from the federation in the areas of legal services, educational programs, research, and social activities.

On the other hand, in the best tradition of Gompers, the federation does not negotiate labor agreements for the affiliated national unions. It is not equipped to render such services; nor do the autonomous national unions desire such intervention. In only one way does a national union directly benefit on the collective bargaining front from its membership in the federation: A framework is provided whereby unions that bargain in the same industry or with the same company can consolidate their efforts. A large company such as General Electric, for example, bargains with many different unions, and affiliated unions that deal with General Electric can thus more easily adopt common collective bargaining goals (such as uniform expiration dates of labor agreements, and the attainment of similar economic benefits) than would be the case without the availability of federation coordination; the joint 1966, 1969, and 1973 bargaining endeavors of eleven major unions with General Electric (and subsequently with Westinghouse) were in fact conducted under AFL-CIO auspices, through the coordinating efforts of the federation's increasingly active Industrial Union Department, and this has been true of several other joint union efforts, which are summarized in the next chapter under "Coordinated Bargaining."

Structure and Government of the AFL-CIO

As the accompanying chart indicates, the supreme governing body of the federation is its convention, held once every two years. Each national union, regardless of size, may send one delegate to the convention, and unions with more than 4,000 members can send additional delegates in proportion to their size. Each national union delegate casts one vote for every member he represents, an arrangement that allows larger unions, such as the Steel Workers and Carpenters, more influence in the affairs of the convention.

Financial expenses of the delegates are defrayed by their individual national unions and not by the federation. Such expenses can at times be quite high and may even dissuade nationals from sending their full quotas of delegates; the convention lasts two weeks, is held in first-rate hotels in a major city, and often involves considerable travel.

The convention reflects any convention of any large group. Federation officers are elected; amendments to the AFL-CIO constitution are proposed and at times adopted; committee reports are rendered; internal policies of the

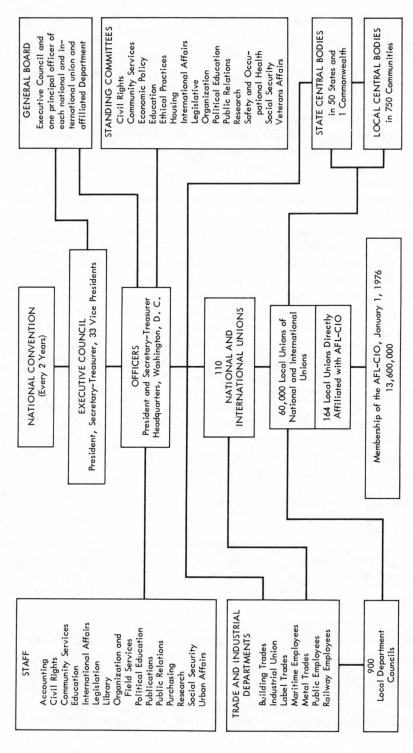

GENERAL BOARD
Executive Council and one principal officer of each national and international union and affiliated Department

STANDING COMMITTEES
Civil Rights
Community Services
Economic Policy
Education
Ethical Practices
Housing
International Affairs
Legislative
Organization
Political Education
Public Relations
Research
Safety and Occupational Health
Social Security
Veterans Affairs

STATE CENTRAL BODIES
in 50 States and 1 Commonwealth

LOCAL CENTRAL BODIES
in 750 Communities

NATIONAL CONVENTION
(Every 2 Years)

EXECUTIVE COUNCIL
President, Secretary–Treasurer, 33 Vice Presidents

OFFICERS
President and Secretary–Treasurer
Headquarters, Washington, D. C.

110
NATIONAL AND
INTERNATIONAL UNIONS

60,000 Local Unions of National and International Unions

164 Local Unions Directly Affiliated with AFL–CIO

Membership of the AFL–CIO, January 1, 1976
13,600,000

STAFF
Accounting
Civil Rights
Community Services
Education
International Affairs
Legislation
Library
Organization and Field Services
Political Education
Publications
Public Relations
Purchasing
Research
Social Security
Urban Affairs

TRADE AND INDUSTRIAL DEPARTMENTS
Building Trades
Industrial Union
Label Trades
Maritime Employees
Metal Trades
Public Employees
Railway Employees

900
Local Department Councils

STRUCTURAL ORGANIZATION OF THE AFL-CIO

federation are deliberated and at times changed; and countless resolutions, ranging from purely trade-union affairs to such weighty topics as United States foreign policy, are voted upon. There are speakers and more speakers. Delegates must be able to sit for long periods and be capable of absorbing rhetoric that is, while occasionally inspirational, far more often soporific.

The decisions and policies adopted by the convention are implemented by the AFL-CIO *executive council,* composed of the president, secretary-treasurer, and 33 vice-presidents of the federation. The vice-presidents are elected at the convention and are usually selected from the presidents of the major affiliated national unions, although the 5,000-member Sleeping Car Porters has constituted a notable exception in this regard—primarily because of the personal respect in which its black president, A. Philip Randolph, is held. Only the president of the federation and its secretary-treasurer devote full time to the affairs of the organization, however; the vice-presidents meet with the executive council at least three times a year, but remain as presidents of their own national unions.

Among its chief duties, the executive council interprets and applies the federation constitution; plays a "watchdog" role in legislative matters that affect the interests of workers and unions; assembles, through a full-time staff of legal and economic experts, the data needed for testimony before congressional committees; keeps in contact with the many federal agencies that have authority in the labor field; and ensures that the federation is kept free from corrupt or communistic influences. If it suspects that a union or its officers are in violation of the federation's constitution, it may investigate the matter, and if it finds that the charges are valid, it may, by a two-thirds majority, vote to suspend the guilty union. It may also recommend the ultimate penalty of expulsion of the union, but only the full convention may actually expel the union from the federation.

The executive council also selects six of its membership who, along with the AFL-CIO president and secretary-treasurer, constitute the federation's *executive committee.* This smaller group meets every two months and has the major function of advising and counseling the president and secretary-treasurer on issues involving the federation and its policies. Only the president and the secretary-treasurer receive a salary for their duties—$90,000 and $60,000 per year, respectively. All other federation officers serve without salary, although they are compensated for their expenses when attending to federation business.

A fourth decision-making body within the federation is the AFL-CIO *general board,* which consists of all members of the executive council and one principal officer of each of the national unions and the affiliated departments (to be described below). Usually, the affiliated national union designates its chief officer as its representative to serve on the general board, which must meet at least once a year and may meet more often at the discretion of the federation's president. Its chief duty is to rule on all questions and issues referred to it by the executive council. An important difference exists between the voting procedure of the general board and that of the executive council, however. General board members vote as *representatives of their unions*, and each may cast a vote based upon the membership of the union. Members of the executive council vote as *individuals*, which means that each member may cast only one vote and that, consequently, the larger unions have less influence than they do in general board meetings.

The federation constitution also requires that the president appoint a number of *standing committees*, and AFL-CIO custom dictates that each committee chairman be president of a national union and that all members be active trade unionists. At present, such committees (which are in all cases supplied with full-time professional staffs) deal with the following issues and problems: civil rights, community services, economic policy, education, ethical practices, housing, international affairs, legislation, organization, political education, public relations, research, safety and occupational health, social security, and veterans' affairs. The growing scope of interests of the federation is illustrated by the character of these committees, most of which are relatively new and virtually all of which clearly extend well beyond strictly trade union affairs.

Seven constitutional departments, which are trade and industrial groupings for unions with strong common interests, are currently in existence: Building and Construction Trades, Industrial Union, Maritime, Metal Trades, Railway Employees, Union Label, and—most recently—Public Employees. National unions may belong to more than one of these departments, and many of them with memberships in two or more areas of interest do exactly that (for example, the International Brotherhood of Electrical Workers, with some members who work in the building trades and others who work in factories), but in each case the national is required to pay to the respective department a per capita tax based upon the number of its members whose occupations or jobs fall under the department's jurisdiction. These dues are in addition to those the national union pays as a condition of belonging to the AFL-CIO.

Each department is concerned with problems of its particular industry. Such problems can involve collective bargaining issues, new organizational drives, legislative matters, or more specialized areas with which the unions of a particular branch of industry are uniquely confronted. Indeed, unlike the AFL-CIO, two of the departments take an active part in collective bargaining: The Railway Employees Department, which represents the members of the craft unions who work in railroad shops, plays a major role in collective bargaining with the railroads; and the Metal Trades Department usually engages in the negotiations where large shipbuilding concerns are involved. The Union Label Department has as its primary objective the education of the consuming public in the desirability of purchasing union-made goods. It is composed of all AFL-CIO affiliates that stress use of a union label to show that union members produced the product; to many union members, such a label is particularly persuasive before a purchase is made.

State and City Bodies

Even though most of the activities of the AFL-CIO are centered in Washington, the federation has also established state and city bodies to deal with problems at the state and municipal level. There are now state bodies in each of the fifty states and one in Puerto Rico; and, on the city level, the federation has created city centrals in about 750 communities.

Note that these state and city central bodies are established *directly* by the AFL-CIO; they are not created by the national unions affiliated with the federation or by local unions that belong to these national unions. Local unions that belong to national unions affiliated with the AFL-CIO may join a state or a city central body, but the national union must be affiliated with the AFL-CIO; and should a national union be expelled from or withdraw voluntarily from the federation, its local unions lose membership in the state and city central bodies. Thus, when the Teamsters Union was expelled from the AFL-CIO, the locals of this union were likewise expelled from the state and city bodies.[5] The same thing occurred when the UAW forfeited its membership in the AFL-CIO. Indeed, the president of the Indiana state AFL-CIO, a UAW member, was deposed from office, since the officers of the federation state and city bodies must be members of an affiliated union. Other points of importance are that national unions do not affiliate with state and city organizations (only their locals may belong to them), and that the federation does not require that the locals affiliate (although most of the national unions require that their locals affiliate with the state and city bodies).

State federations, also, hold conventions at which they elect officers of the state organization. Delegates to such state conventions are elected by the affiliated local unions. Normally these delegates elect a president, vice-president, and secretary-treasurer who devote full time to the organization's business, and, of course, receive a salary for their work. At times, a state central body will also hire full-time representatives who are concerned with special matters, particularly in the field of legislative lobbying.

Similar to the AFL-CIO, also, the state and city bodies have no executive power over their affiliated unions. They do not engage in collective bargaining, call or forbid strikes, or regulate the internal affairs of their affiliated local unions. Instead, the chief concern of the state and city bodies is political and educational activities. They lobby for or against legislation, offer testimony before state legislative committees, and promote political

---

[5] In some cases, however, Teamster locals were allowed to keep membership until the national officers of the AFL-CIO forced the issue.

candidates favored by organized labor. Almost all state organizations now hold schools for representatives of their affiliated unions—the classes being taught by union officials, university instructors, government officials, and, on some occasions, representatives of the business community. The city bodies, in addition to participating in similar legislative and educational activities, engage in a wide variety of community service work—promoting the United Fund, Red Cross, and similar community projects, among other endeavors. In many cities and towns, such bodies have sponsored Boy Scout troops and Little League baseball teams, as well as art institutes, musical events, day-care centers for children of working mothers, and even the purchase of Seeing-Eye dogs for blind people. Although genuine altruism doubtless motivates many of these good deeds, so, too, does the need for an improved public image which is today so keenly felt by many unionists.

Functions and Problems of the Federation

For all that the AFL-CIO voluntarily abstains from doing or is re-stricted by its constitution from attempting, there can be no denying the aggressiveness with which the federation pursues the activities it does under-take. In the political arena, this is particularly true. As do most other major interest groups in the United States, the federation now employs a large corps of full-time lobbyists whose mission is to exert pressure upon members of Congress to support legislation favored by the AFL-CIO and to oppose those bills the federation regards as undesirable. Its principal officers themselves frequently testify before congressional committees and make public decla-rations of federation political policies. And, by its very dimensions, the federation provides a powerful sounding board for all of organized labor. Ostensibly, when the president of the AFL-CIO speaks, he represents more than 13,600,000 union members and their families, 110 national unions, 60,000 local unions, 51 state federations, and over 700 citywide labor bodies. No other labor leader can claim as much attention and exert as much in-fluence. He and other important federation officials are from time to time invited to the White House and are regularly invited by U.S. senators, con-gressmen, and heads of major federal agencies dealing with labor matters to specify labor's position on major issues of the day. It is doubtful that representatives of any other interest group make as many appearances at the nation's presidential residence as do members of the AFL-CIO high command.

At times of federal and state elections, the role of the federation is equally important. The federation has created a Committee on Political Education that coordinates the political action of organized labor during such periods. This political arm of the federation operates on the national, state, and local levels, where (since the Taft-Hartley law, as we know, forbids unions to contribute union dues to political candidates) it raises money on a voluntary basis from union members. Some of this money is given directly to political candidates who are regarded as friends of organized labor; other money is expended for radio and TV programs of a political nature, the publication of voting records of candidates who have previously served in elective offices, the distribution of campaign literature, and kindred activities. Although it is difficult to assess the political impact of the federation upon the nation—the AFL-CIO having had both its successes and its failures—the fact that the federation continues to play an active role in the political affairs of the country would indicate that the victories outweigh the defeats.

The political objectives of organized labor and the federation are varied in character. The AFL-CIO supports legislation that strengthens the role of organized labor in collective bargaining, organizational drives, the strike, picketing, and boycotting. To these ends, the federation has, for example, consistently advocated such measures as the repeal of state "right-to-work" legislation, and lobbied for other changes in the federal and state laws that would strengthen the use of such union self-help methods as boycotts and picketing in labor's direct relationship with business. It has also, however, regularly supported such bills as those favoring national health insurance, low-cost public housing, liberalized minimum-wage laws, more comprehensive unemployment-compensation statutes, and more effective public education—all of which measures are intended to benefit all the workers of the nation and their families, rather than strictly those within the ranks of unionism. The AFL-CIO today fully recognizes that many of these less parochial objectives cannot be achieved through face-to-face union–management collective bargaining and has consequently supported such measures as the ones cited to gain additional leverage in its efforts to improve the status of the American wage earner.

Beyond the legislative and political function, the federation carries out a massive research program—the results of which are embodied in its regular publications, such as the *AFL-CIO News* and the *American Federationist*, as well as in special bulletins, briefs for the courts of the nation, and a series of pamphlets, monographs, and books. Through these varied publications, the federation tries to keep union members and others abreast of labor developments from the union point of view.

Another important function is that of promoting new organizations. Although the basic responsibility for such new organizations falls upon the national unions, the federation does organize on its own, and helps affiliated unions in their organizational drives. When the AFL-CIO organizes a union by itself, it charters such a local union directly with the federation in much the same fashion that the old AFL did in the 1930s. There are 164 such directly affiliated labor unions now in existence, and through its field officers, the AFL-CIO bargains contracts for these local unions and aids them in time of strikes and other difficulties with management. In return, members of such locals pay dues directly to the AFL-CIO. This collective bargaining function for directly affiliated local unions should not, however, be confused with the principle already established: The AFL-CIO does not bargain collectively for affiliated national unions or for locals that belong to such affiliated national unions. Moreover, most of these directly affiliated local unions are themselves ultimately assigned by the federation to a national union that has appropriate jurisdiction over the jobs and occupations of its members.

In recent years, the American labor movement has also demonstrated increasing concern with the labor movement in foreign nations. Two major factors lie behind this development. In the first place, the increasing tempo of international trade, now increasingly also tied into the rise of the "multi-national," has threatened the job security and welfare of American workers. The impact in the United States of products produced by foreign labor under conditions of comparatively lower wages and poorer working conditions makes it more difficult for American unions to retain benefits already secured and to obtain improvements in them. American unions understand full well that benefits secured in their contracts are placed in jeopardy because of such competition from low-wage foreign nations. Hence, by strengthening the foreign labor movement, American unions not only improve the status of workers within foreign nations, but at the same time protect the advances that have been gained through collective bargaining in this country.

The second reason concerns the threat of communist domination of foreign labor movements and, through this tactic, the possible seizure of the governments of foreign nations by communists. Even in the United States, as Chapter 2 has demonstrated, organized labor has been faced with such a threat, although in this country it has been successfully surmounted. The 1949–50 expulsion from the CIO of the several communist-controlled unions, and the establishment of new unions to take over the membership of such unions, dealt a telling blow to the influence of communism in the American labor movement. The AFL, too, when it was the only federation in the nation, waged a continuous and bitter battle against the left and managed to maintain its basically conservative philosophy and objectives. There are today only a handful of American labor unions, all of them relatively minor in strategic power (for example, the Furriers Union), that are even remotely believed to be dominated by communists. But the problem is much more severe in foreign lands: In such nations as Italy and France, communistic elements do have considerable influence in the affairs of the labor movements. And the important officers of America's labor movement, well schooled in the potential consequences of communism, believe with considerable justification that should such totalitarianism spread to the governments of these countries, the first casualties would be the free labor movement, collective bargaining, and the right to strike. For such reasons, the AFL-CIO works hard to help foreign trade unions remain free from communist domination.

At the present time, the AFL-CIO is an active supporter of several international labor bodies. Most notably, it supplies the representation for American workers within the International Labor Organization, now a specialized agency of the United Nations but actually predating the establishment of the UN itself, having been created immediately after World War I with encouragement from Samuel Gompers.

The federation and its affiliates also contribute money to aid in the organization of foreign workers, the training of foreign labor leaders, the education of foreign union members, and the promotion of a variety of similar activities. In addition, the AFL-CIO has representation on various committees of the United Nations, hosts many visiting labor delegates from foreign nations who are sent by their governments or by higher trade-union bodies in their respective nations, and even on frequent occasions itself finances the trips of these foreign labor leaders. The AFL-CIO and many of its affiliated national unions have also financed trips of their own representatives to foreign lands to see at first hand the problems of other labor movements. Under the AFL-CIO constitution, the federation's Committee on International Affairs is charged with the responsibility of coordinating and implementing such activities.

Conflict between Craft and Industrial Unions

If the main benefit associated with federation membership is protection against raiding, one of the most important problems of the AFL-CIO is that of maintaining peace between affiliated unions in their jurisdictional disputes over jobs. Frequently, craft and industrial unions battle each other avidly over such jurisdiction, particularly in establishments where an industrial union holds bargaining rights but where some jobs could be carried out in a more efficient fashion by members of a craft union. Such jobs as those involving the routine maintenance of machinery or other equipment, the major overhaul or installation of equipment, and the construction of new facilities often fall into this category.

What could spark a conflict is the desire of members of craft unions whose members are not employees of the industrial company to do the work that is being performed by the skilled tradesmen on the payroll of the factory. At times, employers find it cheaper to hire these outside craftsmen to perform the work and therefore seek out contractor-employers who control such skilled employees. Upon other occasions, a skilled trade union, through a contractor-employer, makes overtures to the industrial employer. However, the problem could also arise from the other direction. That is, the industrial employer may have customarily subcontracted certain maintenance work to outside skilled tradesmen. To secure this work for its own membership, the industrial union that holds bargaining rights in the factory puts pressure upon the employer to cease this practice and to award the work to his own employees who are, of course, members of the industrial union. It is not difficult to understand that when jobs are scarce, the conflict between craft and industrial unions can achieve major dimensions.

Indeed, the problem became so serious in the recession-marked first months of the 1960s that many observers predicted the imminent collapse of the entire federation through craft–industrial warfare. Remarkably, however, the important leaders of the craft and industrial unions were able to arrive at a workable solution to the problem at the December 1961 AFL-CIO convention and thereby rescue the federation from such a collapse. They adopted an "Internal Disputes Plan," often also referred to as the "Live and Let Live" plan and incorporated it into the constitution of the AFL-CIO. More technically, the constitutional amendment officially preserved the integrity of past practices in work assignments. Henceforth a union's right to jobs would depend on what relevant customs or practices had been in force where it sought such jobs. If the members of an industrial union had held jurisdiction over new construction in the past, this customary work assignment would be respected by craft unions. If an employer had customarily subcontracted out maintenance work, this practice was to be respected by industrial unions, who were not to put pressure upon employers to change it.

An elaborate procedure has been adopted to implement this new constitutional provision. In the event that a union charges that another union is violating the terms of the new policy, the AFL-CIO assigns a federation official to mediate the dispute. If this effort fails, an arbitrator is appointed to make an award. Once the arbitrator hands down his decision, the rival union is expected to abide by the award. However, the losing union has the right to appeal to a three-man subcommittee of the AFL-CIO executive council. This subcommittee may disallow the appeal, in which event the decision of the arbitrator is final and there is no other appeal procedure. But if the subcommittee is not fully satisfied with the arbitrator's award, it may refer the case to the entire executive council, which will decide the issue by majority vote. The council may uphold the arbitrator's award, reverse it, or modify it. In any event, however, the decision of the executive council is final and binding on the unions involved in the dispute.

If a union fails to comply with the decision rendered through this procedure, the amendment to the constitution provides that the federation may impose sanctions (described below) on the noncomplying union, and if the violation persists, the union can be expelled from the federation.

Thus far the plan has worked successfully, and the threat to the federation has abated. The *AFL-CIO News* has detailed the results of the plan from the time of its creation in January 1962 through January 1975. In this time period, 1,546 complaints were filed under the plan. Of these, 875 were settled in mediation, or mediation was still in progress. Arbitrators found violations of the plan in 382 cases. After the arbitrators handed down their awards, unions filed 105 complaints charging noncompliance. Subsequently, non-compliance was found in only 20 cases. There were 6 noncompliance cases pending as of March 1, 1975.

No union has ever been expelled from the federation for noncompliance, although twelve affiliates have been placed under sanctions to be removed upon achievement of compliance. As of March 1975, sanctions were still in effect on two affiliated national unions: the Air Line Pilots Association and the International Typographical Union. When the AFL-CIO imposes sanctions upon a union under the terms of the plan, the union may not file charges under the plan to protest that another union is violating its customary job jurisdiction; the federation will publicly give notice of the union's non-compliance; and the AFL-CIO can deny to such noncomplying union its services and facilities.

With the craft–industrial conflict now having so visibly diminished, it appears that the AFL-CIO will continue to exist as a permanent federation in the United States. At this writing, it is twenty years old, and the old antagonisms of the former members and officers of the AFL and CIO have largely subsided. Even the UAW defection did not result in wholesale withdrawals from the federation, perhaps because in the last analysis this defection was the result of a personal vendetta between the late Walter Reuther and George Meany (Meany asserted on at least one occasion that Reuther was "just a pile of press clippings," for example, and Reuther was no more restrained in his criticisms of Meany), rather than of substantive issues. It is safe to conclude that the federation can overcome future problems, such as the election of new AFL-CIO officers, without falling apart. Moreover, union leaders understand that the collapse of the federation would seriously impair the future of organized labor in this nation. They understand that they had better "hang together" or they will hang separately. Indeed, the collapse of the federation would undoubtedly cause incessant raiding and jurisdictional strikes. Very probably, it would also result in some reemergence of labor violence, a further decline of union membership, a possible resurgence of corruption, and other effects that would adversely affect not only unions and their members, but also employers and the general public. From the point of view of stability in industrial relations, the preservation of the AFL-CIO is a public necessity.

THE NATIONAL UNION

Relationship to Locals

If the national union is quite autonomous in the conduct of its affairs, the story is quite different when one examines the relationship between the national union and its local unions. Although there are many exceptions, most national unions exercise considerable power over their locals. Before a local union may strike, it must normally obtain the permission of the national union. And, should the local union strike in defiance of national union instructions, the national union can withhold strike benefits, refuse to give the local union any other form of aid during the strike, and in extreme cases even take over the local on a trusteeship basis. In addition, consistent with the regulations of many national unions, all local collective bargaining contracts must be reviewed by the national officers before they may be put into force. All national union constitutions today contain provisions that establish standards of conduct and procedures for the internal operation of their con-stituent locals—usually, the dues that the locals may charge, the method by which their officers may be elected and their tenures of office, the procedures for the discipline of local union members, the conduct of union meetings, and other rules of this kind.

Violation of these national union standards can result in sanctions placed upon the local union officers and on the local union itself. Recently, for example, many national unions have been at least as conscious of the problem of racial discrimination within the union movement as has the AFL-CIO, and almost all national constitutions now contain a nondiscriminatory clause, designed to guarantee blacks equal and fair treatment from the local unions. Several local unions have been seized by their nationals when they have discriminated against blacks through such mechanisms as providing segregated local union facilities (such as washrooms and drinking facilities), or when they have failed to afford blacks equal protection in the negotiation of labor agreements or in the grievance procedure.

In addition, within the collective bargaining process, the national union is currently exercising considerably greater control and influence over the contracts that locals negotiate. This is particularly true when the members of the locals work for companies that sell their products in national product markets—an ever-increasing number. Nationals desire that companies over whose employees they have jurisdiction and that compete in national product markets operate under common labor-cost standards. They are less likely to exercise control over the unions whose members produce for local markets—for example, in the construction industry, because the labor costs involved in the construction of a building in one city do not directly compete with those affecting the construction of a building in another.

Service in Collective Bargaining

The national exercises much of its influence over the local in the direct collective bargaining process through the service that the national union provides its locals in the negotiation of labor agreements. To understand this national–local relationship, however, one should not regard the negotiation service of the national union as a function that is performed against the will of the local union. On the contrary, local unions not only generally desire and expect the help of the national union when they negotiate labor agreements with the employer, but should the national union either refuse to provide these services or perform them in an ineffective way, the local union members and their officers can be counted upon to be sharply critical of the national union. The officers of the national could safely assume, in fact, that such a disgruntled local union would attempt to take political reprisal against the officers of the national in the next election of national officers.

The chief reason for the local union's desire for help from the national union in collective bargaining involves the complexities of the contemporary collective bargaining process. As will be made more evident in future chapters, many of the issues of collective bargaining have become increasingly intricate. Most contemporary collective bargaining contracts focus upon such involved items as adjustment to automation, pension plans, insurance programs, supplementary unemployment benefit plans, job evaluation, production standards, time and motion studies, and complicated wage incentive programs. Beyond the complex character of the contemporary issues, moreover, the modern collective bargaining process is obviously made more difficult because of the character of the law of labor relations. In short, it takes an expert to negotiate under current circumstances.

For effective representation, it is necessary to find people who are knowledgeable and experienced, and have a professional understanding of the collective bargaining process; and few local unions are fortunate enough to include such people in their membership. Each local union elects a negotiating committee, but the members of such committees are typically employed in the plant and work full time on their jobs. They simply do not have the opportunity to keep abreast of current developments in collective bargaining and to make a searching study of the problems involved in the negotiation of the difficult issues. On the company side, moreover, there are normally management representatives who are well trained and equipped to handle the contemporary collective bargaining negotiation. Many of them have received special training in labor relations, and some devote full time to the problems of negotiation and administration of collective bargaining contracts.

Indeed, without the services of the national union, there would be a sharp disparity of negotiating talent at the bargaining table. In this light, it is easy to understand why the local union does not regard the intervention of the national union at the bargaining table as an invasion of the rights of the local, but rather views this service as indispensable to the effective negotiation of the labor agreement.

Most national unions have well-qualified people to render this service: the so-called staff representatives, who devote full time to union affairs. They are hired by the national union, paid salaries and expenses for their work, and expected to provide services to the local unions of the national. All of them are union members, and they normally reach their position of staff representative by having demonstrated their ability as union members and local union officers. They are not, however, elected to their jobs, but are hired because of their special talents.

Although the staff representatives perform a variety of duties, such as organizing new plants, engaging in political-action work at times of federal and state elections, directing strikes, and representing the union and its members before the federal and state labor agencies, helping the local unions to negotiate labor agreements constitutes one of their primary functions.[6] Staff representatives gain much bargaining experience because they normally service several local unions, and in the course of one year they may be called upon to negotiate many different labor agreements, thus gaining on-the-job training that serves as an invaluable asset to them when they confront a specific management at the bargaining table. Many national unions also send their staff representatives to special schools, some of which are held on university campuses and are taught by specialists in the labor education field, for additional training. Moreover, the staff representative is invariably backed up by experts within the national union. Almost every national union has several departments that concentrate on the major issues involved in collective bargaining. For example, the United Automobile Workers has departments that deal with pensions, wage systems, insurance, and other critical areas. The specialists assigned to these national departments may be freely called upon by the staff representatives, should their services be needed.

The Regional or District Office

Staff representatives may work out of the headquarters of the national union, but more frequently they are assigned to a regional or district office. Almost every national union divides the nation into regions or districts, and locals of the national union that are located in the geographical area or the district obtain services from their respective district offices. For example, District 30 of the United Steelworkers of America, headquartered in Indianapolis, covers most of Indiana and Kentucky and is administered by a district director elected by the local unions of the district. About twenty staff representatives are assigned by the national union to District 30 and work under the immediate supervision of the district director.

Each staff representative services about seven local unions. He attends the local union meetings, works closely with the negotiating committees, hears the problems of the workers in the plant in which the local holds control, and attempts to understand the values and objectives of the members. He is the liaison between the national and the local union, and in this capacity can do much to influence the local in the acceptance of national union collective bargaining policies. In such a capacity, moreover, the staff

---

[6]A major exception to all these remarks involves craft unions in local-product market industries; here, local business agents are normally elected to perform such duties.

representative can serve as a mediator between local unions and the national when differences arise between them.

A good staff representative wins the confidence of local officers and members, and the local union will thus rely heavily upon his counsel in collective bargaining matters. He can exert great influence upon the local to reject or accept the last offer of an employer. Indeed, frequently he can provoke a strike or prevent one by the way in which he reports to the local union and makes recommendations to the members. He is, in short, often in an excellent position to influence the decision-making process in collective bargaining.

Multiemployer Bargaining

Although most multiemployer bargaining is in relatively small bargaining units in local-product markets, at times national unions bargain with employers on a multiemployer basis. That is, a group of companies band together as a unit to negotiate with the national union. Employers find this structure of collective bargaining valuable because it prevents a given union from "whipsawing" each employer: Usually, under a multiemployer bargaining structure, each employer is comparatively small in size and unimpressive in financial resources, and the companies compete fiercely in the product market; in the absence of multiemployer collective bargaining, the union could pick off one employer at a time. Such employer-association–national-union collective bargaining is found in industries such as clothing, coal, and shipping—all of which contain large measures of the unstabilizing factors noted.

When multiemployer collective bargaining exists and where the product market is not a local one, the national officers themselves typically bargain for the contract, and the local unions play a comparatively passive role—a situation that also holds at the other extreme, when unions bargain with the industrial giants of the nation (such as General Motors and United States Steel). The national unions negotiate the agreement in the latter instance, since no one local union could possibly measure up to the strength of these companies. Bargaining logic dictates that in both cases, the national union rather than the local union play the paramount labor relations role.

Additional National Union Services

Beyond providing considerable help in the negotiating of labor agreements, the national union renders other valuable services to its local unions. The national usually awards benefits to employees on strike, although the actual amount of money paid in strike benefits is usually very minimal—about $25–$40 per week to each member, on the average and this figure is about the same as it was a decade ago. More important, the national union intervenes with the strikers' creditors so that the automobiles, furniture, and other holdings of the union members will not be repossessed. And it ensures that no striking employee or his family goes hungry, even if this guarantee involves the actual distribution of food to the strikers. Management should be aware that unions in these days do not lose strikes because of hunger or unpaid bills. If there are insurance premiums to be paid, doctors to see, rent to be paid, or school tuition to be met, the national unions will see to it that the worker does not suffer. This is true despite the obvious fact that the national unions themselves have financial limitations, for virtually all nationals do under normal circumstances have the resources to assure that the minimum physiological needs of their member-workers are met, and many larger unions are quite amply financed. The Automobile Workers, for example, poured out more than $12 million during the six-year, 1954–60 Kohler strike to aid the members of the local engaged in that conflict. In addition, if a national union does run out of money, labor custom dictates that other national unions will lend it money to finance the strike.

The national union also aids the locals in the grievance procedure and in arbitration, both of which subjects will be discussed in detail in Chapter 6. Normally, the staff representative represents the local in the last step of the grievance procedure. Along with the local union grievance committee, he attempts to settle the grievance to the satisfaction of the complaining worker, and if the case does ultimately go to arbitration, he usually directly represents the grievant. In general, whether they win or lose their arbitration cases staff representatives present the union's case very effectively. This fact is often offered by labor leaders as one reason why unions employ lawyers less frequently than do employers when cases go to arbitration. There is no need to incur the expense if the staff representative can do the job as competently as an attorney.

Of course, at times local unions *are* in need of an attorney, as when the local union has a case that requires testimony in the courts. For example, employers may sue a union for breach of contract, or workers may be indicted because of violence in picketing. When attorneys are needed, the local union can normally obtain the services of the national union's legal staff, whose members, although invariably paid less than comparable lawyers who work for corporations, are frequently highly competent and usually quite dedicated to the union movement. Several prominent attorneys, Clarence Darrow and Arthur Goldberg most notably, made their mark by representing labor organizations.

The fact that the local does so readily receive such services from its national constitutes the reason why the vast majority of local unions belong to a national union. Indeed, less than 2 percent of all locals are not affiliated with a national, and all these "independents" (except for the relative handful of them belonging directly to the AFL-CIO and thus enabled to make use of the federation's services) must rely upon their own resources, whereas the many local unions that do belong to nationals can use the considerable resources of the latter.

Other Functions of the National Union

Although national union officers and staff representatives devote the major share of their time to providing services to the local unions, the range of the national union's activities includes many other important functions. Today, the major concern of all unions is that of increasing membership, in the face of the relative plateau of the past few years. Responsible labor union officials understand that the unorganized must be organized, and the chief burden for this also falls to the national union staff representatives. Although the AFL-CIO does do some organizational work, it does not have the staff to perform this function effectively; nor can the responsibility for the organization of new plants be undertaken by local union officers or members. At times, local union people help in organizational drives, but because they are full-time employees, they do not have much opportunity to carry out this function.

Accordingly, the catalyst for new organization falls to the staff representatives of the national unions, upon whom constant pressure is exerted to organize nonunion plants. Indeed, in some national unions, not only the advancement but even the continued job tenure of the staff representative is determined by his success in organizing such plants.

The task is hardly an easy one. Most nonunion employers can be counted upon to wage a fierce fight against organization. Many employees who are not members of unions do not want a labor union, because management provides them with many of the benefits they would receive if organized. And the staff representative's organizing mission becomes even more difficult if he attempts to organize in the South, or in small communities regardless of sectional location. In any event, the representative must make contacts among the workers, convince them of the value of unions, and dispel notions that unions are corrupt, communistic, or otherwise undesirable institutions. Many workers are ready to believe the worst about organized labor, and staff representatives often admit that these conceptions are difficult to erase.

The staff man is thus forced to use his imagination to the fullest. He may initially attempt to organize "from inside," through the informal leaders in the plant. Then he may visit workers in their homes, distribute leaflets, and arrange organizational meetings (which frequently are poorly attended). Subsequently he must counteract whatever management does to block the organizational attempt; even in today's more enlightened atmosphere, some employers warn employees of dire consequences should they organize, tell their employees that unions exist only to collect dues for the personal benefit of the union "bosses," and—the organizing-tactic laws cited in Chapter 3 notwithstanding—on occasion even threaten workers with loss of their jobs if a union is established, as well as promise them benefits if they reject the union. In 1974, the Farah Manufacturing Company was organized by the Amalgamated Clothing Workers following a $2\frac{1}{2}$-year struggle that included a boycott of Farah products. The victory, however, came only after a National Labor Relations Board administrative law judge had criticized Farah for carrying on "a broad-gauged antiunion campaign consisting of glaring and repeated violations" of the National Labor Relations Act and acting as if "there were no act, no board and no Ten Commandments."[7]

There are other formidable obstacles for the organizer. If the plant is located in a comparatively small community, there may be a concerted attempt among the leaders of the community to keep the union out. The target employer may have good friends who run the newspaper, the radio and TV stations, the Chamber of Commerce, and the local stores, and these power centers may join forces to do what they can to keep the union from gaining a foothold. Indeed, it is not uncommon that the clergy in a town is enlisted in the fight against the union.

The organizational mission of the staff representative is thus a highly challenging one. In recent years, he has probably had more failures than successful ventures. But he is typically persistent, and this tenaciousness occasionally reaps its reward: Illustratively, although clearly also an extreme, the Textile Workers Union of America organized the employees of J.P. Stevens and Co. in seven North Carolina mills in late 1974, after attempting to recruit these workers (in most cases, their predecessor workers) since the 1930s!

Another major function of the national union concerns political action, although national unions differ widely in the vigor they display in this regard. Some, like the Automobile Workers, are constantly engaged in politics; others, like the United Brotherhood of Carpenters, seldom exert much effort to influence elections and the subsequent actions of elected officials. Undoubtedly, however, a larger number of national unions are concerned with political affairs today then were in the past. As has already been noted, their leaders understand that the success of the union depends in large measure upon the fashioning of a favorable legal climate for new organization and for the implementation of traditional trade union weapons when conflicts arise with employers. Moreover, a growing number of national unions share the belief of AFL-CIO leaders that the political programs of organized labor in the areas of Social Security, medicine, low-cost public housing, full employment, and the like are in the best interests of the nation as a whole.

When the national union officers are politically motivated, they are normally aggressive in exerting pressure upon the local unions and their members

[7] *Wall Street Journal*, April 8, 1974, p. 25.

to take an active role in political affairs. Their union newspapers (almost every national union publishes at least one monthly newspaper) are filled with political news, voting records of the candidates, and the union point of view when elections are impending. National unions also arrange political rallies, purchase radio and television time to get the national's story across to the members and the public, and issue a barrage of political leaflets and pamphlets. In some national unions, during the weeks before important elections, the staff representatives are ordered to suspend collective bargaining negotiations, grievance meetings, and arbitrations and devote their full time to political work. The fact that each national union employs many staff representatives—in such large unions as the Automobile Workers and Steelworkers, the numbers run into the hundreds—serves as an important advantage; and if the staff representatives are adroit and hard-working, the favored political candidate can benefit greatly from such support.

Depending upon their sizes and leadership policies, national unions perform other functions. Some arrange educational programs for their staff representatives and local union officers. Most of the courses in these programs deal exclusively with the practical aspects of labor relations—how to bargain labor agreements, the best way to handle grievances, and the like. At times, however, the courses deal with foreign affairs, taxation, economics, government, and other subjects not directly related to the bread-and-butter issues of trade unionism. In addition, some national unions administer vacation resorts for their members, award university scholarships to children of members, organize tours to foreign nations, conduct publicity campaigns to acquaint union members and the public in general with the purpose of the union label, and sponsor a variety of social functions that are similar to those maintained by the state and city labor bodies but more tailored to the specific interests and aptitudes of the particular national union's members.

Government of the National Union

When a national union is formed, a constitution is adopted that spells out the internal government and procedures of the union. Virtually every constitution provides that a convention should be held, and designates this convention as the supreme authority of the union. Under the rules of most national unions, each local union sends delegates to the convention, with the number of delegates permitted to each local being dependent upon the local's paid-up membership totals. Hence, as in the case of the AFL-CIO, the larger locals are more influential than are the smaller units. Within the UAW, for example, the locals range in size from somewhat over 60,000 (the local union representing Ford Motor Company workers at Ford's River Rouge plant) to a literal handful of members in some locals that have contracts with small employers.

Ordinarily, the chief officers of the local unions are elected as delegates, although in the very large locals, which have the opportunity to send many delegates, rank-and-file members are chosen because the quota cannot be filled by the officers alone. Being sent to a convention represents a plum to the delegates chosen. National conventions, again as the AFL-CIO conventions themselves, are usually held in large and attractive cities; when the delegates lose time in the plant because of their election, the local union normally pays their lost wages; and the convention may last as much as a week or so, allowing a welcome relief from the tedium of working in the plant. Many delegates take their wives and children, so that, along with the business of the convention, attendance at the convention may thus become a sort of work–play affair; however, the expenses involved are such that small local unions with limited funds sometimes do not send delegates to the convention even though they are entitled to do so.

Although under the terms of the Landrum-Griffin Act the delegates must be chosen by secret ballot, the officers of the nationals themselves may be selected in either of two ways: In about three-fourths of the national unions, the constitution requires that the principal officers (president, vice-president, and secretary-treasurer) must be elected by the convention. In the others, the officers are elected by a direct referendum wherein each member of the union may cast a ballot. Some of the largest unions in the nation follow the latter procedure, including the United Steelworkers of America, the Amalgamated Clothing Workers, and the International Association of Machinists, but, even among the larger unions, most utilize the convention election system.

In addition to the election of chief officers, the convention transacts the business of the national union. Reports and recommendations of the officers are heard, and the delegates have an opportunity to deliberate upon them and decide whether or not to adopt them. Problems of the various locals are aired, and this provides an excellent opportunity for an exchange of ideas and experiences and for otherwise breaking down the provincialism of the local unions; delegates from a large local union in, say, Chicago can learn of the problems of a small local in a small southern community, for example. The convention also permits local union officers to display themselves to their best advantage. Most of them would like to rise in the union hierarchy, and the convention offers a testing ground for their talents. A rousing speech by a local union president may attract the attention of the delegates, and the consensus may be, "Here is a fellow we should watch."

The actual business of the convention may be initiated either by the national officers or by the delegates. Decision making takes the form of resolutions, proposals, and reports on which the delegates vote. As in any large convention, the officers have a distinct advantage in this respect, since the president appoints the committees that bring important issues before the delegates and is in a position to select members for these committees whom he knows are favorable to the national officers' point of view. On the other hand, a determined local union, or even individual delegates who feel strongly about their cause, can bring to the attention of the convention a resolution, recommendation, or even an amendment to the constitution. There is a limit, in fact, to how far any national president can go in bottling up the resentment of determined delegates. And, particularly if a delegation from a local can enlist the support of delegates from other locals, there is an excellent chance that the entire convention will hear its point of view. For all the authority and control the nationals exert over the locals, if national officers gain the enmity of a sufficient number of local unions, the delegates of these locals can band together and cause an upheaval at the convention; and, if the issues are of extreme importance, the resentment of these locals could result in a change in national union leadership. Thus, the local unions do have a political check against their national officers. There is a line the latter can cross only at the risk of losing their jobs.

In short, as long as the national union holds regularly scheduled conventions, the democratic process has an opportunity of working. The convention provides the forum wherein the policies, behavior, and competency of the national union officers can be evaluated, and the key to the democratic operation of a national union therefore lies in the regularity with which conventions are held. More than half the national unions hold conventions either annually or biennially, and most of the rest hold them every three or four years. A small number of national unions, however, simply do not hold conventions at all, and this clearly eliminates almost entirely any practical opportunity for the local unions to participate in the government of their unions. Nothing in the Landrum-Griffin law, indeed, requires unions to hold regular and reasonably frequent conventions. The law does require that the union membership be afforded the opportunity to elect its national officers at least every five years, but a union managed by autocrats can legally avoid the holding of conventions indefinitely.

National Union Officers

The chief of the national union is, of course, its president. He administers the organization with the assistance of such other major officers as the vice-president (or vice-presidents), secretary-treasurer, and members of the executive board. The latter group is composed ordinarily of the district or regional directors (who, in some national unions, are also called vice-presidents), and its members have a variety of official tasks: enforcing the constitution of the national, implementing its policies, filling a national officer's position when vacant, voting on important matters referred to it by the president, placing items on the agenda for deliberation and voting, and a host of related duties. Normally, the executive board of a national union meets regularly and frequently, according to the provisions of a constitution, and on occasion also meets at the call of the president to deal with some pressing problem. Since the members of the executive board are from all over the nation and have direct supervision of the locals in their particular districts, the board mechanism provides an excellent way for the national union officers to learn of the problems of all locals throughout the country. Likewise, it provides a channel for communicating policies of the national union to its locals and membership.

In some unions, however, executive boards merely rubber-stamp decisions of the national officers. This is true most often when a president, either by union custom or because of his particular personality, is allowed to exercise autocratic leadership. It is safe to say, however, that in most unions the executive board directs the affairs of the union and establishes the union's basic policies, which the president is then obliged to carry out. The exceptions in recent years—James R. Hoffa of the Teamsters and W.A. "Tony" Boyle of the Mine Workers, in particular—have in fact generally been succeeded in office by leaders who appear to have taken extra efforts to alter the old images of power imbalance and to encourage the executive boards to participate more fully in policy-making decisions.

A responsible, devoted, and active national union president has a difficult job. One day he may be negotiating a contract with a major corporation, and the next day speaking at an important meeting of his union, or to the members of some other labor organization. He is also, typically, obligated to testify before congressional committees, preside over the union's executive-board meetings, travel to foreign nations as a participant in international labor organization bodies, take an active role in important national political elections, constantly put pressure upon the staff representatives to organize nonunion plants, mollify companies that are disgruntled because of wildcat strikes or other forms of unauthorized union behavior, and perform a variety of other duties that may either be of major importance or strictly routine in character, but that also take up his time. Indeed, the management of even a small or medium-sized national union is a difficult one; the job becomes immensely more complicated and difficult in a large union.

The union president, moreover, is constantly torn between duties of a pressing character. In many cases, he must make the hard decision by himself and hope it is the right one. As any chief executive, he bears the ultimate responsibility for the organization's efficient, honest, and prudent management. Above all, he must satisfy the membership, and at times this is a much more difficult job than dealing with management.

For all of this, union presidents hardly grow rich on the salaries of their offices. Their average annual pay at the time of this writing was in the neighborhood of $30,000, although this amount was normally supplemented by the payment of expenses incurred while on union business. Latest figures show only one chief executive (Teamster president Frank E. Fitzsimmons, at $125,000) above $80,000, and this extreme can be more than balanced by the aggregative figure for the two top officers of the United Electrical Workers— together they received only some $32,000 in salaries, plus not particularly impressive expense allowances, the paucity of their incomes being explainable by the fact that their union limits its officers to the annual earnings of the highest-paid worker under any of the union's labor agreements.

It is certainly true that a few national leaders have taken things too far, financially speaking, while in office: Before the passage of the Landrum-Griffin Act, for example, President David Beck of the Teamsters succumbed to an urge to buy items of a personal nature in copious amounts and charge them to his union. In more recent times, the authoritarian Mine Worker president Boyle also flagrantly misused union money for his personal benefit. However, the vast number of national officers are scrupulously honest in their expenses, and some, like the late Walter Reuther, have been so almost to a fault. Reuther refused to charge his union with telephone calls that were not totally related to union business, and even absorbed such costs as the pressing of his suit and kindred personal items while he was on union business. Reuther's salary as president of the UAW (a union of 1,400,000 members, and thousands of locals) amounted in 1968 to only $30,861. Clearly, a corporation president managing a business of comparable size would be paid hundreds of thousands of dollars. Indeed, there are even a few college professors who earn $30,000!

Of course, workers pay the national officers' salaries, and the employee who earns $8,000 or less annually may perceive the salary of his national president as being exorbitant. Rather than being too high, however, the verdict of the outside observer must be that the typical national union chief executive is underpaid. When measured by the number of members, the number of locals, and his duties, even the salary of the Teamsters Union president does not seem unreasonable.

Although modestly paid, the national president wants to keep his job. He has power and prestige, and plays an important role in our society. Many presidents do indeed remain in office for considerable lengths of time, and some of them stay in the chief executive chair for so long that memory does not recall another president. William Hutcheson was president of the Carpenters for 42 years; John L. Lewis of the Mine Workers for 40 years; Daniel Tobin of the Teamsters for 37 years; and James C. Petrillo, of the Musicians, gave up his job only when he grew so old and feeble that it is doubtful that he had the strength to play his instrument. A trend, however, may be developing to change this situation. With the demands on the national officers becoming ever more formidable, particularly in the field of new organization, some unions are duplicating the practice of business and requiring compulsory retirement at a certain age. In 1964, the UAW constitution was amended to require the retirement of that union's national officers at 65. Rather than work against compulsory retirement, the national officers of the UAW—including president Reuther, who was 57 years old when this amendment was passed—vigorously upheld the measure, the first to be effected by a major international. UAW actions have frequently influenced the practices of other unions, and in this case the United Steelworkers as well as a number of other, smaller unions have already followed its compulsory-retirement implementation, but it is still too early to say whether or not this will ultimately become the dominant union policy.

There is little doubt that unions need vigorous, young, and dynamic leadership to cope with the problems of modern union affairs. Too many union leaders look with nostalgia at the past and cherish their previous contributions to the union movement, rather than being concerned with their abilities to make future contributions. The election defeats of several union presidents in the past few years—including James Carey of the International Union of Electrical Workers, and David J. McDonald of the United Steelworkers—reflect a growing restlessness among union members and a renewed emphasis on union democracy, and, thus, the possibility that the period of near-lifetime tenure for many national officers may now be ending.

Still, the problem exists, and the median age and years of service of national union officers remain considerable—about 63 years of age and 25 years of service. It is not difficult to explain why national union officers stay in office for so many years. Once in office, incumbent officials possess sufficient power to minimize centralized opposition and to make it extremely difficult for new candidates to present themselves to the membership in an effective manner. The point has been made that when conventions are not held regularly and frequently, it is difficult for a new face to get much backing. In addition, staff representatives are hired by the national union and can usually be removed at the pleasure of the national officers. It would take rare courage for a paid representative to oppose the incumbent president, and the tendency is, in fact, understandably in the other direction. In addition, most incumbent presidents get personal mileage out of their union newspapers. The editor of the national union newspaper is also a hired person, and subject to control of the national officers. Any upstart candidate could not expect much favorable publicity, if indeed he received any publicity at all, in the union press. As Wilfrid Sheed has commented, "The [president] controls the newspaper and assorted promo material, which is likely to feature pictures of himself peering knowingly into a mine face or welding machine, like a bishop at a confirmation. (In the Steelworkers, I'm told, a man could go mad staring at I. W. Abel. It's worse than *Muhammed Speaks*.)"[8]

In short, the incumbent national officers have a political machine that tends to perpetuate them in office. However, it would be incorrect to believe that this is the only reason for long tenure of office. Sophisticated union members understand that frequent changes of national union officers and open displays of factionalism weaken the position of the union against management in collective bargaining. Beyond this, a national union officer may have genuinely earned reelection to office over the years because he has

---

[8]Wilfrid Sheed, "What Has Happened to the Labor Movement?" *The Atlantic*, July 1973, p. 62.

been doing a good job for the membership. A national union president who is devoted, honest, courageous, and competent does not need a political machine to be reelected. Many national union officers fall within this category, and representatives of management should not regard national union officers as incompetent people who hold office only because of political machination.

THE LOCAL UNION

Where the People Are

Although we leave for the last an analysis of the character and functions of the local union, it does not follow that the local union is the least important of the labor bodies in the union movement. On the contrary, it could be argued successfully that, for the individual union member, the local union is the most important unit of all. In a sense, the federation, the national union and its district organizations, and the other labor bodies discussed previously are administrative and service organizations. Although they are vitally important and carry out a variety of significant activities, as we have seen, no union member really "belongs" to such larger bodies. Unionists are members of these organizations only by reason of their membership in a local union, are geographically close only to the local, and largely condition their loyalty toward an image of the total labor movement by what they perceive to transpire within the confines of the local union. Many union members do not, indeed, even know the names of their national and federation officers, but they do know their local union president, business agent, and stewards. They know them because they see them in the plant, and because these are the people who handle the union member's day-to-day problems.

Local Union Officers

Although some locals are formed before the employer is organized, a local union typically comes into existence when there is organization of an employer. After it has organized and secured bargaining rights, a local typically applies for and receives a national union charter. This document establishes the local's affiliation with the national union, entitles the local to its services, and by the same token subjects the local to the rules and discipline of the national union. Depending upon the unit of organization, a local union may be confined to a single plant or several plants of a single company, or may include workers of a single craft, such as electricians who perform their duties in a given geographic area.

Once the local is established, the members, in accordance with their bylaws (which are usually specified in the national union constitution), elect their officers—typically a president, vice-president, secretary-treasurer, and several lesser officials. Since such election procedures almost invariably allow direct participation by all union members, the local union officers are elected on a much more democratic basis than are those chosen to lead the national union. Moreover, the union member knows much more from first-hand experience about the local union candidates for office than he does about the national union officers. The vast majority of local union officers, in fact, work in the plant along with the other union members and are under constant and often highly critical observation by them. Both democracy and a far higher turnover rate for local officers than for the union's national officials also stem from the fact that the local union officer, unlike the national union president, has little if any patronage to dispense. He does not have a paid staff as does his national counterpart; nor, generally speaking, can he make use of any other powers of patronage or the purse, since neither exist in any measure.

In general, the local union officers work without pay. In only the large local unions are such officers reimbursed for their work, and, even then, their salaries tend to approximate the wages that they would have earned from their companies. And in the relatively infrequent instances when the local union president and secretary-treasurer do receive some small compensation for their duties even when they are full-time employees in the plant, the amount of money is comparatively small when measured against the duties they perform.[9] For example, in Bloomington, Indiana, one local's secretary-treasurer receives $600 per year for taking care of the books, making financial reports, answering all correspondence, and assuming a volume of other miscellaneous duties. The size of his job is measured by the fact that the local has over 3,000 members and by the union's requirement that all his duties must be conducted on his own time.

A fair question, then, is why union members desire to acquire and retain local union officer jobs. Despite their nominal or totally nonexistent financial rewards, they must perform a variety of duties and assume considerable responsibility, and they are constantly being pressured by the membership under whose direct surveillance they labor. The question is not an easy one to answer, since the motivations are obviously different with different people. A leading reason, however, is that the local union officers acquire prestige and status in the company and in the community. Virtually all people desire recognition once lower needs have been relatively well satisfied, and the attainment of a local officer's job accomplishes this objective for some workers.

Another reason may involve the local union officer's devotion and dedication to the union movement. If he really believes in unions, he has the opportunity of making the movement work by carrying out his duties in an honest and effective manner. Still other union members may genuinely court the competitive character that is associated with the office: The local union officers deal with the company on a day-to-day basis, and many of the deal-

[9] A few, considerably more notable, exceptions involve the heads of some craft unions operating in local-product markets.

ings regularly involve what some workers view as "the struggle" with management. Finally, the reason may be a political one, involving the future of the local union officer in his national union. As stated, national union officers are elected officials, and staff representatives are union members who are hired by the national union. Thus, to go up the ladder, the union member must normally start at the local union level; a local union officer's job is commonly the first step in the long and hard pull toward the top. The large majority of all current national union officers and staff representatives have held a local union officer's job at some earlier period of their careers.

Functions of the Local Union: Relations with Management

The duties of local union officers are dependent, of course, upon the functions of the particular local union, but unless contracts are negotiated on a multiemployer basis or with a very large corporation, local union officers directly negotiate the labor agreement with the employer. If the national union staff representative often aids the local in carrying out this function and usually plays a highly visible role in the process, the fact remains that the local union officers who are also involved in the negotiations are directly responsible to the members of the local union. The staff representative, a hired hand, does not face political defeat if he exercises poor judgment or fails to negotiate a contract that the membership feels is suitable. Should a contract, however, hurt the local union members, it is very likely that in the next election the local union officers will be changed. Because of its local character, factionalism in the local is, in fact, a constant problem. It is comparatively easy for a dynamic, aggressive, and ambitious newcomer to use a poor contract as a weapon to dislodge an incumbent officer.

Another important function of the local is that of negotiating grievances. Indeed, most of the union's time is devoted to this task; the labor agreement is negotiated only periodically, but, through the grievance procedure, it must be administered every day. To this end, each local union has a number of stewards—usually one steward to a department of the company, elected by the union members of that department—who serve as administrative personnel.

In most plants, the members also elect a chief steward to be chairman of the grievance committee. At the lower steps of the grievance procedure, the worker's complaint is handled by the department steward, and, normally, the local union president or chief steward does not enter the picture until the grievance has reached the higher levels. But at the last step of the grievance procedure, the local union president and the union grievance committee (composed of the chief steward and several other stewards) will negotiate the grievance, typically with the staff representative of the national union also being present. Moreover, if a grievance goes to arbitration, the local union president and the union committee will attend the hearing, and although at this forum the national staff representative usually presents the union's case, he depends heavily upon the local union officers and the committee for the data he will present to the arbitrator.

It is difficult to overestimate the vital importance of the effective use of the grievance procedure as a function of the local union. Indeed, to the union member who has a grievance, the handling of his grievance means more to him than what the union secured in the collective bargaining agreement. This is particularly true when the grievant complains against a discharge or against an alleged company violation of an important working condition.

In this capacity, however, the local union officers are also vulnerable. Take, for example, a grievance that, though important to the employee, does not have merit. If the local union president tells this to the union member, he risks offending a constituent. And if this happens frequently and with many different workers, the union members can demonstrate their resentment in the next election. This appears completely unfair and senseless, but it is what the local union officers have to contend with, and explains why local union officers frequently take up grievances that do not have merit.

At times, too, the local officers are forced to deal with "borderline" grievances—complaints that may or may not have merit but that, for a variety of reasons, the local union officers cannot persuade the company to grant. Often, the local does not want to risk losing the grievance in arbitration. It therefore refuses to handle the grievance, and the job now is to pacify the employee, who may have some justification for being resentful—not an easy mission when the grievance deals with an important issue and has some basis under the labor agreement. Consequently, the local officials may change their minds and take such grievances into arbitration, hoping for the best; if the arbitrator denies the grievance, the local union officers can always use the arbitrator as the scapegoat. However, in spite of an effective presentation at the arbitration hearing, the disgruntled union member may still blame his officers. It is said that victory has many fathers, but defeat is an orphan. Fortunately, unions win their share of grievances in the grievance procedure and in arbitration, and in his campaign before the next election, the local union officer can point with pride to his successes and minimize or explain away his defeats.

Judicial Procedures

Another function of the local union is that of disciplining union members who are alleged to have violated union rules. As does every organization, unions have standards with which members must comply. These standards are incorporated in the national union's constitution and are duplicated in the local union's bylaws. If a union member violates any of these rules, he may be disciplined by the local union membership in the form of a reprimand, a fine, suspension, or, in extreme cases, expulsion from the union.

Commonly proscribed standards of conduct that frequently merit expulsion include the promotion of dual unionism (when a union member seeks to take the local out of one national union and place it in another—true treason in unionism!); participating in an unauthorized or "wildcat" strike; misappropriating union funds; strikebreaking; refusing to picket; sending the union membership list to unauthorized persons; circulating false and malicious reports about union officers; and providing secret and confidential information to the employer. Under the official rules of some unions, a member may also be expelled because of membership in a communistic, fascistic, or other totalitarian group. We may quarrel with the justice or fairness of one or more of these rules, but the fact remains that they must be obeyed, since they have been adopted by the union at large. From the union point of view, each of them pertains to an important area of conduct.

The procedures used at the local level to enforce the rules of the union differ widely, but the following would probably reflect most local union procedures: Any union member may file charges against any other member, including the local union officers. When this occurs, the president has the authority to appoint a so-called "trial committee," composed of union members belonging to the local in question and normally including officers, stewards, and rank-and-file members who take an active role in the affairs of the union. The trial committee has the job of investigating the complaint, holding a hearing if it believes that the charge has substance, and reaching a decision that it will ultimately present to the entire local union body for final determination. To protect against a political situation within the local wherein favorites of the local union officers, or the officers themselves, may not be brought to account for a violation, the union members initiating the charge may appeal to the national union. Thus, a "not guilty" verdict, the dismissal of charges by the local union officers, or the pigeonholing of complaints does not necessarily end the disciplinary process.

After its investigation of the charges, the local union's trial committee holds a hearing at which the accused member is present. He may select another union member to act as his spokesman. As in most other private or semiprivate organizations, the union member may not hire a lawyer to defend him while the case is being processed within the union, but witnesses are called, and cross-examination is permitted. And, although no oath is administered for the same reason (since the hearing is not in a court of law), union members who deliberately lie or who grossly misrepresent the facts may themselves be charged with a violation. After the hearing, the trial committee reports its decision and the reasons for the verdict to the local union membership. At this point, the membership may adopt, reject, or modify the committee's decision. At times, the trial is in effect reheld before the local membership, since some members might desire to review the evidence that the trial committee used to arrive at its decision.

If the decision is "not guilty," the member or members who filed the charge may appeal to the executive board of the national union. By the same token, when the decision of the local goes against the charged union member, he may appeal to the national union and, under the provisions of virtually every constitution, the member can also ultimately appeal the decision of the national union officers to the national convention.

On the surface, this judicial procedure appears fair and calculated to protect the accused union member. It would seem that he receives a full and fair hearing, and gains further protection through provisions for the right of appeal. In practice, however, there have been several instances of serious abuses of the local union judicial procedure, although, with more than 77,000 locals to consider, it is absolutely impossible to make any kind of accurate judgment of the relative extent to which the abuse has existed, and any opinion is sheer speculation.

It was because of such union actions, however, that the Landrum-Griffin Act specified that no member could be disciplined, fined, or expelled without having first received a written list of charges, a reasonable time to prepare his defense, and a full and fair hearing. Today, if these legal standards are violated, a union member may bring suit in the federal courts for relief. Under the law, the union member may not go to court before he attempts to get his case settled through union procedures, although to check dilatory union tactics, the law also specifies that if the internal procedure consumes longer than four months, the union member need not exhaust the internal remedies of the union before going to court.

In 1957, the United Automobile Workers dealt with the problem of abuse in the disciplinary procedure in a different manner. It established a "Public Review Board," composed of seven citizens of respected reputation and impeccable integrity, and having no other relationship with the union. Usually, such citizens have been nationally known members of the clergy, the judiciary, or university faculties. Under the amendment to the UAW constitution that established the plan, the president of the national union selects the board members, subject to the approval of the national union's executive board and ratification by the national convention. Among other duties, this watchdog committee may reverse the decision of the executive board of the national union that has upheld the discipline of a union member, and experience has shown that the board has been quite willing to reverse the national union's executive board on the relatively few occasions when it has believed that such a reversal was justified. To date, however, only the Upholsterers International Union has followed the pattern of the UAW. If each national union were to establish such an agency, and if each agency were allowed the same freedom to act that has been granted the UAW Public Review Board, there would clearly be less need for legislation to protect the status of union members.

Political Activities

Although the AFL-CIO and national union officers and staff representatives play an effective role in lobbying and in supporting candidates in their campaigns for political office, it can be argued with much justification that the political efficiency of the union movement depends above all upon the vigor of the local. After all, the number of the federation and national officers and staff representatives is very small in comparison with the number of local union members. And much of the legwork during the national and state elections must necessarily be performed by local union members if it is to be performed at all on any large scale. Indeed, the success of the union movement in "rewarding its friends and punishing its enemies" depends in large measure on the willingness of local union officers and members to engage in politics.

Nonetheless, the degree to which local unions participate in politics is often determined by the basic philosophy of the national union. If the national union officers do not want their union to engage in politics, or if they merely go through the motions of indicating such a preference, the local unions of the nationals will reflect this kind of leadership. On the other hand, when the national union officers do take an active role in the political affairs of the nation, the local unions typically respond by placing a major emphasis on such political action of their own. However, even when the national unions do cajole their locals into taking this active role in politics, the members themselves may or may not follow the instructions of the national union officers, and the national's efforts must consequently be geared in two directions: toward the local leadership and toward the local membership.

If a constant problem of the national union that is politically inclined is thus to motivate the locals to follow its example, even within the ranks of such unions as the UAW (perhaps the most active national in the political arena), there are many dozens of local unions that either refuse to participate or participate in a lackadaisical way. Locals of less politically conscious nationals often show even greater reluctance. Moreover, just because the AFL-CIO leadership or a national union president supports a candidate for elective office, this does not mean that every union member will vote that way. Some may not vote at all, of course, and postelection analyses of union member districts show that many others vote for the opposite candidate. There is no permanent "labor vote," as is sometimes claimed by people who view the political participation of the union movement as an evil.

Indeed, as long as we maintain secret elections, even the most homogeneous groups in the nation can never rest assured that their members or followers will vote as the organization urges them to. And if members of the most closely knit of unions do not lockstep to the polls and vote in accordance with the recommendations of their leadership, members of less cohesive labor groups are often significantly divided in their election choices.

Our society is, moreover, pluralistic in character, and its countless pressure groups have their own favored candidates. Each group has the right and, indeed, the obligation to participate in the election process. These are the hallmark and the dynamics of a democratic society wherein each group seeks the votes of its members and those of the public. And, under such a system of checks and balances, any one group or organization is prevented from dominating the political life of the nation.

A union member may be a good trade unionist and support with vigor his union's collective bargaining policies and its strikes. He may enthusiastically take his place on the picket line. However, when he casts his ballot for the president of the United States, a senator, congressman, governor, and other political candidates, the vote he casts will reflect his political heritage and his interpretation of the political situation at the time. The union member shares in common with his counterparts in a myriad of other groups the fact that he is not isolated from the multitude of pleas for his vote that arise from countless organizations and sources of political information. The daily press, radio and television, the political candidate, the worker's traditional political affiliation, and many more factors will influence his vote, and his labor organization is only one of many factors that are involved in his political determination at election time.

Nonetheless, a local union that takes an active role in politics can be of great help to a favored candidate, and, in a close election, the support can tip the scales in his favor. The local union will encourage each member to register and to cast his ballot at election time. Prior to the election, it will do all in its power to "educate" the union member as to how to vote, through publications, meetings, house-to-house visits, and other forms of active political activity. In addition, the local union may legally make expenditures from union dues for such purposes as the holding of meetings of a political character and the publication and distribution of politically inspired newspapers and leaflets, although (as stated earlier) only money that is raised on a voluntary basis from the membership can be contributed directly to people running for political office.

Other Functions and Problems

Beyond the major functions discussed above, local unions at times engage in a variety of social, educational, and community activities. Of late, as in the case of higher labor bodies, the last area has become increasingly important. Union leaders realize that the welfare of their members depends in part on a progressive and well-run community. How the schools are run, for example, is of vital interest to the local unionist who must pay taxes to operate the schools and who may have children attending the schools. As in the case of city labor bodies, representation of local union officials on United Fund committees, Red Cross drives, and similar endeavors is also increasing in frequency. Moreover, unions recognize that the public image of organized labor, which has been tarnished in recent years, tends to improve to the extent that unions engage in such community services. Labor's various forms of participation in community-service programs demonstrate that union members are not only collectively a socially oriented group, but also are individually responsible and interested citizens of the community. Likewise, the integration of unions in community work tends to lessen the tensions between management and organized labor. If a union leader can work effectively with the management representatives on the school board or in the Community Chest drive, there is a better chance for harmonious labor relations in the plant.

Many local unions also conduct regularly sponsored and generally effective educational programs for the benefit of their officers and stewards. As noted previously, the need for these programs arises primarily from the complexity of the contemporary labor–management relationship, but it also stems to a great extent from the brisk turnover of the local union officers and stewards. Some of the programs are sponsored by the national unions, although in many cases the local itself arranges the educational program. Indeed, no union is considered modern today unless it has devised a well-planned educational program for its leadership. Such educational programs frequently bring to the surface workers of talent and high native intelligence. Through education, not only are they capable of doing a better job for their membership and acting more responsibly and rationally at the bargaining table, but education tends to make them more useful citizens. Of at least as much practical interest to many workers, union members who acquire such measures of education tend to rise more rapidly to important jobs at both the local and national levels.

One of the most important problems of the local is that of interesting the membership in attending regular monthly meetings of the union. Attendance at these meetings is frequently very poor, and the problem is not easy to solve. The vast majority of union leaders sincerely want their members to turn out at the meeting. They believe that the union has nothing to hide and that, by regular attendance and discussion at meetings, the members become more active, tend to be more devoted, and in general allow the local to deal with both employers and representatives of the public from a considerably stronger position than would otherwise be the case. The fact remains, however, that union members normally stay away from their meetings in droves; for the regular monthly meetings, only about 5 to 10 percent of the membership turns out (even a smaller percentage is common enough, especially in large locals); and one wonders why there has been so much said about union

democracy when the union member himself does not seem sufficiently interested to participate in the affairs of his own union. When unions are poorly
managed, when corruption exists, when leadership is second-rate, the fault
is essentially that of the union member who does not care enough to attend
the regular union meeting.

Thus, although from the days of the earliest unions labor organizations
have undertaken a variety of measures (ranging from more convenient
hours to the incorporation of social activities into the meeting schedule) to
encourage attendance, in 165 years unions have not found the solution to the
problem of worker apathy toward attendance at meetings, and there is every
likelihood that it will persist in the future. The only notable exception
involves meetings at which a strike vote is scheduled to be taken. In general,
the union members will turn out at this time because this issue of striking or
working is, of course, of crucial importance.

On the other hand, management should not interpret poor attendance at
the regular monthly meetings to mean that in crisis situations the members
will not support their union. In a showdown, the typical union member will
actively support his union; a management that makes a decision to chance a
strike solely on the grounds of poor attendance at union meetings makes a
very unwise choice. The members will invariably rally to the union's cause
when there are issues involved that vitally affect their welfare, no matter how
little interest they have demonstrated in the day-to-day operation of their
local at more peaceful times.

UNION FINANCES

As do all other organizations, the union makes many expenditures and
must meet its financial obligations. Chief expenditures of unions include the
payment of salaries for their full-time officers and staff representatives, travel
expenses, clerical help, office equipment and supplies, telephones, telegrams,
postage, arbitration fees, and rent or mortgage payments for office space and
the union hall. Beyond this, the strike fund must be built up to pay strike
benefits when needed.

At the international level, where the lion's share of the dollars is spent,
most of the money paid out goes to staff members who provide direct and
indirect services. It has been estimated that in the case of the United Automobile Workers, for example, about 85 percent of the spending is for this
purpose. The UAW's research budget is roughly $400,000 annually; the un-
ion's 16-member Washington staff also spends about $400,000 per year; its
public relations expenditures are in the vicinity of $900,000 annually; and
this second largest union in the country even finances a six-man staff of
safety experts who fly around the country upon request from local unions to
check for hazards.[10]

[10] *Wall Street Journal*, March 12, 1975, p. 22.

At times, people are impressed by the relatively large amounts that unions collect in dues and initiation fees, forgetting that the union dispenses formidable amounts of money to meet its bills. By some estimates, the annual income of American unions from all sources—special assessments and earnings from investments, as well as the regular monthly dues paid by constituents, and initiation fees—amounts to about $3 billion. And there is little question but that $3 billion looks like a lot of money, particularly when you don't have it. But when one considers the net worth of unions, a more accurate picture is gained. Such worth, for all unions in the United States, still remains under the $1 billion mark and in no way comes close to paralleling the wealth of corporations, at least a dozen of which have net assets that *individually* exceed this billion-dollar figure. Of the General Motors Corporation, it has been written, "In the 1960s, when it had some 1.6 billion dollars in cash and bonds and, embarrassingly, seemed unable to find ventures in which to invest these funds, a General Motors executive, asked by a *Wall Street Journal* correspondent what the corporation planned to do with that vast sum of money, laughed and said General Motors was 'saving up to buy the federal government.'"[11] GM, the world's largest private industrial corporation, is admittedly an extreme, but it is impossible to imagine any labor organization's being placed in the same anecdotal situation.

In general, the dues paid by union members holding semiskilled and unskilled jobs in manufacturing are less than those paid by members who work in the skilled trades. The obvious reason for this is that electricians, plumbers, carpenters, and kindred skilled employees earn higher wages than do employees whose jobs require lesser skill levels. A substantial majority of union members now pay dues that come out to roughly two hours' wages per month, and two major unions—the Steelworkers and Automobile Workers— have in fact officially set their monthly dues figures at exactly this two-hour level, thereby building automatic increases into the dues structure. Initiation fees—by definition, a one-shot affair—tend to be in the $25–$50 range, with only a small handful of unionists (primarily in the building trades, airline pilot profession, and similarly highly remunerated groupings) being charged more than $100 in such fees by their labor organizations.

In the light of all that has been said about the functions of unions, the amount of money the typical member pays is thus comparatively small. Nonetheless, like everyone else, the union member desires maximum and ever-improving services for the least cost possible. Indeed, union leadership must be very careful when it seeks to raise the monthly dues. Even a modest increase of 50 cents per month could cause an upheaval among the membership. With increasing expenses and sometimes declining memberships, unions *must* at times raise dues if they desire to maintain the same level of services to their membership, but this is a step normally taken only as an extreme last resort. Illustratively, during one recent period of declining union member-

[11]William Serrin, *The Company and the Union* (New York: Vintage, 1974), p. 72.

ship, the UAW laid off many staff representatives and otherwise tried to curb expenses drastically before requesting a modest dues increase.

A CONCLUDING WORD

The American labor movement is vast and complicated, but by this time the student should have a firm understanding of the logic of its behavior, structure, and government. Labor's elements fit together in a systematic fashion and provide the framework for the carrying out of the basic functions and objectives of the union movement.

In a day of increasing union dependence upon the sentiments of the general public, particularly as these sentiments are translated into legislative actions, these objectives have increasingly encompassed social and community activities that clearly extend well beyond labor's traditional campaigns for improved "property rights" on the job itself. These more broadly based endeavors can in no way be expected to diminish in the years ahead, for the advantages for the labor movement that can potentially be derived from them are certain to continue.

Yet this newer emphasis should not obscure either the pronounced strain of "bread-and-butter" unionism that has marked organized labor throughout its history or the internal union political considerations that continue to generate this more basic behavior. If unions are, by and large, not democratic, they are nonetheless highly political in nature. The union leader must above all be conscious of the general wishes of his constituents. And these wishes, particularly at the lower levels of the union structure where the collective bargaining process itself takes place, continue to be closely related to wages, hours, and conditions.

Just as internal political considerations have dictated national union autonomy within the AFL-CIO, so too have such considerations led to the complete responsibility of virtually all national union executives to at least the most pressing desires of local unionists, and to such commonly observed phenomena as the high turnover rates of local officers themselves.

It has often been said that a union "is a political animal operating in an economic framework." No one who loses sight of this most fundamental labor relations factor can truly appreciate union behavior, for union members do have the ultimate control of their labor organizations—however much in-practice union *leadership* has been the catalyst of the policies, programs, and operation of the union—and the leadership can never ignore this fact of life.

DISCUSSION QUESTIONS

1. J.B.S. Hardman has described labor organizations as being "part army and part debating society." What considerations on his part might have led to this description?
2. It has been argued in many nonlabor quarters that it is socially undesirable for unions to take the initiative in organizational campaigns and that the public interest

is served only when unorganized workers initially seek out the union. Is there anything to be said for this point of view? Against it?

3. "There are both advantages and disadvantages to AFL-CIO affiliation for national unions." Comment.

4. "The increasing sophistication and enlightenment of modern top business executives in dealing with their subordinates has led to a state of affairs wherein managements today are more democratic than unions." Do you agree? Why, or not not?

5. "Unions are no less private institutions than country clubs or Masonic lodges, and as such, should be no more subject to government regulation of their internal affairs than these other organizations." The present thrust of the laws notwithstanding, is there any validity to this argument?

6. Albert Rees has pointed out that it is "paradoxically true that the presence of strong unions may improve the operation of democratic processes in the general national or state government even if the internal political processes of the union are undemocratic." Explain this paradox.

7. Daniel Bell, the former labor editor of *Fortune* magazine, once commented that in taking over certain power from management, "the union also takes over the difficult function of specifying the priorities of demands—and in so doing, it not only relieves management of many political headaches but becomes a buffer between management and rank-and-file resentments." Is there any justification for such a comment?

SELECTED REFERENCES

BARBASH, JACK, *Labor's Grass Roots*. New York: Harper & Row, 1961.

ESTEY, MARTEN, *The Unions: Structure, Development, and Management*. New York: Harcourt Brace Jovanovich, 1967.

GOULDEN, JOSEPH E., *Meany: The Unchallenged Strong Man of American Labor*. New York: Atheneum, 1972.

HALL, BURTON H., ed., *Autocracy and Insurgency in Organized Labor*. New Brunswick, N.J.: Transaction Books, 1972.

PERLMAN, MARK, *Labor Union Theories in America*. Evanston, Ill.: Row, Peterson, 1958.

ROSEN, HJALMAR, and RUTH A.H. ROSEN, *The Union Member Speaks*. Englewood Cliffs, N.J.: Prentice-Hall, 1955.

SAYLES, LEONARD R., and GEORGE STRAUSS, *The Local Union*, rev. ed. New York: Harcourt Brace Jovanovich, 1967.

SULTAN, PAUL E., *The Disenchanted Unionist*. New York: Harper & Row, 1963.

TAFT, PHILIP, *The Structure and Government of Labor Unions*. Cambridge, Mass.: Harvard University Press, 1954.

PART III
COLLECTIVE
BARGAINING

Chapter 5
At the
Bargaining Table

However much specific unions may differ in their exact structures, governments, and general operations, virtually all labor organizations share at least the same primary objective. Whatever in the way of concrete demands may be sought from the employer, the union's major goal is to negotiate with him a written agreement covering both employment conditions and the union–management relationship itself on terms that are acceptable to the union. But the employer, too, must be able to live with these terms, and it is because of this second requirement that bargaining sessions almost unavoidably contain stresses and strains; more for one party—not only in the economic areas of the contract but, as will be seen, in many of the so-called "institutional" and "administrative" areas—all but invariably means less for the other. Moreover, the labor–management tensions are *recurrent* in their nature, since contracts are regularly renegotiated—most commonly, today, every two or three years. No contractual issue can thus ever be said to have been permanently resolved.

There is always a certain glamor to any interorganizational bargaining situation, particularly when such conflicts as those above can be anticipated. Labor–management negotiations constitute no exception to this rule, and, indeed, the process of arriving at a labor relations agreement has been viewed in a number of rather colorful ways.

Dunlop and Healy, for example, have pointed out that the labor contract negotiation process has been depicted as (1) a poker game, with the largest pots going to those who combine deception, bluff, and luck, or the ability to come up with a strong hand on the occasions on which they are challenged or "seen" by the other side; (2) an exercise in power politics, with the relative strengths of the parties being decisive; and (3) a debating society, marked by both rhetoric and name calling. They have also noted that what men do at the union–management bargaining table has, at other times, been caricatured in a somewhat less dramatic way—as (4) a "rational process," with both sides remaining completely flexible and willing to be persuaded only when all the facts have been dispassionately presented.[1]

In practice, it is likely that *all* these characteristics have marked most negotiations over a period of time. Occasionally, indeed, one such description seems to be extremely apt. Some bargaining sessions within the automobile industry have had all the attributes of the poker game, except that the "losers" and "winners" have not been quite as easily identifiable. No one present at negotiations between the Teamsters and representatives of the over-the-road trucking companies can fail to be impressed by the influence of the relatively far greater economic strength of the union. There are those who see a parallel between bargaining in the men's clothing industry and debating society activities. And the General Electric Company has for years prided itself on its firm resolution to "let the facts govern," although its unions have strongly disagreed that GE has in fact adhered to this policy.[2]

Nor, since bargaining will always by its very nature pit the conflicting interests of the two parties against each other, is there any reason to expect any of these factors to die out. The increasing "maturity" of collective bargaining implies enlargement of the rational process, but it is doubtful that there can ever be such a thing as complete escape from the other elements.

Moreover, a number of additional factors will also, almost inevitably, have a bearing upon the conduct of the negotiations. Items such as the objectives of the parties, the personalities and training of the negotiators, the history of labor relations between the union and management, the size of the bargaining unit, and the economic environment operate to influence the character of collective bargaining negotiations.

Some negotiators try to bluff or outsmart the other side; others would never even think of employing such tactics. Some company or union representatives try to dictate a labor contract on a unilateral basis—"take it or else"— but most bargainers recognize that such an approach is ultimately self-defeating. In most instances, unions presenting their original proposals will demand much more than they actually intend to get, and companies' first counterproposals are usually much lower than the managements are actually prepared to offer. In other situations, however, companies and unions do not engage in these practices to any appreciable extent, and original proposals and counterproposals are relatively realistic. Representatives of companies and labor organizations differ in training, preparation, education, experience, personality, concept and standard of equity, and labor relations philosophy.

There are still other sources of variation. In some negotiations, the predominant feature might be union factionalism; in others, disagreement

[1]John T. Dunlop and James J. Healy, *Collective Bargaining*, rev. ed. (Homewood, Ill.: Richard D. Irwin, 1955), p. 53.

[2]General Electric's unique and controversial bargaining approach, known as "Boulwarism," will be discussed later in this chapter.

between management officials concerning objectives and policies. The history of labor relations in one situation might reveal that each side has had implicit faith in the other. In other negotiations, because of past experience, the bargaining might be conducted in a climate of mutual distrust, suspicion, and even hatred. Certainly, if the objective of the parties is to find a solution to their mutual problems on the basis of rationality and fairness, the negotiations will be conducted in an atmosphere quite different from one in which the fundamental objective of the union is to "put management in its place," or where the chief objective of the company is to weaken or even destroy the union. All these factors, as well as others, will have a profound influence upon the conduct of collective bargaining negotiations.

Two other preliminary remarks are in order. First, because so many variables do have a bearing upon the negotiations, a portion of the following discussion highlights some procedural practices that might help to reduce friction between companies and unions, to minimize the possibility of strikes, and to promote better labor relations. Nonetheless, if labor relations in a company have been harmonious in the past, and if collective bargaining negotiations have been conducted with a minimum of discord, there is little reason to change procedures. "Let sleeping dogs lie" is a sound principle of collective bargaining negotiations. These observations should be kept in mind throughout the following discussion.

Second, there has been a marked change in the general atmosphere of negotiations in relatively recent years. Perhaps 25 years ago, the typical collective bargaining session involved a tussle between tablepounding, uninformed, and generally ill-equipped people. Possibly the side that came out better was the one whose representatives shouted louder or could use overt power threats more effectively. And conceivably the typical negotiation was a matter of each side's taking the adamant position of "take it or else."

At present, however, collective bargaining is most commonly an orderly process in which employee, employer, and union problems are discussed relatively rationally and settled more or less on the basis of facts. There is less and less place in modern collective bargaining sessions for emotionalism, name calling, table pounding, and the like. Not many negotiators use trickery; distortion, misrepresentation, and deceit are not dominant characteristics of the modern bargaining session. Advantages gained through such devices are temporary, and the side that sinks to such low levels of behavior can expect the same from the other party. Such tactics will merely serve to produce bad labor relations and to encourage the possibility of industrial strife. Certainly, one objective of collective bargaining sessions should be the promotion of rational and harmonious relations between employers and unions. To achieve this state of affairs, those to whom negotiations are entrusted should have the traits of patience, trustworthiness, friendliness, integrity, and fairness. If each party recognizes the possiblity that it may be mistaken and the other side right, a long stride will be taken in the achievement of successful collective bargaining relations.

PREPARATION FOR NEGOTIATIONS

By far the major prerequisite for modern collective bargaining sessions is preparation for the negotiations. Both sides normally start to prepare for the bargaining table long before the current contract is scheduled to expire, and in recent years the time allotted for such planning has steadily lengthened. Six months or even a year for this purpose has become increasingly observable in both union and management quarters.

The now-general recognition of the need for greater preparation time rests on the previously cited fact that the contents of the "typical" labor agreement have undergone a major transformation in the comparatively recent past. In recognizing and attempting to accommodate new goals of the parties, contracts have become steadily more complex in the issues they treat.

Take, for example, wage clauses—which have appeared in almost all contracts since the days of the earliest unions. Today, they make anything but easy reading. Where once such clauses noted the schedule of wages (generally the same for all workers within extremely broad occupational categories) and the hours to be worked for these wages, and usually little more than this, over the past few years they have become both far lengthier and considerably more complicated. Today, subsections relating to labor-grade job classifications, rate ranges, pay steps within labor grades, differentials for undesirable types of work, pay guarantees for employees who are asked to report to work when no work is available for them, and a host of other subjects are commonplace in contracts. Moreover, most of these subsections spell out their methods of operation in detail.

Nor can the question of hours any longer be cavalierly disposed of. The extension of premium pay for work on undesirable shifts, holidays, Saturdays, and Sundays has increased the room for further bargaining. In addition, the contract must resolve the question of remuneration for hours worked in excess of a "standard" day or week: All nonexempted workers in interstate commerce today receive, by law, time-and-one-half pay after forty hours in a single week, but an increasing number of contracts have more liberal arrangements from the worker's viewpoint. And having opened these issues to the bargaining process, the parties must now anticipate a whole Pandora's box of further but related issues. Do workers qualify for the Sunday premium when they have not previously worked the full weekly schedule? Where employees are normally required for continuous operations or are otherwise regularly needed for weekend work (firemen, maintenance men, and watchmen in certain operations, for example) can they collect overtime for work beyond the standard week? The bargainers on both the labor and the management side must prepare their answers, and their defenses of these answers, to such questions and many similar ones; all may reasonably be expected to arise during the actual bargaining. And this necessity for anticipation is no less true merely because a previous contract has dealt with these matters, for each party can count on the other's lodging requests for modifications of the old terms in the negotiations.

The same can be said concerning the wide range of employee benefits, from paid vacations to pension plans, which have increased dramatically over the past two decades. This benefit list promises to become even lengthier. Job insecurity in an age of automation should lead to increased income-security devices. Collectively bargained profit-sharing and allied gain-sharing plans have received some impetus from relatively recent single-company developments at American Motors and Kaiser Steel, respectively—and may now, after years of achieving only a foothold in industry, realistically be expected to spread. But it is even more likely that the continuous liberalization in the existing benefits, and the attendant costs and administrative complexities involved in all of them that have marked the histories of each since its original negotiation, will continue. No one is better aware of this fact than the experienced labor relations negotiator.

Finally, increasingly thorny problems have arisen at the bargaining table regarding the so-called "administrative clauses" of the contract. These provisions deal with such issues as seniority rights, discipline, rest periods, work-crew and work-load sizes, and a host of similar subjects that vary in importance with the specific industry. All these topics involve, directly or indirectly, employment opportunities; and, therefore, treatment of them has become ever more complicated in a competitive industrial world that pits a management drive for greater efficiency and flexibility against a commensurately accelerated union search for increased job security.

Fuller discussion of all these areas is reserved for Chapters 7 through 10. Even the cursory treatment offered here, however, offers ample evidence that bargaining the "typical" contract necessitates far more sophistication than in an earlier, less technical age. Labor agreements can no longer be reduced to the backs of envelopes, and ever more specialized subjects confront labor negotiators. Accordingly, the need for thorough and professional preparation well in advance of the bargaining is no longer seriously questioned by any alert union or management.

In today's increasingly data-conscious society, much general information can aid the parties in their advance planning. The U.S. Bureau of Labor Statistics is a prolific issuer of information relating to wage, employee benefit, and administrative clause practices—and not only on a national basis, but for many specific regions, industries, and cities. Many employer groups stand ready to furnish managers with current and past labor contracts involving the same union with which they will be bargaining, as well as other relevant knowledge. International unions perform the same kind of function for their local unions and other subsidiary units, where the bargaining will be on a subinternational basis. And for both parties, there is also no shortage of facts emanating from such other sources as the Federal Reserve Board, the U.S. Department of Labor, private research groups, and various state and local public agencies.

Each bargaining party may also find it advisable to procure and analyze information that is more specifically tailored to its needs in the forthcoming negotiations. Most larger unions and almost all major corporations today enlist their own research departments in the cause of such special data gathering as the making of community wage surveys. On occasion, outside experts may also be recruited to make special studies for one of the parties; much of the bargaining stance taken by the Maintenance of Way Employees a few years ago, for example, rested on a painstaking analysis of employment trends in that sector of railroading, conducted at union expense by a highly respected University of Michigan professor. Many managements have also made major use of the research services of academicians and other outsiders on an ad hoc basis. In multiemployer bargaining situations, whether or not an official employers' association actually handles the negotiations, the same premium on authoritative investigation has become increasingly visible.

The list of uses to which such research can be put is literally endless. Depending upon its accuracy and stamp of authority, it can be used to support any stand, from a company's avowal that certain pension concessions would make it "noncompetitive," to a union's demand for increased cost-of-living adjustments. The management may find support for a desired subcontracting clause in the revelation that the union has been willing to grant the same clause to other employers. The union may gain points in its argument for a larger wage increase by mustering the bright outlook for the industry that has been forecast by the Commerce Department. On the other hand, where poker, power, or debating traits mark the bargaining, and the "rational process" of appeal to facts counts for little, the whole effort may seem a fruitless one. Most frequently, however, negotiators who approach the bargaining table without sufficient factual ammunition to handle the growing complexities of labor relations operate at a distinct disadvantage: The burden of proof invariably lies with the party seeking contractual changes, and in the absence of facts, "proof" is hard to come by.

As painstaking a task as the fact-accumulation process may seem to be, farsighted managements and labor leaders recognize that considerably more must be done to adequately prepare for bargaining.

Increasingly, the top echelons within both union and company circles have come to appreciate the necessity of carefully consulting with lower-level members of their respective operating organizations before framing specific bargaining table approaches. Superintendents, foremen, industrial engineers, union business agents, union stewards, and various other people may never become directly involved in the official negotiation sessions;[3] and the distance separating them from the top of the management or union hierarchy is usually a great one. But the growing maturity of labor relations has brought with it a stronger recognition by the higher levels of both organizations that the success or failure of whatever agreement is finally bargained will always rest considerably upon the acceptance of the contract by such people. In addition, unless the official negotiators are well informed on actual operating conditions in advance of the bargaining, there is every chance that highly desirable modifications in the expiring agreement will be completely overlooked.

On the management side, since the daily routines of the operating subordinates require their close contact with the union, such people are in a position to provide the bargainers with several kinds of valuable information. They can be expected to have knowledgeable opinions as to what areas of the expiring contract have been most troublesome; they can, for example, provide an analysis not only of grievance statistics within their departments but of employee morale problems that may lie behind the official grievances that have been lodged. They presumably have some awareness as to existing pressures on the union leadership, and their knowledge of these political problems can help management to anticipate some of the forthcoming union demands. They may be able to assess how the union membership would react to various portions of the contemplated management demands.

Not to be dismissed lightly, either, is the fact that this process of consultation allows lower managers genuine grounds for feeling some sense of participation in at least establishing the framework for bargaining. The company thus stands to gain in terms of morale, as well as in information.

For the union, the need for thorough internal communication may be even more vital. The trend to centralization of bargaining in the hands of international unions has in no way lessened the need of the union officialdom to be responsive to rank-and-file sentiments. It has, however, made the job of *discovering* these sentiments, and incorporating them into a cohesive bargaining strategy, considerably harder; and "middlemen" within the union hierarchy must be relied upon to perform this assignment. Thus, business agents, grievance committeemen, and other lower union officials can play a key role even where the negotiations themselves have passed upward to a higher union body, for only they are in a position to take the pulse of the rank and file.

The long list of widely varying and frequently inconsistent rank-and-file demands cannot, however, be passed upward to the international level with-

[3]This depends upon the scope of the negotiations, however. Where the bargaining is on the local level (as opposed to areawide, industrywide, or nationwide bargaining), the business agent (for example) will very likely be an active union participant in the formal sessions. The same can be said for many management superintendents.

out some adjustment. Most internationals screen these workers' proposals—inevitably giving more weight to those of important political leaders at the lower levels than to those stemming from totally uninfluential constituents—through committees composed of the subordinate officials at successively higher levels within the union hierarchy. Ultimately, a "final" union contract proposal may be placed before the membership of each local, or at least before representatives of these locals, for their official stamps of approval. And here again, the support of lower union officialdom is vitally needed by the union negotiators—to rally rank-and-file support behind the finalized union demands, and to gain membership willingness to strike, if need be, in support of these demands. Aside from the fact that the local unionists may be as well equipped to help the negotiators plan their strategy as are their management counterparts, local leaders who have been bypassed in the consultation process do not typically make loyal supporters of the union's membership-rallying effort.

Finally, both legal and (on many occasions) public relations considerations now clearly demand a major place in preparation for bargaining. Specialists in both these areas must be engaged and utilized by both sides to ensure that bargaining demands will be compatible with the labor statutes, and that public support (or, at the very least, public neutrality) will be forthcoming, if this is needed. The legal ramifications of present-day trucking contract negotiations, for example, have necessitated for the union the employment of a 400-man corps of lawyers, who have become collectively known as the "Teamsters' Bar Association," and through whose high levels of remuneration former Teamster president Hoffa could claim to have "doubled the average standard of living for all lawyers in the past few years," although the personal legal problems of Hoffa (who mysteriously disappeared in mid-1975, presumably a victim of gangland action) himself undoubtedly accounted for some of the high statistics. And for the importance of public relations to both parties in the railroad industry, one need look no farther than to the myriad of full-page newspaper advertisements placed separately throughout the 1960s and early 1970s by the railroad unions and managements to state their respective labor relations cases to the general citizenry in advance of the bargaining.

For both management and union, bargaining preparation also involves more mundane matters. Meeting places must be agreed upon and the times and lengths of the meetings must be decided. Ground rules regarding transcripts of the sessions, publicity releases, and even "personal demeanor" (a designation that in labor relations can deal with a spectrum extending from the use of profanity to appropriate attire for the negotiators) are sometimes drawn up. Payment of union representatives at the bargaining table who must take time off from work as paid employees of the company must also be resolved. Only on rare occasions have the parties reached a major pre-bargaining impasse on such issues as these, but where relations are already strained between union and management such joint decision-making can be a time-consuming and even an emotion-packed process.

THE BARGAINING PROCESS: EARLY STAGES

No manager who is prone to both ulcers and accepting verbal statements at face value belongs at the labor relations bargaining table. Negotiations often begin with the union representatives presenting a long list of demands in both the economic and noneconomic (for example, administrative clause) areas. To naïve managements, many of these avowed labor goals seem at best unjustified, and, at worst, to show a complete union disregard for the continued solvency of the employer. Although extreme demands, such as the appointment of union officers to the company's board of directors and free transportation in company cars to and from work for all employees, are rarely taken seriously, the company negotiators may be asked for economic concessions that are well beyond those granted by competitors, and noneconomic ones that exhibit a greater use of vivid imagination than that shown by Fellini or Hitchcock.

In the spring of 1974, for example, the local police association in Rockville Centre, Long Island, demanded from its employer municipality 85 concessions, including a gymnasium and swimming pool; 17 paid holidays, including Valentine's Day and Halloween; and free abortions. And these men in blue hold no record for ambitiousness: Walter Reuther used to open automobile bargaining with so many holiday demands that on one occasion his management counterpart at General Motors is alleged to have asked, "Walter, wouldn't it be faster if you merely listed the days on which you would like to work?"

The experienced management bargainer, however, takes considerable comfort in the fact that the union is, above all, the *political* animal that the preceding chapter has depicted: There is no sense in the union leaders alienating constituents by throwing out untenable but "pet" demands of the rank and file (beyond what the various screening committees have been able to dislodge) when the company representatives stand fully ready to do this themselves and thus to accept the blame. This is particularly true when the pet union demands originate from influential constituents or key locals within the international; alienation of such sources is a job for which the company representatives, not being subject to the election procedure, are better suited.

There are other logical explanations for the union's apparent unreasonableness. Excessive demands allow leverage for trading some of them off in return for management concessions. In addition, the union can camouflage its true objectives in the maze of requests and thereby conceal its real position until the proper time—a vital ploy for any successful bargaining.

Beyond this, labor leaders have frequently sought novel demands with the knowledge that these will be totally unacceptable to managements in a given bargaining year, but with the goal of providing an opening wedge in a long-range campaign to win management over to the union's point of view. Only in this light can, for example, Reuther's demand for supplementary unemployment benefits in the early 1950s be understood. Much more recently, "30 and out," or retirement after thirty years of service in the automotive industry regardless of age, had a similar genesis.

Dunlop and Healy furnish further insight on the psychological ramifications involved, and also emphasize the increasing importance of the pre-bargaining research commented upon earlier in this chapter:

> Neither side can ordinarily be expected to concede a new demand the first time it is presented. A new idea may initially produce only opposition from the other party. The demand will be less novel and appear less outrageous a year later. The other side may have had occasion to think it through and to consider administrative problems which need mutual exploration. Thus, a pension or a health and welfare proposal introduced by the union for the first time will ordinarily receive a cool reception. Management may need several years to consider types of plans, to gather data on the age distribution and health distribution of its work force, and to get used to considering this range of issues. New contract demands ordinarily require a period of gestation, and some demands are on the list to be seasoned.[4]

Finally, since contract negotiations frequently extend over a period of weeks (on occasion, months), the union can gain a buffer against economic and other environmental changes that may occur in the interval. Technically, either party can introduce new demands at any time prior to total agreement on a contract, but the large initial demand obviates this necessity.

There is thus a method in the union's apparent madness. Demands that seem to managements to be totally unjustified and even disdainful of the company's continued existence may, on occasion, be genuinely intended as union demands; far more often, however, they are meant only as ploys in a logical bargaining strategy. They are to be listened to carefully, but not taken literally.

In fact, if imitation is the sincerest form of flattery, there is ample evidence that some managements have increasingly come to appreciate the strategic value of the large demand. Many company bargainers have, in recent years, engaged in such "blue-skying" in their counterproposals, and for many of the same reasons as unions have (although other companies have adamantly refused to engage in this process and have even, at least partially, accepted a GE-type approach).

As a result of the premium placed on exaggerated demands and equally unrealistic conterproposals, however, the positions of the parties throughout the early negotiation sessions are likely to remain far apart.

[4]Dunlop and Healy, *Collective Bargaining*, p. 56.

Standing in the way of early agreement, too, is the fact that these initial meetings are often attended by a wide variety of "invited guests," from the ranks of each organization. Given a large and interested audience of rank-and-file unionists, or a union negotiating committee that is so large as to be totally unable (and unexpected) to perform the bargaining function but is nonetheless highly advisable from a political point of view, the actual union bargainers sometimes find it hard to refrain from using creative but wholly extraneous showmanship. Management representatives, too, frequently succumb to a temptation to impress their visiting colleagues as to their negotiating "toughness." And when lawyers or other consultants are engaged by either party to participate in the bargaining sessions, the amount of acting is often significantly expanded.

Even amid the theatrics and exaggerated stances of these early meetings, however, there is often a considerable amount of educational value for the bargainers. The excessive factors still do not preclude each party from evaluating at least the general position of the other side and from establishing weaknesses in the opposing position or arguments. Frequently, indeed, if negotiators are patient and observing at this point, they will be able to evaluate the other side's proposals along fairly precise qualitative lines. Thus, during the first few sessions when each side should be expected to state its position, it can often be discerned which demands or proposals are being made seriously and which, if any, are merely injected for bargaining position. Such information will be of great help later on in the negotiations.

Actually, the principle of timing in negotiations is very important. There are times for listening, speaking, standing firm, and conceding; there are times for making counterproposals, compromising, suggesting. At some points, "horse-trading" is possible; at others, taking a final position is called for. There is a time for an illustration, a point, or a funny story to break ominous tension, and there is likewise a time for being deadly serious. Through experience and through awareness of the tactics of the other side, negotiators can make use of the time principle most effectively.

THE BARGAINING PROCESS: LATER STAGES

After the initial sessions are terminated, each side should have a fairly good idea of the overall climate of the negotiations. The company should now be in a position to determine what the union is fundamentally seeking, and the union should be able to recognize some basic objectives of management. In addition, by this time, each side should have fairly well in mind how far it is prepared to go in the negotiations. Each party to the negotiations in secret internal sessions should establish with some degree of certainty the maximum concessions it will be prepared to make, and the minimum levels it will be willing to accept. Negotiators will be in a better position to bargain intelligently if certain objectives are formulated before the negotiations enter into the "give-and-take" stage. However, even at this stage in the negotiations, it is not wise to take extreme positions and to appear inflexible in the approach to the problems under discussion. Skilled negotiators who are striving to avoid a strike—and this is the attitude of the typical company and union—will remain flexible right down to the wire. It is not a good idea to climb too far out on a limb, since at times it may be difficult, or at least embarrassing, to crawl back to avoid a work stoppage.

Indeed, after the original positions of the parties are stated and explained, skilled negotiators seldom take a rigid position. Rather than take a definite stand on a particular issue, experienced negotiators (often, where negotiation units are large, through the use of subcommittees to focus upon the major bargaining issues individually before these are dealt with at the main bargaining table) "throw something on the table for discussion and consideration." The process of attempting to create a pattern of agreement is then begun. In this process, areas of clear disagreement are narrowed whenever they can be, mutual concessions are offered, and tentative agreements are effected. Counterproposals of companies and unions are frequently offered as "something to think about" rather than as the final words of the negotiators. In this manner, the parties are in a better position to feel one another out as to ultimate goals. By noting the reaction to a proposal thrown on the table for discussion, by evaluating the arguments and the attitudes in connection with it, a fairly accurate assessment can be made of the maximum and minimum levels of both sides.

Actually, flexibility is a sound principle to follow in negotiations, because the ultimate settlement between companies and unions is frequently in the terms of "packages." Thus, through the process of counterproposals, compromise, and the like, the parties usually terminate the negotiations by agreeing to one package selected from a series of alternative possibilities of settlement. The package selected will represent most closely the maximum and minimum levels acceptable to each of the parties. The content of the various packages will be somewhat different, because neither side in collective bargaining gets everything it wants out of a particular negotiation. By the maintenance of flexibility throughout the negotiation, certain patterns of settlement tend to be established over which the parties can deliberate.

The package approach to bargaining is particularly important in reference to economic issues. Once the parties obtain an agreement on a total cost-per-hour figure, it becomes a relatively uncomplicated task to allocate that figure in terms of basic wage rates, supplements to wages, wage inequities, and the like. The more difficult problem, of course, is to arrive at a total cost-per-hour figure. If, for example, through the process of bargaining, the parties established $.50 per hour as the level of agreement, they might finalize the money agreement in terms of a $.38-per-hour basic wage increase, $.06 per hour to correct any wage inequities, $.03 per hour to improve the insurance program, and $.03 per hour to increase pensions. Other subdivisions of the $.50 would be possible depending upon the attitudes of the parties and their objectives in the negotiations.

Trading Points and Counterproposals

In establishing the content of the alternative packages, experienced negotiators employ a variety of bargaining techniques. Two of the most important are trading points and counterproposals. These procedures are best explained by illustrations.

Let us assume that management employs the *trading point* procedure. The first prerequisite in the use of this technique is to evaluate the demands of the union. Evaluation is necessary not only along quantitative lines, but also along the line of the "intensity factor," which requires an assessment of the union demands to determine which of them the union is most anxious to secure. Management representatives should make mental notes of these strongly demanded issues as the negotiations proceed. For example, after a few sessions it may become apparent that the union feels very strongly about securing the union shop. At the same time, the labor organization also demands a $.50-per-hour wage increase and nine paid holidays. The use of the trading point technique in this situation may be as follows: Management agrees to the union shop but insists that, in return for this concession, the union accept a $.23-per-hour increase and seven paid holidays.

Labor organizations also employ the trading point technique, as illustrated by the following example. Assume that, during the course of the negotiations, the union representatives sense that management will not concede to the union demand for a reduction of the basic workweek from 40 hours to 36. Assume further that the union feels that the issue is not worth a strike. Under these circumstances, the union may be able to employ the hours issue as a trading point. Let us say that, along with the hours demand, the union has insisted upon also securing a union shop and a $.40-per-hour increase in pay. After the union presses the hours issue vigorously for some time (as part of the strategy, it may, of course, threaten a strike over the issue), the union negotiators agree to withdraw the hours demand in return for obtaining the union shop and the wage increase.

Counterproposals are somewhat different from trading points. Counterproposals involve the compromise that takes place during the bargaining sessions. As a matter of fact, the use of counterproposals is one element the National Labor Relations Board will consider to determine whether management and labor unions bargain in good faith. However, under the established rules of the board, employers and unions do not have to make *concessions* to satisfy the legal requirement of bargaining in good faith: the implementers of public policy are more interested in whether or not there have been *compromises*. The union may request four weeks' vacation with pay for all employees. Management might counter by agreeing to two weeks' vacation with pay for employees with five years of service and one week for the remainder. A union may demand a $.44-per-hour increase, and management may agree to a $.22-per-hour increase. At times three or four counterproposals may be made before a final agreement is reached on an issue of collective bargaining.

THE BARGAINING PROCESS: FINAL STAGES

There is almost no limit to the ingenuity which skilled negotiators use in attempting to create an agreement pattern. At more sophisticated bargaining tables, even highly subtle modes of communication may do the trick, while at the same time allowing the party making a concession to suffer no prejudice for having "given in." Stevens, for example, points out that

> ... in some situations, silence may convey a concession. This may be the case, for example, if a negotiator who has frequently and firmly rejected a proposal simply maintains silence the next time the proposal is made. The degree of emphasis with which the negotiator expresses himself on various issues may be an important indication. The suggestion that the parties pass over a given item for the present, on the grounds that it probably will not be an important obstacle to eventual settlement, may be a covert way of setting up a trade on this item for some other.... The parties may quote statistics (fictitious if need be) as a ... way of suggesting a position, or they may convey a position by discussing a settlement in an unrelated industry.[5]

Yet, however much the gap between the parties may be narrowed by such methods, even the most adroit bargainers frequently reach the late stages of negotiations with the complete contract far from being resolved. Given the potential thorniness of many of the individual issues involved, this should not be surprising; more than both bargaining sophistication and flexibility is still generally required to bring about agreement on such delicate substantive topics as management rights, union security, the role of seniority, and economic benefits. And the fact that the bargainers seek an acceptable package that in some way deals with *all* these issues clearly makes the assignment a much more complicated one than it would otherwise be.

It is the *strike deadline* that is the great motivator of labor relations agreement. As the hands of the clock roll around, signalling the imminent termination of the old contract, each side is now forced to reexamine its "final" position and to balance its "rock-bottom" demands against the consequences of a cessation of work. And, with the time element now so important, each party can be counted upon to view its previous bargaining position in a somewhat different light.

[5]Carl M. Stevens, *Strategy and Collective Bargaining Negotiation* (New York: McGraw-Hill, 1963), pp. 105–6.

For example, paid holiday demands, which once seemed of paramount importance to the union, may now appear less vital when pursuing them is likely to lead to the complete *loss* of paid holidays through a strike. The labor leaders may also conclude now that, although the union membership has authorized the strike should this prove necessary, a stoppage of any duration would be difficult to sustain—through either lack of membership *esprit de corps* or union resources that are insufficient to match those of management.

On its part, the company may also prove more willing to compromise as the strike deadline approaches. Up until now, it has sought to increase its net income by improving its labor cost position. Now the outlook is for a *cessation* of income if operations stop.

These threats, in short, bring each party face to face with reality and can normally be expected to cause a marked reassessment of positions. The immediacy of such uncertainty generates a willingness to bridge differences that has not been in evidence at the bargaining table before.

The final hours before time runs out are, therefore, commonly marked by new developments. Frequent caucuses are held by each party, followed by the announcement from a caucus representative that his side is willing to offer a new and more generous "final" proposal. Leaders from each side frequently meet with their counterparts from the other side in informal sessions that are more private and have fewer participants than the official sessions themselves. These are also likely to result in new agreements. And issues that are still totally insoluble may be passed on to a newly established long-range joint study committee, with the hope that their resolution can be achieved at some later and less pressure-laden date.

Thus Stevens, in attempting to develop a systematic conceptual apparatus for the analysis of collective bargaining negotiation, examines the implications of the deadline in the following terms:

> The approach of the deadline revises upward each party's estimate of the probability that a strike or lockout will be consequent upon adherence to his own position.... An approaching deadline does much more than simply squeeze elements of bluff and deception out of the negotiation process. It brings pressures to bear which actually change the least favorable terms upon which each party is willing to settle. Thus it operates as a force tending to bring about conditions necessary for agreement.[6]

Paradoxically, the imminence of the deadline can foster positive attitudes, as well as positive actions, between the parties: Its approach dramatically brings home to both groups that each will pay major costs, and thus emphasizes the existence of a common denominator. Walton and McKersie, illus-

---

[6] *Ibid.*, p. 100.

tratively, report an event occurring during the negotiations of a New Hampshire shoe company:

> The atmosphere was tense, and bargaining was definitely an adversary affair until the lights went out. Their common fate was dramatized by this incident, and the parties quickly reached settlement.[7]

Strikes do, however, occur. Sometimes the impasse leading to a work stoppage stems from a genuine inability of the parties to agree on economic or other terms; the maximum that the company feels it is able to offer in terms of dollars and cents, for example, is below the minimum that the union believes it must gain in order to retain the loyalty of its members. Or, where rank-and-file ratification is required to put the contract into effect, the negotiators may misjudge membership sentiments, bargain a contract that they feel will be fully acceptable to the membership, and then see their efforts overturned by the members' refusal to approve what they have negotiated.

On other occasions, inexperienced or incompetent negotiators fail to evaluate the importance of a specific concession to the other side, and refuse to grant such a concession where they would gladly have exchanged it for a strike situation. At times, pride or overeagerness causes bargainers to adhere to initial positions long after these become completely untenable. And, in rare instances, one or even both the parties may actually *desire* a strike—to work off excessive inventories, to allow pent-up emotions a chance for an outlet, or for various other reasons.

The strike incidence has been almost steadily declining in the United States since the beginning of the 1960s, and strikes today, as noted earlier, idle less than 0.2 percent of total available working time. As long as workers are free to strike, however, it is realistic to expect that they will occasionally do it.

CRISIS SITUATIONS

It would be strange, as a matter of fact, if there were not *some* crisis items involved in *any* particular negotiation. In the typical situation, some issues will be extremely troublesome, and they will tax severely the intelligence, resourcefulness, imagination, and good faith of the negotiators. Actually, if both sides sincerely desire to settle without a strike, a peaceful solution of any problem in labor relations can usually be worked out. As previously implied, the possibility of a work stoppage is increased when both sides are not sincere in their desire to avoid industrial warfare, or when one of the parties to the negotiation is not greatly concerned about a strike. If negotiators bargain on a rational basis, keep open minds, recognize facts

---

[7]Richard E. Walton and Robert B. McKersie, *A Behavioral Theory of Labor Negotiations* (New York: McGraw-Hill, 1965), p. 232.

and sound arguments, and understand the problems of the other side, crisis situations can be avoided or overcome without any interruption to production or any impairment of good labor relations.

One way to avoid a state of affairs wherein negotiations break down because of a few difficult issues is to bypass these issues in the early stages of the bargaining sessions. It is a good idea to settle the easy problems and delay consideration of the tough ones until later in the negotiations. In this way, the negotiation keeps moving, progress is made, and the area of disagreement tends to be isolated and diminished. Thus, at the early stages, the parties might agree to disagree on some of the items. If only a few items are standing in the way of a peaceful settlement toward the close of the negotiations, there is an excellent chance for full agreement on the contract. Moreover, what might appear to be a big issue at the beginning stages of the negotiations might, of course, appear comparatively insignificant when most of the contract has been agreed upon and when time is running out.

At times, crisis situations are created not as a result of the merits of certain issues, but because some negotiators make mistakes in human relations. For example, it is good practice to personalize the things that are constructive, inherently sound, and defensible, and depersonalize the items that are bad, destructive, or downright silly. Under the former situation, the union or the company, as the case may be, commends the other party, by saying "That is a good point," or "The committee certainly has an argument," or "Bill certainly has his facts straight." In the latter situation, it is sound policy to deal with the merits of a situation. Thus, in the face of a destructive or totally unrealistic proposal, the reaction of the other side might be something like this: "Let's see how this proposal will work out in practice if we put it into the labor agreement." It is elementary psychology that people like to be commended and dislike to be criticized. If this is recognized, rough spots and danger areas in the negotiations may be avoided.

Another way to avoid crisis situations is to be prepared in advance of negotiations to propose or accept alternative solutions to a problem. For example, suppose that the union desires to incorporate an arrangement in the labor agreement making membership in the union a condition of employment. In mapping its overall strategy for the negotiation, the union committee might decide first to propose a straight union shop, but be prepared, in the face of strong management resistance, to propose a lesser form of union security. Suppose, for another illustration, that the company wants to eliminate all restrictions on the assignment of overtime. It plans first to suggest that the management should have the full authority to designate any workers for overtime without any limitation. At the same time, the company is prepared to suggest some alternative solution to the problem in the event that this proposal appears to create strong resistance. For example, it may propose that seniority be the basis for the rotation of overtime insofar as employees have the capacity to do the work in question. If both sides are prepared in advance to offer or to accept alternative solutions to particular problems, there will be less possibility for the negotiations to bog down. Instead, they will tend to keep moving to a peaceful climax. The momentum of progress is an important factor in reaching the deadline in full agreement on a new contract.

One additional procedure is available to minimize the chances of negotiation breakdowns. It has already been pointed out that many of the issues of contemporary collective bargaining are complicated and difficult. Issues such as working rules, pension plans, insurance systems, and production standards require study and sometimes are not suitable for determination in the normal collective bargaining process. As contract termination deadlines approach, a strike may result simply because not enough time has been allowed for *jointly* attacking these particularly complicated matters in a rational, sound, workable, and equitable manner. All the *unilateral* preparation in the world still does not dispose of this problem. The parties are, however, at liberty to consider such issues by the use of a joint study group, composed of management and union representatives *during the existing contractual period*. At times, the management and union may see fit to invite disinterested and qualified third parties to aid them in such a project. The joint study group does not engage in collective bargaining as such; its function, rather, is to identify and consider alternative solutions. But, by definition being freed from the pressure of contractual deadlines, such a group can gain sufficient time to study these necessarily difficult issues in a rational manner.

To work effectively, the joint study group should be established soon after a contract is negotiated; it should be composed of people who have the ability to carry out meaningful research and the necessary qualities to consider objectively and dispassionately the tough issues confronting labor and management. These are no small prerequisites, but such a procedure has worked successfully in industries such as basic steel, and modified versions of it are also currently being used with beneficial results in the basic automobile, glass, rubber, and aluminum industries. There is no reason to believe that other collective bargaining parties, including those bargaining on an individual plant basis, could not also profit from it in avoiding crisis situations.

Some companies and unions have found the mediation process helpful when crisis situations are reached in negotiations. The Federal Mediation and Conciliation Service of the U.S. government, and state conciliation services, make mediators available to unions and companies. The Federal Service maintains regional offices in New York, Philadelphia, Atlanta, Cleveland, Chicago, St. Louis, and San Francisco, as well as field offices and field stations in many other large industrial centers. It employs several hundred mediators, whose services are available without charge to the participants in the collective bargaining process.

Mediation is based upon the principle of voluntary acceptance. Suggestions or recommendations made by the mediator may be accepted or rejected by both or either of the parties to a dispute. Unlike an arbitrator, the mediator has no conclusive powers in a dispute. His chief value is his capacity to review the dispute from an objective basis, to throw fresh ideas into the negotiations, to suggest areas of settlement, and at times to serve to extricate the parties from difficult and untenable positions. Some time ago, the then general counsel of the Federal Mediation and Conciliation Service, George E. Strong, succinctly stated some of the outstanding features of mediation and the advantages of the use of a mediator in labor disputes, as follows:

> A friend in whom the parties have confidence can emphasize the mutuality of their interests. Such a mediator can assist in deflating extreme ideas and positions and sow seeds of understanding of human as well as institutional rights, duties, needs, and objectives. Of course, the climate of industrial relations created by the parties as well as by the community and the mediator can and does promote the sprouting of these seeds. However, I do not mean to imply that mediation should be utilized in every or even in a majority of negotiations, nor do I suggest that it is always a quick and certain method of avoiding strikes, lockouts, or other coercion. If the parties can settle their disputes without mediation, they should do so, but they should not wait until the situation is frozen before utilizing mediation. Furthermore, if their desire is to destroy each other, they should not seek mediation. If, on the other hand, the parties are willing to be reasonable and seek a fair, just, and peaceful solution of their problems, they will be benefited and assisted by mediation. Fortunately, enlightened self-interest usually suggests that the parties are interdependent. They know that a mutually acceptable agreement is preferable to embittered strife which injures both parties as well as the overriding interests of the non-combatant public.[8]

TESTING AND PROOFREADING

When all issues under consideration have been resolved, the contract should then be drafted in a formal document. Many unions and managements permit lawyers to draft the formal contract. No objection is raised against this practice provided that the lawyer writes the document so that it can be understood by all concerned. A lawyer does not perform this function effectively if he includes in the contract a preponderance of legal phraseology. Such a contract will serve to confuse the people affected by its terms.

Regardless of who writes the final document, the author or authors should draft the agreement in the simplest possible terms. No contract is adequately written until the simplest, clearest, and most concise way is found to express the agreement reached at the bargaining table. Whoever drafts the agreement should recognize the basic fact that unfamiliar words and lengthy sentences will cause confusion once the document is put into force,

[8]From a lecture delivered at Indiana University on October 23, 1956.

and may lead to unnecessary grievances and arbitration. Hence, it is sound practice to use words that have special meaning in the plant or in the industry. Some contracts wisely include illustrations to make clear a particular point in the agreement. And it is of particular value to explain in detail the various steps of the grievance procedure. The contract is designed to stabilize labor relations for a given period. It is not drawn up for the purpose of creating confusion and uncertainty in the area of employer–employee relations.

Before signatures are affixed to the documents, the negotiators should have the contract test-read for meaning. No person who was associated with the negotiations should be used; his interpretation will be colored by his participation in the negotiations. A better practice is to select someone who had no part in the conference. For this purpose, the union may utilize a shop steward or even a rank-and-file member. An office employee, such as a secretary, or a foreman can serve the same purpose for management. If the people who are to administer the contract were not parties to the negotiation, such people should also be used for testing purposes; this is an excellent opportunity for them to determine whether they understand the provisions before they attempt to administer the document. If the testing indicates confusion as to meaning, the author must rewrite the faulty clause or clauses until the provision is drafted in a manner that eliminates vagueness.

The final step before signing is the proofreading of the document by each negotiator. Particular attention should be given to figures. Misplacing a decimal point, for example, can change a sum from 1 percent to one-tenth of 1 percent. Human errors and typographical mistakes are inevitable, and the proofreading of the contract should have as its objective the elimination of any such errors.

The signing of the contract is an important occasion. Newspapers may be notified of the event. Pictures may be taken to be inserted in union and company papers. The tensions of the negotiation terminated, the parties to the conference may well celebrate. They have concluded a job that will affect the welfare of many employees, the position of the labor union, the operation of the company, and, indeed, sometimes the functioning of the entire economy. They have discharged an important responsibility. Let us hope that they did it well!

COORDINATED BARGAINING

When the employer bargains with not just one but a number of different unions, he can frequently capitalize upon a built-in advantage to the situation. There often exists for him the possibility of dividing and conquering the various unions by initially concentrating upon the least formidable of them, gaining a favorable contract from it, and then using such a contract as a lever from which to extract similar concessions from the other unions. Recent corporate trends toward merger have increased such occurrences, not only by bringing together under one company umbrella a large number of unions, but also, generally, by augmenting management bargaining strength as a consequence of the greater resources now provided the company. But even without mergers, many companies have—whether because of historical accident, union rivalry, or planned and successful management strategy—enjoyed this ability to play off one union against another, often gaining even widely divergent contract-expiration dates (thus blunting the strike threat of any one union) in the process.

Increasingly, in recent years, the unions so affected have sought to offset their handicap by banding together for contract negotiation purposes in what has come to be known as "coordinated" or "coalition" bargaining. The concept, which is still so new as to lend itself to no rigorous definition but which universally denotes the presentation of a united union front at the bargaining table and often also involves common union demands, was first applied with any degree of formality in the 1966 General Electric and Westinghouse negotiations (and was reapplied there in both the 1969–70 and 1973 bargaining). By 1975, it had also been used by organized labor as a weapon in bargaining with Union Carbide, Campbell Soup, the major companies in the copper industry, American Home Products, and Olin Mathieson, among others.

Such union attempts to change the traditional bargaining structure had, understandably, been received with something less than enthusiasm by the managements involved. Indeed, most of the endeavors had resulted in rather lengthy strikes. At Union Carbide, for example, eleven different plantwide strikes occurred, with the shortest of them lasting 44 days and the longest going 246 days. The bulk of the copper industry was shut down for more than eight months. And the 1969 General Electric negotiations were marked by a strike of more than three months' duration.[9] Nor could it be said, at the time of this writing, that particularly impressive union victories had been recorded by the new labor strategy. Generally, as Bok and Dunlop have observed, "local unions and internationals which [had] not cooperated previously [had] found it difficult to withdraw their own demands to secure a concession for a relatively unknown partner."[10] In addition, the uncertain legal status of coordinated bargaining had remained a force to be reckoned with for organized labor.

At the moment, cooperation between unions is, at least in the opinion of the U.S. Circuit of Appeals for the Second Circuit (New York), "not improper, up to a point." In a 1969 decision resulting from General Electric's refusal to negotiate with a union's bargaining committee that included—as nonvoting members—representatives of other unions of the company's

---

[9] At Westinghouse, where in recent years the settlements had been patterned after those at GE, work had continued under day-to-day extensions.

[10] Derek C. Bok and John T. Dunlop, *Labor and the American Community* (New York: Simon & Schuster, 1970), p. 258.

employees, the court upheld an earlier NLRB finding that such an inclusion was consistent with the employees' statutory right to select their own bargaining representatives.[11] The court did, however, caution that such a labor strategy would be sanctioned only as long as there was no "substantial evidence of ulterior bad faith" and only if the negotiations were exclusively on behalf of the workers under a specific union contract. Only a few months prior to the ruling, moreover, an NLRB trial examiner had ruled that the ten-union-member bargaining coalition in the copper industry dispute *had* run afoul of the law by insisting upon common expiration dates for the (separate) labor agreements, common terms, and simultaneous settlements.[12] A U.S. appeals court later rejected this NLRB ruling,[13] deciding that the union's demands for similar contracts weren't "evidence of an attempt to merge the bargaining of separate units,"[14] and the U.S. Supreme Court in late 1972 refused to disturb this lower court decision. But consequently, despite these ultimately favorable rulings from the union viewpoint, the somewhat mixed verdicts and absence of a clearcut Supreme Court ruling to dispose of this issue once and for all has meant that the legally permissible boundaries of coordinated bargaining still remain unclear. They will doubtless stay there until, at some later date, an all-but-inevitable definitive Supreme Court decision based on another (as yet nonexistent) case disposes of this issue with more authoritativeness than was offered in 1972.

Generally speaking, spokesmen for those unions that have thus far used the coordinated bargaining approach seem to be encouraged by its results for their specific situations and optimistic about its general growth prospects, but at the same time they appear to be realistic in assessing its general applicability. David Lasser, of the International Union of Electrical, Radio and Machine Workers, is reasonably typical:

> Coordinated bargaining is no panacea for the bargaining process. It is a tool which adapts itself to the facts of modern industry and one which can be used wisely or poorly. . . . Certainly, the development of the skills to use the new tool is in its infancy. With the growing complexity of corporations, the diversity of the unions that deal with them, and the multiplicity of new problems, this instrument will continue to grow and will be perfected.[15]

On the other hand, the continuing failures of the United Steelworkers to form a strong multiunion coalition to bargain with Anaconda, Phelps Dodge, Kennecott, and American Smelting and Refining, because of internal schisms lasting at least to the time of this writing, cannot be overlooked as

[11]*General Electric Co.*, 173 NLRB 46 (1968).

[12]*Business Week*, February 22, 1969, p. 108.

[13]Affirmed by the full NLRB in *AFL-CIO Joint Negotiating Committee* (Phelps Dodge), 184 NLRB 106, 1970.

[14]*Wall Street Journal*, December 12, 1972, p. 10.

[15]Industrial Relations Research Association, *Proceedings of the 1968 Annual Spring Meeting*, p. 517.

a guide to the future, either. As management lawyer Owen Fairweather has accurately observed, "The unions were unable to change the traditional bargaining relationships because it was discovered that employees want to have more involvement in their own destiny and, hence, want the meaningful bargaining to occur at the plant site."[16] Members of the smaller unions have complained of the Steelworkers' "preoccupation with running off carbon copies of its other settlements."[17]

To this point, perhaps all that can be agreed upon by more detached observers of the coalition bargaining concept is that the emergence of this new approach to negotiations does seem, as economist George H. Hildebrand has pointed out, "to sustain the general thesis that bargaining arrangements, as with other institutions, are a response motivated by felt problems and needs and conditioned by ambitions and available power."[18] The certainty of further changes in these problems, needs, ambitions, and power supplies makes the new bargaining arrangements—whether or not coordinated bargaining itself has any assured future—inevitable, assuming only that the institutions involved wish to maintain their existence.

The statements above apply no less to the relationship between American unions and the growing phenomenon of the U.S.-based "multinational," or corporation operating plants in various countries. For several years, the unions have watched fearfully as such firms—attracted by a combination of tax concessions, lower-cost labor abroad, and accessibility to vital materials—have expanded their employment well beyond not only the borders of the United States but, also, quite probably the reach of U.S. labor law. Even as early as 1971, an AFL-CIO study asserted that over 5,000 jobs a week were being exported in this fashion by U.S.-based multinationals,[19] and the figures have only accelerated since then.

The UAW was the first major union to be touched by this threat, long before other labor leaders noted any grounds for alarm, indeed, but Walter Reuther's resulting advocacy of "one big global union" was all but universally believed to be unrealistic. Given the continuing absence of international collective bargaining laws, the wide disparity in union strengths and ideologies throughout the world, the millions of totally unorganized workers and interunion rivalries, it still is. American labor's counterattack to date has been confined essentially only to loose consultation with the unions and union federations abroad. And if the rationales for worldwide bargaining-expiration dates, global strikes and boycotts, and international exchanges of information have all been intensively discussed, to date no move toward

[16]Industrial Relations Research Association, *Proceedings of the Twenty-Sixth Annual Winter Meeting*, 1973, p. 150.

[17]*Business Week*, July 20, 1974, p. 29.

[18]IRRA, *1968 Proceedings*, p. 531.

[19]S. S. Ruttenberg et al., "Needed: A Constructive Foreign Trade Policy," International Union Department, AFL-CIO, October 1971.

meaningful international collective bargaining at the global level can be even remotely detected.

It is not very conceivable that the American labor relations system and its NLRB protection will prove to be of much help to unions even though their target employers are American-based themselves (in most cases). Actions taken by U.S. unions could well turn out to be illegal secondary boycotts, and most American laws could hardly be expected to bind Japanese, British, or German workers in any event. And if this view, recently well defended by Harvard's Arthur S. Leonard,[20] should prove to be warranted, one may well also be drawn to the same author's conclusion that "American unions may [then] have to rely upon the same voluntarist economic resources with which they organized the skilled trades prior to the 1935 Wagner Act to gain a share in international bargaining with multinationals."[21] Hildebrand's general thesis is no less valid here.

RECIPROCAL CHARACTER
OF COLLECTIVE BARGAINING

The fact that collective bargaining is a two-way street is clearly evidenced in negotiation sessions. Some people hold the view that the collective bargaining process involves only the union's demanding and the company's giving. On the contrary, as earlier portions of this chapter have noted, the company will frequently resist and refuse to concede to some issues. And when the company believes that the stakes are extremely important, it will take a strike rather than concede to a particular union demand. Thus, one function of management in collective bargaining is to review union demands in terms of the functions that management must perform in the operation of the plant. It will frequently resist when it believes that the union demands could impair the ability of the company to operate on a dynamic and efficient basis. In addition, most companies play a positive role in the negotiations by making demands on the union. Skilled negotiators on both sides of the table recognize that companies do and should get something out of the negotiations.

Management demands, of course, will be dictated by the character of a particular collective bargaining relationship. In some cases, for example, management will have reason to demand that the labor agreement be negotiated for a longer period than 24 months; that the union be more responsible for the elimination of wildcat strikes; that the company have more freedom in the assignment of workers to jobs; that skilled employees get a larger proportionate increase in wages than unskilled and semiskilled employees;

[20] Arthur S. Leonard, "Coordinated Bargaining with Multinational Firms by American Labor Unions," *Labor Law Journal*, December 1974, pp. 746–59.
   [21] *Ibid.*, p. 759.

that certain provisions of the labor contract that have served to interfere unnecessarily with the efficient operation of the plant or have established "featherbedding" practices be eliminated; or that job descriptions be revised in the light of changing plant technology. Collective bargaining sessions are normally as productive in terms of protecting the basic interests of management as they are in protecting the legitimate job rights of employees. This result, however, cannot be accomplished when management remains constantly on the defensive.

Management demands need not be simulated. Over the course of a contractual period, events will arise that will provide the basis for legitimate management demands. Experienced union negotiators recognize their responsibility to agree to company demands that are sound and fair, just as they expect such behavior on the part of the company representatives in reference to union demands. To the extent that companies and unions recognize in good faith that collective bargaining is a reciprocal process, the negotiation sessions and the ensuing labor agreement will be conducive to serving the interests of all concerned. In this manner, the labor contract will not be a dictated peace treaty, but a document that will establish a rational relationship between the employees, the union, and the employer.

BOULWARISM:
A DIFFERENT WAY OF DOING THINGS

It can be argued with some justification that, for all its ultimate ability to effect a contract with which both parties can live for a fixed future period of time (even on the relatively infrequent occasions when a strike interrupts the negotiations), the conventional bargaining pattern is a highly inefficient one. With its exaggerated opening demands, equally inflated counterproposals, and particularly its seeming inability to motivate the parties into making meaningful concessions until the fixed strike deadline is approached, it consumes the time and talents of many people for weeks, if not months, in a role-playing exercise that is often theatrical and almost always heavily larded with ritual. Could not the parties, it could well be asked, devise a system that comes to the point more quickly and deals with reality from the very beginning? The General Electric Company has had no doubts that such a system could be initiated. It sincerely believes, in fact, that its bargaining approach for almost three decades has attempted to do exactly this.

Since the 1940s, GE has religiously pursued a policy of (1) preparing for negotiations by effecting what company representatives describe as "the steady accumulation of all facts available on matters likely to be discussed"; (2) modifying this information only on the basis of "any additional or different facts" it is made aware of, either by its unions or from other sources, during the negotiations (as well as before them); (3) offering at an "appropriate," but invariably a very early, point during the bargaining "what the facts from all sources seem to indicate that we should"; and (4) changing this offer only if confronted with "new facts." In short, the company has attempted "to do right voluntarily," if one accepts its own description of the process. It has, alternatively, engaged in a ruthless game of "take it or leave it" bargaining, if one prefers the union conclusion.

Aided by a highly favorable combination of circumstances—chief among them the presence of several competing unions, major internal friction within its most important single union (the International Union of Electrical Workers), a heavy dependence of many of its communities on the company as the primary employer, and an abundance of long-service (and thus less mobile) employees—GE was highly successful with this policy, known as Boulwarism after former GE Vice-President of Public and Employee Relations Lemuel R. Boulware, until the late 1960s. With essentially no exceptions, the company offer in its original form was transformed into the ultimate labor contract. Constantly communicating to both its employees and the general citizenry of the various General Electric communities on the progress of the negotiations as these evolved—another major part of the Boulwaristic approach—the company could point with pride to the efficacy of its policy.

For their part, GE's unions attacked Boulwarism not only as an unethical attempt to undermine and discredit organized labor, but as an illegal endeavor in refusing to bargain. Triggered by charges lodged by the IUE following the 1960 negotiations, the NLRB did in fact (in 1964) find the company guilty of bad-faith bargaining in those negotiations. And almost five years later the U.S. Court of Appeals at New York upheld this NLRB ruling, as did the U.S. Supreme Court shortly thereafter by refusing to disturb that decision. But the facts on which these judicial actions were taken were, of course, those pertaining only to 1960, and it appeared that Boulwarism itself was far from dead.

By 1969, however, other changes had started to work against Boulwarism. The long-competitive GE unions had (as mentioned earlier) been able to coordinate their efforts. The IUE itself had been rescued from its intramural warfare by its new president, Paul Jennings. The GE communities had broadened their industrial bases and hence were no longer as dependent as they had been on the company's good will. And the high number of long-service employees on the GE payrolls had, by the normal processes of attrition, been greatly reduced. These factors all served to lessen the company's ability to transfer its offer in pristine form into the final contract. In 1969, indeed, the long and bitter strike (also cited earlier) did motivate GE to adjust its offer somewhat, with the strike itself being the only visible "new fact" in the picture. And in the 1973 negotiations, the original company offer was also modified in the course of the negotiations. But in both 1969 and 1973 the changes were relatively minor and seemed to lie far more in the packaging than in the substance. It appeared at the time of this writing—on the eve of the next round of negotiations between the parties—that GE, having realized so much success for so many years through Boulwarism, would relinquish it only if it had no choice.

SOME FURTHER COMPLEXITIES

Generalizations such as those offered in the bulk of this chapter cannot, of course, do justice in accounting for a *specific* contract settlement or strike. To appreciate adequately the complexities and variations involved in the negotiation process, one must turn to the interdependent variables that are apt to be influential in determining bargaining outcomes.

The *current healths of both the economy and the industry*, for example, have been of major effect in determining the relative settlements of the United Automobile Workers and major car manufacturers in several recent years. In 1955, a boom year, management resistance to union demands was weak, and the UAW gains were consequently significant ones. The strike threat meant relatively little to the companies in 1958, a recession year, and the union could improve the 1955 contract only slightly and after considerable frustration. In 1961, economic conditions were somewhat better than they had been in 1958, and the union demands fared correspondingly better. And in both 1964 and 1967, when automobile-company production and profitability set new all-time records, the management quest for uninterrupted production led the companies to grant Walter Reuther terms that dwarfed even those of 1955. In 1970, company costs were way up and sales (owing primarily to foreign car inroads) were way down at the same time that union members felt themselves badly hurt by inflation. A strike (at General Motors, the target employer of the UAW) was most probably inevitable as a result, and the union, even after 67 days of striking, achieved a settlement that was so relatively unexciting to its members that for a while its ratification was in definite doubt. And in 1973, a rather intermediate year for both the economy and the industry, union gains were moderate.

On the other hand, the shoe industry has been plagued by consistently poor economic conditions for many of its specific employers for years, and, in the face of this variable and its persuasive logic, the Shoe Workers have shown considerable bargaining self-restraint for over two decades.

Technological innovations—running a wide gamut from turbojet aircraft to computerized newspaper typesetting—have been the primary cause of many recent major bargaining stalemates and subsequent strikes, as even the cursory follower of current events is well aware. In turn, job insecurity resulting partly from improved technology in such competitive industries as trucking and the airlines has made railroad workers a particularly touchy group to deal with in the past several years.

The influence of other major variables, all of them noted earlier in this book, can be illustrated. It took years for Swift and Company and the Amalgamated Meat Cutters to establish a *cooperative labor relationship*, but this had been generally effected at the time of this writing, and the most recent negotiations between those two parties had been marked by a statesmanlike joint approach to difficult problems. By contrast, mutual trust is not the case at Armour, and resolutions of Meat Cutter–company differences there have sometimes strained the imaginations of both parties with no noticeable success. The *relative strengths of the two sides* can be decisive in particular negotiations, as in those between the aforementioned over-the-road truckers and the Teamsters Union, and in almost all recent negotiations involving the International Ladies' Garment Workers Union and any of its many highly competitive and marginal employers. Some negotiations have not been easily resolved because of *political problems within the union*: The 1963 bargaining between the International Longshoremen's Association–East and Gulf Coast Shipping Operators was followed by a lengthy strike, owing in large measure to a three-way scramble for leadership within the union and the accompanying jockeying for position of the contenders. Nor have these political problems been confined to top-level unionists. In more recent years, the rank and file of an increasing number of unions—among them the previously cited UAW and Steelworkers—have supported the charges of their local leaders that the bargainers were ignoring local problems, by temporarily refusing to ratify their negotiated settlements. On occasion, they have engaged in protest work stoppages as well.

The *personalities* of labor and management representatives often have a major bearing on the outcome. Despite the greater bargaining power of his union, former Teamster president Dave Beck's avowed philosophy that "for every friend I lose in the ranks of labor, I make two friends in the Chamber of Commerce" won him the wholehearted approval of many of his employers. It also made many Teamster negotiations under his presidency extremely amicable affairs. More commendably, the proven willingness of the late Pacific Maritime Association president, J. Paul St. Sure, and West Coast Longshoreman leader Harry Bridges to subordinate their personal goals to the welfare of their industry resulted, in the early 1960s, in a Mechanization and Modernization Agreement that represents a high level of statesmanship for both parties.

For negotiators whose bargaining can be in any way construed to affect "an entire industry or a substantial part thereof" in such a manner as to "imperil the national health or safety," there may be at least one further possible determinant. Under the Taft-Hartley Act of 1947, as Chapter 3 has explained, the president of the United States has the authority to postpone for 80 days a strike consistent with the specifications above. It will be recalled that other forms of *government intervention* may also be present in such cases: suggestions to uncooperative bargainers that restrictive legislation might be enacted should a strike take place, statements by public officials aimed at throwing the weight of public opinion to one side or the other, mediation by high-level personnel of the Federal Mediation and Conciliation Service or respected private citizens, and a variety of other devices. The possibility that any of these forms of intervention may be used can, of course, influence the actions of the negotiators at the bargaining table. Steelworker Union settlements in the 1960s and early 1970s, for example, were both peacefully arrived at and relatively mild in their economic increases (that is, "noninflationary"). Many observers have explained this situation, somewhat ironic in view of the turbulence accompanying steel negotiations as recently as 1959, by asserting that the government (which did, indeed, play a reasonably active role in all these settlements, with the possible exception of 1962–63) would have it no other way.

And the railroad operating unions, as a second illustration in this area, were widely accused of being unwilling to compromise in their long-standing work-rules dispute of the past decade with the railroads. This was said to be due to their (accurate) belief that government intervenors would ultimately decide these rules anyhow—and possibly on better terms than the unions could extract from their employers.

The preceding examples are only a few of the many that could have been chosen to illustrate each category of variable. In any given contract negotiation, one factor might be of major importance—or of no significance at all. The degree of importance of each also, of course, changes over time. And, clearly, many (or none) of these variables can be at play at one time on the bargainers. Contract negotiation is, in short, no more susceptible to sweeping statements than are the unions and managements that participate in the process.

The foregoing *has* indicated, however, that the negotiation of the labor contract in the contemporary economy is a complex and difficult job. The negotiators are required to possess a working knowledge of trade union principles, plant organization and operations, economics, psychology, statistics, and labor law. They must have the research ability to gather the data necessary for effective negotiations. Negotiators must be shrewd judges of human nature. Often, effective speaking ability is an additional prerequisite. Indeed, the position of the negotiator of the modern contract demands the best efforts of people possessing superior ability. Modern collective bargaining sessions have no place for the uninformed, the inept, or the unskilled.

DISCUSSION QUESTIONS

1. Assume that a large, nationwide company is negotiating a contract at the present time. What economic, political, legal, and social factors might be likely to exert some influence upon these negotiations?

2. It has been argued by a union research director that "a fact is as welcome at a collective bargaining table as a skunk at a cocktail party." Do you agree?

3. Evaluate the statement that "in the absence of a strike deadline, there can be no true collective bargaining."

4. What might explain the frequently heard management observation that "highly democratic unions are extremely difficult to negotiate with"?

5. How do you account for the fact that the joint study approach still remains confined to a relative handful of industries?

6. From the viewpoint of society, is there anything to be said in favor of strikes?

7. Of all the personal attributes this chapter has indicated are important for labor relations negotiators to have, which single one do you consider to be the most important, and why?

8. "Successful labor contract bargaining should no longer be viewed as an 'art.' It is far more appropriate today to refer to it as a 'science.' " Discuss.

SELECTED REFERENCES

BOULWARE, LEMUEL R., *The Truth about Boulwarism.* Washington, D.C.: The Bureau of National Affairs, Inc., 1969.

CHAMBERLAIN, NEIL W., "Strikes in Contemporary Context," *Industrial and Labor Relations Review*, July 1967.

DUNLOP, JOHN T., and JAMES J. HEALY, *Collective Bargaining: Principles and Cases*, rev. ed., pp. 53–68. Homewood, Ill.: Richard D. Irwin, 1955.

LEVINSON, HARRY, "Stress at the Bargaining Table," *Personnel*, March–April 1965.

SCHELLING, T. C., *The Strategy of Conflict.* Cambridge, Mass.: Harvard University Press, 1960.

SERRIN, WILLIAM, *The Company and the Union.* New York: Alfred A. Knopf, 1973.

SLOANE, ARTHUR A., "Collective Bargaining in Trucking: Prelude to a National Contract," *Industrial and Labor Relations Review*, October 1965.

STAGNER, ROSS, and HJALMAR ROSEN, *Psychology of Union–Management Relations.* Belmont, Calif.: Wadsworth, 1965.

STEVENS, CARL M., *Strategy and Collective Bargaining Negotiation.* New York: McGraw-Hill, 1963.

THIEBLOT, ARMAND J., JR., and RONALD M. COWIN, *Welfare and Strikes: The Use of Public Funds to Support Strikers.* Philadelphia: University of Pennsylvania, Wharton School of Finance and Commerce, 1972.

WALTON, RICHARD E., and ROBERT B. MCKERSIE, *A Behavioral Theory of Labor Negotiations.* New York: McGraw-Hill, 1965.

Chapter 6
Administration
of the Agreement

When agreement is finally reached in contract negotiations, the bargainers frequently call in news reporters and photographers, smilingly slap each other on the back (as the cameras snap), and announce their satisfaction with the new contract. The exact performance, of course, varies from situation to situation. In general, however, such enthusiastic phrases as "great new era" and "going forward together for our mutual benefit" are often heard.

There is a minimum of sham in these actions. Public relations are, as has been stressed at several earlier stages in this book, important to both sides; and both management–stockholder and union leader–union member relationships are also not overlooked by the company and union participants, respectively, as they register their happiness with their joint handiwork. But typically the negotiators are genuinely optimistic about what they have negotiated: Compromise and statesmanship have once again triumphed.

It will be some time, however, before one can tell whether this optimism is justified. The formal signing of the collective bargaining agreement does not mean that union–management relations are terminated until the next negotiation over contract terms. After the new labor agreement goes into effect, management and union representatives have the job of making the contract work. The labor agreement establishes the general framework of labor relations in the plant; it spells out in broad language the rights and benefits of employees, the obligations and rights of management, and the protection and the responsibilities of the union. But during the course of the contractual period, many problems will arise involving the *application* and the *interpretation* of the various clauses in the labor agreement.

The application of the contract is, in fact, a daily problem. Representatives of management and the union normally devote a considerably larger share of their time to the administration of the labor agreement than to its negotiation. Moreover, the climate of labor relations in the plant will be determined to a large extent by the manner in which management and union representatives discharge their obligations in the day-by-day application of the labor contract. Whether there will be good or bad labor relations depends to a significant degree on the character of the administration of the labor agreement. For these reasons, it is vital that the parties to a collective bargaining relationship understand thoroughly the problems and the responsibilities that grow out of the application of a contract.

The source of many administrative problems is in the language of the labor agreement. Owing to the conditions under which bargaining takes place, many contractual clauses are themselves written in rather broad terms. The day-to-day job in labor relations is to apply the *principles* of the contract.

Many problems can arise under a single clause of the labor agreement. For example, a contract may limit the right of management to discharge for "just cause." An employee is discharged for talking back to his foreman in harsh terms. Is this just cause within the meaning of the agreement? In another case, a seniority arrangement may provide that the employee with the longer service in the plant will get the better job, provided that he has ability to perform the job equal to that of any other employee who desires the position. Whether or not the employee with longer service *is* awarded the job is an administrative problem. Or the parties may have agreed that employees will be expected to perform jobs falling within their job description. An emergency arises in the plant, and the company directs some employees to work outside their job description. Did the company violate the agreement? Or, as a final example, the labor agreement provides that wage rates of new jobs created in the plant are to be established in a manner that is equitable in terms of comparable jobs. Does a rate established for such a job in fact compare fairly with that for kindred jobs?

These illustrations suggest the multitude of problems that can arise in connection with the operation of a labor agreement on a day-by-day basis. Practically every provision in a collective bargaining contract can be the basis for problems that must be resolved.

GRIEVANCE PROCEDURE

Problems such as those posed above are handled and settled through the grievance procedure of the labor contract. The grievance procedure provides an orderly system whereby the employer and the union can determine whether or not the contract has, in effect, been violated. Only a comparatively small number of violations involve willful disregard of the terms of the collective bargaining agreement. More frequently, employers or unions pursue a course of conduct, alleged to be a violation of the collective bargaining agreement, that the party honestly believes to conform with its terms. In any event, the grievance procedure provides the mechanism whereby the truth of the matter will be revealed. Through it, the parties have an opportunity to determine whether or not the contract has actually been violated. Such a peaceful procedure, of course, is infinitely superior to a system that would permit the enforcement of the contract through the harsh arbitrant of the strike or lockout. Each year, literally hundreds of thousands of grievances are filed alleging contract violations. Indeed, industry would be in a chaotic state if the strike or the lockout were utilized to effect compliance with the contract instead of the resort to the peaceful procedures of the grievance mechanism.

The best way to demonstrate the working of a grievance procedure is through an actual circumstance. For this purpose, a case that actually occurred in industry will be utilized, although fictitious names for the participants will be used.

Tom Swift, a rank-and-file member of Local 1000, had been employed by the Ecumenical Bagel Company for a period of five years. His production record was excellent; he caused management no trouble; and during his fourth year of employment he received a promotion. One day, Swift began preparations to leave the plant twenty minutes before quitting time. He put away his tools, washed up, got out of his overalls, and put on his street clothes. Jackson, an assistant foreman in his department, observed Swift's actions. He immediately informed Swift that he was going to the front office to recommend his discharge. The next morning, Swift reported for work, but Jackson handed him a pay envelope that, in addition to wages, included a discharge notice. The notice declared that the company discharged Swift because he made ready to leave the plant twenty minutes before quitting time.

Swift immediately contacted his union steward, Joe Thomas. The steward worked alongside Swift in the plant and, of course, personally knew the assistant foreman and foreman of his department. After Swift told Thomas the circumstances, the steward believed that the discharge constituted a violation of the collective bargaining contract. A clause in the agreement provided that an employee could be discharged only for "just cause." Disagreeing with the assistant foreman and the front office, Thomas felt that the discharge was not for just cause.

The collective bargaining contract covering the employees of the Ecumenical Company contained a carefully worded grievance procedure. It is through this procedure that Thomas was required to protest the discharge of Swift. The steward was aware that the requirements of the grievance procedure had to be carried out if he intended to take appropriate action to effect reinstatement of the union member. The grievance procedure provided that all charges of contract violation must be reduced to writing. Consequently, the steward and the discharged worker filled out a "grievance form," describing in detail the character of the alleged violation.

The steps in processing the complaint through the grievance procedure were clearly outlined in the collective bargaining agreement. First, it was necessary to present the grievance to the foreman of the department in which Swift worked. Both Thomas and Swift approached the foreman, and the written grievance was presented to him. The foreman was required to give his answer on the grievance within 48 hours after receiving it. He complied with the time requirement, but his answer did not please Swift or Thomas. The foreman supported the action of the assistant foreman and refused to recommend the reinstatement of Swift.

Not satisfied with the action of the foreman, the labor union, through Thomas, the steward, resorted to the second step of the grievance procedure. This step required the appeal of the complaint to the superintendent of the department in which Swift worked. Again the disposition of the grievance by management's representative brought no relief to the discharged employee. Despite the efforts of the steward, who vigorously argued the merits of Swift's case, the department superintendent refused to reinstate the worker. Hence the second step of the grievance procedure was exhausted, and the union and the employee were still not satisfied with the results.

Actually, the vast majority of grievances are settled in the first two steps of the grievance procedure. This is a remarkable record, indicating the fairness of employers and labor unions. The employer or the union charged with a contract violation may simply admit their transgression and take remedial action. On the other hand, the party charged with violating the collective bargaining agreement may be able to persuade the other party that, in fact, no violation exists. Frequently, both parties might work out a compromise solution satisfactory to all concerned. Such a compromise may serve the interests of sound industrial relations, a state of affairs that the grievance procedure attempts to produce.

In the Swift case, however, the union refused to drop the case after the complaint was processed through the second level of the grievance procedure. Accordingly, the union appealed to the third step of the grievance procedure. Grievance personnel for the third step included, from the company, the general superintendent and his representatives; and for the labor union, the organization's plantwide grievance committee. The results of the negotiations at the third step proved satisfactory to Swift, the union, and the company. After 45 minutes of spirited discussion, the management group agreed with the union that discharge was not warranted in this particular case. Management's committee was persuaded by the following set of circumstances: Everyone conceded that Swift had an outstanding record before the dismissal occurred. In addition, the discussion revealed that Swift had inquired of the department foreman whether there was any more work to be done before he left his bench to prepare to leave for home. The foreman had replied in the negative. Finally, it was brought out that Swift had had a pressing problem at home that he claimed was the motivating factor for his desire to leave the plant immediately after quitting time.

The grievance personnel reached a mutually satisfactory solution of the case after all the factors were carefully weighed. Management repeatedly stressed the serious consequences to production efficiency if a large number of workers prepared to leave the plant twenty minutes before quitting time. Recognizing the soundness of this observation, the union committee agreed that some sort of disciplinary action should be taken. As a result, it was concluded that Swift would be reinstated in his job, but would be penalized by a three-day suspension without pay. In addition, the union committee agreed with management's representatives that better labor relations would be promoted if a notice were posted on company bulletin boards stating that all workers would be expected to remain at their jobs until quitting time. Union and company grievance personnel were in agreement that the notice should also declare that violations would be subject to penalty. Thus the grievance procedure resulted in the amicable solution of a contract violation case.

What would have occurred, however, if the company and the labor union had not reached a satisfactory agreement at the third step of the grievance procedure? In this particular contract, the grievance procedure provided for a fourth step. Grievance procedure personnel at the fourth step included, for the company, the vice-president in charge of industrial relations or his representative, and, for the union, an officer of the international union or his representative. It is noteworthy that this particular contract provided four chances to effect a mutually satisfactory disposition of a complaint alleging a contract violation.

All collective bargaining contracts do not provide for the same structural arrangements as the one described in the Swift case. Some contain only three steps; in others, the time limits may be different; or the particular company and union personnel participating at the different steps of the grievance procedure may be somewhat different. If their structural arrangements vary slightly from contract to contract, however, the fact remains that the essential characteristics of grievance procedures are similar. All have as their basic objective the settling of alleged contract violation cases in a friendly and orderly manner. In each there is provided a series of definite steps to follow in the processing of grievances. A certain time limit is placed on each step, and an answer to a grievance must be given within the allotted time. Failure to comply with the time limits could result in the forfeiture of the grievance by the errant party. For example, where a union fails to appeal a grievance within the stipulated time limit, the employer may deny the grievance on that basis. Where such cases go to arbitration, the arbitrator may under appropriate circumstances hold that, since the union did not comply with the time limit, the grievance is not arbitrable. That is, he may deny the grievance on these grounds and without inquiry into the merits of the employee's complaint. (Cases 1 and 2 at the end of this chapter deal with the time limit problem and its consequences. These are the first of fourteen cases offered by this volume to illustrate specific problems of labor relations.)

GRIEVANCE PROCEDURE: ITS FLEXIBILITY

Since company officials and union officers make up grievance procedure personnel, people intimately connected with the plant will decide whether or not a particular pattern of conduct violates the terms of the collective bargaining agreement. Obviously, these people are in a favored position to make such a determination. Frequently, some of them helped negotiate the collective bargaining contract itself. Such participation in the contract-making negotiations should result in a clear understanding of the meaning of particular contract terms. Not only do grievance procedure personnel normally possess a thorough and firsthand knowledge of the meaning of the contract, but they are well aware of the character of the conduct alleged to be a violation. Grievance cases are at times complex in nature. The line dividing "lawful" from "unlawful" conduct under a collective bargaining contract is not always sharply drawn. Clearly, people actually associated with the plant in which the alleged violation occurred can best decide these difficult cases.

The local character of grievance procedure personnel serves to make this contract-enforcing technique highly flexible in character. These people are well aware of the environmental context in which the alleged violation occurred. Weight can be given to human or economic factors involved in alleged violations. This does not mean that an "explainable" violation will go unchallenged. However, the grievance procedure is a peculiarly amenable mechanism. It is probable that grievance procedure personnel might resolve an "explainable" violation in a different manner from one in which no extenuating circumstances were involved.

Since grievance procedure personnel are closely associated with the plant, they are in an excellent position to anticipate the effects of the disposition of a grievance on employers, on the union, on union leadership, and on plant operations. To promote sound industrial relations, management and union grievance procedure personnel, as noted, frequently compromise on the solution of grievance cases. It is not unknown for management to allow the union to "win" a grievance case to bolster the prestige of union leadership in the eyes of union membership; the state of industrial relations may be improved when union leaders have the confidence of the membership. On the other hand, a labor union may refuse to challenge a company violation of a contract when the employer engages in conduct absolutely essential for the operation of the plant. And, in this connection, a circumstance involving an Indiana firm and a labor union might be related.

Contrary to the seniority provisions of an existing collective bargaining contract, the Indiana company laid off longer-service employees and retained shorter-service employees. Such action constituted a direct violation of the particular contract. However, the union representatives agreed with the company, when the case was resolved through the grievance procedure, that the retention of the shorter-service workers was vital to the continued operation of a crucial plant department. Union and management grievance procedure personnel concluded that had the longer-service workers been retained and the shorter-service employees been laid off, the plant, the union, and all employees of the company would have suffered irreparable damage.

It is not intended here to create a false impression of the operation of the grievance procedure. Certainly, the mechanism does not function to condone employer, employee, or union violations of collective bargaining contracts. In the overwhelming number of cases disposed of through the grievance procedure, practices inconsistent with the terms of the agreement are terminated. At times, retroactive action must be taken to implement rights and obligations provided for in the contract. Thus, the employer may be required to reinstate with back pay a worker who had previously been discharged in violation of the discharge clause of the labor agreement. Or perhaps a union caused damage to the company's property while on strike; to comply with a particular contract provision, this union might be required to pay the company a certain sum of money.

Without detracting from the fact that the primary objective of the grievance procedure is to enforce the terms of the collective bargaining contract, it remains true that this mechanism is singularly adaptable for the settlement of contract disputes to the maximum satisfaction of all concerned. Interests of all parties can be considered. Its flexible and personalized character permits compromise when this is deemed the best way to settle a particular grievance. Extenuating circumstances can be given weight. Precedent can be utilized or disregarded, depending on the particular situation. Effects of the manner of disposition of a contract violation case are clearly understood by grievance procedure personnel. In short, the flexible character of grievance procedure is its outstanding merit. Solutions to problems can be reached that will serve the basic interests of sound industrial relations. These observations lead to one conclusion: Resort to the grievance procedure provides management and unions with the most useful and efficient means of contract enforcement.

Grievance Procedure
and Harmonious Labor Relations

As suggested above, the grievance procedure, by providing the parties to the labor contract with an excellent opportunity whereby complaints of workers, employers, and unions can be aired and discussed, may be regarded as supplying the "psychotherapy" of industrial relations. Small problems can be discussed and settled promptly before they become major and troublesome issues in the plant. Serious problems can be analyzed in a rational manner and resolved speedily, peacefully, and in keeping with the terms of the collective bargaining contract. The rights of employees, employers, and unions guaranteed in the labor contract can be protected and implemented in a prompt and orderly fashion. Not only does the grievance procedure serve as a means for the enforcement of the labor agreement; it also provides the parties with the opportunity of establishing the *reasons* for complaints and problems.

Indeed, depending upon the attitudes of the company and the union, the grievance procedure can also be used for functions other than the settlement of complaints arising under the labor agreement. Many parties, for example, use the grievance machinery to prevent grievances from arising as well as to dispose of employee, union, and employer complaints. Major grievances are viewed here as symptomatic of underlying problems, and attempts are jointly made to dispose of these problems to prevent their future recurrence. In other cases, the parties may utilize the scheduled grievance meeting time, after the grievance itself has been dealt with, to explore ways of improving their general relationship and also as an avenue of bilateral communication on matters of interest to both institutions (such as new company plans, the economic prospects for the industry, the upcoming union election).

In the last analysis, in fact, the grievance procedure should be regarded as a device whereby companies or unions can "win" a grievance only in the most narrow of senses. It should also be viewed as a means for obtaining a better climate of labor relations in a company, rather than as the machinery whereby either the company or the union can exercise authority over the other. This does not mean that rights guaranteed in the labor contract should be waived or compromised, but that in discharging obligations under the grievance procedure, the parties should understand the broader implications involved. Company and union representatives who regard the grievance procedure in this light gear their behavior, arguments, and general approach toward the objective of the improvement of labor relations.

This objective is not realized when representatives of management look upon their obligations under the grievance procedure as burdensome chores, as wastes of time, or as necessary evils. Likewise, it is not attainable to the extent that unions stuff the grievance procedure with complaints that have no merit whatsoever under the collective bargaining contract.[1] It cannot be achieved when the parties regard the grievance procedure as a method to embarrass the other side or to demonstrate authority or power. In addition, the opportunities for more harmonious labor relations through the use of the

---

[1]Many unions specifically instruct their stewards and grievance committeemen not to process grievances that have no merit under a labor agreement. Thus, in one union manual: "After you have thoroughly investigated the case, if you decide that no grievance exists, it is your duty to the worker and the union to state this, and to take time to explain why."

grievance procedure cannot be realized to the extent that the system is used to resolve internal political conflicts within the union or the management. If the grievance procedure does not contribute to a better labor relations climate, the fault lies not with the system, but with the representatives of unions and management who either misunderstand or distort the functions that the procedure plays in the industrial relations complex.

ARBITRATION

The vast majority of problems that arise as the result of the interpretation and application of collective bargaining contracts are resolved bilaterally by the representatives of management and the labor organization. Through the process of negotiation, the parties to a contract manage to find a solution to grievances at some step in the grievance procedure. Such a record testifies to the utility of the grievance procedure as a device for the speedy, fair, and peaceful solution of disputes growing out of the application of the collective bargaining contract. It also shows rather clearly that the great majority of company and union representatives understand fully the purpose of the grievance procedure and discharge their responsibilities on the basis of good faith.

Indeed, in healthy union–management relationships, the great bulk of grievances is disposed of at the lower levels of the procedure. This is as it should be; were most such complaints merely bucked up the union and management hierarchical ladders, the time and efforts of the more broadly based officials would be hopelessly drained. Lower-step settlement also helps maintain the status of lower supervision and assures that the grievance is allowed treatment by the people who are apt to be most familiar with the circumstances under which it arose.

Under even the most enviable of labor relationships, however, there will undoubtedly be some grievances that prove themselves completely incapable of being solved by *any* level within the bilateral grievance procedure. Each party genuinely believes that its interpretation of the contract is the right one, or the company and union remain in disagreement as to the facts of the case.

There may also, on occasion, be less commendable reasons for a stalemate. The union leadership may feel that it cannot afford to "give in" on an untenable grievance, because of the political ramifications of doing so. Management may at times prove quite unwilling to admit that the original company action giving rise to the grievance was in violation of the contract, even though in its heart it realizes that the union's allegation is right. The union may, the remarks previously offered in this connection notwithstanding, seek to "flood" the grievance procedure with a potpourri of unsettled grievances, with the hope of using the situation to gain extracontractual concessions from the company. The company may, in turn, seek to embarrass the union leadership by making it fight to the limit for any favorable settlement. And grievances involving such thorny issues as discipline, work assignment, and management rights are sometimes accompanied by emotional undercurrents that make them all the more difficult to resolve by the joint conference method of the grievance procedure.

In short, the amount of challenge that management can expect through the grievance procedure can vary widely, because of the existence of such complex variables as (1) the wisdom and extent of development of the legislated policy that is embodied in the labor agreement itself (and, no less important, the degree of operating policy development which the company has effected to supplement the labor agreement); (2) the political environment and militancy of the local union; (3) the calibre of the company's personnel administration and supervision; (4) the nature of the existing union–management relationship; and (5) economic and related variables affecting employment and working conditions.

Given all these variables, it is, in fact, a tribute to the maturity of labor–management relations that the great majority of all grievances are in fact settled by the joint process.

Nonetheless, some contractual provision must be made by the parties to handle the relatively few issues for which the grievance procedure proves unsuccessful—those occasions upon which the parties to the labor contract are still in disagreement over a problem arising under the contractual terms after all bilateral steps in the grievance procedure have been exhausted. To break such deadlocks, the parties have the opportunity to resort to the arbitration process. An impartial outsider is selected by the parties to decide the controversy. His decision is invariably stipulated in the contract as being "final and binding upon both parties."

Through the arbitrator, the dispute is resolved in a peaceful manner. In the absence of arbitration, the parties might use the strike or lockout to settle such problems, a process that not only is costly to the company, the union, and the employees, but that would tend to foster embittered labor relations. In the light of these observations, it should elicit no surprise that at present some 96 percent of all U.S. labor agreements provide for arbitration as the final step in the grievance procedure. This national percentage is significantly greater than it was in the early 1930s, when fewer than 8 to 10 percent of all agreements contained such a clause. And even by 1944, arbitration provisions had been included in only 73 percent of all contracts.[2]

Not surprisingly, either, the recent statistics involving arbitration caseloads have been of no small order of magnitude. In 1974, for example, arbitrators serving under the auspices of the Federal Mediation and Conciliation Service issued 4,349 awards, compared to 1,887 awards in 1965.[3] In an era of

[2]"Arbitration Provisions in Collective Agreements, 1952," *Monthly Labor Review*, March 1953, pp. 261–66.

[3]Federal Mediation and Conciliation Service, *Twenty-Sixth Annual Report*, 1974, p. 48.

uncertainty as to the future growth of union membership totals, moreover, there is no collective job insecurity in the profession: The case load for arbitrators keeps increasing annually. Much of the most recent impetus for growth was provided by a major judicial decision of the late 1950s: In June 1957, the U.S. Supreme Court held that the federal courts may apply the Taft-Hartley law to enforce arbitration clauses. Under this ruling, an employer may not refuse to arbitrate unresolved grievance disputes when the labor agreement contains an arbitration provision.[4]

The "Trilogy" Cases

On June 20, 1960, the U.S. Supreme Court handed down three other decisions that provide even greater integrity for the arbitration process.[5] These decisions are commonly referred to as the "Trilogy" cases. Each of them involved the United Steelworkers of America, and each demonstrates that the system of private arbitration in the United States has now received the full support of the highest court in the land.

In the *Warrior & Gulf Navigation* case, the Court held that in the absence of an express agreement excluding arbitration, the Court would direct the parties to arbitrate a grievance. To put this in other terms, the Court would not find a case to be nonarbitrable unless the parties specifically excluded a subject from the arbitration process. The Court stated that a legal order to arbitrate would thenceforth not be denied "unless it may be said with positive assurance that the arbitration clause is not susceptible to an interpretation that covers the asserted dispute. Doubts should be resolved in favor of coverage."

More precisely, the courts will not decide that a dispute is *not* arbitrable unless the parties have taken care to *expressly remove* an area of labor relations from the arbitration process. This could be accomplished by providing, for example, that "disputes involving determination of the qualifications of employees for promotion will be determined exclusively by the company and such decision will not be subject to arbitration." But, needless to say, not many unions would agree to such a clause, since management would then have the unilateral right to make determinations on this vital phase of the promotion process.

In so ruling, the *Warrior & Gulf Navigation* decision eliminated a course of action that some companies had followed. When faced with a demand by a union for arbitration, some employers had frequently gone to court and asked the judge to decide that the issue involved in the case was not arbitrable. On many occasions, the courts had agreed with the company, with the effect

[4] *Textile Workers* v. *Lincoln Mills*, 353 U.S. 488 (1957).

[5] *United Steelworkers of America* v. *American Manufacturing Co.*, 363 U.S. 564 (1960); *United Steelworkers of America* v. *Warrior & Gulf Navigation Co.*, 363 U.S. 574 (1960); *United Steelworkers of America* v. *Enterprise Wheel & Car Corp.*, 363 U.S. 593 (1960).

of sustaining the company position in the grievance, and denying the union an opportunity to get a decision based on the merits of the case.

In the instant case, the Warrior & Gulf Navigation Company employed 42 men at its dock terminal for maintenance and repair work. After the company had subcontracted out some of the work, the number was reduced to 23. The union argued in the grievance procedure that this action of the company violated certain areas of the labor agreement—the integrity of the bargaining unit, seniority rights, and other clauses of the contract that provided benefits to workers. On its part, the company claimed that the issue of subcontracting was strictly a management function and relied on the management rights clause in the contract, which stated that "matters which are strictly a function of management should not be subject to arbitration." When the Supreme Court handled the case, it ordered arbitration because the contract did not *specifically* exclude such activity from the arbitration process. It stated:

> A specific collective bargaining agreement may exclude contracting-out from the grievance procedure. Or a written collateral agreement may make clear that contracting-out was not a matter for arbitration. In such a case a grievance based solely on contracting-out would not be arbitrable. Here, however, there is no such provision. Nor is there any showing that the parties designed the phrase "strictly as a function of management" to encompass any and all forms of contracting-out. In the absence of any express provision excluding a particular grievance from arbitration, we think only the most forceful evidence of a purpose to exclude the claim from arbitration can prevail, particularly where, as here, the exclusion clause is vague and the arbitration clause quite broad.

One additional important point must be made relative to the significance of this court decision. It does not mean that private arbitrators do not have the authority to dismiss a grievance on the basis of its nonarbitrability under a contract. Arbitrators before and after the decision have frequently held that a grievance is not arbitrable under the contract. Indeed, the authors, at times after the *Warrior & Gulf Navigation* decision, have upheld the arguments of companies that grievances were not arbitrable under the labor agreement. The major importance of the *Warrior & Gulf Navigation* doctrine is in its ruling that courts may not hold that grievances are not arbitrable *unless* specific and clear-cut language excludes the matter from the arbitration process. The private arbitrator is still fully empowered to dismiss a grievance on the basis of nonarbitrability.

In the second case, *American Manufacturing*, the issue of arbitrability was also involved, but in a somewhat different way from that of *Warrior & Gulf Navigation*. The American Manufacturing Company argued before a lower federal court that an issue was not arbitrable because it did not believe that the grievance had merit. Involved was a dispute involving the reinstatement of an employee on his job after it was determined that the employee was 25 percent disabled and was drawing workmen's compensation. The lower federal court sustained the employer's position and characterized the employee's grievance as "a frivolous, patently baseless one, not subject to arbitration." When the U.S. Supreme Court reversed the lower federal court, it held that federal courts are limited in determining whether the dispute is covered by the labor agreement and that they have no power to evaluate the merits of a dispute. It stated:

> The function of the court is very limited when the parties have agreed to submit all questions of contract interpretation to the arbitrator. It is then confined to ascertaining whether the party seeking arbitration is making a claim which on its face is governed by the contract. Whether the moving party is right or wrong is a question of contract construction for the arbitrator. In these circumstances the moving party should not be deprived of the arbitrator's judgment, when it was his judgment and all that it connotes that was bargained for.

Essentially, this means that the courts may not hold a grievance to be nonarbitrable even if a judge believes that a grievance is completely worthless. It is up to the private arbitrator to make the decision on the merits of a case. He may dismiss the grievance as being without merit, but this duty rests exclusively with him, and not with the courts.

In the third case, *Enterprise Wheel & Car Corporation*, a lower federal court reversed the decision of an arbitrator on the grounds that the judge did not believe that his decision was sound under the labor agreement. The arbitrator's award directed the employer to reinstate certain discharged workers and to pay them back wages for periods both before and after the expiration of the collective bargaining contract. The company refused to comply with the award, and the union petitioned for the enforcement of the award. The lower court held that the arbitrator's award was unenforceable because the contract had expired. The Supreme Court reversed the lower court and ordered full enforcement. In upholding the arbitrator's award, the Court stated:

> Interpretation of the collective bargaining agreement is a question for the arbitrator. It is the arbitrator's construction which was bargained for; and so far as the arbitration decision concerns construction of the contract, the courts have no business overruling him because their interpretation of the contract is different from his.

The significance of this last decision is clear. It shows that a union or a company may not use the courts to set aside an arbitrator's award. The decision, of course, cuts both ways: It applies to both employers and labor organizations. Whereas the other two decisions definitely favor labor organizations, this one merely serves to preserve the integrity of the arbitrator's award. Thus, even if a judge believes that an arbitrator's award is unfair, unwise, and not even consistent with the contract, he has no alternative except to enforce the award.

Thus, the Trilogy cases demonstrate that the private arbitration system has been strengthened by the judiciary. They establish the full integrity of the arbitration process. As a result of these decisions, companies and unions must be more careful in the selection of arbitrators. This is one reason why they have increasingly voiced a desire to use seasoned and experienced arbitrators.

Gardner-Denver and Collyer

In 1974, however, one cloud appeared on the horizon that caused some concern about the efficacy of the arbitration process. At that time, the U.S. Supreme Court decided *Alexander* v. *Gardner-Denver,* and held that an arbitrator's decision is not final and binding when Title VII of the Civil Rights Act is involved.[6] An arbitrator sustained the discharge of a black employee on the grounds that he was terminated for just cause. The employee claimed, however, that he was discharged for racial reasons in violation of Title VII. Lower federal courts upheld the decision of the arbitrator, in line with the Trilogy doctrine. However, the Supreme Court remanded the case to the federal district court to determine whether or not the employee's rights under Title VII were violated. What *Gardner-Denver* means, therefore, is that if an employee loses his case in arbitration, he may still seek relief from the courts, provided that Title VII rights are involved.

One should not believe, however, that the high court intends to undermine the arbitration process just because of its decision in this racial case. At this writing, the Court has not carved out any other exception to the finality of an arbitrator's award. It is stressed that *Gardner-Denver* was decided solely on the grounds that Title VII rights were involved. The case should not be regarded as a signal that the courts intend to strike down arbitrators' decisions on a wholesale basis.

As a matter of fact, the courts have sustained an NLRB policy that makes private arbitration an even more important feature in labor relations.[7] In 1971, the NLRB held, in *Collyer Insulated Wire,* that it would defer some cases to arbitration even though they contained elements of unfair labor practices. In these cases, contractual provisions were arguably involved, and the NLRB believed that private arbitrators could not only decide whether or not the contract was violated but also determine the unfair labor practice issue. Though this *Collyer* decision has been criticized on the grounds that the NLRB should not abandon its statutory duty to enforce the Taft-Hartley Act, the fact remains that the doctrine makes arbitration an even more viable instrument for the settlement of labor–management disputes.

[6]U.S. Sup. Ct. Case No. 72-5847, February 19, 1974.

[7]*Nabisco, Inc.* v. *NLRB* (CA 2) Case No. 72-2073; June 20, 1973; *Electrical Workers* v. *NLRB* (CA, D.C.) Case No. 72-1944, February 28, 1974.

For the arbitrator, the Trilogy and *Collyer* decisions are equally meaningful. Private arbitrators bear an even greater degree of responsibility as they decide their cases. Not only is the post one of honor, in which the parties have confidence in the arbitrator's professional competency and integrity, but the arbitrator must recognize that for all intents and purposes his decision is completely "final and binding" upon the parties. Indeed, if the system of private arbitration is to remain a permanent feature of the American system of industrial relations, arbitrators must measure up to their responsibilities. Should they fail in this respect, companies and unions would simply delete the arbitration clause from the contract and resolve their disputes by strikes or by going directly to court. These are not pleasant alternatives, but the parties may choose these routes if they believe that arbitrators are not discharging their responsibilities in an honorable, judicious, and professional manner. Arbitrators should not feel so smug as to believe that their services are indispensable to labor unions and companies. They are as expendable as last year's calendar.

Limitations to Arbitration

If employers and unions support the arbitration process as an accepted method of disposing of disagreements relating to problems arising under the terms of a labor contract already in existence, there is almost no approval on the part of industry and organized labor for using arbitration as the means of breaking deadlocks in the negotiations of *new* agreements. Most employers and unions would rather have a work stoppage than refer such disputes to arbitration. Many reasons are advanced in support of this position, but the chief consideration lies in the parties' extreme aversion to having an outsider determine the conditions of employment, the rights and obligations of management, and the responsibilities and rights of the union. Employers and unions almost invariably believe that, since the labor agreement will establish their fundamental relationship, they should have the full authority to negotiate its terms. For these reasons, the use of arbitration during the negotiation stage of a labor contract is rare. In only a very few industries do the parties surrender their rights to negotiate new contracts and establish arbitration as the method to break deadlocks.

It is also important to note that in the United States the system is one of *private and voluntary arbitration.* That is, the government does not force the parties to include arbitration clauses in their labor agreements. They do so voluntarily as they negotiate the latter. Either party can refuse to incorporate any arbitration provisions at all, as has been the case in the building construction industry, where the duration of the job is deemed too brief to make use of a neutral feasible, and in much of the trucking industry, where the Teamster hierarchy has traditionally insisted that neutrals "attempt to please both sides and actually please nobody."

Equally significant is the fact that arbitrators are private and not government officials. Most of them are lawyers and college professors. In some nations, such as Spain, arbitration is imposed by government fiat, *must* be used to resolve contractual interpretation disputes, and the arbitrators are government officials or appointees. Let us hope that the American system never takes this route. To follow the pattern of Spain and other totalitarian labor relations systems would mean the demise of the free collective bargaining system.

Characteristics of Arbitration Hearings

Since the decision of the arbitrator *is* final and binding, arbitration is quite different from mediation, a process wherein the parties are completely free to accept or reject the recommendations or suggestions of the mediator. Whether the arbitrator rules for or against a party to the arbitration, his decision must be accepted. This is true even when the losing side believes that the decision is not warranted by the labor agreement, by the evidence submitted in the hearing, or on the basis of fairness or justice. Frequently, an arbitrator's decision will establish an important precedent in the plant that must be followed by the company, the union, and the employees. At times the party that suffers an adverse ruling in an arbitration case will attempt to change, during the next labor contract negotiations, those sections of the labor agreement that proved to be the basis of the decision. Obviously, the side that is benefited by the decision will be reluctant to alter those features of the labor agreement that were interpreted and applied by the arbitrator.

These considerations tend to show the seriousness of arbitration as a tool of labor relations. When the decision to arbitrate is made, the company and union representatives are undertaking a deep responsibility. To discharge this responsibility in a competent and intelligent manner, it is necessary to put the arbitrator in such a position that he can make his decision in the light of evidence and of the relevant contractual clauses. Consequently, the parties have the obligation of preparing fully before coming to the hearing. This means the accumulation of all evidence, facts, documents, and arguments that may have a bearing on the dispute. Careful preparation also means the selection of witnesses who can give relevant testimony in the case.[8] Company and union representatives should leave no stone unturned in preparing for the arbitration.

At the arbitration hearing, each side will have full opportunity to present the fruits of its preparation. Normally, although arbitration hearings are much more formal than grievance procedure negotiations, they are considerably less formal than court proceedings. In addition, the rules of evidence that obtain in the courts of the land do not bind the conduct of the arbitra-

---

[8] A competent elaboration of this topic is contained in Frank and Edna Elkouri, *How Arbitration Works*, 3rd ed. (Washington, D.C.: Bureau of National Affairs, Inc., 1973).

tion.[9] This means that the hearing can be conducted not only more informally but much faster than a case in court. However, the parties should not be deluded into believing that the arbitrator's decision will not be based upon evidence and facts. Even though the arbitration proceedings might be regarded as semiformal, the fact remains that the arbitrator's decision will most likely be based *strictly* on facts, evidence, arguments, and the contractual clauses that are involved in the proceedings. Arbitration cases are not won on the basis of emotional appeals, theatrical gestures, or speechmaking. The arbitrator is interested in the facts, the evidence, and the parties' arguments as they apply to the issues of the dispute. Such material should be developed in the hearing through careful questioning of witnesses and the presentation of relevant documents.

The parties cannot, moreover, take too much care to make sure that they have presented *all* evidence that might support their case. Representatives of unions and companies who have dealt with a problem in the grievance procedure, and who therefore are fully aware of all the facets of a case, will at times not fully present their case because they believe that the arbitrator is likewise familiar with the facts and issues. Unless prehearing briefs are filed by the parties, it should be recognized that the arbitrator knows absolutely nothing about the case at the time of the hearing. It is the responsibility of the parties to educate him about the issues, the facts, the evidence, the arguments, and the relevant contractual clauses. Clearly, if the arbitration process is to have a significant positive value in the area of labor relations, the parties to the arbitration must discharge their obligations fully and conscientiously. Company and union representatives must be indefatigable in their efforts to prepare for the arbitration and must be absolutely thorough in the presentation of their case to the arbitrator.

Responsibilities of the Arbitrator

The arbitrator, of course, is the key man in the arbitration process. His is the cold responsibility for the decision in the case. He decides, for example, whether a discharged employee remains discharged or returns to work, which of two workers gets the better job, whether the company placed a correct rate on a new job, whether an employee worked outside his classification, whether the company rotated overtime correctly, or whether an employee forfeited his seniority under the contract. Indeed, one of the most important jobs a person can receive is the assignment by a company and a union to an arbitration case.

[9]Thus, the rules of the American Arbitration Association provide as follows: "The parties may offer such evidence as they desire and shall produce such additional evidence as the Arbitrator may deem necessary to an understanding and determination of the dispute. . . . The Arbitrator shall be the judge of the relevancy and materiality of the evidence offered and conformity to legal rules of evidence shall not be necessary." *Voluntary Labor Arbitration Rules* (New York: American Arbitration Association, 1965), p. 5.

In discharging his responsibilities, the arbitrator is expected to adhere to a strict code of ethics. His decision must be based squarely on the evidence and the facts presented to him. He must give full faith and credit to the language of the labor contract at the time of the case. It should be recognized by all concerned that the language of the labor agreement binds the company, the union, the employees, *and the arbitrator*. It is not within the scope of the arbitrator's authority to decide whether or not a particular contractual clause is wise or unwise, desirable or undesirable. His job is to apply the language of a labor contract as he finds it in a particular case. To follow any other course of action would not only be a breach of faith to the parties but would create mischief with the labor agreement. The arbitrator must regard the collective bargaining contract as a final authority and give it full respect. If a case goes against a party because of the language of the contract, the responsibility for this state of affairs lies not with the arbitrator but with the parties who negotiated the agreement.

If the language of the contract is clear-cut and unequivocal, the arbitrator's job is not too difficult. Under these circumstances, his award will favor the party whose position is sustained by the precise contractual language. Of course, there are not many cases of this type, since, if the language is clear-cut and precise, the dispute should not have gone to arbitration. It should have been resolved in the grievance procedure on the basis of the contractual language.

What complicates the arbitrator's problem is contractual language that is subject to different shades of meaning. That is, impartial people could find that the language involved may be reasonably interpreted in different ways. Under these circumstances, what is called "past practice" serves as the guide for construction of the ambiguous contractual language. (Past practice is the way the language has been applied in the past. Case No. 3 deals with the language and past practice problem.) The idea behind past practice is that both parties have knowledge of the practice and both expect that the practice will be honored as the basis of administration of the relevant contractual language. Thus, when the arbitrator is confronted with contractual language that is ambiguous, he will normally base his decision on the evidence demonstrating practice. However, if the language is unambiguous and unequivocal, and the practice conflicts with the clear-cut contractual language, the arbitrator will normally base his decision upon the language rather than the practice. That is, unequivocal contractual language supercedes practice when the two conflict.

Also, arbitrators generally recognize that past practice should not be used to restrict management in the changing of work methods required by changing conditions. Thus, past practice is normally not used to prevent management from changing work schedules, work assignments, work loads, job assignments, and the number of workers needed on the job. The key to such an arbitration principle is that changing conditions have made the practice obsolete. Of course, there may be written contractual language that would forbid the management's making such changes in work methods. Under these circumstances, the arbitrator's decision would be based upon the written contractual language; but past practice would not normally be used to block management action when conditions change. Despite these limitations, past practice is frequently used as the basis for arbitrator's decisions, particularly, as stated, when contractual language is subject to different shades of meaning.

Much has been said and written about the necessity of the arbitrator's being "fair" in his decision. A decision is fair only when it is based upon the evidence of a case and the accurate assessment of the relevant provisions of the labor agreement. Furthermore, fairness does not mean charity, compromise, or an attempt to please both sides. At times, a company and a union arbitrate a number of different grievances in one hearing. An arbitrator is not worthy of the confidence of the parties if he deliberately sets his mind to compromise or "split" the grievances. An arbitrator who is a "splitter" not only violates the ethics of his office, but causes untold confusion and damage to the parties. What companies and unions desire in arbitration is a clear-cut decision on each grievance, based upon the merits of each dispute; they do not want splitting. Compromise or "horse-trading" of grievances may be accomplished in the grievance procedure. However, once grievances are referred to arbitration, each and every one of them must be decided on its own merits. Clearly, a "split-the-difference" approach to arbitration can do irreparable harm to the parties, the collective bargaining contract, and the arbitration process. Companies and unions would quickly lose confidence in arbitration if cases were decided not upon their merits but upon the determination of the arbitrator to "even up" his awards.

In fact, before hearing a case, each arbitrator normally takes a solemn oath of office that he will decide the dispute on the evidence, free from any bias. Any arbitrator who transgresses this oath by striving to decide a case on a split-the-difference formula has absolutely no business serving as an arbitrator. A famous and respected baseball umpire once said he called them as he saw them. Even though umpiring a baseball game is quite different from arbitrating a labor dispute, and although the qualifications for baseball umpires are quite different from those for arbitrators in labor relations, the homely statement "call them as you see them" has real significance for arbitration of any kind of dispute.

Additional responsibilities and personal qualities are required in the person serving as an arbitrator. Not only must he be incorruptible, free from any bias, and aware of the principles of arbitration, but he must also have a deep and well-rounded understanding of labor relations. It takes more than honesty and integrity to serve effectively as an arbitrator. Arbitrators who are not trained in labor relations matters, even though they may be paragons of virtue, can cause irreparable damage to the parties by decisions that do violence to the collective bargaining contract.

At the hearing, the arbitrator should treat both sides with the dignity and the respect that is characteristic of the judicial process. He should be patient, sympathetic, and understanding. Experienced arbitrators do not take advantage of their office by being arrogant or domineering. Arbitrators who have a tendency to exaggerate their own importance should be aware of the fact that arbitration, although important, plays a distinctly minor role in the overall union–management relationship. The arbitrator should permit each side to the dispute the fullest opportunity to present all the evidence, witnesses, documents, and arguments that it desires. Experienced arbitrators frequently lean over backwards to permit the introduction of evidence that may or may not be relevant to the dispute. This procedure is better than a policy that could result in the suppression of vital information.

The arbitrator also has the responsibility of keeping the hearing moving. When he notes a deliberate or unconscious waste of time by either or both of the parties, he is obligated to take remedial action. This does not mean that the arbitrator should not permit recesses, coffee breaks, or the occasional telling of a humorous story; what it means is that the arbitrator earns part of his fee by conducting a fair, orderly, thorough, and speedy hearing. To this end, the arbitrator, while at all times demonstrating the qualities of patience and understanding, must remain in full *control* of the hearing. Anyone who unwittingly or by design attempts to take over the hearing must be dealt with courteously but firmly. Of course, if the arbitrator is not experienced, is unsure of himself, or for some reason cannot or will not make definite decisions, the hearing can get out of hand.

The arbitrator also has an obligation to the witnesses called upon to give testimony in the hearing. Even though they should be subject to searching examination, the arbitrator should make sure that they are treated in a courteous manner by the examining party, or by the arbitrator himself if he asks questions of witnesses to clarify a point. He should not permit witnesses to be "badgered" or insulted. Even in cross-examination, where the examining party has more leeway with witnesses than it does in direct examination, they should be treated with decorum.

Finally, the arbitrator has a responsibility to the parties relative to the award. Since one of the great advantages of arbitration is the comparatively fast disposition of disputes that it allows, the arbitrator has an obligation to get his decision into the hands of the parties rather quickly after the termination of the hearing. Unless unusual conditions are involved, such decisions should be forwarded to the parties in not more than 30 days after the ending of the hearing.[10] In discharge cases, the interests of the parties and the grievant may be best served by a decision rendered in about 15 days. Of course, when the parties elect to file post-hearing briefs, the 30-day limit starts from the date of the receipt of such briefs.

---

[10]Thus, the Federal Mediation and Conciliation Service expects arbitrators appointed under its jurisdiction to make their awards within ". . . thirty (30) days from the date of the closing of the hearing, or the receipt of a transcript and any post-hearing briefs . . . unless otherwise agreed upon by the parties or specified by law."

The award should be clear and to the point. There should be no question in the minds of the parties as to the exact character of the decision in the case. If the grievance is denied, the award should simply state that fact. Under these circumstances, some arbitrators in the decision also mention the contract provision or provisions that the company did not violate. For example, in a work-assignment case, the award might read as follows:

> The grievance of Mr. Elmer Beamish, Grievance No. 594, is denied on the basis that the company, under job description for Tool- and Die-makers, Class A, Code 286, and for Maintenance Men, Class A, Code 263, and without violating Article XVI of the Labor Agreement, may properly assign either category of employees to repair the classes of machinery in question in this case.

When a case is decided in favor of the union, the award should clearly and specifically direct the company to take action to bring it into compliance with the contract. In addition, to avoid any misunderstanding, the decision should require the action within a certain number of working days after the receipt of the award. For example, in a "bumping" case, the award might read as follows:

> Within three working days after the receipt of this award, the Company is directed to place the grievant, Reva Snodgrass, into the job of Spray Painter, Class "B," Labor Grade No. 7, and to make her whole for any financial loss that she suffered because of the refusal of the Company to permit her to roll into the aforementioned job on the grounds that the Company violated Article IX, Section 7, Paragraphs A and B of the Labor Agreement.

In addition to the incorporation of a clear award, the arbitrator is charged with the responsibility of writing an opinion to support his decision. Although technically opinions are not required to explain a decision, the fact is that arbitrators almost universally write an opinion. What is more important in this connection, companies and unions expect their arbitrators to write them, and agencies such as the Federal Mediation and Conciliation Service and the American Arbitration Association, which submit to companies and unions the names of arbitrators, likewise tacitly expect the arbitrator to write an opinion.

In the opinion, the arbitrator sets forth the basic issues of the case, the facts, the position and arguments of the parties, and the reasons for his decision. He deals with the evidence presented in the case as it relates to his decision. Arbitrators are frequently extraordinarily careful to deal in an exhaustive manner with each major argument and piece of evidence offered by the losing side. Patently, the arbitrator has an obligation to tell the losing side just why it lost the case. Since normally the losing side will be very disappointed with the decision, the arbitrator should at least indicate in a careful manner the reasons for the adverse ruling. This probably will not make the losing side feel any better, but at least an opinion that is carefully written and covers thoroughly the major arguments and areas of evidence will demonstrate that the character of an arbitration opinion is a guide to the amount of time, energy, and thought the arbitrator puts into the case.

Selection of the Arbitrator

After the parties decide to arbitrate a dispute, the problem of the selection of the arbitrator arises. To solve this problem, most labor agreements provide that the parties will select the arbitrator from a panel of names submitted by the Federal Mediation and Conciliation Service or the American Arbitration Association. When called upon by the parties to an arbitration, these agencies will supply the company and the union with a list of names, and the parties, in accordance with a mutually acceptable formula, will select the arbitrator from the list. Under some labor agreements, the Federal Mediation and Conciliation Service and the American Arbitration Association have the authority to select the arbitrator on a direct-appointment basis in the event that none of the names in the panel is acceptable.

The Federal Mediation and Conciliation Service is administered independently of the Department of Labor under a director appointed by the president of the United States. It maintains a steadily growing roster of experienced professional arbitrators, totalling approximately 1,100 names in 1972.[11] Consistent with the significant growth in arbitration volume in recent years, the requests it has received for approved panels of arbitrators have increased greatly over the past twenty years; in fiscal 1955, for example, the service received 1,240 such requests,[12] but in fiscal 1974, the parties to agreements sought panels on 15,445 occasions.[13] Upon the selection of the arbitrator, the service withdraws from active participation in the case, and the relationship thereafter is strictly between the parties and the arbitrator.

Unlike the FMCS, the American Arbitration Association is a private organization. In its formative years, it devoted itself almost exclusively to the promotion of commercial arbitration, but since 1937 its Industrial Arbitration Tribunal has become increasingly active in labor disputes. In addition to furnishing the parties with arbitrator-selection aid similar to that of the Mediation Service, it administers arbitration hearings in accordance with a number of formalized rules. The association's panel of available arbitrators currently contains about 1,500 names, although most of the work is actually done by fewer than 400 active arbitrators, and the heavy majority of these are exactly the same people as are listed on the FMCS national roster.

Other methods are utilized to select arbitrators. Some parties directly contact one of the almost 400 arbitrators listed in the membership directory

[11]*Monthly Labor Review*, November 1972, p. 16. About 60 percent of the professionals on this panel are lawyers or law professors. Thirty percent are college professors not in law schools. The remainder represent a mixed bag, with clergymen and consultants conspicuous within it.

[12]Federal Mediation and Conciliation Service, *Seventeenth Annual Report* (Washington, D.C.: Government Printing Office, 1965), p. 55.

[13]FMCS, *Twenty-Sixth Annual Report*, p. 48.

of the highly prestigious National Academy of Arbitrators, the major society of the profession and an organization to whose ranks only the most experienced of neutrals are admitted.[14] In some contracts, a person of unimpeachable integrity is designated to select an arbitrator. Under such arrangements, the parties have confidence that the person so designated will select a qualified arbitrator. Thus, under some labor agreements, a federal district judge, the president of a university, or a high-ranking public official will be called upon to appoint the neutral.

Regardless of the method, the majority of labor contracts provide some definite procedure for the appointment of the arbitrator. At times, companies and unions find that in practice they cannot agree on any arbitrator when the contract merely states that an arbitrator "mutually acceptable" to the parties will decide the dispute. It is sound procedure to incorporate some method for the selection of arbitrators by an outside agency when the parties are unable or unwilling to agree on a neutral on a mutual-acceptance basis.

Some companies and unions solve the problem of selection by appointing a permanent arbitrator under the terms of a labor agreement. Under this arrangement, one person will decide each dispute that is arbitrated. However, companies and unions are not in agreement on the use of a permanent arbitrator as against the ad hoc method of selection, in which a different arbitrator may be chosen for each case. Some companies and unions, as a matter of policy, will use a different arbitrator for each dispute; others find it a better practice to use the same arbitrator. The permanent arbitrator is used most frequently when a company has a number of different plants. Such a procedure makes for uniformity of labor policy within the different operating units of the enterprise. Although the permanent arbitrator is not used as frequently in single-plant situations, there is now also a growing tendency for single-plant companies and their unions to use this system.

Actually, there are advantages and disadvantages to each method. Perhaps the chief argument in favor of the ad hoc method is that the parties will not be "stuck" with an arbitrator whom they do not want. The parties can simply dispense with him if he proves incompetent or otherwise unqualified, even though it appears unlikely that a company and a union would have selected such a person to arbitrate on a permanent basis in the first place. Balancing the chief advantage of the ad hoc system are several disadvantages. The time and effort required to select an arbitrator for each case delays the rapid disposition of the grievance, sometimes to the detriment of plant morale. At times, out of desperation, a person who has little or no experience or real qualifications is selected to serve as an arbitrator. Such a choice may be made because he is the only person available who has not handed down an award somewhere at some time that the company and the union do not like. Moreover, because each new arbitrator must be educated as to the local con-

---

[14]Most of the academy's members are also registered with the Mediation Service and AAA, and can be engaged by the parties on this basis as well.

ditions, a comparatively long period may sometimes be required to conduct the hearing.

Perhaps the chief disadvantage of ad hoc arbitration, however, is the fact that this method does not assure consistency in decisions or the application of uniform principles to contract construction. No arbitrator is bound by any other arbitrator's decisions or principles of contractual construction. Consequently, disputes involving fundamentally the same issues could be resolved in as many different ways as there are arbitrators chosen to decide cases. Thus, there is no assurance that a particular decision will bring stability to labor relations. It may have precedent value only until the next time the issues involved in the case are tested before another arbitrator.

The latter consideration indicates the greatest advantage of the selection of permanent arbitrators. The parties have the assurance of consistency and uniformity of decisions and consistent contractual interpretation. As a result, precedent will be established, the parties will know what to expect, and cases dealing with essentially the same issues as contained in a grievance previously decided in arbitration can be settled in the earlier stages of the grievance procedure. In addition, the permanent arbitrator becomes familiar with the labor agreement, the technology of the plant, and the "shop language." This means that cases can frequently be expedited much more effectively than under circumstances of ad hoc arbitration.

Perhaps the chief disadvantage of the permanent selection method is that the parties involved may tend to arbitrate more disputes than are absolutely necessary, rather than first exhausting the possibilities of settling them in the grievance procedure. This is particularly true when the arbitrator is paid a set fee for a year and has the obligation to arbitrate any and all cases submitted to him.

This possibility, of course, is a serious charge against the permanent selection method. As stated before, arbitration should be employed only after the parties have honestly exhausted every possibility of settling disputes in the grievance procedure. One method that might be effective in obtaining the advantages of the permanent method without incurring the possible disadvantages of excessive arbitration would be to compensate the permanent arbitrator on a per diem or a per case basis, rather than on an annual-fee basis. In the last analysis, however, the amount of arbitration needed by a company and a union depends upon the attitudes of the parties rather than on the method of selection or the procedure of payment.

ARBITRATION COSTS
AND TIME LAG

In recent years, arbitration has been criticized as being unduly expensive and involving too much time, but beyond these two criticisms the process has always been criticized for other reasons. Parties complain when they lose a case that they believe should have been decided in their favor. This criticism may not have much validity, but justified censure involves an arbitrator who ignores unambiguous contractual language and thereby rewrites the labor agreement. At times, opinions are confusing, leading to unnecessary discord between the parties; and, indeed, there are instances where the opinion does not even reflect the award. As one dissatisfied party has said, "We won everything except the decision." Some times arbitrators include so-called "dicta" (gratuitous remarks not required for a decision in a case) in their opinions, which could lead to serious problems the next time a labor agreement is negotiated. And, obviously, it is understandable why the losing side believes it has been treated unjustly when the arbitrator does not conduct a fair and impartial hearing, or fails to deal with major arguments, or ignores material evidence.

However, the most vocal criticism recently has pertained to the costs and the delays associated with arbitration. Even though alternatives to arbitration—a strike or court enforcement of a labor agreement—would be far more expensive, arbitration costs, at least on the surface, appear to be quite high. For fiscal 1974, the Federal Mediation and Conciliation Service reported that the arbitrators who served under its jurisdiction charged an average of $180.72 per day. The average cost per case for that year amounted to $601.33, normally shared equally between the parties. This figure included not only the charge for the hearing day and the arbitrator's expenses (travel, hotel, meals), but also payment for the time he devoted to the analysis of the evidence and the writing of his opinion.[15] Beyond the fee and expenses of the arbitrator, there are other costs. Some parties use lawyers, and also may have a stenographic transcript prepared of the proceedings,[16] and there is the payment of plant personnel on both sides who take part in the arbitration hearing.

There are ways to cut arbitration costs. Grievances that are of minimal importance to the parties, particularly those that go to arbitration for political and tactical purposes, should be eliminated from the process. Other suggestions include the use of local arbitrators to save on expenses, elimination of the transcript and attorneys when they are not necessary, and the consolidation of grievances of the same type to be determined in one hearing. To reduce costs, the parties may instruct their arbitrators not to write an opinion but merely to issue an award. The writing of an opinion takes considerable time, even after the arbitrator has carefully reviewed the evidence and has reached a decision. Of course, there is genuine value in a carefully written opinion, as pointed out earlier, but there are cases where the merit of cost saving outweighs the advantages of an opinion.

[15] FMCS, *Twenty-Sixth Annual Report*, p. 48.
[16] At times, the cost of a transcript and lawyer's fees by far exceed the charge of the arbitrator.

One delay is not attributable to arbitrators or the process but to dilatory tactics of the parties. This involves the time before arbitration is requested on a grievance. For example, recently one of the present authors handled a case in which three years had elapsed before the parties invoked the arbitration process. Such an incredible delay is not usual, but grievances commonly vegetate for many months before the parties decide to take them into arbitration. The time-lag criticism properly starts from the point at which the parties request arbitration. For 1974, the Federal Mediation and Conciliation Service reported that, on the average, 173 days elapsed from the time the parties requested a panel of arbitrators until the award was issued.[17] This is far too long, and the parties understandably wonder if in fact the process really constitutes a viable forum for the disposition of grievances in arbitration. One consequence of the delay is the lowering of the morale in the plant, in the same way that the morale of students suffers when their teachers take far too long in returning examination papers. Employees grow impatient waiting for the award; their resentment could have an adverse impact on the quantity and quality of their work, and, frequently, they badger their union representatives about the problem. Employers could also suffer a large financial loss (should they lose their case) if the arbitrator directs a monetary remedy for a contractual violation.

One way to deal with the time problem is for the parties to use comparatively new arbitrators rather than requesting the services of so-called "mainline," or veteran, arbitrators. Since the latter group receives the lion's share of the cases, its members may be unable to provide prompt hearing dates. Indeed, in fiscal 1974, the FMCS reported that 67 days elapsed between the time an arbitrator was appointed and the day of the hearing. It follows that arbitrators with small case loads might be able to offer more prompt hearing dates. The problem, of course, is to convince the parties to use new arbitrators rather than those with considerable experience. It is true that there is no substitute for experience, but it is equally true that new arbitrators could be just as qualified as those who have been in the profession for many years and who have handled a great number of cases. Many veteran arbitrators would agree with this, and encourage employers and unions to provide opportunities for the comparatively newer arbitrators. In the last analysis, however, the decision to use new arbitrators rests with the parties, since, as we know, the arbitrator must be acceptable to both sides of a case.

To avoid the delay associated with the use of arbitrators from the FMCS or the AAA, a growing number of employers and unions are making use of a *permanent panel* of arbitrators. That is, they choose a number (seven is perhaps modal) of arbitrators when they negotiate the labor agreement; when grievances are ready to be arbitrated, one of the members of the panel is selected through some agreed-upon procedure. This could save considerable time, since the use of the traditional agencies for the selection of arbi-

---

[17]FMCS, *Twenty-Sixth Annual Report*, p. 48.

trators necessitates some delay: A letter goes from the parties to the Federal Mediation and Conciliation Service or the American Arbitration Association; the agency then sends a panel of arbitrators to the parties; additional time elapses while the parties decide which one of the arbitrators on the panel is to be used; then they write the appointing agency of the choice; the agency notifies the arbitrator; and then the arbitrator must write the parties to arrange a hearing date. For fiscal 1974, the FMCS reported that 54 days elapsed between the time a request for arbitration was made to the agency and the appointment of the arbitrator. By the use of the permanent panel, most of this delay is avoided. A telephone call or a single letter sent directly to the selected arbitrator is all that is needed.

Not only could costs be reduced by relieving the arbitrator of the responsibility of writing an opinion, but the same practice is a time saver. To reduce the time lag, stenographic transcripts of the proceedings and post-hearing briefs could be eliminated. (Indeed, one of the authors is currently serving on a permanent panel of arbitrators of a major airline and a labor organization, and by contractual agreement transcripts and post-hearing briefs are expressly prohibited.) Transcripts and post-hearing briefs delay the process; it is not unusual to wait a month or longer for a transcript, and then another month for the briefs. In the "normal" case, these are not really needed. The arbitrator simply takes his own notes at the hearing and provides the opportunity to the parties to offer an oral argument at the close of the hearing. To be fair about it, however, there are some cases where a transcript is valuable, and a post-hearing brief could be helpful to the arbitrator in reaching his decision.

Finally, there is the matter of the dilatory arbitrator. As stated before, it is customary, and indeed directed by the FMCS and the AAA, that an arbitrator's decision is due 30 days after the close of the hearing or the filing of post-hearing briefs. Unfortunately, there are arbitrators who take much longer than this allowed time—chiefly because they are handling so many cases that they cannot meet this deadline.

Mini-Arbitration

First started in the basic steel industry in 1971, "mini-" or expedited arbitration has been adopted by other employers and unions, including (in 1974) the U.S. Postal Service and the postal labor organizations. The chief value of the mini-arbitration process is the sharp reduction of the time element and costs. Under the steel plan, the hearing must be held within ten days after the appeal to arbitration is made, and the arbitrator's decision must be made within 48 hours after the close of the hearing. No transcripts or briefs are permitted, and the arbitrator is expected to provide the parties with a short but precise award.[18] Costs are also much lower than in regular arbi-

---

[18]Ben Fischer, "Arbitration: The Steel Industry Experiment," *Monthly Labor Review*, November 1972, p. 9.

tration. A fee is paid only for the hearing day, and this fee is only about $25 to $75 for each party per case.

To provide for such rapid service at an economical charge, the steel corporations and the United Steelworkers of America use a battery of about 200 inexperienced arbitrators, including a significant number of blacks and women. The panel includes relatively young lawyers or a local university's faculty. One advantage of the new process, therefore, is to train new arbitrators. It is said:

> The experimental procedure in steel will increase the flow of new blood into the field because of the instant experience the new steel practice permits. It is a kind of "throw him in the pool" method of teaching swimming, except that the parallel is inexact in that each panel name comes to arbitrate with significant credentials based on background, general competence, and interest.[19]

Indeed, this spin-off from the mini process is of significant value to arbitration. W.J. Usery, Jr., Secretary of Labor, has warned:

> The ranks of active arbitrators are dwindling because of retirement and deaths and are not being refilled by younger, acceptable arbitrators.[20]

Not all cases, however, are disposed of in the mini-process—only, in general, those of the more simple and routine type—with the regular arbitration process still being used for those cases of difficult nature and representing substantial interest to the parties. In addition, either the employer or the union may demand that a case go through the regular arbitration process. Under the steel plan, for example:

> Union district staff representatives or corporate headquarters representatives may veto the local demand to refer a case to the expedited procedure, thereby requiring handling through the grievance procedure and regular arbitration.[21]

In any event, the mini-procedure has worked successfully, at least with the steel industry.[22] Hundreds of cases have been resolved, and the parties continued the process in the 1974 labor agreement. Undoubtedly, there is a place for mini-arbitration within a system of labor relations. It provides a swift and economical forum for the determination of grievances that are well

[19]*Ibid.*, p. 9.

[20]W.J. Usery, Jr., "Some Attempts to Reduce Arbitration Costs and Delays," *Monthly Labor Review*, November 1972, p. 4.

[21]Fischer, "Arbitration," p. 9.

[22]See "Swift Justice on the Job: Expedited Arbitration Works," AFL-CIO, Industrial Union Department, *Viewpoint*, Vol. 4, No. 3 (1974), p. 31. The writer states, "Two and a half years of experience have demonstrated that the expedited system works well. It has helped alleviate some clogged grievance situations. It has improved the reputation of arbitration at the plants where it has been used most. It has aided the grievance procedure's efficiency in a number of plants by providing a means of prompt resolution of grievance disputes."

within the capability of inexperienced arbitrators. It is more than likely that the process will spread throughout the nation. The most difficult problem is to determine which grievances should go the mini and which the regular arbitration route; but this problem is not insoluble, since skilled and mature labor relations representatives on both sides can easily spot those grievances that can best be handled through the expedited procedure.

DISCUSSION QUESTIONS

1. Barbash has offered his opinion that the "handling of workers' grievances on the job is perhaps the single most important function of modern unionism." What considerations might have led to such a statement?

2. It is generally agreed that a low grievance rate does not necessarily prove the existence of good union–management relations, and that a high grievance rate does not necessarily prove the existence of poor relations between the parties. Why might the grievance statistics be misleading as a guide to the quality of the relationship?

3. From the company's viewpoint, what advantages and disadvantages might there be in reducing a grievance to writing?

4. Harold W. Davey has argued that "a genuine grievance requires an airing, even if it is not strictly in order under the existing contract." What considerations, again from the company's point of view, might justify this opinion?

5. Why might (a) a company or (b) a union prefer *not* to have an arbitration provision in the contract?

6. Dunlop and Healy have pointed out that although it is often said that "arbitration is an extension of collective bargaining," it is also frequently held that "arbitration is a judicial process." What are your own feelings regarding these two apparently inconsistent descriptions?

7. Given the fact that arbitrators have no compulsion to follow any other arbitrator's award or line of reasoning, how do you account for the fact that there are available at least three widely distributed publications that feature arbitration awards from all over the country? On the surface, would it not appear that such publications are a waste of time and money, since each arbitrator is in effect a law unto himself?

8. How could the present system of labor contract administration, as described in general terms in this chapter, be improved?

SELECTED REFERENCES

BAER, WALTER E., *Practice and Precedent in Labor Relations*. Lexington, Mass.: Heath, 1972.

ELKOURI, FRANK, and EDNA ELKOURI, *How Arbitration Works*. Washington, D.C.: Bureau of National Affairs, Inc., 1973.

FLEMING, R. W., *The Labor Arbitration Process*. Urbana, Ill.: University of Illinois Press, 1965.

PRASOW, PAUL, and EDWARD PETERS, *Arbitration and Collective Bargaining*. New York: McGraw-Hill, 1970.

SLICHTER, SUMNER H., JAMES J. HEALY, and E. ROBERT LIVERNASH, *The Impact of Collective Bargaining on Management*, pp. 692–806. Washington, D.C.: The Brookings Institution, 1960.

SMITH, RUSSELL A., "The Question of 'Arbitrability'—The Roles of the Arbitrator, the Court, and the Parties," *Southwestern Law Journal*, XVI (April 1962), 1–42.
STONE, MORRIS, *Labor Grievances and Decisions*. New York: Harper & Row, 1965.
————, *Labor–Management Contracts at Work*. New York: Harper & Row, 1961.
TROTTA, MAURICE S., *Labor Arbitration*. New York: Simmons-Boardman, 1961.
WITTE, EDWIN E., *Historical Survey of Labor Arbitration*. Philadelphia: University of Pennsylvania Press, 1952.

As in the eleven other cases that follow in subsequent chapters, the three arbitration cases below are drawn from the authors' own experiences. They demonstrate actual disputes; but since arbitration is a confidential process, the names of the parties and the witnesses have been replaced by initial letters.

Students are urged to read the cases. A great deal can be learned, by faithful study of them, about the dynamics of practical labor relations. The cases provide an insight into the day-to-day disputes that are appealed to arbitration, and they show how a typical arbitrator handles cases submitted to him. Whether or not you agree with the arbitrator is not really important. Rather, the value is to see how arbitrators apply and interpret contractual language, evaluate evidence, and defend their decisions with arguments.

If you desire to read additional arbitration cases, they are available from the Bureau of National Affairs, Labor Arbitration Reports; and Commerce Clearing House, Labor Arbitration Awards. These services have been published for many years, and contain thousands of actual arbitration cases. (In keeping with the confidentiality of the process, the employer and union involved must agree to publication.) The published cases represent only a small percentage of the cases decided by arbitrators; the vast majority are found only in the private files of the arbitrators and the parties.

Each of the fourteen illustrative cases in this textbook is found at the end of the chapter in which the reference to the case is made, and each contains questions to increase your understanding of the dispute.

The first two cases deal with the arbitrability of grievances. In both cases, the employers argued that the grievances should not be decided on the merits because they were not processed in a timely manner in the grievance procedure. In cases of this sort—where arbitrability is involved—the arbitrator must first determine whether or not the grievance is arbitrable under the contract. If he finds that it is not, he will deny it on that basis and make no determination as to the merits of the employee's complaint. If he makes a prior determination that the grievance is arbitrable, he will make a decision on the merits.

Since the same arbitrator reached different conclusions on the arbitrability issue in the two cases, you may speculate as to whether or not his reasoning was consistent in the two disputes.

CASE 1
Arbitrability of a Grievance:
A Case of an Indefinite Answer

Cast of Characters

N   Grievant
L   Her direct supervisor
G   Vice-president of company
M   President of union
T   Company attorney

(*A "Cast of Characters" in this form is, of course, not contained in arbitration cases. It appears here to aid the student in the reading of the cases, since the names of the witnesses have been deleted and initials used.*)

This dispute involved the issue of sick leave pay under the labor agreement. After N had a nine-day illness in June 1974, the company paid her only a half day's sick leave pay. In protest, she filed a grievance, dated August 13, 1974.

Relevant to the dispute were the following provisions of the labor agreement:

ARTICLE X   GRIEVANCE PROCEDURE

Step 1.   The aggrieved employee or the Union Steward initiating the grievance shall attempt to discuss the grievance with the Supervisor of the employee within five (5) working days following the occurrence of the grievance. If the aggrieved is an employee, the Union Steward shall be provided with an opportunity to be present when the grievance is discussed with the Employer's representative.

Step 2.   If the grievant and the Union do not receive a satisfactory resolution within five (5) working days thereafter, the grievance shall be reduced to writing on such fifth day and the Union shall present the written grievance to the person from time to time specified by the Employer. The Employer shall respond in writing to the Union within five days after receipt of the written grievance.

[*Section 4.*]   Failure on the part of the grievant or the Union to comply with the time limits set forth above shall constitute a dropping of the grievance and there shall be no duty to process the matter further.

The basic questions in this case were as follows:

1. Is the grievance arbitrable on its merits?
2. If the grievance is arbitrable on its merits, did the company violate the labor agreement? If so, what should the remedy be?

BACKGROUND

On June 22, 1974, the grievant returned to work after a nine-day illness. In the payroll period ending June 23, she was given a half day's sick-leave pay. She received her paycheck, including the sick leave pay, on June 26, and on this day she complained about her sick pay to L, her immediate supervisor. The grievant believed that she should have received five days' sick leave pay, and she made her position known to her supervisor.

G, vice-president of the company, testified that on June 26, L brought the grievant's complaint to his attention. The vice-president affirmed that he spoke only to L on June 26, not to the grievant.

M, president of the union, testified that on June 26, he phoned G concerning the problem of the grievant's complaint. As a result of this phone conversation, a meeting was held on June 30. As to this meeting, M testified:

> We discussed the problem, and G said we were going into the holiday season, and that he would get her [the grievant's] records and see when her last sick leave was, and that then the company would give us an answer.

M also testified that another meeting was held in the middle of July, at which G stated that "he had no time to go over this with L, and he said there would be no problem on this."

However, during the July meeting, M testified, a company representative phoned the company attorney, T, and reported to the people attending the meeting the results of the phone conversation. M declared:

> We were told that the company attorney stated that no sick leave pay should be paid anybody except as starting on November 9, 1972, the effective date of the contract.

After receiving this information, M testified, he asked G what the union should do about the grievant's complaint. He testified that G said, "Let the lawyers talk about it, and then we will meet and resolve the grievance."

On August 12, 1974, M declared, he again discussed the complaint with G, and was told by the vice-president that the company would pay the grievant only one-half day's sick pay, and that he should reduce the grievance to writing. G confirmed this testimony.

POSITION OF THE PARTIES

The position of the company was that the grievance was not arbitrable on its merits, since a written grievance was not filed in accordance with the time limits specified under Article X, Step 2, of the grievance procedure. In addition, the company position was that the grievance had no merit under the sick leave provision of the labor agreement even if it were found that the grievance *was* arbitrable on its merits. In contrast, the union position was that the grievance was arbitrable and that it had merit under the sick leave provision of the contract.

THE ISSUE OF ARBITRABILITY

The grievant discussed her complaint with L, her immediate supervisor, on June 26, the date upon which she received her pay check that included the one-half day's sick pay. She protested to her supervisor that she was entitled to five days' sick pay, but it was not until August 13 that she filed a written grievance. On this basis, the company argued that the grievance was not filed in time under Step 2 of the grievance procedure, which said that a grievance must be reduced to writing within five working days "if the grievant and the Union do not receive a satisfactory resolution. . . ."

Since more than five working days elapsed between the day when the grievant orally complained and the date upon which she filed her written grievance, the company urged that the grievance be dropped under Article X, Section 4, of the labor agreement.

In this regard, company counsel argued:

Satisfactory resolution of the grievance was obviously *not* received by the Union and the Grievant on such fifth day. Otherwise, why are we here? Thus, the Grievant and the Union were compelled under Step 2 of the grievance procedure to reduce the grievance to writing at that time.

Consequently, the grievance procedure as set forth in the contract must be adhered to and the only matter relative thereto that can be considered by the arbitrator is whether or not that specific procedure was complied with.

The procedure is clear; it was not adhered to; the grievance was dropped under Article X(4); and the grievance is not arbitrable.

The facts leading to the above conclusions are not in dispute.

For the foregoing reasons, the grievance should be dismissed.

The arbitrator's decision included the following statements:

Even though the Company argument is correct as far as it goes, it ignores one basic fact: *The Union and the Grievant did not receive a definite answer from the Company until August 12.*

Note the undisputed facts as testified to by Union President M during the time period under consideration. On June 30, M met with G about the problem under dispute. In this meeting, he was told that G would investigate the sick leave pay record of the Grievant and that *he would give the Union an answer.* What else should the Union believe except that the Company was considering the complaint and would give an answer that might possibly be favorable to the Grievant? Certainly, in the June 30 meeting, the Company did not categorically state that the Grievant's complaint was denied. It was open for further investigation. Since this was the case, why should the Union have filed a written grievance?

Step 2 states that the grievance must be reduced to writing in five working days if the Grievant and the Union do not receive a "satisfactory resolution." Although it is true that the Union did not receive a satisfactory resolution within five days after June 26, it is equally true that in the meeting of June 30, the Union did not receive an *unsatisfactory* resolution of the grievance. The silence of the Company during this five-day period could not possibly be construed by the Union as a denial of the grievance. All that the Union knew was what was told to it by the Company. What the Company told the Union was that the matter would be investigated, and an answer provided the Union.

In the June 30 meeting, the Company did not deny the employee's grievance. Instead, it agreed to investigate the facts, and report back to the Union. To hold that under these circumstances the Union forfeited the grievance under Step 2 of the Grievance Procedure does not appear proper or realistic to this Arbitrator. The Union took the Company at its word, and waited for its answer.

The Union had received no answer by the middle of July and another meeting between the parties took place. Even in this meeting, and despite the counsel of its attorney, the Company again did not categorically deny the employee's complaint. Note the unrefuted testimony of M in this regard: "I asked G what to do about the Grievant's complaint. He said, "Let the lawyers talk about it, and then we will meet to resolve the grievance."

Once again, the Company gave no categorical answer to the employee's complaint, which she orally lodged on June 26. Her complaint was not granted, nor was it denied. If it is argued that here the Company did not give her a *satisfactory resolution*, it is equally true that the Company did not give her an *unsatisfactory resolution*. The matter was still open—the Company's position was not certain—subject to further discussion: "... *then we will meet to resolve the grievance*." [Emphasis supplied.]

It was not until August 12 that the Company categorically denied the grievance, and on the next day the Union filed the written grievance. Until this time, the Company had vacillated and had given no definite answer. Hence, in the light of the Company's posture, the Union had no need to file a written grievance. Until August 12, the Company did not give the Union an *unsatisfactory resolution* to the complaint.

In the past, the Arbitrator has denied grievances wherein a union has not complied with the time limits under a contract. In this regard, the Arbitrator recognizes that clearly defined time limits are to be respected by a labor organization or it faces forfeiture of the grievance. The Arbitrator also understands that many arbitrators have underscored this principle. In the instant case, however, a masterpiece of error would be committed if the Arbitrator held that the Union violated the time limits spelled out in Step 2 of the Grievance Procedure. The circumstances of this case are that the Company failed to provide the Union with a clear-cut answer to the Grievant's complaint until August 12.

In effect, what the Company wants the Arbitrator to do is to apply the language of Step 2 independently and separately from the circumstances of the case.

This would be strictly improper, since, when the conduct of the Company is considered, the Arbitrator is fully satisfied that the Union did not forfeit the grievance under Step 2 of the Grievance Procedure.

After the arbitrator held that the grievance was arbitrable on its merits, he proceeded to determine whether or not the grievant was entitled to additional sick leave pay. After consideration of the evidence and the material contractual language, he granted her five more days. Since the purpose of this case is to illustrate the arbitrability issue, there is no need to present this portion of the case. Of course, the arbitrator could have denied the grievance on its merits even though he held the grievance to be arbitrable.

QUESTIONS

1. Suppose that the company had refused to arbitrate this case, and that the union had gone to federal court requesting an order to direct arbitration. In the light of your understanding of *Warrior & Gulf*, state what you believe the court would have done. Why?

2. Construct a set of facts (other than what actually prevailed in this case) dealing with the meeting of June 30 that would have made the grievance not arbitrable.

3. Given the facts of the case, could you argue with merit that the grievance was not arbitrable on the grounds that in the meetings of June 30 and the middle of July, the union did not receive a "satisfactory resolution" of the grievance within the meaning of Article X, Step 2, of the grievance procedure?

4. Suppose the arbitrator had denied the grievance and the union had gone to court with a request that the court reverse the arbitrator's decision and grant the grievance. In the light of your understanding of *Enterprise Wheel*, what do you believe the court would have done? Why?

CASE 2
Arbitrability of a Grievance:
A Case of a Discharged Employee

Cast of Characters

L	Discharged employee
S	Company attorney
P	Union staff representative
B	Personnel administrator
R	Chairman, union grievance committee
M	Plant manager
J	Doctor visited by discharged employee
A	Industrial relations manager
O	Former staff representative

Effective August 31, 1973, the company discharged L, and on September 3, the union filed the following grievance on his behalf:

> The above employee was wrongfully discharged from his job. . . . The working agreement between the Company and the Union provides better protection than the Company action. . . . The Union demands that the Company pay for all lost time and no loss in seniority.

In denying the grievance on September 8, the company stated:

> In Mr. L's case, every effort was made by the Company to contact him and determine the nature of his illness. A registered letter was sent to him on August 18, in which we informed Mr. L that unless he contacts the Company no later than August 27, he will leave the Company no alternative but to terminate him. Mr. L did not deem it necessary to notify the Company of any details pertaining to his illness to the present date, and consequently, he was terminated on August 31.

Relevant to the dispute were the following provisions of the labor agreement:

ARTICLE 3

Section 1. Except as otherwise specifically provided in this Agreement, the management of the business of the Company and the direction of its employees, including the right to hire, transfer, promote, suspend or discharge for proper cause, to relieve employees from duty because of lack of work, and to maintain discipline and efficiency of employees, shall be vested exclusively in the Company, provided that claims of wrongful promotions and of wrong and unjust discipline shall be subject to the grievance procedure.

ARTICLE 5

Section 2. If, at any time during the grievance, the time periods specified in Section 4, Steps 2, 3 and 4, have elapsed and the next steps have not been taken by the grievant, the Union or the Company, then the grievance shall be considered to have been disposed of, as per the last decision rendered.

Section 4, Step 2: The Grievance Committee or their representative will present the grievance to the Personnel Office within two (2) working days after the Foreman has rendered his decision. Such grievance will be in writing on a regular form provided by the Union and will be addressed to the Plant Manager or his representative and given to the Personnel Department.

Such grievance shall contain a simple statement of facts giving rise to the grievance. Within three (3) working days of receipt of the written grievance by the Personnel Department, a meeting shall be scheduled between the Grievance Committee and the Personnel Director. The Personnel Director or his representative shall answer the grievance in writing within four (4) working days after receipt of the written grievance. The aggrieved employee may be called in by either party. The Personnel Director or his representative shall prepare a written statement of his disposition of the grievance and submit it to the Grievance Committee Chairman within two (2) working days after such hearing.

Step 3: In the event no agreement is reached, the International Union, within ten (10) working days after the Personnel Director's decision, may request a meeting between management, the Shop Grievance Committee and a representative of the International Union. The Company must set a date for such meeting within three (3) working days after such request, and within five (5) working days after such meeting, a written decision will be sent to the International.

Step 4: If the grievance has not been settled, either the Union or management may indicate a desire to arbitrate by written notice to the other party within fifteen (15) calendar days after all prior steps have been taken. Within ten (10) calendar days from the receipt of said notice, an arbitrator shall be selected from a list of five (5) arbitrators submitted by the Federal Mediation and Conciliation Service. . . . However, said arbitrator shall have no power to add to, subtract from or modify any of the terms of this Agreement. The decision of the arbitrator shall be binding upon the Company, the employees and the Union.

Section 8. The Company may discharge any employee, and shall, upon discharge, notify the Shop Committee Chairman within one (1) working day of said discharge. The discharged employee, the Steward or the Committeeman may file a grievance within five (5) working days from the date of discharge, and such grievance shall be presented under Step 2 of the Grievance Procedure.

ARTICLE 7

Section 11. The Company shall recall an employee by sending him a notice by Certified Mail, return receipt requested, or by telegram, to the last known address of such employee. It shall be the responsibility of the employee to keep the Company advised in writing of his correct address. An employee so notified must report for work within three (3) working days of the specified return date, unless reasonable excuse for failure to report for work has been given to the Company, in writing.

Section 12. Sick Leave of Absence will be granted upon written request substantiated by a Doctor's Certificate stating the reason and expected duration of such leave. Renewal of the Leave will be granted upon written request substantiated by a Doctor's Certificate. An employee returning from sick leave of absence will be reinstated upon presentation of a Doctor's release issued within five (5) days from the date of reinstatement.

As will be developed below, there were two basic questions to be determined in this arbitration. The company claimed that the grievance was not arbitrable on its merits because time limits established in the grievance procedure had elapsed. On this issue, S, company counsel, argued:

Based on these undisputed facts adduced at the Hearing in this case, the Employer respectfully submits that, because of the Union's inexcusable failure to abide by the mandatory time requirements contained in the grievance and arbitration procedures of the relevant Collective Bargaining Agreement, the grievance in this case is not arbitrable and should not be considered on its merits by the Arbitrator. Accordingly, the grievance must be denied.

As to the issue of time limits, P, staff representative, stated:

> Mr. Arbitrator, I am going to leave the decision of the timeliness up to you as far as my opening statement is concerned, because I was not here at the time the grievance was filed and at the time it was allegedly untimely. I may just make a worse mess of it than it is presently in. So I will just make an opening statement based on the discharge itself.

As to the merits of the discharge, the company contended that the conduct of the grievant warranted discharge, and the union argued to the contrary.

On these grounds, the arbitrator was compelled to decide the issue of arbitrability before he proceeded to the merits of the discharge. If he were to determine that the grievance was forfeit on the basis of time limits, he would be required to dismiss it on this basis without inquiry into the merits of the discharge. On the other hand, if he were to determine that the union and/or the grievant complied with the time limits established in the grievance procedure, the arbitrator would then decide whether or not under the circumstances of this case the discharge was for proper cause.

In this light, the basic questions to be determined in this arbitration were as follows:

> **1.** Did the union and/or the grievant comply with the time limits established in the grievance procedure?
> **2.** If the preceding determination is in the affirmative, the question is whether or not the company discharged the grievant for proper cause. If the discharge was not for proper cause, what should the remedy be?

BACKGROUND

At the time of his discharge, L was classified as a furnace melter, and he had previously established about 11 years of seniority with the company. Also, at the time of his discharge, he was on the union's grievance committee and served as the treasurer of the union.

Reason for Discharge

In April 1973, the grievant bid on the furnace-melter job, and was awarded it by the company. On August 3, 1973, the company suspended the grievant for three days, from August 4 through August 6, because of excessive absenteeism. However, the company did not discharge him for excessive absenteeism. When evidence demonstrating the absenteeism record of the grievant was offered, the union representative stated:

> Mr. Arbitrator, I would have to object to this, because Mr. L was not discharged for absenteeism as his discharge document states. He was discharged for not obtaining a leave of absence.

As to the specific reason for the discharge, the company attorney's testimony was as follows:

Arbitrator: Now, specifically you discharged the man because he was absent without leave. Is that your position?

S: That is correct.

Arbitrator: He was absent for a certain period of time, which I imagine will be developed in the record, and he did not apply for a medical leave?

S: Correct.

Arbitrator: And this is to show his absenteeism record immediate prior to his discharge?

S: Immediately prior to his discharge.

Arbitrator: But you didn't discharge him for absenteeism, did you?

S: We didn't discharge him for absenteeism. . . .

In short, the record demonstrates that the grievant was not discharged for excessive absenteeism; he was discharged because the company alleged that he was absent from work for a certain period of time without applying for a medical leave of absence. In this light, if the grievance were found to be properly before the arbitrator for a determination on its merits, the grievant's overall absentee record would not be material.

Events after Suspension

The grievant's suspension ended on Friday, August 6. On Monday, August 9, the grievant phoned B, personnel administrator, to advise the company that he was sick and would not report to work. On this point, the grievant testified:

Q: Mr. L, I know we have gone over this quite a bit, but I think we should put it in the record. Did you call in to state, to give reason for your inability to return to work?

A: I called in to report that I was sick.

As to this phone call, B's testimony was as follows:

Q: Do you recall, in this case, Mr. L calling you sometime in August and telling you he was ill?

A: Yes.

Q: Would you explain to us what took place during that conversation?

A: Mr. L called and said that he was ill. I asked him what were the problems. He said back problem. I asked him how long he would be gone and he didn't know.

Q: Did you have occasion to mail anything to Mr. L after your conversation with him, at which time he told you he was ill and did not know when he would recover?

A: I told him I would send him the [medical leave] forms.

Q: Did you mail these forms?

A: Yes.

She also testified that, as a routine matter, medical leave forms were mailed to employees who were ill and not certain as to when they would return to work. In the case at hand, B testified that she mailed the medical leave forms to the grievant with a self-addressed return envelope. This mailing, however, did not contain a letter to the grievant. It included only the medical leave forms and return envelope. B also testified that she had obtained the grievant's address from the company's current employee address file.

As to the return of the medical leave forms sent to L, B testified:

Q: To your knowledge, was that [return] envelope and its contents ever returned to the company?

A: No.

With respect to the initial phone conversation he had had with B, L testified as follows:

Q: When you spoke with Mrs. B, was there any mention about you putting in this form, of your returning a form she was going to send you on leave of absence, sick leave of absence?

A: No, sir. There was no mention of the form and I was completely unaware there was even supposed to be a form that I had to have in at any specific time, until I talked to Mr. R [chairman, Union Grievance Committee], and that was in relation to my discharge. I wanted to know what the reasons were that they had. He told me I had not sent back my form and I told them I didn't send it back because I have never seen it.

Grievant Notification of His Illness

The evidence demonstrated that between August 9 and August 30, the day before the discharge of the grievant, L called the company to report off work as sick on each workday with the exception of August 11, 25, and 27. In this respect, L declared:

Q: How regularly did you call in before you were notified that you had been terminated?

A: Well, I called in almost every day, not every day, and I guess I was calling in on the same day I was terminated or the day after.

After the original phone call, B testified, the grievant called her a second time and requested the phone number of the Codaphone.* After she supplied this phone number, the company witness testified, when the grievant called in to report off work sick, he would use the Codaphone. In this respect, she testified:

Q: Do you have any knowledge as to what is recorded on this Codaphone?

A: Yes.

Q: Can you tell me what he actually said when he called in to say he was sick and wouldn't be in?

A: He gave his name and said, "Sick."

Arbitrator: You listened to the tapes?

Witness: Yes, sir.

Arbitrator: Did he ever talk to you personally after the second time he called you, after you gave him the machine number?

Witness: No, sir. He called several times to ask for the machine number.

Arbitrator: He called several times to ask for the machine number? That was the extent of the conversation, to give him the machine number?

Witness: Before I could say anything, he hung up. . . .

L alleged that when he reported his absences to the company, he used the Codaphone device. In other words, during the period August 9 through August 31, there was no contact between the company and the grievant except through the Codaphone.

Certified Letter Sent to L

On August 18, the company sent the grievant a certified letter that contained medical leave forms. The post office certification number was 445322, and the mailing was sent to the grievant's last-known address. This mailing was returned to the company with the post office designation that it was "unclaimed." As to the return of the mailing, M, plant manager, testified:

A: This is a copy of the envelope sent by certified mail to Mr. L.

Q: And on the copy I have, there is a stamp that has been placed on the envelope and the area marked "Unclaimed" is checked.

A: Apparently the post office attempted to deliver this letter at the proper address and was unable to deliver it because the recipient was not at home. The post office has informed us that in cases of this nature, they leave a notification to have the letter picked up at the post office. If the letter is not picked up within 14 or 15 days at the post office, then the letter is returned to the sender.

*This was a recording device used for employees to leave messages. A tape recorded the information, and the company representative played back the tape to hear the message.

The letter sent to the grievant on August 18 read as follows:

> Enclosed are the medical leave of absence forms for you and your doctor to complete. These forms are to be returned to us no later than August 27th or the company will have no alternative but to terminate your employment.
>
> A stamped, self-addressed envelope is enclosed for your convenience.

L denied that he received the August 18 mailing. At the time the mailing was allegedly sent by the company, the grievant testified, he was living at the same residence where he currently lives. He also testified:

Q: As you know, when you get registered letters sent to you, the mailman, if you are not at home, is supposed to leave a card hanging on your door so you can pick up the letter at the post office. Did you find any such card?

A: Not that I know of. I found the one for the telegram.* I did not find the one for the forms. I was greatly and completely unaware of this.

On August 31, the company sent a telegram to the grievant notifying him of his discharge.

Medical Leave Policy

M testified that there was in effect a company policy dealing with the problem involved in this case:

Q: Does the company have a policy on sick leave?

A: Yes, the company does have a policy.

Q: Has that policy been the same from the time you first came with the company to the present?

A: That is correct. This policy was enforced when I joined the company.

Q: And what is the policy? Explain it to us.

A: The policy is that when an employee calls in and notifies the personnel department that he or she is ill, the personnel clerk will ask about the nature of the illness and the time that the employee estimates he will be off. If the employee doesn't know how long he or she will be off or if the time exceeds five days, we automatically send the forms that have been shown in Company Exhibit 13 to the employee.

Q: Have there ever been employees discharged from this company, since you have been here, for either failing to apply for sick leave within a reasonable time or being absent without renewing the sick leave?

A: Yes, there have been.

Q: Has there been more than one?

A: Yes, there have been more than one.

*Notifying him of his discharge.

L's Illness and Visits to Dr. J.

L testified as follows as to the nature of the illness that he claimed was responsible for his absences following his three-day suspension, and the treatment he received from a physician, Dr. J:

Q: What doctor treated you during your period of illness?

A: Dr. J.

Q: At the time you initially called in sick, on August 9, to the time you recovered from this illness, how many times did you visit that doctor?

A: Every three or four days.

Q: Every three or four days? Did he give you any prescriptions or recommend that you engage in any particular therapy for your illness?

A: He said I was nearly ready to receive some therapy if I did not get some rest. He gave me a prescription for resting and suggested that I just try to relax. When I questioned him about how long, he would just say, come back and talk and see how you are doing. If you are doing any better, I will let you go back to work. I had been to him prior to that, oh, it must have been sometime around September or October of the year preceding and when I began to feel the same way again, that is when I started going back, which is when I got the three-day layoff. I didn't know what to say. I had called I was sick. Everything was wrong and I didn't know what to tell anybody about it. I was sick and didn't know when I could come back to work because he wouldn't say, and the only requirement was that I relax and that was what I was trying to do.

Q: But you visited him and were examined by him every three or four days?

A: Yes, sir.

Q: And when did you recover from this sickness?

A: I don't remember the exact date, but he gave me a release on that day and he says that day I would be able to go back to work. But by then I had already lost the job.

Q: What is the date of the release, do you know?

A: I didn't remember, but I just saw it.

Q: What is it?

A: October 15.

Union Exhibit 1 was a "Certificate for Return to School or Work," dated October 15, 1973. The certificate bore a signature purportedly that of the doctor in question. The substance of the document was:

L has been under my care from Aug. 3 to Oct. 15, and is able to return to work on Oct 15, 1973.

Limitations/Remarks: Above Patient had a nervous hypertension condition and was unable to work during the above dates.

A, industrial relations manager, identified a letter, accepted in evidence as Company Exhibit 16, which carried the signature allegedly that of Dr. J. It stated:

> To whom it may concern:
>
> According to our records, Mr. L was seen in our office on 8/16/73. Subsequently, he received a note to return to work on 10/15, claiming he had been under our care from 8/3 to 10/15, but he was seen only on the above date in our office. We have no record of treatment for nervous hypertension.

A testified that he was present when the doctor signed the letter. He also testified that he spoke to the physician:

Q: You personally talked with this doctor?

A: Yes, I did.

Q: As a result, he checked his records? You told him what you were interested in determining, he checked his records and this [Company Exhibit 16] is what he gave?

A: Yes, sir.

Q: Did you show him a copy of Union Exhibit 1 in asking him to check his records?

A: Yes, I did.

Q: And the doctor told you this [Company Exhibit 16] it was correct to the best of his memory and reference?

A: Yes.

Arbitrator: Did you go to his office?

Witness: Yes, I did.

Arbitrator: And did you show him Union Exhibit 1?

Witness: Yes, I did.

Arbitrator: And did he say he wrote, he executed, that document?

Witness: No, he said he did not execute that document.

Q: Did he sign this letter [Company Exhibit 16] right in your presence?

A: Yes, sir, he did.

Processing of L's Grievance

The grievant was discharged on August 31, 1973; the instant grievance was filed on September 3; and the company originally denied it on September 8. Between September 3 and September 20, M was on vacation, and the parties agreed that this period of time would not count in relation to the time limits established in the grievance procedure for purposes of the case. In this respect, the plant manager testified:

Q: Now, I see, beginning with September 13, a week, a full working-day week and the following Monday, under the dates of which appear the words "grace period." Could you tell me what that has reference to?

A: Yes, I went on vacation on September 13, and Mr. R, the president of the grievance committee, requested a meeting; and the acting plant manager notified them in writing that the company would give the union a grace period of time I was absent on vacation, as we did not know what this case contained.

On September 22, M and R, the chairman of the union grievance committee, held a grievance meeting. In this meeting, R requested to see the certified letter the company had sent to L on August 18. The letter was shown to him. M testified:

Yes, as I explained before, upon my return on September 20, Mr. R requested a grievance meeting. We had meetings normally every four weeks of the local grievance committee. I scheduled this meeting for Wednesday, the 22nd of September. At the meeting, Mr. R talked about the L case. He requested to see the certified letter that he sent to Mr. L, because I told him that I felt the company had done everything in its power to get Mr. L to answer us, including sending a registered letter to him. And he asked me to see that letter and I showed it to him.

On October 1, the company received a letter from P in which the staff representative stated that he was to become the new international union representative and would subsequently service the local union involved in this case. On October 28, O, the former staff representative of the international union, called the company to arrange a meeting to introduce P and to discuss some outstanding grievances.

This meeting was held on November 2, and the L grievance, as well as others, was brought up at that time. As to the L grievance, M testified:

Q: When the union brought up the L grievance on November 2, at the grievance meeting, what was your position at that time?

A: My position at that time was to refuse to discuss the merits of the case, since the grievance was untimely.

Q: Were there other grievances at that same meeting which you considered to be untimely and refused to discuss the merits of?

A: There were three more grievances of that type.

Q: Did you in fact discuss the merits of those grievances, including the L grievance, at that meeting?

A: No, I did not.

P, the new staff representative, sent the company a letter, dated November 12, in which he stated:

This letter is in regard to my understanding at our last meeting that you would send me a letter of the Company's position as it pertains to grievances of the following individuals:

L _____
H _____
W _____
T _____

I would appreciate your letter as soon as possible so that I may formulate some means of expediting the processing of these grievances.

A, the industrial relations manager, responded to P's letter on November 16, stating:

There was no agreement to communicate in writing about the L, H, W, and T grievances.

In the November 2 meeting, the Company took the verbal position that it would no longer consider these grievances, as they were untimely.

Two days later, on November 18, the union invoked arbitration of the instant grievance. In this regard, P wrote A:

This is in regard to your letter of November 16, pertaining to four (4) grievances alleged untimely by the Company.

I would like to reaffirm that Mr. O and I are in agreement that you were to send us a written statement of your position in these matters.

I feel that these grievances have gone unresolved much too long and I would like to impress you with the idea of letting an impartial party settle these four (4) cases, as we have not been able to do so, and appeal all four (4) cases to arbitration.

An arbitrator can determine any question of timeliness and arbitrability. If we cannot resolve these matters in the aforementioned manner, I will have to refer these cases to our Legal Department to be handled by our Attorney.

POSITION OF THE PARTIES

The position of the company was that the grievance should be denied, on the grounds that time limits contained in the grievance procedure were violated; and if found timely, the grievance should be denied on its merits, arguing that L was discharged for proper cause. The position of the union was that the grievance should be granted.

ANALYSIS OF THE EVIDENCE

The arbitrator's decision read in part as follows:

The grievance may not be determined on its merits unless it is found to be properly before the Arbitrator for that purpose. If it is found that the grievance was not processed in the light of the established time limits contained in the

Grievance Procedure, the Arbitrator would be required to deny the grievance on that basis. In other words, the merits of the discharge cannot be reached until the issue of arbitrability is disposed of.

Step 3 Meeting Not Timely Invoked

Under Section 8 of the Grievance Procedure, grievances protesting discharge originate in Step 2. The L grievance was filed on September 3, and denied on September 8. Thus, both the Company and the Union complied with the time limits established at the Step 2 level of the Grievance Procedure.

We know, of course, that the Company denied the grievance in Step 2. To invoke Step 3 of the Grievance Procedure, the "International Union, within ten (10) working days . . . may request a meeting between management, the Shop Grievance Committee and a representative of the International Union."

Excluding the working days between September 13 and September 20 inclusive,* the International Union, therefore, had until September 30 to request a Step 3 meeting. The working days to count for the ten days are September 9, 10, 21, 22, 23, 24, 27, 28, 29, and 30. Nothing in the record demonstrates that the International Union requested a Step 3 meeting on the L grievance during this period of time.

In short, September 30 came and went and there was no request for a Step 3 meeting by the International Union. Under these circumstances, the grievance should be denied, unless there are circumstances involved in this case that would make this provision inapplicable. In other words, we shall make a careful search of the record to determine whether or not there are circumstances that would justify the Arbitrator in finding that the grievance may be considered timely under the Grievance Procedure. He shall do this because the denial of a grievance on the basis of time limits does not permit a decision dealing with the substantive issues of a case. Normally, arbitrators prefer to deal with the merits of a grievance, and denial on the basis of time limits precludes a determination on this basis. This is particularly true in a discharge case, since an employee on the merits may not have been discharged for proper cause.

In other words, in cases of this sort, where the literal language of time limits has not been complied with by a labor union, as in the instant proceeding, the normal procedure is to determine from the evidence whether or not circumstances exist that in the arbitrator's judgment permit a determination on the merits of the grievance. Are there such circumstances involved in this case?

The Meeting of September 22

A meeting was held between the Company and the Local Union Grievance Committee on September 22. It was attended by M, Plant Manager, and R, Chairman of the Union Grievance Committee. In this meeting, the L grievance was brought up. R requested to see the letter the Company had sent L on August 18. Such letter was shown to him by the Company.

Thus, the L grievance was raised in this meeting, and, of course, September 22 was well before September 30, the final date upon which a Step 3 meeting could have been invoked in the processing of the instant grievance. Do these cir-

---

*This was the "grace period," reflecting the time that the parties agreed would not count for time limits.

cumstances permit the Arbitrator to find that the L grievance was properly processed in the light of the Step 3 time limits?

After considerable reflection, the Arbitrator must reply to this question in the negative. This is required not only because of the literal language of the Step 3 provision, but also because of the practice of the Parties. Step 3 language requires that the International Union must request a Step 3 meeting. Obviously, the September 22 meeting was not called by the International Union. It was requested by the Local Union, and, indeed, no International Union Staff Representative was present at this meeting. Without any refutation or contradiction whatsoever, M testified:

Q: ... Did any International Representative contact you to schedule the September 22 meeting?

A: No, sir.

Q: Was any International Representative present at that meeting as required by the contract?

A: No, sir.

Beyond these considerations, the practice has been that Step 3 meetings have been called by the International Union and that a Staff Representative always attended such Step 3 meetings. Again, without contradiction, M declared:

Q: All cases where a Third Step Meeting has taken place, has the International Representative, that being Mr. O or Mr. R, contacted you to arrange the meeting?

A: In all cases, the meeting has been requested by the International Representative.

Q: In all cases where a Third Step Meeting has taken place, has an International Representative been present at that meeting?

A: During the time I was with the Company, yes, sir.

On the basis of these considerations, the Arbitrator must find that the September 22 meeting did not constitute a Step 3 meeting within the meaning of the Grievance Procedure. It was not called by the International Union; no Staff Representative attended the meeting; and there was no representation by the Local Union officers that the meeting constituted a Step 3 meeting.

Change of Staff Representatives

With complete candor, P stated:

P: I don't have any evidence to show. I might as well be fair in my presentation. I don't have any information to show whether it was or was not timely.

Arbitrator: Are you going to present to me some argument as to your position that the grievance was timely filed?

P: Yes, sir. That is the only one I can take.

Arbitrator: Are you going to argue in your brief and orally and persuade me why I should find that as timely?

P: Well, I am going to try, Mr. Arbitrator.

In other words, P tells us that he cannot account for the reason why the International Union did not request a Step 3 meeting in the L grievance by September 30. This is expected, since P did not start to service the Local Union in question until after September 30. What the record shows is that he replaced O as the Staff Representative on or about October 28. It was on October 28 that the former Staff Representative called the Company to arrange a meeting to introduce P as the new Staff Representative.

In other words, as we view the record, the failure of the International Union to request a Step 3 meeting in a timely manner was probably attributable to the change of Staff Representatives. P, of course, does not tell us this, but it appears as the only plausible explanation to account for the failure of the International Union to request a Step 3 meeting for the L grievance. The Arbitrator, however, simply cannot use this reason in mitigation or as an extenuating circumstance to permit him to find that the grievance was timely processed for purposes of the Grievance Procedure. Although the failure may have been understandable, it simply is not sufficient cause to ignore the plain language of Step 3 of the Grievance Procedure.

Even though the responsible International Union Staff Representative fundamentally bears the burden for the failure to request a Step 3 meeting in a timely manner, the Arbitrator has also considered the role of L in this connection. The Grievant was not merely a rank-and-file Union member, who at times may not be aware of the terms of the Labor Agreement, and particularly the technical time limits established in the Grievance Procedure. At the time of his discharge, L was *serving as a member of the Union's Grievance Committee.* As such, he must have been fully aware of the time limits contained in the Grievance Procedure. Clearly, L was partly responsible for the failure to process his grievance in a timely manner. He knew that he was discharged; a grievance was filed on his behalf; and he was knowledgeable of the time limits contained in the Grievance Procedure. In addition, the Grievant appeared to the Arbitrator as a highly articulate and intelligent person.

In other words, L was in a position to act in his own interests. He was in a position to keep abreast of the events involved in the processing of his grievance. Being a member of the Union Grievance Committee, he had access to the Staff Representative in question. Under these circumstances, is it unreasonable to believe that L himself should have made inquiries of the responsible Staff Representative to assure that the Step 3 meeting was held in his case in a timely manner?... In short, the Arbitrator believes that L himself was partly responsible for the failure of the International Union to request a Step 3 meeting in a timely fashion.

No Waiver by Company

At times, an employer by his own actions tacitly waives the time limits established in a grievance procedure. He does this by discussing a grievance on its merits after time limits have expired, and/or failing to inform the labor union that a grievance is not timely before discussing a grievance on its merits. Indeed, in the past, the instant Arbitrator has found that employers tacitly waived time limits by such conduct, even though a labor union failed to conform to time limits spelled out in a labor agreement. Under these circumstances, the Arbitrator has found such grievances timely under the grievance procedure, and proceeded to a determination on the merits of the grievance.

In this case, however, the evidence shows that the Company did not at any time waive the time limits in the L grievance. As M testified:

Q: When the Union brought up the L grievance on November 2, at the grievance meeting, what was your position at that time?

A: My position at that time was to refuse to discuss the merits of the case, since the grievance was untimely.

Q: Were there other grievances at that same meeting which you considered to be untimely and refused to discuss the merits of?

A: There were three more grievances of that type.

Q: Did you in fact discuss the merits of those grievances, including the L grievance, at that meeting?

A: No, I did not.

In other words, we find no evidence that the Company either explicitly or tacitly waived the time limits in question. It was not until November 2 that the International Union brought up the L grievance in a Step 3 meeting. At this time, the Company flatly refused to discuss it on its merits. It told the Union in an unequivocal manner that the Company considered the L grievance as untimely. Beyond these considerations, the Company gave fair warning to the International Union that it expected the applicable time limits to be met. On June 24, 1972, M wrote O the following:

> In reference to your request to table the time limit of grievances, I would like to advise you that I would rather not do so. I am sure that there was a purpose in stating these time limits and inserting them into the contract. I remember only too well that upon my arrival here, I was handling grievances that were six to eight months old, because their time limitations were tabled. I strongly feel that differences between the Union and Management should be resolved in the shortest period of time.
>
> I am sorry that I cannot agree with your request.

In this light, it should not have come as a surprise to the Union that the Company invoked time limits in the L grievance. Both the International Union and the Local Union were given fair warning that the Company expected the time limits established in the Grievance Procedure to be honored.

Conclusions

On the basis of the evidence, the finding must be that the L discharge cannot be determined on its merits. The grievance protesting the discharge was not processed in a timely manner under the Grievance Procedure. It was not timely presented because the evidence demonstrates that a meeting to deal with his discharge was not timely invoked under Step 3 of the Grievance Procedure. In addition, as the foregoing analysis of the evidence demonstrated, we cannot find sufficient cause or circumstances in mitigation or in extenuation for the failure of the Union to invoke a Step 3 meeting in a timely manner. The evidence also shows that at no time did the Company waive the applicable time limits established in the Grievance Procedure. In short, the Arbitrator finds on the evidence that the L grievance is not properly before him for a decision on its merits.

In the last analysis, what is at stake here is the integrity of the Grievance Procedure. The Parties agreed in the most clear language possible in Section 2 of the Grievance Procedure that where time limits have elapsed, a grievance shall be considered as disposed of by the last decision rendered. The language of Step 3 is likewise drafted in unambiguous and unequivocal terms. This is what the Parties agreed to, and under the circumstances of this case, the Arbitrator has no choice except to enforce the language.

Having said all of this, the Arbitrator still regrets that he is unable here to decide the case on its merits. The loss of a job to a worker, of course, to him and to his family is a tragic state of affairs. At the least, he should have the opportunity to have his discharge determined on its merits by an arbitrator to determine whether or not he was discharged by an employer for proper cause.

In any event, the Arbitrator must enforce the Grievance Procedure language as agreed to by the Parties in collective bargaining. Although he admittedly would have preferred to determine whether or not L was discharged for proper cause, the Arbitrator would offend the responsibilities of his office, and betray the confidence that the Parties have reposed in his integrity and professional ability, to find the grievance to be arbitrable on its merits.

QUESTIONS

1. Apparently, the note the grievant offered on his behalf (Union Exhibit 1) from Dr. J was forged, since the physician later denied that he wrote such a certificate (Company Exhibit 16). Does this feature of the case apply to the arbitrability of the grievance or to the merits of the grievance? If you were the arbitrator, would the apparent forgery have had a bearing on your decision as to the arbitrability of the grievance? Why?

2. Is it fair for an employee not to have the merits of his discharge determined in arbitration because a labor organization has not complied with the time limits of a grievance procedure? Explain your position.

3. Do you agree with the arbitrator that the grievant had some responsibility for the failure of the union to request a timely Step 3 meeting? Defend your answer.

4. Would the union's case have been strengthened if O, the former staff representative of the international union, had testified in the arbitration to explain why a Step 3 meeting was not timely called? In your answer, consider the letter that the plant manager wrote to him long before the circumstances of this case arose.

CASE 3
A Case Where Employees
Slept on Their Contractual Rights:
An Exception to a Principle
of the Arbitration Process

Cast of Characters

R—One of the grievants
S—Union committeeman

Normally, arbitrators give full faith and credit to unambiguous contractual language, and almost invariably use such language as the basis for decision. In this case, however, we note an exception to this rule of the arbitration process. Despite an employer policy that conflicted with clear contractual language, employees for many years did not protest until grievances were filed that sparked this arbitration. As you read this case, you will become aware of the dilemma of the arbitrator. On the one hand, he found it very repugnant to depart from unambiguous contractual language. On the other hand, he could not shut his eyes to the fact that the employees had accepted the employer policy for many years without a murmur of protest. Here is a good example of a case in which, no matter what his decision, the arbitrator would be subject to bitter criticism. Unfortunately, arbitration is not a forum designed to make all concerned happy and content. The arbitrator must "bite the bullet," and here is a case where the bullet was particularly hard and wholly unappetizing!

This dispute involved the issue of vacation pay. Alleging that the company's vacation pay policy violated the labor agreement, several employees filed grievances on November 20, 1972. All grievances involved the same issue; the one filed by R is illustrative of the grievances involved in this proceeding. His grievance stated:

> Violation of article ten of the contract. This employee was here ten years Nov. 19th, 1972. The company has refused to pay him vacation benefits for the third wk. as stated in the contract. We ask that the co. pay this employee as called for in the agreement.

Relevant to the case were the following provisions of the labor agreement:

ARTICLE X

(a) Effective October 2, 1970, vacation benefits shall be paid each employee at his basic hourly rate as follows:

Length of Service	*Vacation Pay*
1 year but less than 3 years	5 days (40 hours)
3 years but less than 10 years	10 days (80 hours)
10 years or more	15 days (120 hours)

(b) If the employer desires to close the plant for vacation purposes, he should give the employees a sixty (60) day notice.

(c) If the plant does not close down for vacation purposes, the employees shall be granted vacations in accordance with seniority and the best interests of the company.

As a remedy, the union requested that an award be directed to make not only the grievants whole in terms of vacation pay, but:

all other employees who lost vacation pay over the years where the Company violated the Labor Agreement.

The basic question to be determined by this arbitration was as follows:

Under the circumstances of this case, did the company violate Article X of the labor agreement? If so, what should the remedy be?

BACKGROUND

In 1962, the union obtained bargaining rights. Since that time, the parties had negotiated labor agreements in 1965, in 1967, and on October 2, 1970, when the current labor agreement was put into effect. In each of the former contracts, the parties had negotiated a vacation provision that was essentially the same as Article X in the current labor agreement. There were some changes dealing with the length of service required for vacation pay, but, substantively, the vacation language of the preceding contracts was exactly the same as that in the current one.

According to the testimony of grievant R, each year the company posted a notice on its bulletin board that announced its vacation policy for that year. In effect, such notices stated that for the particular year, *all employees must take their vacations between June and September*, and not at any other time of the year. There was some testimony that in one year, the company may have closed the plant for vacation purposes pursuant to Article X(b) of the labor agreement. However, this plant closing, assuming that it did happen, was not material to the issue involved in this dispute.

The parties were in agreement as to the basic facts that sparked this arbitration. At the core of the dispute was the eligibility of employees to receive vacation pay in the light of their acquired seniority. According to the company vacation policy, if an employee's anniversary date of his seniority occurred after September 30, the employee must wait until the next year to realize the amount of his vacation pay commensurate with his seniority. For example, assume that an employee was hired on October 10, 1971. Since the company required that vacations be taken during the months of June to September 1972, this employee would not have earned one year's seniority by that time. Accordingly, during these months, this employee would not be eligible for 40 hours' vacation pay, since under Article X(a), an employee must have at least one year of service to realize any vacation pay.

Under company policy, our employee hired on October 10, 1971, would therefore be required to wait until June 1973 for vacation pay. He would not receive any vacation pay in 1972 even though he acquired one year of service as of October 10, 1972.

R's grievance cited above also illustrated the basic problem involved in this dispute. He was hired on November 19, 1962, and the anniversary date of his seniority occurred on November 19 of each year. Thus, he acquired ten years of seniority on November 19, 1972. Under Article X, an employee with ten years of seniority is entitled to 120 hours of vacation pay. However, for 1972, the company paid R only 80 hours of vacation pay, because, during the months of June to September 1972, he did not have ten years of seniority. Under company policy, R would be required to wait until June 1973 to collect three weeks' vacation pay, even though he had acquired ten years of seniority on November 19, 1972.

It was the union's position that employees should not have to wait until the next year's vacation period (June through September) to receive vacation pay in accordance with their seniority. In the example of the employee hired on October 10, 1971, the union's position was that this employee should be entitled to a week's vacation as of October 10, 1972, and should not have to wait under company policy until June 1973. In the case of R, it was the union's position that he should have received a third week vacation as of November 19, 1972, and not have been required to wait until June 1973.

As the union argued:

> For several years, the employer posted a notice that employees must take a vacation between June and September. Under this policy, employees who had less than one year's seniority as of September 30 were not permitted to take a vacation in that year, but were forced to wait until the following year for one week's vacation. In the case of R, he qualified for a third week's vacation immediately on November 19, 1972. The Company was approached by the Union Committee on the R problem. But the Company stated that he would have to wait until 1973 to qualify for a third week's vacation. That is when we filed the grievance. We feel the Labor Agreement is clear and unambiguous in its language as to vacation benefits. It says one year service for one week vaca-

tion; three years of service entitles the man to two weeks' vacation; and ten years of service gives him three weeks' vacation pay. . . . Just because the Company says that vacations must be taken during certain months does not relieve the Company of its contractual obligation of providing that amount of vacation pay coming to him under the Labor Agreement.

ANALYSIS OF THE EVIDENCE

Merits of Union Argument

The arbitrator (he said):

feels that there is merit to the Union's basic argument in this proceeding. Under Article X, the language is unambiguous that the amount of vacation pay is commensurate with the length of service stated in the provision. There are no exceptions or modifications contained in the language agreed to by the parties. As the Union argues, the vacation provision states that an employee with one year of service is entitled to 40 hours' vacation pay; this is clear language and does not permit any modifications or exceptions. Additional unambiguous language provides vacation benefits for employees with three years and ten years of service.

Indeed, under the literal language of the Labor Agreement, an employee's vacation benefits become due on the precise date that he acquires the necessary length of service. Article X does not state that such an employee must wait until the following June to receive the amount of vacation pay due him in accordance with his seniority. In the case of R, he acquired ten years of senniority as of November 19, 1972. Under the literal language of the Labor Agreement, he was entitled to three weeks of vacation pay on the date he earned ten years of seniority.

In short, if this case were to be decided strictly on the basis of contractual language, the grievances should be granted. Certainly, at no place in Article X do we find language that authorizes the Company to delay until the following June the vacation benefits of employees who acquire the necessary seniority in the previous year. If an employee acquires one, three, or ten years of seniority between October 1 and December 31 of a year, under the strict language of the Labor Agreement, this employee need not wait until the following June before he realizes the vacation pay due him under the vacation provision. Since there are no exceptions to such language, the employee is entitled to the vacation benefits during the year in which he acquires either one, three, or ten years of seniority.

Arbitration and Unambiguous Contract Language

Under the literal language of the Labor Agreement, there is no question that the Company policy involved in this proceeding violates Article X. Since this is true, it would follow necessarily that the grievances should be granted, and the remedy requested by the Union be directed. Such a decision would be proper under a most familiar rule, which governs the arbitration process: Arbitrators may not subtract from, add to, or modify unambiguous contractual language. Indeed, under Article XI of the Labor Agreement, the Parties instruct their arbitrators that they do not have "the power to add to, disregard, or modify the terms of this agreement. . . ."

As a matter of fact, as the published and unpublished decisions of this Arbitrator demonstrate, he has frequently granted and denied grievances on the very principle that the Union urges in this case. Under these circumstances, it would appear that the Arbitrator should follow this principle in this proceeding and grant the grievances. Indeed, for a considerable time, the Arbitrator believed that this should be his decision despite another feature of the case that we shall consider in the subsequent portion of this Opinion.

We should all recognize that it is repugnant to the arbitration process for any arbitrator to depart from contractual language that is clear and unambiguous. To do so results in a state of affairs whereby an arbitrator denies rights of employees and/or employers gained in collective bargaining. To depart from crystal-clear contractual language also means that an arbitrator usurps the right of employers and labor unions to write their own collective bargaining contracts.

There is no question that Article X is written in a clear-cut manner. There is no question that the Company policy in question violates unambiguous contractual language. There is no question that to deny the grievances would place the Arbitrator in a position of modifying unambiguous contractual language.

Employees Slept on Their Rights

For these reasons, the Arbitrator, as stated, for a prolonged period of time believed that the grievances should be granted. It would be a proper decision based upon the kind of vacation language agreed to by the Parties. Indeed, as his previous observations demonstrate, the Arbitrator fully understands the fundamental arbitration principle urged by the Union. Even now, although the Arbitrator has finally decided to deny the grievances, he wants to state with full candor that he still finds it inherently repugnant to depart from unambiguous contractual language.

Having said all of this, the Arbitrator in good conscience cannot shut his eyes to the incontrovertible fact that the Company's policy in question has been in effect since the Union acquired bargaining rights. No one suggests that the Company kept this policy secret. It was posted for all to see. For many years, employees were paid their vacation benefits under this Company policy. During all these years, no employee raised any protest to the Company or the Union until the circumstances of this case arose. Indeed, until now, the Union had no knowledge that some employees were not receiving vacation benefits as spelled out in the Labor Agreement.

As Union Committeeman S testified:

> We [the Union] were not aware that employees were not receiving their proper vacations. No one complained about it until now. We did not learn about it until now.

If employees had promptly protested against the Company policy, the Union would have had the opportunity to act on their behalf during the contract negotiations of 1965, 1967, and 1970. Obviously, since employees did not protest, the Union was not in a position to take corrective action. A union can go only so far in the policing of a labor agreement. If employees affected by an employer infraction of the contract do not complain to their union, the labor organization, of course, simply does not have the knowledge to take corrective action on their behalf.

R offers an excuse as to why the employees affected by the Company policy in question did not protest. He testified:

> In the 10 years I was with the Company I was not aware that I was entitled to either 2- or 3-week vacations. I did not have a copy of the Labor Agreement, and I did not read it until shortly before I filed my grievance.

In other words, the Grievants and other employees adversely affected by the Company's vacation policy did not know they were entitled to additional vacation pay because they were not aware of their contractual rights. They were not aware of their rights because they did not have and/or read the contracts negotiated by the Parties over the years.

We reject this excuse as being without merit. It is incredible that employees affected by the Company's vacation policy did not have a Labor Agreement to read if they desired to read it. Since 1959, under Landrum-Griffin, employees have had the right to a copy of their collective bargaining contracts. There is nothing in the record to demonstrate that either the Company or the Union violated this feature of national labor policy. Nothing in the record demonstrates that the Union refused to provide its members with copies of the contracts.

In short, we must find that the employees were aware of their vacation rights contained in the contracts, or by reasonable diligence could have learned of these rights. By failing to take prompt action on their own behalf, the employees tacitly agreed to the Company policy in question. Responsibility for this state of affairs rests not with the Union, but with the employees themselves, who slept on their rights. By their failure to protest, the employees acquiesced to the Company policy in question.

In reality, what the Grievants and other employees already affected by the Company's vacation policy request here is for the Arbitrator to rescue them from a state of affairs of their own making. In all candor, their protest comes far too late in the game for the Arbitrator to direct the remedy they request. For many years, during which time three (3) labor agreements had been negotiated, the employees with full knowledge of the Company policy in question did not raise even a murmur of protest. Now, after all these years, the employees request relief from the Company policy. Clearly, the opportunity to raise a timely protest expired a long time ago.

Conclusions

Here we have a valid exception to the rule that arbitrators should apply unambiguous contractual language as the basis of a decision. The Company policy in question was well known to the employees. Indeed, for many years they were paid vacation benefits on the basis of the policy. Either employees were aware of the contractual right, or by reasonable diligence they could have learned of the vacation provision in the Labor Agreement. Instead of protesting in a timely manner, they raised no protest to either the Union or the Company. During this period of time, three contracts were negotiated; each of them contained essentially the same vacation language. The Union could not take prompt corrective action on their behalf because the employees raised no complaint.

Under these circumstances, the employees forfeited rights they had under the Labor Agreement. By their failure to protest in a timely and prompt manner, they acquiesced to the Company policy in question. Therefore, in this case it would not be proper to base a decision on the contractual language in question even though the language is written in a clear and unambiguous manner.

QUESTIONS

1. If you arbitrated the case, and used the unambiguous contractual language as the basis of your decision, explain how you would handle the employer argument that employees did not complain about its vacation policy for many years, during which period of time three labor agreements were negotiated.

2. Appraise the arbitrator's finding that employees' ignorance of contractual language could not be used as a valid basis to explain away their delay in protesting the employer policy.

3. What effect do you believe the arbitrator's decision would have upon the next contract negotiations?

4. Despite the arbitrator's decision, do you believe that the arbitration served a useful purpose?

Chapter 7
Wage Issues
under
Collective Bargaining

Almost all contract negotiations pivot upon, and most grievances and arbitration procedures thus ultimately deal with, four major areas: (1) wages, and issues that can be directly related to wages; (2) employee benefits, or economic "fringe" supplements to the basic wage rate; (3) "institutional" issues, dealing with the rights and duties of employers and unions; and (4) what might be most appropriately described as "administrative" clauses, treating such subjects as work rules and job tenure. In this chapter and the three that follow it, each of these areas will be discussed in turn. As in the preceding chapter, arbitration cases will also be used, where appropriate, to illustrate particular problems.

Probably no issues under collective bargaining continue to give rise to more difficult problems than do wages and wage-related subjects. When negotiations reach a stalemate, they frequently do so because company and union representatives are not able to find a formula to resolve wage disputes. And wage controversies are, for that matter, by far the leading overt cause of strikes: Over the past decade, for example, they have accounted for over 40 percent of all such work stoppages.[1]

This record highlights the vital character of wage negotiations in collective bargaining, and also suggests that in the area of wages much can be done to decrease management–labor conflict substantially. In any area of human relations, ignorance breeds suspicion, distrust, and conflict; this principle of human behavior is fully applicable to wage negotiations under collective bargaining. To the extent that understanding is substituted for ignorance, there will be a greater opportunity for peaceful settlement of wage controversies, even if conflict of interest in such matters never disappears.

It is not difficult to understand why wages do play such an important and controversial role in labor relations. For workers, wages are normally the only source of income, and the standard of living of the employee and

[1]Data furnished by Bureau of Labor Statistics, U.S. Department of Labor.

his family is determined almost exclusively by this source. For workers' families, the weekly paycheck establishes the character and quality of their dwelling, food, clothing, education, recreation, and of all other items that are included in the concept of standard of living.

But if, from the point of view of the worker, wages are income that establishes a standard of living, from the viewpoint of the company, wages are a cost of production. And here is the heart of the wage controversy. On the one hand, employees press for higher and higher wages with the objective of raising their standard of living; on the other hand, employers are confronted with increasing pressures on the cost of production. When wages are a significant element of cost of production, when wage increases are not offset by such economic phenomena as increased efficiency, and when the union has been unable (or unwilling) to extract equal wage concessions from all competitive firms, wage increases tend to place the firm in an undesirable economic position. A company so placed might not be able to survive for long in the competitive struggle. Under such a state of affairs, union wage policy, instead of advancing the standard of living of its members, could plunge them into economic oblivion.

As a result of the difficult and controversial nature of wage problems, it is crucial that they be dealt with in an intelligent and sound manner. As with perhaps no other area of collective bargaining, wage problems test the skill, understanding, and attitudes of negotiators. The latter are, as we know, now confronted with a legion of wage issues, including the establishment of the basic wage rate, wage differentials, overtime rates, and wage adjustments during contractual periods, as well as with the thorny problems involved in the negotiation of the so-called fringe, or supplemental, wage payments, which will be discussed in the next chapter. It is hoped that the following discussion of some of the principles, practices, and trends concerning these several wage and wage-related areas will contribute to better understanding of them.

DETERMINATION
OF THE BASIC WAGE RATE

If union and management representatives are exhibiting an ever-greater willingness to deal with factual information at the bargaining table, there is still no single standard for wage rate determination that has anything approaching a "scientific" base. Both the bargaining parties, indeed, commonly utilize at least *three different* such standards, each of which has definite advantages from the viewpoint of achieving an "equitable" settlement but also significant limitations: the "comparative-norm," ability-to-pay, and standard-of-living criteria.

Comparative Norm

To a great extent, company and union negotiators make use of the "comparative-norm principle" in wage negotiations. The basic idea behind this concept is the presumption that the economics of a particular collective bargaining relationship should neither fall substantially behind nor be greatly superior to that of other employer–union relationships; that, in short, it is generally a good practice to keep up with the crowd, but not necessarily to lead it.

The outside observer would very probably agree with this principle, at least on the surface. When a firm is operating with a highly competitive product or in highly competitive labor markets, there is safety for employee relations in keeping labor costs and wage rates consistent with the local and industrial pattern, but not necessarily any need to exceed this pattern. Unions tend to maintain harmony and contentment among the rank and file as long as wage conditions are uniform; on the other hand, it is at times quite difficult and embarrassing for union leaders to explain to the membership why their economic terms of employment are not at least equivalent to those of other unionists (particularly where one local of an international union falls substantially behind another local of the same international). In short, the comparative-norm principle is often valid for economic, sociological, and psychological reasons.

Thus, companies and unions frequently make a careful and comprehensive study of the community and industry wage structure before negotiations begin and then compare these rates to the rates in existence in the plant involved in the negotiations. The strategic implications of such comparisons, already cited in Chapter 5, are quite obvious. If the plant rates are below the community or industry pattern, the union can be expected to argue for a wage increase on this basis. When the plant rates are in excess of the community or industry pattern, the company has an argument *against* a wage increase.

Notwithstanding these considerations, there are limitations to this approach to the bargaining process. Not all firms have the same capacity to meet economic demands. This is the case not only for firms in different industries but also for companies operating within the same industry. Even though economic forces are at work that tend to place firms operating within the same industrial grouping on the same economic footing, many other factors—such as imperfections in the product market, technological differences, location, stage of economic development, and financial resources—may, at any one time, place such firms on different economic levels. From this it follows that at any one time, firms may be quite different in their individual capacities to meet economic demands and that the optimum wage level for one firm of a particular industry could be quite low (or quite high) in comparison with that of the industry in general.

Negotiations in the steel industry serve to illustrate this point. Most of the basic steel manufacturers, whether large or small, are organized by the United Steelworkers of America. So, too, are most steel fabrication firms, which purchase their steel from the basic steel companies, fabricate it, and then sell the resultant steel products directly to other industrial plants or to private consumers. The membership of the union is, in fact, divided about equally between employees who work in these two sectors of the steel industry.

In negotiations with the basic steel companies, the union's highest national officers deal directly with a small employer committee agreed upon by the larger of these companies (United States Steel, Bethlehem, Republic, Jones and Laughlin, and similar large producers). From this key negotiation, a "pattern" or comparative norm is established. The union then officially tries to gain about the same wage settlement individually from the smaller basic steel plants and the steel fabrication firms. Clearly, however, the financial and market circumstances of the large basic steel producers are quite different from those confronting the other types of managements—and the inevitable result is a wide variety of different degrees of pattern following and pattern deviation in what is nonetheless still referred to as the "steel industry."

Many other examples could be used to demonstrate the same principle. Within the rubber industry, the economic conditions, and thus the wage-paying abilities, of the large firms oriented toward the rubber tire market are quite different from those of the smaller footwear manufacturers. And highly competitive rubber heel plants, for example, normally settle with the Rubber Workers for considerably less than the rubber tire pattern established with Firestone, Goodrich, and similar rubber tire titans, even though many of the latter firms also manufacture footwear. Large meat packers (such as Swift and Armour) are generally in better positions to allow higher wage levels than are their smaller competitors. In the automobile industry, there are obviously significant economic differences between General Motors and American Motors. These considerations must be recognized before one accepts the proposition that the comparative-norm principle of wage determination should used as the exclusive, or the most desirable, standard for wage settlements in collective bargaining.[2]

There are at least four other factors to be considered in regard to the

[2]Recognition of the differences between firms and industries should also be taken into account when the *nonmoney* items of collective bargaining are negotiated. A seniority system, for example, that is suitable for one employer–union relationship may not fit the needs of the employer and employees of another plant. Union security formulas, checkoff arrangements, managerial prerogative systems, grievance procedures, discharge and disciplinary arrangements, and the character of union obligations should be geared fundamentally to the particular collective bargaining relationship. Company and union representatives are at times astonished to learn of the contractual arrangement of another employer–union relationship. The fact is, however, that such a formula can frequently be explained logically in terms of the environment of that firm.

comparative-norm principle. *First*, not only do firms within a given industry at any given time have unequal capabilities to meet economic demands, but frequently it is quite difficult to classify a firm in a particular industrial grouping for wage comparison purposes. Some firms may logically be classified in two or more industries, because of the products they manufacture or the services they provide. Likewise, even if a firm is classified within a particular industry, there are frequently significant subgroupings in each major industrial classification. Within the oil industry, for example, there are large, medium, and small producers of oil, and producers can be classified considerably further in terms of exact product and nature of operations. Such complicating circumstances illustrate the difficulty of classifying a particular firm in a particular industry or in a segment of an industry for purposes of wage determination.

A *second* limitation involved in the use of the comparative-norm wage principle for collective bargaining is the fact that it is at times misleading to compare employees within a particular job classification, because the content of jobs may be substantially different among plants within the same labor market. The duties of an employee classified as a "subassembler, B" in one plant may be quite different from those of an employee classified identically in another plant. The fact is that job classifications within industry have not been standardized. As long as this situation exists, and there is reason to believe that it will continue to exist, the usefulness of the comparative-norm wage principle is proportionately reduced.

This wage criterion is limited in its applicability by still a *third* complication. It is difficult to use the principle when comparing workers who are within the same job classification but who are paid by different systems of wage payments. Some workers are paid on a straight hourly-rate basis, others under an individual incentive system, and still others on a group incentive plan. The kind of wage system in operation can in itself have a significant impact upon wage rates.

Briefly described, incentive wages constitute a method of wage payment by which earnings are geared more or less directly to actual output instead of to time spent on the job. Employees are thus granted a relatively clear-cut financial motivation to increase their outputs, essentially by increasing the effort on which such outputs depend.

On the other hand, determination of the actual rate of pay for each "piece" or unit of output is, of course, open to union–management controversy; the company's conception of an appropriate rate is typically somewhat less liberal than is the union's. And the problem is compounded when the original job on which the rate has been set is in any way "modified" (as virtually all jobs ultimately are, because of a host of factors ranging from worker-implemented short cuts to management job reengineering) and each party seeks a new rate that is beneficial to its own interests.

Some unions have historically opposed such plans from their inception, through fear of management rate-cutting (for example, artificial reconstruction of the job in order to pay it a lower rate) and because of a deeply harbored suspicion that there is nothing "scientific" to *any* established rates. But managements that have yielded too readily to union requests for higher rates have also suffered, in inequities between earnings and effort, and in consequent problems involving not only finances but also employee morale. Increased automation of industry to the point where many workers cannot control their output rates has caused some further deemphasis of incentive plans in recent years. However, about one quarter of all production-plant workers in the United States continue to be paid under such plans, and it is obvious that the presence of such workers can make the comparative-norm principle severely misleading. (Cases 4 and 5 deal with the problem of wage incentive systems.)

Fourth, and finally, consideration must be given to the existence of the wide variety of fringe benefits previously cited. These benefits are not distributed equally throughout industry. Thus it could be wrong to conclude that workers in different plants are not equal in terms of net economic advantage where one group earns a lower basic wage rate but surpasses another group in terms of paid holidays and vacations, retirement, social insurance, and the like.

These considerations do not mean that the comparative-norm principle is of no value in collective bargaining. Its utility is demonstrated by its widespread use. But bargainers who utilize this avenue of wage comparisons without recognition of the several problems and limitations involved in its implementation do so only at their peril.

Ability to Pay

A second leading criterion involved in wage determination under collective bargaining is the ability of the firm or industry to pay a wage increase. The outcome of wage negotiations is frequently shaped by this factor, and many strikes occur where there is disagreement between company and union negotiators relative to the wage-paying capacity of the enterprise. Careful consideration and better understanding of this factor of wage determination is no less imperative for reducing the area of disagreement between industry and organized labor than is familiarity with the comparative-norm factor.

The level of profits is one indicator of the wage-paying ability of the firm involved in the negotiations. If a firm is earning a "high" rate of profit, union representatives will frequently claim that the company can afford all or most of the union wage demand. If the firm is earning a "low" rate of profit, management negotiators will frequently argue that the firm does not have the financial capacity to meet the union's wage demands. But the heart of this controversy is, clearly, the determination of what constitutes a rate of profits sufficient to meet a given union wage demand. Unfortunately, no economic formula can answer this question with precision and exactness.

As in the case of the preceding criterion, the problem is complicated by further considerations. In the *first* place, it is not certain whether a given rate of profits earned by a company over a given time in the past will hold for the future. Future profits may fall or rise depending upon the behavior of a number of economic variables that are themselves uncertain: Changes in sales, output, productivity, price, managerial efficiency, and even the state of international relations will all bear upon the future profit experience of a particular firm or industry. Thus, a wage rate negotiated in the light of a given historical profit experience may not be appropriate in the future. Moreover, if profits are to be used as an indicator of the firm's ability to meet a given wage demand, consideration must be given to anticipated government tax structures. The wage-paying ability of the firm may be quite different before and after the payment of the federal income tax, as many business administrators can testify. There are additional elements of the never-static national and state tax programs that tend to have an impact on the wage-paying ability of industry.

Second, the use to which a company intends to put its profits also has a vital bearing upon this problem. Since profits are frequently used to promote plant growth and improvement, the future plans of the enterprise itself must receive consideration by the negotiators. The problem of whether profits should be used for plant growth and improvement, for lower commodity price, or for higher wages is one of the most troublesome issues in industrial relations. The complexities of the problem involve such highly controversial matters as business-cycle theory, the orderly and sound growth of the economy, adequate purchasing power to buy the goods that industry produces, the varying expansion needs of different firms and industries, the justice or injustice of plant expansion instead of wage increases, the specific amount of the profits that should be used for wages, and alternative methods of financing growth and plant improvement other than the use of profits. These are only some of the secondary problems involved in the use of profits as an indicator of the ability of a company or industry to meet union wage demands. Clearly, the multitude of problems and questions that come to light in this connection demonstrates the difficulty of the utilization of this determinant of wages.

Third, although the level of profits is an important factor in the determination of a firm's ability to pay wages, it is not the only factor. Other considerations that have an important bearing on the problem are the ratio of labor costs to total costs, the amount of money expended for the financing of fringe benefits, the character of the product market in which the firm operates, the degree of elasticity of demand for the firm's product, and the ability of the company to increase productivity.

The ratio of labor costs to total costs particularly conditions the ability of a firm to afford increased wage rates. An employer is in a better position to grant higher wages when the firm's labor costs represent a comparatively small part of the total costs. For example, a 10 percent increase in wage rates will result in a 1 percent increase in total costs when wage costs are 10 percent of total costs (as they are, for example, in portions of the petroleum industry). Where, however, wage costs are 50 percent of total costs (as in segments of the leather industry), a 10 percent increase in wage rates will result in a 5 percent increase in total costs. This illustration, of course, is based upon the assumption that there is no increase or decrease in labor productivity after the wage rates are negotiated. If output increases faster than the wage rise, labor cost per unit of production tends to decrease. The reverse would be true where labor productivity does not increase with higher wages.

Moreover, the ratio of labor cost to total cost cannot by itself be taken as conclusive evidence of the wage-paying ability of a particular firm. Firms with a low labor cost do not necessarily have the capacity to pay higher wages. By the same token, it would not be accurate to conclude that firms with a high labor cost can never afford wage increases. All that can be said with some degree of accuracy is that if all economic variables were held constant, a firm with a low labor-cost ratio could afford to pay higher wages more easily than a firm with a high labor-cost ratio.

As in the case of the comparative-norm principle, it should also be reemphasized that an employer's total wage bill includes not only direct wage costs but costs incurred in providing employees with so-called "fringe" benefits. Even though basic wages constitute the major labor cost, industry each year pays a considerable amount of money in financing supplements to the basic wage bill. Into this category fall such items as sickness, accident, hospital, and dental insurance; pensions; severance pay; and paid holidays and vacations.

Industry's payments for such benefits have been rising rapidly. In a comprehensive survey conducted by the U.S. Chamber of Commerce for 79 identical companies, for example, it was estimated that these benefits rose from an equivalent of about 15.1 percent of total payroll in 1947 to about 30 percent in 1967, an increase of almost 100 percent. Even more impressive were the *absolute* gains revealed by the Chamber: Fringe benefits increased from 21.7 cents per payroll hour in 1947 to about $1.05 in 1967 (or virtually quintupled), and from $439 per employee in 1947 to almost $2,200 per employee in 1967 (for almost an exact fivefold growth in this twenty-year period).[3] By 1971, the percentage of total payroll attributable to fringe costs had increased to about 31 percent, and at this writing it remains at about that figure.[4]

[3] Economic Research Department, U.S. Chamber of Commerce, *Fringe Benefits*, 1967 (Washington, D.C.: U.S. Chamber of Commerce, 1968), p. 28.
    [4] *Ibid.*, 1972.

The ease with which a company can pass on the costs of a wage increase in the form of higher prices to other firms or to the consuming public is still another determinant of its wage-paying ability. Some firms (in the brewing and cigarette industries, for example) operate in a highly competitive selling market. Under these circumstances it is very difficult, if not impossible, for an employer to shift the burden of a wage increase to the consumer. Even a slight increase in price could result in a significant decrease in sales, since consumers would simply buy from other sellers. To the degree that a firm sells its products in a highly competitive market, it will find strong consumer resistance to price increases. In contrast, some companies (for example, newspaper publishers in single-newspaper cities) operate in monopolistic markets. Under these circumstances, companies have a greater degree of freedom to raise prices without experiencing a sharp decrease in sales. This would be particularly true where the product in question is sold under conditions of inelastic demand. Such a demand characteristic would apply to goods that are necessities or to those for which there are few satisfactory substitutes. Thus, if a company is operating in a monopolistic market and selling a product for which the demand is relatively inelastic, it has an excellent opportunity to shift the costs of wage increases to other firms or to the general public in the form of higher prices.

Negotiators at times take advantage of such an economic environment. Wage increases are agreed upon and the result is higher prices. From the public's point of view, it would be much more desirable if unions and employers could work out an arrangement whereby wages could be increased without price increases. Certainly, a wage agreement that increases the prices of basic economic commodities and thereby generates a general inflation of the price level cannot be regarded as socially sound.

Voluntary Wage Guideposts. For a few years in the 1960s, as it had on other occasions in the nation's history, the federal government made its feelings on this latter point abundantly clear. Starting in January 1962, the president's Council of Economic Advisers argued that labor cost increases should be limited to the nationwide annual rise in labor productivity (as measured by output per man-hour). Over the prior few years, according to CEA statistics, this annual productivity increase for the economy had averaged 3.2 percent, and the council consequently urged that contract settlement, through "voluntary restraint" by the bargaining parties, remain below this figure, or at a level that would presumably negate the need for price increases. Consistent with the sentiments of former CEA chairman Walter W. Heller that "the public interest today, more than ever, requires that the stability of our costs and prices be protected,"[5] the council guideposts (or "guidelines," as they were also called) were viewed by government officials as a mechanism for

[5]T. R. Brooks, "A Look Ahead to the Auto Negotiations," *The Reporter*, May 21, 1964, p. 27.

advancing national prosperity, aiding the nation in its balance of payments problems, and generally protecting the broader public interest.

Neither managements nor labor organizations, generally speaking, gave much endorsement to these wage–price guideposts. Managers tended to view them as a not-very-subtle form of government intervention, and even as a harbinger of ultimate price controls. Company spokesmen also argued that the CEA's recommendations would stifle business initiative and that, in addition, the current national levels of unemployment, unused plant capacity, and domestic and foreign competition were sufficient in themselves to ward off inflation. Symbolically, one steel executive commented that the guidelines were "based on the economics of the Potomac, not the economics of the steel industry."

To many unionists, the guideposts appeared to ignore "special situations," such as that existing in the automobile industry prior to the 1964 negotiations there: With auto profits at record highs in that year, the UAW leadership vociferously argued that the industry could pay considerably more than 3.2 percent to its workers and still cut prices, thereby making a settlement noninflationary. The union finally settled for about 4.8 percent. Labor spokesmen also attacked the guideposts as inequitably "freezing" worker shares in the income-distribution pie at their pre-1962 levels, in the absence of a convincing reason why such wage income shares should not be *increased*. And, as their counterparts on the management side, they also viewed with some alarm the increased government intervention implicit in the guideposts. It was said by one leading unionist that the 3.2 percent guideposts were "as welcome to organized labor as 3.2 beer."

Indeed, in February 1966, the AFL-CIO executive council officially condemned the guidelines. At that time, federation president George Meany, in characteristically blunt language, stated:

> Labor does not, cannot, and will not accept the guidelines. We see no way it can be applied equitably in an economy such as we have. We just don't like the guidelines. It destroys our collective bargaining. It works only one way—against us.[6]

Given this wave of opposition, it is doubtful that the guideposts ever had any significant influence on inflation. As President Nixon's Council of Economic Advisers could comment in reviewing these earlier years from the vantage point of 1970, the policy was applied during "years of considerable slack in the economy, relatively high unemployment, and stable or declining farm prices"—conditions that independently tended to favor price stability. When inflationary pressures—owing particularly to the exigencies of the war in Vietnam—increased after mid-1965, the guidepost policy "clearly did not work. . . . Labor and business were being asked to act as if prices were not rising, when in fact they were. As it became evident that steps necessary

[6]*Christian Science Monitor*, February 26, 1966, p. 4.

to keep prices from rising were not being taken, it also became more obviously unrealistic and inequitable to make these requests in specific cases."[7] By late 1965, indeed, settlements reached in the can, aluminum, rubber, textile, oil, and construction industries, among others, had all breached the 3.2 figure in varying degrees, and a few months after this, the guidepost policy, being widely perceived as unsuccessful, was allowed to quietly fade away.

Nixon's Mandatory Wage and Price Control Program. On August 15, 1971, however, Nixon ordered a 90-day freeze on wages and prices. It was followed by a mandatory wage and price control program, a policy that was announced despite previous assurances from the president and high administration officials that such a program would not be put into effect. It was the third time in this century that the federal government set up controls on wages and prices on a national scale, and, as during World War II and the Korean War, the program was adopted to restrain the surging rate of prices.

For, despite Nixon's effort to curb inflation by fiscal and monetary policies, the price level had increased by 5.4 percent in 1969 and by 5.9 percent in 1970. The traditional anti-inflation methods had not been effective because the kind of inflation experienced in those years was not attributable to excessive aggregate demand. It was more a case of *cost-push* inflation than of *demand-pull* inflation, a phenomenon that is not effectively checked by a reduction in demand. As a matter of fact, the pre-1971 Nixon approach had not only failed to stem rising prices, but by common agreement had caused unemployment to increase to 5 percent in 1970 and 5.9 percent in 1971, or to the highest rate since 1961, when the figure was 6.7 percent.

To deal with the unemployment problem (of some political urgency, since by August 1971, the 1972 presidential election was only 15 months away), the Nixon administration reversed its monetary and fiscal policies of the preceding two years and sought to increase aggregate demand. So that the new Nixon policy would not aggravate the inflation problem, the mandatory wage and price control program was put into effect. Despite the criticism (largely from the AFL-CIO) that the price side of the program was not enforced fairly and effectively, the rate of inflation subsided in 1971 and 1972. Prices increased by 4.3 percent in 1971 and by only 3.4 percent in 1972. At the same time, unemployment was reduced to 5.6 percent in 1972.

Policies of the Pay Board. To administer the wage control program, a Pay Board was established, composed of 15 members, divided equally among representatives of business, labor, and the public. However, in March 1972, all labor members except Frank Fitzsimmons, president of the Teamsters, resigned, charging that the wage and price control program was not being administered fairly. George Meany, one of the four labor members who resigned, stated:

[7] *Monthly Labor Review,* March 1970, p. 2.

We will not be a part of the window dressing for this system of unfair and inequitable government control of wages for the benefit of business profits.[8]

The core of Board regulations was a standard of 5.5 percent as the maximum allowable increase in pay. Added to this figure was a 0.7 percent allowable increase in certain fringe benefits. *Thus, the basic standard was a 6.2 percent increase in direct wage and fringe increases.* However, the Pay Board permitted basic wage rates to rise 7 percent as a "catch-up," to cover employees who had received less than a 7 percent increase per year over the preceding three years. In some exceptional cases, the Pay Board permitted increases beyond its maximum standards. Thus, in 1972 it approved a 14.9 percent increase for dock workers; 15 percent in the soft coal industry; 10 percent for many railway employees; and 8.3 percent in the aerospace industry.

One feature of the wage control program, however, particularly irritated labor leaders. Top executive salaries increased by an average of 24.6 percent in 1972, as compared to 9.3 percent in 1971.[9] In a few cases, the increases were particularly high: For example, in 1971, Henry Ford II, chairman of the Ford Motor Company, had his salary and bonuses increased to $689,000, a 37.8 percent jump over 1970; Lee A. Iacocca, president of Ford, enjoyed an increase of 48.3 percent; Lynn Townsend, chairman of the Chrysler Corporation, had his salary increased in 1971 to $225,000, from $200,000 in 1970; and Harold S. Geneen, president of International Telephone and Telegraph, received $812,494 in 1971, compared to $766,755 in 1970.[10] These increases prompted the AFL-CIO to say:

The Pay Board may be doing an excellent job of holding down the wage increase of rank-and-file workers to 5.5 percent, but a different set of rules for the top executives of large corporations [allows] them to receive salary increases [of this type].[11]

Of course, Pay Board allowable increases were not required; they were maximums. Where unions were involved, wage and fringe benefit increases had to be negotiated in collective bargaining within the framework of the Pay Board standards. The record shows that the Pay Board was effective in holding down wage rate increases. Whereas average negotiated wage rates increased by 11.6 percent in 1971, the increase was 7.3 percent in 1972 and 5.8 percent in 1973.

[8]U.S. Department of Labor, Bureau of Labor Statistics, *Monthly Labor Review*, Vol. 95, No. 5 (May 1972), 63. For a detailed account of the Pay Board's policies, see Office of the Federal Register, National Archives and Records Section, General Services Administration, *Code of Federal Regulation—Economic Stabilization*, June 1, 1972.

[9]*Business Week*, May 5, 1973.

[10]*Wall Street Journal*, April 24, 1972; *Louisville Courier-Journal*, May 7, 1972.

[11]*AFL-CIO News*, April 29, 1972.

Beyond its wage rate and fringe benefit policies, the Pay Board established a number of other standards. Wage rate increases based upon promotions were authorized; automatic increases based upon length of service were permitted, provided that the program was in effect prior to the wage control program; and, under certain circumstances, employers were permitted to increase employees' wages on the basis of meritorious performance. On the other hand, the Pay Board did not permit wage increases beyond its standards to be placed in escrow to be paid after the control policy ended.

Beyond holding down employee wage rates, the wage control program had additional effects upon labor relations. Whereas multiyear labor agreements are common in collective bargaining, the impact of the wage control program resulted in the negotiation of one-year labor agreements. The reason, of course, was that unions wanted to be free to negotiate higher wages once the control program ended. Within the construction industry, 81 percent of all contracts were negotiated for one year in 1972, compared with only 7 percent in 1970. In nonconstruction industries, 15 percent of the contracts were of one year duration in 1972, in contrast to 8 percent in 1970.[12]

Their capability in the wage area checked by the control program, many unions also emphasized negotiation in the allowable fringe benefit area.[13] In addition, many unions paid particular attention to the negotiation and the enforcement of employees' job rights, such as protection against arbitrary discharge, promotion matters, and paid time while not actually working. Undoubtedly, the impact of the program resulted in fewer strikes, since the wage issue was largely removed as an item of conflict. Whereas 5,716 strikes involving 3,305,000 workers occurred in 1970, the figure dropped in 1972 to 5,100 strikes involving 1,700,000 workers. The amount of production time lost because of all strikes dropped to 0.14 percent of estimated working time in 1972, as compared with 0.37 percent in 1970. Investigating this trend, one author believes that it was at least partly attributable to the wage control program. He says:

> Even with contruction included in the data, the drop in the number of workers and man-days involved in the strikes appears to be more than accounted for by the drop in workers involved in new negotiations and cyclical factors.[14]

End of Nixon Wage and Price Control Program. In January 1973, following his record-breaking victory in the 1972 presidential election, Nixon abandoned the mandatory wage and price control program. This abrupt change in policy came as a surprise to many people, since the price level had increased

[12]Daniel Mitchell, "Phase II Wage Controls," *Industrial and Labor Relations Review*, Vol. 27, No. 3 (April 1974), p. 373.
[13]AFL-CIO, *American Federationist*, March 1972, p. 12.
[14]Mitchell, "Phase II," p. 373.

by only 3.4 percent in 1972 even though price controls were not enforced with the same vigor as was the program in effect during World War II. With the exception of the food, health care, and construction industries, employers and unions were placed on the honor system to hold down price and wage increases so that overall price level increases would not exceed 2.5 percent for the year.

When the mandatory program terminated, however, George P. Shultz, then secretary of labor, stated that the administration retained an "ability to bring the big stick out of the closet," to enforce unacceptable wage–price behavior. He also stated that the voluntary nature of the program would be aided by "the knowledge that people who don't abide by the program may get clobbered."[15]

Experience proved the voluntary program to be a complete failure. The stick never came out of the closet and no one got clobbered. Indeed, by June 1973, the cost of living increased by about 9 percent. And, embarrassing as it must have been to the Nixon administration, another wage and price freeze was instituted from June 13, 1973, through August 12, 1973. Despite this freeze, prices increased by 8.8 percent for the entire year. Wage rates, however, increased at only 5.8 percent, resulting, of course, in a decline in real income for the average American employee. Inflation surged even higher during the first quarter of 1974, increasing at the rate of about 15 percent!

On April 30, 1974, the entire program terminated when Congress did not renew the authority of the president to impose mandatory wage and price controls. The legislative basis of the program was permitted to die because no pressure was put on Congress. Unions, dissatisfied with employees' experience under the program, cheered at the burial; business, enjoying once again the free market and the capability to increase profits by increasing prices, did not weep; and Nixon himself did not urge Congress to renew his authority to impose mandatory wage and price controls.

But even though these interested parties did not resist the abolishment of the program, the consuming public felt the sting of almost unprecedented inflation in 1974. In that year, the price level increased by 12.2 percent and wage rates increased by 9.8 percent, once again resulting in the decline of real income for the average worker.

Inflation cooled somewhat in 1975, largely as a result of the worst unemployment rate since the Great Depression. It is conceivable that had the wage and price controls been maintained, improved by eliminating the most visible inequalities on the wage side and by more effective enforcement on the price side, the nation might not have suffered simultaneous unacceptable rates of inflation and unemployment.

[15] U.S. Department of Labor, Bureau of Labor Statistics, *Monthly Labor Review*, Vol. 96, No. 2 (February 1973), p. 63.

The Truitt Decision. In April 1956, the U.S. Supreme Court handed down an important and still applicable decision dealing with the legal obligation of employers who argue that they cannot afford wage increases.[16]

At times, a company that is confronted with a wage request by a union will claim that it lacks the financial capacity to meet such a demand. When an employer takes this position, labor organizations will ordinarily request that the company furnish them with information bearing upon the company's wage-paying ability. In the *Truitt Manufacturing Company* case, the Supreme Court held that when the employer argues that he lacks the economic ability to meet a particular wage demand, he must make financial information available to the union. In justifying this policy, the high court stated:

> Good faith bargaining necessarily requires that claims by either bargainer should be honest claims. This is true about an asserted inability to pay an increase in wages. If such an argument is important enough to present in the give and take of bargaining, it is important enough to require some sort of proof of its accuracy.

The *Truitt* decision, of course, does not mean that the company must capitulate to union wage demands. In fact, the company can refuse to meet the union request even if the information elicited by the union shows conclusively that it *has* the ability to pay the wages demanded by the union. In addition, the Supreme Court did not specify that the employer must automatically produce proof in every instance where he pleads inability to pay. The Court held that each case must turn upon its own merits. Thus, in this connection it declared:

> We do not hold . . . that in every case in which economic inability is raised as an argument against increased wages it automatically follows that the employees are entitled to substantiating evidence. Each case must turn upon its particular facts. The inquiry must always be whether or not under the circumstances of the particular case the statutory obligation to bargain in good faith has been met.

Finally, the *Truitt* decision did not establish a hard and fast rule as to the character of evidence that the employer must show when he pleads lack of ability. As is apparent from the general tone of the Court's decision, this determination would also be made on a case-by-case basis, as indeed has been the case in the years since *Truitt* was decided. These considerations, however, do not detract from the important principle established in the *Truitt* decision. The fact is that employers who argue economic inability to meet union wage demands must now generally be prepared either to produce

[16]*NLRB* v. *Truitt Manufacturing Co.*, 351 U.S. 149 (1956).

relevant evidence to substantiate this position or to face charges of unfair labor practice.

Standard of Living

Orientation of the plant wage structure to community and industry levels and ability to pay are not the only criteria utilized for wage determination in contemporary industry. Many management and, particularly, labor representatives are concerned with the problem of the adequacy of wages to guarantee workers "a decent standard of living." Disagreements arise, however, as to what constitutes such a standard.

The problem is most often resolved by personal judgment and opinions of the negotiators. More objective information is, however, at the disposal of the parties, and it has frequently been used to support demands and counter-demands at the bargaining table.

At the present time, the most widely publicized source of standard of living information is that published by the U.S. Department of Labor's Bureau of Labor Statistics. First developed in 1946–47 at the request of Congress, and revised periodically since that time, the BLS's "City Worker's Family Budget" attempts to describe and measure a "modest but adequate standard of living." It is necessarily selective, restricting itself to a measurement of the income needed by a family of four (a 38-year-old employed husband, a wife not employed outside the home, and two children of school age—a 13-year-old boy and an 8-year-old girl), living in a rented dwelling in a large city or its suburbs. By studying the prices of a "representative list of goods and services" presumably purchased by such families, for twenty major cities (weighted according to their populations), the BLS endeavors to show the cost of "a level of adequate living standards prevailing in large cities of the United States in recent years."

To make the "City Worker's Budget" more meaningful, the Bureau of Labor Statistics provides levels for three standards of living—lower, intermediate, and higher. Naturally, employees who earn sufficient wages to live at the higher level enjoy more of the good things of life as compared to the workers whose wages can claim only the goods and services at the lower level. For the spring of 1975, it required $9,469 for the lower budget, $14,800 for the intermediate budget, and $21,442 for the higher budget.[17] The differences in the standards of living are illustrated by the amount of money required for food. The lower budget allocates only $2,440 for food, as compared with $4,020 for the higher budget. At the lower level, this amounts to only $6.68 per day for a family of four. Such a family could hardly be expected to enjoy choice steaks or lobster tails, and if the parents desired

[17]Based on Bureau of Labor Statistics figured for the autumn of 1974 and updated to include the increase in cost of living.

to enjoy alcoholic beverages, they might have cheap wine or an occasional beer, but they surely would not be able to afford Chivas Regal scotch!

As expected, the amount required varies considerably depending upon the city involved. The most expensive city to live in is Anchorage, Alaska, followed by Honolulu, San Francisco, and Boston. Austin, Texas, is the cheapest city in which to live; slightly more expensive are Baton Rouge, Nashville, and Houston. In all cases, however, the overall weighted averages at the time of this writing were sufficiently beyond that earned by most workers to make the budget an attractive bargaining weapon for union negotiators. Labor spokesmen had not been hesitant about arguing the "need" for substantial wage increases to reach the budgeted levels, while also pointing out that the overall weighted average was required to meet the necessities of life, pay taxes, and enjoy a few amenities—but that it contained no allowance for luxuries or savings.

Employers, equally logically, had taken bitter exception to this most recent "City Worker's Budget." They had argued that the items used in computing the budget were far too generous to warrant the description "modest but adequate"; frequently cited in this regard were the budget's annual allowance for gifts and contributions, and certain of its provisions for furniture, appliances, automobiles, and recreation. In addition, they pointed out that wage earners do not have uniform responsibilities in terms of dependents (with many, of course, having no dependents), and that many families have more than one wage earner.

The arguments and counterarguments can be expected to continue indefinitely, without mutual agreement as to their validity; the line of demarcation between "luxury" and "necessity" has never been susceptible to exact location, and the concept of "decency" allows much room for emotion. Moreover, despite the increasingly frequent use of the standard of living criterion at the bargaining table, it does not carry as much weight as the other wage factors analyzed in the previous sections of this chapter. After all, an employer who truthfully cannot pay wages that will realize the "modest but adequate standard of living" may be entirely sympathetic to his worker's needs, but the cold realism of economic life will not persuade him to grant the additional wages. Likewise, a union will not stop at the level of wages required of the budget if it can get more from the employer because of the operation of the other wage criteria; indeed, under these circumstances, the union will probably argue that the items of the budget are too meager.

But use of such standard of living information as that provided by the BLS—and by such other sources as the Census Bureau, Federal Reserve Board, Department of Commerce, and independent studies of the parties themselves—is still to be preferred to total recourse to personal opinion on the subject. The data may not be accepted, but even in rejecting them the recalcitrant party is forced to deal with information that is more objective than mere individual sentiment.

COST OF LIVING: ESCALATOR
AND WAGE-REOPENER ARRANGEMENTS

In addition to the comparative-norm, ability to pay, and standard of living principles, experienced negotiators pay close attention in wage negotiations to the status of the *cost of living*. This economic phenomenon is important because trends in the cost of living have an important bearing upon the real income of workers. Increases in the cost of living at a given level of earnings result in decreased capacity of workers to buy goods and services. By the same token, real income tends to increase with decreases in the cost of living at a given wage level. Real income for a particular group of workers also increases for a time when money wages increase faster than the cost of living.

As a matter of fact, during the soaring inflation in 1973 and 1974, the cost of living was the major determinant for wage negotiations, as union leaders raced to keep up with higher and higher prices to protect the real income of their members. Of course, as explained above, to the extent that wage rates exceeded productivity, negotiated wages aggravated the inflation problem. If the lessons of this period of inflation teach us anything, it is that a stable price level is the way to achieve the negotiation of noninflationary wage rates.

It is beyond the scope of this volume to analyze the multitude of factors that influence the cost of living in the American economy. This cost is affected by a variety of forces, including the general climate of business activity, productivity, the financial and monetary policies followed by financial institutions, the rate of new investment, and the propensity of consumers to spend money, as well as by the wage policies that are followed under collective bargaining itself. Government policies relating to interest rates, tariffs, the lending capacity of national banks, taxation, and agriculture also have an impact upon the cost of living. And, of course, as we well knew in the mid-1970s, rising energy costs constitute another important factor for higher prices. When the Arab nations increased the cost of oil from about $5 per barrel to $11, the effect was felt not only in increasing gasoline prices, but in other goods manufactured by petroleum-chemical industries.

The uncertain character of the forces determining the cost of living makes it very difficult to predict with certainty its future trends. The difficulty inherent in using the cost of living as a determinant in wage negotiations is simply this: Wages are negotiated for a *future* period, whereas cost-of-living data are *historical* in character. It is a comparatively simple task to adjust wages for historical trends in the cost of living if this is the desire of the negotiators. The criterion is of limited usefulness, however, in the attempt to orient wage rates to future trends in the Consumer Price Index. The capricious character of the index makes forecasting extremely hazardous. In any event, for intelligent utilization of this wage determinant, it becomes necessary not only to have accurate information on historical trends, but also to make an assessment of the future trends of the factors that determine the Consumer Price Index.[18] It cannot be emphasized too much that such predictions are fraught with difficulties and uncertainties.

Some companies and unions have, however, adopted one or both of two procedures—escalator clauses and wage reopeners—that take into account the capriciousness of the cost of living and likewise recognize the importance of trends in the Consumer Price Index as they relate to the real income of employees and to the financial position of companies.

Escalator Clauses

The philosophy behind the incorporation of so-called "escalator clauses" in labor agreements is that wages of workers should rise and fall automatically with fluctuations in the cost of living. The escalator arrangement first attained national prominence in the 1950 General Motors–United Automobile Workers collective bargaining agreement. As a result of the anticipated price inflation growing out of the Korean War, many other companies and unions soon negotiated similar arrangements, and by 1952 such arrangements covered about 3.5 million workers—concentrated mainly in the automobile, railroad, textile, aircraft, agricultural implement, and flat-glass industries. They also appeared in a wide variety of other manufacturing and nonmanufacturing industries.

Since 1952, use of the wage escalator clause appears to have depended to a great extent on the upward movement of the cost-of-living index. By 1955, for example, three years of comparatively steady prices had elapsed, and the number of workers covered by such escalator clauses had dropped considerably, to about 1.7 million.[19] In 1956, on the other hand, the Consumer Price Index moved strongly forward, and a study conducted late in that year estimated that approximately 3.5 million workers were once again covered by escalator arrangements.[20] The incorporation of an escalator formula in the 1956 basic steel contract—covering 600,000 workers—alone accounted for almost one-third of this increase.

With relatively modest annual price movements from 1956 through mid-1965, interest in the escalator once more temporarily waned. By 1965, the railroads, electrical industry, and (ironically) basic steel had completely abandoned the device, and only about 2 million workers—concentrated

[18]The Consumer Price Index (CPI) is the index that is almost universally utilized in collective bargaining by employers and unions. It is prepared and published by the Bureau of Labor Statistics and appears each month in the Bureau's *Monthly Labor Review*.

[19]"Wage Escalation—Recent Developments," *Monthly Labor Review*, Vol. 77 (March 1955), 315.

[20]Bureau of National Affairs, ed., "What's New in Collective Bargaining Negotiations and Contracts," No. 300 (November 30, 1956), p. 4.

mainly in automobiles and automobile parts, farm and construction equipment, trucking, and meat packing—were covered by escalator clauses in the latter year.[21] On the other hand, the significant surge in the price level after mid-1965 had brought another half-million employees under coverage by 1969. And the enormous surge of prices in 1973 and 1974 again stimulated the growth of cost-of-living escalator clauses. By the end of 1974, 5.1 million workers were covered by the arrangement.[22] In fact, in the first nine months of 1974, escalator clauses appeared for the first time in 110 major contracts, covering 612,000 workers.[23]

Perhaps the greatest single reason why the figures above are nonetheless not spectacular, even for the pronounced U.S. inflation following 1965, lies in the intense historical management opposition to the escalator concept. Employers have voiced fears that prices could not be commensurately raised without undesirable effects on profits. They have also argued what they view as the inequities of a system that allows workers to benefit without effort of any kind on their part: One mid-1960s increase in the cost-of-living index, for example, was attributed by government spokesmen primarily to increases in sugar and cigarette prices—a situation that even the most sugar-consuming and chain-smoking work force could not noticeably influence. Still other managers have stressed the potential inflationary ramifications of the escalator in opposing its use. Above all, however, employers have attacked the constant "freezing" of cost-of-living allowances into basic wage rates: Most labor contracts ultimately make such allowances a permanent part of rates when the agreements are renegotiated and to many workers the allowances are, consequently, really additional wage increases temporarily couched in other terms.

Managements could, understandably, be expected to generate greater enthusiasm for the escalator in the event of a prolonged national period of markedly *downward* prices, but this appears an unlikely possibility for the foreseeable future. Even in the continuing absence of such a situation, however, and even if one disregards the current aggressive attempts of unions to gain the escalator device in the face of the strong upward price movements now operative, it is possible that some impetus will be provided for the escalator in the general gradual lengthening of the terms of labor contracts.

The evidence that contracts are becoming longer—such temporary regressions in the trend as in the case of the wage controls of the early 1970s notwithstanding—is persuasive. Whereas in 1948 about 75 percent of collective bargaining agreements were for one year or less, by 1963 the proportion

---

[21]"Deferred Increases Due in 1965 and Wage Escalation," *Monthly Labor Review*, Vol. 87, No. 12 (December 1964), 1384. Some employees in chemicals, retail trade, and public transit also remained covered by escalator clauses.

[22]U.S. Department of Labor, Bureau of Labor Statistics, *Monthly Labor Review*, Vol. 98, No. 1 (January 1975), p. 43.

[23]*Ibid.*, p. 7.

of contracts running for longer than one year had increased sharply—to as much as 86 percent, by some estimates,[24] and by 1975 as many as 90 percent of all contracts may have been for more than one year. Longer-term contracts lend greater stability to labor relationships, and by definition they reduce the problems of negotiation and the traumas of frequent strike threats. However, as contracts are negotiated for longer periods of time, negotiators must recognize the necessity of providing some method for the adjustment of wages during the contractual period. Some authorities believe that increasing awareness of this situation, together with the continuation of the trend to contracts of longer duration, will lend greater allure to the escalator formula, even in the face of continuing managerial opposition to the whole idea.

Although there is a wide variety of escalator arrangements, all contain a number of common principles. The most significant characteristic of the escalator formula is its automaticity. For the duration of the labor agreement, wage changes as related to cost of living are precisely determined by the behavior of a statistical index—almost always the Consumer Price Index. Wages are increased or decreased in accordance with comparatively small changes in this index. For example, the labor agreement might provide, as many recent ones have, for a $.01-per-hour adjustment of wages for every 0.4-point change in the CPI.

Escalators frequently work on a quarterly basis. Under this arrangement, used until recently by the automobile industry (among others), the cost-of-living index is reviewed every three months and wages are changed in accordance with the escalator formula. On the other hand, the over-the-road trucking industry currently provides for essentially annual determination, and several other sectors that use the escalator operate it on a semiannual basis. In addition, the escalator arrangement often specifies the floor to which wages can fall in response to changes in the cost-of-living index; However, the escalator formula does not usually contain a *ceiling* on wage increases occasioned by increases in the CPI.

Finally, the escalator principle of wage adjustment is often accompanied by a definite and guaranteed increase in wages on an annual basis. This feature of the wage contract is popularly referred to as the *annual improvement factor*. Under the 1964–67 auto contracts, for example, wages were to be increased in 1965 by $2\frac{1}{2}$ percent or $.06 per hour (whichever was the greater), continuing the same formula for these three-year contracts that had been applied to each year except 1964 (when the formula was suspended to allow increased fringe benefits) of the 1958–61 and 1961–64 automobile contracts. In 1966, however, there was to be a change: The annual increases

<hr/>

[24]See, for example, "Agreement Duration, Renewal, and General Wage Adjustment," published jointly by the School of Business of Indiana University and the Indiana State Chamber of Commerce (Bloomington, Ind., 1963). *Labor Relations Reporter*, June 29, 1959, pp. 198–225, found that even by 1959 only 24 percent of all contracts were for one year or less.

would be advanced to 2.8 percent, with a minimum of 7 cents. And under the 1967–70 contracts a more complicated formula took over; workers with a straight-time hourly rate of less than $3.17 would receive an annual improvement factor increase of 9 cents per hour, those earning between $3.17 and $3.49, 10 cents, and so on. Workers were guaranteed this increase regardless of fluctuations of the CPI during the contractual period.

Wage Reopeners

A second method for wage adjustments during the life of a labor agreement involves a provision that permits either the company or the union to *reopen* labor agreements *for wage issues* at stated intervals. Where such a procedure is employed, labor agreements normally provide that contracts that are negotiated for one year may be reopened for wage issues after six months. Contracts that are written for two-year periods or longer are customarily open for wage negotiations once each year.

Two major characteristics of the wage-reopening clause arrangement distinguish it from the escalator principle as a method of wage adjustment. The most important involves the fact that whereas the escalator arrangement provides for an *automatic* change in wages based upon a definite formula, under wage reopeners the parties must *negotiate* wage changes. This could be an advantage or a disadvantage, depending upon the particular circumstances of a given collective bargaining relationship. In addition, the wage-reopener arrangement can be utilized to take into account determinants of wages other than the cost of living. The fact that both the escalator and the reopener arrangements are frequently found together in industry indicates that both procedures apparently fill the needs of employers, employees, and unions. What may be suitable for one collective bargaining relationship, however, clearly might be unsuitable for another company and union.

To invoke a wage-reopening clause, collective bargaining contracts require that the party which desires to change wages give a written notice to the other party within a specified period. Under the terms of the Taft-Hartley law, as we know, a party to a collective bargaining agreement desiring to modify or terminate the agreement must give 60 days' notice of its intention to do so. Following such notice, the law declares that there may be no lockout or strike "for a period of sixty days . . . or until the expiration date of such contract, whichever occurs later." Employees who engage in a strike during this period lose their status as employees under Taft-Hartley and have no legal right to be reinstated.

These provisions of the Taft-Hartley law are important in connection with this discussion because wage-reopening arrangements invariably provide that a union may call a strike over wage issues if a settlement is not reached during the negotiation period. Such a strike takes place after the negotiation period as provided for in the wage-reopening clause but before the termination date of the entire contract. The question therefore arises as to whether or not a strike under these circumstances is lawful under the Taft-Hartley law. It is stressed that the law provides that no strike may take place during the 60-day notice period or until the date the contract expires, "*whichever occurs later.*"

The National Labor Relations Board in 1954 dealt with this question of whether or not a strike called pursuant to a wage-reopening clause is consistent with Taft-Hartley, and held that such a strike is lawful even though it occurs before the terminal date of the entire labor contract, provided that the 60-day notice requirement of the Taft-Hartley law is met.[25] In reaching this decision, the board was compelled to interpret the portion of Taft-Hartley that forbids a strike during the 60-day notice period or until the date of expiration of a contract, whichever occurs later. It held in this connection that, for purposes of the law, the term *expiration date* refers not only to the terminal date of the entire collective bargaining contract but also to the date agreed upon in the contract when the parties can effect changes in its provisions. On this point, the board declared:

> ... the term "expiration date" as used in Section 8(d)(4) thus has a twofold meaning: It connotes not only the terminal date of a bargaining contract, but also an agreed date in the course of its existence when the parties can effect changes in its provisions.

Upon a review, however, a circuit court of appeals rejected the meaning attributed by the board to the term *expiration date*. In this court's view, the term must be held to mean "termination" date, and all strikes for modification before the contract's actual termination are unlawful. Concluding that the labor agreement had not been "terminated" within the meaning of the Taft-Hartley Act at the time of the strike, the court ruled that the employees in the strike lost their status as employees for purposes of the law and that they could be discharged by the company. Because of the obvious importance of the issues involved in the controversy between the National Labor Relations Board and the circuit court, the board appealed to the Supreme Court for a review of the case. In January 1957, the Supreme Court sustained the position of the board and held that the Taft-Hartley law permits a strike, after a 60-day notice, during the life of collective bargaining contracts that contain wage-reopening clauses. To the date of this writing, labor relations continued to be governed by such a principle.

WAGE DIFFERENTIALS

Under certain circumstances, collective bargaining contracts provide for different rates of wages for different employees performing the same kind of work and holding down the same type of jobs. Such differentials

---

[25]*Lion Oil Co.*, 109 NLRB 680 (1954).

are completely lawful, except when used by the parties to discriminate on the basis of race, color, religion, sex, or national origin; as of July 2, 1965, the latter practices were forbidden under the terms of Title VII of the Civil Rights Act of 1964.[26] To many employers (as well as to unions), moreover, utilization of the "nondiscriminatory" differentials appears mandatory to ensure an adequate supply of willing employees for work under arduous or otherwise unpleasant conditions.

The most common of these differentials involves premium payment for work on relatively undesirable shifts—in the late afternoon, evening, night, and early morning hours. Within industry as a whole, 98 percent of workers in plants running such late shifts were by the mid-1960s receiving extra pay for this work.[27]

In addition, under most contracts there is now a graduated increase in compensation for working the second and third shifts. All but a tiny fraction of workers in establishments where there is a third, or "graveyard," work schedule now receive a rate for it that is higher than that received by second-shift workers. But second-shift workers themselves have received relatively significant premiums for their acceptance of these working hours: Premium rates for second-shift work are now most commonly at least 5 cents per hour, and often as high as 10 percent above first-shift rates. Premiums of at least 15 cents per hour, and often up to 10 percent of second-shift rates, are the general rewards for the graveyard-shift workers.

The rationale for the shift differential is quite easy to understand. When an employee works a less common shift, there is obvious interference with his family life and with his full participation in the affairs of society. In Western society, the school system, recreational activities, cultural pursuits, and the like assume that employees work during the day. Since working the odd hours tends to interfere with the employee's family and societal affairs, the premium is designed to compensate him for this sacrifice. And although it is a fact of industrial life that some employees because of certain conditions may actually prefer to work the afternoon or midnight tour (under these circumstances, the employee reaps a net benefit for the shift differential premium), the overwhelming number of employees prefers the day shift, and thus the shift differential will undoubtedly always be a common feature in the collectively bargained wage package.

Under many collective bargaining contracts, special premiums are also provided for workers who handle certain supervisory or instructional duties, especially demanding tasks, or particularly hazardous, dirty, or undesirable work. For these jobs, extra pay is again granted as a premium to the basic wage rate of the worker concerned. For example, under one current Mid-western agreement, a $1.00-per-hour premium is paid to employees who are

[26]Title VII did, however, grant exemptions to work forces of less than 25 persons.
[27]Bureau of National Affairs, ed., *Facts for Bargaining*, II (Washington, D.C.: Bureau of National Affairs, Inc., June 4, 1965), 522.

engaged in "dirty work." Such work is spelled out in the labor agreement and includes, among other possibilities for premium-rate reimbursement, "work in oil tanks where not cleaned out." Another labor agreement provides for the regular overtime rate for employees engaged in hazardous work. This provision covers employees working at elevations "where there is danger of a fall of fifty feet or more."

In addition to these *premium*-rate practices, many collective bargaining contracts allow *lower* differentials for other situations. A number of agreements provide lower rates for workers who are handicapped, superannuated, temporary, or learners. Such differentials are rooted in the belief that these qualities make workers comparatively less productive, and even the federal government, recognizing the persuasive economic logic involved, has gone along with this employer argument to the extent of exempting such workers from the minimum wage laws. Abuses have occasionally been in evidence, however: Some "temporary" employees turn out, upon closer inspection, to be deserving of 25-year pins; and some "handicapped" employees appear to have nothing more than color-blindness. Such situations notwithstanding, employer good faith in regard to these workers is far more the rule than the exception, and the differential can be defended on the grounds that the alternative to a lower rate of remuneration for such employees is, most often, unemployment.

Until passage and implementation of the Civil Rights Act, some contracts also contained lower wage rates for women than for men and for blacks than for white employees. For women, the practice was traditionally defended on such presumed grounds as a lesser productivity of women than men, a female inability to do all the tasks performed by men in accomplishing a job, and the argument that the employment of women at times involves extra costs not incurred when men are employed. Racial discrimination per se appears to have motivated the black differential, although some of the lower-productivity claims used to defend lower women's wages were also heard. Since mid-1965, neither type of differential is, understandably, promulgated by labor contracts governed by the act, although whether or not the practices involved will continue is subject to employer and union compliance, which goes well beyond the official wording of their agreements. At least for women, one convenient and perfectly legal dodge has been available to recalcitrant managers: the alteration of certain jobs—often by removing some minor portion of the original job sequence—and then re-awarding such work to qualified women applicants as "female work."

OVERTIME PROBLEMS

Collective bargaining agreements invariably establish a standard number of hours per day and per week during which employees are paid their regular rate of pay. For hours worked in excess of the standard, however, employers are required to pay employees overtime rates. By far the most common standards found in labor agreements are eight hours per day and 40 hours per week, with only a fraction of labor agreements establishing standards differing from this formula. In the wearing apparel, printing, and publishing industries, a number of agreements do provide for a basic 7- to $7\frac{1}{2}$-hour day and 35-hour workweek; and in the food-processing, retail, and service industries some contracts establish a standard 44-hour week; but these remain the exceptions.

The fact that Fair Labor Standards Act provides a basic 40-hour week undoubtedly has caused the adoption of a 40-hour standard workweek under collective bargaining. Labor agreements that provide for a basic workweek in excess of 40 hours without premium overtime pay presumably do not fall within the scope of this legislation, or within the reach of the several state wage and hour laws which regulate this activity within certain states for their intrastate commerce. On the other hand, nothing in the federal wage and hour law prohibits employers and unions from negotiating a workweek of *less* than 40 hours, and (although thus far with more potential than actuality) the shorter workweek as a partial answer to the unemployment threats of automation loomed as a new labor relations issue in the 1970s, after years of relative quiescence. In addition, the Fair Labor Standards Act places no restriction on employers who desire their employees to work *more* than 40 hours in a workweek, other than that the employees who work more than 40 hours must be paid at least one and one-half times their regular rate of pay for all hours in excess of 40.

The vast majority of labor agreements provide overtime rates of exactly one and one-half times the regular rate of pay for employees who work in excess of 40 hours per week, thus offering a not surprising conformity to the minimum provisions of the Fair Labor Standards Act, but a relatively small number of labor agreements do call for overtime rates of greater than time-and-one-half pay, most frequently double-time. With respect to hours worked in excess of the *daily* standard, most labor agreements also provide for time-and-one-half, although some labor agreements provide for double-time after a certain number of hours are worked or after a stipulated hour of the day or night. For example, some employers and unions have agreed that double-time rates should be paid if employees work more than four hours' overtime on any one workday. In this connection it should be noted that—since the Fair Labor Standards Act does not establish a basic workday—if employees are to be paid for working hours in excess of a certain number per day, the parties to the collective bargaining contract must negotiate this objective.

In addition to establishing standard workdays and workweeks and providing the rate for hours worked in excess of these standards, collective bargaining contracts deal with other phases of the hours and overtime problem. Most labor agreements prohibit the *pyramiding* of overtime. This means that weekly overtime premiums are not required for hours for which daily overtime premiums have already been paid; moreover, many contracts provide that only one type of overtime premium can be paid for any one day. And in many collective bargaining relationships the company also has the unlimited authority for ordering overtime.

As in the case of the shorter workweek, this issue of overtime scheduling authority also promised to become a major collective bargaining issue at the time of this writing. Because of the economy's growing unemployment totals—which had reached a post–Great Depression high of 9.2 percent by the summer of 1975—and because of the constant menace of ever-greater displacement through automation, some unions were pressing for a flat prohibition against overtime in an attempt to preserve job opportunities. Few unions had thus far succeeded in this goal, although several bargaining units in the wearing apparel industry did enjoy such a situation, but under some other agreements employees did have the right to refuse overtime without any penalty. This development was dramatically highlighted in the 1973 basic automobile industry labor agreement. For the first time in that industry, production employees under certain circumstances now have the right to turn down overtime without being disciplined. Compulsory overtime was a major strike issue, and only by compromise on it did the automobile corporations and the UAW avoid open conflict.

It seemed a reasonable speculation that both the mounting union drive for outright overtime prohibition and sanction for the independent employee refusal to work overtime would grow—despite often fierce employer antagonism to both developments—should the numbers of unemployed not decrease to a more generally tolerable level. Nor, indeed, could one discount the possibility of new governmental action in the overtime arena—perhaps along the lines of an abortive 1964 proposal of the Johnson administration that minimum overtime pay rates in selected industries be increased to double-time (with the goal of lessening the national unemployment figures of that time by encouraging new hiring).

Even without government limitations, moreover, the employer's overtime authority has rarely been an unrestricted one. About half of all collective bargaining contracts provide that overtime work must be shared equally within given classifications of employees, or at least that overtime is to be rotated equally "as far as is practicable." Some agreements limit overtime to regular employees as against seasonal, temporary, part-time, or probationary employees. A number of labor contracts require that the employer give some advance notice of overtime work, the time period of this notice varying from early in the workday in question to early in the workweek during which the overtime is to be done; failure to provide such notice normally relieves the employee of the obligation to work overtime (or at least assures him of special meal pay).

By the same token, however, under many collective bargaining agreements, penalties may be assessed against employees who refuse to work

overtime. Such penalties range from discharge to ineligibility to work overtime at the next opportunity. For all that has been said regarding union
pressures for overtime discouragement, the premium earnings even of overtime at time-and-one-half remain sufficiently attractive to individual employees on most occasions to make the ineligibility penalty a meaningful one.

Indeed, a prolific source of grievances and even arbitration is the employee complaint that the employer has improperly, under the labor agreement, failed to offer him the opportunity to work overtime. Where the
grievance is found to have merit, the employer typically has the obligation
of paying the employee the amount of money he would have earned on the
overtime tour of duty.

The employee, of course, has nothing to lose by filing such grievances,
even if he would have refused the assignment had he been offered the opportunity to work overtime. If the opportunity has *not* been offered him, he can
file his grievance and possibly get paid for work he never intended to do in
the first place. For these reasons, employer representatives are very careful
to assure that eligible employees are afforded the opportunity to work the
overtime. Where a foreman, for example, makes an error in this regard, the
company may be faced with the situation of paying for the same work twice
and at premium rates. To say the least, the company controller would take
a dim view of this state of affairs! (Case No. 6 at the end of this chapter deals
with overtime assignments.)

JOB EVALUATION
AND JOB COMPARISON

Thus far we have been dealing with *general* changes in the level of
wages under collective bargaining. The comparative-norm, ability-to-pay,
standard-of-living, and cost-of-living principles—as well as the principles
relating to wage differentials and overtime rates—rather than affecting any
particular jobs apply either to all jobs within the plant or to all jobs that
fall within certain widely delineated areas (for example, night work, "dirty
work," and overtime work).

Another important problem, however, involves the establishment of
relative wage rates (or rate ranges) for each particular job, so that wage
differentials are rationalized (jobs of greater "worth" to the company are
rewarded by greater pay), and the overall wage structure is stabilized on a
relatively permanent basis.

Essentially, companies adopt one of two methods to achieve this goal:
(1) job evaluation, and (2) what, for lack of a universally accepted descriptive
designation, might be best described as "job comparison."

Job evaluation in its broadest sense is actually used by all companies.
As French argues:

[It] is a universal phenomenon in organizations which pay wages. For example, if the owner of an insurance brokerage decides that the receptionist should be paid more than the typists, job evaluation has occurred. Thus, job evaluation occurs whenever decisions are made about relative worth of jobs and it is therefore an inescapable factor in organizational life.[28]

In the more technical sense in which it is used here, however, job evaluation requires a more systematic approach than that presumably adopted in French's brokerage example. Briefly, job evaluation—through the use of thorough job descriptions and equally detailed analyses of these descriptions —attempts to rank jobs in terms of their (1) skill, (2) effort, (3) responsibility, and (4) working requirement demands on the jobholder. Each job is awarded a certain number of points, according to the degree to which each of these four factors (or refinements of them) is present in it, and the total number of points consequently assigned to each job (usually on a weighted-average basis, depending on the importance of each factor) determines the place at which the particular job falls in the job hierarchy of the plant. Wage rates or ranges are then established for all jobs falling within a single total point spread (usually called a "labor grade") of this hierarchy. All jobs awarded between 250 and 275 points, for example, might constitute labor grade 4 and be paid whatever wages are called for by this labor grade.

Many managements have found the appeal of such a system to be irresistible. In addition to simplifying the wage structure through the substitution of a relatively few labor grades for individual job listings, it allows the company a basis for defending particular wage rates to the union and provides a rational means for determining rates for new and changed jobs (through using the same process for these jobs, and then slotting their point totals into the hierarchy of labor grades). At least three quarters of all American managements probably make use of such a system today.

This growth of job evaluation, at least for unionized companies, has nonetheless been accomplished only in the face of rather adamant union opposition. Only a few unions—most notably the Steelworkers—have done anything but strongly attack the system. Virtually all others have voiced deep suspicion of the technique itself and have decried the reduced possibilities for union bargaining on individual wage rates allowed by job evaluation.

Why, then, has this method of evaluation spread so pervasively to industry? Livernash conveys an authoritative opinion:

In part, unions have been bought off. Objection was not strong enough to turn down evaluation if an increase in the rate structure was also involved. . . . In part, unions became willing to accept less bargaining over individual job rates. . . . Unions found that job evaluation did not freeze them out of a reasonable voice in influencing the wage structure and continuous wage grievances

---

[28]Wendell French, *The Personnel Management Process* (Boston: Houghton Mifflin, 1964), p. 240.

became a union problem. Particularly when accompanied by formal or informal joint participation in the evaluation process, the technique became acceptable.[29]

Thus, as the same observer concludes:

Clearly union practice indicates a far higher degree of acceptance of and tolerance for evaluation than do official [union] pronouncements.[30]

(Case 7 deals with job evaluation.)

Job comparison is, in many cases, the manager's answer to intransigent union opposition to job evaluation where this remains a force. It has also been utilized by many companies whose job structures do not appear complex enough to warrant job evaluation, or (in some cases) where the management itself is divided on the efficacy of the evaluation technique. Although it has certain refinements, it most frequently involves (1) the establishment of an appropriate number of labor grades with accompanying wage rates or ranges, and (2) the classification of each job into a particular labor grade by deciding which already classified jobs the particular job most closely resembles. The systematic approach of the evaluation method is, in short, dispensed with— and so are the many subsidiary advantages of such an approach. By the same token, however, whatever deficiencies the management or unions see in evaluation are also bypassed. The procedure, a not-too-satisfactory compromise between evaluations and individual rates for each job, is not now common in industry and, for the reasons indicated in the discussion of evaluation, can probably be expected to become increasingly less so in the years ahead.

A FINAL WORD

As this chapter has demonstrated, wage rates and allied wage issues pose very difficult collective bargaining problems. But if the resultant complications do make wage controversies the leading overt cause of strikes, the fact remains that such strikes take place in only a comparatively few instances. Although the stakes can be very high and the problems formidable, employers and unions in the vast majority of cases ultimately find a peaceful solution in the wage area as in other areas of bargaining.

Some of the settlements, admittedly, may not be the kind that would be advocated by economists, and some clearly fail to adjust the issues in a way that reflects equity and fairness. But the parties most often do resolve

[29]Sumner H. Slichter, James J. Healy, and E. Robert Livernash, *The Impact of Collective Bargaining on Management* (Washington, D.C.: The Brookings Institution, 1960), pp. 563–64.

[30]*Ibid.*, p. 564.

their wage disputes in a manner that proves generally satisfactory to all concerned.

It should be remembered that these wage problems are not resolved in an antiseptic economic laboratory where wage models may be constructed. If the settlements do, at times, offend the economic purist, it must be appreciated that these issues are dealt with in the practical day-to-day world, wherein pressures, motives, and attitudes cannot be isolated from the negotiations. Given such realities, it is to the credit of both parties that mutual accommodation has become increasingly visible.

DISCUSSION QUESTIONS

1. Both industry A and industry B are extensively organized by militant and honestly run labor unions. Still, since 1953, the wages within industry A have risen at about three times the rate of those in industry B. How might you account for the difference in the wage situation between these two industries?

2. "Even though the actual wage rate that will be negotiated in a particular negotiation is not determinable, it is certain that the set of arguments that union and management representatives will use to support their respective positions will not change from negotiation to negotiation." To what extent, if any, do you agree with this statement?

3. Compare the methods available for the adjustment of wages during the effective period of a labor agreement, and defend what you would judge to be the most desirable arrangement.

4. "From the employer's point of view, it is inherently inequitable—the laws notwithstanding—to require the payment of equal wages to women and to men for performing the same job." Construct the strongest case that you can in support of this statement, and then balance your case with the most convincing opposing arguments that you can muster.

SELECTED REFERENCES

GARBARINO, JOSEPH W., *Wage Policy and Long-Term Contracts*. Washington, D.C.: The Brookings Institution, 1962.

GRAYSON, C. JACKSON, JR., *Confessions of a Price Controller*. Homewood, Ill.: Dow Jones–Irwin, 1974.

LESTER, RICHARD A., *Economics of Labor*. New York: Macmillan, 1964.

MORGAN, CHESTER A., *Labor Economics*, 3rd ed. Austin, Tex.: Business Publications, Inc., 1970.

PHELPS-BROWN, E. M., *The Economics of Labor*. New Haven, Conn.: Yale University Press, 1962.

REES, ALBERT, *The Economics of Trade Unions*. Chicago: University of Chicago Press, 1962.

TAYLOR, GEORGE W., and FRANK C. PIERSON, *New Concepts in Wage Determination*. New York: McGraw-Hill, 1957.

TOLLES, N. ARNOLD, *Origins of Modern Wage Theories*. Englewood Cliffs, N.J.: Prentice-Hall, 1964.

WEBER, ARNOLD R., *In Pursuit of Price Stability: The Wage–Price Freeze of 1971*. Washington, D.C.: The Brookings Institution, 1973.

CASE 4
Incentive Wage System:
A Case of Excessive Earnings

Cast of Characters

B   Foreman
G   Plant superintendent
H   Plant manager
S   Former chairman of union committee
R   Employee in assembler classification
A   Employee in operator classification
L   Chairman of union committee

Among the most difficult cases in arbitration are those that involve the operation of a wage incentive system. Normally, the issues are very complex, and a mass of evidence is introduced by the parties to support their respective positions. In this case, however, the basic issue was quite simple. After an incentive system was established for a group of employees and rates were established for their jobs, employees started to earn what the employer believed to be "excessive earnings." In fact, evidence demonstrated that on some jobs employees earned up to $10 per hour. Faced with this condition, the employer imposed a ceiling on hourly earnings. The union protested, and the case went to arbitration, in which the parties differed sharply on the contractual validity of the ceiling.

This case involved the operation of the wage incentive system governing earnings of shell core operators and shell core assemblers. In protest against the company action in this respect, the union filed Grievance Number 3361, dated August 29, 1972, covering employees in these classifications. The grievance stated:

> The Company have deducted pay from employees of core assembly, and from shell core operators. This is a piece work price cut, in violation of article 7 Section 36 A & B, Section 37 A & B and other parts of the agreement. We ask that all employees who lose pay from this action be compensated for all lost pay.

The grievance was denied by Foreman B in Step 1 of the grievance procedure, and was denied by Plant Superintendent G in Step 2. In denying the grievance, on August 31, G stated:

> Daily earnings are excessive. No foundry could possibly pay this amount for work performed and be competitive. There has to be an error in rates or time,

in method used to attain this amount. I suggest a sincere study be made of both.

Plant Manager H denied the grievance in Step 3 on September 7, and arbitration was instituted for a final determination of the dispute.

Material to the dispute were the following provisions of the Labor Agreement:

ARTICLE VII

Section 33. Wage structure with classifications. (Effective June 5, 1972)

Classification	Rate/Hr.
Core Assembler, Carrier, Heavy	$3.53
Shell Core Operator, 2 mach. simultaneously	3.82

Section 36 **(a).** All piece-work rates shall be set by the employer, using the existing formula on average operators. Any rate may be studied for inequalities and inequities. If any employee claims that the rate is unfair, the job will be restudied and if found unfair an adjustment will be made. If the employee is still dissatisfied with the restudy, he may utilize the grievance procedure.

Section 36 **(b).** Piece-work rates will be set on incentive work as soon as practical. Piece-work rates set will be retroactive to the start of the present production order.

Rates will be temporary until job is in production. Any change in equipment or methods will be cause for rate restudy; Company will negotiate with the Union Committee and make changes on production rates that reflect excessively high or low earnings. Work performed on short orders or temporary jobs will be paid at the present agreed-to rates.

The basic question to be determined in this case was as follows:

Under the circumstances of this case, did the company violate Article VII of the labor agreement? If so, what should the remedy be?

BACKGROUND

As noted, the classifications involved in this dispute were the shell core operators and shell core assemblers. Effective June 5, 1972, the operators received a guaranteed hourly rate of $3.82, and the assemblers $3.53 per hour. Before the current labor agreement went into effect, these classifications were paid on an hourly-rated basis; that is, they were not covered by a wage incentive system.

When the parties negotiated the current labor agreement, they agreed to a wage incentive system for the two classifications in question. This labor agreement was dated June 5, 1971, and the incentive plan went into effect in August 1971. S, former chairman of the union committee, testified:

> The company gave us copies of the standards to use; it was prepared by the company, and the union did not object to it.

Submitted in evidence was Union Exhibit No. 2, which in pertinent part stated:

Proposed Incentive System for Shell Core Makers

1. Schedule for Establishing and Paying of Rates
   (A) Time Study
   1. Each job will be studied and a Standard Hours per 100 core base will be established.
      (a) A job process card will be filled out which will list weight and requirements for good core. Also the card will have a list of functions performed in making of core. . . .
   2. Personal delay allowance will include handling of sand, core trucks, core box release, and core trucks which are full.
   3. Core maker will initial and mark count of cores on truck, in box, or on pallet which he has made.
   4. One Operator on Multiple Machines
      (a) Operator will receive rate for each job. In event of downtime on one machine, operator will receive $\frac{1}{2}$ hourly rate if he is operating two machines, $\frac{1}{3}$ hourly rate if he is operating three machines for the machine which is down. . . .
   5. Downtime will be paid for following only:
      (a) Machine breakdown
      (b) Core box repair
      (c) When shut down by supervisor
      (d) Downtime will be paid at the base rate

Also submitted in evidence was Union Exhibit No. 3; in pertinent part, this document stated:

Proposed Incentive System for Core Assembly and Finishing

1. Schedule for Establishing and Paying of Rates
   (A) Time Study
   1. Each job will be studied and a Standard Hours per 100 core base rate will be established.
      (a) A job process card will be filled out which will list all work to be performed on job (number of chaplets, muddling, filing, etc.). . . .
   2. Personal delay allowance will include moving of cores to and from assembly and finishing area, setting up for job (getting mid-core jigs, chaplets and etc.), except mixing of paste or core wash.

Referring to Union Exhibits 2 and 3, S testified:

> These are the plans the company agreed to use, and did use. These are the two plans presented by the company to the union in August 1971. The union did

not object to them. The union did not submit any changes to the two plans to the company.

R, an assembler, testified that his supervisor had explained the incentive plan to him and showed him an example of how the system would work. The example was submitted in evidence as Union Exhibit No. 4. It contains fictitious names and describes the operation of the system. R declared that "there were no objections to the plan as explained by the supervisor."

In addition, A, an operator, declared:

B showed us how it would work. He used Union Exhibit 4 to demonstrate the operation of the incentive systems. He told us how it would work, and gave us examples. I was the time study man for the union at that time. The plans looked sound to me. We did not object to them. After that, B presented the plans to me as in Union Exhibits No. 2 and No. 3. We did not grieve the plans, or object to them.

For about one year, the union and the company acknowledged that the incentive plan in question operated satisfactorily. H, plant manager, stated in his opening remarks at the arbitration:

Up to August 1972, there were not too many situations which resulted in such drastic events as are involved in this case.

A declared that:

All was OK until August, 1972. The system operated smoothly until then.

Events that arose in August, 1972, however, caused the problems that sparked this arbitration. H provided some examples of earnings of the employees involved in this case during August, 1972. He identified Company Exhibit No. 1, referring to the earnings record of employee K for the week ending August 20. In regard to this document, H declared:

Without the limitation that we imposed, for one day in that week, he would have earned $10.71 per hour.

H was referring to the fact that in August, 1972, the company placed an hourly earnings limit on the employees in the classifications in question. H testified:

We limited the shell core operators to $6.00 per hour, and the shell core assemblers to $5.50 per hour. In the absence of these limitations, employees would have made up to $10.00 per hour.

The plant manager also identified Company Exhibit No. 3, the earnings record of employee W. In reference to this document, H testified that on one day in the week ending August 20, 1972, "he would have made $9.52 per hour if we didn't put on the limitation of earnings."

The company also submitted into evidence Company Exhibit No. 4, which contained the earnings records for August, 1972 of some of the employees involved in this case. This document was purportedly submitted to demonstrate that, were it not for the limitation of earnings, the employees would have made earnings reflecting those of the employees covered by Company Exhibits No. 1 and No. 3.

POSITION OF THE PARTIES

The position of the union was that the grievance should be granted, and the position of the company was that it should be denied. Both parties filed post-hearing briefs; parts of their arguments are quoted below.

L, chairman of the union committee, testified that after the company had imposed the limitations on hourly earnings, the union submitted Grievance No. 3361. He declared:

> We filed Grievance No. 3361 because if a man made $50 in a day under the incentive system, the company would pay him less. This was the main purpose for the filing of Grievance No. 3361.

The union charged a violation of the incentive plan and the material provisions of the labor agreement. It argued that the company did this "without consulting or negotiating with the Union."

In defense of its action, the company argued that the limitations were necessary because of excessive earnings made by the employees. Also, the company argued in its opening statement:

> We put a maximum amount of earnings per man per hour on particular jobs. We had this right because there was more time on the job than was stated on cost cards, and jobs were not done properly. Quality suffered.

In its post-hearing brief, the company also contended:

> The union has a limit on the minimum earnings that an employee can make, which we are obligated to pay. The company's position is that we have the right to set a maximum which we will pay which we consider a fair and just amount. This is the company's position. . . .

> We consider excessive earnings to be 150% times the daily hourly earnings; in this case the employees involved are regarded as having excessive earnings.

> The company would consider 135% times the hourly earnings as being achieved by the average worker. We do consider the earnings of some employees who earn $9.00 or $10.00 an hour excessive when their hourly rate is between $3.44 and $3.83 an hour as indicated on the pay sheets.

> Employees have handed in day work or down time which indicated earnings of $9.85 an hour. The company feels that any employee making anything close to this amount is making excessive earnings when his base rate or day rate is $3.63 an hour.

ANALYSIS OF THE EVIDENCE

The arbitrator's opinion contained the following remarks:

> We reject all these arguments of the Company as being without merit. *Nothing in the Labor Agreement provides the Company with the authority to establish a maximum hourly earnings limit on the employees.* The rules of the operation of the incentive system are clearly outlined in Article VII of the Labor Agreement. Indeed, if the Company believed that earnings are excessive, this provision offers the Company the opportunity to seek relief. Section 36 (a):

> Any rate may be studied for inequalities and inequities.

Section 36 (b):

> Company will negotiate with the Union Committee and make changes on production rates that reflect *excessively high* or low earnings. [Emphasis supplied.]

> Instead of negotiating with the Union Committee for relief from what the Company believed to be excessive earnings, it unilaterally established the limitations in question. Clearly, such action violated the rules agreed to by the Parties as contained in the Labor Agreement which deal with the very problem that apparently confronted the Company. There is no evidence in the record that the Company attempted to negotiate with the Union as to excessive earnings. . . .

> Apparently, the Company believes that because the Labor Agreement guarantees employees a minimum rate—Assemblers, $3.53 per hour, and Operators, $3.82 per hour—it may unilaterally impose maximum earnings limits which it believes to be "fair." The fact is that the Parties in their Labor Agreement agreed to minimum rates of pay. They did not agree to a maximum amount of earnings under the incentive system.

> If the Parties intended to provide the Company with the authority to establish a maximum limitation on earnings, they would have done so in clear and unequivocal contractual language. Not only did the Parties refrain from providing the Company with such authority, but they also provided the Company with the opportunity to bargain with the Union Committee for relief when it believed that rates produce "excessively high . . . earnings."

> The Company did not avail itself of this opportunity, and instead took unilateral action in clear violation of the material provisions of the Labor Agreement.

> Even though it could be argued that an incentive system should produce less than 150% of the base rate, the Company still had no authority under the Labor Agreement to establish maximum earnings limitations.

> There is no need to belabor the obvious. When the Company unilaterally established maximum levels of earnings, it committed a pure and simple violation of the Labor Agreement. For the Arbitrator to approve this conduct of the Company would be a masterpiece of error. No arbitrator worthy of the trust and faith placed in his integrity and competency would permit the Company to engage in a clear-out violation of the Labor Agreement as is involved under the circumstances of this proceeding. To sustain the Company action would result in the destruction of the integrity of the material contractual language.

In this light, the Arbitrator shall direct a remedy for the Company's violation. It shall be directed to award to the employees covered by the grievance the amount of money they would have earned under the incentive systems in question if the Company had not imposed the maximums in question.

QUESTIONS

1. How do you account for the fact that the incentive wage system resulted in earnings that in fact could have been described as excessive?

2. Should the arbitrator have shown sympathy for the employer and helped him out in his problem? Why, or why not?

3. What relief did the labor agreement afford the employer for the problem he faced?

4. Suppose the company and the union negotiated the earnings problem under Article VII, Section 36(b) but could not reach an agreement. Assume further that the company then enforced the ceiling on earnings, and the dispute went to arbitration. Under these circumstances, if you were the arbitrator, how would you handle the case?

CASE 5
Incentive Rates:
The Case
of the Corrected Elk Leather

Cast of Characters

J	Manager of company piece rate department
A	Former shop steward
S	Former business agent
Y	Cutting room foreman
H	Employee
M	Plant superintendent
Z	Another employee

Here is another incentive wage system dispute. It arose in the shoe manufacturing industry, and concerned the kind of elk leather the employees cut. Under the wage rate schedule, employees received a lower rate when the company purchased elk leather that was "corrected" by the tanner. However, the union and employees contended that there was no difference between corrected and uncorrected elk leather. They claimed that it was just as difficult and time-consuming to cut both types of leather.

On September 14, 1973, shoe cutters in the cutting department filed Grievance No. 41026, which stated:

We the shoe cutters are asking for 25% for cutting corrected elk. Our foreman says this leather has been corrected and only pays 15%. Correcting the leather could not change it from being elk end elk is suppose to pay 25% for cutting. The leather is still just about as bad as it could be, even though it is suppose to have been corrected. We are asking for 25% according to our schedule and retroactive to the first of this leather we cut.

Subsequently, the union executive board recommended:

According to schedule, the elk leather is supposed to pay the 25% more. We recommend this 25% be paid these operators as asked.

Material to the dispute was Article IV, Section 5 of the labor agreement, which in pertinent part provided:

Any wage schedule or formula for computing piece rates on individual patterns which has been in effect for as much as six (6) months may not be challenged by either party. The only challenge which may be made is as to the correctness of the piece rate computed from said schedule or formula.

The parties stipulated the following question to be determined in this arbitration:

What, if any, change shall be made in the leather extra of 15% paid for corrected grain elk?

BACKGROUND

Involved in this dispute was the leather extra to be paid for the cutting of elk. As the grievance demonstrated, the shoe cutters requested that a 25 percent extra be paid when they cut elk leather. Prior to December 22, 1970, the company paid the same extra regardless of the character of the elk leather. J, manager of the piece-rate department, testified:

I will say it's entirely possible all the years they had it coming in that category was full grain. It may or may not have been true. On the old schedule there wasn't any difference made between whether it was corrected or whether it wasn't. . . .

On December 22, 1970, the cutters agreed to a schedule for outside cutting that provided for an extra for the cutting of elk leather. The agreement was signed individually by twelve cutters, and also by A, then the shop steward, and by S, then the business agent of the union. In pertinent part, this agreement stated:

> We agree to accept the new Outside Cutting Schedule, which has been offered to us by the Company.

Page 12 of the schedule established a leather extra for various kinds of leathers. As to the leather extra paid for elk, the schedule stated that when such leather was cut as "full grain," the extra would be 25 percent, and that when such leather was cut as "corrected grain," a 15 percent extra would be paid.

In other words, according to the schedule, a lower extra was paid the cutters when the elk leather was received from the tanner companies as corrected grain than when it was received as full grain. Y, the cutting-room foreman, described the difference between full and corrected grain:

Q: Can you explain to the arbitrator and to these men, too, what the difference in full grain and corrected grain is and why we would have a lower percentage on corrected grain?

A: Well, I will take corrected grain first. I will use—well, the tannery terminology is a skin that has been snuffed or buffed or sanded. I will use these terminologies to take the imperfections from the skin, such as whip marks, briar scratches, kickbacks or any other imperfections that might be in the leather.

The full grain, there is nothing done to it, or very little done to it, to remove all your whip marks or kickbacks and your scars are still there.

Your full grain, there is a higher percentage paid for that, and your corrected grain, the surface is better for cutting and there is a lower percentage paid.

The supervisor also testified that the tanner firm made the determination of whether or not the leather was full or corrected grain. Since extra work was done at the tanner's on corrected grain, the company paid a higher price for it as compared with full-grain leather. When elk leather was received from the tanner, Y testified, the company did "not necessarily" check the skins to determine whether the leather was full or corrected grain.

In short, elk leather was received as either full grain or corrected grain; if cutters worked on full-grain leather, they received a 25 percent extra, and if the leather was corrected grain, they received a 15 percent extra. According to union witnesses, however, the leather was the same regardless of whether it was designated as full or corrected grain. As H, a cutter for twenty years, testified:

Q: Tell us if there is any difference in the elk leather now than there was when you were getting 25 percent for it.

A: There is no difference at all. It's the same thing, the same thing as we have been cutting. I had two pieces of leather but I have lost them in the transaction. One of them was elk and one was corrected elk and I carried these two pieces of elk in the office and showed them to M, and he couldn't tell the difference in them.

Q: This is the superintendent?

A: And I don't think there is any difference at all. . . . Full-grain elk, you can take a piece of it and I had two pieces of it, one said corrected elk and one said full-grain elk and they were absolutely the same thing. You can take them up there and look at them and both of them are smooth and both of them looked exactly alike. The backs are alike and all and I took them in there to M and said, "Could you tell me the difference?" And he couldn't tell me the difference to save his life.

Z, a cutter for 22 years, declared:

> And the way I see it, the corrected leather, actually it was bad leather, but it's been buffed down the way I understand and then refinished. Of course, that refinishing over those scars is just about the same as the good place and you can't see it when you're cutting. And when the pressure is put on it then it opens the scars. Actually it makes it worse, and before that you could cut around that and fix it up.

POSITION OF THE PARTIES

The position of the union was that the grievance should be granted, and the position of the company was that it should be denied.

ANALYSIS OF THE EVIDENCE

Scope of Grievance

As union witnesses' testimony disclosed, they alleged that there was no difference between corrected and full grain leather. On this basis, the union requested that the cutters receive 25 percent extra for the cutting of elk leather regardless of whether it was designated as full or corrected grain. Thus, the union argued:

> The fact that the tannery or leather wholesaler sells this leather to the company as being corrected doesn't necessarily have to mean that it is every time. We think that Mr. J's statement, "There is no question in the mind of the company as to whether it's corrected grain or whether it's full grain because they can tell by the purchase price that they pay for the leather," is rather weak, because for one thing, it could get mislabeled, and, of course, many other things could happen.

> The only real way that you can tell the condition of this leather is by the cutters that work on it every day. They are the only ones that really know, because you could not tell by merely looking at it—and again, they say that there is no real difference.

The arbitrator's decision follows in part:

> There could be some merit to this Union argument. That is, the tanner might ship to the Company full grain leather even if the Company had ordered cor-

rected grain leather and paid a higher price for it. Under these circumstances, the Cutters would get a lower extra because of an error on the part of the tanner. What would tend to support this observation is that Y testified that the Company does "not necessarily" check the skins as they are received.

It is possible that an error could be made, and the Arbitrator recognizes this fact. However, the Cutters request 25 percent extra for the cutting of *all* elk leather. In short, the Cutters are not protesting against a particular shipment or skin, but rather the grievance applies to all elk leather they cut. *If the grievance were limited to a particular shipment or skin of elk, a determination would be made as to whether or not that shipment or skin was full or corrected grain.* As stated, however, the scope of the Cutters' complaint embraces much more than that—it covers the cutting of all elk leather.

The Issue of Fraud

To find for the Cutters in this case, the Arbitrator would be compelled to find that the tanner firms are defrauding the Company; that is, that the Company pays for corrected grain, but the tanners constantly ship full grain. On the basis of the evidence in this case, it is not credible that this has been done. There simply is no basis to make a finding of fraud. Equally, there is no basis to find that the Company is not purchasing corrected grain, and that it is not paying a higher price for corrected grain. In other words, it would not be proper on the evidence to hold that the Company is only purchasing full grain elk, and is telling the Cutters that the leather is corrected grain.

Beyond these considerations, there is corroborative evidence that the Company in fact has purchased corrected grain, and that the tanners have shipped corrected grain leather. Without any contradiction whatsoever, Y testified that since the new schedule was put into effect, the Company had paid two extras for elk leather cutting. He testified that between December 22, 1970, and the time the grievance was filed:

Q: That you have had some full grain and some corrected grain.

A: Right.

Q: Now did you pay the 15% on corrected grain all the time since you have been here?

A: Why, yes.

In short, without protest, the Cutters have been receiving a 15 percent extra for corrected grain for about three years. On this basis, it would not be proper to conclude that during all that period the Company had received only full grain leather. If this were true, the Cutters would have protested long before the instant grievance was filed.

Arbitrator Has No Authority To Alter Schedule

In short, there is no sound basis on which to conclude that the Company is purchasing and/or receiving only full grain elk leather. It purchases full grain and corrected grain leather. When the Cutters work on full grain leather, they receive a 25 percent extra, and when they work on corrected grain, they receive a 15 percent extra. This is what the Cutters agreed to under the schedule in question, and these are the extras they are entitled to receive.

On this basis, it would be improper for the Arbitrator to hold that the Cutters should receive a 25 percent extra for the cutting of all elk leather regardless of whether the leather is full or corrected grain. He has no authority to change the schedule agreed to by the Cutters and the Company.

The M Test

Before reaching his final decision, the Arbitrator considered the M test. We have absolutely no reason to doubt the testimony of H that M could not distinguish between a piece of full and corrected grain. On this basis, however, we may not properly jump to the conclusion that there is no difference between these types of leather for purposes of the schedule. One explanation for the M test is that not all imperfections are taken out of the leather when it is processed at the tanner to be sold as corrected grain. He testified:

Q: You are not trying to say, though, that on corrected grain we are going to take out or they are going to take out all the imperfections in that skin.

A: No. It's impossible to do that.

Thus, it is entirely possible that the piece of corrected leather shown to M was a piece from which all the imperfections were not removed. In fact, the particular piece shown to M may have been of comparatively poorer quality than the normal run of corrected skins. Such a selective test, however, does not mean that the entire shipment was of this character. Another explanation could be that by error the entire shipment was designated as corrected grain when, in fact, it was full grain. As noted, the Arbitrator recognizes the possibility that such an error could be made. However, the grievance requests a 25 percent extra for all elk leather, and does not protest against a possible shipping error.

. . . The Arbitrator shall deny the grievance. . . .

QUESTIONS

1. Why did the arbitrator state that he had no authority to alter the rates established in the cutting schedule?

2. What were the economic considerations behind the agreement that cutters should receive a lower rate for cutting corrected leather?

3. What action could the company take to ensure that the skins received from the tanner reflected the higher price and were in fact corrected grain?

4. Do you agree with the way the arbitrator rejected the union argument based upon the so-called "M test"? Why, or why not?

CASE 6
Selection of Employee
for Overtime Work:
A Case of Comparative Ability

CAST OF CHARACTERS

R   Grievant
E   Junior service employee selected for overtime
B   Foreman

Some employees desire overtime work to increase their earnings, particularly since overtime is paid at premium rates. As a result, most labor agreements establish a system of overtime assignments to give employees a fair chance for the extra earnings. However, the prerequisite is that the employee selected must be qualified to perform the available work. In this case, Sunday work was available, but the company bypassed the senior employee and instead selected the junior service employee. Under the circumstances, the company believed that the junior service employee was significantly more qualified. Its position was that the senior employee's ability to perform the job was not reasonably equal to that of the junior employee. The dispute went to arbitration because the senior employee and his union believed that the employer had violated the material provisions of the contract when it selected the junior service employee.

In regard to the assignment of an employee to overtime work on Sunday, May 6, 1973, a grievance was filed by R, who contended that since he had longer length of service than the employee assigned to the work, the company violated the labor agreement. His grievance, dated May 7, 1973, declared:

> The Company violated the Contract under Art. VIII, Par. 69, Page 24. They worked a man in Dept. 5, 2nd Shift on Sunday night. But they would not let the older man, who was R, exercise his seniority rights. They worked a younger man. This younger man was E.
>
> We ask that R be paid 8 hrs. pay at time and one-half for this Sunday night.

Having failed to resolve the dispute in the grievance procedure, the parties instituted arbitration for its final and binding determination.

Relevant to this dispute were the following provisions of the labor agreement:

Paragraph 41—Definition of Seniority

Seniority as used herein shall refer to the length of continuous service, ability to perform the work required and physical fitness. Where ability to perform the work required is relatively equal and physical fitness is not a factor, length of continuous service shall prevail in determining an employee's seniority.

Paragraph 69—Overtime—
Saturday, Sunday, and Holidays

Overtime that is required within a department on Saturday, Sunday or Holidays will first be assigned to the employees working in the department on the basis of their plantwide seniority. Employees will be paid the wage rate of the job classification to which they are assigned.

The basic question in this case was as follows:

Under the circumstances of this case, did the company violate the labor agreement?

BACKGROUND

The circumstances of this case were sparked by the determination of the company to operate a self-spacing fin press in Department No. 5 on the second shift on Sunday, May 6, 1973. Fins produced by this press were needed for the start of the workday on Monday. Under the labor agreement, Sunday was an overtime day, and employees assigned to work on a Sunday were paid at premium rates.

The company selected E for the overtime work in question. At the time of his selection, E was classified as a self-spacing fin press set-up man. The start of his service with the company was established as February 8, 1955.

R, the grievant, was hired by the company on January 1, 1953. At the time of the overtime assignment, R was classified as an assembler, having held also the jobs of machine setter and punch press die setter. Both R and E were assigned to Department No. 5 at the time the overtime assignment was made.

PARTIES' ARGUMENTS

On behalf of the grievant, the union argued that he should have been assigned the Sunday overtime, on the grounds that R was "available, willing, and qualified to perform said overtime work." It also stressed that he had more seniority than E, who was assigned to the job.

Further, the Union claimed that R:

. . . had previously performed the operation of self-spacing fin press operator and had assisted on several occasions in the setting up of said machine and that it was common practice for the Company to assign him to this operation during straight time working hours.

On these grounds, the union requested that the grievance be granted.

In contrast, the company contended that its selection of E rather than R for the overtime work in question was proper under the labor agreement. It argued that:

> The question in the grievance presently before the Arbitrator does not turn on the respective periods of continuous employment or respective dates of hire but turns upon the question of whether or not the ability of R was *relatively equal* to the ability of E. Since the evidence demonstrates that his ability was not relatively equal to E's, there was no violation of Paragraph 69 of the contract in making the overtime assignment.

Therefore, the company requested that the grievance be denied.

EVALUATION OF THE EVIDENCE

The arbitrator said, in his opinion:

> Paragraph 69 establishes the formula for the assignment of overtime work to be performed within a department on Saturdays, Sundays, or holidays. There, the parties agreed that such work will be offered first to employees within the department on the basis of their plantwide seniority.
>
> If the term *seniority* as used in Paragraph 69 meant exclusively *length of service*, R, of course, should have been assigned the Sunday work in question. He had a length-of-service edge over E by about two years.
>
> However, in Article VIII, Paragraph 41 of the Labor Agreement, it is stipulated that "seniority" is a composite concept, referring to length of service, ability to perform the required work, and physical fitness. Note that the provision states "*as used herein*"; by using this phrase, the parties obviously intended that whenever the term *seniority* is used in Article VIII, the "Seniority" article of the Labor Agreement, it should be construed as it is defined in Paragraph 41. Paragraph 69, the overtime provision involved in this case, is part of Article VIII. Therefore, the term *seniority* contained in Paragraph 69 must be construed as it is defined in Paragraph 41, and to hold to the contrary would not be consistent with the unambiguous language contained in Paragraph 41.
>
> On this basis, the Grievant does not have a meritorious claim if he believes that he should have been awarded the overtime work merely because he had longer length of service than E. True, length of service is one element of the concept of seniority, and the Grievant, of course, qualifies ahead of E on this basis. However, the parties by their express language agreed that length of service should be used in the assignment of jobs only when the "ability to perform the work required is relatively equal" among employees.
>
> Accordingly, the fundamental question in this proceeding is the determination of whether or not R's ability to do the work required on that Sunday was relatively equal to that of E. If the evidence shows that his ability was relatively

equal, he should have been assigned to the overtime work in question. On the other hand, if this determination demonstrates that his ability was not relatively equal, his grievance does not have merit, even though he has an edge over E in terms of length of service.

Ability of E and R to Carry Out Overtime Work

No one disputes that at the time of the overtime assignment, E held the classification of "Self-Spacing Fin Press Set-Up." Further, the evidence shows that one of the requirements of this job is the ability to operate the fin press. There is, therefore, no question that the junior service employee was fully qualified to carry out the duties involved in the overtime work.

As stated, the reason for the Sunday work was to produce the fins required for production work to be carried out the following Monday. As such, it would appear on the surface that the only duty would be the operation of the press. However, Foreman B, who made the assignment, testified without contradiction that set-up work would also be required of the employee selected to perform the overtime work. . . . Indeed, the evidence shows that set-up work was performed by E on the day in question. Such set-up work was a prerequisite for the production of the fins. . . .

Consequently, it was a matter of common sense that when B made his selection, he had to choose an employee with the qualifications to set up the press and to operate the press. Both qualities were needed, and B was required to make his selection on this basis.

Moreover, there was another important reason why a fully qualified employee had to be selected for the overtime work. On the Sunday in question, the employee was required to work alone, and without the presence of supervision or a set-up man, . . . relying entirely on his own qualifications. He had no opportunity to get the help of supervision or a set-up man if trouble occurred on the turn, or if set-up work was required. In short, the employee assigned had to sink or swim by himself.

In view of these considerations, it is understandable why the foreman selected E for the job. He was fully qualified to operate the press and to perform set-up work. And, of course, the evidence shows that he did perform the required work successfully.

Does the evidence show that the Grievant's ability was relatively equal to that of E in terms of the work requirements to be discharged on the Sunday in question? At the time of the overtime assignment, R was classified as Assembler, Job 39. Clearly, his experience on that job does not qualify him for the overtime work. The job description of Job 39 states that an employee serving in that classification "performs various manual operations involving only the use of hands and small inexpensive tools." Such work clearly is not relevant to the work required in the set-up and operation of the fin press. R also offers his experience as a machine setter, Job 40, and punch press die setter, Job 47. His experience on these jobs is relevant to the overtime work in question, since set-up work is required on both these jobs. Still, the set-up work in Jobs 40 and 47 appears to be of less complexity and responsibility than the set-up work of the fin press. Note that Jobs 40 and 47 are classified in Wage Group III, while set-up of the fin press is in Wage Group IV. That is, by stipulating a higher rate of pay for the fin-press set-up work, the parties themselves have agreed that such work is of a higher order in terms of complexity and responsibility than that of the set-up work involved in Jobs 40 and 47.

In any event, it should be clear that it would not be reasonable to believe that an employee could step in and set up the fin press merely because he is qualified in Jobs 40 and 47. This is particularly true in the instant case because, as stated, the employee selected for the Sunday work would be required to work by himself and without the help of supervision and/or a fin press set-up man.

Much more relevant to R's experience in Jobs 40 and 47 is his work on the fin press. Both R and B testified that upon occasion, the Grievant did operate the fin press. However, both testified that he never operated the fin press on an overtime basis. That is, when he was assigned to the fin press, R had available supervision and a fin press set-up man. . . .

What, however, is very prejudicial to the claim of the Grievant is the fact that he has never by himself set up the fin press. True, the evidence shows that he has helped the die setter or tool man set up the press.

However, witness this candid declaration of the Grievant: "*I cannot set up the Press by myself.*"

Clearly, since set-up work was expected to be performed, and, indeed, was performed on the Sunday in question, it is impossible to reach a conclusion that the ability of the Grievant was relatively equal to that of E, who was a qualified set-up man. To make a finding in favor of the Grievant on this score would result in a most grievous distortion of clear-cut evidence. . . .

With luck, it is possible that the Grievant may have operated the fin press successfully on the Sunday in question. . . . If nothing unexpected occurred on the overtime tour of duty, it is possible that the Grievant might have been able to produce the required number of fins. However, even on this score, it would appear that the foreman made the correct selection, since problems in the operation of the press could be expected. Since the Grievant has never been alone on the press, we do not know if he could cope with unexpected problems. . . . However, any doubt is eliminated with the selection of E, because he is qualified on the press, and could be expected to cope successfully with any problems that might have occurred on the overtime tour of duty.

However, even if the evidence is viewed in the most favorable way possible for the Grievant, the Arbitrator could not possibly grant his grievance under the circumstances of the case. Let us assume for the moment that R could have operated the press successfully on the Sunday, and by luck nothing unusual occurred in the way of problems or trouble. Or even assume that R was able to deal with unexpected problems that could arise. As stated, this would be the most favorable application of the evidence for the Grievant.

Assuming all of this, what should we do about the set-up work that was expected and was actually performed? Here we cannot possibly read the evidence except the way the events actually occurred. Set-up work was accomplished, and the Grievant himself stated categorically that *without help he could not set up the press.* Here is evidence that cannot be ignored, minimized, or evaded. It is at the root of this entire proceeding, and for the Arbitrator to shut his eyes to it would be inconceivable and a breach of the responsibilities of his office.

Presence of Tool Man

As the evidence shows, there was a "tool man" assigned on Sunday, May 6, and presumably he worked the same tour of duty as did E. Further, from the record, it appears that the tool man is qualified to set up the fin press.

Apparently, what the Grievant suggests is that the tool man would be available to set up the press on the Sunday in question, and, therefore, he should have been assigned to the job. Thus, at one point in his testimony the Grievant declared: "With the help of the tool man I could set up the press."

With all deference to the Grievant and the Union, the Arbitrator cannot grant the grievance on the basis of this argument. After all, the language of Paragraph 41 contemplates that a senior service employee's ability must be relatively equal to that of a junior service employee to claim a job. That is, the ability of the employee *must stand alone* and independent from the ability of some other employee who conceivably could aid him in the performance of required work. Indeed, if the Arbitrator granted the grievance on the basis of the argument herein considered, virtual chaos would result in the application of the seniority provision. Undoubtedly, there would be a vast number of disputes, grievances, and arbitrations based on employees' assertions that they should claim jobs, not on the basis of their own ability, but partly on the ability and help of other employees.

In short, when the facts of the case are reviewed in the light of the seniority provision of the Labor Agreement, there must be a showing that the ability of the Grievant, *his own ability*, is relatively equal to that of E. As the analysis of the evidence has demonstrated, the proofs do not demonstrate this, and, therefore, the Arbitrator has no choice except to deny the grievance.

QUESTIONS

1. Suppose, in the next contract negotiations, that the union desired to nullify the arbitrator's decision by the adoption of new contractual language. What kind of language would the union propose to accomplish this objective, and what do you believe would be the company's reaction to the proposal?

2. What evidence did the arbitrator use to sustain the company's position in this case?

3. How did the arbitrator arrive at the conclusion that the term *seniority* as used in the overtime provision meant more than length of service?

4. Assume that the tool man testified in the arbitration and said he would have been happy to help the grievant set up the process. Under these circumstances, do you believe that the arbitrator would have granted the grievance? Why, or why not?

CASE 7
Job Evaluation:
A Case Where One Point
Was Worth $260 per Year

Cast of Characters

W   Union shop chairman
J   Foreman
M   Employee

Here is a case that involves the evaluation of a job in the light of a job evaluation system. At stake was only one point in the evaluation, but, as you will see, one point made a difference of 13 cents per hour. If the average number of hours an employee normally works in a year is 2,000, the annual amount involved on this basis is $260. So the one point meant a difference of $260 per person in terms of employee earnings and costs to the employer!

As this case demonstrates, judgment is the central feature of a job evaluation system. To this extent, it cannot be called a "scientific" system, as this term is used in, say, a chemistry laboratory, where results found are free from human judgment. In any event, a rate on a new job, or on a revised job, must be established, and job evaluation is one of the two accepted methods used to accomplish this objective.

After you read the case, and assuming that you understand the other method—job comparison—if you are dissatisfied with both methods, try to construct a new system. You would then make an unprecedented contribution to labor relations!

This dispute involved the evaluation of Job M27, styled "Broaching, Filing and Shaping." In protest against the company's evaluation, the union filed Grievance No. M1265, dated November 3, 1973. This grievance stated:

In accordance with Article 20.10 and Article 8.1, step 4, clause (f), we are filing this grievance in 3rd step of grievance procedure. We feel that M27 Broaching, Filing and Shaping was not evaluated properly.

As a remedy, the grievance asked:

Company to place proper values to this job and make employee whole for all losses.

Relevant to the case were the following provisions of the labor agreement:

20.10. The Company shall describe and evaluate on the basis of comparison with factor ratings of other jobs in the plant (a) all new jobs and (b) all jobs the contents of which have been changed. The Company shall notify the Shop Chairman in writing of the description and evaluation of such jobs and on his request supply information pertinent thereto. The Union may grieve concerning descriptions and evaluations of such jobs as provided in Section 8.1, Step 4, clause (f).

8.4 Step 4. Arbitration of job classification, wage rate, merit rating, and incentive rate and allowance questions is limited to the following:

... (e) with regard to jobs the Union claims are new or the content of which the Union claims has been changed within the preceding 6 months, whether the jobs are new or the content has been changed (when the content of a job has been changed within the preceding 6 months, all changes in and prior to said period will be considered); and (f) with regard to descriptions or evaluations of jobs pursuant to Section 20.10 (grievances as to which may be filed by the Shop Committee in Step 3 of the grievance procedure by notice in writing to the Director of Industrial Relations within 6 working days after the Shop Committee is advised of the Company description or evaluation thereof), with respect to descriptions, whether the descriptions are accurate and complete, and with respect to evaluations, whether the Company's factor ratings of the evaluated jobs are proper on the basis of comparison with factor ratings of other jobs in the plant.

The basic question in this case was as follows:

Under the circumstances of this case, did the company properly evaluate the job in question? If not, what should the remedy be?

BACKGROUND

Some time before this grievance was filed, the company changed the content of Job M27. W, union shop chairman, testified to the character of the changes in job content:

The company provided a burring machine to file off burrs, sharp edges, and other things like that. Before this, the operator on the job had to do this work. The filing by him was unskilled work. Also, before, the operator performed broaching on rough blank gears. Now it is finished turned blanks. The operator now has considerably less tolerance to work with. If he now makes an error, he cannot correct his mistakes. It is now a one-shot operation. If he makes an error, the part is ruined.

In the light of these changes, J, a foreman in the machine division, requested a reevaluation of the job on October 22, 1973. The evaluation was conducted by the company under the terms of Section 20.10 of the labor agreement.

The procedure to implement this provision was for the company to select a job evaluation committee composed of at least five high-level management representatives, which would compare a new job, or a job the content of which had changed, with comparable jobs in the light of the job evaluation manual. As provided by this manual, comparison between jobs was evaluated in terms of five factors: mental requirement, skill requirement, physical requirement, responsibilities, and working conditions.

The parties were in substantial agreement as to how the job evaluation committee operated. This procedure was described by the company as follows:

> As in this case, the committee meets whenever a job is changed or a new job is created. It also meets when requested by members of supervision who every two years review all jobs. The members are all high-level supervisors who in the past have held various production jobs and who are thoroughly familiar with all operations in the plant.

> As part of their evaluation process, committee members observe the job to be evaluated if it is in operation. Then, working with a written job specification and other labor-grade and factor-rating references, the committee discusses and analyzes the job, and each member designates the points he thinks should be assigned to each of the five factors in relation to the points assigned to comparable existing jobs in the plant. Further discussion follows, during which members may change their factor-point designations. After the job has been thoroughly discussed and analyzed, the final points assigned by each member to the five factors are averaged and then added together. The total number of points determines the labor grade for the job in accordance with the chart listing the grade limits of evaluation points.

On the basis of the total points awarded a job in terms of the five factors, a job would fall into a labor grade for purposes of wages. Joint Exhibit 11 shows the number of points associated with labor grades. In part, it reads:

Labor Grade*	Points
6	81–88
7	89–96

Schedule 2 of the labor agreement shows the wage rates for jobs falling into the various labor grades. Effective February 15, 1971, the top basic wage rate for a Labor Grade 6 job was $2.48 per hour, and the top basic wage rate for a Labor Grade 7 job was $2.61 per hour.**

Before the reevaluation of the M27 job, as sparked by the change in job content, the job fell in Labor Grade 6. Its point total was 83. After the

*Only these two labor grades and their associated points are needed for purposes of this case.

**Effective February 13, 1972, these rates increased to $2.63 and $2.77 per hour, respectively.

new evaluation, the job evaluation committee increased the point total by five points. The following shows the factors that were increased:

Factor	Point Increase
Working conditions	1
Responsibility	2
Skill	1
Mental requirements	1

Thus, the point total for M27 was increased to 88 points, which left the job in Labor Grade 6. The points for M27 after the new evaluation were as follows:

Mental requirements	20
Skill	19
Physical requirements	18
Responsibility	21
Working conditions	10
Total	88

Under Section 20.10 of the labor agreement, the union had the right to protest the findings of the job evaluation committee under the grievance procedure and arbitration. It elected to exercise this right. For M27, the union protested the ratings assigned by the company to the mental and skill factors; it did not challenge the findings of the committee as to the other three factors.

In the union's judgment, M27 should have carried 21 points for the mental requirement factor and 20 points for the skill factor. If either of these factors were increased by one point, M27 would fall in Labor Grade 7 and thereby claim a higher wage rate. In this respect, the union argued:

Based upon the factor-by-factor comparison of Job M-27 with the aforementioned jobs used for comparison in the respective factors as indicated, the Union submits that the point value of each factor should be as follows:

Mental	Skill	Physical	Responsi-bility	Working Conditions	Total	Labor Grade
21	20	18	21	10	90	7

The company believed that the mental and skill factors of M27 were properly evaluated and argued that neither of them should be increased. In this respect, it stated:

Job M27 was properly evaluated by the Company's Job Evaluation Committee and the grievance herein should be denied.

To justify its position that the mental factor of M27 should be increased by one point, the union offered Job M48, styled "Small Part Layout." Currently, the mental factor for this job carried 21 points, or one point more than the mental factor for M27. And to justify its position that the skill factor for M27 should be increased by one point, the union presented Job M112, styled "Link Boring." Currently, this job carried 20 points for the skill factor, or one point more than the skill factor for M27.

To justify its position that neither the skill nor the mental factors of M27 should be increased beyond the points assigned by the job evaluation committee, the company presented job M30, styled "Keyway Milling and Filing." Currently, the skill factor for this job carried 18 points, or one point below the skill factor for the job in question, and 19 points for the mental factor, one point below the mental factor for M27.

Based upon oral testimony, the job description,* and his inspection of the job, the arbitrator attempted to describe the entire range of duties of the M27 operator, since, under Section 8, Step 4(e), he was compelled to consider the *job as a whole* for purposes of job comparison. That is, he was precluded from considering only the particular changes in a job that resulted in its re-evaluation. Thus, the comparison within the meaning of the labor agreement had to be made in terms of whole jobs, not just of duties that had been changed.

He found that the employee assigned to M27 operated six broaching machines and one shaper. The purpose and function of these machines was to shape, cut keyways, and broach or cut internal splines in the parts which were run through them. Some of these parts were gears, shafts, and spindles. The operator worked from blueprints that spelled out the work to be done for a particular job. He had to set up the machine for a production run for a particular part. In the set-up work, he would select the proper fixtures and also the proper broach for a particular job, according to the blueprint. In his work, the operator used many different kinds of broaches and fixtures, and worked to close tolerances, using a variety of gages, micrometers, and other measuring instruments to ensure that the job was properly performed.

After the operator set up his machine for a particular job, he placed the part in the machine, set the feed to get the proper cut, then engaged the machine, and the machine automatically performed the necessary work on the part.

Some of the machines were horizontal and others vertical; the worker spent most of his time—50 to 75 percent—operating a single horizontal broaching machine. Also, although he ground his own tools, he did not

---

*As agreed in the hearing, job descriptions might not faithfully have reflected the duties of employees. Indeed, the parties agreed that what was not in dispute, and what need not be determined by the arbitrator, was whether or not the job description in all respects was an accurate and complete recital of the duties performed by the M27 operator.

sharpen the broaches. He checked the broaches for wear to determine the need for sharpening.

POSITION OF THE PARTIES

The position of the company was that the grievance should be denied on the basis that the rating of the mental requirement and the skill factor for M27 should not be increased. On its part, the union requested that the grievance be granted on the basis that both the skill and mental factors of the job in question should be increased by one point.

ANALYSIS OF THE EVIDENCE

The arbitrator's decision contained the following comments:

Job evaluation disputes of the kind involved in this proceeding are of critical importance to the internal wage structure in a plant. The purpose of job evaluation is to maintain a proper balance between jobs and wage rates. Where proper balance is disturbed, the effect is to raise serious problems, lessen plant efficiency and worker morale, and present management difficulties. Where a job is given a wage rate higher than it should have, this could provide the basis for the whipsaw of the internal wage structure. Where a job is rated lower than it should be, the effect could be a downgrading of the wage structure. In this light, the Arbitrator well understands the serious nature of the case at hand.

Limitations of Arbitration

No matter how conscientious an Arbitrator may be in cases of this sort, his judgment is inferior to that of the parties. Even though he has carefully considered the available evidence and had a chance to inspect the job in question, it would be presumptuous on his part to state that he knows the job as well as those who live with it on a day-to-day basis. This is why job evaluation cases are best settled by the parties in direct negotiations. They know best the technical characteristics of the jobs in the plant, and no Arbitrator can honestly state that his knowledge on this score is comparable to that of the parties.

Still, it is the Arbitrator's responsibility to decide the dispute on the M27 job. His only advantage is to view the disputed job and those offered in comparison in the spirit of objectivity.

Over the years, this Arbitrator has handled many job evaluation cases, as the parties may suspect. If he has followed one standard in this kind of case, it has been to leave undisturbed an evaluation placed on a job by an employer unless there are significant objective features which indicate that the employer made an error in judgment. This standard follows the principle that in all grievances except those involving discipline, the labor union involved must prove that the employer violated the labor agreement. In other words, in job evaluation cases, as in all arbitration cases except those involving discipline, a union bears the burden of proof.

Findings of Job Evaluation Committee

Applying this principle to the case at hand, we assume that the evaluation of the mental and skill factors of M27 is correct, unless the Union by competent evidence demonstrates that the Company's judgment is in error. In this sense, the proof must be substantial and convincing. In this light, the Arbitrator rejects the Union argument, or at least its inference, that the Company Job Evaluation Committee deliberately and with malice evaluated the factors in question in such a way that the point total of M27 fell one point below that necessary to upgrade it to Labor Grade 7. There is not a shred of objective evidence that the Committee did this, and the inference the Union draws from the results of its work certainly is not evidence upon which to decide this case. In addition, we do not make decisions on the basis of inferences, speculations, or "gut" reactions. Arbitration as a process to determine labor disputes would be worthless if arbitrators decided cases upon such subjective factors. Arbitrators decide cases on evidence, and inferences simply do not stand in the category of hard and solid evidence. . . .

In short, the Arbitrator would do mischief to the job evaluation system, and violate the obligations of his office, if he were to decide this case in favor of the Union because of its inference that the Job Evaluation Committee acted in bad faith. If it made an error in judgment, this error will be corrected in this arbitration. However, we do not equate an error of judgment with bad faith. . . . [For the Arbitrator] to base his decision on the line of reasoning of the Union herein considered would be entirely improper.

Comparison with M112—Skill

It is in this light that the Arbitrator will examine the relevant evidence to determine whether the Committee made an error in judgment. As stated, the Union must prove an error in judgment by substantial and convincing evidence.

As the facts show, M112 carries 20 points for skill, and the Committee placed 19 points on this factor for M27. The Union believes the skill factors for these jobs are comparable, and, therefore, the skill factor for M27 should be raised to the same level as that of M112. On its part, the Company argues:

> Likewise, the *skill* factor rating of Job M112 is properly one point higher than that of Job M27. The skill in operating the link boring machine is in the setups, which take up to two hours according to the operator, and in setting and sharpening the cutting tools. The operator must check the hole size for accuracy at regular intervals and compensate frequently for the slightest deviations caused by inevitable dulling of the tool after boring through a relatively small number of links.

> Unlike the M27 operator, the operator of the link boring machine must hold tolerances of 0.0005. The operator grinds his own multi-angled tools, a task which the operator testified requires considerable skill and judgment. The

foregoing skills are fundamentally different from those required of the M27 operator, which makes comparison difficult.

The Union, not the Company, selected Job M112 as a comparison job. The Company submits that Job M30 provides a much better basis for comparison. Nevertheless, the complexity of the setups, closer tolerances and the tool sharpening requirements justify the slightly higher *skill* factor rating of Job M112.

Each job has some unique characteristics which distinguish it from other jobs. This is particularly true when we attempt to compare jobs which involve considerable skill. Clearly, the M112 and the M27 are skilled jobs in the sense that the operators use complicated machinery, set up their machines, and the result of an error is very costly. Thus, it is difficult to compare any two jobs on the basis of skill, and this difficulty increases as the jobs become more skilled in character. In all candor, what we have involved here is a judgment factor. The judgment of the Job Evaluation Committee is that M27 should remain one point below that of the M112 job. Let us see if its judgment stands the test of objective factors which are involved in the comparison.

In this light, there is one objective factor which is of importance as we compare the two jobs as to skill. The Link Boring (M112) job involves the operation of one machine, while the operator assigned to M27 handles seven machines. This does not necessarily mean that the M27 job requires as much skill. A lot depends upon the complexity of the machines involved and other factors which are material in comparison. It could be that M112 involves more skill even though the operator operates only one machine.

In the judgment of the Arbitrator, the machines the M27 operator handles are comparable in complexity to the one machine operated by the M112 employee. All machines involved are automatic machines in the sense that after the machines are engaged, the machines do the cutting or broaching. Each operator must place his part properly in the machine before he engages the machine. Both operators are charged with the responsibility to make sure that the parts are properly placed before the machines are engaged. In other words, the Arbitrator sees no essential or substantial difference in the complexity of the machines per se. All are complicated pieces of machinery, and the skill factors in their operation are comparable.

In this light, the fact that the M112 operator handles only one machine and the M27 job involves the operation of seven machines becomes of material importance in comparison of the skill factor. It is true that the machines involved in the M27 job are of a kindred type. Still, there are some differences between them, and to this extent it appears a matter of common sense that the skill needed to operate seven separate machines is at least comparable to the skill needed to operate one machine. This finding appears valid even though we recognize that the M27 operator spends a majority of his time on one machine, as the evidence demonstrates. The fact is that from time to time, the operator assigned to M27 must have the skill to operate all the machines covered by his job.

Another factor which permits an objective comparison between the two jobs involves the use of fixtures and cutting tools. Note that the M112 operator only has to select between two fixtures and two boring tools, because he only has to run two different kinds of links. In contrast, the M27 operator must select between many kinds of fixtures and cutting tools. Each different job requires the proper selection of cutting tools and fixtures. True, the blueprints spell out for the M27 operator the kind of fixtures and broaches needed for a particular part. Still, the M27 operator must have the skill to make the correct selection.

Another item for objective comparison involves the set-up of the machines. The M112 operator and the M27 operator must both set up their machines. It is true that the M112 operator spends about two hours in making a set-up. Company Counsel stresses this fact in his argument, and we concede that this is a material factor. However, the set-up on the machines by the M27 operator is likewise complicated even though the set-up time may not be as long. The best evidence of this is the fact that from time to time, the foremen must help a veteran operator on M27 set-ups. This is the case even though the incumbent on the job, M, has held the classification for many years. Beyond this, the M27 operator must know how to set up seven machines and set them up in accordance with the kind of part involved.

In contrast, the M112 operator has only two set-ups to make and these are on the same machine. Thus, although the M112 set-up may take longer, it is important that the M27 operator know how to set up seven different machines and must have the ability to set up these machines for different parts which are far more numerous than the two parts produced by the M112 operator. In this light, the Arbitrator believes that set-up skills on the two jobs in question are comparable.

As stated, while the M112 operator runs only two different products, or two different links, the M27 operator runs many different kinds of parts. On this basis, and since running of different jobs requires different set-ups, the use of different fixtures and cutting tools, it seems safe to conclude that the M112 job is comparatively more routine in character. It would seem that the chance for error would be greater the more varied the job. Thus, the M27 operator must be sure he selects the correct fixtures and broaches from a varied and numerous stock of broaches and fixtures, while the M112 operator need be concerned with only two fixtures and two cutting tools. In this light, the skill between the two jobs on this score appears at least comparable.

Both jobs offer the chance for irrevocable and costly error. If the M112 operator does not align his holes correctly, the part is scrapped, with substantial cost to the Company. But this is also true for the M27 operator. Indeed, a change in the M27 job which sparked the reevaluation is proof of this situation. Without contradiction, W, the union shop chairman, testified:

> Now the M27 operator works on finished turn gear blanks. There is now considerably less tolerance. If he makes an error, he can't correct his mistake. It's a one-shot operation. If he makes an error, the part is ruined.

Thus, both jobs involve the chance of an error which cannot be corrected.

Another point for objective comparison between the two jobs involves the length of time involved in the learning process. Note that the operator on the M112 job, S, told us that in his judgment, it would take several months to acquire the basic skills needed to run his job in an effective way. The job description for the M112 states as follows:

Inexperienced Time To Learn:

Basic: 3 months
Average: 6 months

In contrast, the equivalent times as cited in the job description for the M27 operator are *one year and two years.* In short, when the analysts made a judgment as to learning time as to the two jobs, they concluded that the learning time for the M27 job is substantially greater than that for the M112 job. Foreman J testified in a way which supports the judgment of the analysts who prepared the two job descriptions in question.

Company Counsel stresses that the M112 operator must work to a tolerance of 0.0005, which he says is "unlike the M27 operator." Although this may be true, the fact still remains that the M27 operator also works to close tolerance, even though not as close as that of the M112 operator. It is also true that the M27 operator does not sharpen the broaches he uses. In comparison, the M112 operator does sharpen his boring tools. Apparently he must do this frequently during a day, and if the cutting tools are not properly sharpened, this could result in scrapped parts. We conclude that this gives an edge in skill to the M112 operator; but not a sufficient amount of weight can be ascribed to this function to compensate for the other factors, which establish to the satisfaction of this Arbitrator that the skill needed to operate the M27 job is at least comparable to the skill needed to operate the M112 job.

Conclusions

In short, the Arbitrator believes that the Union has met the burden of proof in establishing that the skill factor of the M112 and M27 jobs is at least comparable. There are objective factors which support this conclusion. Though the Arbitrator concedes that his judgment in this respect may be faulty, he still believes, on the basis of an objective comparison, and with due consideration to the evidence, that the Job Evaluation Committee made an error in judgment in this respect. Therefore, the Arbitrator shall direct that the skill factor for the M27 job be increased by one point.

Since this is the finding of the Arbitrator, there is no need for purposes of this case to compare the M27 job with other jobs presented by the Union and the Company. The Company states that a comparison of the skill factor between M27 and M30 would be "a much better basis for comparison." This may be true, but the Union met the necessary burden of proof by establishing that the skill factor between M27 and M112 is comparable. This is all the proof that the Union need offer to establish the basis for an increase of one point for the skill factor of the M27 job. Of course, the Company in another proceeding may without prejudice raise the skill comparison between M27 and M30. The Arbitrator does not decide this issue, since there is no need to do this for purposes of this case.

Likewise, the Arbitrator for purposes of this case need not compare the mental requirement between M27 and M48. There is no need to do so since, as we all know, the increased elevation of the skill factor by one point for the M27 job elevates this job to 89 points, which is sufficient to place it in Labor Grade 7. Without prejudice, however, should the need arise, the Union may in another proceeding raise the mental requirement comparison between M27 and M48.

QUESTIONS

1. Why did the arbitrator refuse to accept the union argument that the management job evaluation committee in bad faith rated the job in question one point below the figure necessary to put the job in the higher labor grade?

2. Explain why job evaluation disputes illustrated by the present case are particularly difficult for a determination in arbitration.

3. What are the consequences of evaluating a job too high or too low?

4. What specific evidence did the arbitrator use to justify his decision that the skill factor of the job in question should be raised by one point?

Chapter 8
Economic Supplements under
Collective Bargaining

The incorporation of employee supplementary economic benefits—from paid vacations to pension plans—in collective bargaining contracts is widespread throughout American industry. Such benefits have increased dramatically since World War II, in both their value to the employee and in their variety. And, since these supplements to the basic wage rate are now commonly equivalent to over 30 percent of payroll, it is understandable that some managers express hostility when the once accepted designation "*fringe benefits*" is used to describe this area.

Many of these benefits are not new to personnel administration and, indeed, some of them were introduced by employers on a unilateral basis before the advent of unionism. However, such benefits now play a much more important part in labor relations than was ever the case in the past. By the end of World War II, many unions had succeeded in bargaining vacations and holidays for their members; the federal government's regulation of wages during 1942–45 had proven influential in guiding the labor negotiators in this direction. And in the three decades since the war, many other benefits have found their way into labor documents with increasing regularity and employer largesse: pension plans; various health insurance arrangements, including life insurance and hospital and other medical benefits; accidental death and dismemberment payments; and dismissal and reporting pay, among many others. Supplementary unemployment benefit plans, a comparatively recent major collective bargaining issue, also may properly be regarded as a supplement to the basic wage rate.

Beyond all this, many labor agreements contain special benefits, ones that are either absolutely unique or at least not widely prevailing as guaranteed benefits in the working world. Resort hotels in Hawaii grant free use of their golf courses to their International Longshoremen's and Warehousemen's Union members. Clerks at a West Coast supermarket chain can receive almost unlimited use of free psychiatric services and so, too, under certain conditions, can every member of their families. Some employers provide workers with help in filling out their income tax returns; others emphasize tuition subsidization for college-attending children of employees. Some unionists—Steelworkers conspicuously among them—are eligible for comprehensive and meaningful alcohol- and drug-addiction rehabilitation, going well beyond the token benefits offered in many other employment settings. And an increasing but still small number of contracts have in the past few years moved into the area of prepaid group legal service plans, with varying degrees of ambitiousness.

It is, however, to the more widespread and thus costly economic supplements that this chapter devotes its primary attention.

PENSION PLANS

Pension plans became a significant issue in labor relations and collective bargaining in the period immediately following World War II. Many factors operated to make them a major feature of the bargaining process, particularly the 1949 ruling of the United States Supreme Court that held that employers and unions have the obligation to bargain over this issue.[1] The Court rejected the point of view that pensions were not covered as a bargaining issue under national labor law. But other factors, particularly in more recent years, have also contributed to the growth of pension plans: the modest character of the benefits provided under the federal Social Security program; the fact that employees are increasingly expected to live considerably longer and to have more years of retirement after the termination of their industrial lives than in the past; the spread of union-sponsored seniority and related provisions (to be discussed in Chapter 10), making it all but impossible to terminate employment for older employees *except* by pension; and a growing managerial awareness of a company obligation to employees after their retirement. On the last point, even in 1949, one public commission could comment that:

> ... pensions should be considered a part of normal business costs to take care of ... permanent depreciation in the "human machine" in much the same way as provision is made for depreciation and insurance of plant and machinery. This obligation should be among the first charges of revenues.[2]

From a modest beginning in 1946, pension plans in American industry have grown phenomenally. Negotiated pension plans are today found in about 75 percent of all labor agreements. The number of workers covered by negotiated pension plans doubled during the period of 1950–1960, and it is expected to double again by 1980. As of 1973, approximately 22,500,000

[1] *Inland Steel Co.* v. *United Steelworkers of America*, 336 U.S. 960 (1949).

[2] These conclusions were incorporated in the report of the Steel Fact-Finding Board appointed by President Truman in July 1949 to inquire into the facts of and to make recommendations in the dispute that was then taking place relative to pensions between the United Steelworkers of America and the steel corporations.

active and retired workers were covered by negotiated plans.[3] Of this number, about 14.5 million active employees are covered currently by negotiated pension plans.[4]

As might be expected, there is a wide variety of plans in existence, but a number of common characteristics are found in almost all of them.

Whereas the earliest bargaining pensions integrated their benefits with payments received from the operation of the federal Social Security program —and thus, in the late 1940s and early 1950s, enabled employers to realize considerable savings as the benefits of the Social Security Act were liberalized —there has been a distinct trend away from this practice in recent years. One method of passing the statutory increases directly along to the worker has been the establishment of a flat monthly payment per year of service, regardless of the amount the retired worker receives from the federal government. Thus, as of 1974, automobile workers under the Chrysler–UAW agreement, by way of example, were to be credited with $8.75 to $11.50 per month (depending upon their preretirement base wage rate and the date of retirement) for each year of service upon normal retirement, and anything obtained from the public system would be in addition to this amount. For a 30-year service employee, this would amount to $262.50 per month for the retired employee who receives the minimum rate, and $345.00 for the retiree who receives the highest rate. In the same year, the monthly benefits under the Social Security program averaged $166 per month for all retired workers, $155 for aged widows, and $275 for retired couples. If we assume that the retired automobile worker received $345 under the private pension plan and $275 from the public program, he would receive a total of $620 per month in public and private benefits.

However, if the quality of life of retired people as a whole is the issue, these figures are very misleading; the average amount of pension benefits under private plans in 1974 amounted to only about $125 per month, or $1,500 per year.[5] In 1974, it took $4,130 in annual income for a retired couple to live at the lower budget level prepared by the Bureau of Labor Statistics; $5,960 for the intermediate level; and $9,226 for the higher level. Matching these budget levels against the total income (private and public) shows that the average retired couple maintains a very low standard of living.

Recognizing this condition, some unions have made efforts to protect retired people against the ravages of inflation. For example, in 1974, the United Steelworkers of America negotiated a pension plan with the aluminum industry that provides that a retiree's pension will increase as the cost of living increases. As with some wage agreements, an escalator clause for pensions is now contained in that contract. Undoubtedly, other unions and employers

[3] *Monthly Labor Review*, October 1974, p. 10.
[4] *Monthly Labor Review*, January 1975, p. 67.
[5] AFL-CIO, *American Federationist*, Vol. 81, No. 1 (January 1974), p. 2.

will follow this breakthrough in pension plans if inflation continues at a high rate, as it did in the first part of the 1970s.

Under most plans, the mandatory retirement age is set at 65, and although many companies still permit workers, upon mutual annual agreement, to stay on their jobs until they are 70 years of age, there has been some move away from this flexibility in recent years. Many manufacturing employee unions (in steel and rubber, for example), influenced by the size of the unemployment figures in their sectors of the economy, have generally not opposed this increasing trend toward compulsory retirement at 65. In fact, labor organizations have increasingly sought to open up further job opportunities in the face of automation and changing market demands by a new emphasis on early retirement before age 65, and some provision for this benefit is now made under the pension stipulation of many contracts.

By and large, voluntary early retirement (as opposed to retirement necessitated by permanent disability) carries with it reduced benefits for the employee. This typically amounts to a reduction of more than one-third in monthly benefits for a worker retiring at age 60, and of more than 20 percent for an employee who chooses to retire at age 62. On the other hand, under contracts in the automobile, clothing, maritime, and mining industries, to name only four of a fast-growing number, the benefits are identical for all retired workers, regardless of age, subject to their meeting minimum service requirements—which invariably call for at least 20, and most often 30, years.

As these early retirement plans spread in the late 1960s and early 1970s, it was widely believed that they would realize their goal of creating new job opportunities for other workers; when a liberalized plan at Chrysler was implemented in 1965, for example, over five times as many Chrysler workers chose to retire over the next two years as had been true in the two-year period prior to the liberalization.

But by 1975, the picture had changed drastically, owing to the mounting inroads of rapid inflation on fixed incomes. At Chrysler, as at the other major automobile companies, employees could now retire (regardless of age, but after 30 years of service, under the UAW's long-cherished and now-realized dream of "30 and out") with monthly pension benefits of $620—up almost $300 from the 1965 amount. Yet only about one-fifth of the eligible employees were electing to do so in the face of soaring prices.[6] And the story was no different at the other automobile companies, despite similar rises in retirement checks from a decade earlier. It appeared a safe guess that if the inflation rate did not subside considerably, the UAW would, in its next (1979) pension bargaining, aggressively pursue a duplication of the Steelworker cost-of-living escalator formula to link pensions and the Consumer Price Index, effecting an automatic adjustment years earlier afforded active workers.

[6] *Wall Street Journal,* Nov. 11, 1974, p. 1.

Under plans that provide for pension benefits to workers who have been permanently disabled and who have not reached the normal retirement age, it is also usually required that such workers have a specified number of years of service with the company to be eligible for such benefits. Under many of these contracts, 10 to 15 years of service is required before an employee may expect to draw pension benefits because of permanent disability.

The question of who is to finance the pension plans—the employer alone, or the employer and the employee jointly—has been an important issue ever since collectively bargained pensions attained prominence, and it continues to pose problems at the bargaining table. At the present time, in about three out of four plans, employers finance the entire cost of retirement benefits (and the plans involved are therefore called "noncontributory," in recognition of the lack of expense to the employee); the remainder are financed jointly (and thus on a "contributory" basis). Jointly financed plans remain common in some manufacturing industries (notably textiles, petroleum, and chemicals), as well as in the nonmanufacturing area (finance, for example).

In favor of noncontributory plans, the usual arguments are that (1) the average employee cannot afford to contribute; (2) the employee is already contributing toward part of his retirement under the Social Security program; (3) costs of pensions should be borne exclusively by the employer, on the ground that this expense is no less important than depreciation expenses for machinery and plant; (4) the return to the employer from the plan in terms of lower labor turnover rates and increased efficiency justifies the cost; and (5) although employers can charge contributions to pension plans against taxes, employees cannot.

Proponents of contributory pension plans, on the other hand, claim that (1) since there is a definite limit to the economic obligations that employers can assume at any given time, employee contributions ensure better pensions; (2) requiring employees to pay for a share of their pensions tends to educate employees in the knowledge that retirement programs must be paid for by someone; (3) employees will take a far greater interest in plans to which they contribute and hence will advocate better administration, sounder funding, and less waste; and (4) when employees contribute, they have a stronger claim to their pensions as a matter of right.

Regardless of whether pension programs are financed on a contributory or noncontributory basis, however, the program must be financed and funded in a manner that positively guarantees employees the benefits provided for by the plans upon their retirement. There is no need to dwell upon the catastrophe that would befall a worker who upon retirement finds that the pension he expected is not available. Funded plans—those in which pensions are paid from separated funds, isolated from the general assets of the firm—ensure that such benefits are in fact guaranteed, whereas unfunded plans must necessarily depend upon employer ability and willingness to comply with the pension provisions of the labor agreement. In addition, employers may currently minimize their federal income taxes by obtaining tax credits as they make fund contributions, rather than waiting until the pensions are actually paid, and the earnings of the pension trust fund are also exempted from income taxes. Because of these considerations, there is an unmistakable preference among employers and unions for a fully funded and actuarially sound plan; only 7 percent of all workers covered by private pension arrangements belonged to unfunded plans even as early as 1960,[7] and the figure is undoubtedly even smaller today.

Finally, recent contract renegotiations have seen a marked increase in "vesting" allowances for workers covered by pensions—giving, with more or less qualifications concerning years of service and sometimes age, the employee the right to take his credited pension entitlement with him should his employment terminate before he reaches the stipulated retirement age. Only 25 percent of the plans studied by the Bureau of Labor Statistics in 1952 allowed vesting, but 67 percent of those examined in 1963 did so, however much the vesting privilege remained qualified,[8] and by common estimate the figure is probably close to 80 percent today. Considerations of equity, worker morale, and the displacement threats in many industries have given unions the incentive to push hard for the expansion and liberalization of this benefit over the past decade. So, too, has an equally cogent argument for meaningful vesting rights: In the absence of such rights, the individual worker's ever-increasing stake in pension plan entitlement may stifle desirable labor mobility and thus result in the underutilization of manpower. Workers who can take their pension privileges with them are afforded maximum opportunity for employer-to-employer and industry-to-industry movement, a situation that is presumably a desirable one from the viewpoint of our not only efficiency-minded but democratically oriented society.

Experience of recent years has, moreover, demonstrated that a considerable amount of abuse had developed with respect to private pension plans: Many employees who had counted on a pension simply (if tragically) did not receive the benefit. Hearings held by the Senate Labor Committee in the early 1970s disclosed that, in some cases, pension funds were plundered or misused by their administrators. Another abuse involved the requirement that an employee reach a certain age and have a certain number of years of service with an employer to be eligible for a pension; frequently, employees were discharged or laid off permanently just before they qualified under the age and service requirement. In other cases, employers went out of business, or closed a plant, thereby depriving employees of the opportunity to receive a pension. In one case, a plant closed down, laid off 1,000 employees, and:

[7]"Unfunded Private Pension Plans," *Monthly Labor Review*, Vol. 86, No. 12 (December 1963), 1414.

[8]"Vesting Provisions in Private Plans," *Monthly Labor Review*, Vol. 87, No. 9 (September 1964), 1014.

... at least 350 of them were let go short of eligibility requirements—age 40 and 10 years on the job.[9]

In another case, an employee of a company, upon reaching 20 years of service, was discharged at the age of 50, but he did not qualify for a pension because his age plus years of service with the company did not total 80, the minimum requirement for pension plan eligibility.[10] Examples such as these were unfortunately widespread, leading an attorney from a Senate committee investigating the private pension problem to say:

> My very rough guess is that it is possible that one-third of all workers in pension plans will never get anything from them.[11]

Although abuse of the private pension programs was common knowledge for many years, it was not until September, 1974 that Congress finally enacted a law to cover private pension plans. The law, styled "Employee Retirement Income Security Act, 1974," is very long and complex;[12] for our purposes, it will suffice to mention some of its major highlights.

To deal with the abuse involving the age and service requirements, it provides that the employer must select one of three methods for vesting. Under one option, pension rights are vested in the employee starting with 25 percent after five years of service, and increasing with additional years of service until the pension is fully vested after 15 years of service. The second choice is to provide 100 percent vesting after 10 years of service. The third method, called the "Rule of 45," provides that an employee with at least five years of service have a 50 percent vesting right when his age and service add up to 45. The percentage of vesting increases annually by 10 percentage points thereafter, until the 100 percent figure is reached after 15 years of service.

So that funds will be available upon employees' retirement, the law requires that all newly adopted pension plans be fully funded to pay the benefits due retired employees. For those plans in existence before the law became effective, employers have the obligation to fund for past service obligations over a period of specified time. To ensure further that employees will receive the pension benefits upon retirement, the 1974 law establishes a Public Benefit Guaranty Corporation, a government agency that guarantees pensions up to a maximum of $750 per month. To raise the necessary funds to provide the guarantee, employers were initially required to pay annually $1 per worker for single-employer plans and 50 cents for multiemployer plans. Other safeguards, involving the placing of a fiduciary responsibility on the administrators of pension plans, the reporting and disclosure annually

---

[9]*Wall Street Journal,* November 4, 1970.

[10]*U.S. News & World Report,* July 2, 1973, p. 46.

[11]*Wall Street Journal,* November 4, 1970.

[12]See "Pension Reform, the Long, Hard Road to Enactment," *Monthly Labor Review,* Vol. 97, No. 11 (November 1974), 3–12, for a detailed description of the law.

to the Secretary of Labor of financial information showing the operation of the plan, and the right of each employee each year to receive information concerning his vesting and accumulated benefit status, are included in the law.

No law can ever deal with every eventuality and circumstance, but it is safe to say that this legislation will go a long way toward protecting the interests of employees covered by a private pension plan. Undoubtedly, the impact of the law will increase the costs of pension programs and thus probably lead to smaller benefits. However, a smaller but guaranteed pension is better than no pension at all for an employee who has devoted all or most of his working life to a company.

VACATIONS WITH PAY

Vacations with pay for production workers constitute, as was noted earlier, a comparatively new development in American industry. Prior to World War II, only a fraction of workers covered by collective bargaining contracts received pay during vacation periods, and, at that time, other employees were permitted time off only if they were willing to sacrifice pay. At present, vacations with pay are a standard practice in practically every collective bargaining contract, and this has been true for some time. As far back as 1957, in fact, a Department of Labor study of 1,813 agreements, each covering more than 1,000 workers, found that only 8 percent of these contracts did not provide some form of paid vacation;[13] today, the employer not furnishing this type of pay for time not worked is a true individualist.

In addition to the influence of the National War Labor Board's wage controls in spearheading the spread of paid vacations, a growing recognition by employers, employees, and unions of the benefits of such a policy (in terms of worker health, personal development, and productivity) has contributed to the growth.

Paid vacations have also undergone steady liberalization as a worker benefit. In recent years, an annual five-week vacation (normally requiring 20 years of service or more) has been bargained by the parties in some situations, and while this length of paid leisure time is still enjoyed by less than one-third of all unionists, it is relevant that such a vacation was all but non-existent until the late 1960s. Four-week vacations (usually after at least 18 years) are today included in 85 percent of all agreements, or more than triple the 1960 frequency. Of more significance to shorter-term workers is the three-week vacation, provided for in almost 95 percent of contracts (as against 78 percent in 1960) and most frequently requiring 10 years of service (where 15 years was the modal prerequisite a very few years ago). Virtually all employees moreover, can count on a two-week vacation after building up five years of

---

[13]U.S. Bureau of Labor Statistics, *Paid Vacation Provisions in Major Union Contracts, 1957*, Bulletin No. 1233, June 1958.

seniority, and contracts increasingly allow this length of time off after only one or two years of service. The only stagnation that has occurred is, in fact, in the one-week vacation area: One year of service has entitled most employees to a single week of vacation with pay for well over a decade now, and the next frontier relating to the one-week vacation will probably be its total abolition in favor of the two-week vacation after one year—an arrangement that is even now granted by perhaps as many as one-fifth of all agreements.[14]

An innovation that thus far has not spread appreciably beyond the scope of influence of the United Steelworkers of America is considerably more imaginative than the mere liberalization denoted by the statistics above. In 1962, the Steelworkers and metal can manufacturers negotiated a "sabbatical" paid vacation of thirteen weeks' duration, allowed all employees with 15 or more years of service *every five years*, and the basic steel industry incorporated essentially the same agreement for the senior half of its work force the following year. The rationale behind this device is a twofold one: Greater leisure time for employees (with, at least in theory, greater attendant benefits to worker health, personal development, and productivity than under less liberal vacation allowances), and the creation of new jobs through the major immediate need for additional employees brought about the sabbatical. After more than a dozen years, the plan had received mixed evaluations; it was particularly hard to isolate the effects of the plan from such other employment-increasing factors as a strengthened market demand for the products involved in most of those years, and the fact that many eligible employees had exercised an option of accepting extra pay in lieu of some of the time had also to be reckoned with. It was at least apparent that, if the sabbatical was to achieve either of its objectives, employees would be obliged to actually take their vacations—and also to abstain from taking other paid work during the vacation period. It also seemed clear that bargainers in other industries were awaiting more conclusive proof of the benefits of the plan before pushing for its incorporation in their contracts.

In qualifying for vacations, most labor agreements require that an employee must have worked a certain number of hours, days, or months prior to the vacation period, and failure of the employee to comply with such stipulations results in the forfeiture of the vacation benefits. The rate of pay to which the employee is entitled during his vacation is ordinarily computed on the basis of his regular hourly rate, although in a comparatively small number of agreements vacation benefits are calculated on the basis of average hourly earnings over a certain period of time preceding the vacation, and, in some agreements, vacation pay is calculated as a specified percentage of annual earnings; usually this latter figure amounts to between 2.0 and 2.5 percent of the annual earnings.

[14]All information cited in this paragraph is based on data furnished by the Bureau of Labor Statistics, U.S. Department of Labor.

A problem arises involving the payment of workers who work during their vacation periods. In some contracts—as in the case of the steel and can provisions alluded to previously—the employee has the option of taking the vacation to which he is entitled or of working during this period. Other labor agreements allow the company the option of giving pay *instead of* vacations if production requirements make it necessary to schedule the worker during his vacation period. No less than in the case of the sabbaticals, when employees work during their vacation periods either upon their own or the company's option, the principles upon which paid vacations are based (health, productivity, and so on) are, of course, violated. In any event, the question arises as to how to compensate employees for their vacation time when they work during this period. In most labor agreements, employees under these circumstances are given their vacation pay plus the regular wages they earn in the plant. In a few cases, particularly when the employer schedules work during a vacation period, the wage earned by the employee working on his job during his vacation period is calculated at either time-and-one-half or double the regular rate. Such earnings are in addition to the employee's vacation pay.

In a majority of contracts, management has the ultimate authority to schedule the vacation period. Under an increasingly large number of agreements, however, the company is required to take into consideration seniority and employee desires. A fairly sizable number of labor agreements permit management to schedule vacations during plant shutdowns. (Case No. 8 deals with the problem of vacation scheduling.)

An additional vacation problem involves the status of employees who are separated from a company before their vacation period. In some collective bargaining agreements, these employees are entitled to accumulated vacation benefits when they leave the employment of companies under certain specified circumstances, such as permanent layoff, resignation, and military duty. In a comparatively small number of contracts, workers discharged for cause may also claim vacation benefits.

HOLIDAYS WITH PAY

Similar to paid vacations, paid holidays for production workers was not a common practice before World War II. When a plant shut down for a legal holiday, the workers simply lost a day of work. And, also as in the case of vacations with pay, the National War Labor Board permitted employers and unions to negotiate labor agreements providing for paid holidays under its wartime wage regulations. As a result, paid holidays became a common feature in collective bargaining contracts during World War II, and the practice continued after hostilities terminated. By 1948, about 70 percent of all labor agreements provided for paid holidays, and at present nearly 100 percent of all labor agreements incorporate some formula for paid holidays.

The modal number of such holidays granted in 1975 was nine. There was almost universal agreement among the contracts on at least four of these specific holidays: More than 98 percent allowed paid time off for Independence Day, Labor Day, Thanksgiving, and Christmas. And well over 96 percent of all contracts paid for holidays on New Year's Day and Memorial Day. Wider variation takes place where more than six holidays are sanctioned, but half-days before Thanksgiving, Christmas, and New Year's Day are frequently specified, and in an increasing number of cases, a seventh (or eighth, ninth, or tenth) holiday is oriented on an individual basis—such as the employee's birthday. Under this latter arrangement, the company by definition is not penalized with whatever inefficiencies may result from a plant shutdown. Many agreements also recognize any of a variety of state and local holidays, ranging from Patriot's Day in Massachusetts to Mardi Gras in parts of the South. Company—and even union—picnics are declared occasions for paid holidays in a somewhat smaller number of contracts.[15] (The Electrical Workers (IUE) at the Newport, Tennessee, plant of Electro-Voice, Inc., may be absolutely unique, however; in 1974 they won as a new paid holiday February 2, Groundhog Day.)

Most labor agreements place certain obligations upon employees who desire to qualify for paid holidays, with the common objective in this respect being that of minimizing absenteeism. The most frequently mentioned such requirement is that an employee must work the last scheduled day before and the first scheduled day after a holiday. The obligation is waived when the employee does not work on the day before or after the holiday because of illness, authorized leave of absence, jury duty, or death in the family. Under some collective bargaining relationships, illness must be proved by a doctor's certificate, by nurse visitation, or by some other device. (Case No. 9 deals with this aspect of holiday pay.)

Production requirements and emergency situations at times require that employees work on holidays, and such circumstances raise the problem of rates of pay for work on these days. About three-quarters of all labor agreements provide for double-time for work on holidays, and a small number of contracts now call for triple-time. In the continuous-operation industries, such as the hotel, restaurant, and transportation sectors, labor agreements frequently substitute another full day off with pay for a holiday on which an employee worked.

An additional problem involves payment for holiday time when the holiday falls on a day on which the employee would not ordinarily work. For example, if a plant does not normally work on Saturdays, and if in a particular year July 4 (a paid holiday under the collective bargaining agreement) falls on a Saturday, the question arises as to whether employees are entitled to holiday pay. Another aspect of the same general problem involves a paid

[15]Data from Bureau of Labor Statistics, U.S. Department of Labor.

holiday falling during an employee's vacation period. Some unions claim that pay for holidays constitutes a kind of vested benefit to employees, regardless of the calendar week on which the holiday occurs. Thus, if the holiday falls on a regular nonworkday, some unions ask that another day be designated as the holiday or that the employee be given a day's wages; or if the holiday falls during an employee's vacation period, that he receive another day's paid vacation or wages for the holiday. The opposing view holds that payment for holidays falling on a day on which employees do not regularly work violates the basic principle underlying paid holidays, which is protection of employees from loss of wages. Many labor agreements reflect the thinking of labor unions on this issue and designate, for example, another day off with pay if a holiday falls on a nonworkday, but a large number of labor agreements do not treat the problem one way or the other, and frequently because of the nature of the language establishing holidays with pay, controversies in this respect are settled in arbitration.

NEGOTIATED HEALTH INSURANCE PLANS

Health insurance plans are now a common feature of collective bargaining contracts. These plans provide for one or more of the following: life insurance or death benefits; accidental death and dismemberment benefits; accident and sickness benefits; and cash or services covering hospital, surgical, maternity, and medical care. Recently the boundaries of the package have been extended to such areas as major medical insurance (often defraying all such expenses up to 80 percent of their total), dental insurance, and psychiatric treatment benefits. By 1975, the vast majority of workers under collective bargaining contracts were covered, although in widely varying degrees, by some or all parts of this overall insurance mechanism.

A number of factors provide the basis for the spread of insurance plans under collective bargaining. Insurance programs were also a major fringe issue in the period of wage control during World War II, although to a far smaller extent than were vacations and holidays. Many employers and unions have, moreover, increasingly recognized that industrial workers—particularly with health costs rising rapidly in recent years—are not prepared to meet the risks covered by such plans. The Internal Revenue Service has also given incentive to the spread of such insurance, by permitting employers who contribute to these programs to deduct payments as a business expense for tax purposes, where such plans conform to the standards of law for tax relief. In addition, group insurance permits purchasing economies not available to individuals. Finally, the fact that the Social Security program has not provided protection for most risks covered by these insurance plans has made the private insurance system a widely sought one.

Today's typical bargained health and welfare package is of no small dimensions. There is a strong likelihood that it includes: group life insurance for an amount approximating 90 percent of the employee's annual salary; disability and sickness benefits of at least $100 weekly for six months; semi-private hospital room and hospital board for as long as 90 days, together with such add-ons as drugs and medicines, X-ray examinations, and operating-room expenses (under either Blue Cross or a private insurance company plan); surgical expenses up to a $500 maximum for contingencies not covered by workmen's compensation legislation; and coverage for the employee's dependents as well as himself for all or most of these benefits. And, as in the cases of pensions, vacations, and holidays, these emoluments are continuing their own process of liberalization, with discernable trends in recent years involving an increase in the amount and duration of the benefits; the extension of the benefits to retired workers, as well as to those dependents not yet covered; defrayal of the expenses of at least some medically related drugs; and the added protection for catastrophic illnesses and accidents and addition of dental and mental health benefits cited previously.

There has been a commensurately strong trend toward exclusive employer financing of the health benefit package: 21 percent of all unionized employers paid the full cost in 1949; roughly 40 percent did so in 1956;[16] and it is very likely that over 60 percent currently pay all expenses for the greatly enlarged package of the mid-1970s. With the continuing union emphasis on health expense defrayal, no reversal of this trend seems to lie on the horizon.

DISMISSAL PAY

Unlike all the wage supplements discussed above, dismissal, or "severance," pay is still not a common product of collective bargaining. A recent study of 1,339 major (1,000 workers or more) and thus presumably more liberal agreements found only 30 percent of these contracts, or exactly the same percentage as a decade earlier, providing such a benefit.[17] And on an industrywide basis, the practice remains largely confined to contracts negotiated by the Steelworkers, Auto Workers, Communications Workers, Ladies' Garment Workers, and Electrical Workers—although many sectors of the newspaper and railroad industries also have such plans.

Dismissal pay provisions normally limit payments to workers displaced because of technological change, plant merger, permanent curtailment of the company's operations, permanent disability, or retirement before the employee is entitled to a pension. Workers discharged for cause and employees

[16]U.S. Department of Labor, Office of Welfare and Pension Plans, *Welfare and Pension Plan Statistics, 1960* (Washington, D.C.: U.S. Government Printing Office, 1963), pp. 3–4.

[17]U.S. Bureau of Labor Statistics, *Characteristics of Agreements Covering 1,000 Workers or More, 1973*, Bulletin No. 1822, 1974.

who refuse another job with the company normally forfeit dismissal pay rights, as do workers who voluntarily quit a job.

The amount of payment provided for in dismissal pay arrangements varies directly with the length of service of the employee. The longer the service, the greater the amount of money. Ordinarily, a top limit is placed upon the amount that an employee can receive. Although labor agreements vary in respect to the payment formula, as a general rule low-service workers receive one week's wages for each year of service prior to dismissal, with higher than proportional allowances for high-service employees (up to 60 weeks' pay, for example, for 15 or more years of service, and as high as 105 weeks' pay for workers with 25 or more years).

A problem involving dismissal pay is the situation wherein an employee is subsequently rehired by the company. There is little uniformity in collective bargaining contracts relative to the handling of this problem. Actually, a large number of labor agreements that provide for dismissal pay are silent on whether the employee must make restitution to the company upon being rehired or whether he may keep the money paid to him when his employment was originally terminated. Some agreements, however, specifically provide that such an employee must return the money; for example, one telephone industry collective bargaining contract stipulates that such employees must repay to the company any termination payment, either in a lump sum or through payroll deduction at a rate of not less than 10 percent each payroll period until the full amount is paid.

Since the dismissal provision is designed to cushion the effects of employment termination through technological change, merger, and cessation of business (as well as through involuntary retirement due to personal health misfortunes), it is logical to conclude that this benefit, too, will spread in the years ahead. The acceleration of technological and business operations changes beginning in the 1950s and continuing through the 1960s was itself responsible for a considerable increase in the dismissal pay statistics in those years; only 10 percent of labor agreements had such a provision in 1949.[18] Given the continuing presence of these causative factors, there is little reason to believe that the spread of dismissal pay has run its course.

REPORTING PAY

Under the provisions of approximately 90 percent of the collective bargaining contracts currently in force, employees who are scheduled to work, and who do not have instructions from the company *not* to report to their jobs, are guaranteed a certain amount of work for that day or compensation instead of work. Issues involved in the negotiation of reporting pay arrange-

[18]"Dismissal Pay Provisions in Union Agreements, 1949," *Monthly Labor Review*, Vol. 70 (April 1950), 384.

ments are the amount of the guarantee and the rate of compensation, the amount of notice required for the employer to avoid guaranteed payment, the conditions relieving the employer of the obligation to award reporting pay, and the conditions under which such pay must be forfeited by employees.

Labor agreements establish a variety of formulas for the calculation of the amount of the guarantee. Reporting pay ranges from a one-hour guarantee to a full day. About 60 percent of labor contracts dealing with this issue provide for four hours' pay; approximately 10 percent call for eight hours' pay. These rates are calculated on a straight-time basis. However, under circumstances where workers are called back to work by management outside of regularly scheduled hours, such employees are frequently compensated at premium rates, ordinarily at time-and-one-half the regular rate. Such reimbursement, popularly styled "call-in" pay, might be awarded a worker, if, for example, he is called back to work before he has been off for 16 hours. Thus, if he regularly works the first shift and is called back under some emergency condition to work the third shift, the labor agreement might require that he be paid at premium rates. In the event that the employee reports for such work only to find that the company no longer has need for his services, he will still be entitled to a certain number of guaranteed hours of pay calculated at premium rates.

In most agreements providing for reporting pay, an employer is relieved of the obligation to guarantee work or to make a cash payment to employees when he notifies his employees not to report to work. Contracts frequently provide that such notice must be given employees before the end of the worker's previous shift, although in some cases the employer may be relieved of the obligation if he gives notice a certain number of hours before employees are scheduled to work. Eight hours' notice is provided in many labor contracts. In addition, employers are relieved of the obligation to award reporting pay when failure to provide work is due to causes beyond the control of the company. Thus, when work is not available because of floods, fires, strikes, power failures, or "acts of God," in most contracts either employers are fully relieved of the obligation to award reporting pay or the amount of the pay is substantially reduced. Of course, there are many questions of interpretation involved in this situation. For example, does power failure resulting from faulty maintenance relieve the employer of the obligation to award reporting pay? As in so many previous cases, such questions are resolved through the grievance procedure and at times through arbitration.

Under certain circumstances, employees forfeit reporting pay. If employees, for example, fail to keep the company notified of change of address, reporting pay is forfeited under many labor agreements. Other forfeitures might result if employees refuse to accept work other than their own jobs, leave the plant before notice is given to other employees not to report to work, or fail to report to work even though no work is available.

SUPPLEMENTARY UNEMPLOYMENT
BENEFIT PLANS

One of the most interesting developments in relatively recent years in collective bargaining has been the supplementary unemployment benefit (SUB) plan. This area attracted national attention in 1955, when such a plan was negotiated by the United Automobile Workers and the basic automobile manufacturers, and again in 1956 when the basic steel corporations and the United Steelworkers of America included such a plan in their new labor agreement. There is not much evidence of plans protecting workers' income during periods of unemployment prior to 1955, although a few such arrangements had been established in sectors of the consumer goods industries.

Essentially, SUB plans constitute a compromise between the "guaranteed annual wage" demanded by many unions in the late 1940s and early 1950s, and a continuing management unwillingness to grant such relatively complete job security as the "guaranteed wage" designation would indicate. The plans are geared primarily to two goals: (1) supplementing the unemployment benefits of the various state unemployment insurance systems; and (2) allowing further income to still-unemployed workers after state payments have been exhausted. And they implicitly recognize at least one weakness in the state system: Since the states started paying benefits in the late 1930s, the average ratio of these benefits to average wage levels of employees when working has steadily dropped from approximately 40 percent four decades ago to somewhat less than 35 percent today.

About 3 million employees are now covered by negotiated supplementary unemployment benefit plans. By far the largest numbers of these (perhaps one-half) are concentrated in the basic auto and steel industries, but such plans are now also in existence in such other widely divergent sectors of the economy as aluminum, aerospace, glass, farm equipment, retail trade, electrical, can, rubber, apparel, printing and publishing, and the maritime industry, and the vast majority of these plans have some major elements of similarity.

All SUB plans, for example, require that an employee have a certain amount of service with the company before he is eligible to draw benefits; the seniority period varies among the different plans—with a one-year requirement in the basic auto and can contracts contrasting with a five-year prerequisite (the most extreme) in a few contracts negotiated by the Oil, Chemical and Atomic Workers Unions. In addition to seniority stipulations, virtually all plans require that the unemployed worker be willing and able to work. The test in this latter connection is, most often, the registration for work by the unemployed worker with a state unemployment service office; for example, under the automobile plan, a worker is not qualified to obtain benefits unless he registers for work with the appropriate state office and does not refuse to accept a job deemed suitable under such a state system. Beyond this, the plans invariably limit benefits to workers who are unemployed because of layoff resulting from a reduction in the work force by the company. Workers who are out of work because of discipline, strikes, or "acts of God" cannot draw benefits. Nor can workers do so whose curtailment of employment is attributable to government regulation, or to public controls over the amount or nature of materials or products that the company uses or sells.

Under the most prevalent type of SUB agreement, all employees (including those just hired) start to acquire credit units at the rate of one-half unit for each week in which they work. When they complete enough service to qualify for the benefits (the one to five years cited in the preceding paragraph), they are officially credited with these units, which they can then trade off for SUB pay when unemployed up to a maximum unemployment duration. Most plans now have set this maximum at 52 weeks, and consequently, an automobile or steel industry worker with two years of continuous employment has achieved the maximum amount of SUB coverage. Under about half the current plans, however, the ratio of credit units to weeks of benefit can be increased when the SUB fund falls below a certain level, thereby shortening the duration of benefits. Another common variation is to adjust the ratio in such a way that laid-off workers with long service are protected for a proportionately longer length of time than are shorter-service employees.

Almost universally, employees are entitled to draw benefits only up to the amount of credits that they have established, and can receive no benefits—no matter how large the amount of their credits—during the first week of unemployment, a stipulation that is consistent with the one-week waiting period under most state unemployment insurance plans. In addition, credit units are canceled in the event of a willful misrepresentation of facts in connection with the employee's application for either state or SUB income.

Benefit formulas under most layoff plans currently set a normal level of payments at 60 to 65 percent of take-home pay (gross pay minus taxes) for all eligible employees. This level comprises payments from both the negotiated benefit plan and the state system. If, for example, a worker whose normal take-home amount is $180 is laid off, a plan calling for 65 percent of his take-home pay allows him $117. And if his state unemployment compensation totals $65 weekly, the SUB plan would then pay him the weekly sum of $52 to make up the difference. There is some debate even among the most rabid advocates of SUB plans as to whether the level should be pushed much beyond this 65 percent figure, for even at this percentage, several plans have experienced the ironic situation of workers' preferring total layoff to work. The recent experience of the major automobile companies, indeed, has dramatized the potential consequences of liberalizing such a situation: Under UAW contracts since 1967 in that industry, workers with the minimal years of seniority actually received 95 percent of their after-tax wages while on layoff (minus $7.50 for such work-related expenses as transportation, work clothing, and lunches) for up to 52 weeks—and almost invariably preferred

such a well-remunerated enforced leisure period to their normal work assignments! Given the typical influence of auto industry contracts on labor
settlements outside the automobile sector, it seems a safe prediction that
other SUB industries will ultimately experience this problem of unionists'
demanding to be laid off.

To establish the fund for the payment of supplementary unemployment
benefits, most plans require that the company—which invariably exclusively
finances all SUB plans—contribute a certain amount of money per work
hour. Many agreements call for a cash contribution of 5 cents per hour,
although several go as low as 2 cents and about the same number require 14
cents. The payment into this fund most often represents the *maximum*
liability of the company, however. Typically, a maximum size of the fund is
defined, and company contributions for any one contractual period stop
completely when this limit is reached and maintained; the objectives, aside
from relieving the companies of too-rigorous payments, are to prevent too
large an accumulation of fund money and to encourage the companies to
stabilize their employment levels. On the other hand, when fund finances fall
below the stipulated amount, because of SUB-financed payments, the employer must resume payments at the rate required by the plan. In addition,
many SUB plans—including most of those negotiated by the Steelworkers—
require a further company liability: When the SUB fund reaches the "maximum" level, companies continue to make contributions—first to a Savings
and Vacation Plan (to keep its benefits fully current) and then once again to
the SUB fund—until approximately $250 per employee is accumulated. Only
at this point do company contributions cease.

With the passing of time, the impact on the social and economic fabric of
the nation of the operation of plans calculated to protect workers' incomes
during periods of unemployment will become more evident. Since these plans
are still comparatively new and cover a relatively small percentage of the
labor force, there is insufficient empirical data to determine their effects on
the critical elements of the socioeconomic environment. There seems to be
little question that they made some contribution to mitigating individual
hardship, as well as to maintaining consumer purchasing power, during the
general recessions of 1957–58, 1960–61, 1970, and 1974–75. But additional
evidence is needed to establish their impact upon features such as the growth
of industry, the level of employment and unemployment, the mobility of
labor, the incentive of employees to work, the relations between management
and union, the operation and character of state unemployment compensation
plans, and technological changes within industry. Much speculation and
deductive argument has been advanced in this respect. Unfortunately, a large
share of the discussion has been initiated on a purely partisan basis and hence
has served only to confuse and distort the issues. As in other areas of labor
relations, scientific investigation of the effects of this new development of
industrial relations is required.

The fact remains, however, that—in strong contrast to virtually every other economic benefit discussed in this chapter—the growth of SUB plans since their negotiation in the automobile and steel industries in the middle 1950s has been far from impressive. Most craft unions continue to greet such a device with total apathy, preferring to substitute other economic improvements for its introduction. And seniority protection appears to have thus far satisfied workers in many noncraft industries sufficiently so that SUB has not become a major union demand there. But the continuing hold of SUB upon the several major industries in which it was originally negotiated, and the constant improvement of SUB allowances there, remain facts that cannot be ignored, either in assessing the creativity of the collective bargaining process or in judging the potential impact of this "guaranteed annual wage" compromise should the employment instabilities that have always characterized most industries in which SUB has now been implemented spread to other parts of the economy. If SUB extensions have not been impressive in total, SUB today does exist in sectors where it is needed—namely, in cyclical industries.

SUB Plans: When the Money Runs Out

Ironically, a new and unprecedented challenge was confronting SUB at the time of this writing, in the industry where the concept had, two decades earlier, made its first big breakthrough. The continuing unemployment of over 200,000 UAW members in the automobile industry—roughly 25 percent of that sector's overall hourly work force—had emasculated the automobile SUB funds by over $500 million in a 16-month period (by mid-1975). Consequently, benefits could no longer be paid to either General Motors or Chrysler workers, although the two other manufacturers in the industry had not yet reached this condition.

Given the mammoth and long-lasting unemployment in automobiles, this outcome should have come as no surprise. SUB was clearly never designed to cope with anything but normal, short-term plant closings and recessions that were relatively mild in their impact. If the monies had been a major consolation in the three lesser recessions since 1955 and throughout the 16 months this time, it was inevitable that sooner or later the SUB well would run dry in the face of the horrendous layoff statistics of 1974–75. And with Chrysler SUB payments averaging almost $4 million a week with only $220,000 simultaneously coming into the fund, and the GM figures commensurately larger on both sides of the ledger and thus no more fiscally optimistic, it had been obvious to both union and management officials for months prior to the announcements that the end of the SUB payouts for the duration of this recession was in sight.

Yet it was probably also true that few workers had expected the economic downturn to become as pronounced or as durable as it turned out to be, and thus the trauma of benefit termination was hardly minimal. As one UAW leader put it, "We've been rather spoiled by good times in recent years and the promise of 95% of our pay for the duration of a layoff. Now, we are going to be caught with our pants down, and it will be a severe realization."[19]

The UAW could, and did, point out to its members that their fate would have been even bleaker had recent improvements in the automobile SUB plan not been made. As of late 1973, hospital and medical insurance premiums, previously paid out of the SUB fund, had been paid by the company, and these amounts (which would otherwise have cost the average worker $105 per month) would continue to be paid for all laid-off employees. In addition, the employer contribution had at the same time been reduced by 2 cents per hour worked to a maximum of 12 cents, thus preserving the SUB payments for a somewhat longer time period. The union also accelerated its efforts to provide its jobless members with financial counseling, help with creditors, and information on applying for welfare benefits. And it promised to bolster its already-aggressive efforts in the field of legislative lobbying for wide-ranging social reform.

But it was nonetheless clear in the face of this unparalleled depletion of auto's prized SUB program that such benefits could by themselves—even if significantly replenished and liberalized, as expected, in the upcoming 1976 automobile industry bargaining—no longer be viewed by anyone as a guarantee against the ravages of prolonged unemployment, in automobiles or in any other industry. As a valuable (and expensive) segment of the overall employee benefit package, SUB would undoubtedly be of help to the *short-term unemployed* in at least the cyclical industries where it had been established, and perhaps in others where it would be implemented in the years ahead. To make claims that it could do anything more than this, however, would be unrealistic, unfair to the parties who had negotiated it, and a cruel hoax for the many employees covered by it.

SOME FINAL THOUGHTS

Whether or not SUB arrangements will ultimately achieve the universality of pension plans, health insurance, paid vacations, and paid holidays (and such various other widespread but considerably lesser benefits as paid time off for obligations stemming from death in the family, jury duty, and voting) obviously remains an open question. Yet, even in the case of SUB, a broader issue does not. It appears to be all but axiomatic to collective bargaining that *any* benefit, once implemented by the parties, becomes subject through the years to a process of continuous liberalization from the workers' viewpoint. Even supplementary unemployment benefits have undergone this process in the years since 1955, when the automobile industry's maximum of $30 weekly for no more than 26 weeks was considered generous.

[19] *Wall Street Journal*, April 10, 1975, p. 36.

Many of these benefits continue to allow the same cost advantages to the parties, in terms of both "group insurance" savings and tax minimization, that they did at the times of their various inceptions. Generally tight labor markets have further led employers to amass attractive benefit packages, to be placed in the front window as recruitment devices. And considerations of worker retention, productivity, and pure pride have also undoubtedly stirred both managers and union leaders in their bargaining on these economic supplements. As the new worker needs and wants in the benefit area have become active, the collective bargaining parties have clearly responded to the challenge.

However, neither for the bargaining parties nor for the nation as a whole is this situation an unmixed blessing. Increasing caution from both managements and unions will, in fact, be required as the liberalization process continues, and at least six caveats appear warranted.

In the first place, many improvements in the benefit portfolio automatically present potentially troublesome sources of union grievances that would otherwise be absent. Increasing latitude for employee choice of vacation time, by the incorporation of a "seniority shall govern, so far as is possible, in the selection of the vacation period" contractual clause, for example, carries far more potential for controversy than a clear-cut statement reserving vacation scheduling strictly for company discretion. As a second example in this area, with two weeks the maximum vacation allowance, there is usually no question of carryover credit from year-to-year; the worker is not confronted with "too much of a good thing" and normally does not seek to bank unwanted vacation time until it may be worth more to him. Under a more liberal allowance, however, the question does arise, as many companies and unions can testify—and policies must be both established and consistently adhered to if problems on this score are to be averted.

The list of such newly created grievance possibilities could be extended considerably, to virtually all the benefit sectors. Who qualifies as a dependent under an expanded health insurance plan that now accommodates such individuals? What religious credentials must be established to authorize paid time off "as conscience may dictate" on Good Friday or Yom Kippur? Is a suddenly decreed national day of mourning an "act of God," relieving the company of an obligation to grant reporting pay, or do its circumstances compel the employer to pay such amounts? How many hours or weeks of work—and under what conditions—constitute a year, for purposes of calculating pension entitlement within a system granting a flat monthly payment "per year of service"? In a less generous age, these and obviously a myriad of similar questions were automatically excluded.

Second, even on the now-rare occasions upon which the benefits are not formally liberalized, many of them automatically become more costly simply because wages have been increased. All wage-related benefits fall into this category, and a 20-cent-per-hour wage increase will thus inevitably elevate total employment costs by considerably more than this face amount because of the simultaneous rise in the worth of each holiday, vacation period, and any other allowance pegged to the basic wage rate. This industrial relations truism would hardly be worth citing were it not so often ignored in union–management bargaining rooms, in favor of accommodating only wage increases to increases in productivity (for example) rather than wage increases plus wage-related benefit increases. The degree of danger in overlooking these inflationary ramifications, moreover, obviously rises with the increasing value of the benefit itself.

In the third place, one suspects that managements have—at least at times—generated *negative* employee motivation by implementing benefits without either participation or approval of work force representatives in the process. The day of company paternalism, fortunately, now lies far in the past for the large mainstream of American industry. But the arousal of employee ego-involvement is all the more imperative in today's sophisticated industrial world. Few people have dealt with the penalties of oversight in this regard more cogently than has Leland Hazard. Describing a deep and enthusiastic interest in unionization on the part of employees at a large Pittsburgh plant "that was well known as having excellent wages and working conditions, and supposedly had almost perfect employee relationships," he quotes the following remarks of "one attractive girl" to explain the general sentiment:

> It's about time something like this happened. We have got to stand on our own feet. They do everything for you but provide a husband, and I even know girls who they got a husband for. And them what ain't got time to get pregnant, they get foster kids for.[20]

Related to this question of negative motivation, but isolable as a fourth potential problem, must stand the very real alternative possibility of *no* employee motivation whatsoever. Not being masochistic as a class, employers logically expect some benefits from their expenditures in the wage supplement area—particularly, more satisfactory worker retention figures, an improved recruitment performance, and, above all, generally increased employee productivity. Without such returns on the benefit investment, companies would be engaging in clear-cut wastage.

One can readily locate situations where employee benefits have obviously achieved at least some of these desired results. Particularly in those areas where benefit entitlement expands with increasing seniority (pensions and vacations, for example), greater worker retention has undoubtedly often been fostered. Yet there is to this moment no convincing proof that benefits have significantly affected employee motivation on any large-scale basis in American industry—and, for that matter, the few scholarly treatments of this topic

[20]Leland Hazard, "Unionism: Past and Future," *Harvard Business Review*, March–April 1958.

that have cropped up in the literature indicate that the extent of employee knowledge as to exactly what the benefits are is something less than awesome.[21] There is a critical need for far more research into this subject by employers and other interested parties than has thus far been conducted, for the possibility that industry may be undergoing an ever-increasing expense that may be returning very little in the way of concrete worker performance cannot as yet be safely dismissed.

Fifth, it is possible that overall employment has suffered—and conceivably will continue to suffer—from the continuation of benefit expansion of the type described in this chapter. As in the preceding case, the evidence thus far is not fully conclusive. But the increasing cost pressures and personnel administration complexities involved appear to have combined with related factors to push in this direction. Certainly Garbarino, whose exploration of such a possibility for manufacturing employees is perhaps the most thorough of its kind to date, does not dispute this point. He deems it "reasonable to conclude" that the cost and administrative considerations, as well as uncertainty as to future labor requirements and other management problems, have "contributed to minimizing employment expansion without necessarily leading to a major expansion of overtime scheduling."[22] Aside from the basic issues of society's optimum utilization of manpower and the dashed aspirations of the consequently unemployed or underemployed that are always presented by such an outcome, Garbarino's conclusion—if, in fact, "reasonable"—clearly contains further pungent considerations related to urbanized ghetto America today.

Finally, unlike wage increases (which can often be at least partially negated by such mechanisms as job reevaluation and incentive rate implementation or modification), the benefit package has a strong tendency to remain a permanent part of the landscape. Except in extreme cases of corporate financial crisis, it is quite immune from disintegration. And if any significant positive effect of benefits on employee motivation thus far remains to be proven, the annals of industrial history are replete with examples of companies that have encountered surprisingly intense worker resistance in attempting to dismantle even such relatively minor portions of their benefit packages as child-care programs or banking facilities. Downward revisions of the leisure time, health, and pension offerings remain several miles beyond the realm of the conceivable. In short, once the parties introduce a benefit, they can expect to be wedded to it for life, with the only meaningful questions focusing on the timing and degrees of the subsequent benefit liberalizations.

[21]See, for example, James L. Sheard, "Relationship Between Attitude and Knowledge in Employee Fringe Benefit Orientation," *Personnel Journal*, November 1966; and Arthur A. Sloane and Edward W. Hodges, "Employee Benefits: In One Ear and Out the Other?" *Personnel*, November–December 1968.

[22]Joseph W. Garbarino, "Fringe Benefits and Overtime as Barriers to Expanding Employment," *Industrial and Labor Relations Review*, XVII, No. 3 (April 1964), p. 439.

For all the reservations expressed in the paragraphs above, employee benefits hardly warrant an evaluation similar to that given by the old railroad baron James Hill to the passenger train ("like the male teat, neither useful nor ornamental"). They do provide considerable security at minimal cost to the covered employees (whether or not the latter explicitly desire such protection in lieu of other forms of compensation), at least at times abet the employer's recruitment and retention efforts in a tight labor market, and minimize the tax burdens of both company and worker. If there is room for doubt that they also allow the employer any significant return in the form of worker morale and productivity, these other reasons alone are probably sufficient to justify their dramatic spread during the past quarter century.

And because the benefit package has become so relatively standardized among companies in this time interval, too, the wage supplements probably also perform a further (if less constructive) function for managers and the unions with which they deal. Their presence in anything approaching the typical dimensions prevents invidious comparisons by both current and potential employees in evaluating the desirability of the company as an employer. The extent of worker knowledge of specific benefits may fall far short of perfection, but in the late 1970s, because corporate pattern-following has been so prevalent in this area, the absence of seven or eight paid holidays, a three-week paid vacation after no more than ten years of service, significant medical coverage for all members of the family, meaningful pensions, and any of the various other parts of the generally conspicuous benefit protfolio are often grounds for workers' dissatisfaction.

Thus it can be predicted quite fearlessly that the years ahead will see a continuation of the benefit growth. As indicated, it appears to be all but axiomatic to industrial relations that any benefit, once implemented, through the years becomes subject to a process of continuous liberalization from the worker's viewpoint. And, while variety in these economic supplements has now become increasingly difficult to achieve, there is also little doubt but that new ones (perhaps most emphatically in the areas of income stabilization and employment relief) will join the already crowded ranks.

Possibly, however, increasing awareness on the part of fringe benefit implementors as to the various problem areas outlined here will result in some slowing down of the continuous liberalization process and restrain the introduction of new types of benefits until thorough investigation—tailored to the needs of individual companies and unions—has taken place. At the very least, the future demands considerably more research into these areas than has thus far been carried out. And such an omission seems particularly blatant when one realizes that there remain few other aspects of industrial relations that have not been subjected to searching scrutiny. But one must be a pessimist on these scores: Thus far, both the research and the benefit deceleration have been notably absent.

DISCUSSION QUESTIONS

1. Which set of arguments as expressed in this chapter's section on pensions carries more weight with you: the case *for* contributory plans, or the case *against* them?

2. "SUB plans of the type negotiated in the automobile and steel sectors are wholly undesirable. They discourage employees in the incentive to work, replace state unemployment compensation systems, discriminate against the worker not represented by a union, place an undetermined but intolerable burden on management, are financially unsound, and can actually cause permanent unemployment among some workers." In the light of your understanding of the character of these SUB plans, evaluate this statement.

3. Paul Pigors and Charles A. Myers have argued that "management should offer employee benefits and services, not because [it has] to, not only within legal limits, and not as a camouflaged form of bribery, but because such benefits and services are in line with the whole personnel program." Do you agree? Why, or why not?

SELECTED REFERENCES

ALLEN, DONNA, *Fringe Benefits: Wages or Social Obligation?* Ithaca, N.Y.: New York State School of Industrial and Labor Relations, 1964.

BLOOM, GORDON F., and HERBERT R. NORTHRUP, *Economics of Labor Relations*, 5th ed., pp. 613–720. Homewood, Ill.: Richard D. Irwin, 1965.

EHRENBERG, RONALD G., *Fringe Benefits and Overtime Behavior: Theoretical and Econometric Analysis.* Lexington, Mass.: Heath, 1971.

GARBARINO, JOSEPH W., "Fringe Benefits and Overtime as Barriers to Expanding Employment," *Industrial and Labor Relations Review*, XVIII, No. 3 (April 1964), pp. 426–42.

MELONE, JOSEPH J., *Collectively Bargained Multi-Employer Pension Plans.* Homewood, Ill.: Richard D. Irwin, 1963.

SLICHTER, SUMNER H., JAMES J. HEALY, and E. ROBERT LIVERNASH, *The Impact of Collective Bargaining on Management*, pp. 372–489. Washington, D.C.: The Brookings Institution, 1960.

SLOANE, ARTHUR A., and EDWARD W. HODGES, "Employee Benefits: In One Ear and Out the Other?" *Personnel*, November–December 1968.

CASE 8
The Case
of the Forced Vacation Period

Cast of Characters

H   Employee
B   Superintendent

Under most labor agreements, the employer has the ultimate right to schedule vacations so that the production process can be carried out effectively. If too many employees take their vacations at the same time, the orderly and efficient operation of the plant could be jeopardized. Thus, the right of the employer to schedule vacations to avoid this state of affairs is normally superior to the right of employees to select vacation periods on the basis of seniority. In this case, the company forced all employees to take one week of their vacation period during a week of plant shutdown. While you read the case, pay particular attention to the reasons why the employer adopted this policy. Then see how the arbitrator evaluated these reasons in the light of the material contractual language.

In protest against the company policy requiring employees to take one week of their vacations during a plant shutdown period, H filed a grievance, dated June 8, 1973, which stated:

Mr. H was told he would have to retain one week of his vacation for possible plant shutdown next year.

We believe this to be a violation of the Contract between Co. and Union.

Mr. H asks that he not have to save his last week of vacation for (possible) shutdown.

Material to the case were Articles 2 and 8 of the labor agreement:

Article 2. Except as this Agreement expressly provides, the right of the Company to manage its business, operations and affairs, and to establish terms and conditions of employment shall not be impaired. The Company's not exercising rights hereby reserved to it, or its exercising them in a particular way, shall not be deemed a waiver of said rights or of its right to exercise them in some other way not in conflict with the express terms of this Agreement.

Article 8. Employees covered by this Agreement shall be granted vacations in accordance with the following schedule and eligibility requirements:

A.   Employees who have completed one (1) year but less than three (3) years of continuous service shall receive a paid vacation of one (1) week with forty-eight (48) hours straight-time pay.

B.   Employees who have completed three (3) years but less than eight (8) years of continuous service shall receive paid vacation of two (2) weeks with ninety-six (96) hours straight-time pay.

C.   Employees who have completed eight (8) years but less than fifteen (15) years of continuous service shall receive a paid vacation of three (3) weeks with one hundred forty-four (144) hours straight-time pay.

D.   Employees who have completed fifteen (15) years of continuous service shall receive a paid vacation of four (4) weeks with one hundred ninety-two (192) hours straight-time pay. . . .

Employees shall take their vacations during the period or periods the Company establishes and within one (1) year after their qualifying dates. The Company will take seniority into account in scheduling vacations. If, in the Company's opinion, operating conditions make doing so advisable, it may select any time during the year for the scheduling of vacations.

The basic question in this dispute was as follows:

Under the circumstances of this case, did the company violate Article 8 of the labor agreement? If so, what should the remedy be?

BACKGROUND

Depending upon their length of service, employees were eligible for certain lengths of vacation periods, ranging from one week for employees with less than three years of seniority to four weeks for those who had completed fifteen years of service. Vacations were to be taken within one year following the employee's anniversary date of hire. Except when the issue in this dispute was involved, each employee was requested to designate his choice for preferred vacation periods. Based upon these preferences, the company allocated vacation periods for the employees.

B, production superintendent, testified to the operation of this procedure:

Based upon considerations of seniority, knowledge of circumstances in the plant, consultation with employees, vacation periods are allocated. We cannot permit but a certain number of employees to be off from the plant at the same time. There has always been a problem in job classifications as to how many people could be off at any one time. Between April 1 and September 1, this is a frustrating task. Employees desire to plan their vacations. But we cannot positively state when they can take their vacations. There could be last-minute changes, even a week before they planned their vacations. I have asked people to change their vacations because of operating conditions. Their selection as to preference is governed by operating conditions.

The company customarily shut down its production during the week of July 4; maintenance work continued to be carried out, but the prime production machines did not operate. B explained why the company shut down its plant during that week:

Our production is geared to our major customers. They shut down during the week of July 4. That is why we shut down in the same week.

What sparked this dispute was the company policy of requiring employees to take one week of their vacation during the shutdown period. As of August 17, 1973, H was eligible to take a two-week vacation. He elected to take one week of his vacation during the plant shutdown in the week of July 4, 1973. Under the company policy in question, he was required to take his second week of vacation during the pending shutdown of July 4, 1974. In other words, he was forced to "save" one week of his vacation for the contemplated 1974 shutdown period.

Even though the specific issue in the dispute arose with H, the company policy in question affected the entire bargaining unit. As B declared:

> The company policy affects all employees. All are required to take one week vacation in July 1974. If an employee only has one week of vacation coming to him, he must take this week of vacation during the plant shutdown of the week of July 4, 1974.

POSITION OF THE PARTIES

The position of the union was that the grievance should be granted, while the position of the company was that it should be denied. Both parties offered arguments on behalf of their respective positions, and quotations from these arguments will appear below.

ANALYSIS OF THE EVIDENCE

Issue of Past Practice

In its answer to H's complaint in Step 3 of the grievance procedure, the company stated:

> Mr. H had the opportunity of taking one of his two weeks of vacation any time after his eligibility was established, while holding his second week for the period the company established. He was given an option and chose to take it in advance.
>
> *Past practice cannot be an issue; this has been the vacation policy since our first labor contract.* [Emphasis supplied.]

In addition, the company in its concluding argument, offered at the termination of the arbitration, stated:

> Never before had the union questioned the company's right to schedule vacation shutdowns. The union now charges that the company will violate the col-

lective bargaining agreement if it requires H to take the second week of his vacation during the 1974 maintenance and vacation shutdown.

Thus, the company apparently contended that it had been the practice to force employees to take one week's vacation during the July 4 week shutdown. If this were true, this factor would be very significant in the disposition of the dispute. However, the evidence demonstrated that it was during the plant shutdown in the week of July 4, 1973, that the company *for the first time* forced employees to take one week of their vacations during this period of time. Indeed, B testified:

> In 1973, many employees were treated like H. They were told to save a week of their vacation for the following 1974 shutdown. *Before 1973, this was not done.* [Emphasis supplied.]

In addition, at one point in its closing argument, the company stated:

> This is a *new policy*, because the economics of the business has changed. We no longer operate seven days, 24 hours per day. Circumstances have changed.

There was obviously some confusion on the issue of past practice. If the company's argument relating to practice involved its right to shut down the plant each year during the week of July 4, there was no dispute on this point. Apparently, the company had shut down the plant at that time in previous years. Clearly, it was the company's prerogative to shut down its plant on an annual basis.

But the basic issue in this proceeding did not involve the exercise of this company right. There was no evidence that, as a matter of practice, the company had forced its employees to take one week of their vacations during the plant shutdown. If there had been such a practice, it was not made clear by the evidence supplied in the arbitration. What the record demonstrated was that in 1973, the company had for the first time established the policy in dispute in this proceeding.

To find that there was no evidence of practice in support of the company's position, however, was not to conclude that the union's position prevailed on the basis of practice. Indeed, the company argued that its position should prevail on the basis of unambiguous contractual language. Therefore, the dispute had to be determined on the basis of the material contractual language and its construction in the light of relevant facts contained in the record.

Company's Argument: Clear Language

The company's position was that unambiguous contractual language supported its position. It argued:

> Consistently we have replied through every step of our Grievance Procedure that Article 8, Vacations, the provision of the Contract that the Union claims

the Company is violating by directing H to take one week of vacation during this 1974 shutdown, is clear, precise, and unequivocal:

> Employees shall take their vacations during the period or periods the Company establishes and within one (1) year after their qualifying dates. The Company will take seniority into account in scheduling vacations. *If, in the Company's opinion, operating conditions make doing so advisable, it may select any time during the year for the scheduling of vacations.*

In addition, Article 2, Management Clause, stated:

> "Except as this Agreement *expressly provides*, the right of the Company to manage its business, operations and affairs, and to establish terms and conditions of employment shall not be impaired. The Company's not exercising rights reserved to it, or its exercising them in a particular way, shall not be deemed a waiver of said rights or of its right to exercise them in some other way not in conflict with the express terms of this Agreement."

Thus, no language in the Agreement in any way limits the Company's right to schedule H's vacation during a plant shutdown when, in its opinion, operating conditions make such scheduling advisable.

Critical Issue:
Character of "Operating Conditions"

In pertinent part, Article 8 stated:

> The Company will take seniority into account in scheduling vacations. If in the Company's opinion, operating conditions make doing so advisable, it may select any time during the year for the scheduling of vacations.

The arbitrator felt that what these two sentences meant when viewed together was that the company would take seniority into account when scheduling vacations unless operating conditions made it advisable for the company to schedule vacations at *any time during the year*; but when operating conditions made it advisable for the company to schedule vacations at any time during the year, it might properly do so without reference to preference of employees for vacation periods based upon seniority.

There was no question, of course, that when the company scheduled vacations during the July 4 week shutdown period, this period would fall within the phrase "any time during the year"; the shutdown period was obviously a time that fell within the year. However, the arbitrator believed, the last sentence of Article 8 did not provide the company with the unilateral right to schedule vacations at any time during the year, regardless of circumstances. Under this language, the company might schedule vacations at any time during the year, including the July 4 week shutdown, and without reference to the desire of employees to take vacations on the basis of seniority preference, only *provided that operating conditions made it advisable* for the company to do so.

In the case at hand, the company argued that it selected the shutdown period for a week's vacation for its employees because operating conditions made it advisable to designate that week for a vacation period. In this light, what was critical for a sound decision in this dispute was to determine whether or not "operating conditions," within the meaning of the provision, justified the company's decision. If operating conditions were involved in the company's decision, the policy of the company would properly fall within the authority of Article 8. On the other hand, if operating conditions were not involved, it follows that the company violated the provision, because it failed to take seniority into account when it compelled all employees to take a week's vacation during the shutdown period.

Reasons for Company Policy

B testified as to why the company selected the shutdown period for compulsory vacations:

> If we did not designate the plant shutdown period for vacations, we would have to pay overtime to cover jobs vacated by employees on vacations. Also, we would have to hire extra people to take over jobs of those on vacations. Another reason is that some employees would have to work overtime during the hot months of the summer.

It was clear that the scheduling of vacations during the shutdown period served the best interests of the company. As B stated, when vacations were taken outside of a shutdown period, the company covered the jobs of the employees on vacation, either by having other employees work overtime or by hiring new employees. In either case, there was an extra expense to the company; not only was it paying vacation benefits, but it was also incurring overtime and/or new hire labor costs. To save on these costs, it was obviously more economical for the company to require all employees to take one week's vacation during the plant shutdown.

Operating Conditions
and Economic Considerations

The question, therefore, was whether or not these circumstances constituted "operating conditions" within the meaning of Article 8. Was the saving of labor costs synonymous with "operating conditions"? Did the more economical operation of the plant constitute "operating conditions"? The company thought that these questions should be answered in the affirmative. As B testified:

> Operating conditions include excessive overtime. Anything that affects the operation of the plant is included in operating conditions.

In the opinion submitted by the arbitrator were the following remarks:

> With full deference to the Company, the Arbitrator disagrees with this construction of the concept "operating conditions." What the Company really tells us is that the plant can operate *more economically* when it compels vacations during the shutdown period, because there would be a saving on labor costs. However, "operating conditions" are not synonymous with the most economical operation of the plant. If the Parties intended to confer upon the Company the authority it seeks in this proceeding, they could have written the pertinent language of Article 8 to reflect the following:
>
> > If, in the Company's opinion, *economic or financial* conditions make doing so advisable, it may select any time during the year for the scheduling of vacations.
>
> Under language of this sort, the Company could properly bypass seniority preference and schedule vacations during a shutdown period, because under such a scheduling program, the Company's economic and financial situation would be advanced. However, this kind of language does not appear in Article 8. Instead of using terms such as *economic, financial considerations*, or *labor cost savings*, they agreed that the Company may schedule vacations at any time during a year when *operating conditions* made it advisable.
>
> Indeed, the concept "operating conditions" implies that *the plant will be operating* during a vacation period. The dictionary definition of "operate" is this: "To work, perform, or function, as a machine does. . . . To perform some process of work or treatment."*
>
> Beyond the dictionary definition, in common language, "operating conditions" implies that production will be going on—there will be physical operation of the machinery and plant. However, the Company would use as synonymous with "operating conditions" an intangible concept such as economical, financial, or cost savings. Clearly, there is a great difference between the operating conditions of a plant and the economical operation of a plant.
>
> From this analysis, it is clear what the Parties contemplated when they used "operating conditions" as the basis for the Company's authority to schedule vacations at any time during the year. In order to maintain proper operating conditions, the Company may decide when employees may take their vacations. Machines must be operated and work carried out. Not all employees, regardless of their seniority, may take their vacations at the same time, because this would interfere with the operating conditions of the plant. As the Company states:
>
> > It would be chaos to have each employee determine just when he takes his vacation without regard for plant operation.
>
> It was to preserve the integrity of the operating conditions of the plant that the Parties provided broad authority to the Company in the scheduling of vacations. Indeed, the provision permits the Company to decide when the operating conditions of the plant will permit vacations.

*Random House, *Dictionary of the English Language* (1969), p. 1009.

Conclusion

The broad authority conferred upon the Company under Article 8 does not mean that the Company may force employees to take vacations during a plant shutdown. In the last analysis, when the Company uses its proper authority under Article 8, there must be a relation between scheduling of vacations and the proper operation of the plant's production process. To maintain the smooth operation of the productive process, the Company has wide latitude in the scheduling of vacations. To preserve the proper conditions under which production is carried out, the Company may schedule vacations at any time during the year. These observations, however, do not permit the Company to force employees to take vacations during a plant shutdown period. Clearly, such a program has no relation to the conditions under which the plant operates.

QUESTIONS

1. Was the company trying to pull the wool over the arbitrator's eyes by arguing that past practice supported its position? How did he handle this delicate problem?

2. What was the economic motivation behind the adoption of the company policy?

3. Despite the arbitrator's decision, could you argue with merit that "operating conditions" and "economic conditions" mean the same thing?

4. Should a case in arbitration be decided on the basis of valid economic considerations despite the character of contractual language? Why, or why not?

CASE 9
Holiday Pay Eligibility:
The Case of a Doctor's
Certificate Requirement

Cast of Characters

W and R	Grievants
G	Foreman

An important feature of the holiday pay program is related to the eligibility of employees to receive holiday pay. In this respect, almost all labor agreements require that an employee work his last scheduled shift before the holiday and his first scheduled shift after the holiday. In the absence of this requirement for eligibility, some employees might be absent on these holiday pay qualifying days, in order to stretch out their holiday period. Should the number of employees who do this be large, the employer could not operate the plant efficiently. Of course, when the employee has a good excuse for his absence on a holiday pay qualifying day, most contracts will authorize the payment of holiday pay.

In this case, the employer's objective was to make more sure that employees would not improperly use illness as the excuse for not working on the shifts immediately before and after the holiday. As a result, he adopted a policy that required the employee to prove illness by obtaining a doctor's certificate. If the employee did not present such a document, the employer refused to pay him holiday pay.

What makes the case difficult is the fact that the holiday pay clause in the contract did not expressly state that an absent employee had to obtain a doctor's certificate as a prerequisite for holiday pay. Two employees claimed illness and did not work a full shift on the day following the holiday in question. Since they did not present a doctor's certificate, the employer denied them holiday pay.

Involved in this case were two grievances protesting the company action in denying the employees involved holiday pay for Memorial Day, 1974. Grievance No. 13, dated June 11, 1974, filed by W, stated:

Did not receive Holiday Day pay because of being off sick.

Grievance No. 15, dated June 10, 1974, filed by R, stated:

On May 28, 1974, I reported to my foreman that I was sick and could not finish my shift's work, and that I was clocking out. Upon receiving my paycheck on June 7, 1974, I found that I had been docked a holiday's pay for May 27, 1974. Since sickness is a reasonable excuse complying with our contract, and since I do not have a bad absentee record, nor a record of leaving early, I want pay for the holiday that I am entitled to.

Material to this dispute was Article IX, Section 1 of the labor agreement, which in pertinent part provided:

The Company agrees to pay for a maximum of twelve (12) holidays at straight time. In order for an employee to be eligible to receive pay for the holidays, it will be necessary that he work a full shift his last scheduled workday before and a full shift his first scheduled workday after the paid holiday, unless he has a reasonable excuse for not working a full shift. If the employee is required to work on any of these holidays, he will receive pay at the rate of three (3) times his regular rate. The following holidays will be observed:

.

.

.

National Memorial Day (May 30th)

.

.

.

The basic question to be determined in this arbitration was as follows:

Under the circumstances of this case, did the company violate Article IX, Section 1? If so, what should the remedy be?

BACKGROUND

In 1974, Memorial Day, a paid holiday under the labor agreement, fell on Monday, May 27. The company denied the grievants pay for this holiday because each did not work a full shift on Tuesday, May 28. Although this was the reason for denial of holiday pay to both grievants, the facts and circumstances for each grievant were different. W did not report to the Tuesday shift, claiming that he was ill on that day; and R left work early, claiming that he could not continue to work because of illness.

Involved in the dispute was the fact that during the negotiations that resulted in the current labor agreement, the union attempted to eliminate from the holiday provision that portion making eligibility to obtain holiday pay dependent upon an employee's working a full shift on his last scheduled workday before the paid holiday and on the first scheduled workday after it. However, the union was not successful, and it eventually dropped the proposal.

In the same negotiations, the company proposed to the union that a doctor's certificate stating the nature of an employee's illness be required in order that an absence for the purpose be counted as excused. After the negotiations, the company posted the Guidelines for Control of Absenteeism, which contained the company proposal. In pertinent part, it stated that an employee's absence for illness would be counted as excused provided it was "properly certified by a doctor, stating the nature of illness."

POSITION OF THE PARTIES

The position of the union was that the two grievances should be granted, while the company position was that they should be denied. Both parties filed post-hearing briefs, portions of which will be cited below when necessary and appropriate.

ANALYSIS OF THE EVIDENCE

Some General Comments

Article IX, Section 1 of the labor agreement required that, to be eligible for a paid holiday, the employee must work his last full scheduled shift before a holiday and his first full shift after it. The purpose of this requirement was to encourage employee attendance before and after a holiday, so that employees would not attempt to stretch out their holiday periods.

As a study on collective bargaining practices states:

> In some instances [holiday] pay is lost if the employee is absent on the day preceding or immediately following the holiday. This, of course, prevents an undue drop in production during the holiday week.*

And, despite the efforts of the union in this case to eliminate the eligibility requirement, the holiday pay eligibility rule is found in virtually all collective bargaining contracts in the nation.

In adopting the holiday eligibility provision in this dispute, however, the parties agreed that an employee would not be denied holiday pay if he had a reasonable excuse for not working a full shift before and after a holiday. And the union's failure to eliminate that provision did not erase this exception to the requirement.

Each of the grievants failed to work a full shift on Tuesday, May 28. It was on this basis that the company denied them Memorial Day pay, since Tuesday was their first scheduled workday following this holiday. What remained to be determined was whether or not the company properly denied them holiday pay under Article IX, Section 1. Since the circumstances involving their failure to work a full shift on Tuesday were different for each grievant, an analysis of the evidence pertaining to each employee was required, in order to evaluate the company's action in terms of the holiday eligibility requirement.

W

W did not report to work at all on Tuesday, May 28. He explained that he was absent because he was ill. He testified as follows:

Q: Now, you did not work Tuesday, May 28, 1974?

A: Right.

Q: Why did you not work?

A Well, I have a little inner-ear trouble and occasionally it affects me. Not too often. But it just happened that I got up that morning and had an attack. . . .

W testified further that he was advised by his doctor that if an attack was not severe, he need only rest for a couple of hours; but if the attack was severe, he should report to his doctor. On the morning in question, the grievant testified, the attack was not severe enough to go to the doctor. He testified that he rested for a couple of hours or so, and the problem apparently subsided.

*U.S. Department of Labor, Bureau of Labor Statistics, *Union Agreement Provisions*, Bulletin No. 686, p. 107.

The company conceded that illness was a reasonable excuse under Article IX, Section 1, which served to waive the holiday pay eligibility requirement. However, its position was that the requirement would not be waived unless the employee obtained a doctor's statement certifying his illness. W did not obtain such needed evidence, and, on this basis, the company refused to pay him for the holiday. Therefore, at the core of this dispute was a determination of whether or not the company could properly demand that an employee present a doctor's certificate to prove that he was ill on a holiday pay qualifying day.

In its argument, the Union stated:

Regardless of what the Company argues to the contrary, there is nothing contained in Article IX, Section 1, *Holiday Provisions*, that requires an employee to present a certificate from a doctor in order for an absence to be reasonable. The Company did not question the fact that W was sick, only that he did not present a doctor's certificate.

In his decision, the arbitrator wrote:

Purpose of Eligibility Requirement. It is true that the holiday pay provision does not expressly state that an employee must present a doctor's certificate to prove illness. On the other hand, the Union position must be evaluated in the light of the purpose of the eligibility requirement: It is designed to discourage employees from stretching out a holiday period. When an employee knows that he will lose holiday pay if he does not report to work before and after a holiday, he will be more inclined to work on those days; if he knows that he will not lose holiday pay if he misses one or even both of these days, he may be more inclined to stretch out his holiday period.

Suppose a holiday falls on a Monday. If there were no penalty for missing a shift before and after a holiday, the employee may absent himself on Friday and not report to work until Tuesday. Thus, he would be off a total of four consecutive days, which would amount to a sort of minivacation. An employee who would like to enjoy such a mini-vacation might falsely say that he was ill, and on that basis be excused on one or both of the holiday pay qualifying days. Not all employees, of course, would engage in such an abuse of the holiday day pay provision; but it would be naïve not to recognize that some employees would do just that.

The Arbitrator believes that the Company requirement for a doctor's certificate is a reasonable exercise of its authority under the Labor Agreement to prevent abuse of the holiday pay eligibility requirement. Article IX, Section 1 states that an employee need not work on the holiday pay qualifying days provided he has a reasonable excuse for his absence. Where illness is the excuse, it is reasonable that the Company may require verification of the illness. The Arbitrator understands that the requirement will impose some burden on employees, but it is not an unreasonable burden in the light of what the Company seeks to accomplish by the requirement for medical proof of illness. Indeed, in the absence of the doctor certificate requirement, the Parties' agreement that to draw holiday pay employees must work the shift before and the shift after a holiday would not be worth very much. Under these circumstances, to avoid the eligibility requirement, all an employee has to do is claim illness.

By these remarks the Arbitrator does not imply that W was not telling the truth about his illness. However, under the policy, he was obligated to produce a doctor's certificate to verify his illness. He said that he has a family doctor who has treated his inner-ear problem. In this light, it would not have been much of a hardship to him to obtain a certificate showing that he was ill on Tuesday.

W has worked for the Company for 22 years, and apparently all agree that he has a good absentee record. However, a good or bad absentee record has nothing to do with the application of the holiday pay eligibility requirement. Even an employee with a good record must comply with the eligibility requirement by working the shifts before and after a holiday or present a reasonable excuse for his absence. And by the same token, an employee with a poor absentee record still qualifies for holiday pay even if he is absent on one or both qualifying days, provided that he presents a reasonable excuse for his absence.

Even though the Arbitrator believes that the Parties understand this feature of the application of the holiday pay provision, he believes that it is in order to make this observation for future reference. It is stressed that a good or poor absentee record has absolutely nothing to do with the application of Article IX, Section 1. . . .

Conclusions on the W Grievance

In the last analysis, the Arbitrator does not believe that the Company requirement in question is arbitrary, capricious, or unreasonable. It was established to prevent abuse of the holiday pay provision. As stated, to obtain a doctor's certificate to prove illness as the excuse for an employee's failure to work on one or both of the holiday pay qualifying days will impose some burden on the employee. On the other hand, the burden is not unreasonable in the light of the Company objective to discourage abuse of the holiday pay provision.

In the absence of the doctor certificate requirement, any employee could claim illness on one or both of holiday pay qualifying days. Under these circumstances, some employees undoubtedly would take advantage of the reasonable-excuse waiver, and claim illness falsely just to stretch out their holiday period. It is to discourage such conduct that the employee must obtain a doctor's certificate to verify illness. In this light, the Arbitrator is satisfied that such a requirement tends to preserve the integrity of the holiday pay eligibility requirement, and is consistent with the objective of such an eligibility requirement.

R

R reported to work on Tuesday, May 28, at 5:30 A.M. At 8:30 A.M. he informed G, his foreman, that he was leaving the plant, telling him that he was sick. As a result, the company denied him pay for Memorial Day. In this respect, the company argued:

> R left early on May 28 because he was allegedly ill. R, like W, failed to procure the proper doctor's certificate. Without the proper proof, his claim, like W's, must fail.

In other words, the company position was that R was properly denied holiday pay because he failed to obtain a doctor's certificate to prove his illness. Thus, the question here was whether or not the company could properly require a doctor's certificate under the circumstances presented by this grievance.

Excerpts from the arbitrator's opinion follow:

R and W Cases: Distinguishing Characteristic. A significant factor distinguishes the circumstances involved in the R case from those involved in the W case. Note that W did not report to work for his Tuesday shift. Under these circumstances, he had an opportunity to stretch out his holiday period by claiming illness. To prevent such a possible abuse of the holiday pay provision, the Arbitrator held that the Company properly required him to present a doctor's certificate to verify his illness. Thus, the principle was established in the W case that when an employee fails to report to work on a holiday pay qualifying day, the Company may properly require him to obtain a doctor's certificate to verify illness when such an excuse is offered.

In contrast to the W case, R reported to work Tuesday morning. He did not absent himself from work so as to stretch out his holiday period. It was after his shift started that he claimed illness, and he left before his shift was completed.

When an employee does not report to work on a holiday pay qualifying day, a doctor's certificate is necessary to prevent possible abuse of the holiday pay provision. On the other hand, such a document is not needed to prevent abuse when an employee actually reports to work on a holiday pay qualifying day. As a result, the Company violates Article IX, Section 1 when it requires a doctor's certificate to prove illness when an employee, such as R, actually reports to work on a holiday pay qualifying day.

In the absence of a doctor's certificate, however, there must be adequate showing in the record that an employee is genuinely ill when he leaves early, before his shift ends. He loses holiday pay if he feigns illness on a holiday pay qualifying day, and on this basis does not complete his shift. Although the Company may not require a doctor's certificate to prove illness when an employee leaves his shift early, this does not mean that every employee who works a short shift on a holiday pay qualifying day, and who claims illness for his early leaving, is entitled to holiday pay. In cases of this sort, his right to holiday pay turns upon the credibility of the employee's testimony and upon any other material evidence.

In this respect, after a careful examination of R's testimony, the Arbitrator is confident that R was ill when he left his shift early on Tuesday morning. He stated that on Memorial Day he had used a poison compound to spray under his house. The aftermath of this procedure was illness. He said:

Well, I felt bad at my stomach when I went to bed, but the next morning, you know, I got up and I was nauseated and everything but I came on to work because usually—I have done it before. You know, get sick and then work awhile and then it goes away. So, I figured that I would do it this time.

In other words, although feeling ill, R reported to work and obviously had the intention of completing his shift. Why else would an employee get up early enough to meet a 5:30 A.M. shift starting time?

Beyond his testimony, which, as stated, appears credible to the Arbitrator, there exists an objective fact to show that R told the truth when he said he was too ill to finish his shift. He reported to the nurse before he left the plant. R declared:

Q: Did you go to see the nurse before you left?

A: Yes. She gave me some Pepto-Bismol.

Unless we ascribe to R a Machiavellian tactic to secure holiday pay, his visit to the nurse is corroborating and objective evidence that he was sick when he left the plant. R does not appear to be the kind of a person who would go to the nurse in order to set the stage for claiming illness so as to secure holiday pay in a deceitful manner. His testimony about his illness has the ring of truth to it, and his visit to the nurse makes his declarations more credible.

Under the Absentee Guidelines, an absence for illness is not counted as excused unless it is supported by a doctor's certificate showing the nature of the illness. Thus, the Company apparently counted that portion of the day which the Grievant missed as unexcused. Since it is unexcused under the Absentee Guidelines, the Company understandably argues that R's absence for illness on Tuesday, May 28, may not properly be regarded as a "reasonable excuse" under the holiday pay provision. How can an absence be for a reasonable excuse when it is not excused? the Company asks.

There is, of course, a certain appeal to this Company argument. It does appear logical that if an employee's absence is not counted as excused for one purpose, the basis for the absence should not constitute a reasonable excuse for another area of the Labor Agreement. In any event, and recognizing that his judgment might be subject to criticism, the Arbitrator believes that the eligibility rule for holiday pay may be read and applied separately and independently from the Work Rules, which involve employee discipline. As mentioned in the W grievance, the holiday pay provision does not per se call for a doctor's certificate to prove illness as a reasonable excuse for an employee's absence on a holiday-pay qualifying day. In the W grievance, the Arbitrator, however, held that such a document may properly be required to prevent holiday period stretchouts and thus abuse of the holiday pay provision. As abundantly demonstrated above, such a certificate is not needed to prevent abuse when an employee, as did R, reports to work on a holiday pay qualifying day. Under these circumstances, an employee may show illness without offering a doctor's excuse even though the same absence is counted as unexcused for disciplinary purposes.

With full deference to the Company, the Arbitrator is satisfied that the holiday pay provision and the Absentee Guidelines can be read and construed as separate and independent entities. One deals with holiday pay eligibility and the other deals with employee discipline. Even though it can be argued, as the Company does, that both provisions should be merged and read as a whole for purposes of holiday pay eligibility, the fact remains that the objectives of the two provisions are quite different in character.

R Grievance: Conclusions

As distinguished from the W case, the early leaving of R on the holiday pay qualifying day in question did not involve the possibility of abuse of the holiday pay provision. Since R reported to work on the day following Memorial Day, he did not seek to stretch out his holiday pay period. Since there was no abuse of this kind to be prevented, the Company under Article IX, Section 1 improperly required him to submit a doctor's certificate to prove his illness.

In addition, the Arbitrator regards the testimony of R as credible. His visit to the nurse before leaving the plant underscores the truthfulness of his declaration that he was sick when he left the plant early. When R reported to the plant at 5: 30 A.M., he obviously intended to work the full shift. It is not reasonable to believe that any employee would get up that early in the morning unless he in good faith intended to complete his shift.

Finally, just because his absence for the balance of the Tuesday shift is properly counted as unexcused for purposes of employee discipline, it does not follow that R did not have a reasonable excuse for his absence within the meaning of the holiday pay provision. Since the Absentee Guidelines and the holiday pay eligibility requirement are designed to realize different objectives, they may properly be read and applied separately. It would impair the employees' right to holiday pay to engraft upon Article IX, Section 1 the system for excused absences established in a document which deals exclusively with employee discipline.

QUESTIONS

1. Why did the arbitrator grant holiday pay to one employee and deny it to the other?

2. What was the chief argument presented by the union to urge that both employees should have received holiday pay? How did the arbitrator handle this union contention? Do you believe that his reasoning in this respect is sound?

3. If you were the arbitrator, and if the employee who left his shift early claiming illness had not reported to the nurse, would you have granted him holiday pay? Why, or why not?

4. Do you believe that the arbitrator was deliberately trying to please both sides by denying holiday pay to one employee and granting it to the other? Defend your answer.

Chapter 9
Institutional Issues
under
Collective Bargaining

The modern collective bargaining contract encompasses many issues that do not fall into the general category of wages or fringe supplements. Such subjects, rather, deal with the rights and duties of the employer, the union, and the employees themselves. Some of them—such as seniority and discharge—most directly serve to protect the job rights of workers and might be most appropriately thought of as "administrative" concerns. They will be treated in such a manner in Chapter 10.

Other subjects, however, tend to supply the institutional needs of either the labor organization or the particular management—through "compulsory union membership" clauses, for example, or by provisions explicitly allowing the company the right to make decisions for the direction of the labor force and the operation of the plant. These matters will be dealt with in the paragraphs that follow in this chapter.

In considering this institutional dimension of collective bargaining, it must be recognized that the topics it encompasses can on occasion give the negotiators considerably more trouble than do the wage or fringe issues. There can, indeed, be deeply rooted conflict over basic philosophies of labor relations, the rights of management, and the rights and obligations of unions. And it is, for example, at times infinitely easier to compromise and settle a wage controversy than to resolve a heated difference of opinion as to whether or not a worker should be compelled to join a union as a condition of employment. For all the thorniness of many wage and wage-related issues, some of the longest and most bitter individual strikes have had as their source conflicts dealing with the institutional issues of collective bargaining.

This chapter will inspect, in turn, union membership as a condition of employment, the so-called "checkoff" mechanism, union obligations, and managerial prerogatives.

UNION MEMBERSHIP
AS A CONDITION OF EMPLOYMENT

Prior to the passage of the Wagner Act in 1935, there was essentially only one way in which a union could get itself recognized by an unsympathetic management: through the use of raw economic strength. If the labor organization succeeded in pulling all or a significant part of the company's employees out on strike, or in having its membership boycott the production or services of the company in the marketplace, it stood a good chance of forcing the employer to come to terms. Lacking such economic strength, however, the union had no recourse—even if all the company's workers wanted to join it— in the face of management opposition to its presence.

The 1935 legislation, as we know, greatly improved the lot of the union in this regard. It provided for a secret-ballot election by the employees, should the employer express doubt as to the union's majority status. It also gave the union the exclusive right to bargain for all workers in the designated bargaining unit, should the election prove that it did indeed have majority support. As Chapter 3 has indicated, these new ground rules for union recognition continue to this day.

Legally fostered recognition has not been synonymous with any assured status for the union as an institution, however. Indeed, in the many years since the Wagner Act, unions have still been able to find three grounds for insecurity. For one, the law has given the recognized labor organization no guarantee that it could not be dislodged by a rival union at some later date. For a second, there have still been many communication avenues open to antagonistic employers who choose to make known to their employees their antiunion feelings in an attempt to rid themselves of certified unions after a designated interval following the signing of the initial contract. And for a third, the government has not granted recognized unions protection against "free riders"—employees who choose to remain outside the union and thus gain the benefits of unionism without in any way helping to pay for those benefits. Under the law, the union clearly has not only the right but also the obligation to represent all employees in the bargaining unit, regardless of their membership or nonmembership in the union. Unions have particularly feared that the "free-rider" attitude could become contagious, resulting in the loss through a subsequent election (in which nonmembers as well as members can vote) of their majority status and thus of their representation rights.

Consequently, organized labor has turned to its own bargaining-table efforts in an attempt to gain a further measure of institutional security. By and large, such attempts have been successful: By the 1970s, possibly as high as 83 percent of all contracts contained some kind of "union security" provision.[1]

---

[1]Based on unofficial information furnished by the Bureau of Labor Statistics, U. S. Department of Labor.

Such provisions, which are frequently also referred to as "compulsory union membership" devices, essentially are three in number: the closed shop, the union shop, and the maintenance-of-membership agreement. Brief reference has already been made to each of these mechanisms. A common denominator to all is that in one way or another membership in the union is made a condition of employment for at least some workers. They differ, however, in the timing for the requirement of union membership and in the degree of freedom of choice allowed the worker in his decision about joining the labor organization.

The closed shop and union shop are dissimilar in that under the former the worker must belong to the union *before* obtaining a job, whereas the latter requires union membership within a certain time period *after* the worker is hired. Under a maintenance-of-membership arrangement, the worker is free to elect whether or not he will join the union. Once he does join, however, he must maintain membership in the union for the duration of the contract period or else forfeit his job.

These forms of compulsory union membership can also be viewed as differing with respect to the freedom of the employer to hire workers. Under the closed shop, he must hire only union members. This allows the union in effect to serve as the employment agency in most situations, and to refer workers to the employer upon his request. Under union shop and mainte-nance-of-membership arrangements, the employer has free access to the labor market. He may hire whomever he wants, and the union security provision becomes operative only after the worker is employed.

A final significant feature of union security is, of course, that it has received considerable attention from both Congress and the state legislatures. The laws these bodies have enacted must be taken into account at the bargaining table, and union security provisions that disregard these relevant public fiats do so only at a definite risk.

As in many other areas of collective bargaining, there are several different approaches to the union security problem. The elasticity of the process is clearly demonstrated in the varied methods that employers and unions have adopted to deal with the issue.

The *closed shop*, obviously the most advantageous arrangement from labor's point of view, appeared in 33 percent of the nation's agreements in 1946.[2] Prohibited for interstate commerce by the Taft-Hartley Act of 1947, it visibly decreased in its frequency in the years immediately thereafter, and an elaborate study of 1,716 collective bargaining contracts that was conducted by the Bureau of Labor Statistics in 1954 revealed that by then less than 5 percent of all agreements researched contained such a provision.[3] No exhaustive investigation on the subject has been conducted since 1954, but there is reason

[2]Theodore Rose, "Union Security Provisions in Agreements, 1954," *Monthly Labor Review*, Vol. 78, No. 6 (June 1955), p. 646.

[3]*Ibid.*

to suspect that the closed shop's decline is somewhat exaggerated in the bureau's figures. Not only was the study confined primarily to agreements governed by the Taft-Hartley Act and hence not completely representative, but—as Slichter, Healy, and Livernash could argue even in the 1960s— "many enterprises subject to the Taft-Hartley Act, which nominally have the union shop, in fact have the closed shop, either because the employer finds it advantageous or because the union is too strong for the employer and dictates the terms of the contract."[4] Even some industries subject to Taft-Hartley, moreover, have refused to accept the law's closed shop verdict—notably building construction, which bluntly flouted it until 1959, when the Landrum-Griffin Act recognized the special characteristics of that sector and officially allowed it a stronger form of union security that approximates the closed shop.

Nonetheless, there can be no denying that closed shop arrangements received a severe setback with the passage of Taft-Hartley, and that presumably, at least, the bulk of the closed shop provisions that continue in force have been negotiated by companies and unions that are not within the scope of the national labor law.

With the decrease in usage of the closed shop, the *union shop* became the most widespread form of union membership employment condition. After being part of only 17 percent of all contracts in 1946,[5] it appeared in about 64 percent of all labor agreements in 1959, and the figure is at about the 70 percent level today.

The *maintenance-of-membership* arrangement, originating in the abnormal labor market days of World War II, is still fully legal, but is utilized relatively infrequently. After appearing in about one quarter of all contracts in 1946, it had steadily lost ground thereafter, and only 3 percent of all contracts studied in 1973 made provision for it.[6] Much of the loss was undoubtedly absorbed by the gains of the union shop, which maintenance-of-membership employers, having already taken this step toward accommodating the union, have rarely resisted very adamantly.

Two other brands of union security, both relatively infrequent, constitute compromises between the union's goal of greatest possible security and the management's reluctance to grant such institutional status. Under the *agency shop*, nonunion members of the bargaining unit must make a regular financial contribution—usually the equivalent of union dues—to the labor

---

[4]Sumner H. Slichter, James J. Healy, and E. Robert Livernash, *The Impact of Collective Bargaining on Management* (Washington, D.C.: The Brookings Institution, 1960), p. 29.

[5]Rose, "Union Security Provisions."

[6]U.S. Department of Labor, Bureau of Labor Statistics, "Characteristics of Agreements Covering 1,000 Workers or More, July 1, 1973," Bulletin 1822, p. 12. Part of the decline is, however, not entirely real: Some arrangements have adopted the name of "union shop" but been modified in practice to equate or nearly equate to maintenance of membership.

organization, but no one is compelled to join the union. The money is, in fact, at times donated to recognized charitable organizations. Nonetheless, the incentive for a worker to remain in the "free-rider" class is clearly reduced in this situation, and the union thus gains some measure of protection. The *preferential shop* gives union members preference in hiring but allows the employment of nonunionists, and its efficacy seems to depend on how the parties construe the word *preference*.

Although the straight union shop thus appears to be the most popular form of union security, some employers and unions have negotiated variations of this species of compulsory union membership. Under some contracts, employees who are not union members when the union shop agreement becomes effective are not required to join the union. Some agreements exempt employees with comparatively long service with the company. Under other contracts, old employees (only) are permitted to withdraw from the union at the expiration of the agreement without forfeiting their jobs. Under this arrangement, a so-called "escape period" of about 15 days is included in the labor contract. If an employee does not terminate his union membership within the escape period, he must maintain his membership under the new arrangement. Newly hired workers, however, are required to join the union.

Whether the straight union shop or modifications of it are negotiated, the Taft-Hartley law forbids an arrangement that compels a worker to join a union as a condition of employment, unless 30 days have elapsed from the effective date of the contract or the beginning of employment, whichever is later. In administering this section of the law, the National Labor Relations Board has held that the 30-day grace period does not apply to employees who are already members of the union.[7] However, it interprets the provision literally for workers who are not union members on the effective date of the contract or who are subsequently employed. Thus, in one case, a union shop arrangement was declared unlawful because it required workers to join the union on the twenty-ninth day following the beginning of employment.[8] Another union security arrangement was held to be illegal because it compelled employees to join the union if they had been on the company's payroll 30 or more days; in invalidating this agreement, the board ruled that it violated the law because it did not accord employees subject to its coverage the legal 30-day grace period for becoming union members *after the effective date* of the contract.[9]

Whereas some negotiators have adopted variations of the straight union shop, others have devised a number of alternatives to the maintenance-of-membership arrangement. Only at the termination of the agreement are employees under most maintenance-of-membership arrangements permitted to withdraw from the union without forfeiting their jobs, and usually only a

[7] *Charles Krause Milling Co.*, 97 NLRB 336 (1951).
[8] *Chesler Glass Co.*, 92 NLRB 1016 (1950).
[9] *Continental Carbon, Inc.*, 94 NLRB 1026 (1951).

15-day period is provided at the end of the contract period during which time the employee may terminate his union membership. But many agreements have a considerably less liberal period of withdrawal, from the worker's viewpoint, and some contracts allow more than the modal 15 days. If an employee fails to withdraw during this "escape" time, he must almost invariably remain in the union for the duration of the new collective bargaining agreement.

Under some labor agreements, maintenance-of-membership arrangements also provide for an escape period after the *signing* of the agreement, to permit withdrawals of existing members from the union. Other agreements do not afford this opportunity to current members of the union but restrict the principle of voluntary withdrawal to newly hired workers.

These modifications are fully consistent with the law in all but the 19 "right-to-work" states, which ban any form of compulsory union membership, but certain other arrangements are not. Reference has already been made to the terms of Taft-Hartley under which an employee cannot lawfully be discharged from his job because of loss of union membership unless he loses his membership because of nonpayment of dues or initiation fees. In spite of the existence of an arrangement requiring union membership as a condition of employment, expulsion from a union for any reason other than nonpayment of dues or initiation fees *cannot* result in loss of employment. The National Labor Relations Board will order the reinstatement of an employee to his job with back pay where this feature of the law is violated. Depending upon the circumstances of a particular case, the board will require the employer or the union, or both, to pay back wages to such an employee.

The board has, in fact, applied a literal interpretation to this feature of Taft-Hartley. In one case the board has held that a worker actually does not have to join a union even though a union shop arrangement may be in existence.[10] His only obligation under the law is his willingness to tender the dues and initiation fees required by the union. In this case, three workers were willing to pay their union dues and initiation fees but they refused to assume any other union-related obligations, or even to attend the union meeting at which they would be voted upon and accepted. As a result, the union had secured the discharge of these workers under the terms of the union security arrangement included in the labor agreement. The board held that the discharge of workers under such circumstances violated the Taft-Hartley law, ruled that both the union and the company engaged in unfair labor practices, and ordered the workers reinstated in their jobs with full back pay.

The "right-to-work" laws themselves, of course, serve as formidable obstacles to union security arrangements in the primarily Southern and

---

[10] *Union Starch & Refining Co.*, 87 **NLRB** 779 (1949).

Southwestern states in which, through 1975, they remained on the books. On the other hand, not only has their effect on labor relations in these states been highly debatable, but in its 1965–66 sessions Congress came close to repealing the relevant Taft-Hartley Act passage permitting the enactment of such state laws (Section 14b),[11] and there was at the time of this writing some likelihood that the repeal efforts would soon be resumed on Capitol Hill.

Were Congress to remove Section 14b, this action would nullify all right-to-work laws as far as these laws apply to interstate commerce, because of the *federal pre-emption* doctrine, which forbids states to pass laws in conflict with a federal statute. And in this event the right-to-work laws existing in Alabama, Arizona, Arkansas, Florida, Georgia, Iowa, Kansas, Mississippi, Nebraska, Nevada, North Carolina, North Dakota, South Carolina, South Dakota, Tennessee, Texas, Utah, Virginia, and Wyoming would have application only in the area of intrastate commerce. They would cease to have any effect upon firms engaged in interstate dealings.

Regardless of the fate of right-to-work legislation, however, it seems very likely that the question of whether union security provisions should be negotiated in labor agreements will remain a controversial one for some time to come—among the general public and some direct parties to collective bargaining, if not among the large segment of unionized industry which has already granted such union security.

This controversy actually contains three major elements: morality, labor relations, and power.

Whether or not it is *morally* right to force an employee to join a union in order to be able to work is not an easy issue to resolve. Unions and supporters of unionism often argue that it is not "fair" to permit an employee to benefit from collective bargaining without paying dues, given the fact that the union must under the law represent all workers in the bargaining unit. And the argument is not without logic. Improvements obtained in collective bargaining *do* benefit nonunion members as well as union-member employees, and the union *is* compelled by law to represent nonunion bargaining unit employees, even in the grievance procedure, in the same fashion as it represents union members. Against this argument stands the equally plausible one that employees should not be forced to join a union in order to work. Such compulsion seems to many people to be undemocratic, immoral, and unjust. Almost everyone, however, has different ideas on what is "morally" correct in this controversy. Indeed, even the clergy has been drawn into the fight, and its members have exhibited the same lack of unanimity in their opinions as

[11]The repeal measure passed the House by a 20-vote margin, but a filibuster led by the late Sen. Everett M. Dirksen of Illinois prevented the bill from being formally considered by the Senate. AFL-CIO officials, nonetheless, claimed that as many as 56 Senate votes, or more than the majority needed, would have been forthcoming in favor of repeal had the measure been brought to a vote.

have other people. If these stewards of God are not certain what is morally correct, how can two college professors make a judgment that will once and for all resolve the moral issue?

Some observers claim that union security is the key to *stability in labor relations*. It is argued that a union that operates under a union shop arrangement will be more responsible and judicious in the handling of grievances and in other day-to-day relations with its employers because of its guaranteed status. Again, there is some strength to this argument. At times, conflict between union members and nonunion employees does hamper the effective operation of the plant, and on this basis, some employers may welcome an arrangement that forces all employees to join the union, as a way of precluding such conflicts. Moreover, unions can also claim that in the absence of a union security provision, the union officers must spend considerable time in organizing the unorganized and keeping the organized content so that they will not drop out of the union. Proponents of this position justifiably declare that if union officers are relieved from this organizational chore, they can spend their time in more constructive ways, which will be beneficial not only to the employees but also to the company.

On the other hand, other debaters point out with equal justification that unions which do enjoy a union security arrangement sometimes use this extra time to find new ways to harass the company. The solution to this particular controversy appears to an outsider to depend upon the character of the union involved and on its relationship with the employer. Clearly, no one would blame an employer if he resisted granting the union shop to a union that had traditionally engaged in frequent wildcat strikes, continually pressed grievances that had no merit, and, in short, sought to harass management at every turn.

At times, finally, employers and unions themselves argue along morality and labor relations lines to conceal a different purpose—their respective desires for *power* in the bargaining relationship. It is self-evident that the union does have more comparative influence in the negotiation of labor agreements and in its day-to-day relationship with the employer when it operates under a union shop. And, by the same token, the employer has more comparative influence when employees need not join the union to work and may terminate their membership at any time. Or, in short, the parties may speak in terms of morality merely as a smokescreen to conceal an equally logical but less euphemistic power issue.

But "power" still remains a rather nebulous term. Depending upon the assumptions one makes, a union could have infinitely more power than a company, and the reverse would be true under a different set of assumptions and circumstances. Given this elusiveness, as well as the unhappy connotations often placed on the word, it is perhaps not surprising that the verbal controversy over union security continues to be waged along the other lines described as well as those of power.

THE CHECKOFF

Checkoff arrangements are included in the large majority of collective bargaining contracts. This dues-collection method, whereby the employer agrees to deduct from the employee's pay his monthly union dues (and in some cases also his initiation fees, fines, and special assessments) for transmittal to the union, has obvious advantages for labor organizations, not only in terms of time and money savings but also because it further strengthens the union's institutional status. For the same reasons, many managers are not enthusiastic about the checkoff, although some have preferred it to the constant visits of union dues-collectors to the workplace. Once willing to grant the union shop, however, employers have rarely made a major bargaining issue of the checkoff per se. And the growth of this mechanism has been remarkably consistent with that of the union security measure: Where in 1946 about 40 percent of all labor agreements provided for the checkoff system of dues collection, by 1954 this percentage had increased to about 75 percent,[12] and the figure is, as we know, somewhat over 80 percent today.

Taft-Hartley, as was also pointed out earlier, regulates the checkoff as well as union security; under the law, the checkoff is lawful only on written authorization of the individual employee. It is further provided that an employee's written authorization may be irrevocable for only one year or for the duration of the contract, whichever is shorter.

Soon after the Taft-Hartley law was enacted, the question arose as to the lawfulness of a collective bargaining provision under which an employer deducts initiation fees, special assessments, and fines as well as regular monthly membership dues. In addition, a question was raised as to whether it was required under the national law that each employee personally sign a new authorization card each year. In 1948, the assistant solicitor general of the United States issued an opinion that has served to clarify these questions somewhat.[13] He ruled that the term *membership dues*, as utilized in the law, includes initiation fees and assessments as well as regular periodic dues. On the other hand, he made no reference to fines assessed against union members for the violation of union rules. The assistant solicitor general further offered as his opinion the ruling that checkoff arrangements that provide an employee the annual opportunity to rescind a written authorization did not appear to be a "willful" violation of the Taft-Hartley law. This meant that arrangements between employers and unions that give such an opportunity to employees but do not actually involve the signing of a new authorization each year are valid.

---

[12]Rose, "Union Security Provisions," p. 657.
[13]"Coverage of Checkoff under Taft-Hartley Act," *Monthly Labor Review*, Vol. 67 (July 1948), p. 42.

As a result, many checkoff provisions now allow for the deduction of initiation fees and assessments as well as for regular monthly membership dues. In addition, it is a common practice in industry for employees to sign one authorization card. However, under the latter arrangement, both the collective bargaining contract and the authorization card clearly state that the employee has an annual opportunity, usually lasting for 15 days, to rescind his written authorization. If he does not avail himself of this opportunity, the authorization card remains in force for another year.

Checkoff provisions frequently deal with matters other than the specification of items that the company agrees to deduct. Some arrangements specify a maximum deduction that the company will check off in any one month, require each employee to sign a new authorization card in the event that dues are increased, indemnify the company against any liability for action taken in reliance upon authorization cards submitted by the union, require the union to reimburse the company for any illegal deductions, and provide that the union share in the expense of collecting dues through the checkoff method. Not all these items, of course, appear in each and every checkoff arrangement; many labor agreements, however, contain one or more of them.

From the foregoing, it appears rather clear that although the checkoff is an important issue of collective bargaining, it does not normally constitute a crucial point of controversy between employers and unions. It does not contain the features of conflicting philosophy that are involved in the union security problem, falls far short of other problems of collective bargaining as a vexatious issue between the parties, and has rarely by itself become a major strike issue, since the stakes are not that high. As a matter of fact, even though the checkoff serves the institutional needs of the union, employers often find some gain from the incorporation of the device in the collective bargaining agreement. This would be particularly true where the labor contract contains a union security arrangement. Not only does the checkoff obviate the previously noted need of dues collection on company premises, with the attendant impact upon the orderly operation of the plant, but it avoids the need of starting the discharge process for employees who are negligent in the payment of dues. Frequently, without a checkoff, an employee who must belong to a union as a condition of employment will delay paying his dues, and the employer and union are both faced with the task of instituting the discharge process, which is most commonly suspended when the employee, faced with loss of employment, pays his dues at the last possible minute. The checkoff eliminates the need for this wasted and time-consuming effort on the part of busy employer and union representatives.

Even when the union shop is not in effect, moreover, the checkoff need not necessarily be given permanent status. The employee obligates himself to pay dues for one year only, and if he desires to stop the checkoff he may do so during the "escape period." But under any circumstances, if the management believes that the union with which it deals is so irresponsible as not to deserve the checkoff, it need not agree to it as its part of the renegotiated contract, and the mechanism is consequently also revocable from the company's point of view.

UNION OBLIGATIONS

The typical collective bargaining contract contains one or more provisions establishing certain obligations on the part of the labor organization. By far the most important of these obligations involves the pledge of a union that it will not strike during the life of the labor agreement. Most employers will, in fact, refuse to sign a collective bargaining contract unless the union agrees that it will not interrupt production during the effective contractual period.

The incorporation of a no-strike clause in a labor agreement means that all disputes relating to the interpretation and the application of a labor agreement are to be resolved through the grievance and arbitration procedure in an orderly and peaceful manner, and not through the harsh arbiter of industrial warfare. The pledge of the union not to strike during the contract period stabilizes industrial relations within the plant and thereby protects the interests of the employer, the union, and the employees. Indeed, a chief advantage that employers obtain from the collective bargaining process is the assurance that the plant will operate free from strikes or other forms of interruption to production (slowdowns, for example) during the contract period.

Companies and unions have negotiated two major forms of no-strike provisions. Under one category, there is an *absolute and unconditional* surrender on the part of the union of its right to strike or otherwise to interfere with production during the life of the labor agreement. The union agrees that it will not strike for any purpose or under any circumstances for the duration of the contract period. Employers, of course, obtain maximum security against strikes by this approach to the problem.

Under the second major form, the union can use the strike only under certain *limited* circumstances. For example, in the automobile industry the union may strike against company-imposed production standards. Such strikes may not take place, however, before all attempts are made in the grievance procedure to negotiate production standard complaints. Other collective bargaining contracts provide that unions can strike for any purpose during the contract period but only after the entire grievance procedure has been exhausted, when the employer refuses to abide by an arbitrator's decision, or when a deadlock occurs during a wage-reopening negotiation. The union cannot strike under any other conditions for the length of the contract.

In the vast majority of cases, labor organizations fulfill their no-strike obligations, just as most unionized companies fulfill all their contractually delineated responsibilities. However, in the event that violations do take place, employers have available to them a series of remedies. In the first place, under the terms of the Taft-Hartley law, employers can sue unions for violations of collective bargaining contracts in the U.S. district courts. And, although judgments obtained in such court proceedings may be assessed only against the labor organization and not against individual union members, additional remedies are provided for in many collective bargaining contracts. Under some of them, strikes called by a labor union in violation of a no-strike pledge terminate the entire collective bargaining contract. In others, the checkoff and any agreement requiring membership as a condition of employment are suspended.

In addition, the employer may elect to seek penalties against the instigators and the active participants, or either group, in such a strike. Many contracts clearly provide that employees actively participating in a strike during the life of a collective bargaining contract are subject to discharge, suspension, loss of seniority rights, or termination of other benefits under the contract, including vacation and holiday pay. The right of an employer to discharge workers participating in such strikes has been upheld by the Supreme Court.

Finally, arbitrators will usually sustain the right of employers to discharge or otherwise discipline workers who instigate or actively participate in an unlawful strike or slowdown. Such decisions are based upon the principle that the inclusion of a no-strike clause in a labor agreement serves as the device to stabilize labor relations during the contract period and as a pledge to resolve all disputes arising under the collective bargaining contract through the orderly and peaceful channels of the grievance procedure.

In June 1970, the Supreme Court provided employers with a powerful legal weapon to deal with strikes that violate a no-strike clause contained in a collective bargaining contract. At that time, the high court by a 5–2 vote in *Boys Markets* v. *Retail Clerks* (398 U.S. 235) held that when a contract incorporates a no-strike agreement and an arbitration procedure, a federal court may issue an injunction to terminate the strike. This decision permits employers to go into court to force employees back to work when a labor agreement contains these features. The idea behind the decision is that the grievance procedure and arbitration should be used to settle disputes that arise during the course of a collective bargaining contract.

Even though the decision of the Supreme Court could be defended on the grounds that employees should not strike to settle their grievances when arbitration is available, the 1970 decision astonished many observers of the labor relations scene, because in 1962 the Court had ruled that federal courts could not issue an injunction to stop a strike called in violation of a no-strike clause (*Sinclair Refining* v. *Atkinson*, 370 U.S. 195). In the 1962 decision, the high court held that injunctions could not be issued because the Taft-Hartley law did not make such strikes illegal. Since they were not made illegal, the Court reasoned, such strikes, although in violation of the labor agreement, constitute a labor dispute within the meaning of the Norris-La Guardia Act. We have learned from the study of this law that federal courts are forbidden to issue injunctions when a labor dispute exists within the meaning of the statute.

Thus, after an eight-year period, the Court reversed its position. Some people believe the Court was wrong in this switch of policy, because Congress did not seek to change the 1962 decision through legislation. As the *Wall Street Journal* observed on June 5, 1970:

> As a matter of fact such legislation was introduced, but Congress so far has not seen fit to act. Congressional action, of course, would have been much the better way. However desirable the result, the Supreme Court still should restrain itself from assuming the tasks that properly belong to the legislators.

Such criticism of the *Boys Markets* decision does not, of course, mean approval of strikes in violation of no-strike agreements. As a matter of labor relations stability, and to preserve the integrity of agreements made at the bargaining table, employees and unions should resort to arbitration, not to the street, to settle disputes with their employers. Rather, the source of the criticism is the change in Supreme Court policy after an eight-year period during which Congress did not see fit to reverse the 1962 *Sinclair* decision. As the minority opinion stated:

> Nothing at all has changed except the membership of the court and the personal views of one justice.

Regardless of one's judgment of the Supreme Court change in policy, the fact remains that it has provided employers with a potent weapon to stamp out strikes that violate no-strike agreements.

At times, strikes and other interruptions to production that are not authorized by the labor organization occur. These work stoppages, commonly known as "wildcat strikes," are instigated by a group of workers, sometimes including union officers, without the sanction of the labor union. Under many labor agreements, the employer has the right to discharge such employees or to penalize them otherwise for such activities.

A special problem has been created by the Taft-Hartley law in reference to wildcat strikes. Under this law, a labor union is responsible for the action of agents even though the union does not authorize or ratify such conduct.[14]

---

[14]Section 301(e) states: ". . . For purposes of this section, in determining whether any person is acting as an 'agent' of another person as to make such other person responsible for his acts, the question of whether the specific acts performed were actually authorized or subsequently ratified shall not be controlling."

Thus, an employer may sue a union because of a wildcat strike even though the union does not authorize or ratify the work stoppage. As a result of this state of affairs, unions and employers have negotiated the so-called "nonsuability clauses" that were mentioned in Chapter 3. Under these arrangements, the company agrees that it will not sue a labor union because of wildcat strikes, provided that the union fulfills its obligation to terminate the work stoppage. Frequently, the labor contract specifies exactly what the union must do in order to free itself from the possibility of damage suits. Thus, in some contracts containing nonsuability clauses, the union agrees to announce orally and in writing that it disavows the strike, to order the workers back to their jobs, and to refuse any form of strike relief to the participants in such work stoppages.

Other features of some collective bargaining contracts also deal with strike situations. Under many labor agreements, the union agrees that it will protect company property during strikes. To accomplish this objective, the union typically pledges itself to cooperate with the company in the orderly cessation of production and the shutting down of machinery. In addition, some unions agree to facilitate the proper maintenance of machinery during strikes even if achieving this objective requires the employment of certain bargaining unit maintenance personnel during the strike. Finally, it is not uncommon for unions to agree in the labor contract that management and supervisory personnel entering and leaving the plant in a strike situation will not be interfered with by the labor organization.

Many collective bargaining contracts place other obligations upon unions, extending well beyond the area of strikes and slowdowns. Under many agreements, for example, the union obligates itself not to conduct on company time or on company property any union activities that will interfere with the efficient operation of the plant. The outstanding exception to this rule, however, involves the handling of grievances: Meetings of union and company representatives that deal directly with grievance administration are usually conducted on company time. Some agreements also permit union officials to collect dues on company property where the checkoff is not in existence. And another exception found in many contracts involves the permission given to employees and union officers to discuss union business or to solicit union membership during lunch and rest periods.

Another frequently encountered limitation of union activity on plant property involves restrictions of visits to the company by representatives of the international union with which the local is affiliated. Still another denies unions permission to post notices in the plant or to use company bulletin boards without the permission of the company. Where the union is allowed to use bulletin boards, many labor contracts specify the character of notices that the union may post; notices are permitted, for example, only when they pertain to union meetings and social affairs, union appointments and elections, reports of union committees, and rulings of the international union.

Specifically prohibited on many occasions are notices that are controversial propagandist, or political in nature.

MANAGERIAL PREROGATIVES

That collective bargaining is in many ways synonymous with limitations on managerial authority is an observation that was offered in the earliest pages of this book. A fundamental characteristic of the process is restriction on the power of the company to make decisions in the area of employer–employee relations, and much of the controversy about collective bargaining grows out of this factor. On the one hand, the labor union seeks to limit the authority of management to make decisions when it believes that such restrictions will serve the interests of its members or will tend to satisfy the institutional needs of the union itself. On the other hand, the responsibility for efficiency in operation of the enterprise rests with management. The reason for the existence of management, in fact, is the overall management of the business, and executives attempt to retain free from limitations those functions that they believe are indispensable for the successful operation of the business. Since the responsibility for efficiency of the enterprise rests upon the shoulders of management and not of the union, companies feel that they must retain for themselves the authority to make certain decisions free from control of the bargaining process. Consequently, controversy in collective bargaining occurs when the desire of unions to achieve an objective through the bargaining process is in conflict with the determination of management to exercise a particular function on a unilateral basis.

The problem is, moreover, hardly disposed of simply because most union leaders assert—and normally, in good faith—that they have no intention of interfering with the "proper functions of management." Years of witnessing official union interest expand from the historical wages and hours context into such newer areas as those outlined in this portion of the book have led managers understandably to conclude that what is "proper" for the union depends on the situation and the values of the union membership.

Nor do employers find much consolation in the fact that the managerial decision-making process is already limited and modified by such economic forces as labor market conditions, by such laws as those pertaining to minimum wages and discrimination, and by the employee-oriented spirit of our society. If unionism is not by any means the only restriction on company freedom of action in the personnel sphere, it is nonetheless a highly important one for companies whose employees live under a union contract.

Beyond this, finally, the controversy is hardly confined to the personnel area, for managers can point to numerous (although proportionately infrequent) instances of strong union interest in such relatively removed fields as finance, plant location, pricing, and other "proper" management functions. In recent years, for example, some railroad unions have constantly blamed their employers' high degree of bonded indebtedness for depriving railroad workers of "adequate" wage increases; legal representatives of the Ladies' Garment Workers as well as those of several other unions have become familiar faces in courtrooms, to protest plant relocations of their unions' employers; and the United Automobile Workers' interest in the pricing of cars is now all but taken for granted in automobile industry bargaining rooms (although the UAW's freely offered advice on this subject has yet to be accepted by the automobile manufacturers). Given the present state of the government's "legal duty to bargain" provisions, as Chapter 3 has indicated, no one can assert with complete confidence that such examples will not multiply in the years ahead.

In many ways, in fact, ramifications of the subject extend far beyond the two parties to collective bargaining. There is justification, indeed, for arguing that the "managerial rights" issue really pivots upon the broader question of what the appropriate function of labor unions in the life of our nation should be.

Managements have frequently translated their own thoughts on the subject into concrete action. Approximately 60 percent of all labor agreements today contain clauses that explicitly recognize certain stipulated types of decisions as being "vested exclusively in the Company."[15] Such clauses are commonly called "management prerogative," "management rights," or (more appropriately, to many managers) "management security" clauses.

Fairly typical of management prerogative provisions is the following, culled from the 1973–76 agreement of a large Midwestern durable goods manufacturer:

> Subject to the provisions of this agreement, the management of the business and of the plants and the direction of the working forces, including but not limited to the right to direct, plan, and control plant operations and to establish and to change work schedules, to hire, promote, demote, transfer, suspend, discipline, or discharge employees for cause or to relieve from duty employees because of lack of work or for other legitimate reasons, to introduce new and improved methods or facilities, to determine the products to be handled, produced, or manufactured, to determine the schedules of production and the methods, processes, and the means of production, to make shop rules and regulations not inconsistent with this agreement and to manage the plants in the traditional manner, is vested exclusively in the Company. Nothing in this agreement shall be deemed to limit the Company in any way in the exercise of the regular and customary functions of management.

Some rights clauses, by way of contrast, limit themselves to short, general statements. These are much more readable than the one above, but considerably less specific—for example, "the right to manage the plant and to direct the work forces and operations of the plant, subject to the limitations of this Agreement, is exclusively vested in, and retained by, the Company."

[15]Bureau of Labor Statistics, "Characteristics of Agreements," p. 15.

No matter which way management injects such clauses into the contract, however, two industrial relations truisms must also be appreciated: (1) The power of the rights clause is always subject to qualification by the wording of every other clause in the labor agreement; and (2) consistent administrative practices on the part of the company must implement the rights clause if it is to stand up before an arbitrator.

According to one point of view, moreover, the inclusion of such a clause in a labor agreement is unnecessary, and, of course, many agreements do not make any reference to managerial rights. This practice of omission is often based upon the belief that the employer retains all rights of management that are not relinquished, modified, or eliminated by the collective bargaining contract. Thus, in the absence of collective bargaining, according to this view, the employer has the power to make any decision in the area of labor relations that he desires (subject to considerations of law, the marketplace, and so on). This right is based upon the simple fact that the employer is the owner of the business. For example, the employer's right to promote, demote, lay off, make overtime assignments, and rehire may be limited by the seniority provisions of the collective bargaining contract. And the contract may stipulate that layoffs be based upon a certain formula. However, to the extent that such a formula does not limit the right of the employer to lay off, it follows that management may exercise this function on a unilateral basis. (Case No. 10 deals with management rights in a dispute that involved an overtime assignment.)

This concept of management prerogatives is sometimes called the "residual theory" of management rights. That is, all rights reside in management except those that are limited by the labor agreement or conditioned by a past practice. Where a management embraces the residual theory, it most commonly takes a stiff attitude at the bargaining table relative to union demands that would tend to further limit rights of management. With more elements of an "Armed Truce" than an "Accommodation" philosophy, it views the collective bargaining process as a tug of war between the management and the union—management resisting further invasions by the union into the citadel of management rights, which are to be protected at all costs as a matter of principle.

Such companies are not particularly concerned with the merits of a union demand; *any* demand that would impose additional limitations on management must be resisted. For example, such a management, regardless of the merits of a particular claim, would typically resist the incorporation of working rules into the labor agreement—rules dealing with such topics as payment to employees for work not actually performed, limitations on technological change or other innovations in the operation of the business, the amount of production an employee must turn out to hold a job, and how many workers are required to perform a job. One can also safely predict that a residualist management would strongly resist any demand that would limit its right to move an operation from one plant to another, shut down one plant of a multiple-plant operation, subcontract work, or compel employees to work overtime. In addition, such a management would quite probably try aggressively, when the occasion seemed appropriate, to regain "rights" that it had previously relinquished.

Indeed, today many employers are striving to reclaim the right to make unilateral determinations of working rules. The 116-day steel strike of 1959 (as well as many other important strikes of more recent years) was waged because management desired to erase from the bargaining relationship working rules to which it had agreed in previous years. It is understandable why labor organizations resist these attempts of management: With the elimination of working rules, employees could more easily be laid off, for example. Since automation and changing market demands constitute in many relationships constant threats to job security, it is no mystery why some unions would rather strike than concede on this point.

The opposing view of the theory of residual rights is based upon the idea that management has responsibilities other than to the maximization of managerial authority. It proceeds from the proposition that management is the "trustee" of the interests of employees, the union, and the society, as well as of the interests of the business, the stockholders, and the management hierarchy. Under the "trusteeship theory," a management would invariably be willing to discuss and negotiate a union demand on the merits of the case, rather than reject it out of hand because it would impose additional limitations on the operation of the plant. Such a company would not necessarily agree to additional limitations, but it would be completely amenable to discussing, consulting, and ultimately negotiating with the union on any demand that the latter might bring up at a collective bargaining session. Exhibiting an attitude of "Cooperation," the trusteeship management does not take the position that the line separating management rights from that of negotiable issues is fixed and not subject to change. Rather, it attempts to balance the rights of all concerned with the goal of arriving at a solution that would be most mutually satisfactory. As such, the "trusteeship" and "residual" theories are poles apart in terms of management's attitude at the bargaining table, and even in the day-to-day relationship between the company and the union.

There is no "divine right" concept of management in the trusteeship theory, a statement that cannot be made for the residualist camp. No better summary of the differences between the two theories on this score has ever been made than that offered many years ago by the eminent Arthur J. Goldberg, then general counsel of the United Steelworkers of America:

> Too many spokesmen for management assume that labor's rights are not steeped in past practice or tradition but are limited strictly to those specified in a contract; while management's rights are all-inclusive except as specifically taken away by a specific clause in a labor agreement. Labor always had many

inherent rights, such as the right to strike; the right to organize despite interference from management, police powers, and even courts; the right to a fair
share of the company's income even though this right was often denied; the
right to safe, healthful working conditions with adequate opportunity for rest.
Collective bargaining does not establish some hitherto nonexisting rights; it
provides the power to enforce rights of labor which the labor movement was
dedicated to long before the institution of arbitration had become so widely
practiced in labor relations.[16]

It is impossible to determine how many companies follow the residual
theory of management rights and how many follow the trusteeship theory.
Crosscurrents are clearly at work: the previously mentioned management
attempt to regain work-rule flexibility, and the equally visible trend to more
employee-centered management that was described in Chapter 1. The relative
infrequency of Cooperation philosophies would, however, indicate that
trusteeship managements remain in the distinct minority. Moreover, there is
no universal truth as to which would be a better policy for management to
follow, or whether some compromise between the two might form the optimum arrangement. The answer to this problem must be determined by each
company in the light of the climate of the particular labor relations environment.

CONCLUSIONS

If unions and management are viewed as institutions, as distinct from the
individuals they represent, the issues considered in this chapter take on special
meaning. Institutions can survive long after individuals have perished, and in
a real sense the problems of union security, union obligations, and management rights are related to the *survival* of the bargaining institutions. Union
security measures preserve the union per se (although in so doing they may
also allow it to do a better job for the members of the organization). Similarly, to survive and function as an effective institution, management must
be concerned with its prerogatives to operate the business efficiently. It must
also be concerned with union obligations as these might affect its continued
effectiveness.

In principle, therefore, the devices of collective bargaining that feed the
institutional needs of the union and the firm are cut from the same cloth.
They are designed to assure the long-run interests of the two organizations.
The objectives of labor unions and companies are quite different, but the
fact remains that to carry out their respective functions both need security of
operation. Business operates to make a profit, and thus must be defended
against encroachments of organized labor that might unreasonably interfere

[16]"Management's Reserved Rights under Collective Bargaining," *Monthly Labor
Review*, Vol. 79, No. 10 (October 1956), p. 1172.

with its efficiency as a dynamic organization in the society. And although firms clearly differ in their philosophical approach to this problem, as witness the sharp differences between the residual and trusteeship concepts of management rights, the typical management position is the fundamental one that the business unit must be permitted to operate as efficiently as possible within the collective bargaining relationship. Its insistence upon management prerogatives stands as a bulwark of defense in this objective.

But unions also justify themselves as institutions on the American scene in their attempting to protect and advance the welfare of their members, and union security arrangements are an important avenue toward the realization of this objective. Although there may be philosophical objections to compulsory union membership, there cannot be any question that union security arrangements serve the long-run survival needs of organized labor.

If we view in retrospect the labor relations environment over the years, the conclusion appears irrefutable that business and unions have been relatively successful in reconciling these fundamental objectives, however much the verbal controversies continue to rage. Businesses that have engaged in collective bargaining relationships have by and large not only been able to survive but have often flourished. Many of the most influential and prosperous firms in this country (the automobile companies and the airlines come immediately to mind) have, as we know, been highly unionized for years. Likewise, organized labor has not only survived but has grown appreciably in strength over the years, the contemporary unexciting performance of union membership totals being accountable chiefly by causes other than management destruction. Moreover, if institutional survival and growth of unions is measured by the quality of employee benefits, one would have to conclude that in most relationships, unions have succeeded in defending and promoting the welfare of their members. Although the objectives of the two institutions are quite different, and although occasional major impasses are reached by unions and managements in their bargaining on these issues, meaningful protection for both organizations has been provided in the vast majority of unionized industry.

DISCUSSION QUESTIONS

1. Arguing in favor of "right-to-work" laws, a publication of the National Association of Manufacturers has expressed the view that "no argument for compulsory unionism—however persuasive—can possibly justify invasion of the right of individual choice." Do you agree or disagree? Why?

2. "From the viewpoint of providing maximum justice to all concerned, the agency shop constitutes the optimum union security arrangement." To what extent, if any, do you agree with this statement?

3. Which of the two management prerogative concepts, residual or trusteeship, do you personally tend to favor, and why?

4. Evaluate the opinion of former Steelworker Union president David J. McDonald that "nothing could be worse than to have . . . management appease the union, and nothing could be worse than to have the union appease management," relating these remarks to the areas of management rights and union security.

SELECTED REFERENCES

CHAMBERLAIN, NEIL W., *The Union Challenge to Management Control*. New York: Harper & Row, 1948.

CHANDLER, MARGARET K., *Management Rights and Union Interests*. New York: McGraw-Hill, 1964.

MCDERMOTT, THOMAS J., "Union Security and Right-to-Work Laws," *Labor Law Journal*, November 1965, pp. 667–78.

MEYERS, FREDERIC, *Right To Work in Practice*. New York: Fund for the Republic, 1959.

PULSIPHER, ALLAN G., "The Union Shop: A Legitimate Form of Coercion in a Free-Market Economy," *Industrial and Labor Relations Review*, July 1966, pp. 529–32.

STONE, MORRIS, *Managerial Freedom and Job Security*. New York: Harper & Row, 1963.

CASE 10
A Case of Management Rights

Cast of Characters

L and C	The grievants
F	Foreman
S	Plant manager
W	Another foreman
U	Steward

On the surface, it would appear that this case is one that involved an overtime assignment. Actually, as you read the case, it will be evident that at the heart of the dispute was the issue of management prerogatives. The union argued that in making the assignment, the employer violated past practice and provisions of the labor agreement. The employer denied both these contentions, and rested its case on the principle of management rights. The issue, therefore, was whether or not the employer's right to make the assignment in question was limited by past practice or by contractual language.

When the company did not offer two employees in the shipping department the opportunity to work overtime on August 22, 1972, the employees filed grievances. L, classified as a packer-checker, in his grievance, dated August 30, 1972, stated:

> Work was given to men in another department that should have been given to men in Department 10. Pay me for the time the man from the other department spent doing packer/checker work. Offer the men in Dept. 10 the extra work instead of giving it to another department.

C, classified as a warehouseman, also filed a grievance dated August 30, 1972, which stated:

> Overtime. Want pay for time they worked. We want the overtime they are giving to other departments.

Material to the case were the following provisions of the labor agreement:

ARTICLE VI

Section 4. Overtime work will be distributed as equally as possible among the qualified employees in the classification, within the department, and on the shift where it occurs. . . .

Section 13. When employees are temporarily transferred to other jobs for which the rate is higher, they shall receive the higher rate for all time spent in such job. When employees are temporarily transferred to other jobs for which the rate is lower, they will be paid the rate of their regular job. Such temporary transfers will not be made for more than fifteen (15) workdays. The Company will not exercise this right for the purpose of avoiding the job promotion procedure. . . .

ARTICLE XVIII

The Company shall manage the plant and direct the working forces. Among the exclusive rights of management, but not intended as a wholly inclusive list of them, are the following:

> The sole right to manage its business, including the right to decide the machinery and tool equipment, the products to be manufactured, the method of manufacturing, the schedules of production, the processes of manufacturing and assembling, together with all designing, engineering, and control of raw materials and finished parts which may be incorporated into the products manufactured; to maintain order and efficiency in its plant and operations; to hire, lay off, assign, transfer and promote employees; to discipline and discharge employees for cause; to make and enforce reasonable shop rules and regulations; to relieve employees from duty because of lack of work or other legitimate reasons; to introduce new production methods, materials or facilities; and to change existing production methods, materials, or facilities. Such authority shall not be applied in a manner that would violate any of the provisions of this Agreement.

The basic question to be determined in this arbitration was as follows:

> Under the circumstances of this case, did the company violate the material provisions of the labor agreement?

BACKGROUND

The two grievants were classified as a warehouseman and a packer-checker. They were assigned to the shipping department, designated as Department No. 10. L described the duties of a packer-checker:

> I fill orders, load trucks, check off orders, and perform warehouse work.

C detailed the duties of a warehouseman:

> I haul material to the warehouse from the production department, and bring the material to the warehouse with a forklift truck. I also get material ready for shipping by moving the material from the warehouse to the shipping dock. Also, I help to make up orders for shipping.

During the afternoon of August 22, 1972, C and L were moving material from the warehouse to the shipping dock in preparation for the filling of orders for the company's customers. This warehouse was located upstairs from the dock, and to move the material they were using an elevator or a conveyor. Their shift was scheduled to end at 4 P.M. Sometime between 2 and 3:45 P.M., the elevator broke down, and it became apparent that they would be unable to complete the work to which they were assigned before the shift ended.

Aware of this problem, F, the first-shift shipping department foreman, told S, the plant manager, of the difficulty. In this regard, S testified:

> F told me about the problem with the elevator. He told me that there would be a bind on the shipments for the next day. I asked him for a list of the material that was needed for these shipments. I told him that I would see to it that the material would be moved to the shipping dock.

At 4 P.M., the grievants left the plant in accordance with their regular schedule. Neither they nor anyone else assigned to Department No. 10 was asked to work overtime to complete the job in question. Instead, W, the second-shift shipping department manager, assigned three second-shift employees from Department No. 4, a production department, to the shipping department to complete the work the grievants were doing before they left the plant. W testified that the plant manager instructed him to transfer these men. These three employees were assigned to the job at 4 P.M., and completed the task at 7:45 P.M.

Becoming aware of the company's conduct the next morning, the grievants contended that they should have been held over on an overtime basis to move the material from the warehouse to the dock. Their grievances alleged that the company violated the labor agreement by assigning Department No. 4 employees to the job in question instead of providing them with the opportunity to work overtime.

POSITION OF THE PARTIES

The union requested that the grievances be granted, and the company requested that they be denied. Both parties offered arguments to defend their respective positions, and excerpts from these arguments will be cited below when necessary and appropriate.

ANALYSIS OF THE EVIDENCE

The Matter of Exclusive Jurisdiction

One way in which this dispute could be resolved in favor of the grievants would be for the proof to show that, as a matter of practice, no employees except those assigned to Department No. 10 had performed work falling within the scope of the grievants' classifications. If the evidence demonstrated such a state of affairs, it would follow that Department No. 10 employees held exclusive jurisdiction over all duties that were carried out in the shipping department. Under these circumstances, it would be reasonable to conclude that the company was obligated to schedule the grievants for overtime on the day in question rather than transfer Department No. 4 employees to perform the work.

Apparently, the union believed that the Department No. 10 employees held exclusive jurisdiction over all work carried out in the shipping department when it argued:

> We feel the Company violated Article VI, Section 4 when the Grievants were refused the opportunity to work overtime on that day, and let employees in Department 4 on the second shift do the work. These employees [the grievants] do this work as part of their normal duties, and have frequently worked overtime.

In short, the question here was a determination of whether or not the evidence showed that Department 10 employees had in the past exclusively performed all work falling within the classifications held by the grievants. Even if company testimony that Department 10 employees did not hold exclusive jurisdiction over all work performed in the shipping department were disregarded, the evidence did not support the apparent contention of the grievants that they did. There was the testimony offered by the grievants themselves. C declared:

> On other occasions, employees have been temporarily transferred into Department 10 on the day shift. At times, not very often, Department 4 and 6 employees have moved material to the warehouse.

L testified:

> Department 4 people have moved finished material from the assembly line to the warehouse, but they do not move finished material from the warehouse to the shipping dock. Department 4 employees, when the warehouse is full, would take finished goods from the assembly line to the shipping dock. Department 3 people at times move finished goods from the assembly line to the dock area, but not from the warehouse to the dock for shipping purposes.

So both union and company witnesses testified that it was not uncommon for the company to temporarily transfer employees into shipping to perform some work normally carried out in that area of the plant.

Interdepartmental Transfers and Past Practice

In the light of such evidence, the union could not realistically argue that the grievance should be sustained on the basis of exclusive jurisdiction. Instead, it attempted to distinguish the circumstances of this dispute from other occasions when the company temporarily transferred employees into Department 10. In this respect, the union argued:

> We believe that the work in question belongs in Department 10. The Grievants normally perform this kind of work. We have had grievances dealing with interdepartmental transfers before this time. We dropped these grievances because the employees in the other departments did not have work to do, and they were transferred to Department 10 because of absenteeism. We have been fair with the Company in these instances. In this case, Department 4 employees had work to do. They were told that the Department 10 work was more important to do. This is the first time that a case of this sort has been called to the attention of the Union.

In other words, the union said that it had dropped grievances dealing with interdepartmental transfers when the facts showed that the employees temporarily transferred had no work to do, and that there was a need for their services in the other departments. For example, the union dropped the B grievance on these grounds. In that case, the company answer at Step 2 of the grievance procedure stated:

> Due to the high absenteeism in Dept. 4 and the temporary lack of material and work in Dept. 6, the 2 employees in Dept. 6 were put in Dept. 4 to perform work. No overtime was worked by the 2 employees from Dept. 6. Therefore no article of the contract was violated and the grievance is denied.

When the Union dropped the grievance, it stated:

> Under the circumstances in this case, the Company is not in violation of the contract as claimed. Grievance denied.

As to the B grievance, the union now argued:

> We dropped it because of absenteeism in Department 4 and lack of work in Department 6. But the B grievance is distinguished from this case because there was no absenteeism in Department 10 and there was no lack of work in Department 4.

In short, the union distinguished the instant case from other times when the union dropped grievances, or did not file grievances, involving interdepartmental transfers. However, Department Manager W testified:

> I have assigned men from Department 4 to Department 10 where they performed warehouse work. I did this even when there was no lack of work in Department 4 and where the warehouse people had too much to do.

On the other hand, U, steward on the second shift of the shipping department, testified:

> The company never did make an interdepartmental transfer to Department 10 from other departments after the first-shift Department 10 people went home. On the second shift, Department 4 people do not take material from the warehouse to the dock.

It would appear that there was a conflict of testimony between the company and union witnesses as to the matter of practice dealing with the specific facts of this case. As stated, the facts seemed to be these:

1. There was no lack of work in Department 4 when the transfer was made.
2. There was no absenteeism in Department 10 when the transfer was made.
3. The transfer was made because Department 10 personnel could not get the work done without additional help.
4. The transfer was made after the grievants had left the plant.
5. Department 4 employees moved material from the warehouse to the shipping dock.

Company testimony was that such circumstances existed in the past when employees were temporarily transferred to Department 10. Union testimony was that such a practice did not exist, or, if it did exist (the union argued):

> This is the first time a case of this sort has been called to the attention of the union.

Application of Temporary Transfer Provision:
Avoidance of Overtime

For purposes of this case, however, the apparent clash of testimony as to practice, in the light of the specific facts of the case, was deemed not of significant importance. In the final analysis, the determination of this dispute depended upon the correct application of the temporary transfer provision. If the company violated the language of this provision under the facts of this case, the practice described by company witnesses would not erase or expunge the violation.* If the company did *not* violate this provision, the union testimony as to practice would not supersede the contractual language, and lack of knowledge by the union as to the practice described by company witnesses would not be of material importance. Lack of union knowledge would be of material importance only if the language of the provision supported the union's case.

In short, the crux of this case involved the application of the temporary transfer provision to the facts of the case. In the last analysis, what the company conduct amounted to in this dispute was to avoid overtime payments by making a temporary transfer.

As the union argued:

> The grievants have normally performed this work. They have done it on over-time. The company found a way to get around paying overtime. By doing this, the company violated the temporary transfer clause. This clause was not intended to permit the company to avoid paying overtime. If the company feels that they should have a right to use this clause to avoid paying overtime, they should negotiate this right in collective bargaining. They should not use this provision this way in the middle of a contract period.

If the arbitrator found that the company violated the temporary transfer provision under the circumstances of this case, it would mean that employees would have to be held over and paid overtime rates to finish a job, and the company would not be able to avoid paying such overtime by the means of a temporary transfer. If the grievance were denied, it would mean that the opportunity for employees to increase their earnings by working overtime would be diminished. In short, there was a lot riding on the arbitrator's decision, and, needless to say, he had to take this into consideration in his analysis of the provision in question.

Interdepartmental Transfers Permissible

The arbitrator's opinion read, in part:

> As we read the temporary transfer provision, one feature becomes readily apparent. The Company has the right to temporarily transfer employees between jobs for a maximum of fifteen (15) working days. Since the phrase "temporarily transferred to other *jobs* . . ." [emphasis supplied] is not qualified, limited, or circumscribed, it follows that the Company may use this provision to temporarily transfer employees between departments. If the Parties intended to limit temporary transfers only to jobs within a single department, they would have used appropriate language to accomplish this objective. As the language stands, the word "jobs" is not limited, and it would be improper for the Arbitrator to

---

*The principle here is that normally practice does not supersede clear contractual language.

read into the provision a limitation that the provision could only be used to transfer employees between jobs on an intradepartment basis.

In short, the Company did not violate the provision when it transferred Department 4 employees to Department 10. The transfer by itself is permitted by the provision. This observation, of course, does not deal with the substantive issue involved in the case, since interdepartmental transfers could be used in a way which would not necessarily diminish employees' opportunities for overtime work.

Further Analysis of the Language

What about, however, the use of this provision to avoid overtime payment as demonstrated by the facts of this dispute? As we said, this is the critical issue involved in this proceeding. It could be argued that the Company may not use the provision to avoid overtime because the language does not expressly state that the Company may use it in this fashion. For example, the provision in literal terms does not state, "The Company may use temporary transfers to avoid overtime." No such express language appears in the provision, and on this basis it could be possible for the Grievants' claim to prevail. Upon reflection, however, the Arbitrator must reject this construction of the temporary transfer provision.

In the first place, we must read the temporary transfer provision along with material language in the management rights provision. In pertinent part, Article XVIII states that the Company has the authority "to hire, lay off, assign, *transfer* employees [unless] such authority would violate any of the provisions of this Agreement." [Emphasis supplied.]

Nothing in the temporary transfer provision expressly states that the Company may not use the provision to avoid overtime payments. In the light of the Company's authority to transfer employees under Article XVIII, it follows that for the Company to violate the temporary transfer provision, there would have to be an express statement in the provision which would forbid the Company to use the provision to avoid overtime. To put it in other terms: Under the management rights provision, the Company has the right to transfer employees unless this right is limited by other provisions of the Labor Agreement. We find no language in the temporary transfer provision which forbids the Company to use it to avoid overtime. The Parties did not see fit to place such a limitation on the Company's right to transfer employees.

In the second place, the Parties in the temporary transfer provision did restrict the right of the Company in other ways. They agreed that when the Company uses the provision, the employees so transferred must get the rate of the new job if it is higher than the rate on their regular jobs. In addition, the Parties agreed that the provision can be used to transfer employees only for a maximum of fifteen (15) work days. Also, and of particular importance, the Parties agreed that the Company may not temporarily transfer employees for the purpose "of avoiding the job promotion procedure."

In short, even though the Parties took care to place three (3) significant restrictions on the right of the Company to transfer employees under the provision, they did not limit the right of the Company to transfer employees between jobs to avoid overtime payment. Clearly, the matter of restriction of the Company's use of the provision was a subject of discussion when the provision was negotiated. As a result of the discussion, the Parties did agree to restrict the Company's use of the provision. What is critical is that they did not restrict the Company in its use of the provision to avoid overtime payments. Clearly, the Arbitrator would violate the limits of his authority if he read into the provision such a restriction.

Conclusions

In its argument, the Union says:

> As far as taking work away from one group and giving it to another group, this denies the employees their seniority rights on overtime work. If the Company gets away with this, the seniority and overtime clauses in the Labor Agreement would mean nothing. We are not trying to get something that we did not get in collective bargaining.

With full deference to the Union, on the basis of the reasoning in the foregoing section of this Opinion, the Arbitrator must deny the grievances because in negotiations the Union did not secure language in the temporary transfer provision which would prohibit the Company in its use for the purpose of avoiding overtime. As noted, the Arbitrator would seriously violate the limits of his authority if he placed into the provision the restriction which the Union seeks in this case.

QUESTIONS

1. Why did the arbitrator hold that the apparent contradiction of testimony showing practice was not of material importance for purposes of this case?

2. Assume that the management rights provision, Article XVIII, did not contain the word "transfer." Under these circumstances, how would you decide the case?

3. What were the economic implications of this case to the employer and the employees?

4. What do you believe to be the most important principle of arbitration presented by the case?

Chapter 10
Administrative Issues under Collective Bargaining

Provisions relating to seniority, discipline, employee safety, and the various other "administrative" areas of the labor relationship have, as in the case of institutional provisions, the common characteristic of falling into the noneconomic classification of collective bargaining. It should not, however, be concluded that they do not have a profound influence upon the economic operation of the plant or the economic status of the employees.

The character of a seniority clause, for example, can have a vital impact upon the efficient operation of the productive process. Similarly, the protection afforded an employee as a result of the discharge clause can be of much greater importance than any of the rights he enjoys as a result of the negotiation of wage rates or fringe benefits. It matters little to the worker who has been discharged for an obviously unfair reason that the wages called for by the labor contract are very generous.

Moreover, at the present time, the problem of automation rivals the importance of most wage issues for many collective bargaining relationships. In a real sense, in fact, the adjustment to automation through contract negotiations cuts across the entire gamut of bargaining. Currently, the overriding concern of many employees and unions is with job security, a posture resulting from the fact that each day many hundreds of jobs are eliminated by innovations in the technological structure of industry. Already there has been mention of union demands that are rooted at least partially in the automation problem—early retirement of workers, severance pay, and supplementary unemployment benefit programs, for example. As will be demonstrated, many administistative demands of unions also flow from worker fears that jobs are vulnerable because of automation.

In short, as important as the negotiation of economic issues may be, one cannot ignore these nonwage administrative issues of collective bargaining. Both are interwoven in the contemporary labor relations environment, and to ignore or slight either—or, clearly, the institutional area of the contract, as well—would represent a distortion and an incomplete picture of present-day labor relations in the United States.

The following discussion indicates the nature of these problems, the manner in which employers and unions handle them in collective bargaining, and recent trends in administrative clause negotiations.

SENIORITY

The principle of seniority, under which the employee with the greater length of company or company subunit service receives increased job security (and, commonly, greater entitlement to employee benefits), is not a new one for American industry. The railroads and printing trades, for example, have emphasized it for many decades.

For at least four reasons, however, seniority has received increasing stress in labor contracts over the past three decades.[1] In the first place, both management and employee representatives have become convinced that there is a certain amount of justice to the arrangement, especially in terms of work contraction or recall opportunities after layoffs. Second, the application of seniority is an objective one, calculated to avoid arbitrariness in the selection of personnel for particular jobs and consequently less irksome for the labor negotiators to deal with than alternative devices. Third, the employee benefit programs that have mushroomed in these years have been geared almost exclusively to seniority—often, to make them more acceptable to the companies by restricting the number of employees entitled to the benefits. And fourth, outside agencies, notably government labor boards and impartial arbitrators, have tended to weigh seniority heavily in their decisions.

Almost every labor agreement now includes some seniority formula, and this practice has become a deeply imbedded feature of the collective bargaining process. It is a chief method whereby employees obtain a measure of security in their jobs. It also limits the freedom of management to direct the labor force and influences considerations of plant efficiency. A seniority structure that approaches the ideal would be one that affords protection to employees in their job rights and at the same time does not place unreasonable restrictions on the right of management to make job assignments without sacrificing productivity and efficiency in the plant. This objective can best be realized to the extent that a seniority system is constructed to fit a particular plant environment. It must be tailored to fill the requirements of the technology, the kinds of jobs, the skills and occupations of the employees, and the character of labor relations of a specific company. A seniority formula that might be desirable in one industrial situation might not be suitable

---

[1]For an excellent full description, see Sumner H. Slichter, James J. Healy, and E. Robert Livernash, *The Impact of Collective Bargaining on Management* (Washington, D.C.: The Brookings Institution, 1960), pp. 104–41.

to another plant environment. In addition, perhaps no other phase of the collective bargaining relationship demands so much of company officials and union leaders in terms of common sense, good faith, and reciprocal recognition of the problems of management, the labor organization, and the employees.

As a result of the nature of the seniority principle, many problems are inherent in the formulation and application of a seniority structure. Among the major problems, beyond the crucial determination of the phases of the employment relationship that are to be affected by the length-of-service principle, are: establishment of the unit in which employees acquire and apply seniority credits; identification of circumstances under which employees may lose seniority; determination of the seniority status of employees who transfer from one part of the bargaining unit to another, or who leave the bargaining unit altogether; and the fixing of certain exceptions to the seniority system. As can be expected, these problems are handled in a multitude of fashions in collective bargaining relationships. Some labor agreements, moreover, attempt to cover all these issues, and some deal with only certain ones of them.

Virtually all labor agreements, for example, provide that seniority play a part in the determination of layoffs, in rehiring, and in promotions. But, as discussed below, the same labor agreement might use one seniority system to govern layoffs and rehiring and a different one in connection with promotions (where considerations of ability and physical fitness are often as important as, and in many cases more important than, length of service). Where a fixed-shift system exists in a plant, labor agreements may permit workers their choice of shifts on the basis of seniority, and factors such as personal convenience, wage or hour differentials, and the kind of job itself may dictate the senior worker's choice in this respect. Under other contracts, however, seniority plays no role in shift assignments.

Units for Seniority

There are three major systems relating to the unit in which an employee acquires and applies his seniority credits: company- or plantwide, departmental or occupational, and a combined plant and departmental seniority system.

Under a *company- or plantwide seniority system*, the seniority status of each employee equals his total service with the firm. Thus, transfers from job to job within the establishment or transfers from one department to another have no effect on an employee's seniority standing. Subject to other features of the seniority structure, an employee under the company- or plantwide system will apply his seniority for purposes covered by the seniority system on a strictly company- or plantwide basis. In actual practice, this system is not used in companies in which it would be necessary for an employee to undergo a considerable training period when he takes a new job to replace a worker with less seniority. It is practicable only for companies where the jobs are more or less interchangeable. A companywide system obviously gives the greatest protection to employees with the longest length of service. On the other hand, depending upon the other features of the seniority structure, it could serve as a deterrent to the efficiency and productivity of the plant.

Under *departmental* or *occupational seniority systems*, separate seniority lists are established for each department or occupational grouping in the plant. If such a system does not have any qualifications or limitations, an employee can apply his seniority credits only within his own department or occupation. Such a system facilitates administration in large companies employing a considerable number of workers. It minimizes the opportunity for large-scale displacement of workers from their jobs in the event of layoffs or discontinuation of particular jobs because of technological innovations, or because of permanent changes in the market for the products of the company. On the other hand, additional problems arise as the result of the use of this kind of seniority system. If layoffs in one department become necessary, or if certain jobs in such a department are permanently discontinued while other departments are not affected, a state of affairs could develop wherein employees with long service in a company would find themselves out of a job while employees with less seniority were working full time. In addition, under a strict departmental seniority structure, transfers between departments tend to be discouraged because a transfer could result in complete loss of accumulated seniority.

As a result of the problems arising from a strict company or departmental seniority system, many companies and unions have negotiated a number of plans combining these two types of seniority structures. Under a combination system, seniority may be applied in one unit for certain purposes and in another unit for other purposes. Thus, seniority may be applied on a plant-wide basis for purposes of layoffs, whereas departmentwide seniority is used as the basis of promotion. A variation of this system is to permit employees to *apply* their seniority only within the department in which they are working, but to *compute* such seniority on the basis of total service with the company. In addition, although the general application of seniority is limited to a departmental basis, employees laid off in a particular department may claim work in a general labor pool in which the jobs are relatively unskilled and in which newly hired employees start out before being promoted to other departments. At times, a distinction is drawn between temporary layoffs resulting from lack of business or material shortages, and permanent layoffs resulting from changes in technology or permanent changes in the products manufactured by the company. Under the former situation, seniority may be applied only on a departmental basis, or seniority might not govern at all (as in autos), whereas under the latter circumstances, employees have the opportunity to apply their seniority on a plantwide basis. Other variations of the combination system are utilized within industry as determined by the circumstances of a particular plant.

Limitations upon Seniority

Regardless of the type of system under which seniority credits are accumulated and applied, many collective bargaining agreements place certain limitations and qualifications upon length of service as a factor in connection with layoffs. Possibly as many as one-third of all agreements in existence may include such limitations. In some cases, seniority systems provide for the retention of more senior employees only when they are qualified to perform the jobs that are available. In considerably fewer labor agreements, a senior employee will be retained in the event of layoffs in a plant only when he is able to perform an available job "as well as" other employees eligible for layoff.

Although a large number of labor agreements permit employees scheduled for layoff to displace less senior employees, limitations on the chain displacement or "bumping" process are also included in many labor agreements. Employers, unions, employees, and students of labor relations recognize the inherent disadvantages of seniority structures that permit unlimited bumping. Such disadvantages are manifested in many ways. Bumping could result in serious obstacles to plant efficiency and productivity to the detriment of all concerned, could cause extreme uncertainty and confusion to workers who might be required to take a number of different jobs as a result of a single layoff, and could result in serious internal political problems for the labor organization.

For these reasons, careful limitations are usually placed on the bumping process. Many labor agreements allow an employee to displace a less senior worker in the event of a layoff only when the former employee has a minimum amount of service with the company. Other contracts circumscribe the bumping process by limiting the opportunity of a senior employee to displacement of a junior worker from a job that the employee with longer service has already held. Under this system, the worker comes down in the same fashion that he went up the job ladder. Under other seniority systems, the area into which the employee may bump is itself limited: It may be stipulated that employees can bump only on a departmental or divisional basis, or can displace workers only within equal or lower labor grades. In addition, the objective of limiting the displacement process is achieved by permitting the displacement of only the *least* senior employee in the bumping area and not of any other less senior employees.

Most labor agreements provide for rehiring in reverse order of layoffs—the last employee laid off is the first rehired. In addition, laid-off employees are given preference over new workers for vacancies that arise anywhere in the plant. However, such preferences given employees with longer service are frequently limited to the extent that the employee in question is competent to perform the available work. In this connection, the problem of the re-employment of laid-off workers becomes somewhat complicated when a straight departmental seniority system is used. In such a case, although a labor agreement might provide for the rehiring of workers in the reverse order of layoffs, production might not be revived in reverse order to the slack in production, and thus employees with shorter service might be recalled to work before employees with greater seniority. To avoid such a state of affairs, some labor contracts provide the older employee in terms of service with the opportunity of returning to work first, provided he has the ability to carry out the duties of the available job.

Length of service as a factor in promotion is of less importance than it is in layoffs and rehiring, and in only a relative handful of contemporary labor agreements is length of service the sole factor in making promotions. The incidence is low because all parties to collective bargaining realize that a janitor, for example, in spite of many years of service in this position, is not qualified to be promoted to, say, a tool- and-die-maker's job. But if such a criterion is rarely the sole factor in the assignment of workers to higher-rated jobs, the vast majority of labor agreements now require that seniority along with other factors be given *consideration*. In many contracts, seniority governs promotions when the senior employee is "qualified" to fill the position in question. Under others, seniority becomes the determining criterion in promotions when the senior employee has ability and physical fitness for the job in question "equal to that" of all other employees who may desire the better job. Under the latter seniority structure, length of service is of secondary importance to the ability and physical fitness factors, however.

In practice, management makes the decision about which worker among those bidding for the job gets the promotion; and in the heavy majority of cases, this decision of the company is satisfactory to all concerned, usually because the senior employee *is* best qualified for the job in question, or because the company is completely willing to give preference to him when ability differences among employees are not readily discernible. At times, however, when the company passes over a senior employee in favor of an employee with shorter service in making a promotion, the union may protest the action of the company through the grievance procedure. For example, the union may argue that the senior employee bidding for the better job has equal ability to that of the worker whom the company tapped for the promotion. The problem in such cases is to evaluate the comparative abilities of the two workers. Such a determination involves the study and appraisal of the entire work record of both workers. Consideration here is usually given to such items as the previous experience of the workers on the actual job in question or on closely related jobs; the education and training qualifications of the workers for performing the job in question; production records of the employees; and absenteeism, tardiness, and accident records, when relevant. Ordinarily, such disputes are resolved between the union and the company on the basis of these considerations. At times, however, the parties are still in disagreement, and the matter is then most often referred to an impartial arbitrator, who will make the decision in the case. (Case No. 11 deals with this kind of issue.)

Seniority in Transfers

Another seniority problem involves the seniority status of employees who transfer from one department to another. As stated above, interdepartmental transfers do not create a seniority issue under a straight plantwide seniority system. To the extent that seniority is acquired or applied on a departmentwide basis, however, the problem of transfers becomes important to employers, unions, and employees; reference has been made to the fact that interdepartmental transfers are discouraged when employees lose all accumulated seniority upon entering a new department. Some contracts deal with this problem by allowing a transferred employee to retain his seniority in his old department, while starting at the bottom of the seniority scale in the new department; under these circumstances, such an employee would exercise seniority rights in his old department in the event he were laid off from his new department. Some contracts even permit such an employee to further accumulate seniority for application in his old department in the event that he is laid off from his new department. Another approach to the problem permits the transferred employee to carry his seniority acquired in the old department to the new department. This is a common practice where the job itself is transferred to a new department, where the job or the department itself is permanently abolished, or upon the merging of two or more departments.

Still another seniority problem arises under the circumstances of an employee's transferring entirely out of the bargaining unit. This issue is particularly related to the seniority status of workers who are selected by management to fill foremen's jobs. There are three major approaches to this problem. Under some contracts, a rank-and-file employee who takes a supervisory job simply loses accumulated seniority. If for some reason his supervisory job is terminated and he desires to return to a job covered by the collective bargaining contract, he is treated as a new employee for purposes of seniority. Another method is to permit such an employee, when he serves as a foreman, to retain all seniority credits earned earlier. Under this approach, if the employee transfers back to the bargaining unit, he returns with the same number of seniority credits he had when he left. Finally, under some contracts, an employee taking a supervisor's job accumulates seniority in the bargaining unit while he serves as a foreman. If he returns to the bargaining unit, he comes back not only with the seniority credits that he acquired before he took the supervisory job, but with seniority credits accumulated while he served as a foreman. Rank, at times, does have its privileges.

Obviously, the seniority status of foremen is not a problem when management fills its supervisory posts by hiring outside the plant. On the other hand, the problem is a real one when the company elects to fill such jobs from the rank and file. It is apparent that a worker with long seniority in the bargaining unit would hesitate to take a foreman's job if he would lose thereby all his accumulated seniority. In recognition of this situation, many employers and unions have agreed that workers promoted from the bargaining unit to supervisors' jobs may at least retain the seniority they accumulated while covered by the labor agreement. Whatever approach unions and companies take to this problem, it would generally be desirable to spell out the method in the labor agreement. Confusion, uncertainty, and controversy could arise when the contract is silent on this issue.

Exceptions to the Seniority System

Under many collective bargaining contracts, there is provision for some exemptions from the normal operation of the seniority structure. One of these involves the issue of "super-seniority" for union officers. Some companies and unions have agreed that designated union officers may have a preferred status in the event of layoffs. Such employees are protected in employment regardless of their length of service with the company. They are entitled to such consideration strictly by virtue of the union office they hold, however, and lose their super-seniority status when their term of office is terminated.

One obvious problem involved in the negotiation of a super-seniority clause is the designation of the employees who are to have this status. Frequently, labor agreements limit this protection to the comparatively major local union officers. If too many employees are covered by a super-seniority status, the effective and fair operation of the seniority structure might be prevented. In any event, it is common practice to specify exactly which officers of the union are to be included under the super-seniority clause.

Another problem concerns the bumping rights of employees protected under such an arrangement. Contracts are usually clear as to just what job or jobs such employees are entitled to when they are scheduled for layoff. In addition, it is common practice to make clear the rate of pay that the employee will earn in the new job. Thus, if a worker protected by super-seniority takes another job that pays a lower rate than his regular job to avoid layoff, the contract specifies whether or not he will get the rate of the job that he is filling or the rate of his regular job. Obviously, when these problems are resolved in the labor agreement, there is less chance for controversy during the hectic atmosphere of a layoff itself.

Some labor agreements also permit management to retain in employment during periods of layoff a certain number of non-union-officer employees regardless of their seniority status. Such employees are designated as "exceptional," "specially skilled," "indispensable," or "meritorious" in collective bargaining contracts. As in the case of super-seniority, problems growing out of this exception to the seniority rule are normally resolved in the collective bargaining contract. Problems in this connection involve the number of employees falling into this category, the kind of jobs they must be holding to receive such preferential status, their bumping rights (if any), and the rate of pay they shall earn in the event that they are retained in employment in jobs other than their regular ones.

Another general exception to the normal operation of a seniority system involves newly hired workers. Under most labor agreements, such workers must first serve a probationary period before they are protected by the labor agreement. Such probationary periods are frequently specified as being from about 30 to 90 days, and during this period of time the new worker can be laid off, demoted, transferred, or otherwise assigned work without reference to the seniority structure at all. However, once such an employee serves out his probationary period, his seniority under most labor agreements is calculated from the first day of hire by the company.

Under the terms of many collective bargaining contracts, employers may lay off workers on a *temporary* basis without reference to the seniority structure. Such layoffs are for short periods of time and result from purely temporary factors, such as shortages of material, power failures, and the like. It is, of course, vital in this connection that the labor agreement define the temporary layoff. At times, contracts incorporate the principle that employers may lay off without reference to seniority on a temporary basis but fail to specify what is meant by the term *temporary layoff*. Some agreements define the term as any layoff for less than five or even ten working days. Other contracts, however, specify that the seniority structure must be followed for any layoff in excess of 24 hours. Whatever time limit is placed on the term, the labor agreement should specify the duration of a temporary layoff. By this means, a considerable amount of future argument will be avoided.

Finally, virtually all seniority structures specify circumstances under which an employee loses his seniority credits. All employees should fully understand the exact nature of these circumstances and the significance of losing seniority credits. Under the terms of most collective bargaining contracts, an employee loses his seniority if he is discharged, voluntarily quits, fails to notify the company within a certain time period (usually five working days) of his intentions to return to work after he is recalled by the company after a layoff, fails to return to work after an authorized leave of absence, neglects to report to work within a certain period of time (usually 90 work-ing days) after discharge from military service, or is laid off continuously for a long period of time, usually from about 24 to 48 months.

An Overall Evaluation

However qualified it may be in particular situations, there can be no denying the current acceptability of the seniority criterion in regulating poten-tial competition among employees for jobs and job status. The traditional arguments that seniority fosters laziness, rewards mediocrity, and crimps individual initiative are no longer automatically brought into play by man-agers to oppose this length-of-service criterion. And the on-balance benefits of seniority, both in improving employee morale and in minimizing admin-istrative problems, are no longer seriously questioned by progressive com-panies, *if* length of service is limited by such other factors as ability when these are meaningful. Although it is probably true that in general a seniority system tends to reduce the efficiency of the plant operation to some extent, if care is taken to design a system to the needs of the particular company, and if length of service is appropriately limited in its application, the net loss to plant efficiency is normally not very noticeable.

Beyond this, many would argue that efficiency, despite its obvious importance, should not be the only goal of American industry. The advan-tages of providing a measure of job security to employees, and thereby relieving them of the frustrations of discrimination and unfair treatment, cannot be easily quantified. But human values have become the increasing concern of modern management, and the judicious use of seniority clearly serves the human equation.

Seniority under Fire:
A Special Situation

In the first half of 1975, the following statements were made, all by observers in a position to register informed opinions, and all with passion: (1) "If anybody succeeds in altering the seniority system to help blacks keep their new-found jobs, I guarantee you, you'll see the biggest damn race war this country has ever had";[2] (2) "There is no way I would stand for bypassing seniority. That's how the union was built";[3] (3) "It's a real problem. The economy is messing over women and minorities";[4] and (4) "Legislation? Are you crazy? We're not kamikazes over here."[5] Respectively, the com-ments were offered by two labor officials who had often been described as "liberal," a representative of a public-interest group representing 15 low-

---

[2]*New York Times*, March 9, 1975, Section 4, p. 1.
[3]*Business Week*, May 5, 1975, p. 67.
[4]*Ibid.*
[5]*New York Times, loc. cit.*

seniority patrolwomen who had recently been laid off by the Cleveland Police Department, and a member of Congress. All of them referred to the mass layoffs being experienced by the economy during this time and to the fact that minority group and women workers—generally having been last hired—were now being, in accordance with seniority, first fired.

Equal opportunity had, of course, finally come to such workers over the previous decade. It had had many causes—among them, certainly, more progressive mores of society and more enlightened attitudes on the part of the new breed of industrial leader. But, patently, one factor had been paramount: Title VII of the Civil Rights Act of 1964, with its ban on job discrimination by race, sex, color, religion, or national origin and its application to all corporations, state and local governments, labor organizations, and employment agencies having more than 15 employees. Following this landmark legislation, blacks and other minority group members, as well as women, had been hired and promoted, often in some abundance, into jobs for which previously they had been given only two kinds of chances: (1) none, and (2) fat.

To the Equal Employment Opportunity Commission, charged (together with the Justice Department) with enforcing Title VII and, as of March 1972, empowered to sue the title's violators, what employers should do in the face of the need for layoffs was clear: Give special protection to the newly recruited groups to compensate them for past discrimination. At least as clear, however, was the fact that union contracts commanded respect for the seniority principle and its "last in, first out" principle. And, all but universally, the second of these Hobson's choices was embraced by the management community as the economy sank to its lowest levels since the Great Depression of the 1930s.

Thus, within a matter of months, many workplaces became once again as white and as male as they had been prior to 1964. At the huge General Motors installation in Linden, New Jersey, for example, all 350 women who had been hired since 1970, following a change in hiring policies, were laid off. At a Pittsburgh-based conglomerate, while 15 percent of the 30,000 total employees were released, 26 percent of the black workers and an even higher proportion of the women were let go. At a Louisiana can plant, the number of blacks was reduced from 50 out of 400 to 2 out of 151. And the story was much the same elsewhere, as seniority was applied across the nation as the safer of the two layoff options.

As court dockets became clogged with consequent affirmative action vs. seniority suits (with the EEOC lending its full weight to minorities and women, and the U.S. Department of Labor generally supporting seniority), most experts felt that seniority would ultimately triumph—at the U.S. Supreme Court level, where the issue would inevitably wind up. For one thing, the 1964 Civil Rights Act itself specifically approved "bona fide" seniority systems in layoffs (although it omitted any helpful interpretations as to what was "bona fide"). For another, with only one exception prior to mid-1975, the lower courts had already consistently upheld the seniority system, most notably in the case of *Jersey Central Power and Light Co.*, where a U.S. appeals court judge ruled that Congress had not mandated such a sweeping remedy as that proposed by the EEOC and that only Congress could do so. And for a third, layoff by seniority was specifically sanctioned even on the occasion of the EEOC's most conspicuous victory: in 1973, when, by a consent decree, the American Telephone and Telegraph Company agreed to pay $51 million in back wages and raises.

On the other hand, predictions as to the ultimate judicial fate of this critical issue would also have to take into consideration the March 1976 Supreme Court decision (in *Franks* v. *Bowman Transportation Company*) that if victims of hiring prejudice later were hired by the offending employer and could prove the original discrimination, they must be granted seniority retroactive to the date of their original rejection for the job. The decision, relating as it did only to victims of bias who were (1) later hired and (2) could prove the original action, is clearly limited in its application, however, and may or may not be a harbinger of future Supreme Court action.

Whatever the judicial outcome, however, and whatever one's personal views on the subject, it was hard to disagree with the opinion of UAW general counsel Stephen I. Schlossberg that "remedying past discrimination is hard enough without pitting worker against worker during a recession. That is not the way you make progress. You have to do it when the economy is expanding."[6] The expanding economy in the decade following 1964 had certainly made the employment progress of the now-laid-off groups easier. And it was equally to be hoped by all of good will that the economic recovery would build on this solid base to ensure that the next business downturn would see women and minority group members so firmly established on the typical seniority ladder as to make this burning issue of the mid-1970s no longer a relevant one.

DISCHARGE AND DISCIPLINE

In the absence of a collective bargaining relationship, an employer may discharge or otherwise impose penalties upon an employee without any limitations except those imposed by law. An employee may be discharged for any reason, or, indeed, for no reason. The power of discipline in a nonunion situation remains fully and completely in the hands of the employer.

Once a collective bargaining relationship is established, however, the employer's prerogative to discipline employees is invariably limited by the labor agreement. The nature of such a restriction is not that the company loses its right to discharge or otherwise discipline employees; rather, it is

---

[6]*Business Week, loc. cit.*

that the employer's right in this connection is restricted to the extent that he can inflict discipline on employees only for sufficient and appropriate reasons.

Thus, most collective bargaining contracts contain the general statement that an employee can be discharged only for "just cause." And the critical interpretation of just cause is accomplished through industrial practice, through the results of the grievance procedure existing in the particular plant, through common sense, and through arbitration decisions.

Frequently, companies and unions agree that a particular infraction by an employee constitutes a proper reason for discharge, and there is no litigation on the issue. On the other hand, in many cases the employer and the union are in disagreement as to whether an offense by an employee constitutes a valid basis for discharge. Under these circumstances, the issue is discussed and debated between the company and the union in the grievance procedure. If the parties fail to reach an agreement through this process, the dispute is frequently submitted to an arbitrator for final decision.

It is understandable that a large percentage of arbitration cases involve discharge. Discipline, of course, is required to run an efficient business. If every worker were free to do what he wanted, the productive process could hardly be carried out effectively; such a state of affairs would operate to the distinct disadvantage of the employees, the employer, and the union. Accordingly, the right of the employer to discipline becomes an indispensable prerequisite to the operation of a successful business. On the other hand, to the worker and to his family, the loss of a job by discharge is very serious. Not only does it result in the loss of a person's immediate livelihood, but the stigma of discharge is likely to make it more difficult for him to find another job. From this point of view, a discharge has much more serious consequences to the worker and his family than does a permanent layoff. In addition, a discharged employee frequently loses part of his coverage under most state unemployment compensation laws. Thus, because the implications of discharge are so profound, this feature of collective bargaining has frequently proven both highly challenging and quite controversial for both labor relations parties.

Although the majority of contracts contain only the previously noted general and simple statement that discharge can be made only for just cause (or "proper reason"), many labor agreements list one or more specific grounds for discharge: violation of company rules, failure to meet work standards, incompetence, violation of the collective bargaining contract (including in this category the instigation of or participation in a strike or a slowdown in violation of the agreement), excessive absenteeism or tardiness, intoxication, dishonesty, insubordination, and fighting on company property. Labor agreements that list specific causes for discharge normally also include a general statement that discharge may be made for "any other just or proper reason."

In addition, many contracts distinguish between causes for immediate discharge and offenses that require one or more warnings. For example, sabotage or willful destruction of company property may result in immediate discharge, whereas a discharge for absenteeism may occur only after a certain number of warnings. In recognition of the fact that not all employee infractions are grave enough to warrant discharge, lesser forms of discipline are imposed at times under collective bargaining relationships. Into this category fall oral and written reprimand, suspension without pay for varying lengths of time, demotion, and denial of vacation pay. Frequently, union and management representatives in the grievance procedure will agree upon a lesser measure of discipline even though the employer presumably has the grounds to discharge an employee for a particular offense. At times, the union and the employee in question will be willing to settle a case on these terms rather than risk taking the case to arbitration.

A very large number of collective bargaining contracts specify a distinct procedure for discharge cases. Many of them require notice to the employee and the union before the discharge takes place. Such notification is generally required to contain the specific reasons for the discharge. A hearing on the case is also provided for in many labor agreements, typically requiring the presence of not only the worker in question and an appropriate official of the company, but also a representative of the labor organization. Frequently, collective bargaining agreements provide for a suspension period before the discharge becomes effective. The alleged advantage of this procedure is that it provides for an opportunity to cool tempers and offers a period of time for all parties to make a careful investigation and evaluation of the facts of the case.

In 1975, the U.S. Supreme Court decided a case that has an important bearing on the right of employees to union representation when discipline is an issue.[7] In *Weingarten*, the Court held that an employee has a right to the presence of a union representative at investigatory interviews conducted by an employer which the employee may reasonably believe could lead to disciplinary action. At times, employers conduct a "fact-finding" interview with an employee to determine whether or not such action should be imposed. In such a session, the employer does not impose a penalty, but obtains information to decide whether the employee should be disciplined. Since it is an investigation session, some employers have refused requests by employees for union representation. However, under the Court's rule, the employer must grant an employee's request for union representation in such a session. Failure of an employer to obey this doctrine violates the rights of employees protected by Taft-Hartley, and the National Labor Relations Board may direct the reinstatement of the employee to his job with back pay despite his offense.

[7] *NLRB* v. *J. Weingarten*, U.S. Sup. Ct. No. 73–1363, February 19, 1975.

Part of the procedure for discharge cases is provided for in the general grievance procedure of the collective bargaining contract. As suggested, almost every labor agreement provides for appeal of discharge cases, and this appeal is taken through the regular grievance procedure, since the appeal is looked upon as a grievance. If, for example, the labor agreement provides that the employee or the union must appeal a discharge within a certain number of days, such appeal must be made during this period or the discharge may become permanent regardless of the merits of the case. Likewise, a company that neglects its obligation to give an answer to the appeal within the stipulated number of days may find that it has lost its right to discharge the worker regardless of the justice of the situation.

Frequently, labor agreements also provide that a discharge case has a priority over all other cases in the grievance procedure. Some of them even waive the first few steps of the grievance procedure and start a discharge case at the top levels of the procedure. In these arrangements, companies and unions recognize the fact that it is to the mutual advantage of all concerned to expedite discharge cases. The worker wants to know as quickly as possible whether or not he has a job in the plant. The company also has an interest in the prompt settlement of a discharge case, because of the disciplinary implications involved and because labor agreements normally require that the company award the employee loss of earnings where a discharge is withdrawn.

From the foregoing, it should be clear that under a collective bargaining relationship, the employer does not lose his right to discipline or discharge; it is, however, more difficult for management to exercise this function. There must be just cause, a specific procedure must be followed, and, of course, management must have the proof that an employee committed the offensive act.

If a case does go to arbitration, in fact, the arbitrator will be particularly concerned with the quality of proof that management offers in the hearing. On many occasions, employers have lost discharge cases in arbitration because the evidence they have presented is not sufficient to prove the case for discharge. At times, the company's case against the employee has simply been poorly prepared; at other times, the management has not been able to assemble the proof despite the most conscientious of company efforts. (One difficulty in this latter regard, as all arbitrators are well aware, is that employees dislike testifying against other employees who are charged with some offense.)

If the arbitrator did not demand convincing proof before sustaining discipline, however, the protection afforded employees by the labor agreement would be worthless. The same situation prevails in our civil life, wherein juries have freed criminals because the state has not proved its case. Such courses of action reflect one of the most cardinal features of our system of justice, the presumption that a man is innocent until proven guilty, and this hallmark of our civil life plays no less a role in the American system of industrial relations. This situation has undoubtedly resulted in the reinstatement to their jobs with full back pay for employees who are in fact "guilty," but it is beyond argument that an employer bears the obligation to prove charges against employees it has displaced. In the absence of such an obligation, this most important benefit allowed employees under a collective bargaining contract, protection against arbitrary management treatment, is obviously negated. (Cases 12 and 13 at the end of this chapter involve the discharge of employees.)

SAFETY AND HEALTH
OF EMPLOYEES

Few people would argue that employees do not have a real interest in the area of industrial safety and health. After all, it is the worker and his family who suffer the most devastating consequences of neglect in this area, in terms of accidents, sickness, and even death. And although most employers can sincerely claim that they, too, are deeply interested in safe and healthy working environments, such concern cannot restore to life a man killed on the job, or restore an employee's limbs, or succor his family when an employment-caused accident or illness disables him for long periods of time. Indeed, this consideration is at the root of a long-standing policy of the National Labor Relations Board that safety and health demands of unions are mandatory subjects of collective bargaining. Thus, employers must bargain on these issues even though company working conditions are also subject to the many safety regulations imposed by federal and state statutes.

Not surprisingly, then, most collective bargaining contracts contain explicit provisions relating to the safety and health area, although such provisions take one of two routes, depending upon the particular contract.

On the one hand, many contracts merely state in general terms that the management of the plant is required to take measures to protect the safety and health of employees. At times, the term *measures* is qualified by the word *reasonable*. When a contract contains such a broad and general statement, the problem of application and interpretation is obviously involved, and disagreements between the company and union in this regard are commonly resolved through the regular grievance procedure, or by the operation of a special safety committee.

The second category of contracts provides a detailed and specific listing of safety and health measures that obligate the company. Thus, many agreements stipulate that the company must provide adequate heat, light, and ventilation in the plant; that it will control drafts, noise, toxic fumes, dust, dirt, and grease; that it will provide certain safety equipment, such as hoods, goggles, special shoes and boots, and other items of special clothing; and that it is responsible for placing guards and other safety devices on machines.

In addition, under many contracts, the company must provide first-aid stations and keep a nurse on duty. Of course, whether or not a collective bargaining contract contains safety rules, a company must comply with the federal and state safety and health laws applicable to its plant.

Many labor agreements impose obligations on employees and unions as well as on employers in the matter of safety. Such provisions recognize the fact that safety, despite the individual employee's crucial stake in it, is a joint problem requiring the cooperation of the company, employees, and the union. Under many labor agreements, employees must obey safety rules and wear appropriate safety equipment, and employees who violate such rules are subject to discipline. In some labor agreements, the union assumes the obligation of educating its members in complying with safety rules and procedures of the plant. And some agreements, in the interest of safety, also establish a joint union–management safety committee. Many of these committees serve as advisory bodies on the general problem of safety and health; others, however, have the authority to establish and enforce safety and health rules, allowing the union a considerably more active role.

The Occupational Safety and Health Act and Its Consequences to Date

A high point in the area of employment safety and health was reached in the last days of 1970, with the enactment of the Occupational Safety and Health Act, generally referred to (as is the federal agency primarily charged with administering it) as OSHA. Under it, the federal government assumed a significant role in this area for the first time in history, and individual states were allowed to share jurisdiction if their plans for doing so could meet with the approval of Washington. OSHA inspectors were granted authority to inspect for violations (without prior notice to the employer) at the nation's 5 million workplaces and to issue citations leading to possibly heavy fines and even, as a last resort, jail sentences.

AFL-CIO president Meany applauded OSHA's enactment as "a long step down the road toward a safe and healthy workplace"; Richard M. Nixon, in signing it, referred to the act as "a landmark piece of legislation"; and the normally unemotional *Monthly Labor Review* passionately proclaimed it a "revolutionary program."[8] Great expectations, in short, accompanied passage.

Yet disillusionment was quick to set in and, within a very few years, OSHA appeared to be all but friendless, its critics coming in almost equal numbers from the ranks of labor and management. The following statistics, valid after almost four years of OSHA's operation and not substantially different at the time of this writing, largely explain why: (1) With less than 800 inspec-

[8]George Perkel, "A Labor View of the Occupational Safety and Health Act," *Labor Law Journal*, August 1972, p. 511.

tors available to visit the 5 million places of work, the average employer could expect to see an OSHA agent roughly once every 66 years; (2) penalties for violations had averaged $25 each, and, after all this time, only two companies had been convicted of criminal violations; (3) OSHA's 325 pages of safety and health standards were so technical as to be unintelligible to the vast majority of employers without professional (and thus costly) help; (4) the standards themselves were under any conditions expensive to satisfy, OSHA's noise-control demands alone potentially costing management anywhere from $13 billion to $31 billion (depending upon the final severity of these rules); and (5) only 16 states had opted to administer their own federally approved programs, and even these were generally viewed as inadequate.[9]

For all these sobering considerations, however, OSHA has had an impact, and in fact a very significant one, on employee health and safety. On the management side, the very presence of OSHA's formidable standards (with many more undoubtedly to come) has generated enormous expenditures on capital investments linked to this area: in 1973, $2.6 billion; in 1974, an estimated $3 billion; and by 1977, a predicted $3.4 billion.[10]

From organized labor, the activity has been even more pronounced. As former Federal Mediation and Conciliation Service Director W. J. Usery has commented, "Occupational safety and health comes up in almost every negotiation now in one way or another. You always would have a few people in a union that were safety-conscious. But now the [growing dissatisfaction with the enforcement of OSHA] has added impetus. I think it's the wave of the future."[11] To this impetus can be traced literally hundreds of recent major contract innovations—ranging from the establishment in Oil, Chemical and Atomic Worker–oil company agreements of local joint health and safety committees with not only access to company data but the right to arbitrate unresolved safety controversies, to the training of local UAW officials as full-time, paid health and safety monitors in the automobile industry, to a $2 million steel company–financed research fund to study the effects of coke-oven emissions on worker health. In the words of an AFL-CIO observer, "The rank and file are really awake and they believe the leaders' complaints about the inadequacy of federal enforcement of the law. So they're saying, 'Okay, let's get some protection in our own contracts.' "[12]

Many unions—possibly most—are still not much more active than they have historically been in the area of safety and health. Others do no more than the minimum required to prevent membership outbursts. And the AFL-CIO, with its safety staff of three people (who are also entrusted with other affairs), clearly can also be accused of not yet becoming sufficiently active

[9]All statistics in this paragraph are from the *Wall Street Journal*, August 19, 1974, p. 1.

[10]*Wall Street Journal*, August 20, 1974, p. 1.

[11]*Wall Street Journal*, August 19, 1974, p. 1.

[12]*Ibid.*

in this vital area. But the momentum set in motion, first by the high hopes for OSHA and then by the fears of the act's inadequacies, shows no sign of abating. Most probably, then, the years ahead should see even more activity and expenditure both at the bargaining table and (from all concerned groups) in lobbying efforts toward a goal that all but the most selfish segments of society can applaud: the minimization of occupational hazards in the American workplace.

PRODUCTION STANDARDS AND MANNING

Certainly one of the most important functions of management is that of determining the amount of output that an employee must turn out in a given period. So important is this area to management's objective of operating an efficient plant that employers will at times suffer long strikes to maintain this right as a unilateral one.

It is easy to understand why employers have such a vital interest in production standards. To the degree that employees increase output, unit labor costs decline. With declining labor costs, employers make a larger profit, or else they can translate lower labor costs into lower prices for their products or services with the expectation of thereby increasing the total volume of sales and strengthening the financial position of the company.

There is still another way to look at production standards in the operation of the firm. If employees produce more, the employer will have to hire commensurately fewer additional employees, or may even be in a position to lay off present employees on a temporary or permanent basis. Indeed, with a smaller labor force, the management could also save on the number of foremen needed to supervise the work of its employees.

Production standards are thus directly related to the manning of jobs, or to the question of how many employees are needed to carry out a specific plant assignment. But even where contractual commitments or past practices obligate the company to assign a certain minimum number of workers to a given operation at all times, significant economies can be realized by management if it is able to impose higher production standards upon this inflexible crew.

If the interest of management in production standards is understandable, however, it is no less understandable that employees and their union representatives have an equal interest in ensuring "reasonableness" and "fairness" in this phase of the firm's operation. Before the advent of unions, employers could require employees to produce as much as management directed. Failure to meet these production standards could result in the summary dismissal of the employee. At times, employees suffered accidents, psychological problems, and a generally shortened work life in meeting the standards of the employer. And although modern and enlightened management does not normally impose production standards that employees cannot reasonably attain, unions and employees are nonetheless still vitally concerned with the amount of production that an employee must turn out in a given length of time because of the patent ramifications for job opportunities and union membership.

There is no simple solution to the problem of how much an employee must produce to hold his job or to earn a given amount of pay. At times, the determination of a solution is purely subjective in character; a foreman's or superintendent's individual judgment is the criterion adopted to resolve the problem. To this, unions argue that the judgment of employees or labor union officers is as good as that of the management representatives.

More sophisticated methods of determination are available, but these techniques, too, are hardly so perfect or "scientific" as to end the controversy. Such techniques fall under the general title of time and motion studies. That is, having been shown the most efficient method of performing a job, so-called "average" employees, who are presumably thus working at average rates of speed, are timed. From such a study, management claims that the typical employee in the plant should at least produce the average amount in a given period. Where incentive wage systems are in effect, as we know, the employee receives premium pay for output above the average. However, production standards are important even when employees are paid by the hour, since failure to produce the average amount could result in employee discipline of some sort—ranging from a reprimand to discharge, with intervening levels such as a suspension or a demotion to a lower-paying job. Unions are far from convinced that time and motion studies constitute the millennium in the resolution of the production standards problem. They claim that the studies are far from scientific, since they still involve human judgment, and that employees who are timed are often far better than average, so that their rate of speed is consequently unrealistically fast.

With few exceptions (most notably in the garment industries), unions have pressed for an effective means of review of employer establishment of production standards, rather than toward seeking the right to establish such standards initially. Organized labor has generally believed that employee and union institutional interests are served as effectively, and without the administrative and political complexities of initial standard establishment, if there is a union opportunity for challenge of the management action, either through arbitration or by the exercise of the right to strike during the contractual period in the event of unresolved production standards disputes.

Some unions have historically preferred the right to strike to arbitration in this area. The United Automobile Workers has, for example, steadfastly refused to relinquish its right to strike over production standards disputes, and although the UAW now agrees to arbitration on virtually all other phases of the labor agreement, it is adamant in its opposition to the arbitration of standards. The international neither distrusts arbitrators nor challenges their professional competency. Rather, it believes that a union cannot properly prepare and present a case in arbitration that can successfully challenge production standards. It contends that the problems are so complicated, the proofs so difficult to assemble, and the data so hard to present in meaningful form that arbitration is not the proper forum for resolving production standards disputes. In essence, it claims that employers have an advantage in any arbitration dealing with production standards, and the union does not intend to turn to this process because it would jeopardize the interests of its members.

On the other hand, most unions have now agreed to the arbitration of production standards. Beyond reflecting the general contemporary acceptance of the arbitration process itself, this course of action has behind it a highly practical reason: Frequently, production standards are protested by only a small group of employees in the plant. For example, the employer may have changed the standards in one department (because of improved technology, equipment, or methods), but left unaltered at least temporarily the standards in all other departments. Without arbitration, the only way in which the affected employees could seek relief would be for the entire labor force to strike—at times, a politically inopportune weapon for the union to use, because the employees in the other departments are satisfied and do not care to sacrifice earnings just to help out employees in a single department. Arbitration avoids this situation, while still allowing a final and binding decision on the grievance of the protesting employees.

There is, however, probably no area of labor relations wherein management and organized labor still stand any further apart than in production standards. There is no magical solution to such controversies when they arise. Standards lie at the heart of the operation of the plant and are vital to the basic interest of the employees and unions. To say that they should be established "fairly" and "reasonably" is a most idle statement to make, falling in the same category as "we should all love our mothers." In the give and take of day-to-day operations, wherein production standards may be changed, deep and bitter conflicts are perhaps even bound to arise. The stakes are very high, and as long as management seeks efficiency and the union seeks to protect the welfare of its members, there exists no easy way out of the problem. Certainly nothing approaching a panacea for it has yet been discovered by the parties to collective bargaining.

At least, however, if companies and unions fully recognize the apparent inevitability of standards disputes, the fact that no dispute in this area will perhaps ever be settled in such a way that all involved in it will be fully satisfied, and the high degree of sensitivity of this labor relations issue, the point of realism will have been reached. Once these basic propositions are understood, the parties are in a position to fashion workable production standards compromises without jeopardizing the broader collective bargaining relationship.

AUTOMATION

As stated at the beginning of this chapter, the problem of automation cuts across much of the contemporary collective bargaining process. Most of the methods the private parties have employed to ease the adjustment to this new technology are administrative and institutional in nature, insofar as they deal with the job rights of workers, the institutional needs of labor organizations, and the rights of management in directing the work force. But such previously discussed "economic" issues as severance pay, pension-rights vesting and supplemental unemployment benefits are also increasingly being geared to cushioning the labor-saving and displacement effects of automation. It is thus quite unrealistic to view this problem as falling exclusively within one descriptive category. Indeed, one is fully justified in looking at this final portion of the chapter as a synthesizer of many current trends in collective bargaining, providing the capstone of the "administrative" segment but actually extending well beyond it.

Broadly defined, automation is the control of the elements of production through a system of automatic devices that integrate the entire productive process. Not only is the human hand not needed, but the process also makes less necessary a major feature that distinguishes human beings from animals: judgment. Automated computers are now able to determine optimally what product to produce in the first place, the color and design of the product, where the goods should be sold, and even the pricing of the product.

Even today, automation affects, to some extent, almost all segments of the work force. Although the industrial blue-collar worker, and particularly the unskilled and semiskilled factory worker, has thus far been hardest hit, examples abound to show the impact of automation, even at this relatively early stage in its history, in other sectors of the economy. In railroading, for example, robot track-laying equipment and the automatic handling and dispatching of freight cars have made many jobs obsolete. The same can be said of many forms of retail trade, as symbolized by one mail-order house in which a computer now handles 90,000 tallies each day, keeping an automatic inventory record of the 8,000 items sold by the firm in the process. Nor has government employment been immune from automation's inroads: The 450 U.S. Treasury clerical workers who were recently replaced by a computer designed to accommodate the 500 million checks issued by the federal government every year are far from unique among the casualties of automation in that sector.

The fact remains, however, that the blue-collar worker in mass production industry—unionism's strongest bastion—has been the most visible victim of the advent of automation. In the modern automobile plant, 154 engine blocks now run through the production line in one hour, requiring 41 workers; under older methods, the same amount of production required 117 men. In the typical automated radio-manufacturing establishment, only two employees produce 1,000 radios per day, where standard hand assembly required a labor force of 200. And, perhaps most dramatic of all, 14 glass-blowing machines, each operated by a single worker, have for some time produced 90 percent of all glass light bulbs used in the United States, as well as all the glass tubes used in radio and television sets except for the picture tubes!

For all these labor-displacement and related skill rating and wage payment effects, there are clearly offsetting advantages offered by automation. Certainly, the automating employer benefits, either by gaining a competitive edge or by closing a competitive gap, in making this form of technological change. Of far more general benefit, national living standards are raised immensely by the increased productivity allowed. It is now estimated, for example, that the average family income in the United States at constant dollars will be $20,000 annually in the year 2000, up from only about half that figure today.

There are, moreover, still other advantages to automation: greater safety, resulting from the use of modern methods of materials handling and from the elimination of other hazardous jobs; a frequent improvement in product quality, since the automatic machine has little room for human error; and even an improved defense posture for the nation, modern methods of warfare having as their common denominator an automation base. Most important of all, it can be argued with considerable justification that everyone, in the long run, benefits from the needs and wants created by improved technology. There are infinitely more men working in the automobile production and servicing industries than there ever were blacksmiths, for example. And the number of employees associated with the telephone industry vastly exceeds the highest labor force totals ever achieved by the town-crier profession.

All these arguments, however, are of small consolation to the employee actually being displaced or threatened by automation. Just as logically, he can echo the irrefutable statement of Lord Keynes that "in the long run, we are all dead." And he can often balance the fact that automation has generally improved working conditions by pointing to undesirable features of the problem that have an impact upon the workers in the plant: greater isolation of employees on the job, with less chance to talk face to face with other workers and supervisors; a greater mental strain, particularly since mistakes can now be much more costly; the deterioration of social groups, since it requires considerably less teamwork to run the modern operation; and the fact that jobs in the automated plant (or office) are fast becoming much more alike, with less on-the-job variety also often the case, and attendant psychological and social implications stemming from this situation.

But most worrisome of all to the industrial worker is the threat of displacement, or at least of severe skill requirement downgrading, through *future* automation. The results of one employee survey with which the authors are personally familiar showed that almost three-quarters of all respondents, asked whether they believed that "automation is a good thing for workers" replied in the negative (and many of them added that the new methods constituted a "real job threat"). Such findings have been echoed in countless other studies.

The fears appear to be well grounded. If automation undeniably creates new jobs and even industries, the possibility remains that at the present time, it is destroying more jobs than it creates. Even placing all government and private estimates at their rock-bottom minima, it is likely that 4,000 jobs are eliminated *each week* in this manner. And however many of the displaced are ultimately reabsorbed into the employed labor force, the increasing skill requirements of an automated world leave little room for at least the unskilled worker to join their ranks; at the time of this writing, with a national rate of unemployment seemingly inflexibly fixed in the 7 to 8 percent range, the rate for unskilled workers has steadily exceeded 15 percent in recent years.

Thus, while by far the greatest organizational problem of unions involves the organization of the white-collar sector in the face of the automation-caused changing complexion of the work force, within the current arena of collective bargaining, organized labor—both as the blue-collar worker's representative and for its own institutional preservation—has inevitably been forced toward the promotion of *measures minimizing job hardship for blue-collar workers.*

Accordingly, unions have in recent years pushed hard, and with much success, for several devices geared explicitly to cushioning the employment impact of automation. In addition to such previously discussed areas as SUB, pension vesting, severance pay, extended vacation periods, and early-retirement provisions (which have frequently been negotiated for reasons other than adjustment to automation), several such devices deserve attention.[13]

1. Advance Notice of Layoff or Shutdown. Such advance notice, impracticable for management in the case of sudden cancellation of orders and

---

[13]Some of the following exposition is based upon information provided in a comprehensive 1964 review by the U.S. Department of Labor's Bureau of Labor Statistics, *Methods of Adjusting to Automation and Technological Change.* See also Gerald G. Somers, Edward L. Cushman, and Nat Weinberg, eds., *Adjusting to Technological Change* (New York: Harper & Row, 1963); and Edward B. Shils, *Automation and Industrial Relations* (New York: Holt, Rinehart & Winston, 1963).

various other contingencies, is far more feasible where automation is involved, since many months may be required to prepare for the automated equipment and processes. An increasing number of agreements now call for notice considerably in excess of the few days traditionally provided for in many contracts, with most of the liberalizations now providing for three to twelve months.

Managements independently have often agreed with the advisability of such liberalization—to maintain or improve community images, to dispel potentially damaging employee rumors, and, frequently, because of a desire to develop placement and training plans for displaced workers. Very often, in fact, the actual notice given by management exceeds that stipulated in the contract. There seems to be little doubt, however, that unions have been instrumental in inserting longer advance-notice provisions in some contracts —as in portions of the meat-packing and electronics industries—that might otherwise not have modified traditional practices.

2. Adoption of the "Attrition Principle." An agreement to reduce jobs solely by attrition—through, in other words, deaths, voluntary resignations, retirements, and similar events—by definition gives maximum job security to the present jobholder, although it does nothing to secure the union's long-run institutional interests. As a compromise, it has appealed to many employers as an equitable and not unduly rigorous measure. Managements have proven particularly amenable to this arrangement when the voluntary resignation rate is expected to be high, when a high percentage of workers is nearing retirement age, or when no major reduction of the labor force is anticipated in the first place (and the number of jobs made obsolete by automation is consequently small to begin with). In other cases, unions have been the major force behind introduction of the principle—usually, however, with some modifications more favorable to the union as an institution placed upon it. Thus, the current agreement between the Order of Railroad Telegraphers and the Southern Pacific Railroad places an upper limit of 2 percent upon the jobs that can be abolished for any reason in a given year. Good faith is obviously required in such cases, however; as Bok and Kossoris comment:

> If [employers] are bound to follow attrition by agreement, temptation may arise to hasten the departure of employees by imposing more onerous working conditions or otherwise making the job less attractive. Further controversy may result if the agreement does not answer such questions as whether employees must agree to transfer or to accept more demanding positions and assignments in order to remain on the payroll.[14]

3. Retraining. An expanding but unknown number of bargaining relationships now provides opportunities for displaced employees to retrain for

---

[14]Bureau of Labor Statistics, *Methods of Adjusting to Automation*, p. 5.

another job in the same plant or another plant of the same company. The same protection is also increasingly being extended to employees for whom changes in equipment or operating methods make it mandatory to retrain in order to hold their current jobs. Often, such retraining opportunity, which is most commonly offered at company expense, is limited to workers who meet certain seniority specifications. General Electric workers, for example, must have at least three years of continuous service in order to qualify. At other times, preference but not a promise for retraining is granted senior workers, as in one Machinist union contract that provides that such employees "shall be given preference for training on new equipment, provided they have the capabilities required."

Where such provisions have significantly mitigated displacement, not unexpectedly, they have been implemented by companies whose operations have been expanding in areas other than those causing the initial displacement. "Retraining for *what*?" is a meaningful question when such expansion is not in evidence, or at least is not highly likely. Lack of employee self-confidence or lack of worker intelligence levels sufficient to meet the new skill requirements have also been known to make the retraining opportunity an essentially valueless one for employees permitted to utilize it. Yet, there is much to be said for retraining in the absence of such adverse factors; as the personnel director of Inland Steel has stated:

> Retraining makes maximum use of manpower and contributes to the long-range security of the individual. . . . We think this is smart because it minimizes resistance to change, enables us to get up production faster than when people fear they won't keep their jobs, and gives us a quicker return on our investment.[15]

4. Automation Funds.   Ironically, the several "automation funds" that have sprouted in a variety of industries in the recent past do little or nothing to aid employees who are actually displaced. They do, however, tend to make it easier for management to implement change, both by gaining the cooperation of the retained workers and by strengthening the union's institutional status through providing benefits for present and future union members. Such funds as those negotiated by the United Mine Workers, American Federation of Musicians, West Coast Longshoremen, New York Longshoremen, and Amalgamated Meat Cutters with various employers are essentially devices for sharing the savings of automation with retained employees— through such means as free medical care, guaranteed weekly pay provisions, early retirement allowances, and lump-sum "bonus payments."

In addition to the political and public relations advantages they allow to the various unions, there are specific advantages in the funds from manage-

---

[15] *Wall Street Journal*, August 23, 1961, p. 6.

ment's point of view. Kennedy believes that perhaps the major such advantage:

> ... is that it impresses more strongly on the employees the reason for the benefits which they are receiving. When the benefits are paid from an "automation" fund, it is clear that they are being paid out of the savings of automation and that the employees are expected to cooperate with the automation process in return for such benefits. On the other hand, when the savings of automation are shared through higher wage rates or through improved fringe benefits without a fund, the service of the benefits as well as the reason for giving them may not be so evident in the beginning and are much more easily forgotten with time.[16]

On such a pragmatic basis, automation funds can probably be expected to continue their spread.

5. Restrictions on Subcontracting. *Subcontracting*, the term that stands for arrangements made by a company (for reasons such as cost, quality, or speed of delivery) to have some portion of its work performed by employees of another company, can obviously have major work-opportunity ramifications for the first company's employees. There is probably no completely integrated company in the nation, and some measure of subcontracting has always been accepted by all unions as an economic necessity. But when the union can argue that union member employees could have performed the subcontracted work, or that such work was previously done by bargaining unit employees, it can be counted upon to do so. And when disputes do arise over this issue, they are, as Chapter 4 has pointed out, often of major dimensions. In the face of automation-caused job insecurity, there has been an observable recent trend toward union control over many types of subcontracting; the battle has tended to move from open interunion competition to the union–management bargaining table.

So thorny is the subcontracting problem that more than 75 percent of all major contracts still make no direct reference to it in a special contractual section. But an increasing number of contracts are incorporating in various of their other sections (ranging from union recognition clauses to seniority articles) or in separate "memoranda of understanding" certain limitations on the procedure.

The limitations are of several kinds: (1) agreements that subcontractors will be used only on special occasions (for example, "where specialized equipment not available on company premises is required," or "where peculiar skills are needed"); (2) no-layoff guarantees to current employees (as in "no Employee of any craft, which craft is being utilized by an Outside Contractor, shall be laid off as long as the Outside Contractor is in the plant

[16]Thomas Kennedy, *Automation Funds and Displaced Workers* (Boston: Harvard University, Graduate School of Business Administration, 1962), pp. 351–52.

doing work that Employees in such craft are able to do"); (3) provisions giving the union veto power over any or all subcontracting; and (4) requirements that the company prove to the union that time, expense, or facility considerations prevent it from allowing current employees to perform the work.

Slichter, Healy, and Livernash some time ago summed up the subcontracting situation as follows:

> [Unlike many other collective bargaining areas] subcontracting remains an area of conflict in labor relations. Where adjustment has been achieved by the adoption of workable contract language, it has usually had the effect of limiting management's flexibility to a considerable extent. Seldom has explicit language been adopted affirming management's right to subcontract without challenge from the union. The trend has been in the opposite direction.[17]

These words were no less valid as this was written; only when more adequate solutions to the problems of automation are formulated can one expect the conflict in this area to abate. (The final case in this book, 14, involves the subcontracting issue.)

6. Other Measures. Unions have also unilaterally attempted to minimize the administrative, institutional, and other problems of automation through increasingly successful, if still limited, bargaining table campaigns for (1) shorter workweeks, often with a prohibition against overtime work when qualified workers are on layoff or where the overtime would result in layoffs; (2) the requirement of joint labor–management consultation prior to the introduction of any automated change; (3) the overhauling of wage structures with job upgrading to reflect the "increased responsibility" of automated factory jobs; and (4) special job and wage provisions for downgraded workers, to minimize income losses suffered by such workers, or to offset them entirely. In addition, unions have in some cases sought to facilitate new employment through the development of their own training, placement, and referral services. And, perhaps most visibly, they have often waged highly ambitious political lobbying campaigns (both on the international and AFL-CIO levels) for: a vast array of employment-generating public works programs; far-reaching tax programs and expanded Social Security benefits (to increase consumer purchasing power and lessen the burden on those most likely to be displaced); and innovative federal and state training programs.

As judged by short-run goals—the insertion of the various contract provisions within labor agreements and, in the latter case, the enactment of the lobbied-for legislation—unions have achieved a considerable measure of triumph. And the fact that they have frequently been aided in such campaigns by increasingly social-minded employers in no way detracts from

---

[17]Slichter, Healy, and Livernash, *The Impact of Collective Bargaining*, pp. 315–16.

this success. Although union aggressiveness and creativity has varied widely, there can be no denying that many unions have considerably alleviated the burdens of automation for many workers.

Yet neither singly nor in combination have these measures, or the host of other automation-adjustment methods cited earlier, provided anything approaching a full solution for the basic problems with which they deal. The displacement and displacement threats continue, now actually in accelerated form, as automation continues to prove that it is both a blessing and a curse for society. Indeed, a case can be made that a vicious circle is involved: Virtually all these measures increase labor costs for the companies concerned, giving the employer even further motivation for automating, and often thus causing the represented employees to lose jobs all the more rapidly.[18]

There appears to be rather general agreement among all segments of our society on at least three relevant points, however. First, most of us concede that automation is a product of society. It is not caused only by individuals, single firms, or groups of firms, but rather it is an expression of our cultural heritage, of our educational system, and of our group dynamics. As such, unlike other problems affecting collective bargaining, it requires not only a private (labor–management) solution but a supplementary public (government) one. Second, we are essentially in agreement that no single group should bear the entire burden of automation. Rather, we admit that we should all bear the burden by making sure that the benefits of the increased productivity allowed by automation are shared by all. Without such a philosophical basis, automation would mean that some would make spectacular gains, and others would shoulder the full burden. We do not want automation to divide the nation into "haves" and "have nots." Third, we share general unanimity that this is a time for daring innovation in social dynamics and social engineering and that, although the problem is great, we fortunately have within our capacity the power to deal with the issues within a system of free enterprise. Since old methods will not work, we must innovate and pioneer.

The increasing attention being given to automation at the bargaining table (and by the bargaining parties in the public arena) can thus be viewed as recognition of a great but not necessarily insurmountable challenge.

A CONCLUDING WORD

The mutual accommodations and adjustments to the hard issues of collective bargaining that the parties have displayed in regard to wages, employee benefits, and institutional issues is no less in evidence when one inspects the current status of the administrative issues in our labor relations

---

[18]This is, of course, true only if the costs are incurred in any event. If they occur *only* if one automates, they reduce the saving and in some cases could make automation unprofitable.

system. Management has increasingly recognized the job-protection and working-condition problems of the industrial employee and has made important concessions in these areas. At the same time, however, there has been reciprocal recognition on the part of unions that the protection of the employee cannot be at the expense of the destruction of the business firm. The axiom that employees cannot receive any protection from a business that has ceased to exist appears to have been fully appreciated by all but the extreme recalcitrants of the labor movement, and workable compromises have been possible with respect to the areas of seniority, discipline, and the various other dimensions discussed in this chapter no less than in the case of previous topics.

Clearly, there is considerable room for future progress, and, on occasion, the conflicts between the parties on the administrative issues can be very serious. Production standards and subcontracting remain two highly visible sticking points. And strikes do, of course, at times result. There should be no illusion that the sensitive matters of collective bargaining are adjusted without painful struggle. Such an observation would not be realistic and would run contrary to the contemporary scene. Even standing alone, however, this chapter demonstrates rather irrefutably that managers and unionized employee representatives have increasingly recognized each other's positions. It offers additional evidence of the growing maturity of the American labor relations system.

DISCUSSION QUESTIONS

1. It has been generally agreed that the increased use of the seniority concept in industrial relations has lessened the degree of mobility among workers. What can be said (a) for, and (b) against, such a consequence?

2. "The typical labor agreement's disciplinary procedures contain as many potential advantages for management as they do for unions and workers." Comment.

3. Jack Barbash has commented that "management's perception of technological change is producing an offensive strategy; the union's perception is in general producing a defensive strategy." Confining your opinion to automated changes, do you agree?

4. The several devices noted in the last section of this chapter constitute the major existing avenues for minimizing employee resistance to automation. Can you suggest other measures that might be utilized in an attempt to realize this goal?

SELECTED REFERENCES

BRODEUR, PAUL, *Expendable Americans*. New York: Viking, 1974.

GERSUNY, CARL, *Punishment and Redress in a Modern Factory*. Lexington, Mass.: Heath, 1973.

KENNEDY, THOMAS, *Automation Funds and Displaced Workers*. Boston: Harvard University, Graduate School of Business Administration, 1962.

PHELPS, ORME W., *Discipline and Discharge in the Unionized Firm*. Berkeley: University of California Press, 1959.

SIMLER, NORMAN J., "The Economics of Featherbedding," *Industrial and Labor Relations Review*, October 1962.

SLICHTER, SUMNER H., JAMES J. HEALY, and E. ROBERT LIVERNASH, *The Impact of Collective Bargaining on Management*, pp. 104–371, 624–62. Washington: The Brookings Institution, 1960.

SOMERS, GERALD G., EDWARD L. CUSHMAN, and NAT WEINBERG, eds., *Adjusting to Technological Change*. New York: Harper & Row, 1963.

THOMIS, MALCOLM I., *The Luddites: Machine-Breaking in Regency England*. New York: Schocken Books, 1972.

U.S. Department of Labor, Bureau of Labor Statistics, *Methods of Adjusting to Automation and Technological Change*. Washington, D.C.: U.S. Government Printing Office, 1964.

WEINSTEIN, PAUL A., ed., *Featherbedding and Technological Change*. Boston: Heath, 1965.

CASE 11
Filling a Promotion:
The Case of the Bypassed
Senior Employee

Cast of Characters

L	Grievant
B	Employee who was awarded the job
F	Manager of department
W, M, Z, K, and O	
	Other employees who bid on the job
H	Union business manager
G	Supervisor
A	Another supervisor

Length of service or seniority is not the only criterion used to fill a promotion. Normally, the senior employee must have qualifications reasonably equal to those of a junior service employee who also bids on the higher-paying job. It is a distortion of the facts to believe that length of service is normally the sole factor in the awarding of promotions on the labor relations scene. In this case, the employer awarded the better job to a junior service employee. Its position was that the senior employee lacked the qualifications for the job. The union argued that the senior employee did have the qualifications, and the case proceeded to arbitration. Note that the job in question was a "white-collar" or professional job—senior cost accountant. Note also that under the labor agreement the employer had the right on a unilateral basis to establish the qualifications for the job.

Involved in this dispute was the filling of a vacancy in the job classification styled "Senior Cost Accountant, T & D" (transmission and distribution). L and B entered bids for the job. Even though L was senior to B, the company filled the job with the junior service employee. L filed a grievance, and this arbitration was instituted to test the merit of his claim.

Material to the dispute were the following provisions of the labor agreement:

ARTICLE 13

Section 5. . . . Vacancies subject to bidding shall be filled on the basis of seniority, ability and qualifications being sufficient. First claim shall be had by employees employed in any classifications in the promotional series in which the vacancy occurs, on the basis of Promotional Series Seniority. Second claim shall be had by all other employees coming under this Agreement, on the basis of Local Union Unit Seniority. . . .

Section 10. For the purpose of defining ability and qualifications, it is agreed that: (a) Ability shall mean the capacity of an employee to satisfactorily perform all of the duties of the job as set forth in the job specifications, as demonstrated by his previous work record; (b) qualifications shall generally mean those set forth in the job specifications. In determining the sufficiency of qualifications, the Company will be guided by the qualifications set forth in the job specifications. In instances where the Company does not promote a candidate because of lack of sufficient qualifications, the Union shall have the right to question, through the grievance procedure, the reasonableness of the qualification requirement for the job as set forth in the job specifications.

If the Company and the Union cannot agree as to the sufficiency of the ability and/or qualifications of a senior candidate for a job to be filled, the disagreement may be handled as a grievance. . . .

The parties submitted the following question to be determined in this arbitration:

Did the Company violate Article 13, by disqualifying L in his bid on the Senior Cost Accountant, T & D job, and should L be awarded this position and be reimbursed the difference between his current pay and the pay of the Senior Cost Accountant, T & D job from a date 30 days after the date of his disqualification?

BACKGROUND

On May 2, 1960, the company established a job description for the senior cost accountant. In this document, the duties of the job were listed as follows:

Organize, accumulate, prepare, and maintain cost and expenditure data in a form usable for review, budget preparation, and comparison.

Assist in the preparation of the annual Transmission and Distribution Budget.

Collate cost information from accounting records and interpret results.

Make continuing special studies of work performance and cost results in various Transmission and Distribution work groups.

Devise methods and procedures for better cost analysis and cost control.

Prepare reports on the above as assigned.

On September 19, 1972, the company posted a notice to fill a vacancy in the job of senior cost accountant, T & D. The notice stated:

Job Title	Dept. or Div.	Location	Salary (per month)
Senior cost accountant, T & D	Transmission and distribution clerical, order processing and cost control	Main office	$1,042.11 to $1,356.14

Duties:

Under direct but not constant supervision, to perform the more difficult assignments in connection with accumulating, computing, and analyzing cost information as related to work performance and budgetary requirements in the Transmission and Distribution Division. Also, as required, to serve as leader in assigning and reviewing the work of Cost Accountants, clerks, and other employees.

Qualifications:

Must have a degree from an accredited college or university with the major field of study in accounting, business administration, or economics, with at least 12 hours' credit in elementary and intermediate accounting plus four years of experience in accounting work.

Twenty-five employees bid on the job in question. For purposes of this case, it is necessary to list only the seven most senior employees who desired the job. In order of seniority, these employees were W, M, Z, K, L (the grievant), B, and O.

F, the department manager, had interviewed these employees, and testified as to the results of these interviews. With respect to W, M, and Z, he declared that each of them qualified in terms of education, but did not possess the necessary accounting work experience. K qualified in terms of education and accounting experience, but elected not to take the job.

With respect to his interview with L, F testified:

Q: What did you find upon interviewing Mr. L?

A: I found that Mr. L had the educational qualification, but insufficient experience, accounting experience.

Q: What experience did Mr. L have, accounting experience?

A: The information I had at the time I interviewed Mr. L was that he had worked for approximately two and a half years as an accountant.

Arbitrator: In what department was that?

A: In the comptroller's function.

When I informed Mr. L that this did not meet the qualification for a senior cost accountant's job, he offered his experience as a payroll clerk and as a console operator programmer, offering the opinion that this should qualify as accounting experience. Having some knowledge of the work of the payroll clerk and of the console operator programmer, I informed him that I could not consider this as accounting experience. I explored with him if he had any other experience that could qualify as accounting experience, and he informed me that he had worked for some time in tax work, and further questioning brought out that he had worked for a firm which he identified as Tax Teller, doing income tax returns. And I told him that there was a possibility this could qualify, and asked him to submit a statement from his former employers about what kind of tax work he did with them and the period of time it covered.

We further explored this, and he told me that this covered one tax season, approximately three months, and he thought most of his work was on personal tax returns. I informed him that I doubted that that could qualify if it was limited to personal tax returns, but I again asked him to submit a record from his former employer of the work he did there, and how much time he had in it. Mr. L then told me that he thought his work as a payroll clerk and a console operator programmer should qualify as accounting experience, and that if I refused to accept that, he would grieve the matter.

Q: So then did you refuse to accept his payroll clerk's work and console operator programmer?

A: I did, and I disqualified him.

O qualified in terms of education and accounting experience, and F offered the job to him. However, this employee requested time to consider whether or not he would take the job, and in the meantime, B submitted a bid for the job. After an interview, the job was offered to him, and B accepted it. F testified:

Q: . . . What did you find when you interviewed Mr. B?

A: I found that Mr. B was educationally qualified, and qualified as to accounting experience. He had sufficient ability to do the job. I offered it to him, and he accepted.

Since L was senior to B, he filed a grievance alleging that the company violated the labor agreement when it refused to award him the job.

Between December 15, 1959, and April 1, 1963, L had served as a payroll clerk. After holding a draftsman's job for a period of time, on July 11, 1966, he was classified as an accountant in the comptroller's department. He held that job until March 19, 1969, when he was classified as a console operator programmer, and he was serving in this job at the time of the arbitration.

On June 4, 1966, L was awarded a bachelor of science degree in commerce by St. Louis University. His major was accounting. The following demonstrates the accounting courses the grievant took while at St. Louis University:

Course	Hours
Elementary accounting	6
Intermediate accounting theory	6
Advanced accounting theory	6
Cost accounting	6
Auditing	3
Federal income tax	3
Total hours	30

ANALYSIS OF THE EVIDENCE

Four Years' Experience in Accounting Work

As the record showed, the company unilaterally prepared job specifications. For the job in question, the company specified that to be eligible to fill a vacancy in the classification, an employee must have a college degree with a major field in accounting, business administration, or economics. It also required that the employee must have at least twelve hours' credit in elementary and intermediate accounting. On this basis, the grievant satisfied the educational qualification for the senior cost accountant's job; as a matter of fact, he had completed far more accounting courses than the specification required.

In this light, this case boiled down to a determination of whether or not the grievant qualified in terms of the necessary experience in accounting work, independent of courses taken in a university. The company required that to be qualified for the job in question, the employee must show "four years of experience in accounting work," and it was on this basis that the company disqualified the grievant.

The union apparently did not argue that the four-year accounting work experience was an unreasonable qualification. Thus:

Arbitrator: ... You don't challenge the job specification?

H (union business manager): That's correct. ...

Arbitrator: ... I asked that question, remember, way back. I said as I understood it, the job specifications are prepared unilaterally by the company.

H: That is true.

Arbitrator: I asked that question. And, in other words, you are bound by those job specifications. Your quarrel is with the interpretation of the specifications, not the writing of the specifications.

H: Well, yes. And my quarrel—and if it's objected to, fine—but my quarrel is, if the company meant it as an accountant, they should have stated so, instead of the words "accounting work."

Also, the union stated:

> It should be noted here that the Union is not questioning "the reasonableness of the qualification requirement for the job as set forth in the job specifications" (Article 13, Section 10), but has filed its grievance under the provisions of the second paragraph of Section 10, "If the Company and the Union cannot agree as to the sufficiency of the ability and/or qualifications of a senior candidate for a job to be filled, the disagreement may be handled as a grievance."

In short, the union did not protest against the four-year accounting work experience requirement. Instead, its argument was that the grievant qualified in this respect in the light of the jobs he held while employed by the company. In this respect, the arbitrator found that the job specification did not say that an employee must have been classified as an accountant for four years. The grievant had served in this capacity for only about two and one-half years while employed by the company, but this did not necessarily disqualify him from the job, because the job specification stated, "four years of experience in *accounting work*" [emphasis supplied], and an employee could thus conceivably obtain experience in accounting work even though he might not be classified as an accountant.

F testified as follows:

Q: I am saying that from your testimony, and concerning your interviews with those people who bid on the job, and also your testimony concerning those people who have held that job, that I got the impression, and perhaps wrongly, and that's why I'm asking you, that you considered in your determination for someone to fill that job, that in order to fulfill the qualification statement on the job specification of four years of experience in accounting work, that that must be derived from work as an accountant? . . .

A: I don't see that you can assume that, because I testified that I did explore with Mr. L, for instance, when I interviewed him, if he had any other experience that he felt could qualify as accounting work. And we did explore his work in doing tax work, in that regard.

In any event, the arbitrator found that the material language of the job specification in question did not require that an employee must be classified as an accountant to meet the four-year work experience requirement.

Article 13, Section 10:
Deviation from Job Specification Requirements

In this provision of the labor agreement, the parties agreed that:

> . . . qualifications shall *generally* mean those set forth in the job specifications. In determining the sufficiency of qualifications, the Company shall be guided by the qualifications set forth in the job specifications. [Emphasis supplied.]

In this respect, the union argued:

> If the Labor Agreement required that the necessary qualifications for a successful bidder for promotion be those specifically spelled out in the Job Specification and that no deviation was allowable, then the Company's position could be upheld. The fact is that the Labor Agreement makes no such requirement. Instead, the Labor Agreement's language is quite contrary to that position and notes that ". . . qualifications shall *generally* mean those set forth in the job specifications. In determining the sufficiency of qualifications, the Company will be *guided by* the qualifications set forth in the job specifications." [Emphasis added.]

The arbitrator's opinion read, in part:

> There is validity in this Union argument, since Section 10 does not require that the employee must exactly possess the qualifications stated in a Company-prepared job specification. Instead, the provision contains the word *generally* and states further that the Company will be *guided by* the qualifications set forth in the particular job specification. In other words, the parties agreed that under appropriate circumstances, there could be a deviation from the specific qualifications spelled out in a particular job description.

> Although the aforecited Union argument has merit, the Arbitrator is somewhat puzzled. Unless the Arbitrator has misread the Union presentation, he understands that the Union does not per se challenge the four (4) year accounting work experience. As the Arbitrator understands the basic Union argument, it is that the Grievant, in the light of the totality of his work record in the Company, fulfills the four (4) year accounting work experience requirement. . . . The Arbitrator has already held that such experience is not limited to work as an Accountant. Hence, the Grievant's total work experience in the Company would be of evidentiary value. This feature of the case is dealt with in a subsequent portion of the Opinion.

> On the other hand, the Arbitrator rejects the Union argument herein considered if it suggests that the four (4) year accounting work experience requirement should be watered down. Let us assume here that the Union's reference to the material language of Section 10 ("generally" and "guided") in effect requests the Arbitrator to ignore the four (4) year accounting work experience requirement spelled out in the job specification. If this is the thrust of the Union's argument, the Arbitrator rejects such a request. *The major reason for this finding is that the record shows that the Company has uniformly required such experience before it has promoted an employee to the Senior Cost Accounting classification.*

> In the Comptroller's Office, there exists an Accounting Department. About twenty-four (24) or twenty-five (25) Senior Cost Accountants are assigned to this department. With respect to this group, H testified:

Arbitrator: Well, I think the crunch question is in the Comptroller's Department, are there any Senior Accountants who, before they became Senior Accountants, had less than four years' service as an Accountant?

A: No.

In the Transmission and Distribution Department, four (4) employees hold the job of Senior Cost Accountant. With respect to these employees, F testified:

Arbitrator: Let me pin this down. Is it your testimony, subject to verification of Company Exhibit 8, that all of these people actually were classified as Accountants before they became Senior Accountants, for four or more years?

A: That is correct.

In short, there has been no deviation from the four (4) year accounting work experience requirement as a prerequisite for a promotion to Senior Cost Accountant. Whether in the Comptroller's Department or in the Transmission and Distribution Department, each employee who held the job previously had at least four (4) years' experience in accounting work. . . . Since no exception has been made in the past to this requirement, no exception is warranted in the case of the Grievant. In fact, to make an exception for the Grievant would result in discriminatory treatment of the employees who had four (4) years' accounting work experience before they were promoted to the Senior Cost Accountant classification.

In this light, for the Grievant's case to prevail, the Union must show that he had four years' accounting work experience during his tenure in the Company. If the evidence demonstrates that he had this experience, the grievance shall be granted. If the evidence demonstrates that he lacks this experience, the grievance shall be denied.

Original Payroll Clerk Job Specification

On April 3, 1957, the Company prepared a job specification for Payroll Clerk in the Transmission and Distribution Department. Among other qualifications for this job, the Company specified, "some knowledge of accounting practices."

As the record shows, the Grievant held this classification for about three (3) years and four (4) months. If this experience is added to his two and one-half ($2\frac{1}{2}$) years as an Accountant, the Grievant would have qualified on this basis for the Senior Cost Accountant's job.

In about April 1969, the Company centralized its payroll function and discontinued the original Payroll Clerk job in the Transmission and Distribution Department. It prepared another job description styled "Central Payroll Clerk." In this job description, the Company did not specify "some knowledge of accounting practices."

Since the original Payroll Clerk job specification contained such a qualification requirement, it could be argued that while the Grievant served in that classification he performed accounting work. As H testified:

Q: I call your attention to the bottom of the page where the qualifications are, under the heading "Qualifications." I assume that is the entry qualifications for the job?

A: For the Payroll Clerk job, yes.

Q: Would you read those, please, for the Arbitrator?

A: "Graduation from high school, or the equivalent. One year of clerical experience in the company. Some knowledge of accounting practices. Ability to handle multiplication and division."

Q: Now, in your discussion with the Company in the grievance procedure, were any of these qualifications significant to the Union's contention that Mr. L's time as a Payroll Clerk should be considered as qualifying him under the terms of the job description for the Cost Accountant?

A: Well, as I testified to, yes, that we had contended that this was one of the jobs which would help to qualify Mr. L in Accounting work, yes.

Q: And what part of that job description was significant in your mind in making that determination?

A: Well, the qualification is one of the significant things. . . .

On the surface, this would appear to be a reasonable and convincing position for the Union to take in this dispute. Why would the Company specify some knowledge of accounting practice if the Payroll Clerk did not actually engage in accounting work? If accounting work was not to be performed by the Payroll Clerk, it would follow that the Company would not have specified knowledge of accounting practice as a requirement for promotion to this job. Note that when the Company centralized its payroll position, it dropped such a requirement for entrance to the Payroll Clerk classification.

When asked why the Company originally specified a knowledge of accounting practice as a requirement for the Payroll Clerk job, G, one-time Supervisor of the T & D Payroll Section, could not produce a satisfactory answer. He testified:

Q: Would you know, then, from your knowledge of this particular job, why knowledge of accounting practices was required as an entry qualification for a payroll clerk?

A: No. I really couldn't say, in fact, what that meant, because I know from experience, as just an example, that people were promoted into the Payroll group that had no prior accounting experience. And I believe that was possibly put in there to try to get some Company experience wherein they would learn the routines of the various functions so that this would be a help to them when they came into the department.

Now, I'm only surmising this, I don't know for a fact. But I can state for a fact that many of the clerks promoted into the Payroll group had no prior accounting experience. It wasn't really necessary, this was strictly copy work.

On the other hand, *the Union did not refute* the explicit declaration of G that employees were promoted to the Payroll Clerk job who had had no prior accounting experience. In other words, the Company ignored the accounting practice qualification when it awarded Payroll Clerk jobs to employees. It was in the job description, but it was ignored.

In this light, the fact that the Payroll Clerk job specification contained an accounting practice knowledge qualification does not demonstrate proof that the Grievant engaged in accounting work when he served in that classification. If the Grievant actually had performed accounting work duties, this must be proved by evidence separate from the character of the original Payroll Clerk job specification.

Payroll Clerk Duties
and Accounting Work Experience

It is the Union's position that the Grievant's duties as a Payroll Clerk and as a Console Operator Programmer qualify as accounting work experience.

This argument, of course, raises the essential problem involved in this dispute. If the Grievant's experience as a Payroll Clerk and/or as a Console Operator Programmer is related to accounting work, he would have had sufficient qualifications for the Senior Cost Accounting job.

What then does the evidence demonstrate relative to the Grievant's work as a Payroll Clerk in terms of accounting work experience? In this respect, H testified that in his opinion, the Grievant's duties as a Payroll Clerk constituted accounting work within the meaning of the job specification in question. In this regard, he testified:

> The second part of it is I performed work as an auditor for [the Company] for several years, and during this time I performed the payroll on it within this department, and I further performed audits of the costs as they are established within the T & D Department. In my payroll audits, or my experience with that, I was able to note that all of the information which starts out within the Payroll Department culminates within the cost structure that is used by the senior accountant within that department. I feel that this is significant because it is a training, it is a training of the source information that every senior would have to go through in order to be able to make the determination within that job of what his results are and where his problems are when there is an error within that department.
>
> The job that we are discussing is the cost accountant's job, and his job basically is to pull together the costs of the T & D Department. Now, this is, of course, our linemen and our crews and the material that is used by these individuals, and to make the determination as to whether a crew, et cetera, is functioning under the—I guess you could call it the guidelines as set out by the Company, the standards that the Company attempts to have these crews meet.

And:

A: My opinion is that to understand the basic methods under which you account for your payroll, your cost of your payroll, the determinations that the amount of time as reported by the crews is in balance with the overall work-order structure of the department, is a very significant and important part of the accounting work that is done within the department.

Q: Is that why the Company would require some knowledge of accounting practices as an entry qualification into this job?

A: Yes.

Arbitrator: Well, to put it in a nutshell, your opinion is that work as a Payroll Clerk within the T & D Department constitutes accounting work within the meaning of the job specification?

A: Yes. And to go just one step further, based upon my experience and my opinion, I want to quote it as opinion that work within the department that you are going to be the Cost Accountant of is very important and very significant.

With full deference to the Union, the Arbitrator is fully satisfied, based on the evidence, that the Grievant's duties as a Payroll Clerk do not constitute accounting work within the meaning of this concept. It may have been helpful to an Accountant to be familiar with the duties performed by a Payroll Clerk. However, in all candor, to equate the Payroll Clerk's duties to accounting work would be entirely improper. . . . As we know, the Company in practice did not require prior knowledge of accounting when it promoted employees to the Payroll Clerk classification. Clearly, this was done because the day-to-day work of a Payroll Clerk did not require any knowledge whatever of accounting principles and/or practices.

What did the Grievant do as a Payroll Clerk when he served in this classification? Company Exhibit 9 and the testimony of G thereto establish what the Grievant did on a day-to-day basis.* Field employees prepare "Daily Time Reports." These reports show the kind of work performed by each employee, and the number of hours devoted to each job. Each day the Grievant prepared an "Intermediate Report" based upon the Daily Time Reports. To do this, he copied material data contained in the Daily Time Reports into the appropriate column printed on an Intermediate Report form. Then L added the number of hours spent on each job performed by the field employees. Based upon the Daily Time Reports, the Grievant also recorded each man's time into a payroll voucher, and also copied the number of vehicle hours into a transportation report.

Each month, the Grievant prepared a Monthly Payroll Distribution Summary. This report was based upon the Intermediate Reports. On the monthly report, the Grievant copied the number of hours devoted during the month to particular jobs. He then added the number of hours spent on each job to get a monthly time total. L added the total hours spent on each job on each day across the page to get a total monthly hourly record, and then added down the page the hours associated with each job for each day. To do this, the Grievant used an adding machine. After he completed the monthly report, it was forwarded to the General Accounting Office.

G explained the purpose of the Intermediate Report and Monthly Payroll Distribution Summary. He testified:

Q: So, then, what he is doing is summarizing the daily time reported accounts in an intermediate report.

A: That's true. And the purpose of that was to balance the hours as shown on the intermediate report to the paid hours on the payroll. Once that is balanced, then the accounts indicated on the intermediate distribution were copied to the appropriate date on the monthly distribution. At the end of the month, this is totaled and forwarded to the payroll section of the General Accounting Department.

Q: So the monthly distribution, then, he copies from his intermediate totals onto pages 8 and 9 of this Exhibit?

---

*Beyond the duties described in the following discussion, the grievant also handled absentee and overtime reports. These duties, of course, have no relation to accounting work.

A: Yes.

Q: Did he do anything with the handling of these accounts other than copy them from one page to the other?

A: No, he had no knowledge.

Q: Is this a typical illustration of the work that the Payroll Clerk did?

A: Yes, it is. It's typical.

Arbitrator: He would fill out pages 8 and 9, right?

A: Yes. This is right.

Arbitrator: Make all the totals down at the bottom of the page?

A: Yes. They are provided with adding machines, and they just do this account by account, strike a total, and then enter that on the intermediate distribution and balance to the paid hours.

In all candor, these duties are not accounting work. What L's work amounted to was the copying of hours in appropriate columns on the daily and monthly reports and the addition of these totals. It is true that he was required to make sure the hours were entered correctly as to the kind of job performed; to be neat in his work; and to make sure that his addition was correct. Such tasks, however, are clearly clerical in nature and in no way could be termed accounting work.

An Accountant does more than enter figures in proper columns and make additions. Note, for example, the job duties of a Cost Accountant (not *Senior* Cost Accountant). These duties are:

> Under direct but not constant supervision, to perform responsible assignments in connection with accumulating, computing, and analyzing information as related to work performance and budgetary requirements in the Transmission and Distribution Division. Also, as required, to serve as leader in assigning and reviewing the work of clerks and other employees. In this connection to perform details of work, such as:
>
> > Accumulate, prepare, and maintain cost, expenditure, and statistical data. Assist in the preparation of the annual Transmission and Distribution Budget.
> >
> > Collate information from accounting and statistical records.
> >
> > Assist in making special studies of work performance and cost results in various Transmission and Distribution work groups.
> >
> > Prepare reports on the above as assigned.

How can it be argued reasonably that the work the Grievant did compares with the duties performed by a Cost Accountant? Among other items of difference, perhaps the outstanding one is that an Accountant must *analyze* data. In no way did the Grievant analyze data when he served as a Payroll Clerk.

In short, accounting work requires much more than the mechanical recording of data and the addition of various series of figures.

The Arbitrator simply cannot find that work the Grievant performed as a Payroll Clerk constituted "accounting work" in the commonsense and professional meaning of the concept. Clearly, to perform effectively as a Payroll Clerk, an employee did not require academic training in accounting. At the very best, a high school education only was required. Whereas accounting work puts a significant intellectual demand upon an individual, involving the exercise of discretion and judgment, the work L performed was routine and mechanical in nature, and required a minimal amount of intellectual effort.

Console Operator Programmer Duties and Accounting Work

The Union also believes that the duties the Grievant performed as a Console Operator Programmer constituted accounting work. In this respect, H testified:

> The Console Operator Programmer job that Mr. L had within the Data Processing Department involved two areas of application. One was the stores section, and the other was the T & D section. Now, I have discussed this in my investigation for my third-step meeting, and in connection with today's hearing, and the knowledge and accounting background L possesses, I will admit that he is not required to have it to program. If the individual's department establishes exactly what the program is, there is no need to understand the accounting that is required. However, Mr. L, in his job and in his function as a programmer, and when he operated within the T & D Department, certainly had to be exposed to, and to work with, the accounting principles that are established within that department. And I feel that this, in itself, in working with these procedures, and some of the jobs of the Senior Cost Accountant, as an example, of working on the rejects list, and making determinations of what the predetermined accounts—the accuracy of the predetermined accounts, which must all be programmed by the individual doing the program in the Data Processing Department.

On the other hand, A, Supervisor of Data Processing, explained the exact duties of the Grievant as a Console Operator Programmer. There is no need to detail his testimony for purposes of this case. In no way does the Grievant's work as a Console Operator Programmer constitute accounting work. He works with computers, and such duties simply are not equated in any way whatsoever with accounting work. To find otherwise would be highly improper, and would constitute a breach of the Arbitrator's responsibilities.

Conclusions

The facts show that the Grievant lacked the necessary experience in accounting work when he bid on the job in question. Whereas he performed accounting work for about two and one-half (2½) years, the job specification requires four (4) years. Over the years, the Company applied this requirement uniformly and consistently. As the previous discussion has abundantly demonstrated, the work the Grievant performed as a Payroll Clerk and Console Operator Programmer is in no way comparable to accounting work. The Union made a valiant effort to substitute such experience for actual accounting work. Though he respects its judgment, the Arbitrator cannot possibly find on the evidence that such duties constitute accounting work as the concept is used in its professional sense.

Under the facts in this case, the Arbitrator simply cannot hold that the Grievant had sufficient qualifications to claim the job within the meaning of Article 13, Section 10. The Union has not demonstrated by competent proof that the four-year accounting work qualification is unreasonable or that it was not uniformly applied. Under these circumstances, the Arbitrator would exceed the powers conferred upon him under the Labor Agreement to reduce the qualifications for the Senior Cost Accountant job. In effect, the Union requests that the Arbitrator should award the job to the Grievant even though he substantially lacks the work experience required by the job description. If he did this, it would be the same in principle as if in another proceeding the Arbitrator would hold that a senior employee would be required to show more qualifications than established in a job specification. In either case, the Arbitrator would abuse the authority he derives from the Labor Agreement.

QUESTIONS

1. How did the arbitrator handle the union argument that under the material provision of the labor agreement, Article 13, Section 10, an employee must possess qualifications "generally" set forth in the job specifications?
2. Why was the union adamant in its position that the grievant's work as a payroll clerk be counted as experience in accounting? What reasoning did the arbitrator employ to reject this argument?
3. Do you believe that, as in this case, the employer should have the unilateral right to establish the qualifications for a job? Why, or why not?
4. What major principle of the arbitration process is demonstrated in this case? Explain your answer.

The following two cases involved the discharge of an employee. Discharge cases are obviously very important to all concerned, and are among the most difficult for an arbitrator to decide. No type of case exceeds discharge disputes in terms of human drama and of employers' rights, since what is at stake is an employee's livelihood and his reputation, and the employer's right to discipline so as to maintain an orderly plant operation.

Both cases involve the question of theft, Case 12 dealing with the issue of attempted theft, and Case 13 with the charge of actual theft. Unauthorized removal of employer property is a leading problem in industry, but, as these cases show, arbitrators normally demand evidence that proves the offense beyond a reasonable doubt—a higher level of proof than is required in other discharge cases—since the sustaining of a discharge based upon an offense involving moral turpitude gravely injures the employee's reputation and would seriously affect his opportunity to be hired by another employer. As you analyze these cases, determine in your mind whether or not the employers had sufficient evidence to prove conclusively that the employees were guilty of the offenses for which they were discharged.

CASE 12
Attempted Theft
of Drums of Paint:
A Case of Conspiracy To Steal

Cast of Characters

B	Discharged employee
F	Industrial relations manager
H	Plant production manager
W	Another employee (forklift driver) involved in incident
P	Security guard
S	Pickup truck driver (not a company employee)
Z	General foreman
M	Superintendent
Y	Foreman
L	Another foreman
G and A	Union stewards

This case involved the discharge of B, charged by the company with the offense of "attempting to take unauthorized material from the plant." In protest against the discharge, B filed Grievance No. 087-351, dated October 10, 1972, which stated:

> On Monday of this week, F and H accused me of taking paint. On a situation before I had taken the same steps in obtaining a pass for three drums of paint. I had no intentions of possessing the material without a pass. H had given me a pass before for three drums. These drums, in the last situation, were loaded on a truck with the understanding that a pass would be got from the proper source. They had not and were not going to leave the plant without a pass. The driver of the truck agreed to do me a favor in hauling the drums for me. I asked W to load the drums for me. I had joked with the guard about taking them without a pass. Joking was the only purpose, knowing that the guard required a pass before anything leaves the plant. I had not taken anything from Company property and had no intention to do so. We were not hiding from anyone or concealing anything that belonged to the Company. Men were working in the area where the loading took place and a pass was to be obtained. I feel the Company is trying to place and pin a case on me because they say material has been stolen.

As a remedy, the grievant requested reinstatement in his job, with full back pay and restoration of his seniority rights.

Under Article III of the labor agreement, the company had the right to "discharge for cause."

Also material to the case was the following notice, posted by the company on March 16, 1971 (for convenience, referred to hereafter as the Company Rule):

PERMANENT NOTICE

TO: ALL EMPLOYEES

SUBJECT: Passes for Material Taken from the Plant

Previous bulletins on this subject were issued on August 29, 1955, November 1, 1960, and August 17, 1965. Since many new employees have been hired since then and older employees may have forgotten the contents of these bulletins, it is being reissued.

Employees taking paint, tools, equipment, or any other Company-owned material from the plant *must* have a pass signed by a supervisor in the department *giving or issuing the material*. Passes will be filled out in ink and will show the employee's name and department and the material being taken out. The pass should be dated the day the material is taken from the plant.

Passes are to be presented to the guard at Gate #2 as you leave the Company's premises with the material. If the guard is not on duty, the pass should be presented to the Personnel Department. A record of passes will be maintained by the Personnel Department.

Gate #2 or through the Manufacturing Offices Building are the only two (2) authorized exits to be used for taking materials from the plant. Employees from the Main Office and from Product Development may use the street or sidewalk to approach Gate #2, but passes must be presented for materials.

Any person using any plant exit other than those outlined above with material will be dismissed.

Any material taken from the plant is for your own use, and *is not to be sold or given away*. It is the privilege of the guard and/or the Personnel Department to inspect any package to determine its contents. The package contents must agree with the pass. All scrap paint, solvents, resins, etc., that are given to employees must have a "scrap paint" label.

Any employee that obviously abuses the privilege will become ineligible to receive further passes.

Stealing is a violation of Company Rules, and any guilty person will be dismissed.

The basic question to be determined in this arbitration was as follows:

Under the circumstances of this case, was B discharged for cause? If not, what should the remedy be?

BACKGROUND

Before his discharge, the grievant had worked for the company for about three and one-half years. At the time of his discharge, he was classified as a pumper-receiver. He testified that he was earning $14,000 per year before the discharge.

On October 9, 1972, at about noon, the grievant and P, a security guard and an employee of the company, had a conversation in the guardhouse. As to this conversation, P testified:

> B asked me to do him a favor. He said he wanted to take two drums of scrap paint from the plant. He told me the drums were in the dump,* and that the paint was no good and would be thrown away anyway. He said that he couldn't get a pass for the material, and asked me to let him take the material out without a pass.

Thereupon, the guard declared:

> I said "no." I told him I didn't want to get mixed up in a deal like this, and told him that he would have to get a pass.

To this, the grievant said "OK" and started to walk away. However, P declared:

> B called me back again, and told me that he could sell the paint for $25 per drum. He offered me $25 to let him take the material out without a pass. I told him that I would have to think about it, and would give him my answer after lunch.

According to P, the grievant returned to the guardhouse at about 12:30 P.M. and the guard agreed "to go through with the plan." He was advised by the grievant that S, an independent hauler, would remove the drums in a pickup truck.**

B also testified as to the content of the conversation he had with P on October 9. In this respect, he declared:

> At first it was my intention to take the drums out without a pass. I offered him the $25 at first. But then I spoke to P and he said it was not worth it. I agreed with him. I agreed with him that it was not worth it to take the drums out without a pass. I told him that I got a pass for material like this before, and that H† was not in his office, but I was sure that I could get a pass because I got one before. I told him that I agreed with him that it was not worth it before I made arrangements with S to haul the drums.

After the grievant left the guardhouse, P called F, the industrial relations manager, and told him of the conversation he had had with the grievant. After F received this information, he testified, he checked with Z, the general

---

*This was a plant area where drums of scrap paint were stored prior to being removed to an authorized landfill area outside the plant.

**S had hauled liquids for the company in his tank truck for about fifteen years.

†H was the plant production manager. Under Company policy, he was authorized to sign passes for employees to remove paint drums from the plant area.

foreman, and M, superintendent of traffic and purchasing, to determine whether or not either of them had issued a pass to the grievant for the drums in question. He declared that neither of them had given B a pass for the material.

Thereupon, F and H went to a building that overlooked the area in which scrap drums of paint were stored. Their purpose was to observe the grievant. They observed that a pickup truck (eventually identified as the one S drove into the plant) stopped at Building 38, a building not located at the scrap dump area. They saw the grievant pedal his bicycle to the same location. F testified that then they observed the truck and the grievant headed for Building 52, located in the area where paint drums were stored when they were returned from customers because of some deficiency in the product. Both supervisors were following the truck and the grievant when they made this observation.

At this point, F testified:

> We saw the grievant jump down from the pickup truck. We also saw an unidentified person with a forklift and S near the pickup truck. We approached the vehicle, and the forklift driver left hurriedly and went into a warehouse. H followed him into this building. On the pickup truck, there were four drums of paint.

According to F's testimony, he approached the grievant and asked to see the pass for the material. To this, B said, "I am going to get a pass." F asked, "From whom?" and B replied, "From Y."

F declared that he told the grievant, "You know damn well that Y is not authorized to give you a pass for drum lots," to which B replied, "L will give me a pass."

F and B proceeded to the supervisor's office and, on the way, met Y. When asked about a pass for the grievant to take out the material, Y said that he knew nothing about it. Meanwhile, the grievant seemed to have decided that he did not want to see L, and, continuing toward the office, said that about a year previously H had given him a pass to take two or three drums of paint out of the plant, and that H would give him a pass.

As to the encounter between the grievant and the two supervisors, B testified:

> We loaded the four drums in the truck when they came. I told them I was going to get a pass. I did not have an opportunity to get a pass because F demanded that I go to his office.

A meeting was then held in F's office, attended by company representatives F, H, and M. Besides the grievant, the union was represented by G, alternate chief steward, and A, steward. F declared that when A asked what was going on, the grievant replied:

> W* [the forklift driver] and me were loading scrap paint, and F and H came running up and took us.

F testified that he told the union representative what he had seen, and that W and B were suspended for "attempting to remove property from the plant."

On October 17, 1972, B's suspension was converted to a discharge in a letter written by F. It stated:

> On October 9, 1972, you were observed attempting to take unauthorized material from the plant. You were suspended indefinitely pending investigation of the case.

> As a result of this investigation, you are hereby terminated for violation of plant rules and established procedure for material passes, effective October 9, 1972.

> Please consider this the third-step answer to Grievance Number 087-351.

ANALYSIS OF THE EVIDENCE

The Critical Issue

The critical issue in this proceeding was to determine whether or not, on the basis of the evidence, the grievant intended to remove the four drums of paint from the plant area without authorization. As the Company Rule stated:

> Employees taking paint, tools, equipment, or any other Company-owned material from the plant *must* have a pass signed by a supervisor in the department giving or issuing the material.

It followed, therefore, that removal of or the intent to remove material owned by the company from the plant without a pass constituted a violation of the Company Rule. The company discharged the grievant because he was "observed attempting to take unauthorized material from the plant."

As the facts showed, the grievant did not take the drums from the plant area. On this basis, union counsel argued:

> The Grievant was discharged by the Company for attempting to remove four drums of paint from the premises of the employer without the necessary special permission so to do.

*After W was identified by the grievant, he was located by H. At first, W denied that he had anything to do with the drums, but when he was told that he had been identified by B, he came to the meeting but remained mute. Subsequently, W was reinstated on his job, but without back pay.

By memorandum from the Company dated October 17, 1972, the employer stated his position for the discharge, which is, "you are hereby terminated for violation of plant rules and established procedure for material passes, effective October 8, 1972."

The plant rule referred to, I presume, is the notice to all employees dated March 16, 1971. It provided for dismissal under two circumstances: (1) "Using any plant exit other than those outlined above," to wit, Gate #2 or through the manufacturing office building; (2) stealing.

The quick answer to either of the above grounds for dismissal is that B did not use an exit other than those described. He, in fact, used no exit at all.

As for stealing, the traditional definition is depriving a person of property with the intent to convert said property to the use of the person so taking.

B did not deprive the Company of its property, and whatever his intention may have been, the overt act of taking from the possession of the Company did not occur.

If B is guilty of any infraction, it would be that of violating "established procedure for material passes." Such procedure seems to be ill-defined and indefinite.

Under the belief that we should not go on the intent, but the actual fact, it is our position that B should not have been discharged and that he should be reinstated, and, since he seems to have violated no plant rules, with full seniority and back pay.

In the arbitrator's opinion, he wrote:

As lucid as this argument may be, the fact remains that if the evidence demonstrates that the Grievant intended to take the drums from the plant without permission, the Grievant violated the Company Rule. With full deference to Union Counsel, we reject his argument.

Clearly, if his intent to remove the paint without authorization is established beyond reasonable doubt, the Grievant stands in violation of the Company Rule, even though he did not actually remove the paint from the Company's premises. We understand that a person may have a subjective intent to do wrong, but take no overt action to commit the offense. Under these circumstances, an employee would not be properly disciplined. On the other hand, when the evidence establishes beyond a shadow of doubt that the employee took overt action to carry out his intent, he may be properly disciplined under the Company Rule. This remains true even though he does not actually remove the material from the Company premises because of interference by Company supervision.

In short, we must carefully search the evidence to determine whether or not the Grievant intended to remove the drums in question from the Company's premises without first attaining the necessary authorization. What does the evidence demonstrate in this respect?

Repeatedly, the Grievant testified in the arbitration and in his written grievance that he did not intend to remove the drums without first securing a pass. He tells us that he merely loaded the drums, and then he was going to obtain a pass. We agree with Union Counsel when he argues:

> There is no provision in the notice which provides that an employee must have a pass before he picks up the material. It is only that he may not take material off the premises without presenting a pass to the guard.

If what the Grievant tells us is true, the Grievant would be blameless. It could be that an employee would first load material on a truck, and then secure the proper pass. This procedure would not necessarily violate the Company Rule in question. If this were all there was to B's conduct, there would be no evidence that he intended to remove the paint without permission. The Grievant testified that about a year ago, he loaded some drums in a truck, and then secured a pass from H. After he received the pass, the material was hauled from the plant area. In other words, the Grievant tells us that what he did on October 9 was the same as he did a year ago. He loaded the drums on the truck, and then he was going to secure a pass. Therefore, he did not intend to remove the drums in an unauthorized manner. If his explanation holds up, there would be sufficient grounds to grant his grievance. As Union Counsel argues:

> B's testimony was that he had in the past gone to select the materials that he desired, and would then go get a pass. This does not seem unreasonable, since it is necessary to go through what you want before you ask for a pass describing it with the specificity required in the notice. That it was loaded on a truck before B was to go ask for a pass is not unreasonable in view of the fact that it is necessary to procure help from someone with a tow motor, in this case, to help load.

The Conspiracy

If the Grievant's explanation for his actions holds water, how do we account for the fact that a few hours or so before the drums were loaded on the truck, B offered P a bribe to permit him to remove the drums without a pass? As to this hard and obvious question, the Grievant testified that after he offered the bribe to P, the guard told him that it "was not worth it, and I [Grievant] agreed with him."

Thus, the Grievant admits that he tried to bribe the guard but that, upon the advice of the guard, he abandoned his intention to remove the paint without a pass. On this point, Union Counsel argues:

> There remains the conversation between B and the guard, P. B acknowledged that he offered to give the guard $25 if he would let him out the gate without a pass. B's testimony is that he and the guard decided that it was risky and foolish, and that the conspiracy was abandoned without an overt act. An abandoned conspiracy does not constitute stealing, and therefore, would not be grounds for dismissal.

> It is submitted that B was telling the truth with relation to these instances in full, if for no other reason than no one could make up such a story.

In short, it is the Grievant's testimony that he abandoned the conspiracy after he offered the guard a bribe. In the light of the evidence, we simply cannot credit the Grievant's testimony. In the first place, P does not corroborate the Grievant's testimony in this respect. As to this, the guard testified:

Q: You heard the Grievant's testimony where he said you told him that it was not worth it, and he agreed with you. Do you agree with that?

A: There was no such conversation to my recollection.

Added to this is the *objective fact* that after the Grievant left the guardhouse, P called F to inform him of his conversation with the Grievant. Clearly, if the Grievant had told P that the conspiracy was abandoned and that he was going to get a pass, how do we account for P's call to F? There is nothing in the record to demonstrate that P bore any animosity against the Grievant before the events of October 9 took place. Indeed, would P jeopardize his own job by passing false information to a Company official? What obviously occurred is that after P told B that he would go along with him in the conspiracy, the guard had second thoughts on the matter. At this point, P called F so as to extricate himself from the conspiracy. This, of course, was not known to the Grievant, and he proceeded on the basis that the drums would leave the plant under the conspiracy arrangement. Once P made the call, the trap was sprung, and B fell into it. This is the risk, however, anyone takes by engaging in a conspiracy. There is always the chance that one of the conspirators will get cold feet and blow the whole plan, with dire consequences to the others.

Beyond these considerations, there is another reason why we cannot credit the Grievant's testimony that he abandoned the conspiracy. Without refutation, P testified that he had a phone conversation with the Grievant a day or two after the events of October 9. The Grievant was in the arbitration room when the guard testified to the substance of the phone conversation. There was no separation of witnesses. As to this phone conversation, P declared:

He told me that I had nothing to worry about. He told me that my name had not been mentioned yet. He told me that he believed that he and the other fellow [W] were in the clear.

Indeed, if the conspiracy had been abandoned, why would it have been necessary for the Grievant to reassure the guard that he had nothing to worry about? Why would the Grievant have to tell the guard not to worry if, in fact, the conspiracy was abandoned?

Clearly, B tried to reassure the guard because as far as he knew the guard was implicated as much as he was in the plan to remove the drums without authorization. There is no other plausible explanation for the Grievant's comment to the guard that P "had nothing to worry about."

Also, it is curious that nothing in the record demonstrates that the Grievant told the Company, or for that matter the Union, that the conspiracy had been abandoned before he testified in this fashion in the arbitration. In his grievance, written one day after the events in question, there is no mention that the conspiracy was abandoned. Likewise, there is no showing that at any time before the arbitration, the Grievant told anyone that the conspiracy had been abandoned.

If there was evidence to demonstrate that the Grievant promptly told the Company that the conspiracy was abandoned, there would be a better basis to believe the Grievant's testimony in this respect. As far as the record shows, it is at the arbitration that we hear about the abandonment explanation for the first time. In all candor, B's testimony in this regard was to overcome the damaging testimony of the guard.

Overt Conduct To Implement Intent

In short, we find on the evidence that B and P arranged a conspiracy to get the drums out of the plant without permission. When B loaded the drums on the truck, he believed that the plan he had devised with the guard would be carried out. Clearly, this shows that B intended to take the drums out without the necessary pass. He did not know that P had called the Company to alert it about the plan. When he loaded the drums, he believed that P would play his part in the conspiracy.

Here we have evidence that the Grievant intended to carry out an unauthorized act in defiance of the Company Rule. It was not just a subjective intent, not to be carried out, but overt conduct to implement the Grievant's intent. Union Counsel, as noted, argues, ". . . we should not go on the intent, but the actual fact. . . ." The actual fact is that the Grievant offered the guard a bribe to permit him to take out the drums, and loaded the drums on the truck in preparation to get the drums out of the plant without authorization. He did not remove the drums, because the Company, informed of the conspiracy by P, prevented him from doing this.

No Pass Needed if Conspiracy Held Up

At one point in his testimony, B declared:

> If I did not get a pass, S* could not get out of the gate. I would have unloaded them if I didn't get a pass.

To the contrary, if P had kept up his end of the bargain, no pass would have been necessary. P would have permitted the removal of the drums without a pass. It is true that S testified:

> I know that you must have a pass to get out. I would not have left the area without a pass. I know a pass is needed.

This could have been arranged simply by the Grievant's telling the driver that he had given the pass to P. If the conspiracy held up, all that P had to tell S was that the Grievant had given the pass to him.

In any event, even if S had refused to move the drums unless he (S) physically saw a pass, this does not make the conduct of the Grievant any less offensive. By devising the conspiracy with the guard, and by loading the drums on the truck, the Grievant made an attempt to remove the drums from the plant area without authorization. This attempt stands separate and independent from whatever S may or may not have done.

*As noted, the grievant made arrangements for S to haul the drums in his pickup truck.

Contradictory Testimony

A sharp contradiction between the testimony of S and that of the Grievant indicates further that B intended to remove the paint without a pass. S testified:

> I asked B a number of times if he had legal authorization to take the paint out. He said, "I am authorized to remove the paint." I asked him this a number of times.

On the other hand, the Grievant testified:

> I told S that I would obtain a pass before the paint went out. I told him that I was sure that I would get a pass.

Note the difference in the testimony. The driver testified that the Grievant told him that he was authorized to take the paint out. The Grievant testified that he told the driver that he would obtain the pass. S's testimony is credible because it is consistent with the conspiracy that the Grievant had arranged with the guard. We have already established on the evidence that the Grievant did not abandon the conspiracy. When he spoke to S, he did not know, of course, that the guard had withdrawn from the plan, and had reported it to the Company. Hence, believing that the conspiracy was in effect, it follows that the Grievant would tell the driver that he was authorized to remove the drums. In short, S's testimony as to what the Grievant told him fits into the conspiracy plan, and this is added evidence that the Grievant intended to remove the paint without authorization.

The Issue of Mitigating Circumstances

On the basis of the analysis of the evidence, we find that beyond a reasonable doubt the Grievant intended to remove the paint in question from the plant premises without a pass. The Company proved that the Grievant committed the offense for which he was discharged. Without a shadow of doubt, the evidence conclusively demonstrates that the Grievant attempted "to take unauthorized material from the plant." This is a violation of the Company Rule. Indeed, the Company Rule has as its objective the prevention of removal of material by employees from the plant without authorization. This is the purpose of the Company Rule, and it was clearly violated by the Grievant.

What remains, therefore, is to determine whether or not the penalty of discharge is too severe under the circumstances of this case. At times, arbitrators, including the instant Arbitrator, reduce the penalty of discharge to a suspension even though an employer has proved the charges which resulted in an employee's discharge. This is done where there exist material mitigating circumstances which would make the penalty of discharge too severe. Are there such mitigating circumstances involved in this dispute?

As the record shows, the four (4) drums in question were located in an area used to store returned paint from the Company's customers because of deficiencies in quality. Such paint drums are distinguished with a letter "E," followed by a serial number. After testing in the laboratory, drums are then transferred to the scrap dump area provided it is determined that the paint cannot be worked over and brought up to the necessary standard of quality.

One of the drums involved in this case was designated "E-1799" and the other three were marked "E-1877." Each of the drums contained fifty-five (55) gallons of paint, and was of the baking enamel variety used for high-heat areas. F testified that the labor and material involved in the four drums of paint in question amounted to $980. He declared that the drum marked "E-1799" was recycled and eventually sold. As to the other three drums of paint, he declared:

> I don't know about the other three drums. If they went to the scrap dump, they would be of no value to us. If the drums in the scrap dump are hauled outside the plant to the authorized landfill area, this would be an expense to us.

On this basis, Union Counsel argues:

> The drums that were loaded into S's truck were rejected material that had been returned to the Company by the customer. The drums bore some sort of markings, known to B, indicating that they were unsatisfactory. My notes do not disclose it, but I think it is the letter "E" before a number. One drum bore the number E-1799 and three of them were E-1877. F, for the employer, was uncertain as to the final disposition of the four drums in question, but his recollection seemed to be that three of the drums were "dumped" and that one was recycled, but he was not sure.

In other words, the Union argues that the paint was of no value to the Company,* and that this should stand in mitigation of the Grievant's offense. If we give the Grievant the benefit of the doubt, the finding is that three drums went to the scrap dump and one drum was eventually sold. Using F's figure of $980 as the value of all four (4) drums, the remaining drum which was recycled amounted to $240 in terms of labor and material. From this figure, there should be deducted the cost (not established in the record) for hauling the three scrap drums from Company property.

In the last analysis, however, the value of the drums is not material to the case. The Company Rule in question applies to all Company property regardless of value. It does not say that employees may remove Company property which has no value from its premises without authorization. It makes no distinction between scrap paint and salable paint. The Rule states that no Company property shall be removed from its premises without a pass.** Therefore, the value of the paint the Grievant intended to remove from the Company premises without authorization may not be held to be in mitigation of his offense.

B testified that he desired the four drums of paint for use on a farm owned by himself and his brother-in-law jointly. It was to be used to paint barns and other buildings. Even though P testified that the Grievant told him that he intended to sell the paint, we need not for purposes of this case establish the motivation for the Grievant's conduct. Even if we credit the Grievant's testimony that the

*Note, however, that F testified that one drum was worked off and eventually sold.
**The Company Rule in this respect was not arbitrary or capricious. In the matter of paint, F explained why the Company does not desire its scrap paint to be sold or given away by its employees. The Rule is designed to control the disposition of scrap paint; that is why it required authorization to remove scrap paint. Beyond this, the simple fact is that the scrap paint is Company property, and the Company had full right to determine the disposition of its own property.

paint was only to be used on the farm and not sold, he still violated the Company Rule in question. It does not state that Company property can be removed without authorization when the employee intends to use the material on a personal basis. Therefore, we do not hold as a mitigating factor the use to which the Grievant intended to put the paint.

Nor do we find in mitigation the fact that about a year ago the Grievant received a pass to remove 2–3 drums of paint from the Company's premises. It would seem that the Union argues that all that B did on October 9 was what he did a year ago. That is, he loaded the paint and then was to secure a pass. We established beyond a reasonable doubt that the Grievant intended to remove the paint without authorization. A year ago he obtained a pass; on October 9 he did not intend to obtain a pass for the material.

We also considered whether or not the Company discriminated against the Grievant. As the record shows, W helped the Grievant load the paint on the truck. It developed that W was not discharged, but was reinstated without back pay.* This was a reasonable judgment on the part of the Company, since the roles of the Grievant and W were quite different. It was the Grievant and not W who conceived the plan to remove the drums. Also, we have the Grievant's testimony that "I asked W to load the truck for me. He did what I told him to do." Apparently, on the day in question, W, assigned to the forklift job on a temporary basis, was under the control of B.

After his services were suspended for about a week while the Company conducted an investigation, S returned as an independent contractor to haul for the Company. There is no evidence that S was part of the conspiracy. Note that the Grievant testified that he told him that he would get a pass for the material. Also, note the testimony of S that he asked the Grievant if he had the authority to remove the paint, and that the Grievant assured him that all was legal.

In short, we do not find that the Company discriminated against the Grievant, and this factor cannot be held in mitigation of his offense.

Conclusions

On the basis of the evidence, the finding must be that the Grievant intended to remove four (4) drums of paint from the Company's premises without authorization. His conduct, therefore, is in violation of the Company Rule in question. We find no mitigating factors which could be used to lessen the penalty. The Company exercised its right under the Labor Agreement to discharge for cause in a proper manner. Its proof was sufficient to demonstrate that the Grievant did commit the offense for which he was discharged.

At the heart of the Arbitrator's decision is the finding that the Grievant never did abandon the conspiracy he arranged with the guard. Beyond his own testimony in this respect, there is not a scrap of evidence which corroborates his story. On the other hand, there is sufficient evidence to corroborate the guard's testimony that the conspiracy was not abandoned by the Grievant. Such corroboration consists of the guard's phone call to F; the Grievant's assurance to P that the guard had nothing to worry about; S's testimony that

---

*Surely, W believed that there was something wrong. Why else did he flee when H and F arrived on the scene? The Union said that he did this because he was frightened. If all was sweet innocence, he had no need to be frightened or to flee.

the Grievant said he had authorization to remove the paint when in fact he did not; and the fact that nothing in the record demonstrates that the Grievant told anybody in the Company or Union that he had abandoned the conspiracy until he told this story at the arbitration.

We recognize, of course, the seriousness of the Grievant's discharge under the circumstances of this case. The Arbitrator takes no personal joy in this decision, since he fully understands the significance of the discharge to B and his family. On the other hand, the Grievant committed a very serious offense, and to exonerate the Grievant or reduce his penalty under the evidence would be a masterpiece of error. If justice is to be tempered by mercy, this action must come from the Company and not the Arbitrator.

QUESTIONS

1. Since the company did not discharge W, the forklift driver, shouldn't the arbitrator have reinstated the grievant without back pay so that the penalties between the two employees would have been the same?
2. Do you believe that P, the guard, was telling the truth when he testified that the conspiracy between the grievant and himself was not abandoned?
3. Unlike the arbitrator, do you find mitigating circumstances that should have been used to reduce the penalty from discharge to suspension?
4. If the company believed the grievant was guilty of attempting to steal the paint, why did it not have him arrested and charged with the offense under criminal law?

CASE 13
The Case
of the Stolen Wieners

Cast of Characters

K	Discharged employee
P	Employee (owner of car in which wieners were found)
L	Personnel manager
W	Foreman
S	Supervisor
D	Employee who reported theft
M	Another supervisor
N	Union steward
R	Another union steward

This dispute involved the discharge of K, charged with the theft of two boxes of company wieners. In protest against his discharge, K filed a grievance, dated September 15, 1971, which stated:

On Monday September 13, 1971, I was arrested on a complaint from the Company and discharged by the Company for alleged theft.

I am innocent of this charge.

I was unjustly discharged by reason of my innocence.

As a settlement to this grievance, I demand that I be reinstated with full seniority rights and all pay lost as a result of my dismissal be restored to me.

Relevant to the case was the following provision of the labor agreement:

ARTICLE 16

Nothing in this Agreement shall be construed as preventing the Employer from discharging an employee for just cause, but no employee covered by this Agreement shall be discharged by the Employer except for just cause.

The basic question in this dispute was as follows:

Under the circumstances of this case, was K discharged for just cause? If not, what should the remedy be?

BACKGROUND

The circumstances of this case took place in the company's sausage plant at about 11 P.M. on Saturday, September 11, 1971. K, the grievant, reported for work that evening at 7:30 P.M. At about 11 P.M., K left the plant on break time through a door located in the shipping and loading-dock area. He entered a car belonging to P, another employee who was working the same shift. This vehicle was stationed in the company's parking lot, a portion of which was located adjacent to the shipping and loading-dock area and illuminated by two large spotlights. In this respect, L, the personnel manager, testified:

Q: And are there any spotlights, some lighting?

A: Yes. There is a double set—or I should say a set of spotlights is located at the top of the building right at the corner of the building. And then there is another set in about this area of the building. And there are a few small lights dotted in between, three of them actually. But these are the giant-size floodlights that light up certain areas of the parking lot. Particularly the areas right here at the corner and from the—these are parking spaces. . . .

K declared that P's car was located under one of the two large spotlights.

K remained in P's car for five or six minutes and then returned to the plant. To enter the plant, he had to go to the main entrance, because the shipping-area door locked from the inside. While returning to the plant, K encountered W, a foreman.

This supervisor left the employment of the company about one month before the arbitration and did not testify in the proceedings. However, S, another supervisor, questioned W about the circumstances of the night in question and related the results of their conversation. S testified that W said all he saw was K getting out of the car.

D, another employee, was working the same shift as K. D was scheduled to end his shift at 11:30 P.M., but he finished his work shortly before 11 P.M. and received permission from his foreman to leave the plant.

Without changing clothes, D left the plant through the main entrance. He established that he left the plant "about two or three minutes to eleven, something like that."

D proceeded through the parking lot to a staircase adjacent to a driveway located next to the parking lot, because his wife was scheduled to pick him up there at 11:30 P.M.

The substance of D's testimony was that he observed K placing two boxes of company wieners into P's automobile. He reported the incident to Foremen S and M, who were inside the plant. D testified as to why he reported the incident:

Q: Mr. D, why did you—when you got into the parking lot there, why did you go back into the plant to report what you saw?

A: Well, for one thing I care about my job. For one thing. I mean I feel that although I'm in the union and he was in the union it was just bad business. That's all there was to it.

As to his identification of K, D declared:

Q: You are sure it was K?

A: I am sure it was K.

Q: Was there anybody else in the parking lot besides you?

A: Nobody but me. I was the first one out. Everybody else was changing clothes.

And:

Q: Did you, on September the 11th, 1971, about 11 P.M., see K in the parking lot?

A: I did.

Q: Did you see him put something in a car?

A: I did.

Q: Is there any question in your mind on that?

A: No, there's no question in my mind.

And further:

No, there was no doubt in my mind. If there was, I wouldn't be here.

After D reported the incident to supervision, he accompanied S to the car in question. On the way to the car, D and S passed K and W. D and S arrived at the car, and in this respect, S testified:

Q: Now, you said "by the car." What kind of a car was it?

A: Well, it was a blue Oldsmobile. I'm not sure of the year now.

Q: How did you know what car to stand by?

A: Well, D took me up there and showed me the area. And I walked over to the car and looked in the window and could see some boxes on the floorboard.

Q: Just describe what you saw when you looked in the window.

A: Well, I couldn't see much of anything. I could see the corner of a cardboard box with the general shape and dimensions of a wiener box.

Q: And was the box fully visible or was it covered?

A: No. It was covered by a rag or a blanket or something.

Q: And where was it in the car?

A: On the back floorboard behind the driver's seat.

At this point, S gave permission to D to leave the plant area, and he left with his wife. W joined S at the car, and S asked him to remain at that location while he went into the plant to get K. S declared:

> Well, I went back in the building to get K. I went back in the building and found him and asked him if he would come with me. And he agreed and came back to the automobile. I asked him to open the door and he did open the door. And then I pointed to the wieners and asked him how they got there. And he said he didn't know and stood there just a minute longer. . . .

And:

Q: Do you recall him saying something about what he was doing in the car?

A: The only thing I can recall is he said he went to the car to get something.*

After these events, S asked K to remain at the car while he called a security guard. K refused, insisting that he wanted the services of his union steward. S declared that K started "to walk fast or run back into the building."

S remained by the automobile, and a guard arrived at the scene. Shortly after, K returned with his union steward, N. Also, P and his union steward, R, arrived at the car. After some conversation between S and the guard, the police were called. Upon their arrival, the police officers asked some questions of the persons who were at the scene of the car. S testified that the police

---

*As will be developed below, K testified that he went to P's car to look at some magazines.

gave him the wieners and that the two boxes were marked and put into the cooler in the laboratory.

On Monday, September 13, 1971, the police arrived with a warrant for the arrest of K. Subsequently, he was tried in county court and acquitted of the charge of theft of the wieners in question.

K was discharged by the company effective September 13. In this respect, L declared:

Q: When was K discharged?

A: He was discharged in the conference room in the presence of a number of individuals. . . .

Q: When was he discharged?

A: As he reported for work.

Q: And the grounds for discharge?

A: Removing property from the premises, company property.

Q: Stealing wieners? Theft?

A: Theft.

POSITION OF THE PARTIES

The position of the company was that the grievance should be denied, while the position of the union was that it should be granted. Portions of their post-hearing briefs, where necessary and appropriate, will be cited below.

ANALYSIS OF THE EVIDENCE

Some General Observations

In a discharge case, the employer bears the burden of proof. The rule is that the employee is not required to prove himself not guilty, but rather the employer, by competent evidence, must prove that the employee committed the offense charged by the employer. It is also recognized that when the offense charged against the employee involves an act of moral turpitude, such as theft, professional and experienced arbitrators require proof that is beyond a reasonable doubt. In *How Arbitration Works*, a standard and authoritative study of labor arbitration, we find the following:

> In fact, arbitrators have often recognized that proof beyond a reasonable doubt should be required where the alleged offense involves an element of moral turpitude or criminal intent. Moreover, where the offense is of this type, management may be required to prove, by a high degree of proof, both the commission of the act and the existence of criminal intent. When, however, the alleged offense is not one that is recognized by the criminal law or does not otherwise involve moral turpitude, Arbitrator Benjamin Aaron has urged

vigorously that proof beyond a reasonable doubt should not be required by arbitrators.*

In this case, since the charge involved theft, the company had to produce the quality of proof that would establish the guilt of K beyond a reasonable doubt. And if it did, the fact that the value of the wieners amounted to only about $24 wholesale and $33 retail would not stand in mitigation of the grievant. The value of the stolen material is not material to the penalty.

In addition, if the company sustains its burden of proof, it is not material that the grievant had a clean record as an employee and was not previously charged with theft or dishonesty. Under proper circumstances, an employee may be discharged, and his discharge sustained in arbitration, even though he has had no previous disciplinary record.

As the record showed, K was tried and acquitted in the county court of the offense involved in this proceeding. Counsel differed widely as to how the arbitrator should consider this feature of the case. Union counsel argued:

> This brings us back, then, to where we began and where the case ends for the Company—the uncorroborated word of D against that of his fellow employee K. This was not good enough in Criminal Court. D was not believed over K there either, and K was acquitted of the criminal charge brought by the Company.

> The Company understandably objected to the evidence offered by the Union showing the acquittal of grievant in the criminal proceeding brought by the Company. The arbitrator correctly admitted this evidence for his consideration. Where, as here, the Company was the charging party which sponsored and actively pursued the criminal charges, definite weight must be given the Court acquittal. Where further, as here, the same evidence was presented by the same key witness, D, in an attempt to convict the grievant, the matter reaches a point where the acquittal itself raises reasonable doubt as to the guilt of the grievant.

On his part, company counsel argued:

> Nor should the determination in the criminal case brought against K have any bearing on this arbitration proceeding. With regard to any contention that this arbitration should be governed by the outcome of the criminal proceeding, it is respectfully submitted that the issue presented here [i.e., whether the company had "just cause" for discharging the grievant] was not the issue in the criminal proceeding. In addition, the criminal proceeding was between the State and the grievant. The Company was not a party to that proceeding and could exercise no control over the prosecution of the grievant.

Each attorney cited convincing arbitration precedent for his argument on this feature of the case. As to this issue, the arbitrator found that the court

*Frank Elkouri and Edna A. Elkouri, *How Arbitration Works* (Washington, D.C.: Bureau of National Affairs, 1960), p. 418.

proceeding in question was not binding upon him. An arbitration is not the same as a court proceeding. In this case, the issue was whether the company had *just cause* to discharge the grievant; in the court proceeding, the issue was whether the state could convince the court to *imprison and/or fine* the grievant. The decision that a previous court proceeding should not be given weight in an arbitration protects the interests of the employee and the employer.

> Indeed [wrote the arbitrator], if the Court had found K guilty, Union Counsel would undoubtedly have argued that the Court action should not be binding upon this Arbitrator. In short, if there exists reasonable doubt that K was guilty of theft, such doubt is not established from the Court proceeding.

The Case against the Grievant

In this case, therefore, the basic question was whether there existed reasonable doubt that the grievant stole the merchandise in question. If there was no reasonable doubt, the arbitrator would sustain the discharge; if there was reasonable doubt, he would grant the grievance.

Several elements in the record served to establish the guilt of the grievant. He had the opportunity to steal the product. As he testified, on his walk through the plant to leave through the shipping-department door, he passed the cooler where the products of the company were stored:

> I walked back through the kitchen area, through the packaging area, and out into the cooler to go out the back way.

Also, the grievant admitted that he was in the same automobile in which the wieners were found. It could be argued that it was not just coincidental that K happened to be in the very car that contained the stolen merchandise. Why should he have been in this car to spend his break?

Added to these circumstances was the testimony of D, who declared unequivocally that he saw K put the wieners into the automobile. The arbitrator was satisfied that D told the truth as he saw the truth. His motive in reporting the incident to supervision was not involved. He testified that he saw K commit the theft and that he felt he had an obligation to report the incident to the company. On the record, the arbitrator had no cause to impute any other motive to D. Would D risk perjury penalties in his appearance before the court and in this arbitration if he had fabricated his story?

In addition, the record showed that after S called the wieners to the grievant's attention, K refused to wait at the car until the supervisor called a security guard. Instead, he either walked fast or ran into the plant to get his union steward. Although it may be that K panicked when S showed him the wieners, the grievant's conduct in this respect did not add up to innocence.

Thus, there was evidence pointing to the guilt of the grievant even though, of course, he denied the theft.

The "Girlie" Magazines:
The Grievant's "Alibi"

If the grievant did not offer any plausible explanation for his presence in P's car at the time in question, there would have been substantial reason to believe that he had entered the automobile for the purpose of placing in it the two boxes of wieners. According to K, however, he entered the car for an innocent purpose—to view some "girlie" magazines that P kept in the vehicle.

K testified that at about 10:45 P.M., he requested permission from P to view his collection:

Q: So then we come up to a quarter till eleven. And please describe your conversation with P, and who was present or about.

A: Okay. Well, I walked back through the packaging area and back into the kitchen where they were cleaning up. And I knew where P was or where he worked. So I naturally went right to him. And R just happened to be over there. I don't know exactly, you know, what he was doing. He just happened to be there. And I asked P if he had any magazines out in his car. And he said somebody had been looking at them and he doesn't know for sure, you know, whether they put them back or not but I could go out and take a look if I wanted to.

Q: R was nearby?

A: Yes, sir.

Q: All right. Then what did you do?

A: I asked if it was locked. He said, "No, it isn't." He said, "I never lock my car."

Q: All right.

A: So I just immediately turned and went on out. I went through the kitchen through the packaging area, and through the back of the cooler, and out the rear entrance, which was close to where P's car was. Because he had told me previously where it was.

In another portion of his testimony, the grievant described the character of the magazines contained in P's car:

Q: After you got in the car— What kind of books? Just casually describe the girlie books. I wish you would have brought them.

A: Well, they were just women, you know, in various stages or poses, dresses, undressed, you know. Some with guys, some with other girls. You know. They were just dirty books. That's all.

R corroborated the grievant's testimony that he asked permission of P to enter his automobile to view the magazines. He testified:

A: Well, sir, K had come back where P was working when I was standing there talking to P. . . .

Q: You heard K ask P?

A: Yes, sir.

Q: What did you hear K ask P?

A: If he had the magazines. . . .

Q: And what did P say? Or relate the conversation as you heard it.

A: Really, I can't remember exactly whether P said they were or not. But he did say, he said, "Go look."

P did not testify in the arbitration, but there was additional testimony that he granted permission to K to enter his car and look at his magazines. When the police arrived at the car, there were present P and R, as well as other persons. R testified as to the issue:

A: They walked— First I believe it was the sergeant of the police force came up and wanted to know whose automobile it was. And P—at this point was the first time P had ever said one word. And he said, "It's my car." He asked him, he said, "Do you have the keys to your car?" He said, "Yes, sir." He said, "Was it locked?" He said, "No, sir." He asked him, he said, "Do you know anything about the articles in the car?" He said, "No, sir." He asked him if he did give K permission to go to his car. And he said, "Yes, sir."

Arbitrator: This is the police sergeant you are talking about?

A: Yes, sir.

Q: He said, "Yes, he gave K permission to go to his car?"

A: Yes, sir. . . .

K testified that he entered the car and found the magazines under the front seat. He declared further that when he was in the car, he did not look back to the rear area. In any event, K declared that he remained in the car for five or six minutes viewing the magazines.

In short, K offered a plausible explanation for his presence in the car in question. However, his explanation in this respect would be meaningful only if the analysis of other features of this case shed doubt upon his guilt. And the arbitrator would wonder why the grievant decided to view P's collection *at the very time that P's car proved to be the depository for the stolen merchandise.* It could have been a mere coincidence, and perhaps K's penchant for viewing pornographic literature made him an innocent victim of circumstances, but it appeared very strange. In any event, it remained to be seen whether or not a reasonable doubt existed as to his guilt in terms of the evidence offered by the company to prove its charge.

D's Delay in the Identification of K

Even though the arbitrator was fully convinced that D told the truth as he saw the truth when he identified K as the thief, there were elements to be considered before his identification could be accepted as the proof needed by the company to establish the guilt of the grievant beyond a reasonable doubt.

According to the testimony of D, he observed the grievant placing the wieners in the car when he was in the parking lot. D testified that he had left the plant by the main entrance, which was located about 255 feet from the location of P's automobile, and had walked about 150 feet when he observed K placing the stolen merchandise into P's car.

On this basis, D was about 100 feet from the car when he saw K placing the wieners in the car. As stated, the area was illuminated by two large flood-lights, sufficient for K, according to his testimony, to look at the magazines. Also, K testified that the lighting condition was sufficient for a person to see somebody else between 100 and 200 feet away.

On this basis, the conclusion was clear that D saw a person put the wieners into P's automobile. This person, D declared without any doubt in his mind, was K.

In this light, the arbitrator wondered why *D did not immediately identify K when he reported the incident to Foremen S and M*. Note the testimony of D in this respect:

A: Well, I came back in the front door where I came out, you know, the first time. And I cut through this door right here, which is the main office. And I went through another door here, which is the foremen's office. And that's where S and M was doing the paper work.

Q: And then what happened?

A: Then I told S that there was *a fellow* out there *putting wieners in his car....* [Emphasis supplied.]

Note also the testimony of S:

Well, I was in the foreman's office. About eleven o'clock, D came in the office and told M and I that there was *someone* in the parking lot stealing wieners. [Emphasis supplied.] And we talked for a second and tried to clear it up. I didn't understand whether he meant they were doing it now or they had done it a few minutes before. And he said, "No. If you go out there now you'll probably catch him."

At this point, D did not specify that it was K whom he saw. Rather, he identified the person he observed putting the wieners in the car as "a fellow" and/or "someone." The obvious question was this: If D was positive beyond a reasonable doubt that it was K whom he observed, why did he not tell the supervisors that it was K? D was anxious that the guilty party be apprehended. He was positive that it was K. So why use terms such as "a fellow" or "someone" instead of stating it was K?

The failure of D to name K as the thief when he originally reported the incident to the supervisors tended to establish some doubt in the arbitrator's mind as to D's identification of K.

Indeed, it was not until D and S were proceeding to the car, and passed W and K returning to the plant, that D identified K. This was *after* D had reported the incident to the supervisors. S testified:

> ... I proceeded out of the building with D. And we walked up the sidewalk. And as we walked up the sidewalk walked past W and K. And we proceeded on up to the area, well, to the area where D was taking me.
>
> And I said, "Where is he? I don't see anybody now." And he said, "Well, there he goes there." And I turned around and I said, "You mean W?" And he said, "No. No." And then I said, "You mean K?" And he said, "Yeah. That's the guy."

In other words, after D first identified the guilty party to S as "a person" and/or "someone," he then saw K face to face. At this point, he identified K as the person he saw putting the wieners in the car. He did not identify K when he originally reported the incident, even though he had no reason to conceal the guilty party's name at that time. This bothered the arbitrator, creating doubt as to whether or not it was K whom D saw putting the wieners into the car.

A Case of Mistaken Identity?

In the last analysis, the company's case rested upon the identification by D of K as the thief. Without such identification, the company had no case. In this regard, note the testimony of S:

Q: It is true, isn't it, Mr. S, that the only thing you have to link K to putting those wieners in the car is the word of D?

A: Yes, sir.

The arbitrator's decision read, in part:

> In cases of this sort, there is always a problem when an employer bases a discharge upon the identification by a single witness. The problem is that the witness could be mistaken in his identification even though he believes in his own mind that the person he identified committed the theft. Hence, the possibility exists that some other person had committed the theft. After all, we are involved with artificial lighting, no matter how brightly the spotlights illuminated the area; and D was about 100 feet away from the car when he saw the theft being committed. He was not at as close range as when he saw K face to face when he passed K going to the car with S.
>
> These observations are not to be taken lightly under the circumstances of this case. Note that the wieners were found in P's automobile. If K in fact is the guilty party, the Arbitrator wonders why he would have put the wieners in P's automobile. Nothing in the record demonstrates an adequate explanation for this strange event. It would seem reasonable that as part of its proof the Company would offer a plausible explanation. ... The Company did not, and the Arbitrator is at a loss to understand why K would do this, if, in fact, K was

the thief. Unless there was a conspiracy between P and K, we frankly wonder why the Grievant would have selected P's car as the depository for the stolen merchandise. With candor, S testified:

Q: Did you ever suspect P?

A: After I found out whose car it was, yes.

We know for a fact that the stolen merchandise was discovered in P's automobile. We also know that the physical characteristics of P and K are quite similar. Without refutation, R testified that P is of the white race, 5'9" tall, weighs about 184 pounds, and has dark brown wavy hair. K is 5'8" tall, weighs 190–195 pounds, has dark brown hair, and is of the white race.

These observations are not made in Perry Mason fashion to exonerate the Grievant and pin the crime on someone else. They are made only to establish that under the circumstances of this case D could have been mistaken in his identification of K as the guilty person.

What W Did Not See

Although W did not testify in the arbitration, the record shows that he was outside the plant when D saw a person put the wieners into P's automobile. By an analysis of the pertinent testimony, we can establish with a degree of certainty what this supervisor saw and did not see on the night in question. To place this feature of the case in perspective, we must examine other elements of D's testimony. In this respect, he declared:

Q: And when you got to the center of the parking lot, what happened?

A: Well, I seen him [K] make two trips over this terrace here. Each time carrying a case of wieners.

Q: What did you then observe?

A: Well, I observed him setting them on the curb of the parking lot beside the sidewalk.

D then told us that after K set the wieners beside the sidewalk, W came out of the front entrance of the plant and started to walk toward the car in question. At this point, the supervisor was about 200 feet or so from the two boxes of wieners deposited on the sidewalk. D then testified that K picked up both boxes of wieners and crossed the sidewalk so as to get to P's automobile:

Q: Do I also understand that while W was on the sidewalk, K crossed the sidewalk?

A: That's right.

Q: With a box?

A: The box was on the curb. Right here. [Indicating.]

Q: Oh, K crossed the sidewalk?

A: That's right. And picked them up and put them in the car.

Q: And picked the boxes up from the curb?

A: That's right.

Q: And put them in the car?

A: That's right.

In other words, D identified W as on the sidewalk, *walking toward K,* when the Grievant crossed the sidewalk with the two boxes of wieners. D also testified that there was no obstruction on the sidewalk which would have prevented the supervisor from seeing down the length of the sidewalk. . . .

On the basis of D's testimony, therefore, it would seem reasonable that W would have seen K crossing the sidewalk with the wiener boxes. At least, it appears that he would have been in the physical position to see *someone* crossing the sidewalk with the wiener boxes. However, S testified that W told him that he did not see K carrying the wiener boxes. In this regard, S testified:

Q: And the word of someone else on the scene at the same time, W, when you talked to him, was that he didn't see K with any wieners, all he saw was K getting out of P's car, right?

A: Well, not exactly. He didn't say that he didn't see him with any. He said that— I just can't remember the exact words. To the effect that he hadn't seen him carrying any wieners.

Q: Well, you testified that W said all he saw was K get out of the car. Now, is that right or not?

A: Yeah. That's right. What I was trying to clarify is I don't remember W's exact words.

Q: I understand.

A: One way or the other.

Q: You are clear though that W never said he saw K with wieners?

A: Yes, sir. Yes, sir.

W, who could have corroborated D's identification of K as the guilty party, told us through S that he did not see the Grievant carrying the wieners. And, as stated, it is reasonable that W was in a physical position to see K if in fact he had picked up the two boxes of wieners and had crossed the sidewalk. It follows, therefore, that other elements of doubt arise as to whether the Grievant was the thief. Here was a supervisor who could have played a vital role in establishing the Company's proof beyond a reasonable doubt against K. He did not do so, and, indeed, what he *did not see* tends to weaken considerably the Company's case against the Grievant.

Conclusions

On the basis of the entire record, the Arbitrator finds that the Company did not sustain the burden of proof required to demonstrate the validity of its position. It was required to prove that K was the thief beyond reasonable doubt. We find that there is reasonable doubt that the Grievant committed the theft. As we have demonstrated, D did not promptly identify the Grievant when he first reported the theft to supervision. Instead, D identified K only when he saw the Grievant face to face as he passed him on the way to the car in question. If he was so positive that K had placed the stolen wieners in the car, we find no reasonable explanation as to why he delayed his identification of K. This sequence of events establishes doubt that K was the person whom he observed stealing the wieners.

In addition, there is the possibility that D could have been mistaken in the identity of K. There were about 35 to 40 employees of the white race employed on the shift in question, and at least P, in weight, height and color of hair, resembles the Grievant in appearance. Except that the Grievant admits that he was in the car which contained the stolen wieners, there is no corroboration to D's identification of K. When an employer bases its case against an employee charged with an offense of moral turpitude upon the identification of only one witness, this witness's testimony should be supported by convincing corroborative evidence. Such corroborative evidence, not found in the instant case, would tend to rule out the possibility of mistaken identity.

Although W was reasonably in a physical position to see the Grievant carrying the wieners across the sidewalk, he declared to S that he did not see K do this. The supervisor's failure to identify the Grievant in this respect tends to establish substantial doubt that K was the person whom D observed putting the wieners in the automobile in question.

Finally, the Company offered no plausible explanation as to why the Grievant would have selected P's car in which to place the wieners. As part of its proof, the Company was obligated to explain to the Arbitrator this strange feature of the case. Even at this late stage in this inquiry, and after considerable reflection, the Arbitrator still wonders why the Grievant would have selected P's automobile to deposit the wieners, if in fact K is the thief.

We do not, of course, find that K did not steal the wieners. It is entirely possible that he did. If he did, this decision deals a terrible injustice to the Company. However, in a case of this sort, it is not required to find the accused person innocent of the offense. The grievance is granted merely because on the evidence the Company did not establish K's guilt beyond a reasonable doubt. . . .

On this basis, the Arbitrator shall direct that K be awarded back pay, to be reduced by any earnings or unemployment compensation he received during the period of his discharge.

QUESTIONS

1. Despite the arbitrator's decision, do you believe that the company proved beyond a reasonable doubt that K had stolen the two boxes of wieners?

2. What were the major reasons upon which the arbitrator based his finding that the evidence was not sufficient to prove that K had stolen the wieners?

3. Comment upon the arbitrator's finding that the county court decision involving K was not binding upon him.

4. What are some principles of the arbitration process contained in the arbitrator's discussion of the case?

CASE 14
Subcontracting:
The Case of the Displaced
Entomologist Helpers

Cast of Characters

B   President of local union
S   Vice-president of traffic

This case deals with the employer's right to subcontract. Cases of this sort are among the most difficult that confront arbitrators. Normally, the stakes are very high in terms of plant efficiency and job protection for the employees. Language adopted to deal with the problem requires construction in the light of the material facts presented in the particular case. Frequently, contractual language dealing with the problem is ambiguous. It seems that the character of the problem precludes the adoption of language that is clear-cut and unequivocal, thus adding to the arbitrator's difficulty in arriving at a sound decision.

As you read the case, pay particular attention to the evidence that the arbitrator used to guide him in the interpretation of the contractual language, which was inherently ambiguous and vague.

After a number of entomologist helpers were removed from their classification as a result of a subcontracting arrangement, they filed a grievance, dated May 25, 1972, which stated:

> Violation of Article I, Section 2, paragraph 2 of Contract and all other articles, sections, and paragraphs pertaining to this grievance. Company subcontracting job duty #16.

> Company taking job duty #16 away from Entomologist Helpers and allowing it to be done by others on the outside and laying Ent. Helpers off from the Misc. Dept.

> We are demanding the Entomologist Helpers be returned to their dept. immediately and allowed to perform job duty #16 as in the past.

> We also demand that everyone in the Dept. (Entomologist Helpers) and Local Union members laid off from the plant as a result of this irresponsible act of management be reimbursed for any time lost, straight premium or time and $\frac{1}{2}$ as stated in the contract.

The company denied the grievance, stating:

> There is no violation of Article I, Section 2, Paragraph 2 of the local contract. Services being provided by railroad are in accordance with their obligation as a carrier.

Relevant to the dispute was Article I, Section 2 of the labor agreement, which stated:

> The operation of the plant and the direction of the working force employed therein, including the right to hire, promote, demote, suspend, lay off, transfer, discharge, or discipline for cause, and the right to determine how many men it will employ or retain, as well as to maintain discipline and efficiency, are invested exclusively with the Company subject to the provisions of this agreement.

> In the event of subcontracting of any Bargaining Unit work within a production classification, no employee within the affected classification shall be laid off as a result thereof.

Involved in the dispute was the job description of the entomologist helper classification. Of the job duties spelled out in the job description, No. 16 was material to the case. Job duty No. 16 stated:

> Reconditions cars for safe and sanitary loading, including cleaning, coopering, strapping, papering, removing nails and other damaging effects.

The basic question to be determined was as follows:

> Under the circumstances of this case, did the company violate Article I, Section 2 of the labor agreement? If so, what should the remedy be?

BACKGROUND

Cleaning and Coopering:
The Work in Question

At issue was the cleaning and coopering of railroad cars used by the company to ship its products. As described in the arbitration, this duty included the sweeping of the cars; pulling out any nails and cardboards; determining whether or not the walls and floors of the cars required that they be lined with cardboard and paper; removing from the cars any debris from a previous shipment; fumigating the cars when required before installing the necessary cardboard or paper; and, when necessary, vacuuming the edges and floors of the cars. In short, the job involved the cleaning of the car and the installation of required cardboard and paper so that the car would be in suitable condition before it was loaded with grain products.

For many years, entomologist helpers, pursuant to their job description, performed this duty. As cars were obtained from a railroad carrier, employees in this classification performed the cleaning and coopering. As their job description demonstrated, employees in this classification also performed other duties. However, what sparked this arbitration was the decision of the company to subcontract the coopering and cleaning of the cars. As a result of the subcontract, between ten and eleven entomologist helpers were removed from their classification. However, they were not laid off from employment in the company, but exercised their seniority to bump to other jobs within the plant. According to the testimony of B, president of the union, the displaced entomologist helpers:

> . . . exercised our seniority rights to bump to other jobs. We bumped into jobs which paid less money. We were not laid off from the plant. We were denied employment in the entomologist helper classification.*

The Decatur Precedent

S, vice-president of traffic, detailed the circumstances that resulted in this arbitration. He testified that it was the carriers' responsibility to furnish cars that were suitable for grain products. Under Interstate Commerce Commission rulings and court decisions, carriers were directed to provide cars suitable for the shippers' products. However, he testified that frequently (if not always), cars were received that were not suitable for the company's products. Accordingly, in 1956, Track 6 was constructed, and cars were moved to this track and were cleaned and coopered by entomologist helpers.

S testified that this function constituted a growing cost item for the company:

> This has always been a cost to us. Each year, our costs for cleaning and coopering kept going up.

As early as 1963, S made inquiries of the railroads about supplying the company with cars that were properly cleaned and coopered. The carriers refused, and the company dropped the matter for many years. In 1969, S testified, he again attempted to prevail upon the XYZ Railroad to cooperate with the company in the matter of suitable cars. This additional effort failed, and the matter was not revived until July 1970, when the company learned that the ABC Railroad agreed, with the approval of the ICC, to defray a part of the costs for cleaning and coopering at its Decatur terminal.

Carriers' Agreement To Defray Portion of Costs

With this precedent established, S again approached the XYZ Railroad in an effort to have the Decatur policy apply here. After negotiation, the

---

*B also testified that when the displaced entomologist helpers bumped into other jobs, employees so bumped were laid off from the plant. He was, however, unable to name specifically all of these employees. B further testified that these other employees were laid off from the plant about two weeks after the subcontract was arranged. At this time, he declared, there was a "sizable" plant layoff involving about 35 employees.

carrier agreed to work out an arrangement with International Cleaning Corporation whereby its employees would clean and cooper cars for the company. In February 1972, the other carriers that serviced the company agreed to defray a portion of the cleaning and coopering charges. With the approval of the ICC, the arrangement became effective on May 22, 1972.

Cost Savings under the New Arrangement

In short, the carriers entered into an arrangement with International Cleaning whereby the carriers would pay a portion of the costs for cleaning and coopering. Even though there was no legal or government compulsion that the company must have cars assigned to it cleaned and coopered by International Cleaning, the company implemented the arrangement to take advantage of the cost savings. Under the arrangement, the company paid the carrier $4.50 for cleaning and coopering a car for bulk loading. The carrier then added $1.70 per car and paid the total amount to International Cleaning. If a car was to be used for bag loading, the carrier paid International $3.50 per car, and the company paid $14 per car when the car measured 40 feet and $15 if it measured 50 feet. With respect to hopper cars, the carriers defrayed none of the costs for car preparation, but the company paid International $6.50 per car for whatever preparation work was required on these cars.

As stated, the new arrangement went into effect on May 22, 1972. Thereupon, the entomologist helpers covered by this grievance were removed from their classification and were bumped into other jobs.

S testified to the cost savings accruing to the company by the subcontract arrangement. He declared that if the arrangement had been in effect for 1971, the company would have saved $44,084.50; and that for June and July 1972, the company saved $6,694 in cleaning and coopering costs as compared with the same two months in 1971.

Indirect Cost-Saving Benefits

Beyond these dollar savings, S testified, under the new arrangement there were several indirect cost-saving features. One of these involved costs saved when products were lost or damaged. When the company's own employees cleaned and coopered the cars, a question existed as to whether the company or the carriers were responsible for the losses. S testified that each year, the company had filed about $100,000 in claims against the railroads. Under the new arrangement, since the company's employees did not clean and cooper the cars, the carriers and/or International Cleaning bore the burden for these losses.

S also testified that, under the new arrangement, the company saved on demurrage charges. Under the old arrangement, the company paid a car charge to the carrier at the precise moment the car was delivered to the company's premises. Since time was consumed in the cleaning and coopering of the cars by its own employees, the company paid a charge for the time involved for this process. Under the new arrangement, the car was delivered to the company prepared for immediate loading and the company no longer paid the demurrage charge caused when its own employees cleaned and coopered. However, S did not translate this savings into a dollar figure.

In addition, S declared that, under the new arrangement, space problems on the company's premises were alleviated. Formerly, a backlog of cars would be on the company's premises while they were being cleaned and coopered, and this made for congestion. Under the new arrangement, the company called for a car when needed, and the car arrived cleaned and coopered and ready to load.

The A Award

On July 25, 1967, Arbitrator A had handed down a decision involving a dispute between the company and the union. The case arose because the company had subcontracted the work involved in rodent, bird, and weed control. Like the instant case, the job classification involved was entomologist helper. The union had grieved on the basis that these duties were covered by the job description of the classification. Arbitrator A had denied the grievance, stating:

> The evidence also clearly established that there was no reduction in the number of employees in the entomologist helper classification nor any reduction in the number of overtime hours worked by them since the outside contractor activities were undertaken. Hence the contracting-out did not reduce the size of the bargaining unit or impair the Union's position in the plant.

> There is no express provision limiting the Company's right to contract out work except one which places a penalty on the Company if certain maintenance work is contracted out. That provision is not applicable here. Moreover, the Company asserted, and the Union did not deny, that in several negotiations the Union sought provisions to limit the Company's right to contract out work but was not successful in its efforts. This bargaining history indicates that the question of contracting-out received the parties' attention and that the Company reserved the right to do so.

> On the basis of all the evidence, the Arbitrator concludes that there are no express or implied limitations on the Company's right to contract out the work in question. Moreover, there were bona fide production, safety and economic reasons for doing so. Therefore, the Company did not violate either the letter or the spirit of the Agreement by contracting out rodent, bird and weed control activities outside the plant, and the grievance must be denied.

Negotiation of the 1967 Labor Agreement

In August 1967, the parties were involved in negotiations of a new labor agreement. During these negotiations, the union proposed a limitation on the company's right to subcontract. Its proposal stated:

Section 2. Right to Manage Plant—Add to the first paragraph:

All work now being subcontracted will be returned to the proper classifications within the Bargaining Unit.

All future work shall be performed by employees within the recognized Bargaining Unit and in the event the Company desires to subcontract any work to outside contractors, such work, if it cannot be performed by Bargaining Unit employees, shall be presented to the Union first for its approval before being contracted out.

The company refused to agree to this proposal. B, then the chairman of the union bargaining committee, testified:

We originally asked for a provision which would have prohibited the company to subcontract anything without our approval. The company would not go along with it.

Thereupon, the union offered another subcontracting proposal. B testified that it was drafted by R, international union representative, and that it was proposed and agreed to by the company "at the ninth hour."

In addition, B testified:

When we made the proposal, L, vice-president of personnel, said, "We have no intention to lay off people from a job classification. We will give it to you because we have no intention to lay off anybody from the job classification."

In any event, the parties agreed to the union's proposal, and stipulated that the language adopted for the first time in the 1967 contract be the same language appearing in Article I, Section 2:

In the event of subcontracting of any Bargaining Unit work within a production classification, no employee within the affected classification shall be laid off as a result thereof.

POSITION OF THE PARTIES

The position of the union was that the grievance should be granted, and the position of the company was that it should be denied. Both attorneys filed post-hearing briefs, and portions of the arguments contained in the briefs will be cited below where necessary and appropriate.

ANALYSIS OF THE EVIDENCE

The Basic Problem

As the facts demonstrated, the entomologist helpers covered by the grievance were displaced from their job classification as a result of the subcontract in question. The record further demonstrated that the employees were not laid off from the plant. When they were displaced from their classification, they exercised their seniority and bumped into other jobs. In the light of these facts, the arbitrator was called upon to determine whether or not the company violated the subcontract provision.

In the final analysis, the outcome of this dispute depended upon the proper construction of the phrase "laid off" as contained in this provision. If it were construed to mean only *laid off from the plant*, the position of the company would prevail and the grievance would be denied. If it were held to mean *laid off from their classification*, the union's position would prevail and the grievance would be granted.

Both parties argued a construction of the subcontract language consistent with their basic positions in this dispute. Union counsel argued:

> The term "laid off" as used in Article I of the Contract in light of the negotiating history can only mean laid off from an individual's job classification.

On the other hand, company counsel contended:

> The union's claim of a contract violation is based solely upon their unique interpretation of the familiar term "laid off." They argue that simply moving or being transferred from one job classification to another constitutes a layoff and, hence, violates Article I, Section 2 of the contract. There is no basis for applying such a construction of the term to this clause. . . .

> Had the term "laid off" been used in Article I, Section 2 in other than the traditional and accepted meaning, this new and broader meaning would have been spelled out with particularity and a specific definition would have been stated. No such defining language is found anywhere in Article I, Section 2.

The Subcontract Language

The first guide in the construction of a contract provision is its language. If contractual language is clear, unequivocal, and unambiguous, the language of the provision is applied as written. Under these circumstances, the job of an arbitrator is very easy: He applies the provision in the light of its language, and there is no need for interpretation or construction. Indeed, when contractual language is crystal clear, requiring only the automatic application of its terms, what was said in negotiations about such language does not become a proper standard for the construction of the language. As has been stated:

> . . . if the writing is clear and unambiguous, parol evidence will not be allowed to vary the contract.*

Both attorneys argued that the subcontracting language standing alone supported their respective positions. Union counsel stated:

---

*Frank Elkouri and Edna A. Elkouri, *How Arbitration Works* (Washington, D.C.: Bureau of National Affairs, 1960), p. 241.

Paragraph 2 refers only to work within a production classification and that employees within the affected classification shall not be laid off. Because the paragraph makes a specific reference to only the classifications, we can reasonably conclude, based on the rule of *ejusdem generis*, that this provision in referring to layoffs meant classification layoffs and not plant layoffs.

In contrast, company counsel argued:

Mr. B quoted L, the Company's Personnel Manager, as stating at the time the present language was agreed upon that "the Company had no intention of laying off employees within the classification." Certainly such a statement is consistent with the Company's position that it agreed that no employee within the affected class would be deprived of employment as a result of the subcontracting. This statement, however, in no way supports the Union's interpretation that the Company agreed that no employee would be shifted from one classification to another as a result of the subcontracting as the Union now contends. Indeed, even if this statement, made during the course of negotiation, did tend to support the Union's interpretation of the word "layoff," which it does not, it would not be controlling in the face of the clear language of the contract.

Ambiguity in Provision

The arbitrator found that the language in question was not as clear as the attorneys contended. Indeed, he found ambiguity that precluded a decision one way or the other based strictly upon the subcontract language. With reference to the union argument, the language did not positively and squarely protect an employee in his job classification following a subcontract. This would have been accomplished if the language had read as follows:

In the event of subcontracting of any Bargaining Unit work within a particular classification, no employee within the affected classification shall be laid off *from his classification* as a result thereof.

If the italicized words had been contained in the provision, the language standing by itself would have been clear enough to grant the grievance.

With respect to the company's argument, the express language did not by itself protect employees affected by a subcontract only from being laid off from the plant. This would have been true if the language had read as follows:

In the event of subcontracting of any Bargaining Unit work within a production classification, no employee within the affected classification shall be laid off *from the plant* as a result thereof.

If the italicized words had been incorporated in the provision, the language standing by itself would have been clear enough to deny the grievance. In fact, under either of these circumstances, it is extremely doubtful that the case would be in arbitration.

In contrast to the subcontracting language, which merely stated "laid off," was the clarity of the concept in other areas of the labor agreement. Under the terms of Article IV, Section 4, when a reduction in force was required involving nonskilled employees, probationary employees were first to be laid off *from their classification*. After this, the provision said, employees would be laid off *from their classification* based upon plantwide seniority. Such laid-off employees would then have the opportunity to exercise their seniority to bump into other jobs. In Article IV, Section 5, the language said clearly that when there was need for a reduction of force in a skilled classification, the employees would be reduced by laying off employees *from the classification* on the basis of plantwide seniority. In addition, under Article IV, Section 7, the parties defined layoffs for purposes of recall. The provision stated that employees who were laid off *from the plant* would be eligible for recall on the basis of plantwide seniority.

Under these provisions, there was no doubt as to the concept of "laid off." By the use of unambiguous language, the parties defined the concept in terms of layoffs from classification or from the plant. In contrast, under the subcontract language, there was only the term "laid off," without establishing unequivocally whether, for purposes of the provision, the concept referred to layoffs from a classification or from the plant.

In short, the subcontract provision was not so clear and unequivocal as to permit the application of its terms in an automatic manner. In this light, there existed the problem of construction and interpretation of the subcontracting language.

What caused the ambiguity in the language? Perhaps it resulted from the haste in which the provision was adopted. As the record showed, the subcontract language was agreed to by the parties shortly before the previous contract expired. It was apparently adopted at the last minute—just before the "zero hour"—to preclude a possible work stoppage. In any event, whatever caused the ambiguity, it would have been improper to apply the subcontract provision on the basis of its language standing alone. Construction and interpretation were required in order to reach a sound decision in this dispute.

"Within the Affected Classification"

As to the problem of construction and interpretation, the company offered one possible solution, which would result in a finding that the concept "laid off" meant *laid off from the plant;* that is, that the provision permitted removal of employees affected by a subcontract from their classification, but protected them against being laid off from the plant. Other employees—those who were not directly affected by the subcontract—could be laid off from the plant. This interpretation would mean that the company properly removed the entomologist helpers from their classification, and that the employees they bumped were properly laid off from the plant, since it was the entomologist helper classification and no other that was directly affected by the subcontract.

In this respect, company counsel argued:

> If the union's unique definition were intended to be applied in Article I, Section 2, the phrase "within the affected classification" would not have been included. By definition, subcontracting will have an impact only upon employees within the affected classification. Only these employees might move to another classification. Since such movement would be a layoff under the union's special definition, "within the affected classification" would be rendered mere surplusage. Only if "laid off" refers to something other than mere movement between job classifications does this phrase have any real meaning as used in Article I, Section 2. As noted above, there is nothing in the contract to indicate that "laid off" should not be accorded its traditional definition. If this is done, each word in Article I, Section 2 will have meaning. This result is to be favored as a rule of construction.

In other words, what the company argued was that by incorporating in the provision the phrase "within the affected classification," the parties intended that only those employees directly affected by the subcontract receive job protection, and this protection was limited to plant layoffs. Since the provision stated "within the affected classification," the company argued, some employees could be laid off. In the case at hand, this would mean that the employees whom the entomologist helpers bumped after this classification was directly affected by the subcontract were properly laid off from the plant. In short, under the company construction, the provision protected only those employees directly affected by a subcontract against losing jobs in the plant, even though they might properly be removed from their classification.

Phrase Redundant?

There was obviously some merit to this construction and interpretation of the subcontract provision. It was seriously considered by the arbitrator, in the light of the arbitration principle cited by company counsel. It is true that all words contained in a contractual provision should be considered, and it is not proper to hold that words contained in a provision were placed in there merely as surplusage.

After serious and prolonged reflection, however, the arbitrator rejected the company's argument, even though he agreed that its construction was reasonable and made sense. When contractual language is ambiguous, there must be a construction of its terms that precludes other reasonable and logical interpretations. It was necessary to construe the subcontracting language as it read, without any reference to what went on in negotiations when the provision was adopted, and to limit the analysis only to the language of the provision to determine whether or not the language standing by itself provided a compelling and exclusive meaning to the concept of "laid off."

As stated, the heart of the company's argument was that by the incorporation of the phrase "within the affected classification," the provision meant that employees within that classification could properly be removed from their classification and be permitted to bump other employees out of the plant; but it was equally possible that the parties did not repeat the phrase "within the affected classification" after the words "laid off" because it would have been redundant; that is, that there was no need to write the provision this way:

> ... no employee within the affected classification shall be laid off *within the affected classification* as a result thereof.

It was reasonable that the parties did not repeat the phrase because it was previously incorporated in the provision. In other words, it is possible that the phrase was omitted on this basis, and that the provision should be construed and interpreted in this fashion.

Conflict with Other Layoff Provisions

Of greater importance, however, the company's construction of the subcontract provision could have resulted a state of affairs that would conflict with other layoff provisions established in the labor agreement. The essence of the company's construction was that the provision protected the employees in a classification affected by a subcontract from being laid off from the plant, not from being removed from the classification.

Suppose, however, that a classification was directly affected by a subcontract and resulted in the removal from this classification of a number of employees, and that the employees in the classification directly affected by the subcontract *did not have either the seniority or the qualifications* to bump to other jobs.

After all, the subcontract provision could not possibly be construed to override and supersede the layoff language contained in the labor agreement. Under Article IV, Section 4, for example, the parties agreed that an employee in a classification could bump a junior service employee, provided the bumping employee was "able to handle the work in his new classification." Now, what would happen to an employee displaced from a classification directly affected by a subcontract when he did *not* have the seniority or the qualifications to bump?

Under the company's construction of the subcontracting provision, the employee would be protected from being laid off from the plant; but Section 4 said that if he did not have the seniority or the qualifications to bump, he would of necessity be laid off from the plant. Thus, there existed an obvious inconsistency between the company's interpretation of the subcontract provision and the layoff procedure established in other areas of the labor agreement. If the company's interpretation of the subcontract provision were accepted, a basis might be established for an irreconcilable conflict between that provision and the layoff procedures incorporated in the labor agreement.

The arbitrator's opinion, proceeding from this point, read:

> We recognize, of course, that this conflict did not happen in the instant case, since the Entomologist Helpers removed from their classification did have the seniority and qualifications to bump into other jobs. We recognize further that an Arbitrator should construe contractual language in the light of the facts of the case, and it is not proper to go beyond the facts which are involved in a particular dispute.
>
> However, these considerations do not apply in this dispute. We are called upon to construe the subcontract provision so as to establish what the language means as a permanent feature (unless changed in contract negotiations) for contractual application. Even though the Company's construction fits the facts of this case, it is reasonable that other circumstances could arise when its construction if affirmed by the Arbitrator would lead to a state of affairs which would be irreconcilable with the layoff provisions of the Labor Agreement. Clearly, the Arbitrator would create mischief with the Labor Agreement if he adopted a contractual construction and established a precedent which could conflict squarely with other contractual provisions. When an alternative contractual construction is reasonably possible, should we select the one which would establish a precedent which provides the basis for direct conflict with other provisions of the same contract?
>
> Indeed, the Company's construction of the subcontract provision establishes a cul-de-sac. It permits no solution from a set of circumstances wherein the employees within a classification directly affected by a subcontract do not have the seniority or the qualifications to remain in the plant. The Company argument is that these employees are protected in jobs within the plant, but not in their classification. Other provisions of the Labor Agreement provide, however, that these employees could be laid off from the plant. What happens under these circumstances?
>
> Surely, the Arbitrator would establish this very set of circumstances if he adopted the Company's construction of the subcontract language. He would establish an arbitration precedent which would provide the basis for irreparable conflict between contractual provisions. Should he do this where there is available an alternative construction of the subcontract provision which would not result in such a conflict? No conflict, of course, would exist if we held that the subcontract provision protects employees from removal and/or layoff from their classification. We do not affirm this construction of the subcontract provision at this point in our inquiry, but merely point it out to show there is an alternative construction of the provision which would eliminate any conflict with other provisions of the Labor Agreement.

Traditional Meaning of "Laid Off"

As we have detailed, the concept "laid off" as contained in the subcontract provision is not expressly defined by the language as meaning laid off from the plant or laid off from the classification.

On this basis, the Company urges that we should construe the words "laid off" in the light of the customary and ordinary usage of the term. The Company is correct in its contention that unless there are compelling reasons to the contrary, the term "laid off" means layoff from employment—that is, a layoff from the plant.

To buttress the argument, Company Counsel could have cited arbitration decisions which run parallel to its contention. Indeed, it might have referred to the definition of "layoff" contained in a U.S. Department of Labor publication:

> Separation from employment for a temporary or indefinite period, without prejudice, as a result of slack work or other reasons.*

In short, unless there are compelling reasons to the contrary, we recognize that "layoff" means separation from employment. The concept does not mean in its traditional usage "removal from one classification and assignment to another classification." . . . To this extent, the Company's argument has merit, and on this basis, we should construe "laid off" to mean layoff from the plant.

There are, however, compelling reasons which make inapplicable such a construction of the term "laid off" for purposes of the subcontract provision. The first of these reasons has been abundantly demonstrated in the earlier portion of this Opinion. If we hold to the customary and common usage of the term, we would establish the basis for a conflict of the subcontract provision with the layoff provisions. The second reason involves the circumstances of the negotiation of the subcontract provision, a matter to which we now direct our attention.

Negotiation of Subcontract Provision

As we have stated earlier, if the subcontract provision was unambiguous as to its meaning, it would not be necessary to establish the circumstances under which this provision was negotiated. If the provision was written in unequivocal fashion as to the meaning of "laid off," the only job of the Arbitrator would be to apply the language as it was written. Indeed, as mentioned previously, it would be improper under the parol evidence rule to consider the circumstances of the negotiation of a contractual provision when it is written in crystal-clear and unequivocal terms.

With respect to the subcontract provision in question, however, we have found that it is inherently ambiguous as to its essential meaning. . . . It does not tell us in an unequivocal manner whether the Parties meant protection from layoff from the classification or only protection from layoff from the plant.

Under these circumstances, not only is it proper that we consider whatever evidence is available as to the negotiation of the provision, but it is indispensable that we do so in order that we reach a sound decision in this case. We simply cannot detect the intent of the Parties from the language standing alone.

In this respect, it should be clear to all concerned that the spark which caused the Union to demand protection against subcontracting resulted from the A award referred to in an earlier portion of this Opinion. In his case, Arbitrator A stated that one of the contentions of the Company was that:

> None of the employees in the classification [Entomologist Helper] was laid

*Labor-Management Relations in the United States, Bulletin No. 1225, U.S. Department of Labor, Section 4, p. 13.

off or suffered any reduction in the amount of overtime because of the Company's action.

Also, as part of his reasoning in the denial of the grievance, Arbitrator A stated:

> The evidence also clearly established that there was no reduction in the number of employees in the entomologist helper classification. . . .

After an unsuccessful attempt by the Union to secure its original subcontracting provision, the Parties agreed to the language incorporated in Article I, Section 2. In the light of one of the Company's contentions in the A case, and in the light of one of the reasons used by A to deny the grievance, as quoted above, there is at least some reason to believe that the Union presented its final proposal to protect employees from being displaced from their classification because of a subcontract. Of course, this does not mean that the Company agreed with this intention, if, in fact, the Union presented its proposal to accomplish this objective.

After all, we may not determine the meaning of contractual language on the basis of what a Party may have in mind when it proposes a provision. We are not in the business of mind-reading, and it would be improper for the Arbitrator to reach a decision in this case on what either Party had in mind when it agreed to the subcontract provision.

What is material in the determination of the intent of contractual language is what is said by Parties when they are in the process of negotiating contractual language. Declaratory statements, and not subjective intent, constitute a proper basis for the determination of the intent of contractual language.

What Was Said in Negotiations

In this light, we make reference to the testimony of Union Witness B, who was Chairman of the Union Bargaining Committee when the instant provision was adopted in the 1967 negotiations. In this respect, he testified:

> We put it in there so no one would be laid off from their job classification. When we negotiated the subcontract provision, we referred to department [classification] layoffs. The employer did not say "no" to this. The Company did not say it [the subcontract provision] applied to plant layoffs.

What is significant is that the Company did not present a witness to refute the testimony of B. Indeed, the Union witness was the only person who testified as to what was said and/or not said in the negotiations.

A fair reading of B's testimony demonstrates that the Union communicated to the Company at the bargaining table that the provision was designed to protect employees within a classification from being laid off from their classification as a result of a subcontract. It was in the light of this Union explanation that the Parties adopted the instant subcontract provision. In the absence of evidence to the contrary, we must of necessity conclude that it was the mutual intent of the Parties to protect employees from layoffs from their classification. If this was not the intent of the Company, it would be expected that it would have presented a witness to refute B's testimony.

In other words, the ambiguity of the subcontract provision is resolved by reference to the explanations which took place when the provision was adopted. These explanations, as demonstrated by the unrefuted testimony of B, lead to the finding that it was the intent of the Parties that a subcontract was not to result in the layoff and/or removal of employees from the classification affected by the subcontract.

We stress that under the record of this case there simply exists no other basis on which to establish the intent of the Parties when they adopted the language in question. If B did not relate accurately what was said and what was not said in the negotiations, if he did not tell it as it happened, if he distorted or left out any material statement, it was the obligation of the Company to present evidence to refute his testimony. This the Company did not do, and under the record the Arbitrator has no choice except to conclude that the Parties mutually agreed and understood that employees in a job classification affected by a subcontract are not to be laid off and/or removed from their classification.

Additional Company Arguments

Before reaching his final decision in this dispute, the Arbitrator considered two additional arguments offered by the Company. One of these concerns the comparison of the original Union subcontract proposal and the one the Parties adopted. . . . Even though the instant subcontract provision does restrict the Company's opportunity to subcontract, it is not correct to argue that the provision adopted is as limiting on the Company's right to subcontract as the one the Company refused to accept. Under the Union's original proposal, the Union would have obtained a veto power over any subcontract. Indeed, the Company would not have any right to subcontract unless the Union agreed. Note the contractual language of the Union's original subcontract proposal:

> . . . in the event the Company desires to subcontract any work to outside contractors, such work, if it cannot be performed by Bargaining Unit employees, *shall be presented to the Union first for its approval before being contracted out*. [Emphasis supplied.]

What this language tells us is that even if the Company's employees are not qualified or available to perform some kind of bargaining unit work, the Company *still may not subcontract such work unless the Union agrees*. In short, if the Company agreed to such language, it would have lost any power to subcontract on a unilateral basis. In this light, it is understandable why the Company rejected the original Union proposal.

Under the subcontract language adopted by the Parties, the opportunity for the Company to subcontract on a unilateral basis still exists. Circumstances still could exist where a subcontract would not result in layoffs. For example, this could occur when there are not sufficient employees in a classification to perform the necessary work, or where the Company subcontracts for other reasons, provided that employees are not laid off from their classification. Indeed, these circumstances occurred in the A case. The Company subcontracted for the control of rodents, birds, and weeds. It did so without reducing the number of employees in the job classification.

Under the subcontract provision adopted by the Parties, the Company still has the right to subcontract work under similar conditions without requiring Union approval or violating the provision. Indeed, there is no per se limitation on the Company's right to subcontract under the provision. What Article I, Section 2 tells us is that no employee will be laid off in the classification directly affected by the subcontract. Of course, this is a practical limitation on the Company's opportunity to subcontract. However, this is something different from a provision which would provide the Union with veto power over Company decisions to subcontract. That was the idea behind the original Union proposal rejected by the Company. Under the provision as adopted by the Parties, the Union has no power to veto a subcontract. The protection it provides employees is not that the Union may forbid a subcontract; rather, the protection is that no employee will be laid off from his classification after the subcontract is made.

Actually, the subcontract provision adopted by the Parties reflects what is quite common in collective bargaining. Many labor agreements provide job protection to employees from the subcontracting process. As a matter of fact, some labor agreements establish a much more restrictive limitation on the employer's right to subcontract as compared to the subcontracting provision agreed to by the Parties. In the light of contemporary collective bargaining practices, the Company did not make such a "bad bargain," as suggested by Company Counsel's argument. It was forced to agree to an important practical restriction on its opportunity to subcontract—that was the result of the practicalities of the collective bargaining negotiations. However, it is not correct to argue or to imply that under the instant provision the Company has surrendered its right to subcontract, or that the Union has the veto power to block subcontracts as would be true under the Union's original proposal.

The Matter of Efficiency

Having said all of this, the Arbitrator does not mean to minimize the restriction on the Company's opportunity to subcontract. There certainly does exist an important practical restriction. One would be naive to make an observation to the contrary.

As Company Counsel argues, the subcontract provision, as applied in this decision, will tend to diminish the Company's opportunity to maximize efficiency. We need go no further than the case at hand to establish this point. As a result of the Arbitrator's decision, the Company probably will not find it to its advantage to continue the subcontract in question. If it terminates the subcontract, the Company will lose the carriers' subsidy. As S's testimony demonstrates, the Company undoubtedly stands to lose a considerable amount of money as a result of this decision. S declared that under the subcontract, the Company would save about $40,000 in direct wages per year, and would benefit from other cost-saving features of the arrangement.

Certainly, the Arbitrator is fully aware of the amount of money involved in this case. Indeed, if Company efficiency measured in dollar savings were the only standard for decision in this dispute, the grievance would be denied. We also recognize that some of the Company's competitors are taking advantage of the carriers' subsidy. Since the grain business is fiercely competitive, there is no question that the market position of the Company will be injured as a result of this decision.

Although we recognize all these considerations, the Arbitrator still has no choice except to grant the grievance. Once he became convinced that the Parties intended the provision to protect employees from layoff from the classification affected by the subcontract, the duty of the Arbitrator became clear and mandatory. In the final analysis, the Company agreed to the provision, and was aware of its intent and purpose. It is, of course, the privilege of the Company to hold the Arbitrator fully responsible for a decision which will undoubtedly cause it to operate less efficiently. On the other hand, the Arbitrator believes that if the Company objectively reflects upon the evidence and the provision, it would agree that the Arbitrator has applied the provision exactly as the Parties intended.

The Remedy

In any event, the Arbitrator finds that the Company violated Article I, Section 2 under the circumstances of this case. All that remains is to direct the proper remedy for the violation. In this regard, the Arbitrator directs that the Entomologist Helpers removed from their classification as a result of the subcontract be reinstated to their classification. He also directs that they be awarded back pay in the amount of wages they lost as a result of the layoff from the classification to the extent that the subcontract resulted in their displacement.

For reasons expressed earlier, the Arbitrator, however, shall not direct that the Company terminate the subcontract. To comply with the Arbitrator's Award, the affirmative action to be taken by the Company is to return the displaced Entomologist Helpers covered by the grievance to their classification and to award them appropriate back pay. The violation by the Company is not that it subcontracted the work in question. The violation by the Company is that it laid off employees from their classification. As we pointed out, the language of Article I, Section 2 does not per se forbid the Company to subcontract. It is up to the Company to determine whether or not it desires to terminate the subcontract.

Also, the Arbitrator shall direct back pay to any other employee who was laid off from the plant as the result of the bumping process caused by the subcontract. A back pay award is proper for these employees because if the Entomologist Helpers had not been removed from their classification, the presumption is that these employees would not have been laid off from the plant. However, there was additional testimony that these other employees might have been laid off even if the subcontract and the bumping process did not take place. The basis for this observation was testimony that after the subcontract and the bumping process, there was a general plant layoff in the plant. It is possible, therefore, that the employees bumped by the displaced Entomologist Helpers might have been laid off from the plant in the general layoff even if they had not been bumped by the Entomologist Helpers.

Since the evidence dealing with this issue is not conclusive, the Arbitrator shall hold jurisdiction of the case to resolve any disputes covering back pay for a period of thirty (30) calendar days. The Arbitrator hopes that the Parties will settle any disputes involving back pay through direct negotiations. In the event that they do not, the Arbitrator will determine any such dispute provided that a request is made by the Parties within thirty (30) calendar days from the date of this Award.

QUESTIONS

1. What was the fundamental problem in contractual interpretation presented by this case?

2. Why did the arbitrator say that to accept the company's construction of the sub-contract language could result in an irreconcilable conflict with other provisions of the labor agreement?

3. Was the arbitrator justified in giving considerable weight, as a basis of his decision, to the events of the negotiations that resulted in the subcontract language? Defend your position.

4. Why did the arbitrator state that, even though nothing in his decision per se prevented the company from subcontracting, it did place a partial limitation on its right to subcontract?

PART IV
SOME
FINAL THOUGHTS

Chapter 11
Concluding Statement

The productive potential of the United States depends upon many factors, including the status of employer–employee relations. Our nation has been extremely fortunate in being endowed with a highly favorable natural environment for the encouragement of the productive process. Its virtually inexhaustible stores of natural resources, advantageous geographic location, and population growth constitute a sound basis for an expanding and dynamic economy. Despite these considerations, the fact remains that the fruitfulness of the productive process of our nation depends fundamentally upon the creativeness of the managerial function, the economic and political systems in which business and labor operate, and the industry and the spirit of the labor force. Other nations that have not attained the level of industrial development of the United States can match to some extent our natural resources. Few people, however, equal the vigor and the creativeness of Americans in implementing the productive process. In the last analysis, the level of the standard of living of a nation depends not so much upon its stores of iron ore, coal, oil, and the like, as upon the motivation and the energy of its people, and the system of government and economics within which the productive process is accomplished.

A fundamental if implicit thesis of this volume has been that an important prerequisite for the increasing productivity of the American nation is the status of its employer–employee relations. Since we are a nation practicing free enterprise, what has thus far remained (despite a highly visible trend to increasing government interest in labor relations) an essentially private employer–employee relationship is by far the dominant characteristic of the industrial relations environment. The character of this relationship determines to an important extent our productive capabilities. A wholesome labor relations environment that encourages maximum efforts of labor and management will do much toward improving our standard of living. In contrast, the productive process will be obstructed to the extent that the employer–employee relationship is implemented in a hostile framework. From this it follows not only that the best interests of employers and employees are dependent upon the establishment of a harmonious industrial relations climate, but that the entire nation likewise has a stake in the accomplishment of this objective.

In retrospect, the evidence is clear that collective bargaining relations in the United States have improved remarkably over the years. It is well to recall in this connection that widespread collective bargaining is a comparatively recent development in this country. The earliest unions date from 1800, and unionism can hardly be viewed as a new phenomenon, but even 45 years ago only a relatively few employers and employees were involved in the process, virtually none of the vital industries of the nation were characterized by collective bargaining, and unionism had not yet penetrated the major mass-production sectors. During the period of growth of collective bargaining, union–employer relations in these industries were far from satisfactory and not conducive to high levels of industrial productivity. Since the process was new and virtually untried, there was much distrust and suspicion on both sides of the bargaining table. Many employers questioned the methods and the ultimate objectives of labor unions and, in general, aggressively resisted the development of unions. In some cases, unions moved too fast in their development and failed to take into consideration the legion of problems involved in establishing collective bargaining within new industries. On a number of occasions, labor–management relations deteriorated into prolonged and violent strikes resulting in loss of life, in physical injury, and in destruction of company property. It may be argued with some validity that these events were probably unavoidable because of the newness of the collective bargaining process. Such happenings might be regarded as the "growing pains" of a new and potentially important area. Notwithstanding these considerations, the fact remains that some of the history of the development of industrial relations—particularly prior to the 1930s, but even as late as World War II—is not pleasant to recall.

With the passage of time, labor relations handled under the collective bargaining process have improved enormously. As noted earlier, violence during strikes has virtually disappeared from the American industrial scene. To appreciate this, one has only to compare the bloody Memorial Day, 1937, Little Steel incident with the Ford Motor Company strike in the fall of 1967. In the steel industry strike, ten lives were lost, scores of people suffered serious physical injury, and there was severe damage to property. In the automobile strike, only token picket lines were manned by the union, and there was no violence and no damage to property. The latter strike was so "civilized," indeed, that some of the plants involved in it supplied power for the TV sets viewed by employees serving on picket-line duty.

The virtual demise of the role of violence is, however, only one of many developments attesting to the greatly improved state of labor relations in recent years. The earliest pages of this volume indicated that there has been similar progress along almost every basic labor–management dimension, and it is hoped that, by this point in the book, the reader stands in fundamental agreement. The facts show not only that in an overwhelming number of instances the parties have been able to negotiate under a strike deadline without reaching a stalemate, but that with respect to unauthorized, or "wildcat," strikes, the record is similarly impressive. Instead of resorting to industrial warfare as the means of adjusting and settling disputes arising over the interpretation and application of an existing contract, employers and unions settle these problems through the grievance and arbitration procedure, thereby lending considerable further stability to their relationships.

Running through the preceding pages are testimonials to other types of success—from a stress on considerably more informed bargaining sessions to the attainment of a far larger measure of contracts that constitute "good compromises," and from the almost complete disappearance of Conflict philosophies to the great growth of Accommodation (if not Cooperation) ones.

Indeed, under some management–union relationships, there is now a genuine feeling of mutual trust and respect between the parties. Although contract negotiations, grievances, and arbitration cases are treated with vigor by both the company and the union, the problems are handled within a general framework of friendliness and of bilateral trust and confidence. It is obvious that such a state of development of industrial relations fosters high levels of productivity, profits, wages, and quality of product. It means that all parties to the collective bargaining process, including the public, derive benefit.

Such progress in labor relations did not develop by accident. There are cogent reasons for the great strides that have been made in the union–management relationship. Developments in management and union attitudes, in philosophy, and in procedures have been responsible for this trend.

On the part of employers, there is general acceptance, even if this is in many cases given begrudgingly, and even if at times it might appear not to be given at all in some public sector relationships, of the process of collective bargaining. In contrast to the state of affairs three decades ago, the typical management today has no open quarrel with the existence of collective bargaining. However much it might prefer a nonunionized work force (and however greatly it might continue to oppose the union in theory), it is now preoccupied with the practical problem of getting along with its labor organization on a day-by-day basis, while preserving at the same time those managerial prerogatives needed to operate an efficient and productive enterprise. Many companies operating under collective bargaining contracts sincerely believe that the protection of job rights of their employees by a labor agreement is desirable. Even though at times protection of job rights obtained through collective bargaining might diminish plant productivity, most companies and unions have found the collective bargaining contract sufficiently elastic to accommodate the objectives of both efficiency of production and the protection of job rights. The pliability of the collective bargaining process has thus far provided chances for the reconciliation of both objectives, and it is to be suspected that even the thorny problems of automation will ultimately be resolved in the same way (although, here, most likely in conjunction with government actions). So, too, if history is any guide at all, will the still-primitive relationships that are perhaps the inevitable birth and growth pains in some (but far from all) of the public sector.

In addition, many managements have taken a realistic approach to the institutional character of unionism. They are aware that, to an extent, the collective bargaining process tends to supply the needs of the union as an institution, as well as to provide the mechanism whereby the terms of employment of workers are established. Many contractual provisions are agreed to by management on the theory that a union secure in its status may be more judicious in its behavior at the bargaining table and in grievance negotiations.

Management's recognition of the problems and needs of employees is likewise an important element in the establishment of sound relations under collective bargaining. Relations between companies and unions are bound to be more harmonious as management exhibits a genuine understanding of the problems confronted by the individual employee. A union will tend to be more aggressive and attempt to impose more limitations on the managerial function to the extent that a company, through its general behavior and personnel policies, demonstrates an unsympathetic attitude toward employees' problems and objectives. Indeed, one major reason for the establishment and the expansion of unions is that in the past, some companies did not give sufficient attention to the needs of employees. At present, the evidence is quite clear that the business community in general is vitally concerned with the welfare of its workers. One of the primary bases of the science of personnel management is the development of techniques and procedures that have at their core the sympathetic consideration of employee problems. In many companies, the needs of employees are given equal weight and attention with the problems of finance, production, sales, and quality control. And executives are, in fact, assigned to personnel departments to no small extent because of their ability to understand sympathetically employees' problems and to deal with employees on the basis of sound human relations. This development means that a solid foundation exists for more harmonious relations between companies, unions, and employees.

There is also a growing tendency on the part of industry to place the operation of labor relations in the hands of qualified and professional managers. There is scarcely a major company in existence that has not established a department to handle labor relations and personnel problems. More important, in many companies, the industrial relations department has equal prestige and status with any other division or department within the enterprise. Such a development likewise fosters better relations at the bargaining table. But because collective bargaining negotiations and the administration of labor agreements constitute a most difficult and highly responsible job, it is necessary that companies entrust such a function to executives who are qualified in terms of training, motivation, skill, and personality. Companies that delegate these duties to unqualified personnel, or impose the duties as additional responsibilities on already busy executives, cannot expect to acquire a labor relations climate conducive to high levels of productivity.

It is also noteworthy that companies are increasingly conducting classes and other training programs involving the problems of contract administration for first-line supervisors. This appears an indispensable part of a sound company industrial relations program. Frequently, grievances arise because first-line supervision has not been adequately trained in the principles of labor relations and in the meaning and application of the collective bargaining contract. With the growth of the science of industrial relations, and particularly as this is cast within the framework of collective bargaining, it is imperative that a company's labor relations program be executed and administered correctly by all levels of supervision. To the extent that this has been recognized by the business community, the cause of harmonious and sound labor relations has been proportionately advanced.

Not only does the evidence, finally, reveal that employers in increasing numbers are giving sympathetic understanding to the problems of employees and unions, but there is also a growing awareness by union members and their leaders of the problems of management. At present, many union leaders, although they are representatives of organizations that are, above all, political, are fully conscious of the fact that in the last analysis the welfare of employees depends upon the economic prosperity of the firm. The leaders understand further that the collective bargaining process is conditioned by the economic framework surrounding the particular negotiations, and that the overall economic character of a firm or an industry relative to its competitive position, sales, profits, capital equipment, expansion requirements, and quality of production necessarily determines the economic benefits that can be provided to employees. There is increasing awareness that a company has obligations not only to its employees but also to its investors, management, and customers. These considerations do not mean that unions are less militant in collective bargaining. Negotiations are not conducted in a tea-party atmosphere. What these observations do mean is that labor relations generally improve to the degree that collective bargaining negotiations are based upon factual information and rationality, and are carried on in a general atmosphere of reciprocal recognition of problems and in a spirit of genuine good faith and mutual respect. Clearly, guesswork, emotionalism, preconceived notions of equity, and intransigence, whether displayed by a company or by a union in collective bargaining negotiations, are not conducive to good labor relations.

Collective bargaining literally means the joint determination of the terms of employment. The process does not *create* the problems of the employment relationship; issues such as wages, hours and overtime, vacations, holidays, discipline, job classification, promotions, and employee safety and health exist with or without collective bargaining. Problems growing out of the employment relationship must be solved, in one way or another. In the absence of collective bargaining, they are handled and determined by the employer on a unilateral basis. His decisions in this respect are final; they have as their frame of reference his own standards of fairness and are limited only by the marketplace and the law.

But if collective bargaining does not create the problems of the employment relationship, it does establish a definite procedure wherein they are handled and resolved. Employers and employees, through their respective representatives, negotiate the terms of employment and provide the mechanisms by which these terms can be administered throughout the contractual duration. Whatever deficiencies remain in the present system, the considerable progress that has been made in the past few decades augurs well for the future productive potential of the nation, assuming only that we can exercise sufficient patience in having our expectations for collective bargaining translated into action.

Appendix

Mock

Negotiation Problem

The purpose of this problem is to familiarize students with the negotiation of a labor contract. The problem is strictly a hypothetical one and does not pertain to any actual company or union. It is designed to test in a practical way the student's understanding of the issues of collective bargaining studied during the semester and the strategy of the bargaining process. The strategy and techniques of negotiations are treated in Chapter 5, and the issues of collective bargaining are dealt with primarily in Chapters 7 through 10. Before the actual mock negotiation, the student should carefully reread these chapters.

PROCEDURE AND GROUND RULES:

1. Class will be divided into labor and management negotiation teams. Each team will elect a chairman at the first meeting of the team.

2. Teams will meet in a sufficient number of planning sessions to be ready for the negotiations. Each participant will be required to engage in necessary research for the negotiation.

3. In the light of the following problem, each team will establish *not more* than 8 items *nor less* than 6 that it will demand. *All demands must be based upon the problem. No team will be permitted to make a demand that is not so based.* For purposes of this problem, a union wage demand and all fringe issues, if demanded, will be considered as only *one* demand.

4. Each team should strive to negotiate demands that it believes to be most important. This requires the weighing of the alternatives in the light of respective needs of the group the team is representing.

5. Compromises, counterproposals, trading, and the dropping of demands to secure a contract will be permitted in the light of the give and take of the actual negotiations.

6. Each team should strive sincerely and honestly in the role playing to do the best job possible for the group it represents. This is a *learning situation*, and to learn there must be sincere dedication to the job ahead.

7. *Absolutely no consultation with any of the other teams, regardless of whether* *company or union, will be permitted. Each team must depend entirely upon its own resources.*

8. Chairmen should coordinate the planning of each team, decide on the time and place for planning sessions, and assign work to be done to members of the team. Chairmen, however, are not to do all the talking in the actual negotiations. To maximize the learning situation, each member of the team should positively participate in the negotiations.

9. There must either be a settlement of all issues in the negotiation or a work stoppage. *No extension of the existing contract will be permitted.* It is a question of either settlement or work stoppage.

10. Someone on each team should keep track of the settlements. Do not write out the actual contractual clauses agreed to. It will suffice only to jot down the substance of agreements.

11. There will be a general discussion of the problem after the negotiation. Each team chairman or his representative will make a brief statement to the entire class as to the final outcome of the problem.

Herein follows the problem upon which the demands will be based and which provides the framework for the negotiations. *Read the problem very carefully to size up the situation. Base your demands only upon this problem.*

Representatives of the Auto Products Corporation of Indianapolis, Indiana, and Local 5000, United Metal Workers of America, are in the process of renegotiating their collective bargaining contract. The current contract expires at the close of today's negotiations. *(Instructor should set the date of the mock negotiation, and the exact clock time that the contract expires.)* The negotiations cover the Indianapolis plant.[1] Auto Products also owns a plant in Little Rock, Arkansas, but the southern plant is not organized and is not a part of the current negotiations. The current contract, which covers only the Indianapolis plant, was negotiated for a three-year period. *The time of the negotiation is the present, and, accordingly, the parties are conditioned by current elements of economic trends, patterns of collective bargaining, and labor relations law.*

The Indianapolis plant has been in business for 56 years and has steadily grown in size. At present, 3,800 production and maintenance employees are in the bargaining unit for the plant.

Except for the depression years, 1929–36, the financial structure of the company has been relatively good. For the current year, the sales of the Indianapolis plant amounted to $56 million. Sales totaled $52 million in the preceding year, and $53 million for the first year of the current contract period. During the last fiscal year, the Indianapolis plant's profits amounted to $4.2 million after taxes; $3.9 million the preceding year; and $4.1 million in the first year of the labor agreement. At present, its assets in the Indianapolis plant amount to $18 million, including an inventory of $400,000 of

[1] The location of the plant may be shifted to your own area to provide more local relevance.

unsold goods. Over the three-year period, the company distributed 75 percent of its net profits in dividends; 20 percent was held as retained earnings; and 5 percent was used to improve and expand facilities in the Indianapolis plant. (All the financial data above apply exclusively to the Indianapolis plant.) The company's stock is listed on the New York Stock Exchange. It has no bonded indebtedness, although last year it borrowed $4.3 million from the Hoosier National Bank. The rate of interest on the loan amounts to 6.9 percent. The proceeds of the loan were used to expand the Little Rock plant. The loan is scheduled for liquidation in ten years.

The company manufactures a variety of auto accessories. These include auto heaters, oil pumps, fan belts, rear-view mirrors, and piston rings, and in the last year the company has also started production of auto air conditioners. About 65 percent of its sales are to the basic auto companies (General Motors, Ford, Chrysler, and American Motors); 25 percent to auto-repair facilities; and the rest to government agencies. The plant operates on a two-shift basis. A 3-cent-per-hour premium is paid to employees who work the second shift.

The employees of the company were unionized in 1937, as a result of the CIO campaign to organize the mass-production industries. In August of that year, the union was victorious in an NLRB election. As a result of the election, certification was awarded, on August 17, 1937, to Local 5000, since which time Local 5000 has represented the production and maintenance workers of the company. The first collective bargaining agreement between the company and Local 5000 was signed on November 14, 1937.

Only one contract strike has taken place since the union came into the picture. It occurred in 1940; the issues were the union's demands for a union shop, increased wages, and six paid holidays. The strike lasted six weeks. When it terminated, the union had obtained for its members a 4-cent hourly wage increase, retroactive to the day of the strike (the union had demanded 7 cents), and four paid holidays. The union failed in its attempt to obtain any arrangement requiring membership in the union as a condition of employment. Also, the current contract does not include a "checkoff." At the time of these negotiations, all except 400 workers in the bargaining unit are in the union.

The average wage for the production workers in the Indianapolis plant is $4.90 per hour. Of the 3,800 employees, there are 175 skilled maintenance employees (electricians, plumbers, carpenters, mechanics, and tool and die makers), and their average rate is $6.20 per hour. The existing contract contains an "escalator" clause providing for the adjustment of wages in accordance with changes in the Consumer Price Index. It provides a 1-cent increase in wages for each 0.5-point change in the CPI. During the past three years, employees have received a 12-cent increase in wages as a result of the escalator clause, and a 5-cent-an-hour wage increase in each of the past two years from the operation of the so-called "annual improvement" feature of the contract.

The current wage rates in the plant include the increases generated from the escalator clause and the annual improvement factor.

The Little Rock plant was built five years ago. It started with a modest-size labor force, but during the past three years the southern plant expanded sharply, and it now employs about 1,500 production and maintenance workers. Efforts to organize the southern plant have so far been unsuccessful. The union lost an NLRB election last year by 300 votes. Of the 1,500 employees, 1,300 cast ballots, with 800 voting against the union and 500 voting for it. The average wage in the Little Rock plant is $3.90 per hour. During the last eight months, 300 employees in the Indianapolis plant have been laid off. It is no secret that one reason for this has been the increase of output in the Little Rock plant. Another reason was decrease in sales at the Indianapolis plant. In Little Rock, essentially the same products are made as in Indianapolis.

In general, the relations between the management and the union have been satisfactory. There have, of course, been the usual disagreements, but all in all, relations have been quite harmonious. However, last month there was a "wildcat strike," the first one since the union came into the picture. It occurred in the Oil Pump Department, and the alleged cause was the discharge of the steward of the department on the grounds that he shoved a foreman while he was discussing a grievance with him. The union disclaimed all responsibility for the strike, and its officers stated that they did all they could to get the men back to work. However, the employees in the Oil Pump Department picketed the plant, and the incident, which lasted two days, shut down all production in the plant for these two days. There is a no-strike clause in the contract that states:

> There will be no strikes, slowdowns, or other interruption of production because of labor disputes during the contract period. Employees who engage in such prohibited activity are subject to discharge.

The company threatened to sue the union for damages under the Taft-Hartley law, but finally decided not to go to court after the employees returned to work. No employee was disciplined because of the strike; however, at present, the steward remains discharged, and the union has demanded his return to his job. Under the contract, the company has the right to discharge for "just cause." The steward is 63 years old, and was one of the leading figures in the organization of the union.

The existing contract contains a standard grievance procedure and provides for arbitration for all disputes arising under the contract, except production standards, which management has the unilateral right to establish. During the last contractual period (three years), 275 written grievances were filed by employees protesting "unreasonably" high production standards. As required by the contract, the company negotiated the production standard grievances, but the union did not have the right to appeal to arbitration or to strike over them. In three cases sparked by the production standard grievances, the company reduced the standards. In all other cases, the company denied the grievances. The management rights clause states in effect that the company retains all rights except as limited by express provisions of the labor agreement.

Provided in the contract are a series of fringe benefits: eight paid holidays; a pension plan that is exactly the same as in basic auto; a very good hospitalization and surgical benefits insurance plan; and a vacation plan wherein employees receive one week's vacation for one year of service and two weeks' for five or more years of service. The total costs of all these fringe benefits amount to 90 cents per hour. The current contract does not require that employees retire when eligible for pension.

With respect to the seniority clause, it provides for promotions based on length of service and ability. That is, seniority governs when the senior employee has qualifications reasonably equal to those of junior employees who bid on the job. During the contract period, 21 grievances were filed by employees who protested against the company's filling jobs with junior service employees. The company's position in these grievances was that the junior employees had far more ability than the senior employees. Five of these grievances went to arbitration, the company winning four and the union winning only one. Promotions are bid for on a departmental basis.

The seniority area of the existing contract provides for plantwide application of seniority credits for layoffs and recalls. During the recent period in which layoffs occurred, the company, as required by the contract, laid off many junior employees rather than senior employees because of the plantwide system. Foremen have complained to management that, in many cases, the junior employees who had been laid off were more efficient than the senior employees who had to be retained because of the plantwide system.

Also, the current contract provides that an employee whose job goes down, or whose job is preempted by a more senior employee, may bump any junior employee in the plant, provided he has the qualifications to fill the job. During layoff periods, the company became aware that this situation caused a great deal of expense because of an unreasonable amount of job displacement. Also, the current contract does not contain a temporary layoff clause. This means that a displaced employee may exercise his bumping rights based upon his plantwide seniority regardless of the length of the layoff. Foremen have complained to the management that employees should be laid off without regard to seniority when the layoff is for a short period of time.

The existing contract provides for "super-seniority" for stewards and other union officials. This provision protects the stewards and union officials only from layoffs. There are 60 stewards in the plant. Last year, stewards spent, on the average, about ten hours each per week on grievance work, for which they were paid by the company. There are no limitations on stewards for grievance work. Foremen have complained that some stewards are "goofing off," using "union business" as a pretext not to work. All stewards deny this. In fact, the stewards claim that it is the unreasonable attitude of foremen that provokes grievances and complaints. Also, the stewards claim that there cannot be a true measure of their time on the basis of the number of written grievances filed (a total of 185 were filed last year), since a good share of their time is spent discussing grievances on an oral basis with employees and supervisors before a written grievance is filed. There is no record to show how many of these oral discussions ended problems without written grievances being filed.

Last year, because of an unexpected order from the government, the plant worked Saturday and Sunday overtime for a period of two weekends. Under the existing contract, the company has the right to require overtime. About 200 employees refused to work overtime, and did so only because the company threatened to fire them if they refused. These 200 employees have been raising a lot of trouble in the union about this overtime affair. Also, the company has the right to select the employees to work overtime. Some employees have claimed that foremen are not fair, giving their personal friends the opportunity to earn the extra money and discriminating against the other employees.

For many years, by custom, each skilled tradesman has worked only within his trade. There are five maintenance trades: mechanics, carpenters, tool and die workers, plumbers, and electricians. Five months ago, the company required a mechanic to do a job normally performed by a plumber. The employee and union filed a grievance, and the case went all the way to arbitration. The arbitrator sustained the position of the union on the basis of the "past practice" principle.

Some maintenance people have been affected by the current layoff, with 25 laid off. They charge that the company has been subcontracting out skilled work that could be done by them. Last year, for example, the company subcontracted out electrical work while three electricians were on layoff. The subcontract job lasted six days. Under the current contract, there is no restriction on the company's right to subcontract.

The present contract, as stated, was negotiated for a three-year period. Both sides have indicated that in the future they may want to move away from this long-term arrangement for a variety of reasons. However, there is no assurance of whether this attitude indicates the parties' sincere position or is merely an expression of a possible bargaining position.

With respect to the current layoffs, the facts show that of the 300 employees laid off, 75 have exhausted their benefits under the Indiana Unemployment Compensation Act. The present contract does not provide for a supplementary unemployment benefit program.

Automation has been a problem in the company for several years. About 250 workers have been permanently separated because of automation. Union and management meetings to deal with the problem during the past several years have proved fruitless. Previous discussions have centered around the rate of automation, the problem of income for the displaced employees, and training of employees for the jobs created by automation. All indications are that the next wave of automation will cost about 390 bargaining unit jobs. The 250 employees who have been permanently separated are in addition to the 300 employees who are currently on layoff because of the southern situation and the drop in sales.

There has been considerable controversy over the problem of temporary transfers. Under the existing contract, the company may not transfer an employee to a job not in his job classification.

There are also problems regarding other working rules. These now include a 15-minute rest period every four hours; a stipulation that no supervisor may perform bargaining unit work regardless of circumstances; paid lunch periods of 20-minute duration; and paid "wash-up" time for 10 minutes prior to quitting time. The company contends that these "working rules" are costing it a lot of money. Whenever this issue has been brought up in the past, the union has refused any change.

Company records show that 60 percent of the workers have seniority up to 10 years; 30 percent, between 10 and 20 years; and 10 percent, more than 20 years. The average age of the employees in the plant is 39. About 5 percent are over 65 years of age. About 20 percent of the bargaining unit are women, and 15 percent are blacks. Some black employees have complained that they have not been given equal opportunity to get better jobs. They have threatened to file complaints against both the company and the union under Title VII of the Civil Rights Act and Taft-Hartley. They have retained an attorney for this purpose.

FOR THE INSTRUCTOR: HOW TO USE
THE MOCK NEGOTIATION PROBLEM

We have used the preceding mock negotiation problem with great success for several years. Students are uniformly enthusiastic about the problem, and there exists a friendly rivalry among the students during the weeks before the negotiation. Here are some suggestions on how to use the problem most effectively:

    1. The class should be divided into union and management negotiation teams about the middle of the semester. Each management and union team should include from three to five students. The teams could be selected in random fashion, but a better method is to distribute the better students among the different teams; by the middle of the semester, the instructor should have a good idea of the capability and the potential of the students. Each student should be assigned to a specific team, and each team should elect a chairman as rapidly as possible.

    2. The teams should be instructed to conduct the research necessary to collect the data and formulate the arguments to be used in the negotiation. The chairman of each team should be encouraged to divide the research among the members of each team. For example, one member may be responsible for the problem of wages; another for answering the other team's demands for changes in the seniority structure; and so on. Depending upon the number of students on each team and the number of issues that are likely to be negotiated, one student may be required to research more than one issue. The idea here is that each member of each team should be involved in the research, and the task of research should be divided as equally as possible among all members of the team. The instructor should advise students where the information can be found. The more helpful sources include the *Monthly Labor Review* of the U.S. Department of Labor; the Bureau of National Affairs' *Collective Bargaining Negotiations and Contracts;* special reports of the U.S. Department of Labor; existing collective bargaining contracts; the AFL-CIO *Federationist;* the *AFL-CIO News*; publications of the American Management Association and other management sources; *Labor Law Journal; Industrial and Labor Relations Review; Business Week;* and the *New York Times* and *Wall Street Journal.*

3. Experience has shown that each team should meet in its private planning sessions about five times, for about two to three hours for each session, before the negotiation. This is in addition to research conducted on an individual basis. Because of the time involved, the negotiation could be used instead of the traditional term paper.

4. The instructor may, if he desires, attend some of the planning sessions, although in recent years we have not been doing this on the grounds that the full responsibility for planning should be assumed by the students. If visits are made, the instructor should not shape the overall strategy of the team but merely consult with the team on particular problems.

5. We have found that the negotiation session should last about four hours. It could be held on an evening or a Saturday morning. Announce the date well in advance of the actual negotiation—at least six weeks.

6. The negotiation should be held toward the end of the semester so that the students can use the knowledge gained during the semester. We have usually scheduled the exercise during the second-to-last week of the semester.

7. The number of negotiations depends upon the number of students in the class. In one semester, the class included 66 students, and, hence, there were six negotiations going on simultaneously. Be sure to arrange well in advance of the exercise for the rooms in which the negotiations are to be held. If possible, the room should be of the conference type, although any room will do, provided that chairs can be arranged around a table so that the teams face each other.

8. The instructor should visit each negotiation, and his time should be divided equally among the groups. If some technical problem arises during the negotiation, the instructor should deal with the issue. Other than this, the instructor should remain silent as he observes the negotiation. *Do not give any help to any team while the negotiation is under way.* At times, we have had management and organized labor representatives visit the negotiations. Uniformly, they have been impressed with the success of the students and their competence at the bargaining table.

9. *The teams should be instructed that the sessions must end promptly at the specified time. If the negotiations are to end at 10 P.M., they should end at 10 P.M. Do not extend the time, since to do so would result in lack of uniformity for the different teams.*

10. When the negotiations are over, all students should meet in one room for a wrap-up session. Each chairman should report on whether there was a strike or a settlement, the major difficulties and problems of the negotiation, and other highlights. The chief purpose of this session, however, is for the instructor to make observations based on his visits to the negotiations. This session should not exceed 45 minutes. This meeting is usually charged with emotion, some horseplay, and friendly criticism of each other by the students. If there is not a definite time limit, it could go on indefinitely. In the instructor's analysis, the students should be treated kindly. They have worked hard and deserve congratulations and a pat on the back. Remember that this is their first experience and mistakes will be made. These should be pointed out, but in a strictly impersonal manner.

11. Other suggestions are that (1) some arrangements should be made for the students to have coffee during the negotiations; (2) if possible, smoking should be permitted; (3) to pacify the janitorial staff, the rooms should be cleared of debris, and chairs and tables rearranged, when the negotiations are ended; (4) the instructor should permit some poetic license during the actual negotiation, but cut off a student or a team that invents too much; and (5) he should not discourage some of the fun the students develop during the negotiations.

Index

A

Abel, I. W., 36
Administration of Labor Agreement, 217–45
  arbitration, 226–45
  grievance procedure, 216–25
  language of, 217–18
Administrative Issues under Collective Bargaining, 405–34
  automation, 426–33
  contract negotiation of, 191
  discharge and discipline, 416–20, 447–74
  production standards and manning, 423–26
  safety and health of employees, 420–23
  seniority, 406–16
Agency shop, 379–80
Air Line Pilots Assoc., 94, 157
Alexander v. *Gardner-Denver*, 230
Alioto, Joseph, 45–46
Amalgamated Assoc. of Iron and Steel Workers, 71
Amalgamated Clothing Workers, 97, 164, 166
Amalgamated Meat Cutters, 213–14, 430
American Arbitration Association, 237–38
American Federation of Government Employees, 39
American Federation of Labor (AFL)
  CIO challenge to, 81–84
  early history, 67–81
  exclusive jurisdiction, 99
  "federal locals," 81
  founding principles, 68–70
  growth of, 72–81
  Knights of Labor and, 67–68

American Federation of Labor (AFL) (*cont.*)
  leadership in, 78–79
  merger with CIO, 86–88
  nonskilled workers and, 81
  organized labor and, 115
  United Mine Workers and, 146
  World War II, 84–85
American Federation of Labor–Congress of Industrial Organizations (AFL–CIO)
  advantages of affiliation
    coordinated bargaining, 147
    political power, 146–47
    protection against raiding, 144, 146
  biannual convention, 147–49
  black workers, 90–91, 94, 145, 150
  Building and Construction Trades Dept., 92
  business conglomerates and, 143–44
  characteristics of, 48
  collective bargaining and, 153–54
  Committee on International Affairs, 155
  Committee on Political Education, 152–53
  communism and, 154
  community service, 152
  craft and industrial union warfare, 155–57
  dues, 144, 150, 153
  effect on organized labor, 157
  employee safety and health, 422–23
  expulsion weapon, 144–46
  federation rules, 144
  foreign labor movements, 154–55
  functions, 152–55
    new organizations, 153–54
    political activities, 152–53, 432
    research program, 153

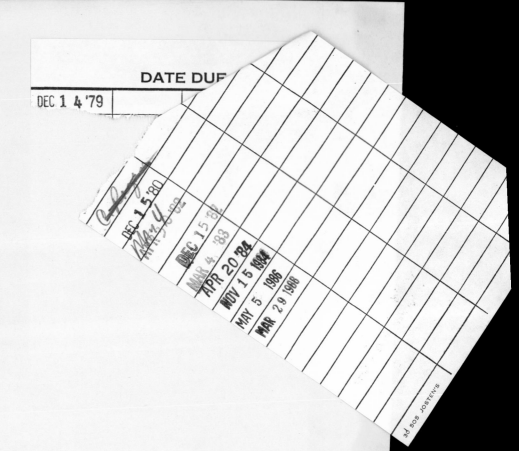